Be lud,

gary Wild

RACING POST
RACING ALMANAC

Five Centuries of History in 366 Dates

This edition first published in Great Britain in 2009 by
Racing Post Books
Compton, Newbury, Berkshire, RG20 6NL

1 3 5 7 9 10 8 6 4 2

A catalogue record for this book is available from the British Library.

ISBN 978-1-905156-64-1

Designed by Fiona Pike

Printed in the UK by CPI William Clowes Beccles NR34 7TL

www.racingpost.com/shop

RACING POST
RACING
ALMANAC

Five Centuries of History in 366 Dates

Graham Sharpe

FOREWORD

Almost the earliest date in this book is January 10, 1511 – I'll leave you to discover what happened on that date, and to locate the one a few centuries earlier than that.

But over the next five hundred years from 1511, a considerable amount happened in the ever expanding racing world – and you definitely will not find absolutely all of it listed in these 366 pages.

But here you will find many of the significant events of that half a millennium set out on the very date on which they occurred, along with a veritable treasure trove of births, deaths, achievements, records, feats, unusual happenings, comic capers, worthwhile words and notable turf topics.

Space limitations mean that the majority of entries are designed to pique your interest, and supply you with the bare bones of a story, leaving you free to investigate full details of what happened should you wish to delve further into the event or occasion.

I apologise in advance for the inevitable glitch or two, which invariably creeps in to the best proof-read of books, but the contents here have been checked, double checked, and frequently triple checked for accuracy, and where written records differ, mention has been made of that fact.

As racing is a sport in which the participants seem always to be looking towards tomorrow and the next race, rather than spending much time concentrating on what has happened today, I hope this book will help put events into perspective and act as an aide memoire so that when you read or dip into it and spot an entry which interests or intrigues you, you will firstly enjoy recalling what it was and, secondly, express surprise that it was either so recent or, and this is more likely, so long ago – whereas, in your memory it seems as fresh as the moment you saw it happen or heard about it.

Don't cheat and look it up – but just ask yourself now – when was Shergar kidnapped? When did Arkle last race? When did Lester Piggott retire for the first time? When did Ascot racecourse first open for business?

You'll find all the answers inside, along with thousands more, and if you do think your own favourite racing moment has gone unrecorded for some reason, well, write or email and let me know, so that I can include it in subsequent editions of the book.

GRAHAM SHARPE
gsharpe@williamhill.co.uk

1 JANUARY

SIGNIFICANT EVENT
1920 The 15-year-old Gordon Richards arrived at Foxhill, Wiltshire to start his first job in racing as stable lad to Martin Hartigan.

STRANGE EVENT
1924 The three runners in a 1m4f Flat race at Calcutta were shocked to find a set of hurdles left on the track from the previous race. All three negotiated the jump successfully and the result was allowed to stand despite an objection from third-placed Trezidella's jockey.

OTHER EVENTS
1834 Racehorses at Newmarket began to celebrate their official birthdays on this date each year, with the rest of the country following suit from 1858.
1925 Later to win two Cheltenham Gold Cups, Easter Hero saw a racecourse for the first time, finishing unplaced in the Killeston Plate at Baldoyle in Ireland.
1934 Top Irish hurdler at 1m4f (a popular distance then), Millennium won the Feltrim Handicap Hurdle at Baldoyle – carrying an astonishing 13st 12lb.
1973 Charmian Hill, later owner of Champion Hurdle-Gold Cup heroine Dawn Run, became the first lady to compete against men in Ireland, finishing third in a Fairyhouse bumper.
1991 For the first time a husband and wife finished first and second in a Group Race as Jim Collett on Star Harvest, at 46/1, beat off wife Trudy on Shugar in New Zealand's NZ$400,000 Auckland Cup.
1994 Eight-year-old Tempering won for the 18th time at Southwell, a post-War record, for trainer David Chapman.
1994 Frankie Dettori rode the first winner of the year – Tiddy Oggie at Lingfield.
1996 The minimum Flat weight was raised from 7st 7lb to 7st 10lb.
1998 Ladbrokes announced they were to take over Coral; deal never completed.
1999 Racecourse bookmakers were required to 'operate from a standardised plastic pitch'.
2008 Betting shop pictures provider Turf TV, with exclusive rights to 31 courses, launched its full service .
2009 Clerks of the course were required to release information and readings about their racecourse's going conditions gleaned from the Turf Trax-pioneered 'GoingStick'.

QUOTE OF THE DAY
When his Vintage Crop won the 1993 Melbourne Cup, the Irish stewards sent a fax saying: *'Irish racing is basking in your glory,'* to trainer Dermot Weld, who on this day in 1972 sent out his first jump winner when Peter Russell rode Spanner to victory at Baldoyle.

BIRTHDAYS
1859 Seldom mentioned when 'best jockey ever' discussions begin, black jockey Isaac Murphy, born in Kentucky today, rode 628 winners from 1,412 rides – a 44 per cent winning rate. He was paid a $10,000 per year retainer to ride for owner Lucky Baldwin. He died of pneumonia aged 37.
1951 Lambourn trainer Duncan Sasse, whose 28/1-shot Roland Gardens won the 1978 2,000 Guineas.

DEATHS OF THE DAY
1831 Jockey John Mangle, 81. Known as 'Crying Jackie' after his habit of bursting into tears after losing, he rode five St Leger winners and became a trainer.
2004 Jockey Johnny East, who won the inaugural Whitbread Gold Cup on Much Obliged in 1957, died aged 79.

CELEBRITY OF THE DAY
1960 Jockey-turned-actress Kelly Marks was born today. She rode in England, California, Holland and Belgium before turning to acting, appearing in the movies *Champions* (1984) and *A View To A Kill* (1985).

2 JANUARY

SIGNIFICANT EVENT
1965 Having held a permit for 13 years, Donald 'Ginger' McCain finally got off the mark when San Lorenzo was a 3/1 winner at Liverpool – where Ginger's Red Rum would go on to land his immortal Grand National treble.

STRANGE EVENT
1992 A day after announcing he was launching the first jockey testimonial year, 36-year-old Steve Smith Eccles broke an ankle at Lingfield.

OTHER EVENTS
1939 Arthur 'Fiddler' Goodwill rode Khordad to win the Charlton Hurdle for Tom Leader at Manchester.

1955 Panamanian president, José Ramon Antonio Rémon Cantera was assasinated at Juan Franco racetrack.

1989 27-year-old jump jockey Micky Hammond, runner-up to Peter Scudamore in the 1987-88 title race, retired with 231 winners to his credit.

1990 Ayr trainer John Wilson saddled his first treble after 12 years, when Impecuniosity, 20/1, Persuasive, 11/8 and Young Miner, 33/1, landed odds of 1,695/1 at his home course.

1990 Bruce Raymond rode his first winner on the all-weather at Southwell – the same course at which he'd ridden his only jump winner over hurdles 25 years earlier.

1993 Despite returning at 25/1, few should have been shocked when Rapporteur won on the all-weather at Lingfield. After all, it was the Charles Elsey-trained 7yo's 14th win there.

QUOTE OF THE DAY
'Mostly unprintable.' Irish trainer and prolific winning amateur rider John Fowler, born on this day in 1946, when asked what were his favourite recreations.

BIRTHDAYS
1951 Navan trainer Noel Meade, who describes his riding career as 'short' and whose first training licence was taken out in 1972. He has dominated the champion trainer title in Ireland, on a winners and money-won basis, since 1999. His best horses include Harchibald and Harbour Pilot.

1946 Welsh trainer Edward Owen Jr. (Monte Ceco, Rupertino), who also rode nine winners under NH Rules.

DEATHS OF THE DAY
1983 Sam Armstrong, rider of 50 jumps winners, and trainer of Classic winners Sayajirao (1947 St Leger) and My Babu (1948 2000 Guineas) died aged 78.

2002 Armando Martinez, Cuban jockey for legendary gangster Al Capone, died aged 88. He partnered 5,000 winners in five different countries after fleeing the Castro regime in 1958, and rode for the last time aged 76.

CELEBRITY OF THE DAY
1920 Andrew Robert Buxton Cavendish, 11th Earl of Devonshire, P.C., M.C. was an Old Etonian, born this day. He served in the Coldstream Guards during the Second World War and was notoriously unlucky with his racehorses until acquiring the great mare Park Top for just 500gns. The Duchess made him keep her in training until she was six and she won 13 races and £136,440, including the 1969 King George VI and the Queen Elizabeth stakes plus a second in the Prix de l'Arc de Triomphe. The Duke wrote *A Romance of the Turf* (1976) about her.

3 JANUARY

SIGNIFICANT EVENT
1984 The two events may or may not have been connected – the Prince of Wales fell off his horse whilst out with the Cottesmore Hunt in Leicestershire and Buckingham Palace announced that women would not be allowed into the Royal Enclosure at Royal Ascot 'if their hats are too small.'

STRANGE EVENT
2009 Namu 'pi**ed' up in the 2.35 at Kempton, run on the all-weather. The 6yo was about to enter the stalls when she stopped and relieved herself copiously, causing jockey Adam Kirby to declare he had never seen such a thing, trainer Teresa Spearing to reveal the mare normally did it in her box and John Francome to brand it 'extraordinary.' It worked, though – she romped home in the 6f sprint handicap.

OTHER EVENTS
1990 Optician-turned-jockey Andy Orkney caught the eye when, the day after opening a practice in Leyburn, he rode his first double on The Maltkiln and Kersil at Sedgefield.

1992 US rider Angel Cordero Jr broke an elbow, three ribs and damaged his spleen in a fall at Aqueduct racecourse, New York. He never raced again and retired later in the year with 7,076 winners to his credit.

1993 Ed Carvalho, a 10lb claiming apprentice, rode his first winner at the 42nd attempt on Majestic Moran at Tampa Bay Downs, at the age of 43.

1993 Former Surrey-based trainer Robin Gow went through the card at Seeb racecourse in Oman, saddling all six winners on the thoroughbred, Arab and harness racing card.

2008 Melbourne Cup-winning trainer Graeme Rogerson became the winningmost trainer in New Zealand when Minno Noir gave him his 1,878th winner there.

QUOTE OF THE DAY
1993 *'I have to ride out every morning and do odd jobs in the afternoon to keep afloat,'* said jockey Gee Armytage when rides were drying up. Whether she was doing one of those odd jobs on this day in 1988 when she appeared on TV sports quiz 'Sporting Triangles' and asked Manchester United and England footballer Bryan Robson which sport he was involved in is unclear.

BIRTHDAYS
1924 Trainer Reg Hollinshead born in Longdon, Staffs. Ace developer of apprentices like Steve Perks, Kevin Darley, Walter Swinburn, Paul Eddery and Willie Ryan, he saddled Remainder Man to be runner-up in the 2,000 Guineas and third in the Derby in 1978.

1940 Epsom trainer John Sutcliffe Jr, whose Right Tack won the 1969 2,000 Guineas.

1967 Jockey Robert Bellamy, whose first winner was Molojec for Jenny Pitman on Grand National day in 1987.

1967 Jockey Gerald Mosse, who won the 1990 Arc on Saumarez and partnered 'wonder horse' Arazi as a 2yo.

1983 Hayley Turner, the first female jockey to ride 100 winners in a year.

DEATHS OF THE DAY
1913 US financier and owner James R Keene, whose Foxhall, trained by William Day in Wiltshire, won the 1881 'Autumn Double', both the Cambridgeshire (10/1) and Cesarewitch (named in honour of Emperor Alexander II of Russia, 9/2).

1946 Canadian jockey George Woolf, 35, fell at Santa Anita and died the next day. Woolf, who won 721 races including the 1936 Preakness Stakes, was diabetic and was believed to have fainted or suffered a dizzy spell.

CELEBRITIES OF THE DAY
King George and Queen Mary, who on this day in 1912 were centre of attraction at Calcutta races.

4 JANUARY

SIGNIFICANT EVENT
1990 The Shanahan Bay became the first, but far from last, horse to win four races on the all-weather when the Eric Eldin-trained 5yo scored over 6f at Lingfield.

STRANGE EVENT
1997 Jenny Pitman's Master Tribe (Norman Williamson) was the 18/1 winner of the Ladbroke Hurdle – but Leopardstown bookies were on strike so prices were returned by an off-course survey of Irish and UK bookmakers.

OTHER EVENTS
1991 Henry Cecil's former wife Julie sent out her first runner as a trainer. Ferox finished last on the all-weather at Southwell.

1992 Jockey Steve Cauthen, 32, wed 25-year-old law student Amy Rothfuss.

2008 Figures showed that the 2007 Pari-Mutuel betting turnover was a record 8.841bn euros.

2008 Still not ready to race, Great Leighs racecourse handed seven more scheduled fixtures to BHA – making a total of 102 thus far.

2008 16yo Ben Morris, son of Newmarket trainer Dave, rode his first winner, 5/2 favourite Cragganmore Creek, at Southwell, trained by dad.

QUOTE OF THE DAY
1992 *'They told me it was not a fast-food store,'* said Frankie Dettori after stewards at Sha Tin, Hong Kong, cautioned him – for chewing gum! He'd been called in with local rider Jackie Tse who had taken exception when Frankie's mount had hindered him during the race, and had lashed out with his whip.

BIRTHDAYS
1927 Trainers Robin Dun and Peter Asquith.

1936 Jump jockey Tommy Jennings, who would win a Scottish Champion Hurdle and partner Sempervivum and Mugatpura, was born.

1944 US Hall of Fame jockey, Jacinto Vasquez.

1954 Flamboyant, later somewhat overweight US trainer Roger Stein was born in Detroit. The handler of the useful Forty Niner Days brought that horse over to contest a race at Ascot, and there were sharp intakes of breath all over the course as Stein appeared in the parade ring sporting a blue tracksuit and, horror of horrors, no tie.

1974 Five time German champion jockey, Andrasch Starke.

2006 1994 Melbourne Cup winner Jeune, aged 16. He sired 210 winners, 14 of which won stakes races.

DEATHS OF THE DAY
1967 Former trainer Colin Laidler, whose Stenquill won Manchester's Emblem Chase in 1962, died after a lengthy illness.

1995 Chris Leonard, who rode Peter O'Sullevan's Attivo to win a Tote Roll-Up Handicap in 1973, died aged 44, having never properly recovered from injuries sustained in a fall at Ostend in 1981.

CELEBRITY OF THE DAY
1993 Tragedy struck for Sir Andrew Lloyd Webber's wife, Madeleine, on this day, when the horse he bought her for £80,000, Champion Hurdle hopeful Al Mutahm, was destroyed after severing a tendon during Newbury's Ramsbury Hurdle.

5 JANUARY

SIGNIFICANT EVENT
1961 Josh Gifford rode his first winner for Ryan Price as Cantab won at Stratford.

STRANGEST EVENT
1920 Both runners in a Plumpton novice chase fell. Longerline was remounted to win and a spectator caught and rode the other horse in to finish second. As Mr. Dale made the weight he was officially placed second.

OTHER EVENTS
1842 They raced for the first time at Epsom – Epsom, near Auckland, New Zealand, that is.

1963 The awful weather meant there had been no racing since December 21 and would be no more until March 8, but a brief respite at Ayr saw Tommy McGinley ride three winners.

1968 Weather again played havoc with racing and Les Kennard's Eastern Delight, ridden by claimer Ken Begley, won a hurdle at Sandown, the first race run anywhere in Britain since November 25.

1987 Tot won the first race at the first jumps meeting at Edinburgh (now called Musselburgh).

1988 Ravinella became the first filly to top the European 2yo rankings since the awards were introduced in 1978.

1989 The 100-1 shock winner at Ayr, Allerlad, went unbacked by owner-trainer David MacDonald, but Raceform journalist Alan Amies invested £20 each-way on the horse at an early 200/1 and collected £4,800.

1992 After a horse collapsed and had to be destroyed before racing started in Bombay, Indian police launched an investigation into criminal involvement in horse doping. Drugs and syringes were uncovered at the track.

1993 Gay Kelleway saddled her first winner as a trainer, Aberfoyle, at Lingfield, where new-style hurdles were introduced, with Josh Cadell riding Faynaz to win the first race over them.

QUOTE OF THE DAY
'I've decided I don't want to be cremated. I'm going to be buried – there's a slight chance I might get out again,' revealed veteran trainer Mick Easterby, whose Welcome Sight had to be rescued from the River Rye near Malton on this day in 1983.

BIRTHDAYS
1935 Milton Bradley, trainer of smart sprinter The Tatling.

1938 Jump jockey-turned-starter Gerry Scott. His first winner came on Kiddleywink at Sedgefield on 10 March 1956 and he won the 1960 Grand National on 13/2 shot Merryman II for his guvnor, Neville Crump.

1973 Glamorous TV presenter Alice Plunkett, former GB eventer and amateur jockey.

DEATH OF THE DAY
1993 Former trainer Jack Morris, one of only two people to survive when a plane carrying broodmares from Deauville crashed at Heathrow in 1968, died of cancer, aged 68.

1997 Francois Doumen's brother, jockey-turned-trainer Christian, died aged 64.

1998 58-year-old trainer David Morley, whose Celeric won the 1997 Ascot Gold Cup, died of a heart attack.

2000 Younger brother of Fred, trainer John Winter, died aged 70. His Spaniards Mount won the 1966 Wokingham Stakes.

CELEBRITY OF THE DAY
1965 Vinnie Jones, labourer-turned-footballer-turned-actor, and pal of Frankie Dettori, born this day. An owner with John Gosden, his first horse, Sixty Seconds, won at Leicester for him. Jones was captain of the Great Britain and Ireland team at the 2001 Shergar Cup.

6 JANUARY

SIGNIFICANT EVENT
1945 After a gap of almost three years, jump racing resumed after the war with a meeting at Cheltenham.

STRANGEST EVENT
1991 After a five-year layoff during the Civil War, racing resumed in Beirut, Lebanon, with 25,000 turning up to see the four races.

OTHER EVENTS
1987 A Mars bar which was held responsible for De Rigueur's disqualification from Ascot's 1986 Balmoral Handicap, announced this day in 1987. The horse's post-race sample showed traces of a prohibited substance, attributed to a Mars Bar chocolate snack he had consumed, pre-race.

1996 Myjinka won for 88-year-old trainer Jack O'Donoghue, his last runner after a 50-year career in which he won the 1951 Grand National with Nickel Coin.

1999 Violet at Wolverhampton was the last winner as a trainer for Lord Huntingdon, who was formerly known as William Hastings-Bass.

2008 *The Racing Post* reported that triple Gold Cup winner Best Mate's owner Jim Lewis had removed his horses from trainer Henrietta Knight. She said: 'It's disappointing when loyalty flies out of the window'.

QUOTE OF THE DAY
1992 Tony Murray once said: *'When you lose a race, it's a matter of passing the buck; the owner blames the trainer, the trainer blames the jockey, and the jockey blames the*

poor old horse.' Sadly, the dual Classic-winning rider, son of a jump jockey, was found dead at his Wiltshire home aged just 41 on this day. Tony won the Oaks on Ginevra in 1972 and the St Leger on Bruni in 1975, both for Captain Ryan Price, and won over 1,100 races.

BIRTHDAYS
1938 Scottish jockey Duncan Keith. He won the 1965 2,000 Guineas on Niksar, at 100/8, and was runner-up on Linden Tree when Mill Reef won the Derby. Twice disqualified in the Ascot Gold Cup on Rock Roi, who passed the post in front, only for the horse to to fail a dope test in 1971 and in 1972 to be demoted for interfering with Erimo Hawk. He retired in 1973.

1951 US trainer Shug (well, you might want another name if your given one was Claude – sorry, Mr Duval!) McGaughey. His Easy Goer won the 1989 Belmont Stakes.

1966 US champion jockey Chris Antley born in Florida.

1975 Jockeys Aimee Cook and J. D. Smith.

DEATHS OF THE DAY
1998 Ternimus became the first equine victim of new-look all-weather hurdles when breaking his neck in a Southwell selling hurdle on this day in 1993.

CELEBRITY OF THE DAY
2008 Former West Ham skipper and FA Cup winner, Billy Bonds, presented the trophy to connections of Ironside, the 25/1 winner in Plumpton's Sussex National.

7 JANUARY

SIGNIFICANT EVENT
1968 El Mighty won an obscure hurdle race at Cagnes-Sur-Mer. The previous year he had started as a leading fancy for the Derby, having been backed from 200/1 to 22/1 after a story was published that a punter had 'dreamed' the Dave Hanley-trained, Paul Cook-partnered outsider would win the big race. He didn't. Noel Murless-trained Royal Palace did.

STRANGEST EVENT
1995 Confusion all round as a problem with Don't Ask Mike's passport saw the horse officially declared a Naas non-runner – only to be reinstated. This came too late for the Tote to include the Michael Hourigan-trained runner for betting purposes, so he raced as a 'non-runner' – fortunately finishing unplaced.

OTHER EVENTS
1972 Irish trainer Jim Dreaper sent out his first winner when Straight Fort won at Sandown – and the very next day registered his first in Ireland when Geordie Hugh won at Naas.
1993 An enormous gamble on Big Ben Dun at Punchestown came off big time as the farmer John O'Neill-owned, Sean Donovan-trained runner put the form of his last race – 16th of 19 in a hurdle event – well behind him to win the Carrick Hill Handicap Chase by ten lengths, having been backed from 100/1 to 3/1 favourite and taking a reported IR£500,000 out of the ring.
1994 16-year-old schoolboy Mattie Kneafsey took the day off to ride his dad's Sporting Spirit at Southwell – and won at 50/1.
1999 Over 1,000 Italian trainers, owners and jockeys staged a protest outside the Agriculture Ministry in Rome demanding urgent measures to help the sport. Demonstrators carried an effigy of a jockey hanging from a noose.

QUOTE OF THE DAY
'Aubrey's up, the money's down; the frightened bookies quake/Come on, my lads and give a cheer – Begod, 'tis Cottage Rake.' This piece of doggerel was hugely popular when the dual-purpose jockey Aubrey Brabazon, born on this day in 1920, was riding Vincent O'Brien's triple Cheltenham Gold Cup-winning Cottage Rake (1948-49-50). He also partnered triple Champion Hurdler Hatton's Grace.

BIRTHDAY
1833 John Osborne, who became the most popular northern-based jockey of the Victorian era, was born in Derbyshire. Nicknamed 'Old Pusher' for his persistence with lost causes, he won 12 Classics including six 2,000 Guineas and the 1869 Derby on Pretender before becoming a trainer at Middleham, winning the 1898 Manchester Cup and Northumberland Plate with King Crow. He rode out until the age of 88, a year before he died.

DEATH OF THE DAY
1949 Albert 'Snowy' Whalley, who rode his first winner in India, aged 23, and won the 1919 1,000 Guineas on Roseway and the 1920 Oaks on Charlebelle, died in Newmarket, aged 63.

CELEBRITY OF THE DAY
1788 Dennis O'Kelly, who died 28 December 1787, owner of the first equine superstar, Eclipse, was buried at Cannons Church, Whitchurch in north-west London. He was outlived by Eclipse.

8 JANUARY

SIGNIFICANT EVENT
1992 Jockey Brendan Powell and Blue Danube became the first fallers in a British all-weather chase when they took a tumble in Southwell's Huntsman's Handicap Chase.

STRANGEST EVENT
1996 Reg Hollinshead saddled Loch Style and Taniyar for races at Southwell – sadly, though, putting each in the other's race! Both were unplaced.

OTHER EVENTS
1993 An official crowd of 4,000 attended the Racing for Miners meeting at Southwell – the first meeting to be used as a political platform. Politicians and racing personalities made speeches and races were named after pits threatened with closure.
1994 Wolverhampton staged Britain's first all floodlit meeting on its all-weather track.
1994 Indian Derby and St Leger winner Astonish, 10/1, was the first such import to score on his debut in Hong Kong, when Alan Munro rode him to win at Sha Tin.
2008 Charges of conspiricy to defraud Betfair customers against trainer Alan Berry over the running of Hillside Girl in 2003 were finally dropped as the City of London Police investigation ended.

QUOTE OF THE DAY
'In 1773 I could ride horses in a better manner in a race than any person ever known in my time. In 1775 I could train horses for running better than any person I ever yet saw,' declared the rider of four Oaks and one Derby winner, Sam Chifney senior. He died on this day in 1807, in Fleet prison to which he had been committed for owing a saddler £350.

BIRTHDAYS
1928 Dual code jockey-turned-Flat trainer Matt McCourt.
1934 Jump jockey-turned-starter Bill Rees, son of 1922 National winning jockey Bilby. Bill won the 1960 Cheltenham Gold Cup on Pas Seul and won 51 races for the Queen Mother.
1937 Sally Ann Bailie, who rode over jumps in England, then trained in the USA where she was the first woman to win $100,000 and $200,000 stakes races, and the first to saddle a Japan Cup runner.

DEATHS OF THE DAY
2008 One of the great Australian jockeys, George Moore, died aged 84. He teamed up with trainer Tommy Smith in the 1940s and rode champion Tulloch in 19 of his 36 wins. He rode in Europe and won the 1959 Arc on Saint Crespin, and the 1967 2,000 Guineas and Derby on Royal Palace. He retired in 1971, with 119 Group One wins and became a trainer in France, Australia and Hong Kong, where he was 11 times champion.
2009 Aspiring jockey Jamie Yeates, 15, known as 'Spencer' after his hero Jamie and who worked for trainer Alison Thorpe, was stabbed to death (see 15 January).

CELEBRITY OF THE DAY
The Queen Mother, who enjoyed her first double, Double Star and Sparkling Knight at Hurst Park for trainer Peter Cazalet and jockey Arthur Freeman in 1959.

9 JANUARY

SIGNIFICANT EVENT
1987 Schweppes announced that they were to end their sponsorship of the oft-abandoned Gold Trophy at Newbury.

STRANGEST EVENT
1990 Jockey Dean Gallagher won on Last House at Newton Abbot – and lost his claim – again. He had done so before a revision in the rules which allowed him to become the first rider to claim 3lb for a second time.

OTHER EVENTS
1969 Arctic Coral won at Warwick to give David Nicholson his first winner as a trainer.

1986 A racecourse worker at St Moritz, where they race on ice and snow, narrowly escaped death when his Snowcat tractor sank under the ice.

1993 Only 250 paying customers attended a Lingfield card (average crowd 1,000 at the time) in atrocious weather.

1994 Jacqueline Freda finished second in the Italian Jockeys' Championship with 125 winners – the first European woman to ride over 100 winners in a season.

2008 Brazilian jockey Jorge Ricardo, 46, rode a five-timer at San Isidro, Argentina, to become the first rider to score 10,000 career wins.

QUOTE OF THE DAY
'You little ba*tards, you thought you were going to get me, but you didn't,' said troubled three-times Irish champion jockey Bobby Beasley to the optics in the pub he bought after overcoming alcoholism. He partnered Roddy Owen in 1959 and Captain Christy in 1974 to win the Cheltenham Gold Cup and landed the National on Nicolaus Silver in 1961 and the Champion Hurdle a year earlier on Another Flash. Died this day in 2008.

BIRTHDAYS
1820 Legendary Flat trainer Mathew Dawson, who sent out 28 Classic winners, from Catherine Hayes in the 1853 Oaks to St Visto in the 1895 St Leger.

1930 Geoff Wragg, son of jockey Harry Wragg, who trained Teenoso to win the 1983 Derby.

1948 Lightweight jockey Ernie Johnson, who won the Derby on Blakeney in 1969 and lost it by inches to Roberto on Rheingold in 1972.

DEATHS OF THE DAY
1968 The Dorothy Paget-owned 1943 Derby winner Straight Deal, aged 28.

1976 Legonotis, who returned at 400/1 when winning at Randwick, Sydney.

2009 Joe Hirsch, who wrote for the Daily Racing Form in the United States for 55 years and became the only racing writer to win both an Eclipse Award and a Lord Derby Award, died aged 80.

CELEBRITY OF THE DAY
1944 Comedian Freddie Starr, whose Miinnehoma won the Grand National after he bought the horse at auction for 35,000gns by sticking out his tongue, was born today.

10 JANUARY

SIGNIFICANT EVENT
1511 Order of the Corporation of Chester decreed that the prize of a silver ball, value 3s4d (17p), should be run for by horses on the Rood Eye (later Roodee) course at Chester. Some sources dispute this date – see 9 February.

STRANGEST EVENT
2008 Four of the five jockeys ignored a recall flag at Southwell, completing the 1m course with 2/1 chance Jord 'winning'. Only Chris Catlin on 10/1-shot Rebellious Spirit pulled up. The rest were ineligible for the re-run having already passed the post, so Catlin and his mount were able to go round in splendid isolation to walk over.

OTHER EVENTS
1975 Aldaniti, then owned and trained by Josh Gifford, won at 33/1 over hurdles on his debut at Ascot, partnered by Bob Champion, who rode the horse to victory in the 1981 Grand National.

1988 The successful partnership between trainer Vincent O'Brien and stable jockey Cash Asmussen was dissolved.

1994 Southwell staged the first all-weather stand-by fixture.

1995 After refusing to start in four consecutive races, Azureus did it again at Leicester – with the slight difference that he condescended to set off 100 yards behind the rest. 'I'm finished with him,' said trainer Henry Kavanagh.

QUOTE OF THE DAY
2009 *'The last time the Queen tapped me on the shoulder was to complain about the ride I had given one of her mum's horses,'* said John Francome, congratulating the Injured Jockeys' Fund's Serena Oxley on receiving the OBE.

BIRTHDAYS
1942 Jump jockey turned Colchester-based trainer, Jim Scallon.

1959 Flat trainer Christian Wall. His Rotherfield Greys won the 1988 Stewards' Cup, landing a £500,000 touch for his owner, Ealing publican Tony Gleeson. On the same day, but a year later, Rotherfield Greys' jockey Nigel Day was born.

1961 Flat jockey Philip Robinson, the first British jockey to become Hong Kong champion. He won both the English 1,000 Guineas on Pebbles and the Irish 1,000 Guineas on Katies in 1984.

1963 Jockey Tony McGlone, who would win the 1987 Kuwait Derby on Saare.

DEATHS OF THE DAY
1967 Former jockey Arthur Waudby, aged 70. He rode four successive winners at Wetherby in October 1928.

1969 Ronald Blindell, 63, owner of Stalbridge Colonist, who beat Arkle in the 1966 Hennessy Gold Cup.

1998 Former jockey Tommy Wyse, associated with Bishop Auckland trainer Denys Smith for 40 years, aged 78.

FIRST OF THE DAY
1995 Persistence paid off for 79-year-old retired meat trader F Jackman who gained his first win after 30 years as an owner when Bon Secret won Lingfield's Victory Auction Stakes.

11 JANUARY

SIGNIFICANT EVENT
1994 For the first time at such short notice, the BHB gave permission for a switch of venue for a major race when the Victor Chandler Chase, scheduled for Ascot on 15 January, was permitted to move to Warwick if Ascot was off – which it was.

STRANGEST EVENT
1991 The Dean of St Paul's Cathedral officially opened a new betting shop at Old Bailey, London..

OTHER EVENTS
1919 Derby winner Captain Cuttle, named after a character in Dickens' Dombey and Son, was foaled. If he had been foaled 12 days earlier he would have been a yearling when a day old!

1982 Owners of Ireland's Kildangan Stud paid undisclosed compensation to owners of two mares after it was proved resident stallion Tap On Wood did not cover them as stated. It later emerged that they had been covered by a 12 hands high Connemara pony.

1991 Trainer Len Lungo saddled his first winner, Cumbrian Ceilidh, at Edinburgh.

1997 Jenny Pitman won the Ladbroke Hurdle at Leopardstown with Master Tribe, the first British victory in the race for ten years.

2002 Tony McCoy won on Native Man at Huntingdon to achieve the fastest ever double century in a single season.

QUOTE OF THE DAY;
'A right ba*tard and a miserable old sod.' Celebrating his 68th wedding anniversary with wife Betty on this day in 2008, champion jump jockey of 1946-47 Jack Dowdeswell recalled the trainer to whom he was apprenticed, Ted Gwilt.

BIRTHDAYS
1857 Frederick James Archer, son of a jump jockey, was born in Cheltenham. He shot himself in 1886, by which time he'd been Champion jockey 13 times and ridden 2,748 winners from 8,084 mounts, including 21 Classic winners. He left £60,000 in his will.

1943 Henry Richard Amherst Cecil, one of the all-time great trainers with four Derbys, six Oaks, six 1,000 Guineas, three St Legers and two 2,000 Guineas so far to his credit.

1937 Walter 'Wally' Swinburn, the first jockey in Irish racing to achieve over 100 winners in a year; father of jockey-turned-trainer Walter.

1937 Trainer Brian Swift, who rode 200 winners from 1951-61. He had Flat and jump winners including the Triumph Hurdle and Stewards' Cup.

1962 Trainer John Best.

1964 Trainer Nicolas Clement, whose Saumarez won the 1990 Prix de l'Arc de Triomphe.

1973 Richard Hughes, son of trainer Dessie, who rode his 100th winner on the popular Persian Punch, who he rates as one of the best he has ridden, along with triple Arc runner-up Youmzain.

DEATHS OF THE DAY
1987 Trainer Syd Woodman, 67, and owner Sir David Robinson, 82. The latter once owned Kempton, and his Our Babu won the 1955 2,000 Guineas.

1990 Charmian Hill, 70, owner of Dawn Run.

2004 Co. Kildare trainer Arthur Bunyon, whose Local Whisper won the 1991 Tattersalls Gold Cup at Punchestown, aged 74.

CELEBRITY OF THE DAY
1994 Two jackets belonging to the showman tipster Ras Prince Monolulu were sold at auction for a total of £760 to the National Horseracing Museum.

12 JANUARY

SIGNIFICANT EVENT
1994 Ascot caved in to protests and announced that they would retain the Queen Alexandra Stakes as it was and not shorten its length of 2m 6f 34yds, the longest race in the Flat programme. After the redevelopment of Ascot, the race is now 2m 5f 159yds long.

STRANGEST EVENT
1993 Not one Tote punter found 66/1 winner Starmine at Leicester. Just one bet would have produced a dividend of 1,530/1.

OTHER EVENTS
1983 Harry Wragg, champion jockey of 1941, retired from training, having ridden 13 Classic winners (the Derby three times) and trained five more – including Psidium in the 1961 Derby.

1990 Riding Gospel Rock at Wetherby, Graham Bradley was thrown, the horse bolted, smashed down a concrete post, crashed through a fence and hedge, raced down the main road and ended up in the car park of local pub The Swan.

1991 A mega-gamble was landed in Leopardstown's Ladbroke Hurdle as The Illiad, backed from 33/1 ante-post to 7/1, won connections a reported seven-figure sum, including £400,000 for owner Noel Furlong.

1991 Partnered by Richard Dunwoody, Desert Orchid was fourth of five in the Victor Chandler Chase at Ascot – the seventh time that trainer David Elsworth's head lad Rodney Boult had seen Dessie run, and the seventh time he'd lost. He never beat the jinx.

1991 16-year-old part-time art student, Emma O'Gorman rode her first treble, at 267/1, on the all-weather at Lingfield.

1993 James Fanshawe landed his first jumps double – Perfay and Fired Earth at Leicester.

1993 Once secretary of the Lady Jockeys' Association, Yvonne Stapleton became the first woman appointed to the investigating team of the Jockey Club security department.

QUOTE OF THE DAY
'I can't make a living out of this game any more', declared jockey Dale McKeown on retiring aged just 28 in February 1993, with 138 winners to his credit. On this day in 1990 trainer Brooke Sanders and McKeown teamed up for their first trebles, with Don Keydrop, Solitary Reaper and Oublier L'Ennui at Lingfield.

BIRTHDAYS
1934 Dual code trainer Michael John Bolton. His Magic Boy was the 20/1 winner of the 1958 Wokingham Handicap.

1960 Flat jockey Alan Mercer, whose best season was 1979 when he rode 30 winners. Married Mhairi Jane.

DEATH OF THE DAY
1983 Francois Mathet, an outstanding French trainer and ex-cavalry officer, aged 74. Sent out winners of four Arcs, six Prix du Jockey Clubs, two Derbys, a 1,000 Guineas and four Coronation Cups.

CELEBRITY OF THE DAY
On this day in 1994 it was announced that Sir Andrew Lloyd Webber had purchased a £200,000, five per cent share in Newbury racecourse – for his wife, Madeleine.

13 JANUARY

SIGNIFICANT EVENT

1990 Redundant Pal won Ireland's richest hurdle race, The Ladbroke, at 20/1 for trainer Paddy Mullins. He had been asked for an explanation of the horse's defeat at 1/5 in a two-horse race a fortnight earlier, after which stewards confirmed that they had accepted Mullins' explanation that he 'had no explanation'.

STRANGEST EVENT

1995 Jockey Jacqui Oliver was acquitted of helping to mastermind a £2.5m conspiracy to defraud by selling counterfeit credit cards.

OTHER EVENTS

1965 A record 229 runners contested eight races at Worcester.

1988 Friday the thirteenth proved lucky for Peter Niven, who rode four winners for four different trainers at Edinburgh in a 318/1 accumulator.

1988 Park Slave was laid at 3,000/1 for the Whixley Hurdle at Wetherby, perhaps the longest odds quoted on a British racecourse. He finished seventh.

1990 Lambourn trainer Captain Mark Smyly's last runner, Answers Please, fell at Newcastle. His Yanuka was third at 33/1 in the 1979 1,000 Guineas.

1992 US jockey Mike Smith rode six winners from seven mounts at Aqueduct – and did it again 17 days later.

1993 Racing in Bombay was cancelled due to political riots.

1993 Irish Derby winner St Jovite rated a controversial 10lb above Derby winner Dr Devious in 3yo classifications.

1994 Perhaps uniquely, bookies Victor Chandler opened a book on where their sponsored Chase would take place, offering 2/5 Ascot – where it was scheduled to be run; 5/2 Warwick – where it would go if Ascot was unfit; 6/1 no race. It was run at Warwick.

QUOTE OF THE DAY

'There are no fallers, so every horse finishes the race and no horses or jockeys get injured,' enthused ubiquitous TV face and voice Derek 'Tommo' Thompson on this day in 2009, extolling the virtues of, er, 'Virtual Racing.'

BIRTHDAYS

1920 John Hislop, respected rider, writer and owner-breeder of Brigadier Gerard.

1953 Bob Baffert, top US trainer. White-haired Baffert is not everyone's favourite – a disgruntled punter set up the website page IHateBobBaffert on which he gave these reasons why: 'He's a snob; Got too much money; He's a snob; Never takes off his glasses; He's a snob.'

1966 Trainer Nigel Hawke. He rode Seagram to win the 1991 Grand National and trained Kendal Cavalier, 14/1 winner of 1998 Welsh Grand National.

DEATH OF THE DAY

1862 Jockey Luke Snowden, already with three Classic winners to his credit, aged just 22.

CELEBRITY OF THE DAY

1927 England cricketer Ted Arnold was owner of Bubbly, beaten odds-on favourite on this day in at Tenby racecourse as stablemate Oyster Maid, owned by Arnold's pro punter pal, Ben Warner, won at 100/6, landing a huge off-course gamble. 'The result concealed the biggest and most bitterly resented betting coup National Hunt racing has ever known,' said Dick Francis. Many bookies refused to stand at the track again in protest.

14 JANUARY

SIGNIFICANT EVENT

1997 The 71-year-old trainer Charlie – real name, Arthur – Moore sent out his final runner, Kingsdown Trix, at Lingfield, having held a licence for 36 years. The horse finished sixth and the track marked the occasion with a commemorative cake. However, Moore was nowhere to be seen – he had an appointment with his heart specialist.

STRANGEST EVENT

1991 For the first time, the Jockey Club hinted that Derby day could be switched from Wednesday to Saturday.

OTHER EVENTS

1970 The 30-year-old jockey Charlie Patton was forced to retire, having fallen from Toy Soldier at Ascot the previous summer and suffered internal injuries.

1984 Newspaper *The Irish Field* revealed that during 1983 there was £5.5m available in prize money, up by £1m on 1982. A million was contributed by sponsors in 1983 and half that in 1982.

1991 All weather racing at Southwell was called off becuase of the weather: frost.

1992 Trainer Martin Pipe completed his sixth successive century as Ambassador won at Folkstone.

1993 Sabin du Loir won for the 21st time in 41 races, signing off aged 14 at Wincanton after winning a total of £250,000 in prize money and beating Desert Orchid on four of the five occasions they met.

QUOTE OF THE DAY

1993 '*When there is no admission, desirable persons remain away, because they do not want to be present with the sort of people who attend only because it is free,*' sniffed *The Blood Horse* magazine on this day when Jefferson Park racecourse in New Orleans experimented with free admission. Towcester, take note!

BIRTHDAYS

1948 John Williams, the dual Grand National winner in Norway who also won the Ayr Gold Cup and Stewards' Cup on Green Ruby in 1986. He celebrated his 45th birthday by riding a double at Lingfield.

1967 Alan Munro, winner of the 1991 Derby on Generous, a karate black-belt and once dubbed 'the Cocky jockey'.

DEATHS OF THE DAY

1985 Lincolnshire trainer William Barrett, aged 49.

1991 Billy Parvin, 86, who rode in 16 (second only to Michael Scudamore's 17) consecutive Grand Nationals – best placing, runner-up in 1935.

1995 Murray Lindley, champion trainer in Zimbabwe, died in a car crash near Harare.

FIRST OF THE DAY

1992 Gay Kelleway took time off from regaling *Sunday Sport* 'readers' with her tips to celebrate her first winner as an owner, Aberfoyle, at Lingfield.

15 JANUARY

SIGNIFICANT EVENT
2009 Set to collect over £200,000 for his £400 Tote Super7 wager, pro punter Dave Nevison was cheering Topless home at Taunton when, with yards to run, jockey James Davies, 24, – son of Hywel – fell off. 'I don't want to start slagging off the jockey, but he could have just sat on it and it would have won' said Nevison, slagging off the jockey.

STRANGEST EVENT
1998 There was no trophy for connections of Indian Arrow, winner of the Lillo Lumb Chase at Wincanton, to receive because the Queen Mother had mislaid it. She won it in 1996 with Norman Conqueror and the 1997 running was abandoned. When asked for the return of the trophy spokesman Alastair Aird admitted, 'We think as the trophy was won in the West Country it is probably at Windsor Castle.'

OTHER EVENTS
1925 Hialeah racecourse, USA, opened its doors for the first time – to 17,000 racegoers.
1945 Newmarket stable hands' wages are to rise by 10/- (50p) per week to £3 10/- reported *The Sporting Life*.
1978 Paul Webber rode his first winner, Weeny Bopper at Chepstow.
1995 Tweseldown point-to-point in Hampshire became the first meeting to take place on a Sunday with on-course betting. William Hill supplied a mobile facility for 4,000 racegoers; 83-year-old bookie Pip Sims died at the meeting.
1998 Alex Greaves rode her 200th winner, Sihafi at Lingfield.
1998 After 18 months out with diabetes, Jonathon Lower returned to the saddle, becoming the first diabetic to ride in the UK and finishing second on Martin Pipe's 2/7 favourite Totally Yours at Wincanton.
1999 Folkestone's Foreland Hurdle was delayed by 12 minutes when one of the seven runners dislodged Chris Maude and ran loose. He was caught and remounted, but bucked and kicked again, unseating Maude once more and running off. Finally withdrawn, the horse's name was... I Ain't Misbehavin.

QUOTE OF THE DAY
'Life's precious, and he was a young lad,' said Jamie Spencer after winning on Dishdasha at Great Leighs in 2009. He was wearing a black armband and waving his whip to the memory of aspiring jockey Jamie Yeates, 15, who was stabbed to death a week earlier, and who rode for the trainer of the winner, Alison Thorpe (see 8 January).

BIRTHDAYS
1935 George Renilson, owner-trainer of the 1978 Scottish National winner, King Con.
1944 Trainer Robert Armstrong, whose Moorestyle and Never So Bold were probably his biggest stars.

DEATHS OF THE DAY
1992 Argentinian-born trainer Angel Penna Snr, who was based in France and responsible for 1974 Arc winner Allez France, aged 68.
1995 Rubstic, the first Scottish-trained (by John Leadbetter) winner of the Grand National (at 25/1 in 1979).

CELEBRITIES OF THE DAY
Actor James Nesbitt, owner of the winning hurdler, Riverside Theatre, trained by Nicky Henson was born today in 1965. Twenty years earlier Princess Michael of Kent, an owner with Barry Hills, was born.

16 JANUARY

SIGNIFICANT EVENT
2009 The racing world was shocked as Britain's newest racecourse, Great Leighs, having staged just 48 fixtures, was placed into administration, and future meetings cancelled.

STRANGEST EVENT
1995 Raahin became one of the few dead horses to win a race. He actually 'died' for six minutes whilst under anaesthetic in February 1994, but today won a Fontwell handicap hurdle, aged ten.

OTHER EVENTS
1987 William Hill announced they woould no longer sponsor the Dewhurst Stakes.

1991 As Iraq prepared for war, and the final deadline for the country to pull out of Kuwait passed, the Iraqi authorities permitted racing to take place in Baghdad.

1992 Deep Flash became the first runner to be declared a non-runner for betting purposes after the 150/1 shot refused to race at Taunton having come under orders.

1993 Sprinter, Schillaci set the Australian 1000m record of 55s in Australian $60,000 Rubiton Stakes at Sandown.

1994 Suzhou, a 4yo debutant, recorded the greatest ever winning margin in German history when scoring by 42 lengths in a Dortmund Flat race.

1999 Amateur rider Keith Loads wed Kate Heynes at Lingfield, then contested a race named in honour of the wedding day. He finished tailed off on 25/1 shot Badrinath – having put up 18lb overweight.

QUOTE OF THE DAY
'If this had happened on grass it would have been unbelievable, but because it is Fibresand people think it's a fluke. I don't.' Trainer David Barron reflects on Alex Greaves – without a winner before December – taking her tally to nine winners from 14 rides at Southwell with a double on this day in 1989, making her the track's leading jockey.

BIRTHDAYS
1941 Ivan Allan, former champion trainer in Singapore.

1969 Jockey-turned-TV racing pundit Norman Williamson.

DEATH OF THE DAY
1983 Frank Cundell, 73. He sent out Crudwell to win 50 races on the Flat, over hurdles and fences – including the 1956 Welsh Grand National under Dick Francis. Crudwell placed in 32 more of his 108 races.

CELEBRITY OF THE DAY
1959 Radio and racecourse TV presenter Rupert Bell, born today.

17 JANUARY

SIGNIFICANT EVENT
2004 Tony McCoy notched up his 2,000th win over jumps in Britain on Corporate Player at Wincanton.

STRANGEST EVENT
1994 Despite an earthquake registering 6.6 on the Richter Scale in nearby Los Angeles, Santa Anita raced as usual, although 'after-shocks during the afternoon caused the press box high in the grandstand to sway.' Trainer Roger Stein's home was badly damaged – but 19,000 turned up as his Southern Truce won at 11/1.

OTHER EVENTS
1890 Swindler, Windscales and Zelotes won on the first day of two at Plumpton – and all won again the next day.
1968 Bob Champion rode his first winner, Altercation, at Plumpton.
1984 The graded stakes panel of the Thoroughbred Owners and Breeders Association announced that all seven races would have Grade 1 status at the inaugural Breeders' Cup Championship later in the year.
1970 Il Tempo, seven, set the 2m world record time of 3m 16.75sec carrying 130lb (9st 4lb) at Trentham, NZ.
1988 John Reid appointed stable jockey to Vincent O'Brien.

QUOTE OF THE DAY
'If you'd been beaten on an odds-on favourite, some of those fellas were ready to dig your mother up out of the grave and throw her at you,' recalled Ted Walsh of his days riding at Leopardstown. On this day in 1991, he had his first winner as a trainer, with Roc de Prince at Gowran Park.

BIRTHDAYS
1916 Sir David Llewellyn, who was far better known as *The Sporting Life* columnist 'Jack Logan'.
1939 North Yorkshire trainer Sarah – known as Sally – Hall. Winner of the Newmarket Town Plate twice as an amateur rider, she began training in 1969, with Hallgate, Cool Decision and Key To My Heart amongst her best.
1962 Tony Mullins, Irish jump jockey-turned-trainer, who rode the great mare Dawn Run to a sequence of wins but lost the ride in the Champion Hurdle and Gold Cup to Jonjo O'Neill.

DEATHS OF THE DAY
1987 Graham Burrows, a stable lad for Michael Dickinson, killed in a car crash.
1993 Northern owner Clifford Atkinson, 78. He bred his own runners and had horses for 30 years. Lady Mere was sold to Robert Sangster and won the Princess Elizabeth Stakes.

CELEBRITY OF THE DAY
1945 BBC rugby union correspondent Ian Robertson, born this day. He retained an oval ball link when naming his runners Rugby Special and Twickenham, both winners, the latter 11 times.

18 JANUARY

SIGNIFICANT EVENT
2009 Tony McCoy rode his 3,000th winner when Kilbeggan Blade won at Towcester – but the total included three on the Flat in Britain and six more on the level in Ireland.

STRANGEST EVENT
1992 Judge Jonathan Dimsdale confirmed 6/4 favourite Major Ivor as the winner at Catterick – only to change his mind minutes later and give it to 8/1 shot Blackdown.

OTHER EVENTS
1952 France's popular Tierce bet was launched: punters had to find first, second and third in a weekly race.
1988 One of the greats, Yves St Martin, who won the 1963 Derby on Relko, retired after two rides in San Francisco.
1991 Nashwan's first foal, a chestnut colt out of Ashayer, was born at Shadwell Stud, Norfolk at 10pm.
1991 Alex Greaves became the first woman to ride a four-timer in Britain when she did it at Southwell. A 212/1 accumulator, all trained by David Barron.
1993 Her trainer John Hill and another bidder both offered £4,011 for Southwell claimer winner Nikki Noo Noo – lots were drawn and Hill won.
1994 Bobby Elliott, 52, retired from the saddle with over 1,000 Flat winners while jump jockey Hywel Davies (won the Grand National on Last Suspect at 50/1) did likewise with 761 winners – only to make a quick return (see 17 March).
1995 Richard Dunwoody was given a record 30-day ban for 'careless riding; intentional interference' in a Uttoxeter race 12 days earlier. It was the longest ban for an offence since Lester Piggott got three months in 1954.
1996 Martin Pipe completed his tenth consecutive century of winners with a Taunton double.
2008 Three-times champion jump jockey Richard (born Thomas) Dunwoody conquered new territory as he reached the South Pole 49 days after setting out on the 650-mile expedition along with US explorer Doug Stoup. It was the 44th birthday of the man who would contest Strictly Come Dancing in 2009.

QUOTE OF THE DAY
'I just think it's a load of bo**ocks,' declared Richard Dunwoody, dismissing, with the confidence of a champion, criticism of his riding in 1994.

BIRTHDAYS
1947 David Maitland, who won the 1975 Royal Hunt Cup on Ardoon.
1950 Beckhampton trainer Roger Charlton. He rode Pride of Kentucky to win the 1969 Kim Muir Memorial at Cheltenham and won the 1990 Derby with Quest For Fame, 7/1, having received his first licence in February of that year.
1975 Xavier Aizpuru, British-born former US champion jump jockey.

DEATHS OF THE DAY
1997 Neville Crump, 86, who refused, reasonably enough, to train for bookies. Won three Aintree, five Scottish and two Welsh Nationals.
1999 Frankie Barlow, leading Flat jockey of the 1950s. He won the 1956 2,000 Guineas on 50-1 Gilles de Retz, trained by Helen Johnson Houghton (although the licence was in the name of Charles Jerdein). His wife's sister wed Frankie Durr who died a year to the day later.
2000 Frankie Durr, 74. Won two St Legers and two 2,000 Guineas and trained top sprinter Ahonoora. Amateur sailor.

CELEBRITY OF THE DAY
Carlo D'Alessio, high profile Italian owner, born on this day in 1915. Owner of consecutive 2,000 Guineas winners Bolkonski and Wollow (becoming the first Italian to own a Classic winner since 1908) and dual Ascot Gold Cup winner Le Moss. Died 5 September 1994.

19 JANUARY

SIGNIFICANT EVENT
1993 Home Secretary Ken Clarke announced that Britain's 9,400 betting shops could open until 10pm from 1 April to 31 August.

STRANGEST EVENT
1996 Controversial but brilliant Kiwi jockey Chris Johnson, who had a lengthy disciplinary record on the track and had also been jailed for driving while disqualified and refusing to give a sample, used his left elbow to halt a challenge from David Wadley. Wadley complained to stewards he had been elbowed 'eight or nine times' during a Greymouth race. Johnson was suspended for six months.

OTHER EVENTS
1957 Devon Loch, infamous for collapsing under Dick Francis with the 1956 Grand National at his mercy, broke down in the Mildmay Chase at Sandown. He still finished fourth but it was his last race.

1990 Jockey Paul Cook – with two Classic victories to his credit – injured at Doncaster in September when Madraco fell on the Flat, announced his retirement.

1994 French ruling body GIE-GALOP voted to close the Maisons-Laffitte and Chantilly tracks to save £1.2m per annum.

2006 Legendary US jockey Jerry Bailey retired aged 48 with 15 Breeders' Cup wins to his credit, and 5877 others.

2009 Cheltenham announced they would name a Festival race in honour of 15 times champion trainer Martin Pipe. 'Martin is, quite simply, a legend' said course MD, Edward Gillespie.

2009 Uttoxeter racecourse announced discounted admission to members of the British armed forces, after the track signed up to the 'Value for Valour' campaign.

QUOTE OF THE DAY
'It ain't right. I know I ain't did it', but Sylvester Carmouche was a lone voice as the jockey was banned from this day in 1990 until April, after stewards ruled that he had hidden his mount in thick fog for a circuit of a race at Delta Downs, before rejoining on 23/1 Landing Officer and winning by 24 lengths.

BIRTHDAYS
1940 Chris Collins, owner and rider of prolific hunter chaser Credit Call with 37 wins. Old Etonian Collins was the first Brit for over 50 years to win the gruelling Czech 'Pardubice' Chase, on Stephen's Society.

1951 Jump jockey-turned-trainer Martin Blackshaw, who rode 300-odd winners in the UK before moving to France to become 1978 champion. He turned to training in 1980 and died tragically in a 1989 car crash (see 23 January).

1993 The first foal by Derby winner Generous born to Water Woo, at Newmarket's Stetchworth Park Stud.

DEATHS OF THE DAY
None recorded.

CELEBRITIES OF THE DAY
1993 Football internationals Ian Rush (Wales), Bobby Robson (England) and Jan Molby (Denmark) teamed up as their Boogie Bopper, trained by Martin Pipe, was a 9-2 winner at Folkestone.

20 JANUARY

SIGNIFICANT EVENT
1931 Golden Miller, who would win a record five Cheltenham Gold Cups, landed his first victory, an £83 Leicester maiden hurdle – amazingly, on the same day, 31 years later, the other candidate for the accolade of greatest chaser ever, Arkle, also won for the first time, 20/1, at Navan.

STRANGEST EVENT
1994 Midlothian trainer Robin Dun ended his spell on the 'cold list', sending out Coqui Lane to win at Ayr – almost 13 years after his last winner.

OTHER EVENTS
1931 Dual Gold Cup winner and Grand National runner-up, Easter Hero, won Leicester's Wigston Chase for the second successive time.

1951 Thirty-six and 40 went to post for two divisions of a Wetherby novice hurdle; 158 runners contested six races.

1987 The Jockey Club launched a campaign to introduce Sunday racing.

1988 Graham Bradley was fined a hefty £500 after dropping his hands and losing the Ludlow race he should have won on Trout Angler.

1990 Neil Graham, who took charge of Dick Hern's West Ilsley stable during his 1988 illness, sent out the first winner from his new Newmarket base, Silken Lines at Southwell.

1992 Merrick Francis, son of Dick, sent out his last winner as a licensed trainer with his last runner, Alkinor, at Lingfield.

1993 John Fowler scored his first treble, sending out Deep Inagh, Jennycomequick and Will This Do, all at Fairyhouse.

2008 Having had horses with the top French trainer Andre Fabre since 2005, the Aga Khan removed his 30 strong team due to what the handler branded as 'operational disagreements'.

QUOTE OF THE DAY
'Balls of steel' was how trainer Eddie O'Grady described Charlie Swan's ride on 1994 Cheltenham Festival winner Time For A Run.

BIRTHDAYS
1922 Lord Hanson, who would sponsor the Derby via Ever Ready.

1931 Major Dick Hern, who won every Classic and had Brigadier Gerard, Henbit, Troy and Nashwan in his yard.

1962 Harry 'The Dog' Findlay, mega punter, and part owner of Denman and many more.

1968 Trainer Charlie Swan, nine times Irish champion jockey, partner of triple Champion Hurdler Istabraq.

DEATH OF THE DAY
1995 Ivan Parke, 86, top US jockey-turned-trainer, who sent out 1945 Kentucky Derby winner Hoop Jr.

CELEBRITY OF THE DAY
Racing was cancelled from this day in 1936 until 29 January to mark the death of King George V.

21 JANUARY

SIGNIFICANT EVENT
2006 Paul Nicholls became the first jumps trainer to win six races on one card when he achieved the feat at Wincanton.

STRANGEST EVENT
2000 Having never really existed, Charles Croft died aged 87. The name was an alias used by pioneering racing writer Dorothy Laird when she worked at the Racing Information Bureau. She helped found the Lady Jockeys' Association in 1972, becoming President. It merged with its male equivalent in 1976.

OTHER EVENTS
1950 Lord Mildmay of Flete's Cromwell won the Prince's Chase at Sandown, but four months later champion amateur Mildmay, who rode Cromwell, went missing after going for a morning swim, never to be seen again. The Prince's Chase was renamed the Mildmay Memorial Chase in 1952 – and won by Cromwell.
1983 First time over hurdles, Desert Orchid fell at Kempton, lay winded and was down for 12 minutes. He got up and the rest is history.
1992 Adrian Maguire was disqualified 12 times in a day – after the Jockey Club confirmed he had been incorrectly claiming 3lb when riding the 'winners'.
1996 Master Smudge, awarded the 1980 Cheltenham Gold Cup and once sold to travellers for a case of whisky, died aged 25.
1998 Footballer-turned-trainer Micky Quinn sent out his first winner, Miss Dangerous, 3/1, at Wolverhampton. Football commentator John Motson sponsored a race on the same card for his wife's birthday.
2008 Unusually for a trainer, Don Cantillon claimed to have won £30,000 after his 9/4-shot My Mirasol won at Wolverhampton.

2008 The first race at Kempton was delayed after geese had to be removed from the track, prompting commentator Mike Cattermole to tell racegoers: 'Some geese have decided to stage a sit-in.'

QUOTE OF THE DAY
'470 winners and 5,000 losers.' A self-deprecating description of his career by jockey-turned-TV commentator/writer Richard Pitman, former husband of Jenny, born today in 1943. Best known for riding a loser – magnificent front-running jumper Crisp, narrowly beaten when Red Rum won his first National in 1973. Recreations – 'dog walking and water-skiing' but not, we hope, at the same time.

BIRTHDAYS
1917 The owner of Bollin Eric, Bollin Emily, Bollin Knight, Bollin Patrick and Royal Bollin – not, strangely enough, Mr Bollin, but Sir Neil Westbrook.
1937 Francois Boutin, trainer of wonder horse Arazi, as well as Nureyev and Miesque.
1959 Flat jockey Walter Wharton (25 winners in 1977). He once described his hobbies as 'eating and cigars' – not, one trusts, together.

DEATHS OF THE DAY
1968 Henry Morgan Bletsoe, 84, who rode 66/1 shot Rubio to win the 1908 Grand National.
2005 US handler Ivor Balding, 96, uncle of English trainers Ian and Toby, and farm manager for wealthy US owner C V Whitney in the 1930s.

CELEBRITY OF THE DAY
2003 Equestrian artist Lionel Hamilton-Renwick, whose painting of the Queen's 1954 King George VI & Queen Elizabeth Stakes winner Aureole was hung in Buckingham Palace, died aged 85.

22 JANUARY

SIGNIFICANT EVENT
1993 Amrullah, feted as the least successful horse in training, and without a win in 74 races, was led into the winner's enclosure at Kempton to mark his retirement.

STRANGEST EVENT
1994 Lady Broker won at Wolverhampton but jockey Danny Wright had weighed out 6lb light due to a mix-up over a penalty incurred for winning at Southwell the day before. Stewards knew before the race but decided it was 'too late to take action'. The horse remained the winner for betting purposes but was later disqualified.

OTHER EVENTS
1819 Four runners contested a chase for gentleman riders at Lismore, Ireland. All fell at least once, the winner four times.

1972 Geoff Prowse beat Frankie Dettori to it, riding seven winners from as many mounts at Elwick, Tasmania, Australia.

1991 Coalite became sponsors of the St Leger.

1993 British girl Georgina Frost rode a 31/1 treble at Aqueduct, USA.

1993 Kent Desormeaux won on his first ride back in the saddle, at Santa Anita, just a month after sustaining 14 skull fractures at Hollywood Park.

1993 Prime Mover won at Southwell – the horse was minus one hip, carrying a hole where the left one had been.

2008 Perhaps owner John Fretwell summed up the standard of the all weather racing at Southwell in the depths of winter when, after his So Sublime won the 7f seller. he sold him

and commented: 'I've had enough on him to cover my expenses. It was a poor race and thanks to a good trainer we've won a moderate race with a moderate horse'. I think he was happy.

2008 Cheltenham announced the 138th running of the Festival's 4-miler as the Peter O'Sullevan National Hunt Chase in honour of the legendary broadcaster.

QUOTE OF THE DAY
'I obviously feel let down to some extent.' Remarkably understated response to being sacked in 1990 as stable jockey to his father Barry, by Michael Hills, born today in 1963.

BIRTHDAYS
1948 Yorkshire trainer Thomas Tate, who trained Ask Tom.

1963 Jockey twins Michael and Richard, sons of trainer Barry Hills. Michael rode his first winner some ten weeks before Richard, both in 1979.

1991 69 today, West Virginian jockey Willie Clark was still riding – with 1,141 winners from 10,613 mounts, the first in 1947.

DEATH OF THE DAY
1991 Tommy Lowrey, 79, who rode one of the greatest ever 'coincidence' winners, backed by numerous ex-RAF personnel coming so soon after the end of the War, 50/1 shot Airborne in the 1946 Derby.

CELEBRITY OF THE DAY
1940 Actor/owner John Hurt, born today, who also starred in the 1984 movie Champions about jockey Bob Champion and the Grand National-winning horse Aldaniti.

23 JANUARY

SIGNIFICANT EVENT
1795 Admiral Henry Rous was born, one of the great 'dictators' of the English turf. He was elected a Jockey Club steward in 1838. Published *On the Laws and Practice of Horse Racing* in 1850.

STRANGEST EVENT
1993 The Jimmy George Final Fling Hurdle at Warwick was the first race named in honour of a stag night – that of the advertising manager of racing magazine *Pacemaker*.

OTHER EVENTS
1907 W Kirk rode four winners at Wairoa County, New Zealand to take his winning streak to 11 straight victories.
1980 Trainer Mark Tompkins saddled his first winner, Timmatemma, at Market Rasen.
1982 G'day for sure for Aussie trainer Colin Hayes who saddled ten winners in one day – seven at Victoria Park, Adelaide, three at Caulfield.
1992 1,470 days since seeing a racecourse last, Barry Window, partnered by Peter Scudamore for Martin Pipe, won at Newton Abbot. On the same day jockey Jason Titley rode his first double, on Grand Habit and Bishops Hall at Gowran Park.
1994 Pat Day, 40, became the tenth jockey to ride 6,000 winners, on Miss Popsnorkle at Oaklawn Park, USA.
1997 Possibly getting out at the right time – 29-year-old Roger Marley retired having ridden over 100 winners, never having missed a ride or broken a bone.
2001 Nintendo revealed details of the Derby-based horse racing Game Boy product.
2006 Maywood Park, Illinois racetrack president Duke Johnston predicted the end of the road for the 60 year old course after proposals to permit restaurant and bar gambling in the district were advanced, calling it: 'The final nail in the coffin'. It was still going at the end of 2009.

QUOTE OF THE DAY
1993 *'Their back ends are similar,'* declared owner Tony Hill after his Ann Hill – named after his wife – won at Lingfield.

BIRTHDAYS
1919 Owner-jockey Dick Smalley.
1940 Everton footballer Brian Labone, who called his first racehorse Goodison.

DEATHS OF THE DAY
1918 Jacob Pincus, 79, died in the USA. As a Newmarket trainer in 1881 his Iroquois, Fred Archer up, became the first American-bred Derby winner.
1989 Martin Blackshaw, 38, jockey-turned-trainer in France, killed in a car crash near Chantilly.
1995 Irish trainer Barry Kelly, 35, with fiancée Sandra Clifford, in a tragic car crash two weeks before their scheduled marriage. His Eliogarty won the 1993 Christie's Foxhunters' Chase at Cheltenham.

CELEBRITY OF THE DAY
1998 Clare Balding made her debut as main presenter of BBC TV's racing coverage, at Ascot.

24 JANUARY

SIGNIFICANT EVENT
2009 Kevin Tobin closed his career as a jockey with winner Mr Big at Uttoxeter – prior to departing for the USA to train as an addiction counsellor.

STRANGEST EVENT
1994 Betting shop customer Terry Garrett, 50, suffered concussion after glass fell out of the TV he was watching in his Mannings shop in Bethnal Green, London, and hit him on the head.

OTHER EVENTS
1948 BBC televised racing began with three jump races broadcast from Sandown.

1959 *The Irish Field* magazine held a vote to nominate the most popular horse in training – Havasnack won from Roddy Owen.

1994 Raymylette was the first winner owned by Madeleine, wife of Andrew Lloyd Webber, scoring at Leicester 48 hours after her Joe Gillis died at Kempton and a year after Al Mutahm died at Newbury.

1996 Peter Easterby's 45-year training career came to an end as the handler's Balhernoch won at Sedgefield.

1974 US jockey Chris McCarron finished last on his first career mount – then rode a record 546 winners during the season.

1988 Stable lads' basic weekly pay broke through the £100 barrier for the first time.

1990 Having retired in 1971, trainer Jim Dreaper returned to the saddle on Sir Bumble at Fairyhouse – to finish 23rd of 25 in the bumper.

1991 After a ten-week lay-off for a broken leg, Peter Scudamore returned to win on Outside Edge at Newton Abbot.

1991 Unusual for 11yo mare Hopeful Waters, who gave birth to a Monsanto colt on the same day as Lingfield winner Comedy River became the first of her progeny to win.

1992 Quest For Fame won a race at Santa Anita to become the first Derby winner of the century and the first for 97 years – since Isinglass in 1895 – to win as a 5yo.

1998 Optician Alistair Dinsmore landed a probably unprecedented double for an owner as his Prince Ashleigh won at Wolverhampton and his Al Shaab won at Kenilworth, South Africa.

2009 68yo New Yorker, John Coste won $500,000 as he was crowned Daily Racing Form Handicapper (Punter) of the Year, with an overall 'profit' of $228 overall on his selections.

QUOTE OF THE DAY
'The longer a young rider goes on without a winner, the better. Too much success early on and they begin to think their job's easy,' said jump jockey Hywel Davies some years after he'd broken his own duck on this day in 1977 on well named Mr Know All.

BIRTHDAYS
1915 Gainsborough, the first Derby winner owned by a woman – Lady James (!) Douglas – was foaled.

1928 Peter Twite. Cheap shot, yes, but was there ever a more appropriately named Jockey Club controller of rules than he?

1954 Trainer John McConnochie, former assistant to Fred and Mercy Rimell.

1988 Derby winner Slip Anchor's first colt born, out of Doumayna.

DEATH OF THE DAY
1956 Bahram, undefeated Triple Crown winner of 1935, died in Argentina.

CELEBRITY OF THE DAY
Racehorse owner, presenter of Zoo Time and 'Horsewatching' author Dr Desmond Morris, born today in 1928.

25 JANUARY

SIGNIFICANT EVENT
1993 On-course physios were introduced to the racecourse for the first time as Mary Bromiley and Grant Downe were at Leicester to administer to jockeys as part of a Jockey Club experiment.

STRANGEST EVENT
1983 Trainer Nelson Guest had to stump up £125 for a cab to drive from Newmarket to Chepstow after his Noblissimo arrived without his passport. The taxi made it in time for John Francome to compete in – and win – a 3m hurdle.

OTHER EVENTS
1941 Cidade Jardim racecourse opened in Sao Paolo, Brazil.

1990 Yorkshire trainer Tim Etherington had a lucky escape when a 50ft pine tree crashed through his roof as gales swept the country, demolishing the room he was in. Seamus O'Neill also got lucky returning from abandoned Taunton when a tree crushed his car.

1994 Rapporteur's 18th win at Lingfield equalled Tempering's post-war record of 18 Southwell wins.

1994 Carl Lewellyn became the first jockey to wear a sponsor's logo on breeches and boots when partnering Earth Summit at Chepstow, wearing advertising for trainer Nigel Twiston-Davies' Grange Hill yard.

1996 The Thatcher Limited Stakes at Lingfield was won by the 7/2 chance, Carrolls Marc.

1997 'My wife got a ride on our honeymoon', revealed champion jockey Richard Dunwoody on Channel 4's Morning Line – meaning to explain how Carol had ridden a winner while they were in Jersey.

1997 Chris Maude went out to ride Daraydan for Martin Pipe at Cheltenham with a sign attached to the back of his silks reading 'Please get me to the church on time'. He finished unplaced before dashing off to nuptials with fiancée Clare 'Dolly' Pegna.

2008 Brave Inca, the 2006 Champion Hurdle winner, returned from injury, aged 11, to win the Irish Champion Hurdle at Leopardstown at 11/4 under Ruby Walsh for trainer, Colm Murphy.

QUOTE OF THE DAY
'It's not a tragedy you know. Far from it. There's no doubt I'll bounce back. It's very silly of people to talk of retirement. I'm young at heart and have many years left', declared Kieren Fallon, after being banned from riding for 18 months by France Galop on this day in 2008 after failing a drugs test.

BIRTHDAYS
1947 West Country trainer Malcolm Saunders, whose Indian Maiden won 15 races and Repertory 13.

1954 Trainer James Toller. Must like a row, as Duck Row and Teapot Row were amongst the best from a stable which has won the Irish 2,000 Guineas, July Cup and Wokingham.

DEATHS OF THE DAY
1992 Jump jockey Tommy Cullen, 86, who rode Copper Court to win the 1932 Grand National.

2002 Amateur jockey Dick Saunders, 68, who became the oldest winning rider of the race at 48 when winning the 1982 Grand National on Grittar, 7-1, the first clear favourite to win for 22 years.

CELEBRITY OF THE DAY
Former Arsenal and Everton striker Francis Jeffers teamed up with fellow Arsenal player Ray Parlour and golfer Ian Poulter to become an owner; born this day in 1981.

26 JANUARY

SIGNIFICANT EVENT
1986 The somewhat ill-fated but talented Royal Gait raced for the first time – fourth over 1m1f in Seville, Spain. Went on to 'win' the Ascot Gold Cup in 1988 but was disqualified; then survived a stewards' inquiry to win the 1991 Champion Hurdle; dropped dead after a Leopardstown hurdle in 1992.

STRANGEST EVENT
2009 Kempton MD Amy Starkey announced a jet-ski would be moored in the course's lake in response to an incident when a horse broke loose, ran through the rails and plunged into the water, having to be rescued.

OTHER EVENTS
1892 Manifesto fell at Manchester in his first chase but soon got the hang of things – he went on to run eight times in the Grand National, winning in 1897 and 1899, also finishing third three times, fourth and sixth, falling once.
1938 Two Champion Hurdlers won under 12st 7lb at Newbury – Victor Norman in a chase and Free Fare in a handicap hurdle.
1968 Crack US jockey Bill Shoemaker broke his right thigh at Santa Anita; he was out for over a year. On the same day the first three home in the 5½f sprint at Hialeah were former British-trained runners, Polyfoto (who'd been with Eddie Reavey); On Your Mark (Sam Armstrong) and Reet Lass (Snowy Gray).
1970 There was a riot at Calcutta racecourse after a hot favourite was beaten by an outsider. Racing was cancelled for a fortnight to repair damage.
1983 Stuart Murless, whose Nocturnal Spree won the 1975 1,000 Guineas, retired aged 65.
1994 Martin Pipe entered a record 17

horses for the Grand National – of which Miinnehoma did best when winning.
2008 7/10 favourite, Pocket Power, ridden by Bernard Fayd'Herbe for Leicester-born trainer Mike Bass, became the first horse since Politician in 1978 and 79 and only second ever to win consecutive 10f J and B Met race in the 125 year history of Kenilworth, South Africa, event.

QUOTE OF THE DAY
'Sue Lawley explained that no other living creature is allowed – I opted for snorkelling equipment instead.' Peter Scudamore chose favourite horse Sabin du Loir as his luxury item when appearing on Desert Island Discs – he might also have nominated Capability Brown, on whom he fell three out when well clear on the 8/15 novice chase favourite at Chepstow this day in 1993. Remounted, the horse blundered again at the last, but still won the nine-runner event.

BIRTHDAYS
1924 Jockey Johnny Greenaway.
1964 Trainer David Loder, who handled Sheikh Mohammed's favourite horse, Dubai Millennium.

DEATHS OF THE DAY
1994 US jockey Ron Hanson, who had been reported missing, was found dead.
1996 Trainer Eric Cousins, 74, found dead on holiday in Barbados. He won the Ayr Gold Cup three times and was Robert Sangster's first trainer.

CELEBRITIES OF THE DAY
Ice hockey star Wayne Gretzky, born today in 1961, part owner of 1990 Arc winner Saumarez; while on this day in 2009 actor James Nesbitt was at Kempton to see his Riverside Theatre win a hurdle.

27 JANUARY

SIGNIFICANT EVENT

2009 'Ten years ago in the book *A Century of Champions* I ranked Fred Winter as the greatest jump jockey since 1900, with Tony McCoy at number seven. Now McCoy is clearly the greatest of all time', wrote *Racing Post* 'anorak'/racing historian John Randall.

STRANGEST EVENT

1994 Lingfield's Thatcher Stakes was won by jockey A. Tory.

OTHER EVENTS

1871 The Royal College of Surgeons was presented with a skeleton of the great Eclipse by the New Veterinary College of Edinburgh, which had paid £105 for it.

1907 Organised horse racing began on the frozen lake at St Moritz.

1934 As a result of the prevailing financial situation the Kentucky Derby's added prize money, which had stood for 12 years at $50,000, was to be cut to $30,000, announced race director Col. Matt Winn, 72, who had seen every running since its 1875 inception.

1967 Confusion in a novice hurdle at Windsor when two fell at the first and set off the wrong way round the track, meeting the rest of the field head on and bringing down three more.

1967 The first UK victory by a Russian-bred horse when the Peter Cazalet-trained Sirius III won a Windsor hurdle.

1990 Husband and wife Patrick and Anthea Farrell both contested a Doncaster chase – he was second, she pulled up.

1993 Amenable was withdrawn from the Lincoln in a fit of pique by trainer David Barron, who didn't even own the 1991 winner, claimed for 10,500gns by current owner Andrew Millar and moved to handler Roger Spicer after a Southwell race. Miffed Barron was able to use an arcane Jockey Club rule which meant the horse's entries were still under his control.

1994 Chantilly racecourse, earmarked for closure, was reprieved.

1995 Southwell's meeting was switched to Wolverhampton, as approach roads were affected by adverse weather conditions. The switch was made with just 24 hours' notice – the first time such a thing had happened in Britain in that timescale.

1997 Married two days earlier, Chris Maude interrupted his honeymoon to ride at Plumpton winning on Pomme Secret.

QUOTE OF THE DAY

'It was just an ordinary handicap, but he did it in an amazing way. Conduit has come from being a bridesmaid that day to become a king.' When the horse won a US Eclipse Award on this day in 2009, Peter Reynolds, general manager for Ballymacoll Stud, got his genders in a twist whilst commending Conduit's rise from a 0-105 handicap to 2008 Breeders' Cup glory.

BIRTHDAYS

1949 Former champion jump jockey Graham Thorner. He won the 1972 Grand National on his guvnor Capt. Tim Forster's Well To Do.

1965 Cornelius Lysaght, BBC radio racing correspondent.

DEATHS OF THE DAY

1993 Lady Murless, nee Gwen Carlow, 77, wife of trainer Sir Noel. She also trained – her first winner was chaser Golden Crown in 1934.

2006 Syd Dale, aged 90, the first trainer to handle great chaser Mill House. His Plummer's Plain won the 1960 Whitbread Gold Cup.

CELEBRITY OF THE DAY

Chester Barne – youngest English table tennis player champion ever in 1963, representing his country 250 times – who became assistant to Martin Pipe, was born this day in 1947.

28 JANUARY

SIGNIFICANT EVENT

1961 Mill House made his debut at Naas – finishing fourth. He would go on to win the Oberstown Hurdle there, then improved to be one of the all-time great chasers, winning the 1963 Gold Cup and taking on Arkle in a number of stirring battles.

STRANGEST EVENT

1993 Winner of Lingfield's Albert Handicap was the 3/1 favourite – Albert.

OTHER EVENTS

1988 Lester's wife, Susan Piggott, was granted a trainer's licence.

1992 Two-year-old Arazi was awarded top weight of 9st 4lb in the US Experimental Free Handicap – 1lb higher than legendary Secretariat and the second highest rating ever, behind 1942's Count Fleet who won the Kentucky Derby the following year, who was rated at 9st 6lb.

1995 Zadok landed a A$600,000 plunge when winning at Randwick, Sydney, backed down from 150/1 pre race. The trainer later revealed the horse, listed as a colt, had been gelded shortly before the race.

2008 Liberal Democrat MP Mike Hancock tabled a written question in the House of Commons calling for jockeys to be banned from using the whip. He said: 'I feel the police should be looking into cases of excessive use of the whip by jockeys.'

2010 Scheduled date for the first meeting of Dubai racecourse, Meydan.

QUOTE OF THE DAY

'When he was found by his owner Jacques Van't Hart he was lying on a thin carpet of wet snow, a barely moving little black shape contrasting with the white background.' Henrietta Knight, recalling this date in 1995 when future triple Gold Cup winner Best Mate was born in Co. Meath.

BIRTHDAYS

1904 Leading US jumps owner Mrs Miles Valentine whose Cancottage won the Maryland Hunt Cup three times; while Deaux Coup and Down First both won the US Grand National.

1919 Paddy Mullins, Irish trainer of Champion Hurdle and Gold Cup winner Dawn Run.

1934 Trainer Ray Peacock, who shortly before his 74th birthday broke a seven-year losing run when Komreyev Star won at Southwell, on 17 January 2008.

1943 George McGrath, dual Irish champion jockey in 1965 and 1970.

1962 Jockey Tony Clark, Ile de Chypre's partner when they won the Juddmonte International in 1989.

1964 Jockey Martin Bosley, who won for the first time when Bit Bent scored at Folkestone in May 1980.

DEATHS OF THE DAY

1989 Dunfermline, 15, the Queen's 1977 Oaks and St Leger winner, of a twisted gut.

2008 Trainer John (middle name Read) Bosley, 77, whose Eyecatcher was twice third in the Grand National in 1976 and 1977. He won the 1954 Aintree Fox Hunters' Chase on Dark Stranger.

FIRST OF THE DAY

1982 Jeff King's Stephouette was a 50/1 winner on an objection at Huntingdon to get the former successful jockey's training career off the mark.

29 JANUARY

SIGNIFICANT EVENT
1969 The first swimming pool for racehorses opened at Caulfield racetrack in Australia, where the £12,000 training aid was 300ft long by 6ft wide and 9ft deep.

STRANGEST EVENT
2009 Nick Luck used a word rhyming with his surname when Racing UK coverage switched from Wincanton to Dubai, catching the presenter off guard as he exclaimed 'f***ing Nad Al Sheba'.

OTHER EVENTS
1925 All four runners in the Ringmer Novice Chase at Plumpton refused. Race voided.

1980 Ben de Haan's first winner as a jockey was Arctic Princess at Chepstow.

1982 The Irish Turf Club passed a rule allowing horses considered not to have run on their merits to be suspended for up to three months.

1993 Brr – not before time, central heating was fitted into Doncaster's weighing room.

1993 The first Racing Hall of Fame was launched at Cheltenham. Inductees included the Queen Mother, Vincent O'Brien, Fulke Walwyn, Fred and Mercy Rimell, Golden Miller, Arkle, Sir Ken, Dick Francis, Dawn Run, Jonjo O'Neill and Fred Winter.

1994 Richard Dunwoody became the fourth jump jockey to reach 1,000 winners, on Flakey Dove at Cheltenham, after Stan Mellor, John Francome and Peter Scudamore.

1994 Vet Harry Hobson of Hertfordshire had his first winner, Who's Next at Ampton point-to-point, 26 years after becoming an owner.

2008 Johnny Murtagh was unveiled as Aidan O'Brien and Coolmore's new retained jockey.

2008 Jockeys Paul Doe and Adrian McCarthy began wearing black instead of white breeches on the all-weather. 'They are 100 per cent waterproof and windproof and you don't feel the kickback through them,' said fashion guru Doe.

QUOTE OF THE DAY
'If Jesus Christ rode his flaming donkey like you just rode that horse, then he deserved to be crucified.' Great trainer Fred Rimell, inducted into the first Racing Hall of Fame at Cheltenham on this day in 1993, gave then amateur jockey Jim Old a hard time.

BIRTHDAYS
1879 Equine artist Gilbert Holliday, who became famous for painting horses from unusual angles and would also paint sitting in a saddle!

1937 Nick Embiricos, owner of Grand National winner Aldaniti.

1965 Jump jockey Dale McKeown.

1971 Clare Balding, BBC face of racing and champion lady rider of 1990.

1989 *The Directory of the Turf* would have you believe he was born in November, but Willie Carson's jockey grandson William was in fact born on this day.

DEATHS OF THE DAY
1993 Sir John Carew, 90, oldest member of the Jockey Club and owner of 1950 Valentine Chase winner at Liverpool, Prince Brownie.

1997 Jack Leach, jockey and author of *Sods I Have Cut On The Turf*, who rode 20/1 shot Adam's Apple to win 1927 2,000 Guineas, aged 70.

2007 Barbaro, the 2006 Kentucky Derby winner, lost his gallant fight for life after an eight-month battle to overcome injuries sustained in the Preakness Stakes.

CELEBRITY OF THE DAY
John Forsythe, actor, director at Hollywood Park, Eclipse awards host, racehorse owner/breeder and 'Dynasty' star, born in 1918. Also outspoken professor Germaine Greer, once an owner with Mark Tompkins, born 1939.

30 JANUARY

SIGNIFICANT EVENT
1976 Muriel Naughton was the first woman to ride over fences in Britain, finishing sixth on Ballycasey at Ayr.

STRANGEST EVENT
1891 Bookies were outlawed on-course in New Zealand after a meeting at Takapuna, where 29 paid £12 10/- fee to operate. The last race was won by Sir Artigel, ridden by Albert Whittaker, who was killed shortly after in a race fall at Peaeroa.

OTHER EVENTS
1956 Triple Champion Hurdler Sir Ken lugged 12st 8lb to victory in a Nottingham chase.

1982 Stuart Shilston rode his first winner for the Queen Mother, Sindebele (F. Walwyn) at Cheltenham. On the same day there, Cima gave trainer Captain Jim Wilson his 150th winner.

1990 Alex Greaves became the first woman to ride a Flat-race treble at a single meeting, at Southwell.

1991 The only trainer whose name is a London Underground station saddled his first winner, Dramatic Event, at Windsor – well done Stan Moore.

1993 Leanne Isherwood became the first Aussie woman to ride the winner of New Zealand's prestigious Wellington Cup when partnering outsider Dancing Lord to win £67,797 event.

2009 Canadian Pari-Mutuel Agency announced it would 'implement testing for veterinary approved anabolic steroids' from June 1, 2009. Trainers were reminded of 'thresholds and withdrawal' guidance for pre-race use of substances.

QUOTE OF THE DAY
'If I have to limp a little it's worth a trade-off for being able to ride', declared Julie Krone after nine months off from an ankle injury in 1994, showing she was the real deal as a rider. the 4ft 10in rider also made her public debut on well named runner-up Tiny Star at Tampa Bay Downs this day in 1981.

BIRTHDAYS
1939 Trainer Nick Gaselee. He won 90+ races as an amateur rider, and won the 1992 Grand National with Party Politics.

1948 Trainer Lord Huntingdon, namely William Hastings-Bass, alias Lord William Edwards Robin Hood.

1951 Trainer Jim Dreaper, who finished second on Black Secret in the 1971 Grand National and sent out Ten Up to win the 1975 Cheltenham Gold Cup. Serial winner of the Irish Grand National.

1966 Newmarket jockey Michael Tebbutt.

DEATHS OF THE DAY
1917 Galtee More, Triple Crown winner of 1897, died in Germany.

1972 Trainer Harvey Leader, months after retiring. He rode on the Flat from the age of 12 and trained the 1920 St Leger winner Caligula.

2001 Cyril Mitchell, 85. Trained both dual-purpose Triumph Hurdle winner, Attivo and sprinter Be Friendly for Sir Peter O'Sullevan.

2007 Irish trainer Con Collins, 82. His Princess Pati won the 1984 Irish Oaks. His daughter Tracey took over the licence.

FIRST OF THE DAY
1987 Jonjo O'Neill saddled his first winner when Shelbourne won at Ayr.

31 JANUARY

SIGNIFICANT EVENT
2008 England striker Michael Owen spent 150,000gns on 4yo filly Blue Rocket, previously owned by Newcastle team-mate Joey Barton and a daughter of Rock of Gibraltar, a big-time winner for Sir Alex Ferguson.

STRANGEST EVENT
1991 Riding 30/1 shot Quilma in a Flat race at Gulfstream Park, Julie Krone had to ask her mount to jump an unexpected obstacle – a fox sunning itself on the track. That may have cost them the race, which produced a record 96,751-1 trifecta dividend, as they finished second to 46-1 chance Hero's Lover with a 31/1 shot in third.

OTHER EVENTS
1883 Fred Archer, superstar jockey, wed Helen Rose, daughter of his trainer Mathew Dawson's brother, John. She died just a year later after giving birth to a daughter.
1957 Dick Francis announced his retirement from the saddle.
1984 Jockey Billy Newnes was warned off for three years because of his involvement with pro punter Harry Bardsley, who received a 15-year sentence. Newnes admitted to receiving a £1,000 'bribe' from Bardsley.
1988 Dancing Brave's first foal was born – a colt out of Lady Moon.
1997 Martin Pipe sponsored a meeting at Taunton, naming the last race the 'Am I That Difficult?' Handicap Hurdle.
2005 In only his second UK race, Kauto Star fell at Exeter, but Ruby Walsh got back on to finish second, sparking a review of remounting rules.
2008 Legendary trainer Vincent O'Brien's colours were back in the winner's enclosure as Lord Admiral, trained by his son Charles, won at Nad Al Sheba, Dubai.
2008 Conrad Allen, 48, with some 250 winners to his name, bowed out

of training. On the same day sprint specialist trainer David Chapman, 74, saddled his final runners of a 40-year career. Soba and Chaplin's Club were both prolific winners for him.
2009 An anonymous Scoop6 syndicate laid out £18,800 and won a record £1,541,739 payout.

QUOTE OF THE DAY
Unwanted publicity for the sport as a *Daily Mail* sensationalist article today in 2009 alleged: '*The racing industry is indulging in wholesale slaughter – foals are being killed at birth; mares shot in the field; pregnant horses aborted; healthy prize-winners butchered in abbatoirs.*' Zoe Brennan's article seemed to have no input from the paper's racing writers.

BIRTHDAYS
1928 Scottish-based trainer Harry Bell. His Sebastian V (1977) was one of three Scottish Grand National winners, along with Quick Reply (1972) and Astral Charmer (1981). In 1985 he was found guilty of causing unnecessary suffering to one of his horses and banned for seven months. In 1988 he was given a six-month jail sentence for similar charges.
1933 Jockey-turned-trainer Herbert Jones, who won in England, India, Sweden, Denmark and Norway. Won the 1952 Ayr Gold Cup on Vatellus, 10/1, and the Ebor on 10/1 shot Signification.
1954 Former champion lady rider Diana Grissell.

DEATH OF THE DAY
1941 Lady James Douglas, 87, the first woman to own a Derby winner – Gainsborough.

CELEBRITY OF THE DAY
Ken Barlow in Coronation Street, actor Bill Roach in real life, saw his 20/1 shot Let's Go Sabo win at Southwell this day in 1992.

1 FEBRUARY

SIGNIFICANT EVENT
1999 US philanthropist (he gave away $600m) Paul Mellon, owner/breeder of the great 1971 Derby winner, Mill Reef, died aged 91. He became a racing fan at Cambridge University. Had his first winner at Gatwick in 1936; his last at Lingfield in 1999. Arts And Letters, 1969, and Fort Marcy, 1970, were US Horses of Year for him. His colours were black, gold cross front and back.

STRANGEST EVENT
1983 Unbeaten in five starts, juvenile hurdler The Grey Bomber was electrocuted whilst out on the road near Denys Smith's stables after gales brought down electric cables, and contact between horseshoe and road surface created sparks which triggered a current. Rider Tommy Nevin was saved by his rubber-soled boots.

OTHER EVENTS
1967 David Nicholson rode a 2,952/1 four-timer at Haydock.
1986 Californian Craig Phillips won $1,906,491.90 with a 'Pick Nine' bet at Santa Anita.
1992 94 yo Fred W. Hooper, owner of 1945 Kentucky Derby winner, Hoop Jr, received the Eclipse Award of Merit.
1993 Kovalevskia completed a quick fire treble, winning over 2m on flat at Southwell, having won over hurdles at Lingfield on grass on Jan 25, and on Southwell all weather hurdle course, Jan 27.
1996 Tim Easterby took over the training licence from his father Peter, and won with Bridle Path, his second runner, in a Sedgefield novice hurdle.
1996 Frank Pasero jr set a record for a North American trainer when he saddled two winners at Gulfstream Park, to take his consecutive run of winners to ten.
2008 Russell Baze became first North American jockey to ride 10,000 winners, reaching the total on Two Step Cat at Golden Gate.
2009 Having never been there in his 30-year career, Nicky Henderson visited Musselburgh – and saddled a double with Giorgio Quercus, 11/8, and Bellvano, 1/2.

QUOTE OF THE DAY
1993 '*The work of disgruntled Taiwanese investors who have lost a fortune since the track opened,*' declared a caller to a Chinese newspaper after a bomb blast rocked Taipa racecourse in Macau.

BIRTHDAYS
1914 Trainer Ken 'The Benign Bishop' Oliver. He rode 1950 Scottish Grand National winner Sanvina and saddled five winners of the Ayr race too, but was second four times in the Aintree equivalent.
1929 Ace snapper, Gerry Cranham.
1961 Jockey Mark Rimmer, who won the 1979 Cesarewitch on Sir Michael and the 1988 Lincoln on Cuvee Charlie.

DEATHS OF THE DAY
1927 Runner-up in both the 1925 and '26 Grand Nationals, 13yo gelding Old Tay Bridge dropped dead at exercise whilst preparing for another attempt.
1995 French trainer Francois Boutin, 58. He won the 1987 1,000 Guineas (Miesque) and the 1974 (Nonoalco) and 1982 (Zino) 2,000 Guineas in England, while Miesque was a dual Breeders' Cup winner in 1987 and '88.

CELEBRITY OF THE DAY
1996 Former member of top 1960s pop band The Monkees, singer Davy Jones won for the first time as a jockey, partnering Digpast, 10/3, a recent 50th birthday present from daughter Sarah, in an amateur riders' race at Lingfield.

2 FEBRUARY

SIGNIFICANT EVENT
1999 Seventy-something owner John Stevenson watched his 10/1 shot Gunner Mac win at Musselburgh – then collapsed in the winner's enclosure with a heart attack. His heart stopped for several minutes but he was resuscitated by course doctor Britt-Marie Crawford.

STRANGEST EVENT
1993 Skeletal remains were discovered near Lexington, Kentucky, believed to be those of missing jockey James A Kratz who vanished aged 24 in 1973 having told his wife he had been offered $2,000 to pull a horse. Kratz was declared legally dead in 1980. Examination of the remains suggested blows to the head as the cause of death.

OTHER EVENTS
1968 Frank Cundell saddled Kempton treble – French Kilt and Grey Venture ridden by Stan Mellor; Rope Ladder by John Cook.
1983 The Tote announced a £1 minimum bet in all enclosures – it had been 50p since 1975.
1991 Jump jockey Richard Rowe rode his 554th and final winner, Super Sense at Sandown.
1992 Laffit Pincay rode five winners at Santa Anita to overtake Bill Shoemaker as the California track's leading rider with 2250 victories.
1997 Ireland's favourite horse, Danoli, 6/1, won the Hennessy Cognac Gold Cup at Leopardstown, beating Gold Cup winner Jodami – who suffered a career-ending injury – into second.
2007 Cheshire cleaner Agnes Haddock won £688,620 on the Tote Scoop6.
2008 Trainer Peter Grayson saddled six of the nine runners in a 5f maiden at Lingfield, winning with 40/1 shot Stoneacre Pat having indicated to punters that Stoneacre Chris was his best hope – the 20/1 shot finishing second.

QUOTE OF THE DAY
1993 *'I can't make a living out of the game any more,'* said jumps jockey Dale McKeown as he retired, aged 28 with 138 wins.

BIRTHDAYS
1941 Three-times champion jump jockey in the 1960s Terry Biddlecombe, now wed to trainer Henrietta Knight.
1948 US trainer whose Strike The Gold won the 1991 Kentucky Derby, Nick Zito.
1966 Former co-champion conditional jump jockey with 100 winners-turned-trainer Richard Fahey.
1967 Jump jockey-turned-starter Robbie Supple.

DEATHS OF THE DAY
1986 Mill Reef, brilliant winner of the 1971 Derby.
1992 Amateur jockey Maurice 'Mossie' O'Neill, 38, after suffering severe head injuries at Ireland's Carrigtwohill point-to-point.
1992 The Queen's 1974 1,000 Guineas and French Oaks winner, Highclere.
1994 Jockey Matty Curran, 51, who rode Irish Grand National winners Vulpine (1967) and Dim Wit (1972).
2004 Trainer Norman Bradley, father of jockey Graham, aged 72.

CELEBRITY OF THE DAY
1995 The Dowager Lady Beaverbrook's (widow of *Sunday Express* founder and politician Lord Beaverbrook) beaver brown and maple leaf green colours were carried to victory for the first time since her death when 13/8 Peutetre won at Lingfield – her executors continued to race her horses under the Dayspring Co Ltd banner.

3 FEBRUARY

SIGNIFICANT EVENT

1990 All-time great rider Bill Shoemaker, 15 times US champion, retired with 8,833 winners from 40,350 mounts after finishing fourth on Patchy Groundfog in the 'Legend's Last Ride' Handicap at Santa Anita. He took up training but in April 1991 suffered a broken neck and fractured pelvis in a car crash. He was confined to a wheelchair but still enjoyed training success.

STRANGEST EVENT

1852 A hunters' Flat race at Lincoln saw the 'winner' disqualified for being a thoroughbred; the runner-up likewise, for having won more than the stipulated total of prize money. The race was awarded to Loddington, who had finished 'a bad third of four'.

OTHER EVENTS

1924 The first Grand Prix de St Moritz was run on the Swiss frozen lake track.
1968 Chaos at Taunton where part of the starting gate failed to rise properly in a hurdle race. The recall man missed the starter's signal and failed to stop the race, which Indamelia 'won'. Inevitably it was later voided.
1938 Anthony Mildmay won on Davy Jones at Gatwick – the course is now part of the airport. The same combination had led over the second-last fence in the Grand National two years earlier, only for the reins to break and the horse run out at the last.
1991 Lester Piggott rode in India for the first time in 22 years. He won over 6f in Bombay on Scorpio.
1996 Kieren Fallon was fined £100 and banned for one day for 'pushing and kicking' another rider after finishing runner-up in the Calcutta St Leger.
2007 Halsion Chancer, 3/1, won on debut at Lingfield. Chris Powell, who persuaded the boss at Halsion company to buy horse, put £20 on him – and

celebrated by having horse's name tattooed on his chest.
2008 Racing at Santa Anita was cancelled due to continuing drainage problems on the synthetic cushion track, set to be 'amended' by Australian Pro-ride synthetic polymer and binder.
2009 The Maryland Racing Commissioner John McDaniel condemned the decision of the *Washington Post* to cease reporting horse-racing related stories on a regular basis.

QUOTE OF THE DAY

'It may have been the only time during his long career that Shoemaker was cheered for finishing out of the money on a favorite,' said writer William Murray, one of 65,000 present as Bill Shoemaker, 58, rode for the last time.

BIRTHDAYS

1949 Former Norwegian triple champion jockey Walter Buick, whose son William is tipped to emulate him in the UK. Some punters snapped up 500/1, for him ever to be champion.
1950 Three times champion jumps trainer Michael Dickinson, whose feat of saddling the first five home in the 1983 Cheltenham Gold Cup has yet to be emulated. He moved to the US to ply his trade, saddled Breeders' Cup winners and invented Tapeta, a new artificial surface.
1971 At the Races presenter Matt Chapman.
1991 Taipa racecourse, Macau.

CELEBRITY OF THE DAY

1914 The only female owner-breeder of two Derby winners, Psidium (1961) and Henbit (1980), Countess Wurmbrand, aka Etti Plesch. Her Sassafras won the 1970 Arc and her maternal grandfather Aristides Baltazzi won the 1876 Derby with Kisber. Married six times, she died in 2003. Her fascinating *Horses & Husbands* memoirs were published in 2007.

4 FEBRUARY

SIGNIFICANT EVENT
2008 Trainer Mark Johnston got to 2,000 winners faster than any other British Flat trainer when Leamington won at Southwell. He started as a trainer in February 1987, and his stable motto is 'always trying' –chosen, observed Clare Balding, 'in wry recognition that not everyone is'.

STRANGEST EVENT
1862 Ace of Hearts and The Rug – did he start at 'double carpet'?– dead-heated in a 4m chase at Carmarthen. So a run-off was staged – in which they dead-heated again.

OTHER EVENTS
1887 After a blank year due to financial problems, Plumpton returned and The Nightingale, 1/15, was an easy winner of the Naval and Military Cup.

1937 George Owen, who would train the 1949 Grand National winner Russian Hero, 66/1, rode both Go Canny and Russian Sentry to win big chases at Haydock.

1938 Playman, a 2000 dollar claimer, won first race at Santa Anita returning $673.40 for two dollar stake.

1956 Willie Shoemaker rode Terrang to Stakes Race win at Santa Anita – and did the same thing at the same place on Tempest II in 1959, and again on Cedar Key in 1965.

1977 Richard Rowe's first mount, Royal Rudolf, was third over hurdles at Sandown.

2000 Martin Pipe became the first trainer to saddle 2,989 winners when he overtook Arthur Stephenson to become the most prolific jumps handler of all, as Through The Rye won at Folkestone.

QUOTE OF THE DAY
'Completely poisoned by the all-weather track' was trainer John Panvert's novel excuse after his Toughnutocrack finished last of twelve at Lingfield this day in 1994.

BIRTHDAYS
1937 Welsh dual purpose trainer Dai Burchell, who rode three winners as an amateur, and whose best horses include Maamur and Castle Secret. Once declared: 'If somebody is telling me their horse has a good chance, it's because they ain't trying. If they really think it's going to win, they tell nobody.'

1941 Trainer Susan Davenport.

1949 Jockey Georges Doleuze.

1950 Top amateur jockey Jim Wilson, who won the 1981 Gold Cup on Little Owl, 6/1, in his brother Robert's colours. His local pub, the New Inn, had its name changed to the Little Owl. Jim, who gave up riding in 1985, had been champion rider at the Festival the previous year.

1955 Jockey Steve Knight, who started out on the Flat, won the 1987 Grand National on 28/1-shot Maori Venture, on whom he also twice won Newbury's Mandarin Chase. Ninety-two-year-old owner Jim Joel left the horse to Knight in his will.

1957 Chris Pimlott, jumps jockey who became a jockeys' agent.

FIRST OF THE DAY
2000 Martin Pipe became the first trainer to saddle 2,989 winners when he overtook Arthur Stephenson to become the most prolific jumps handler of all, as Through The Rye won at Folkestone. Pipe doesn't seem to believe that the sport he dominated will always be around, commenting once: 'I can honestly see the time when there won't be any jump racing, or only a very limited amount. People are anti-whips, anti-jumps, what next?'

5 FEBRUARY

SIGNIFICANT EVENT

1926 Sceptre, the only winner of four Classics – in 1902 when she missed out only on the Derby, in which she was fourth – died at Exning Stud, Newmarket. Only Formosa, in 1868, came close – winning 1,000 Guineas, Oaks and St Leger, and dead-heating in 2,000 Guineas.

STRANGEST EVENT

1996 Twenty-three-year-old conditional rider Darren Salter was banned for 21 days for testing positive for cannabis in a random test at Chepstow. He claimed he was the victim of a trick after eating a cake containing the drug at a party.

OTHER EVENTS

1945 Big Racket clocked a record 43.26mph in a 2f race in Mexico City.

1993 Belmont Stakes winner A. P. Indy, winner of 8 of 11 starts, worth $2,979,815, was named US Horse of the Year, 1992.

1993 Lester Piggott's comeback following a Breeders' Cup fall the previous October was delayed, as a downpour and the death of a member of Dubai's ruling family caused the postponement of a meeting there.

1993 Nine-year-old Jinxy Jack, 1/8, became the first recorded example of a horse winning a hurdle race for four consecutive seasons, Kelso's Morebattle Hurdle. He was trained by Gordon Richards and ridden by Neale Doughty.

2007 Brazilian rider, Jorge Ricardo, 45, went ahead of US rival Russell Baze as winning-most jockey ever, with his 9591st winner.

2009 Charlie Mann's Lambourn stable was snowbound and he faced the possibility of not getting his runners to Taunton – so he hitched the horsebox to a tractor and dragged it to the M4

from where he drove to the course – and both his horses won, Fair Point, 3/1, and Borero, 8/1.

QUOTE OF THE DAY

1998 *'Slow.'* After nine years during which the going was officially 'Standard', Lingfield's ground was declared 'Slow' today.

BIRTHDAYS

1904 Goodwood owner the Duke of Richmond.

1917 Owner-breeder of Derby winner, Reference Point, Louis Freedman.

1950 Rider of over 100 winners, and once Martin Pipe's first jockey, Dumfries & Galloway trainer Len Lungo's best horses have been The Bajan Bandit, Crazy Horse, Freetown, Celtic Giant and Mirjan.

1960 Jockey Dean McKeown, three times winner of the Cambridgeshire, in 1987 (Balthus, 50/1), 1989 and 1992, (both Rambo's Hall, 15/1, 9/2) all for trainer Jeremy Glover.

1960 Former jockey, until paralysed in a fall at Bangor, turned writer, Sharron Murgatroyd.

DEATHS OF THE DAY

1967 Lord Penrhyn, 101, who, as Major Frank Douglas-Pennant, owned the 1908 Grand National winner Rubio.

2003 Irish jump jockey Anthony Powell, 43, who rode Maid of Money to win the 1989 Irish Grand National, died in a car accident.

CELEBRITY OF THE DAY

1942 *Daily Mail* racing writer Colin Mackenzie was born. He has been an 'enthusiastic owner of a variety of slow, quick, quick, slow horses' including Welsh Oak, 16 NH wins, and Garrylough, seven wins.

6 FEBRUARY

SIGNIFICANT EVENT
1992 Riding at Sha Tin, Hong Kong, for the first time, Mick Kinane rode a treble.

STRANGEST EVENT
1992 Old-timers ruled at Santa Anita where 80-year-old trainer Noble Threewit saddled the first two winners, both owned by fellow octogenarian W R Johnson, 85.

OTHER EVENTS
1885 Northampton won under W Nightingall at Plumpton – then did it again under Mr Abington.

1985 Former footballer Francis Lee sent out his first winner as a permit trainer when Miramac won a novice hurdle at Ludlow.

1992 The *Racing Calendar*, essential reading for those in the business, was printed in white from 1773 to 1969 when it changed to yellow. Today it reverted to white.

1992 A case of passing the bucks, as car park tipsters Alexander Buck (one year), and son Clifford (three years) were warned off all racecourses and Jockey Club properties.

1993 Hamanaka won at Wetherby, partnered by Chris Grant, to give Middleham-based trainer Micheal Hammond's 100th winner.

1993 Rosemary Henderson, 50, rode and trained 7/2 shot Fiddlers Pike to win the Grand National Trial at Chepstow.

1993 Julie Cecil's first runner over jumps – Aremef – won at Stratford.

2000 Cat Thief had won the $5m 1999 Breeders Cup Classic at 19/1, beating Budroyale, 26/1 into second. Today those placings were reversed at Santa Anita in the $300,000 San Antonio Handicap with 7yo gelding Budroyale won over 9f by one and a quarter lengths from Cat Thief.

2009 'Docu-soap', 'Jockeys', chronicling the lives and careers of seven jockeys based at Santa Anita racecourse, USA, premiered on the Animal Planet TV.

QUOTE OF THE DAY
1992 *'Do something about them ,or I'll do it myself. It's happening all the time and I shouldn't have to put up with it.'* Aussie jockey Jim Cassidy, beaten on a string of short-priced favourites at Warwick Farm, Sydney, threatening punters who gave him a hard time, via the stewards, who passed the matter to course security.

BIRTHDAYS
1952 Hampshire-based trainer Lindsay Bower.

1961 Jockey Stuart Morris – champion apprentice in Hong Kong, and fan of tropical fish.

1963 Jockey Steve Dawson. He rode the 1984 Cesarewitch winner Tom Sharp.

DEATHS OF THE DAY
1889 1864 Derby-winning (Blair Athol) jockey Jem (aka Jim or James) Snowden died in poverty near Doncaster, aged 45. Alcohol proved his downfall and only a subscription organized by Middleham trainers raised money for a funeral and memorial.

1952 King George VI died – racing was cancelled until February 16.

1999 US Hall of Fame trainer Henry Clark, 95, who was still sending out winners in late 1998 when his first had been saddled when he was 29.

CELEBRITY OF THE DAY
1940 Jimmy Tarbuck, comedian and owner with Mick Channon, born.

7 FEBRUARY

SIGNIFICANT EVENT
1591 George, Earl of Huntly, recorded in his memoirs that horseracing was taking place at Leith, Scotland.

STRANGEST EVENT
1994 *The Sporting Life* reported that 'the wife of Christophe Le Scrill, one of France's top young jockeys, has admitted strangling him.' The promising 24-year-old had been missing since early January.

OTHER EVENTS
1796 *The Sporting Magazine* reported matches and sweepstake races taking place in Hyde Park.

1976 Diana Thorne became the first lady to ride a winner under NH rules, on Ben Ruler at Stratford.

1989 Peter Scudamore completed what was then the fastest ever 150 winners in a season, wiping out Jonjo O'Neill's record of 149 winners in season, set in 1977-8. The horses Scudamore booted home for Martin Pipe were always fit, but 'Scu' once commented: 'Punters are being taken for a ride when they back horses that are not fit – and some trainers run their charges at a level of fitness that does not allow them to run at their best.' Surely not!

QUOTE OF THE DAY
1994 *'It was excessive, but you don't think of that during the Gold Cup and I wouldn't have won otherwise.'* Adrian Maguire, who was fined £400 for riding a finish a circuit too soon at Fontwell on this day, highlighted the Catch 22 of jockeys' whip use after winning the 1992 Gold Cup on Cool Ground.

BIRTHDAYS
1947 Rider of Supermaster, John Enright.

1950 Further proof that Americans have the best names – Churchill Down's star trainer, Burk Kessinger, a former stockbroker.

1951 Panamanian jockey in the US, Ricardo Lopez.

1952 Jockey Tony Ives, (who called his Newmarket house, ahem, Linga Longa) rider of Provideo and Teleprompter. He rode successfully in Hong Kong and Macau.

1965 Perhaps Americans don't have all the best names after all – jockey Mickey Flynn slipped into the world today.

1966 Racecourse commentator Richard Hoiles.

1973 David Pipe, son of serial champion jumps trainer Martin. He rode 22 point-to-point winners and two under rules, including Bonanza Boy in the Ludlow Gold Cup. Learned the training trade in South Africa, France and the USA, then sent out 164 pointing winners in six seasons before breaking into the big time.

DEATHS OF DAY
1982 US trainer Burly Cocks, 82.

1988 Trainer John Frederick Watts, 77. Won the 1960 Cesarewitch with Alcove and the 1964 St Leger with Indiana. Son of dual Classic-winning trainer John E Watts; grandson of John Watts, trainer of 19 Classic winners; father of Classic-winning trainer Bill (well, John William) Watts.

1989 Eddie Dempsey, 77, who rode 100/1-shot Caughoo to win the 1947 Grand National. The race was run in thick fog, which led to accusations that he only went round once!

CELEBRITY OF THE DAY
1829 The foundation stone for the Aintree Grandstand was laid by Lord Molyneux, who placed a full bottle of sovereigns inside the footings.

8 FEBRUARY

SIGNIFICANT EVENT
1983 Derby winner Shergar was kidnapped, never to be seen again, despite a request for a £2m ransom.

STRANGEST EVENT
1993 Tony Charlton almost managed to object to himself after winning at Fontwell. Believing that his mount Metal Oiseau had been beaten in a photo-finish by Gallant Effort, he lodged an objection to 'the winner', only to discover that the photograph revealed he'd won.

OTHER EVENTS
1886 Tattersalls' rules on betting were introduced. The committee was empowered to settle betting-related matters, queries and disputes.

1938 Breeder of the brilliant Brigadier Gerard, John Hislop, and Olympic show jumper-to-be, Sir Harry Llewellyn, both won at Warwick – on Overseas and Talybont respectively.

1970 After winning 85 races between them, with the likes of Green Drill and Snaigow, trainer Verly Bewicke and owner Lord Cadogan ended their 14-year partnership after a 'disagreement.'

1978 Sweet Millie won at Haydock to give Jonjo O'Neill the fastest century of winners in a season by a jump jockey.

1989 Chris Antley rode a winner at Aqueduct, USA – then did exactly that for 64 successive racing days there, including a March 27 5-timer, before finally drawing a blank on May 1.

1990 An anonymous bidder paid £10,900 at auction for five green leather armchairs used by the Queen, Prince Philip and other Royals to watch racing at Newbury. The auctioneers had reckoned on £1,000 at best.

2004 Bookmakers attended the 'Great Noojee Mountain Horse Races' in Victoria, Australia, to make bets on the eight uphill races.

2008 Scottish Grand National-winning jockey, trainer and starter John Leech retired after half a century in the game, on his 70th birthday after acting as starter at Bangor.

QUOTE OF THE DAY
'It was like going into someone's bedroom after they've died. You have just been to the funeral and you come back to look at their empty bedroom. It's a terrible feeling, believe me.' Vet Stan Cosgrove, part-owner of Shergar, kidnapped this day in 1983, on viewing the horse's empty box.

BIRTHDAYS
1945 Jockey Myrddin Lloyd 'Taffy' Thomas. He rode his first winner at Hurst Park in 1961 and was a frequent winter rider in India, Malaysia and Singapore.

1960 Trainer Alex Scott, who was tragically shot dead in 1994. His Possessive Dancer won both the Oaks D'Italia and Irish oaks. He was an old Etonian.

1980 Jump jockey Tom Doyle. He rode his first winner, aged 17, as an amateur on Blackburn at Fairyhouse. He moved from Ireland to England winning on his first mount, Petasus, a 25/1 outsider, at Plumpton on September 13, 1999. In 2007 he returned to Ireland.

DEATHS OF THE DAY
1995 Jump jockey John Burke, 41. He won the 1976 Cheltenham Gold Cup on Royal Frolic and, in the same season, the Grand National on Rag Trade.

CELEBRITY OF THE DAY
The bravest, perhaps; the most foolhardy, almost certainly, jockey to ride in the Grand National, Spanish nobleman Beltran, Duque de Albuquerque, died this day in 1994, aged 74. He completed the National once in seven attempts and eventually was prevented from competing for his own good.

9 FEBRUARY

SIGNIFICANT EVENT
1540 Some historians assert that this day, Shrove Tuesday, marked the first racing at Chester where a silver bell (some say 'ball') worth 111 shillings was competed for. (See 10 January.)

STRANGEST EVENT
1809 Trainer Tom Dawson, born today, became the first handler to dispense with the entrenched process of 'sweating' horses by giving them strong gallops whilst wearing heavy rugs and hoods. As he sent out 1869 2,000 Guineas/Derby winner Pretender and three other Classic winners from his Tupgill, Middleham stable, he was doing something right.

OTHER EVENTS
1974 Jockey Chris McCarron rode his first winner, Erezev, at Bowie, Maryland. He was inducted to Hall of Fame and became tv analyst after retiring with nine Breeders Cup and six Triple Crown race victories.

1988 Cash Asmussen confirmed as stable jockey to Andre Fabre. As Cash admitted: 'To some people I am over-priced and they use other people. But I ride quality horses for quality people.'

1991 All racing – jumps, Flat, all-weather, – was called off in Britain and Ireland because of frost and snow.

2009 Tony McCoy rode his 3,000th jumps winner in Britain and Ireland, the Nicky Henderson-trained Restless D'Artaix at Plumpton.

QUOTE OF THE DAY
1987 *'As a jockey you never allow yourself to take a break because you're scared someone else will get your winners,'* said Walter Swinburn, perhaps helping to explain how he came to get a two-year driving ban, later cut to six months.

BIRTHDAYS
1938 Ron Boss, who rode 18 winners as a jockey then turned trainer, sending out Olwyn to win the 1977 Irish Oaks.

1951 Jump jockey Peter Haynes.

1956 *Racing Post* writer and Channel 4 presenter Alastair Down.

1972 Jockey-turned-At The Races presenter Jason Weaver. Champion apprentice of 1993, he became stable jockey to Mark Johnston and in 1994 reached 200 winners in a season, including 2000 Guineas on Mister Baileys. He retired in 2002 with weight problems.

1974 Jockey Paul Carberry who won the 1999 Grand National on Bobbyjo – following his dad Tommy's win on L'Escargot in 1975. They were the first such father-son winning combination.

2008 First foal out of great mare, Ouija Board, a colt by Kingmambo, named Voodoo Prince.

DEATHS OF THE DAY
2005 Five-times champion jockey in South Africa Gerald Turner, 58.

2006 Budget airline pioneer Sir Freddie Laker, 83. His Blarney Beacon won the 1965 Triumph Hurdle, while Spartan General won many Flat races. He served as a steward – racecourse not air – at Brighton and Lingfield in the 1980s and was a Jockey Club member.

CELEBRITY OF THE DAY
1943 Actor/owner Joe Pesci was born on this day. He starred in the *Goodfellas* movie and owned the useful filly, Pesci.

10 FEBRUARY

SIGNIFICANT EVENT

1849 Great US trainer William Ransom Johnson died this day, aged 67. In 1807-8 he started horses in 63 races and won 61 of them, acquiring the nickname 'Napoleon of the Turf', and was recognised as 'the' authority on racing of his day.

STRANGEST EVENT

1990 Tim Reed rode one of the longest-odds doubles when 100/1-shot Wrekin Melody and 20/1 chance Alistair's Girl both won for him at Catterick – paying 2,120/1.

OTHER EVENTS

1940 Aussie track Williamstown, near Melbourne – where all-time great Phar Lap won during 1931 – closed after almost 60 years to become an army training camp.

1945 192 runners contested eleven races at Windsor.

1992 The Aga Khan sold his disqualified 1989 Oaks 'winner' Aliysa and ten other mares to Sheikh Mohammed.

1993 Lester Piggott made his comeback following a fall from Mr Brooks in the Breeders' Cup Sprint in October 1992. He rode two runners-up and two unplaced horses at Nad Al Sheba, Dubai.

1993 Peter Scudamore reached his eighth consecutive century of winners.

1996 Three-times Austrian champion jockey Jean-Pierre Lopez rode his first British winner, on Greenspan, 12/1, at Southwell.

2008 A proposal to close New York's Aqueduct racecourse after a meeting on this date was averted. The track, opened in 1894, was rebuilt in 1959 by noted racetrack architect, Arthur Froehlich.

2009 13yo horses Fancy Dancer and Yankee Ruler were granted special dispensation to race at Fonne Park, Nebraska, subject to 'examination prior to entry'. An unusual example of ageism?

QUOTE OF THE DAY

1983 '*Why was it a slow time? Because we went too fast.*' Comments like this one, 'explaining' a 1996 defeat, underline why Willie Carson has always had a slightly edgy relationship with the racing public – who really want to like him, but are never quite sure about him – although on this day few would have begrudged him his trip to Buckingham Palace to collect his OBE.

BIRTHDAYS

1908 Owner-jockey Arthur Harris of Tipperary, who rode his last winner 10 days before his 50th birthday and still played cricket aged 81. Best horse, Avondale, winner of six flat, three hurdle and three chase races.

1948 Owner-Jockey Club member, Anthony Mildmay-White, whose Merry Maker won 13 jump races.

1948 Influential racing figure and Coolmore Stud kingpin, John Magnier.

1949 Flat and jumps trainer Roger Curtis. His best horses included Brave Hussar, The Yomper and Mister Ed.

DEATH OF THE DAY

1983 Former trainer Ricky Vallance, 74. He won the 1958 Imperial Cup with Flaming East and the 1973 Hennessy with Red Candle.

FIRST OF THE DAY

1899 The first jumps meeting was staged at Haydock.

11 FEBRUARY

SIGNIFICANT EVENT

1884 The first race meeting at Plumpton. Harry Escott rode a treble, two of the wins coming on the same horse, hurdler Cowslip.

STRANGEST EVENT

1998 Jonothan Lower became the first diabetic jockey to ride a British winner – 6/1 Serendipity at Ludlow.

OTHER EVENTS

1981 Aldaniti, out through injury since November 1979, won the Whitbread Trial Chase at Ascot – next stop Aintree for a history-making tilt at the National.
1984 Edward Hodson of Wolverhampton beat odds of 3,956,748/1 when his 5p yankee bet came up – sadly, he placed his wager with a bookie whose payout limit was just £3,000.
1988 Breeders' Cup Distaff shortened from one and quarter miles to 9f.
1991 Morley Street was voted Champion US chaser in the Eclipse Awards, but was returned to hurdling in England after three chase failures – then won the 1991 Champion Hurdle.
1991 Peter Scudamore rode his first two all weather winners, Vigano and Tom Clapton, on the fibresand track at Southwell.
1993 Lester Piggott rode his first winners – a double in Dubai – since returning from a broken collarbone and two broken ribs in October.
1995 The 1994 US Horse of the Year, Holy Bull, broke down at Gulfstream Park when 1/5 favourite and was retired aged four, having won 13 of his 16 starts and $2,481,760 prize money.
1996 Walter Swinburn was in intensive care after a fall from Liffey River at Sha Tin. He had a broken left shoulder, three fractures of the left collarbone and multiple fractures to ribs.

QUOTE OF THE DAY

'Conventional wisdom will tell you that the breed is not as sound today as it was 30 years ago, 50 years ago and 75 years ago. Conventional wisdom is almost never right,' declared John R Gaines, the man who founded the Breeders' Cup and who died on this day in 2005.

BIRTHDAYS

1942 Jump jockey Bob (R A) Davies, who rode for Gay Kindersley – not to be confused with triple champion jump jockey Bob (B R) Davies – see May 14, 1946; or jump jockey Barry (B W) Davies, born September 12, 1946; or jump jockey Clive (C G) Davies, retained by Ryan Price, born June 15, 1945; or jump jockey Roy (R F) Davies, born March 2, 1948, who rode for Mick Easterby; or jump jockey Tom (T F O) Davies, born Dec 2, 1962 who rode for W Manners and won Teesside's £1,000 Rosebowl Chase; or jump jockey T G Davies, born Feb 29, 1950, who rode for R C Armytage – or even Martin Davis, born 1946, who rode for R Vibert. Then there was trainer Colin (C H) Davies, who trained triple Champion Hurdler Persian War. (That's enough Davies's – Ed).
1966 Flat jockey Dana (real first name Alison) Mellor, daughter of legendary jockey/trainer Stan.

DEATHS OF THE DAY

1994 One of the first women permitted by the Jockey Club to work in racing stables, Ann Argyle, 76, who was a work rider for Capt. Sir Cecil Boyd-Rochfort.
2005 Scottish-born dual-purpose trainer Dave Thom, 79.

CELEBRITY OF THE DAY

England international footballer and owner of Seebald and Auetaler, Steve McManaman was born on this day in 1972.

12 FEBRUARY

SIGNIFICANT EVENT
1981 Record-breaking female jockey Julie Krone rode her first winner, Lord Farkle, at Tampa Bay Downs.

STRANGEST EVENT
2008 The most expensive horse ever, $16m 4yo The Green Monkey, was retired. Bought for that sum by Coolmore at the 2006 Florida Fasig-Tipton sales, he managed a third and two fourth places for trainer Todd Pletcher.

OTHER EVENTS
1556 The oldest reference to what is claimed to be England's oldest race, the Kiplingcotes Derby, when Thomas Carter of Helperthorpe said on oath that he 'chauncinge to be at a horse running at Kiplingcotes Ashe about Shrovetide last'. The race, held over the Yorkshire Wolds each year on the third Tuesday in March, is believed to have been first run in 1519 and is open to any horse. Uniquely the second horse can often win more than the winner as first prize is funded by the interest on the original prize fund, while second prize is the entry fees of those entered.
1856 Fisherman, owned and trained by Tom Parr, was beaten in his first race of the season at Lincoln. He soon made up for it, winning 23 of 34 starts during the season and 70 of 121 during his career, ending up at stud in Australia.
1983 Trainer Jack Calvert retired, 65, with 530 winners to his name including Dieppe, who won 17.
1994 Dorset trainer Richard Barber set point-to-point record with six winners from nine runners at the eight-race South Dorset meeting, with Polly Gundry winning on four – a female record.
1996 Jockey Mark Perrett retired with 370 jumps winners to his credit, and 17 on the flat. His highlight was the 1985 Topham Chase win on Smith's Man.
2009 Hayley Turner had become the first racing figure short-listed for the *Sunday Times* Sportswoman (or any other category) of the Year, but she missed out to Olympic gold medal-winning cyclist Nicole Cook. Perhaps Hayley didn't fancy her chances – she went instead to ride at Kempton, unplaced on three mounts.

QUOTE OF THE DAY
2009 *'It was a desperate race. If I could have found a pair of running shoes I could have won it,'* observed trainer Stuart Williams after his Itshim won at Kempton.

BIRTHDAY
1949 Eight times Sydney's top trainer, John Hawkes.

DEATHS OF THE DAY
1929 Lily Langtry, beauty and actress, 75, in Monaco. She raced under the pseudonym Mr Jersey (her birthplace) and won the Cesarewitch with Merman in 1897 and Yentoi in 1908.
1969 Bobby Jones, 64, who rode Flares to win the Ascot Gold Cup for Sir Cecil Boyd-Rochfort in 1938. He won the 1922 St Leger on 33/1 Royal Lancer when still an apprentice, and also won both Guineas and the Oaks.
1989 Trainer William (Henry Gatehouse) Hide, 81, father of jockey Eddie and trainer Tony Hide. He sent out some 500 winners.
1993 Trainer Michael Marsh, whose Larbawn won consecutive Whitbread Gold Cups in 1968 and '69, plus three Golden Miller Chases; aged 77.
1998 Major Peter Nelson, 84, trainer of the 50/1 Derby winner of 1974, Snow Knight.

CELEBRITY OF THE DAY
1948 Politician and owner Nicholas Soames, born. Suggested in Parliament that wounded British soldiers should be invited to race meetings 'so that people can see them, welcome them and give them appropriate recognition for their astonishing acvhievements.'

13 FEBRUARY

SIGNIFICANT EVENT
1997 John Holmes, who would launch the ill-fated Great Leighs racecourse there, purchased what had been Essex County Showground.

STRANGEST EVENT
1959 Lester Piggott rode his 20th and last hurdles winner, 6/4 favourite Jive at Sandown.

OTHER EVENTS
1968 19yo Roger Rowell rode his first winner, Vaux-le-Vicomte, 5/1 at Plumpton.

1971 Jockey Ridley Lamb rode his first winner, White Speck, at Catterick.

1988 Saros's fourth place at Santa Anita pushed jockey Jorge Velasquez's career winnings past $100m.

1993 King Credo, 10/1, bred by actor James Bolam, and owned by him and his actress wife Sue Jameson, won the Tote Gold Trophy at Newbury.

1993 Trainer Kevin Morgan celebrated his first treble, all partnered by Adie Smith, at Catterick.

2008 State officials announced a deal to extend New York's state horse racing franchise for another 25 years, with the New York Racing Association running Aqueduct, Belmont and Saratoga for the next quarter of a century.

2008 Heavy snow forced cancellation of racing at Penn National racecourse in the US, where the new $310m Hollywood Casino was due to open in conjunction with the racing. Despite the lack of live racing, simulcast racing was shown from around the country.

QUOTE OF THE DAY
1993 *'You couldn't see the last hurdle, I was convinced the meeting would be abandoned. Luckily it wasn't. Scribbler was in front after the first and, after an interminable wait, emerged from the fog and won by five lengths. We won about £100,000.'* Despite thick fog descending as the race began, pro punter Dave Nevison landed his 'best ever bet', backing his own Teenage Scribbler at Catterick. He organised a team of betting shop punters to pour £20 bets on the horse, which drifted out on course to 14/1.

BIRTHDAYS
1954 Jump jockey-turned-stipendiary steward, Paul Barton.

1964 One time-rider of Sea Pigeon, turned Yorkshire trainer, Steve Muldoon.

1966 Trainer since 1999, Jacqui Doyle. She won the 2000 Winter Derby at Lingfield with Zanay. Mother of jockeys James and Sophie.

DEATHS OF THE DAY
1993 Former Northern jump jockey Phillip James, 55.

2006 Bicycle importer, Sam Rubin, 91, owner of twice Horse of the Year, in 1981 and 84, John Henry, who won 39 of 83 races and $6,591,860. Rubin was voted the 'Person who did most for racing' and 'Outstanding owner' by New York Turf Writers Association in 1981.

CELEBRITY OF THE DAY
1938 Actor, hell-raiser, and owner of Gawnmysun, Oliver Reed was born.

14 FEBRUARY

SIGNIFICANT EVENT
2003 The death of English-born jockey Johnny Longden, 96, the first man to both ride and train Kentucky Derby winners. Rode a career total of 6,032 winners, almost all in the US. Was born – also on Feb 14 (most sources say 1907, some 1910) in Wakefield before emigrating to Canada, (his parents reportedly booked to go on the Titanic but missed the sailing) aged five. He won five US champion jockey titles, and the 1943 Triple Crown on Count Fleet. He took up US citizenship in 1944 and rode 320 winners in 1956. Retired from the saddle in 1966 and three years later sent out Majestic Prince to win the Kentucky Derby. His trainer son, Vance, had died aged 72 in January 2003.

STRANGEST EVENT
1965 Colourful racecourse tipster Ras Prince Monolulu, catchphrase 'I gotta horse', died, believed to be 80. He was really Peter Carl McKay, originally from the West Indies.

OTHER EVENTS
1950 Jockey Pat Taaffe rode his first winner as a pro, Oberstown's Sister over hurdles at Thurles, for father Tom.
1951 Tim Molony rode Arctic Gold, 8/1, to win Doncaster's Great Yorkshire Chase. The 6yo started favourite for that year's National but fell at the Canal Turn.
1976 Val Greaves became the first lady rider to compete against pros and to ride over hurdles, when she was unplaced on Silver Gal at Catterick.
1989 Avionne at Newton Abbot would have been Peter Scudamore's 1000th winner, had an earlier 'winner' not subsequently been disqualified.
1991 Red Rum was on the move as Ginger McCain moved yards from Southport to Cholmondeley.
2009 Lord Oaksey's Carruthers, a 6yo, won a chase at Ascot, encouraging His

Lordship to dream of Gold Cup glory and thus land the 1,000/1 odds I laid to a tenner on his behalf to his racing writer pal, Sean Magee.

QUOTE OF THE DAY
1989 'Only human beings can be made a freeman.' The response to David Preston of Elmbridge, who wrote to the Town Clerk requesting Desert Orchid be made a freeman of Elmbridge for his exploits at the borough's Sandown track. Town clerk David Jenkins responded: 'Perhaps he could be granted common grazing rights', but the request was eventually turned down.

BIRTHDAYS
1929 One of Timeform's driving forces, Reg Griffin. Since he died, a memorial race has been run at York in June in his honour.
1942 Trainer of Champion Hurdler Alderbrook on the Flat, Julie Cecil, former wife of Henry.
1972 Former champion lady rider Emily Jones.

DEATHS OF THE DAY
1966 Trainer Capt. Charles Elsey CBE, 84. He trained six Classic winners including Musidora (1949 1,000 Guineas and Oaks) and Cantelo (1959 St Leger.)
1988 Irish jumps trainer Peter McCreery, 57. His Hilly Way won Cheltenham's 2m Champion Chase in 1978 and '79 and Daring Run won the Irish Champion Hurdle and Sun Templegate Hurdle.
2008 Hall of Fame trainer Sid Waters jr, in Maryland, 90. He had big winners over jumps and on the Flat – his Hoist The Flag, 1970 juvenile champion, sired the great Alleged and his Slew O'Gold was 1983 champion 3yo.

CELEBRITY OF THE DAY
1951 Some-time owner/breeder of Funfair Wane, Kevin Keegan born.

15 FEBRUARY

SIGNIFICANT EVENT

1971 Ben Dearg (Roddy Armytage/
Stan Mellor) won a 2m chase at
Wolverhampton, making history as the
first modern day winner returned at
decimal odds – 13/10.

STRANGEST EVENT

1995 Rumours that the horse had been
'got at' swept the racing world after the
gambled-on Lobilio collapsed and died
on the way to the start at Hereford. He
had run in Dr Devious' Derby but slipped
down the ladder to contest low-grade
hurdles. Trainer Dai Burchell dismissed
the gossip – 'I believe he died from a
problem with his heart'. Won't we all!

OTHER EVENTS

1941 The Plumpton racecard warned
racegoers – 'In case of an air raid the
public is requested to act promptly
on the instructions of the police. The
presence of enemy aircraft in the vicinity
will be notified to the public by short
blasts on police whistles.'
1957 Irish trainer Kevin Prendergast
wed Lesley Daly. He listed one of his
business interests as 'breeding' – and the
pair had seven daughters.
1964 Rosyth, 10/1, Josh Gifford up,
won the Schweppes Gold Trophy at
Newbury. The horse was considered by
the stewards to have made abnormal
improvement since his previous race, and
trainer Ryan Price was disqualified until
the end of the season while Gifford's
licence was withdrawn until March 31.
1983 Music City won at Newton Abbot,
trainer John Mailes' first winner for 20
years.
1989 Peter Scudamore became the third
jockey to ride 1,000 jumps winners, on
15/8 favourite Baluchi at Worcester.
1992 A double tragedy for point-to-
point rider Jill Dawson at the Badsworth
meeting as Sweet Diana and Herman
Blake died under her in successive races.
Adding insult to injury the unfortunate

latter was also posthumously
disqualified.
2009 With the race at his mercy, 4/6
Cousin Vinny crumpled at the last in a
Leopardstown novice hurdle, sending
jockey Patrick Mullins crashing to
the floor. As he leapt up, Mullins was
knocked flying by the onrushing runner-
up, Western Charmer. He lived to tell
the tale.

QUOTE OF THE DAY

2008 *'These young 'uns have got no idea.'*
Former London docker Fred Farrow, who
won an amateurs' charity Flat race at
Fakenham on Ballyowen – aged 70.

BIRTHDAYS

1917 Racecourse commentator
Cloudesley Marsham.
1986 Jockey Amy Baker. On her fourth
birthday the local paper reported 'when
she grows up Amy wants to be a jockey.'
By 2008 she had been Jersey champion
lady jockey for three successive years,
planning to win again to keep the trophy
but she lost it to Kylie Manser in 2009.

DEATHS OF THE DAY

1983 Jockey/trainer Ted Leader, 80.
He rode Sprig to win the 1927 Grand
National and won the Gold Cup in 1925
on Ballinode and in 1932 on Golden
Miller. Champion jockey 1925/6.
2001 Dave Dick, the jockey who
partnered ESB, winner of the 1956
National after Devon Loch capsized on
the run-in, to land a rare Spring double
having already clinched the Lincoln on
Gloaming, aged 17 in 1941. Dick was a
six-footer with weight problems.
2004 Aussie jockey Pat Glennon, 76,
rider of 1965 Derby/Arc winner Sea Bird
II. Won two Melbourne Cups.

FIRST OF THE DAY

2009 The first 300 racegoers through
the gates at Hereford received a free pie
and a pint.

16 FEBRUARY

SIGNIFICANT EVENT
1993 Super Impose, the biggest stakes winner in Australian racing history, was retired. The colt raced 74 times, winning 20 races worth a total of A\$5,659,290. In his first race at Benalla he won the equivalent of £200, but his last, the W S Cox Plate, yielded A\$1.75m. Trained by Lee Freedman.

STRANGEST EVENT
1999 Three horses died at Sedgefield when, during a race, loose horses careered back into runners.

OTHER EVENTS
1998 Erintante, 1/5, from the Francois Doumen stable (ridden by Thierry), was the first French-trained winner at Plumpton.
2008 US Throughbred Racing Association agreed to testify to a congressional panel investigating doping in sport: 'I think the perception is that drug use in racing is worse now than maybe it's ever been' said Congressman Ed Whitfield.
2009 19yo Brazilian rider Maylan Studart won on Trillion at Aqueduct, New York, but also attracted attention by being pictured modelling lingerie whilst 'riding' a merry-go-round horse, and being included in website Sports Climax 'Hottest Female Athletes Gallery'. 'Horse racing is in my blood, its my addiction' she said. Maylan's career suffered a setback when she broke a leg in June 2009 when a horse reared up and landed on top of her.
2010 'Breakfast with Charlie Mann' was on offfer at £69 per person for this date to racing fans wishing to purchase a trip to the unconventional Upper Lambourn trainer's yard.

QUOTE OF THE DAY
'The vets did exhaustive tests but couldn't find an explanation. It's a bit like cot deaths in infants.' Aussie trainer Colin Hayes, born today in 1924, after two of his horses from the same stallion, Sir Tristram – National Gallery, valued at A\$2m, and Frame – both collapsed and died during big races in 1984.

BIRTHDAYS
1924 Champion trainer Colin Hayes, in Adelaide. He rode 52 winners as an amateur and had his first winner as a trainer in 1947. He once sent out ten winners in a single day. His At Talaq finished fourth behind Secreto in the 1984 Derby before winning the Melbourne Cup. Hayes received OBE for racing in 1980, and died in 1999.
1930 Welsh trainer Bryn Palling. A modest type never taking more than two lines to describe his set-up in the annual *Directory of the Turf*.
1953 Jockey champion apprentice, Robert Edmondson 1972. The story is told – possibly apocryphal, of Edmonson cutting across Lester Piggott during a race at Doncaster, after which Piggott objected to Edmonson winning, telling stewards it was on the grounds of 'attempted ****ing murder'.
1955 The trainer of Double Schwartz and Minstrella, Charlie Nelson. He boasted wins in the Prix de l'Abbaye, Fred Darling Stakes and Palace House Stakes.
1956 Trainer and former jockey, Paul D'Arcy, whose first winner came in 1975 at Pontefract, before he spent time riding in Belgium.

CELEBRITY OF THE DAY
1954 Fast-bowling West Indies cricketer, lover of racing and owner (Vallani, trained by Walter Swinburn) Michael 'Whispering Death' Holding, born today. 'When possible,' says Holding, who has a home in Newmarket, 'I spend most mornings at Michael Stoute's (keen cricket man) stables. Racing is first and cricket comes second!'

17 FEBRUARY

SIGNIFICANT EVENT
1968 Tom Dreaper trained the winner of the Leopardstown Chase for the seventh consecutive year as Peter McLoughlin rode Fort Leney to victory.

STRANGEST EVENT
1993 Bidding for a record 17th win in 18 outings at Southwell, Suluk went off at 1/14 – and was beaten, becoming the biggest odds-on loser since 1/14 chance Arum Lady at Haydock in December 1988 – slightly disappointing the punter who tried to 'buy' £200 for £3,200 – so didn't even get the best price!

OTHER EVENTS
1968 Carrying 11st 13lbs, the Colin Davies-trained triple Champion Hurdler Persian War, partnered by Jimmy Uttley, won the 33-runner Schweppes Gold Trophy at Newbury.

1987 The previous year's Arc winner, Dancing Brave, came off second best when hit by a car in Newmarket. Some bright spark described his condition as 'stable'.

1990 Phil Tuck, 33, rode Midland Glenn 5/4 favourite to win at Newcastle – and promptly retired with 423 winners to his credit. Perhaps the highlight of his career was a run of ten straight wins from Aug 23-Sept 3, 1986.

1990 Almost two years after being retired, triple Champion Hurdler, See You Then, returned finishing 6th of 8 in a handicap hurdle at Nottingham. Three disappointing races later he retired again – for good.

2005 California Horse Racing Board outlined plans to make minimum weight to be carried in races 116lbs, excluding 'jockey attire and equipment'. In the board's annual report, 306 racehorse fatalities were reported in California between July 1, 2007 – June 30, 2008.

QUOTE OF THE DAY
1898 'He's fourth, Mrs Genter, he's third, Mrs Genter ... he's second, Mrs Genter, he's taking the lead, Mrs Genter, he's a winner, he's a winner, you've won the Kentucky Derby, Mrs Genter. I love you, Mrs Genter.' Not Mr Genter, but trainer Carl Nafzger to 92-year-old wheelchair-bound owner Frances Genter – born this day – as her Unbridled won the 1990 Kentucky Derby. She became involved with racing after receiving literature from a tipster. Husband Harold invented the pop-up toaster.

BIRTHDAYS
1944 Jockey Philip Hewitt.
1949 Jockey David Atkinson, who partnered Party Man to five wins in one season.
1973 Epsom dual-licence trainer Jim Boyle, whose riding career consists of finishing fourth in a Salisbury charity race. His stable boasts an equine spa to help with horses' lower-limb injuries.

DEATHS OF THE DAY
1985 Jockey-turned-trainer Brian Swift, 48, who rode 200 winners from 1951-61 including the King's Stand Stakes. He won the Triumph Hurdle and Victor Ludorum Hurdle as a trainer.
2006 US businessman Bob Lewis, 81, whose Silver Charm won the 1997 Kentucky Derby and Preakness Stakes; his Charismatic did likewise in 1999. Lewis was entered in US Hall of Fame. It was a bad day for owners of Kentucky Derby and Preakness winners, as Roy Chapman, whose Smarty Jones also won those two races in 2004, died aged 79. 'Smarty Jones was some of the best medicine he had as the excitement of his Triple Crown campaign gace him a new lease of life when he was already deathly ill' said his widow, Patricia.

FIRST OF THE DAY
1981 Sixteen-year-old Richard Dennis rode his first winner, Snowdrop Wonder, at Newton Abbot.

18 FEBRUARY

SIGNIFICANT EVENT
1967 Controversy raged after the Ryan Price-trained Hill House, ridden by Josh Gifford, won the Schweppes Gold Trophy at Newbury. A dope test showed a high concentration of cortisone and a 171-day enquiry concluded that the horse manufactured his own cortisone. Hill House ran in 23 more races, never winning again and often refusing to start.

STRANGEST EVENT
1880 Trainer of five Classic winners, Thomas Dawson, 70, died after leaving his sickbed to watch a trial on his training gallops.

OTHER EVENTS
1857 Did anyone care that the first champion jockey Nat Flatman rode the first winner of the season at Lincoln, on Apathy?

1976 The Queen Mum's 300th winner over jumps, Sunyboy at Ascot, ridden by Bill Smith, trained by Fulke Walwyn.

1991 Jump jockey Richard Rowe who won the 1982 Whitbread Gold Cup on Shady Deal for Josh Gifford, announced his retirement.

1993 The David Nicholson-trained Stylus, first winner for jockey Robert Massey, at 150/1 was the longest-odds winner since 250/1-shot Equinoctial at Kelso two seasons previously.

1995 Tony McCoy rode his first treble – Top Spin, 7/2; Treasure Again, 7/4, and Benjamin Lancaster, 5/4, at Chepstow.

2008 Alan Munro returned to riding after an 18 month sabbatical – winning on 8/1 fav, General Butcher at Lingfield

QUOTE OF THE DAY
'We weren't unlucky, she was ridden by an asshole who didn't follow instructions,' fumed owner Alec Wildenstein after his Vallee Enchantee, ridden by Dominique Boeuf, was beaten. He sacked the rider two days later. Wildenstein, 67, who owned 2005 Ascot Gold Cup (run at York) winner Westerner, died this day in 2008.

BIRTHDAYS
1948 Racing writer Geoff Lester. He once tipped Arazi to win a race, naming him as the third certainty in life, after death and taxes. The horse lost.

1950 Jockey Tony Murray born at Wantage Hospital, Berkshire, where Lester Piggott also entered the world.

1951 Cumbria jockey-turned-trainer Maurice Barnes. Her rode Rubstic to win the 1979 Grand National at 25/1.

1953 Jump jockey John Burke, who rode 1976 Cheltenham Gold Cup (Royal Frolic) and Grand National (Rag Trade) winners.

1969 Jockey Dean Gallagher, who rode successfully over jumps in Britain and France.

DEATHS OF THE DAY
1991 Legendary trainer Fulke Walwyn, 80. He rode Reynoldstown, 10/1, to win the 1936 Grand National and trained four Cheltenham Gold Cup winners, six Hennessy Gold Cup winners and seven Whitbread Gold Cup winners.

1995 Irish trainer Denny Cordell-Laverack, 52. His Baba Karam was the highest-rated Irish 2yo colt of 1986. The second string to his bow was the record business in which the Argentinian-born producer was responsible for the huge hit 'A Whiter Shade of Pale' by Procol Harum.

CELEBRITY OF THE DAY
1933 Former England manager and racing fan and owner Sir Bobby Robson born. He told of the time when boss of England that '(Peter) Shilton was mad on horses, so was (Bryan) Robson. So we produced a video and had racing evenings, with Shilton as the bookie.'

19 FEBRUARY

SIGNIFICANT EVENT
1909 Anti-betting legislation introduced into California killed off racing in the State – which only returned in 1933 to boost state revenue during the Great Depression.

STRANGEST EVENT
1966 Determined to bring his campaign for the banning of whips to a wider audience, Walter Hoystead held up runners for Flemington, Melbourne's Fulham Hurdle at gunpoint. This bizarre hostage-taking delayed the start for 16 minutes as police reasoned with Hoystead, who was arrested and later fined A$80.

OTHER EVENTS
1910 Albert Whittaker rode seven winners from seven mounts at Huntley, New Zealand.

1968 Cousins, Willie and Arthur Stephenson each sent out three winners – Arthur at Doncaster, Willie one at Doncaster, two at Newbury.

1988 Peter Scudamore and Bruce Dowling were each given 21 day ban for reckless riding after becoming involved in a mid-race fracas.

1993 Jockey Tim Reed wore spurs as he won at Edinburgh on 8/1 Palanquin.

1993 Despite a 1032 day injury lay-off, Dick Allen-trained 4/1 shot, Tough Cookie lived up to his name at Edinburgh.

2009 A modern-day record of 216 entries were received for Cheltenham's newest Festival race, the Martin Pipe Conditional Jockeys' Handicap Hurdle.

2009 Huntingdon's Sidney Banks Memorial Hurdle took place; it has been lost to the weather twelve times since its introduction in 1976. Banks, who died in 1974, was an owner, trainer, steward, farmer, corn merchant and master of foxhounds who won the 1947 Cheltenham and Liverpool Foxhunter's races. His stable jockey Tony Pipe was uncle of Martin. Time For Rupert produced a 20/1 shock for Paul Webber, ridden by William Kennedy.

QUOTE OF THE DAY
'I always thought there were 200 ways you could lose a racehorse. This was 201.' Owner of the 1992 Irish Derby winner St Jovite, Virginia Kraft Payson, born today in 1932, after her Uptown Swell drowned in 1990 during swimming exercise – having reportedly been stung by a bee.

BIRTHDAYS
1916 US jockey Eddie 'Banana Nose' Arcaro. His 4,779 wins included five Kentucky Derbys. His real first name was George. He won the Triple Crown on Whirlaway in 1941 and Citation in 1948.

1957 Jockey Stuart Webster – most famous for being dragged from his mount by at-the-time unknown flat jockey Kieren Fallon, in a unsavory 1994 incident, which resulted in a six month ban for the future champion.

1974 Northants trainer Alex Hales.

1983 Joint champion apprentice – with Hayley Turner – Saleem Golam.

DEATH OF THE DAY
1993 Leading stallion Dominion, 21. He produced 13 European Pattern-race winners including Primo Dominie.

CELEBRITY OF THE DAY
1993 Prominent owner and Jockey Club member, Sir Robin – born Robert – McAlpine, chairman of the Sir Robert McAlpine construction company, died aged 86. His Circus Plume won the 1984 Oaks. He left estate valued at over £17m.

20 FEBRUARY

SIGNIFICANT EVENT

2009 As the credit crunch began to bite, Irish radio station RTE revealed that due to 'economic difficulties' they would be unable to send popular racing correspondent Colm Murray to the Cheltenham Festival – the first time he would not be reporting from there for 18 years.

STRANGEST EVENT

2009 Having escaped from prison, convicted fraudster Terry Kirby, whose speciality was impersonating jockeys, was captured. He was serving eight months for car robbery having previously impersonated Dean Gallagher, Graham Lee, Timmy Murphy, Shay Barry and Leighton Aspell, amongst others.

OTHER EVENTS

1883 Racing began at the premier Indian track, Bombay.

1993 US jockey Bill Shoemaker reportedly negotiated an out-of-court $1m settlement with Ford, who built the car he was driving on the night of the crash which paralysed him.

1993 A record Hong Kong tierce – 1,2,3 – dividend at Sha Tin paid HK$390,697 for HK$10 when a 140/1-shot beat 12/1 and 100/1 chances.

1993 Beat Them Up did just that to Lester Piggott at Sha Tin, gashing him over the left eye when he reared up, and putting Lester, just back from another injury, back in hospital, having earlier ridden his first Hong Kong winner since 1986 on the equally well named 7/1-shot So Easy.

1993 Punters who backed the 7/2 chance Spring Hill Spirit to win the race at South Durham point-to-point were not best pleased when it transpired that the horse hadn't even made it to the course. The stakes were eventually refunded.

2008 Tony McCoy revealed he had been literally freezing himself in a 'kriotherapy' unit, introduced into the country by former trainer Charlie Brooks, and which aims to increase recovery time by putting the subject in a -125C° temperature environment. AP did two sessions of two and a half minutes as he battled to get over a back injury from a Warwick fall in mid-January in time for Cheltenham.

2008 Britain's newest racecourse, Great Leighs, was given yet another potential opening date – one of several since its scheduled opening in October 2006 – of Friday April 4, 2008.

QUOTE OF THE DAY

'No business that is closed down, as racing was at Sandown Park by a group of its participants – the jockeys – striking for the dubious human right of ringing their punters from the weighing room, can see itself as very far from a laughing stock.' Brough Scott, who broke his arm when National Hitch fell at Doncaster on this day in 1968, commenting on a 2003 incident, in which jockeys objected to a mobile phone ban.

BIRTHDAYS

1883 Trainer Reg Day who sent out Solario to win the 1925 St Leger and Sweet Solera to win the 1961 1,000 Guineas and Oaks.

1926 Owner of Dahlia, Empery and Youth, Nelson Bunker Hunt.

1931 Newmarket trainer David Ringer.

1935 Yorkshire trainer Ernie Weymes.

DEATHS OF THE DAY

2008 One of three fillies to win the Kentucky Derby – in 1988 – Winning Colors was put down, 23.

2008 Gabriel 'Squibs' Curran, 58, who partnered 1977 2,000 Guineas winner Nebbiolo to victory.

CELEBRITY OF THE DAY

1993 Jockey Maxine Juster, who wed Kent cricketer Graham Cowdrey.

21 FEBRUARY

SIGNIFICANT EVENT
2009 The small matter of £2,755,923 was riding on 7/2 favourite Big Fella Thanks, owned by Harry Findlay, in the Racing Post Chase at Kempton, after an anonymous Suffolk man who won the previous week's Scoop6 worth £669,465.50 pledged to donate his Bonus payment to the Royal British Legion should he win. In the event the horse finished third – but the donor then handed over £200,000 of his previous winnings.

STRANGEST EVENT
1989 After novice hurdler Hello Rocky jumped atrociously and fell at Huntingdon, jockey Barrie Wright claimed to the stewards that the horse was deaf and this was a contributory factor.

OTHER EVENTS
1860 Harry Grimshaw rode a treble at Nottingham. He won the 1865 Derby on Gladiateur, but died the next year when the trap he was driving at night overturned.

1911 Jump racing ceased at Doncaster, but was revived in 1946.

1987 Record-breaking jumps trainer Michael Dickinson flew out to launch his new training career in Maryland, USA, declaring he had 'no plans to train again in England', which he has not done.

1967 The Isle of Man parliament voted to permit cash betting 'with grave misgivings.'

1990 Peter Scudamore rode his his 1200th winner, Run For Free, 5/2, at Warwick.

1992 The Jockey Club confirmed that security officers were investigating the running of some all weather races.

1993 Vincent O'Brien's son, Charles, saddled his first runner, Yukon Gold at 7/1, coming fourth in the Punchestown Hurdle.

1993 Returning after a heart attack, US trainer Gary Jones appeared to be offering Santa Anita punters a real coincidence bet by saddling Cardiac on his first day back. Punters ended up broken-hearted as it could only manage second.

1994 *Daily Star* tipster Tony Lewis went through the card at Wolverhampton for a 10,022/1 accumulator, having set a world record of 45,044/1 when doing the same thing at Lingfield in 1993.

QUOTE OF THE DAY
'Because every time he comes on the telly and gives an interview he tells the truth,' declared owner Harry Findlay, revealing why he had named his 8/13 Kempton novice chase winner of this day in 2009, Herecomesthetruth, in honour of trainer Paul Nicholls.

BIRTHDAYS
1905 Eccentric but very wealthy owner Dorothy Paget born. She owned great chaser Golden Miller, five-times Gold Cup winner, and 1943 Derby winner Straight Deal.

1967 Triple Crown winner Nijinsky (by Northern Dancer out of Flaming Page).

DEATH OF THE DAY
1998 Ridden by Robbie Supple for permit holder Lavinia Taylor, Domaine de Pron won the Eider Chase at Newcastle – but collapsed and died seconds later.

CELEBRITY OF THE DAY
1596 The fifth Earl of Rutland, keen racehorse owner during reign of Elizabeth I, recorded the fact that his runner won the 'forest race of Galteresse.'

22 FEBRUARY

SIGNIFICANT EVENT
2008 With a 50p, eight-horse accumulator, starting with Isn't That Lucky, 10/1, at Sandown, and ending with A Dream Come True, 2/1, at Wolverhampton, Thirsk man Fred Craggs became a millionaire after William Hill waived their £100,000 limit on bets including foreign races – three of his winners were at Nad Al Sheba.

STRANGEST EVENT
1992 With two to jump 8/11 favourite Plat Reay was clear in a Stratford chase. Jockey Carl Llewellyn rode him into the fence, there was a flash from a camera and the horse fell. After something like that had developed, it seemed likely the jockey might snap, but he didn't and put everyone in the picture.

OTHER EVENTS
1960 Lester Piggott married Susan Armstrong, daughter of trainer Frederick Armstrong. They had two daughters, Maureen and Tracy.

1993 One time 'wonder horse', Azari, commenced stud duties at Newmarket's Dalham Hall stud.

1994 Aussie jockey Mark Sestich, four times top rider in Western Australia, was banned for six months for betting offences, which also resulted in two of WA's biggest bookies, Kim Hunter and Keith Dixon, being stood down for twelve months.

1995 After 111 years of continuous use, Hong Kong's Happy Valley closed for refurbishment with a record 51,892 spectators attending final meeting.

1999 The previous year's champion 2yo filly and ante-post favourite for the 1,000 Guineas, Mick Channon's Bint Allayl, fractured her shoulder, a fatal injury, on the Lambourn gallops.

2003 12yo gelding, Leaping Plum won the same race – the 4f Grasmick Handicap – for an astonishing eighth time since 1995, at Fonner Park, Nebraska. He came back in 2004 but finished fourth.

QUOTE OF THE DAY
'I threw a kiss to the heavens because I knew Vinny would be looking down on us,' said 1992 Cheltenham Gold Cup-winning jockey Adrian Maguire, dedicating his win on Cool Ground to his brother, killed in a hit-and-run accident. On this day in 1997 Maguire rode a 355/1 accumulator of five winners at Kempton.

BIRTHDAYS
1938 Australian Hall of fame jockey Ron Quinton. Several times champion in Sydney, he rode often for Robert Sangster. He tried his luck in England but only managed four placings from ten rides before returning home.

1939 Owner of One Man and Azertyuiop, John Hales.

1955 Jump-jockey-turned trainer Ridley Lamb, who rode The Thinker to win the 1987 Cheltenham Gold Cup.

1965 Champion jockey Kieren Fallon, at Crushee, Co Clare.

DEATHS OF THE DAY
1989 Jump jockey Albert Power, 68, who rode Overshadow to win the 1953 Irish Grand National.

1994 Owner-breeder of Brigadier Gerard, John Hislop, 82. Rode 102 Flat winners and was champion amateur for eleven straight years. He partnered 48 jumps winners and was third in the 1947 Grand National on Kami.

1999 Newmarket trainer Tom Waugh, 83, who won the 1962 2,000 Guineas with Privy Councillor. Younger brother of trainer Jack.

CELEBRITY OF THE DAY
1990 England footballer-turned-trainer Mick Channon sent out his first runner, the unplaced 66/1 Dear Miff, at Wincanton, in a novice hurdle.

23 FEBRUARY

SIGNIFICANT EVENT
1968 Derby, Eclipse, King George VI & Queen Elizabeth Stakes, Arc and Coronation Cup winner Mill Reef born in the USA, bred by his owner Paul Mellon. Mill Reef sired the 1978 Derby winner, Shirley Heights.

STRANGEST EVENT
2009 Will Biddick rode 7/2 chance Chopneyev into third at Plumpton despite dropping his whip when he began his drive for home. Fortunately, he apparently suddenly acquired another which, he said, landed in his lap after being hurled into the air when another jockey came a cropper earlier in the race. Sounds plausible, wouldn't you say?

OTHER EVENTS
1935 The oldest continually run $100,000 stakes in the USA, the Santa Anita Handicap, was run for the first time.

1939 Five-times Cheltenham Gold Cup winner Golden Miller ran his final race, unplaced in a Newbury handicap chase.

1963 Belmont Stakes winner, Chateaugay, a son of 1955 Kentucky Derby winner Swaps, made a winning 3yo debut at Hialeah, over 7f, beating the champion 2yo Never Bend, in the process.

1972 Triple Grand-National winning jockey Brian Fletcher fell at Teesside and was unconscious for ten days. He was advised never to ride again.

1993 Mansfield House, trained by Peter Upson at Folkestone, raced on an unfamiliar surface when his horsebox crashed on the A604 dual carriageway near Huntingdon. The horse charged off along the road but was caught before damaging himself.

2001 With Northern Californian horses being 'lured' to other racing jurisdictions to compete because of higher prize money and more frequent racing, state racing commissioners called on racing leaders 'to stem the exodus and prevent fields from shrivelling to disastrous levels'.

2009 Australia's Victoria Racing Club announced it would donate gate receipts and catering profits, worth over A$500,000, to the Country Fire Authority, following recent bushfire tragedies. Sheikh Mohammed donated a further A$1m.

QUOTE OF THE DAY
2009 *'You wouldn't want him to run unbacked'* explained owner Craig Watts after revealing he had a tenner each way at 100/1 on his 66/1 at Wolverhampton winner Just Timmy Marcus.

BIRTHDAYS
1904 Trainer Marcus Marsh. He sent out 1934 and 1952 Derby winners Windsor Lad and Tulyar, having been dismissed by his uncle, trainer Fred Darling, for not placing all his bets via him!

1927 Jocelyn Reavey, who became a trainer following the death of husband Eddie in 1981.

1948 Trainer Sue – wife of Harvey – Smith.

1968 Jockey Peter Hutton, who won the 1988 German St Leger on Goodbye Fancy.

DEATH OF THE DAY
1995 Dual Melbourne Cup winner Think Big (1974/5), aged 24.

CELEBRITY OF THE DAY
1992 The Queen opened the new grandstand at Randwick, Australia, and presented the Queen's Cup to connections of the Tommy Smith-trained Aquidity.

24 FEBRUARY

SIGNIFICANT EVENT

1994 Amidst concerns that all-weather hurdling was proving too dangerous, the BHB cancelled the season's four remaining meetings. Thirteen horses had died on such cards. On the same day War Beat died in a Lingfield hurdle race while the last all-weather hurdle there was won by Royal Circus 100/30, ridden by David Bridgwater who quit at 27 on this day in 1998 when told his injured arm would not recover. He won the Scottish National on Earth Summit.

STRANGEST EVENT

2009 Top trainer Mark Johnston resumed work following a skiing holiday – with the unwanted souvenir from St Moritz of a broken leg.

OTHER EVENTS

1947 13 French horses were entered for the Lincoln – quoted at 5/1 for any of them to win at first call-over of prices at the Victoria Club. It was won by the 100/1 chance Jockey Treble.

1964 Canada's best 2yo of the previous year, Northern Dancer, won at Hialeah en route to winning the Kentucky Derby and Preakness before finishing third in the Belmont Stakes.

1979 Trainer J C Williams set a world record when sending out eight winners at Waterford Park (since re-named Mountaineer Park), West Virginia on a twelve-race card.

1982 Hollywood Park, California, was announced as the venue for the inaugural Breeder's Cup meeting in November that year.

1992 A foal out of grey 7yo mare Halvoya, and sired by Indian Ridge, was born two months early at Campbell Stud, Bury St Edmunds, reportedly becoming the earliest premature thoroughbred in Britain to survive.

1993 Police launched an investigation after wheels fell off horseboxes belonging to trainers Philip Mitchell and Mick Naughton in separate incidents.

1996 Trainer Micky Hammond ran 13 horses at Musselburgh (last four winners) and Haydock (two), and had a 64,259/1 six timer.

2008 Lough Derg was the 5/1 winner of Fontwell's National Sprint Hurdle, partnered by Tom Scudamore, who was boosted into the big time by the victory – repeated in the 2009 running when they were 5/2 favourites. 'Every jockey needs a horse to define his early career. My father (Peter) had Broadsword and I've got Lough Derg' said the jockey, of the David Pipe trained horse.

QUOTE OF THE DAY

'Over the years, I've been very lucky,' said jockey Brendan Powell, who broke his leg at Doncaster today in 1992, apparently overlooking the small matter of a ruptured stomach, internal bleeding, another broken leg, a broken arm, broken wrist, and broken collar bones.

BIRTHDAYS

1911 The splendidly named US trainer Noble Threewit, responsible for the equally excellently nomenclatured Cuzwuzwrong.

1938 Trainer of 1981 Kentucky Derby and Preakness winner Pleasant Colony, John Paul Compo.

1944 Lewes trainer, Roger Hoad.

FIRST OF THE DAY

1985 Simon Sherwood won on his first ride in France, the Philip Mitchell-trained Duelling, at Cagnes-Sur-Mer.

CELEBRITY OF THE DAY

1968 High-profile owner Charles St George, who served in the Coldstream Guards from 1943-49 and became an underwriting member of Lloyds. Owner of 1972 Oaks winner Ginevra and 1975 St Leger winner Bruni, he celebrated his first jumps winner, Marcus Brutus at Lingfield, 16 years after his first Flat winner.

25 FEBRUARY

SIGNIFICANT EVENT
1993 The Jockey Club revealed that the Geoff Lewis-trained Flash Of Straw, backed from 25/1 to 4/1 favourite at Yarmouth on August 20 the previous year, but unplaced, had been doped.

STRANGEST EVENT
1997 Adrian Maguire broke his arm at Leicester – meaning for the third successive year he would miss the Cheltenham Festival. The previous year he had suffered a broken collar bone; in 1995 he was in mourning for his mother.

OTHER EVENTS
1956 Kentucky Derby and Belmont Stakes winner, Needles, won at Hialeah in Florida.

1988 Triple Champion Hurdler (1985-7) See You Then was retired after pulling up at Wincanton. An unsuccessful comeback two years later produced no wins from four outings.

1988 Richard Guest came down to earth with a bump at Wincanton – recording his eighth fall in five days.

1993 Charlie Swan rode his first four-timer, at odds of 400/1, at Tipperary.

2004 'He is pretty irresponsible sometimes, and too loud for the BBC.' Just who could Clare Balding have been discussing in today's *Times*? You're right – John McCririck.

2009 Bangor-on-Dee racecourse – reportedly Dick Francis' favourite track – celebrated its 150th anniversary – and there were probably still people managing to go to the 'wrong' Bangor!

QUOTE OF DAY
'Sleeping' answered jockey Hywel Davies when asked to name his favourite recreation, but on this day in 1984 he was nearly doing that permanently when he 'technically died' following a fall from Solid Rock at Doncaster. He rode there once more, fell, and decided never again.

BIRTHDAYS
1905 Oaklawn Park racecourse which opened for buisness today in Arkansas, with 3000 turning up as the Mayor declared a half-day holiday to mark the occassion.

1947 Moscow Flyer's trainer Jessica Harrington.

1954 Trainer Michael Blanshard – hobby archaeology – who dug up winners like Ardrox Lad and Lemhill.

1958 Patricia Cooksey, at Newton Falls, USA. The first female jockey to ride in the Preakness Stakes, the second to ride in the Kentucky Derby, the first to ride stakes winner at Churchill Downs where she was the all-time leading female, winning on 144 of her 1,126 mounts there in 1991, for prize money of $1,791,053.

1973 Seven-times champion UAE jockey Ted Durcan.

DEATHS OF THE DAY
2001 John Tammaro jr, 75. A top US jockey who rode nearly 1,000 winners before becoming a successful trainer for 35 years.

2005 Four-times Polish champion jockey Tomasz Dul, 54, in a car accident. He rode almost 1,300 winners.

FIRST OF THE DAY
1938 Bryan Marshall, champion jump jockey of 1947-8, Grand National winner in 1953 and '54, rode his first winner over jumps, Carlore, for Noel Murless in a Manchester selling hurdle.

26 FEBRUARY

SIGNIFICANT EVENT
1839 Some say it was the first Grand National, others that that happened three years earlier. Whatever, the Grand Liverpool Steeplechase was run at Aintree and was won by the best chaser of the day, Lottery, partnered by Jem Mason. During the race Captain Becher fell/jumped/took refuge into the ditch subsequently named after him and secured immortality.

STRANGEST EVENT
2008 Racing at Catterick was abandoned even as runners circled before the opening race, because of 75mph winds battering the track.

OTHER EVENTS
1789 Unbeaten Eclipse died of kidney failure aged 24 at 7pm – although some sources, including Nicholas Clee in his excellent 2009 book, *Eclipse*, suggest it happened on February 27.
1985 Racing's jockey-optician, Andy Orkney, made a spectacle of himself by winning for the first time when partnering Golden Ty at Nottingham.
1955 Nashua won at Hialeah, Florida, only to lose out to Swaps in the Kentucky Derby before bouncing back to win both the Preakness and Belmont Stakes.
1998 Trainer Lynda Ramsden, husband Jack and jockey Kieren Fallon were awarded libel damages of £195,000 in the High Court over allegations they had conspired to cheat racegoers. They brought libel action against *The Sporting Life* over a 'savage verbal onslaught' in an unsigned comment piece published after their Top Cees won the Chester Cup at 8/1, alleging they conspired to deceive the public by deliberately not trying with the horse in a race three weeks previously.

QUOTE OF THE DAY
2008 *'From the back of the nostril forwards, rather than the old margin of a short head'* explained racecourse judge Felix Wheeler, after awarding Coral Shores, ridden by Adrian McCarthy at Lingfield, the first ever win by the newly introduced shortest margin of 'a nose'. Any the wiser? No, me neither.

BIRTHDAY
1909 Trainer Paddy Sleator, who won the 1960 Champion Hurdle with Another Flash. He caused controversy in the early 1960s by sending a string of fit horses from his Co. Wicklow stables to Arthur Thomas' Warwickshire yard from which they farmed good autumn and early-winter races until outraged English trainers intervened and the authorities clamped down.

DEATHS OF THE DAY
1839 Dictator became the first horse to die in the Grand National, falling at the second brook.
1918 A stand collapsed and caught fire at Happy Valley, Hong Kong, and some 600 died.
1991 Jockey Tommy Burns, 92. He rode 21 Irish Classic winners, the first aged 17.
2009 Four-times winner of the Aintree Hurdle, twice winner of the Breeders' Cup Chase and 1991 Champion Hurdler, Morley Street, 25. He raced 45 times, won 20, and collected win/place prize money of £589,589.

CELEBRITY OF THE DAY
1937 The King George VI Chase, inaugurated as a tribute to the newly installed monarch, was run for the first time at Kempton. It was won by Southern Hero, ridden by Jack Fawcus, trained by Gwyn Evans at Druids Lodge Stables, Salisbury.

27 FEBRUARY

SIGNIFICANT EVENT
1952 Federico Tesio's broodmare Romanella, in foal to Derby Italiano winner Tenerani, gave birth at the National Stud, West Grinstead, to dual Arc winner Ribot, named after an obscure 19th century French painter.

STRANGEST EVENT
1993 Believed to be the oldest active jump jockey in the country, 56-year-old George Turner rode Rathmichael to win at the Lemalla point-to-point in Cornwall – the first winner he'd ridden there in 25 years of trying.

OTHER EVENTS
1973 Brantridge Farmer won at Fontwell, making Auriol Sinclair the first woman trainer to send out 100 winners.
1978 Love From Verona, ridden by Nicky Henderson, gave Barry Hills his first winner over jumps as a trainer.
1988 Son of Secretariat, Risen Star, won the Louisiana Derby Trial Stakes. He went on to win the Louisiana Derby, then finished third in the Kentucky Derby, winning both Preakness and Belmont Stakes.
1993 Veteran trainer Noble Threewit, 82, saddled Devoted Brad to win the San Raphael Stakes at Santa Anita.
1996 Steve Wynne lived up to his name on Eastern River, 16/1 at Leicester. The 25-year-old registered his first success since smashing his leg so badly at Haydock on December 16 that surgeons considered amputation.
2001 Horse racing was suspended following today's meetings, shortly after the outbreak of foot and mouth disease. Cheltenham Festival was amongst the casualties.

QUOTE OF THE DAY
2008 An earthquake of 5.2 on the Richter scale, the strongest for 25 years, hit England – its epicentre at Market Rasen, where racecourse MD Pip Kirkby commented: *'We've been telling everyone for years that Market Rasen is the epicentre of the world.'* No other racing damage was reported.

BIRTHDAYS
1901 Argentinian trainer in the US, Horatio Luro. His Decidedly and Northern Dancer both won the Kentucky Derby. He lived to 90.
1915 Trainer Cyril Mitchell, who trained Attivo and Be Friendly for Peter O'Sullevan.
1934 Triple Grand National-winning trainer and world-class pessimist, Captain Tim Forster.
1970 Top US jockey Kent Desormeaux, who rode a record 598 winners in 1989; has won three Kentucky Derbys and was the first foreign jockey to win a Japanese Classic.

DEATHS OF THE DAY
1992 Former Epsom based jockey and trainer, Albert Patrick 'Munch' Taylor, 77.
2000 The man who bred Desert Orchid, James Burridge, 78.
2000 Pioneer of transporting racehorses by air in the in USA, H E 'Tex' Sutton, 78. He started his business in 1969, prior to which horses moved around by rail or road.
2003 US jockey with 2,450 career wins, Jimmy 'Cowboy' Nicholls, 74.

CELEBRITIES OF THE DAY
1932 National Velvet star, actress Elizabeth Taylor born.
1951 Steve Harley, owner with Jeff Pearce, punter, racegoer, rock star and inspiration for the name of 2,000 Guineas winner Cockney Rebel.

28 FEBRUARY

SIGNIFICANT EVENT
1938 Dorothy Paget's Golden Miller, perhaps the greatest ever chaser, won for the final time in an optional selling chase at Birmingham, starting the 8/100 favourite.

STRANGEST EVENT
1991 Hellenic Prince threw John McLaughlin during the three-runner Tarragon Hurdle at Lingfield and raced back to the unsaddling area. The jockey remounted there and returned to the course for third prize money of £231 but by then the hurdles had been removed and the judge had departed, so to no avail.

OTHER EVENTS
1699 Diarist John Evelyn noted 'The Duke of Devon lost £1900 at a race horse race at Newmarket.' A substantial wager today, let alone 300 years ago.

1844 Discount won the Grand National – thus named after owner Mr Quartermaine negotiated down the price requested by Mr Payne for the horse.

1936 Wheatley won a £317 hurdle race at Gatwick, trained by Walter Nightingall – his first for owner Dorothy Paget for whom he would eventually train 210 winners.

1980 18yo Sonny Somers won over fences at Lingfield to register his second success at an age seldom equalled and never exceeded.

1987 Princess Anne made her NH debut, finishing last of four at Kempton. She had won on the flat aboard Gulfland the previous August.

2001 No UK racing from today because of foot and mouth outbreak.

2009 The Reverend won a Kelso chase at a Sunday meeting – possibly with divine help, as the horse was owned by the Reverend Fiona Sample, 53, whose churches were in the parishes of Whalton, Hartburn, Meldon, Bolam and Netherwhitton in north-east England.

QUOTE OF THE DAY
'The great joy of jump racing is that everyone with whom you rub shoulders in the stands in a bitter November rain is a true believer', which is just what keen racegoer, tipster, close pal of John McCririck, and former Labour foreign secretary, Robin Cook, born today in 1946, was.

BIRTHDAYS
1920 Owner Priscilla Hastings, whose Taxidermist stuffed the opposition in both the Whitbread and Hennessy Gold Cups in 1958.

1933 Trainer (Hubert) Pat Rohan, who ended up in Bahrain. He won consecutive July Cups with Right Boy and Tin Whistle in 1959 and 1960.

1958 Trainer Nigel Tinkler – by the age of 16 he had ridden winners on the Flat, over hurdles and over fences.

1943 Twice champion jump jockey Ron Barry, who won the 1973 Gold Cup on The Dikler. Later became an inspector of courses.

DEATH OF THE DAY
2008 Jockey-turned-trainer George Vergette, 87. He rode the first of 50 winners on the Flat aged 15 then switched to jumps and rode 67 more. Began training in 1944, sending out 42 Flat and 298 jumps winners, while Purple Silk was runner-up to Team Spirit in the 1964 National.

CELEBRITY OF THE DAY
2003 Founder of the London Marathon, Gold Medal-winning athlete (3,000m steeplechase, Melbourne) and pacemaker for Roger Bannister in the first four-minute mile, Chris Brasher, died aged 74. An owner from 1990, notably with Heart and Non So who both won Kempton's Lanzarote Hurdle, and Maid For Walking, winner of the Redcar 2yo Trophy in 1995

29 FEBRUARY

SIGNIFICANT EVENT

1984 John Francome rode his 1,000th winner over jumps in Britain, Observe at Worcester. Albert Fuller of Mottingham, London had £100 on it in his local William Hill branch, to mark his 100th birthday.

STRANGEST EVENT

1992 Hereford staged a candidate for worst race ever. The February Novice Selling Hurdle had 13 runners. None had ever finished in the first three of any race. Six were pulled up. Two fell. One unseated rider. Last of the four to finish was tailed off. The 50/1 third finished 'at one pace', the runner-up, 20/1, who completed in 29.8s slower than average, found 'no extra on flat'. The winner Arr Eff Bee had form figures of PPPB, was returned at 50/1, and attracted absolutely no bids at the after-race auction.

OTHER EVENTS

1996 Nottingham's last day as a jumping course. Dominie, ridden by Timmy Murphy and trained by Kim Bailey, was the final winner in a hurdle race at 7/1. Graham Bradley won the final chase on Andre Laval at 4/1 for Charlie Brooks.
2008 South Australian Jockey CLub announced that it was 'financially irresponsible' to continue racing at the 160 year old Adelaide track, Victoria Park. It closed in the August of that year.
2008 Expect Money lived up to its name for punters at Oaklawn, Arknasa, winning at 54/1.
2008 Reflecting on little known but but record breaking Canadian born jockey Russell Baze, with over 10,000 wins to his credit, LA Times writer called him 'the most famous non-famous jockey ever to be lifted up on a thoroughbred.' Most of Baze's winners have been at Bay Meadows and Golden Gate in North California.

QUOTE OF THE DAY

'It's quite easy to explain. I was christened in a small Catholic church in Kent, and there must have been a mistake. There is absolutely no doubt about it. I was born on July 29.' His birth certificate says he was born on February 29; but Irish-based trainer Dermot Weld, who has won Group races on four continents, and has a full set of Irish Classics, insists he was born on July 29, 1948.

BIRTHDAYS

1916 Rider of consecutive Grand National winners in 1953/4, Bryan Marshall.
1940 US trainer of Seattle Slew, Billy Turner.
1950 Jump jockey T.G. Davies, who rode for R C Armytage.

DEATH OF THE DAY

1988 Nan(cy) Kennedy, 78, one of the first women trainers, albeit she had been doing the job for half a century before being allowed to hold a licence in her own name in 1977. She won the Schweppes Gold Trophy and Welsh Champion Hurdle with Ra Nova in 1984.

FIRST OF THE DAY

1836 William Lynn staged the first Liverpool Grand Steeplechase at Aintree, won by The Duke and ridden by Captain Becher. Was this the first Grand National? Ten went to post, with The Duke favourite at 3/1 behind Laurie Todd, 2/1. Becher almost completed a notable double, but his mount Ironsides was an unlucky second in the other chase on the card, having been remounted, after coming down because of a poorly filled hole in the course.

1 MARCH

SIGNIFICANT EVENT
1843 For the first time the fledgling Grand National, aka the Liverpool and National Chase, became a handicap, framed by William Topham. Vanguard won under 11st 10lbs with Peter Simple lugging top weight of 13st 1lb. Winning jockey Tom Olliver became the first to win the race in successive seasons.

STRANGEST EVENT
1839 R Ackermann published a set of four prints purporting to depict the 'first steeple chace on record' allegedly run overnight in 1803 by the 3rd Dragoons, stationed at Ipswich, who raced from their barracks to Nacton Church.

OTHER EVENTS
1906 In a forerunner of the now famous St Moritz frozen lake races 12 riderless horses contested a race there.
1944 Cottage Rake was unplaced on his racecourse debut on the Flat at Thurles. He improved to win three Cheltenham Gold Cups from 1948-50.
1969 What A Myth warmed up for a tilt at the Cheltenham Gold Cup by winning a hunter chase at Market Rasen by 20 lengths, landing another at Newbury a week later before winning the big one.
1969 Tuesdee Testa, 27, became the first female to win at a major US course when she rode Buz On to win at Santa Anita.
1989 Martin Pipe became the first National Hunt trainer to saddle 150 winners in a season, courtesy of Beau Ranger, 40/85, at Worcester.
1991 Bill Shoemaker, Laffit Pincay, Angel Cordero, Chis McCarron, Jorge Velasquez – now Pat Day, finishing second on Wild Sierra at Oaklawn Park, became only the sixth jockey to win $100m prize money.
1994 Richard Dunwoody was suspended for 14 days for 'intentional interference' with Adrian Maguire's Mr Geneaology, 4/5 fav, at Nottingham. Dunwoody was

also disqualified and placed last.
2000 Professional punter Dave Nevison described his activities as 'a very hard way to make easy money'.
2008 The largest field for 25 years, of 14, as Heatseeker, 7/1, won the $1m Santa Anita Handicap. Trained by Jerry Hollendorfer.

QUOTE OF THE DAY
1940 *'Ron, if you get a new owner, don't win a race for two years. Get them used to losing first.'* Interesting advice proferred by former jockey-turned-permit trainer John Gambler to fellow handler Ron Hodges, winner of both the Ayr Gold and Silver Cups, born on this day.

BIRTHDAYS
1941 Trainer of Japanese equine phenomenon and disqualified Arc third, Deep Impact, Yasuo Ikee.
1959 Jockey-turned-trainer in France, Stuart Cargeeg.
1977 Irish dual-licence jockey Ross Geraghty.

DEATHS OF THE DAY
1992 Jockey Davy (D.L.) Jones, 84, who rode Red Power to win the 1945 Cheltenham Gold Cup. He won the Kenya Derby aged 62 and continued to ride there until prevented when he reached 65.
1994 Somerset dual-purpose trainer Richard Holder, 61, who won the 1989 Triumph Hurdle with Ikdam and the 1987 Lincoln with Star of a Gunner.
1996 36-year-old US trainer Rodney Rash died 'from complications of a rare blood disorder'. His Urgent Request won the Santa Anita Handicap in 1995 to give him his biggest victory. Trained 143 winners from 1,061 starts, worth $8,707,331.

CELEBRITY OF THE DAY
1945 Rock star-turned racehorse owner, Roger Daltrey of The Who born.

2 MARCH

SIGNIFICANT EVENT
2004 Keiren Fallon and fancied 15/8 chance Ballinger Ridge were caught and beaten on the line at Lingfield, having been well clear at one stage. The race would spark wild rumours and allegations of race fixing. 'I've never made a mistake like that, before or since' declared Fallon.

STRANGEST EVENT
1954 The opening race at the Cheltenham Festival was the Birdlip Selling Hurdle, won by Mull Sack – ridden by up and coming jump jockey ... Lester Piggott.

OTHER EVENTS
1781 The minutes of Doncaster Corporation recorded that Mr John Carr should receive 100gns 'for his trouble in architecting and directing' the work of constructing Doncaster racecourse's grandstand, which cost them £2,637.
1938 Front running Airgead Sios won the second King George VI Chase for trainer Vic Tabor, beating three opponents.
1948 National Spirit won his second successive Champion Hurdle for trainer Vic Smyth, who had changed the horse's name from Avago.
1985 Hieronymous at Haydock was jockey Peter Scudamore's first ride, and first winner, for trainer Martin Pipe.
1986 The Santa Anita Handicap became the first such race with a guaranteed value of $1m.
1996 Women were permitted to compete at major courses in Japan for the first time. Yukiko Makihara, 18, finished fourth in the first race on the card at Tokyo track Nakayama on 33/1-shot Daiwa Asahi. Maki Tamura, 18, rode at the same course, Junko Hosoe, 20, at Chukyo.
1997 Willie Carson announced his retirement – in the News of the World.

QUOTE OF THE DAY
'Beating John Francome in a photo-finish the day before my 21st birthday'. Highlight of Lorna Vincent's – born today, 1959 – riding career in which she also won on her first rides over hurdles and fences.

BIRTHDAYS
1838 Trainer of seven Derby winners, John Porter, at Rugeley, Staffs. He took over at Kingsclere stables in 1868 and retired in 1905 having won 1,063 races worth £720,021 over 43 seasons. He also helped found Newbury racecourse.
1959 Clwyd trainer Cathie Lloyd-Jones who claims to have been the youngest trainer granted a licence – she was 21 when she received it.
1971 Jockey Jason Titley, who won the 1995 Grand National on Royal Athlete.

DEATHS OF THE DAY
1994 Matty Curran, who won Irish Grand Nationals on Vulpine and Dim Wit, 51.
2009 The 1993 Arc winner and top stud mare, Urban Sea, 20. Amongst her sons were 1998 Derby winner Galileo, and Sea The Stars who won the Epsom Classic in 2009.

CELEBRITY OF THE DAY
1947 Football manager and owner with Jamie Osborne and Bryan Smart, Harry Redknapp born.

3 MARCH

SIGNIFICANT EVENT
2009 Hayley Turner, who had ridden 100 winners in 2008, was hospitalised after suffering head injuries from a stalls injury in Newmarket whilst schooling Old Sarum. The injury threatened to keep her out all year.

STRANGEST EVENT
1974 Owner-trainer-breeder John Thorne rode his Woodland Wedding, 10/1, to dead-heat with that horse's sister Flying Timber, 20/1, who he also bred, at Warwick.

OTHER EVENTS
1847 The first race named the Grand National Handicap Chase was run at Liverpool, won by 9yo Mathew.

1959 The Ryan Price-trained Fare Time won the Champion Hurdle, one of Fred Winter's then record five Festival winners.

1984 7lb-claiming amateur Richard Dunwoody rode a 1,628/1 four-timer at Hereford.

1985 Bill Shoemaker became the first jockey to reach $1m career earnings as Lord At War won the Santa Anita Handicap.

1987 Birmingham Turf Club, the first thoroughbred track in America's 'Deep South' opened, despite objections from local religious leaders. After a 175 day season during which operators lost over $50m, the Turf Club went bankrupt. The course re-opened in May, 1989.

1991 Lester Piggott rode the 10/1 shot Delage to win the Indian Turf Invitation Cup in Madras.

1992 Peter Scudamore became the first jump jockey to ride 1,500 winners when Slavi won a novice hurdle at Warwick.

1995 Sheikh Mohammed had his first all-weather winner when 13/8 favourite Warluskee won a Southwell maiden. On the same card the East Midlands Electricity Handicap was won, shockingly, by A Million Watts, 6/1.

1997 Horses ready; jockeys ready: racegoers ready – but no sign of judge Nick Haynes, who finally arrived late at Southwell, delaying the racing by six mintues.

2009 Sporting form figures POPPFP, Teeming Rain, running in just that at Exeter, was a 20/1 winner for AP McCoy.

QUOTE OF THE DAY
'I pulled a masterstroke, because I fell off my horse onto my head and landed in the back of an ambulance. This is absolutely what you should do if you want to find out whether a girl is remotely interested in you'. Old Etonian trainer-turned novelist Charlie Brooks, born today in 1963, on his first date with his now wife, *Sun* editor Rebekah Wade.

BIRTHDAYS
1918 Sir Peter O'Sullevan, CBE, who named his autobiography *Calling The Horses*. He might have become a jockey but on the eve of his debut in Plumpton novice chase during WWII he contracted pneumonia, saving himself from 'an excursion which neither horse or rider could reasonably have been expected to survive'.

1923 Aussie-born, Irish-based jockey Garnie Bougoure.

1924 US Hall of Fame trainer Elliott Burch.

1948 Trainer Sir Mark Prescott, he of the politically incorrect love of cigars, coursing and bull fighting – and putting one over the handicapper.

1952 Newmarket trainer Lord John Fitzgerald, whose riding career of 104 mounts resulted in two victories.

DEATH OF THE DAY
2000 Canadian Hall of Fame trainer Donald Campbell, 88.

CELEBRITY OF THE DAY
Born today in 1946, snooker star-turned commentator and owner of Jokist, John Virgo.

4 MARCH

SIGNIFICANT EVENT
1840 With bullock trucks as grandstands, a clothes prop as the winning post, with bets struck and settled in rum – it was the second day of the first race meeting at what became known as Flemington in Melbourne.

STRANGEST EVENT
1995 Having deliberately forgotten to tell girlfriend Zoe that he had paid £350 plus VAT – cost of a modest honeymoon – to sponsor the Zoe Hurworth Will You Marry Me? Stakes at Lingfield, Jason Brautigam faced the ordeal of awaiting her answer. She said yes ... but they never did wed.

OTHER EVENTS
1846 Horse names don't come much odder than Hornihiharriho, a 33/1 shot who fell in today's Liverpool and National Chase. The winner, Pioneer, was such a no-hoper that he was returned unquoted in the betting.

1868 Grand National favourite Chimney Sweep broke a leg without jumping a fence – when he hit course-marking rock.

1978 Red Rum was unplaced in his 110th and last race, the Greenall Whitley Brewers Chase at Haydock. Rummy won three Flat races, three hurdles, 21 chases and £115,234 prize money.

1985 Jonothan Lower rode his first winner, Silver Ace, at Wetherby.

1989 Martin Pipe sent out two runners at Hereford, two at Newbury and two at Haydock – and they all won.

1993 Following a spate of doping cases, the Jockey CLub announced a reward of £5000 for information leading to convictions.

2009 *The Irish Times* reported that internet punters in Ireland were being turned down for mortgages by banks taking a 'negative view of regular gambling outgoings.'

QUOTE OF THE DAY
'I left England for New Zealand for a holiday, but loved the place so much, I decided to stay' explained former Household Cavalryman Steven Cooper, 52, who on this day in 2009 trained 8yo 57/1 outsider Spin Around to win the £250,000 Auckland Cup at Ellerslie.

BIRTHDAYS
1946 Racing writer/tipster Tony Stafford, who once received a letter from a *Daily Telegraph* reader – 'The coup de grace came when you featured seven out of eight runners in a race – needless to say, the unmentioned nag won.'

1954 Trainer Lydia Richards. Dancing Brig won 14 races for her.

DEATH OF THE DAY
2004 Dick Whitford, 93, first of the modern handicappers, whose ratings appeared daily in *The Sporting Life*, and who worked with founder Phil Bull in the early days of Timeform.

CELEBRITY OF THE DAY
1980 The Prince of Wales finished second on Long Wharf at Plumpton in a Flat race – beaten by the ubiquitous Derek 'Tommo' Thompson on Classified.

5 MARCH

SIGNIFICANT EVENT
2009 The final foal born to the legendary Storm Cat was delivered at Town and Country Farms in Paris, Kentucky. The filly, out of the Grade 3-winning mare Richwoman, was one of just three foals from Storm Cat's final crop.

STRANGEST EVENT
1845 Cure-All walked from Grimsby to Aintree to win the Grand National – then walked back. He and groom, Kathy Crisp, were greeted by church bells on their return to Lincolnshire.

OTHER EVENTS
1840 The final day of the inaugural three-day meeting at Flemington, Melbourne – the track reportedly being named after local butcher Bob Fleming.
1840 When Weathercock fell at Becher's in the Grand Livepool Steeplechase, his jockey known only as Barker, who was concussed, was taken to a nearby farmhouse – and left there for three days until someone remembered him!
1855 Riccarton, in Christchurch, New Zealand, staged its first meeting.
1968 Having been announced as 'lame, unable to run', Veronica Bell was nonetheless backed from 7/1 to 9/2 for a Doncaster chase – and duly won after what trainer Gordon Richards described as 'a misunderstanding.'
1983 No SPs were returned as the Michael Dickinson-trained top class chasers, Bregawn at Hereford, and Silver Buck at Market Rasen, scored bloodless wins.
1993 Pontefract racecourse was reunited with an oil painting by David Dalby of the 1824 Badsworth Gold Cup which hung at the club stand entrance until the early 1960s when it went missing, only to turn up at a Sotheby's auction, valued at £20-£30,000.
1994 Irish champion Mick Kinane and Arc-winning French jockey Eric Saint-Martin were 'warned about their future conduct' after a weighing room 'fracas' at Sha Tin, Hong Kong. The two had been involved in a 'bumping duel' during a race won by Kinane.

QUOTE OF THE DAY
'We all spend every day racing around going about our business. When something like this happens you ask yourself why. This has shown me the value of life and makes things you would normally worry about very small fry.' Declan Murphy, born this day in 1966, suffered life-threatening injuries from a May 1994 Haydock fall. He came back briefly some 17 months later and won a race but quit shortly after.

BIRTHDAYS
1943 Fanatical Manchester United supporter who once risked and lost £1m on them, and who ended up having his own Betfred betting shops in Old Trafford, bookmaker Fred Done.
1948 Staffordshire trainer of Aonoch, Sally Oliver.
1952 French trainer Ellie Lellouche, in Tunisia.

DEATH OF THE DAY
1994 'Mr Scottish Racing', Bill McHarg OBE, 75, former clerk of the course at Ayr, Bogside, Kelso and Perth.

LAST OF THE DAY
1959 Clear at the last in the Cheltenham Gold Cup, Pas Seul fell, handing the race to the Bobby Beasley-ridden Roddy Owen.

6 MARCH

SIGNIFICANT EVENT

1968 20/1 South Rock at Chepstow gave Tony Dickinson his first winner as a trainer and 17-year-old Michael Dickinson his first winner as a jockey at the fourth attempt.

STRANGEST EVENT

2009 The first four runners home in the opening race at Ayr were disqualified for taking the wrong course, leaving the fifth, Seraphin at 6/1, partnered by Graham Lee, the winner. Five jockeys reeived 10 day bans.

OTHER EVENTS

1858 Little Charley won the Grand National, ridden by William Archer – whose son, 14 months old at the time, would become one of the finest jockeys of all – Fred.

1951 Hatton's Grace won his third Champion Hurdle.

1990 Shaston, 8/1, at Warwick was jockey Hywel Davies' 600th winner, while at Sedgefield Sir Jest was trainer Arthur Stephenson's 250th at the track.

1992 12yo Amrullah was beaten for the 73rd time in 73 races in the Sandown novice chase. 'If he were mine I'd retire him, but the owner likes to see him run' said trainer John Bridge of the horse who had become a cult figure on the turf. He would have one more race, which he also lost.

1993 78 year old Scobie Breasley saddled his third consecutive winner of Barbados' premier race, the Cockspur Gold Cup, then he announced his retirement. He died, aged 92, in Deember 2006

1994 Tom – son of Pat – Taaffe, 30, retired after riding 9/4 favourite All The

Aces to win a chase at Leopardstown.

1995 Jockey Steve Williams, nine times stable lads' boxing champion, made his debut as a pro, drawing with Shaun Hall in a flyweight bout.

1995 French jockey Dominique Boeuf, recently convicted for possession of drugs, receiving a one-year sentence, won at Saint-Cloud on Sharpest Image. Boeuf had appealed the sentence.

2009 Fakenham gave Tony McCoy an unusual gift to mark his recent achievement of notching his 3,000th winner – an apple tree.

QUOTE OF THE DAY

'Lester, if you do that to me again, I'll put my foot so far up your backside it will take me a week to get it out.' Fellow jockey Scobie Breasley proving that he took few prisoners when he rode; he later trained and on this day in 1993 aged 78 sent out 39/1-shot Chou-Chou Royale, his third consecutive winner of the Cockspur Gold Cup, the premier race in Barbados.

BIRTHDAYS

1907 Gladys 'Posy' Lewis. Probably the first woman trainer, she owned and trained the 1959 and '61 Welsh Grand National winner, Limonali.

1963 US Hall of Fame jockey Gary Stevens, in Idaho. Won the 1988 Kentucky Derby on Winning Colors.

FIRST OF THE DAY

2009 Sally Randell, Lance Bombardier turned sports coaching student, 24, became the first female winner of Sandown's Grand Military Gold Cup, on 5/2 favourite, Oakfield Legend.

7 MARCH

SIGNIFICANT EVENT
1964 Arkle, 7/4, beat Mill House, 8/13, by five lengths to win his first Cheltenham Gold Cup. 'The 1964 Gold Cup defies the laws of perspective; the further it recedes into history, the greater it appears' wrote racing historian John Randall.

STRANGEST EVENT
1934 This type of race is no longer run here – the National Hunt Juvenile Chase for 4yos, run at Cheltenham, won by Fred Rimell on Captain's Choice, trained by his father Tom.

OTHER EVENTS
1661 No open-top buses for the first Epsom Downs meeting – but King Charles II was there.
1691 Diarist of the Chester Recorder may have seen history made when he noted, 'We rode to Farne race where I run against Sir Edmund Ashton, Mrs Morte, Mr Mackworth and Capt Warburton. Mrs Morte won the race.' Whether they were the owners and/or riders is not clear.
1967 Andy Turnell rode his first winner over fences, Sweeney Todd at Plumpton, trained by Brian Trafford.
1985 The first race confined to owners who had never had a winner, a novice hurdle at Wincanton, was won by Stevasa, ridden by Hywel Davies.
1987 Future Japanese champion jockey Yutaka Take rode his first winner, Dyna Bishop at Hanshin.
1990 Jockey Reg Crank, 35, rode his 250th winner, 11/4 favourite Sally's Dove at Bangor – then quit.
1993 Frankie Dettori won the Young Jockeys World Championship in Japan for second year in succession.
2001 Cheltenham Festival was postponed due to foot and mouth outbreak – it never took place.
2009 *Racing Post*'s 'Pricewise' writer, Tom Segal, hit bookies for an estimated £4m headache when he tipped 12/1 Imperial Cup winner Dave's Dream at 20/1, and 9/4 Flipando at Wolverhampton, backed from 5/1.

QUOTE OF THE DAY
'It's the most ridiculous thing I've ever heard. We are in 1947 with a Labour Government and there will be no rich people. Nobody will be able to afford racehorses.' Tory MP father Ronald was scathing when his son, Old Etonian Jeremy Tree, revealed that he intended to go into racing. Tree, who died today in 1993, trained four Classic winners and, according to Richard Griffiths of *The Independent*, became 'the personification of a racing aristocrat.' His Rainbow Quest won the 1985 Arc.

BIRTHDAYS
1916 Canadian owner Donald G. Willmot, whose West Approval won that country's Triple Crown in 1898 – followed by his Izvestia a year later.
1950 Trainer Michael Oliver, whose West Tip won the 1986 Grand National.
1959 Former South African champion jockey Felix Coetzee.
1960 Former jockey, Martin Fry.
1974 Frankie Dettori's wife Catherine.

DEATHS OF THE DAY
1970 Former trainer Cyril Harty, father of jockey Eddie. He trained Knight's Crest to win the 1944 Irish Grand National.
1982 Amateur jockey John Thorne, 55, following the fall of Bend A Knee at Mollington point-to-point. He was runner-up in the 1981 National on his own Spartan Missile.
2007 Trainer Paul Davey, 81. Best known for My Swallow, winner of four top juvenile French races in 1970 before finishing third behind Brigadier Gerard and Mill Reef in the 1971 2,000 Guineas.

CELEBRITY OF THE DAY
Top rugby union international and owner Ronan O'Gara, born today in 1967.

8 MARCH

SIGNIFICANT EVENT
1622 The first recorded race at Newmarket, a match between horses owned by Lord Salisbury and the Marquess of Buckingham for £100.

STRANGEST EVENT
1997 Having announced his retirement six days earlier, Willie Carson returned to the saddle for his most bizarre race. Over 180yds at Wolverhampton, Carson rode a hack called River – rumoured to be recent sprint winner Royal Cascade – against greyhound bitch Gorgeous, four-time winner at East Anglian tracks and 4/11 favourite. Carson's mount had a five-second start to enable the horse to get into his stride – which was enough to enable him to ride another winner, after which he performed a flying Dettori dismount to celebrate.

OTHER EVENTS
1900 The previous year's Triple Crown winner Flying Fox was sold for a record 37,500gns when Duke of Westminster's stable was sold off.
1949 Fifth the year before, Hatton's Grace won the first of three consecutive Champion Hurdles. Ridden by Aubrey Brabazon and trained by Vincent O'Brien, he started at 100/7.
1950 The Vincent O'Brien-trained Cottage Rake completed a Cheltenham Gold Cup treble.
1983 Michael Dickinson set the record for the fastest ever Century when Sir Wimpy won at Warwick.
1993 After 48 hours' intensive chiropractor treatment on a slipped disc, Aussie jockey Mick 'Enforcer' Dittman won the A$650,000 Gp 1 Australian Cup at Flemington on Vendercross to become the first jockey since Pat Hyland in 1970 to complete the Newmarket Handicap-Australian Cup double.
1994 '*I never bet*' claimed trainer John Manners, admitting only to having

'a pound each-way' on his 100/1, 25 lengths, Leicester winner Killeshin, a first victory for jockey Gary Brown. One of the most eccentric of trainers, Manners once bought a horse called Manners purely because of its name. He died, aged 83, in September 2009.
2009 Richard Hughes rode favourite Autonomy to win the Indian 2,000 Guineas in record time at Mahalaxmi, Mumbai.

QUOTE OF THE DAY
2009 '*Earlier this season, a racegoer dressed as a jockey rushed into the parade ring at Cheltenham when the mounting bell was ringing and leaped onto the first horse he came to. I had to be all disapproving at the time.*' But now Cheltenham Managing Director Edward Gillespie was telling *Racing Post* readers this was the funniest thing he'd seen at a racecourse.

BIRTHDAYS
1890 Wetherby trainer Percy Vasey, who also played cricket for Malaya.
1939 Jockey Jean Cruguet.
1952 Jockey-turned-trainer, and father of Ryan and Jamie, Gary Moore.
1958 Trainer Annabel King – also breeder of ornamental chickens.
1966 One of a rare breed – an MP racehorse owner Gregory Baker with trainer Diana Grissell.

FIRST OF THE DAY
2009 Rockwithacaveman, trained and ridden by Polly Gundry, became the first British point-to-pointer to collect a four-figure prize in one race when winning a mixed open at Buckfastleigh – first prize of £700 plus a £360 sponsor bonus.

CELEBRITY OF THE DAY
1996 The 95-year-old Queen Mother was at Sandown to see her 3/1 Norman Conqueror win her a fifth Grand Military Gold Cup, ridden by Major Ollie Ellwood.

9 MARCH

SIGNIFICANT EVENT
1993 The Jockey Club introduced the Raceguard Line, inviting anyone with information about dodgy doings to ring a 24/7 line, 071 935 7151.

STRANGEST EVENT
1989 The Stewart Tory Chase at Wincanton was won by 4/1 chance Sirrah Jay – ridden by Stewart Tory's jockey grandson, Anthony, 27.

OTHER EVENTS
1870 The Colonel's Grand National victory was a record fifth in the race for jockey George Stevens, who died the next year when thrown by his hack at his Cheltenham home.

1982 Dual Champion Hurdler Sea Pigeon was retired by trainer Peter Easterby after working disappointingly. The great dual purpose veteran won £275,687.22 prize money.

1991 Jockey Jill Dawson won the Ladies' Open point-to-point race at Brocklesby Park for an extraordinary eighth successive year, on Sweet Diana. Her first three wins were on Witchin, the next three on Sweet Diana, then Roscoe Boy.

1992 Hywel Davies booted home his 700th winner as 100/30 shot, Unique New York won at Plumpton.

2009 Son of the legendary Australian trainer, Bart Cummings, Anthony Cummings saddled 6yo Zavite to win the Group 2, A$400,000 Adelaide Cup, beating 19 opponents.

2009 Aussie trainer Lee Freedman who was watching television in Melbourne had to ring hs stable lad Sam Pritchard-Gordon at Morphetville to find out whether their Pluralism had won the A$200,000 BMW Magic Millions Classic, after all power, including radio and tv feeds, went down. The horse had won.

QUOTE OF THE DAY
'The verbal attack and the way in which it was delivered was so severe and threatening

as to be violent and improper,' chided the Disciplinary Committee on this day in 1995 as Champion trainer David Nicholson was fined £1,500 after a row on King George day at Kempton with photographer Edward Whitaker. He was found guilty of 'violent and improper conduct and bringing racing into disrepute.' The incident was sparked when Whitaker tried to snap the trainer consoling jockey Adrian Maguire after the last-fence fall of Barton Bank. There were unproven allegations that a punch was thrown.

BIRTHDAYS
1920 Florida trainer Warren A (Jimmy) Croll jr. Had his first winner in 1940, and trained 1987 Belmont Stakes winner Bet Twice.

1945 French jockey Henri Samani, partner of Kalamoun and Blushing Groom.

1961 Jockey Peter Bloomfield.

1978 Jockey Fergal Lynch, who won the 1996 Ebor on 17/2 shot Clerkenwell, trained by Michael Stoute, the year he was champion apprentice.

DEATHS OF THE DAY
1988 The 1972 2,000 Guineas winner and successful sire High Top was put down, aged 19.

2000 Jumps trainer and owner Geoff Hubbard, 81. He earned a fortune from the refrigeration business which he poured into racing, owning 1982 Whitbread winner Shady Deal and Mildmay of Flete winner Gee-A.

FIRST OF THE DAY
1991 Welsh racing history was made as brother and sister Tim Jones and Pip Nash became the first such pair to ride doubles on the same day at the same meeting, doing so at Llanfrynach point-to-point. The feat was first achieved anywhere by David Turner and Josie Bothway at Ampton in 1977.

10 MARCH

SIGNIFICANT EVENT
1896 The man who invented the totalisator, American electrical engineer, Harry Strauss born – he came up with the ide at Havre de Grace races in Maryland in 1927.

STRANGEST EVENT
1870 Jockey Arthur Yates told his friend, popular gentleman rider George Ede, 'Don't ride the brute, he'll kill you' before Ede went out to partner Chippenham in Aintree's Sefton Chase. Ede died after he and the horse fell at the water jump.

OTHER EVENTS
1959 Magic Wind breezed in at odds of 300/1 when winning at Doomben in Brisbane, Australia.

1986 Televisions were permitted in betting shops for the first time since shops were legalised on May 1, 1961.

1992 Disqualified as winner of the 1988 Ascot Gold Cup, Royal Gait won the Champion Hurdle after a 20-minute Stewards' Inquiry. He was the first novice to win for 36 years.

1993 Trainer Nigel Twiston-Davies reached his first half century of winners when 3/1 Dandy Minstrel won at Folkestone.

1993 Eddy Delahoussaye, 41, became the 14th jockey in North America to ride 5000 winners when Ackler won at Santa Anita.

1994 Newcastle clerk of the course David Parmley was fined £600 for giving a 'misleading report' on conditions for Fighting Fifth Hurdle day at the track, saying the meeting would go ahead, only for frost and snow to cause abandonment.

2009 6/4 favourite, Binocular, (Tony McCoy) was beaten into third place in the Champion Hurdle by stablemate Punjabi at 22/1, partnered by Barry Geraghty for Nicky Henderson, whose pair were divided by Celestial Halo, ridden by Ruby Walsh, in a race featuring four previous winners. Later, a man called Elliot Shortt claimed in the *News of the World* that he had won £1.5m laying Binocular in this race, and a total of £20m betting over a year with Betfair. No, I didn't believe him either!

QUOTE OF THE DAY
'Now is the time to bet like men.' *Guardian* and *Observer* writer Richard Baerlein commanded readers after seeing Shergar win the Classic Trial at Sandown, and being offered at 12/1 for the Derby. Baerlein named his house 'Shergar' as a result. He died this day in 1995.

BIRTHDAYS
1951 Legendary owner, punter, bookmaker JP (John Patrick) McManus, nicknamed 'The Sundance Kid' by writer Hugh McIlvanney. JP's first bet was £4 on 100/8 winner Linden Tree at Newmarket in 1970. He was diagnosed with prostate cancer in 2008, but later given the all clear.

1989 Future Derby winner Dr Devious foaled.

DEATH OF THE DAY
1953 Arthur Wragg, 41, brother to Harry and Sam. He rode 46 winners in 1933, his best season. In a 1934 Newcastle race the brothers filled the first three places.

FIRST OF THE DAY
1919 Wild Aster became the first and only horse to win three races at the age of 18, when he won at Warwick.

11 MARCH

SIGNIFICANT EVENT
1995 Cardiff bookie John Lovell claimed to be the first in Britain to use an Australian computerised system to record bets on course. He had Aussie computer expert Greg Cook clerking for him at Chepstow.

STRANGEST EVENT
1965 Stoney Crossing, third to Arkle in the Cheltenham Gold Cup, was a former Australian Olympic show-jumper which had never raced in the UK before.

OTHER EVENTS
1961 Victorian Totalisator Agency Board set up the Commonwealth's first legalised off-course betting system in Melbourne.
1980 Talon gave jump jockey Graham Bradley his first success, at Sedgefield.
1989 Pat Eddery rode his first Australian winner – Concordance, at Rosehill, Sydney.
1989 Scobie Breasley, 75, the former Champion jockey, sent out Sandford Prince to win the Cockspur Gold Cup in Barbados where he was based, for the first of three occasions.
1992 Sportscast, which broadcast horse and dog racing to pubs and clubs, went off air after parent company British Aerospace pulled the financial plug.
1992 Thirty-four years after his first success there, Jim Joel, 97, had his twelfth Cheltenham Festival winner when 5/2 favourite Keep Talking, ridden by Marcus Armytage, won the 4m National Hunt Chase.
1993 Tenesaint, 8/13, was the third succesive winner of Towester's John Wrathall Memorial Chase for trainer Caroline Saunders, for whom Wrathall rode until his untimely death in a road accident in France.
1997 Martin Pipe's Make A Stand, 7/1, won the Champion Hurdle in record time, ridden by AP McCoy; BBC presenter John Inverdale was left with mixed feelings, having once owned 'a leg' of the horse. Pervious year's winner,

Collier Bay, pulled up.
2007 *Racing Post* revealed that Aidan O'Brien's Holy Roman Emperor, second favourite for the 2000Gns was to be retired to stud at Coolmore to replace stallion George Washington who had fertility problems and would resume racing.
2007 Alison Thorpe saddled her first treble as Valiant Shadow, 13/2, and Cusp, 9/4, won at Market Rasen; Scarlet Mix, 10/3, at Warwick.
2008 Robert Thornton won the Champion Hurdle at 10/1 on the Alan King trained Katchit. Nina, Paul and Philip Carberry all rode in the race. On the same day JP McManus became the clear record holder for the number of Festival winners, 29, as Captain Cee Bee, 17/2, and Garde Champetre, 4/1, won.
2009 4/1 Master Minded won the Queen Mother Champion Chase for the second successive year, ridden by Ruby Walsh for Paul Nicholls.

BIRTHDAYS
1922 Jockey Russ Maddock.
1933 Trainer Alistair Charlton.
1947 Hang-gliding jockey Gordon Holmes, also an equine dentist.

DEATHS OF THE DAY
1988 Successful sire Busted, 25, following a heart attack. England's Horse of the Year in 1967, he sired 1974 St Leger winner Bustino.
1994 The great chaser Crisp, remembered for his gallant front-running display in the 1973 Grand National when caught on the run-in by Red Rum, died aged 21 in Yorkshire.
2003 Winner of the 1942 Kentucky Derby on Shut Out, jockey Wayne D Wright, 86.

FIRST OF THE DAY
1954 After 15 unsuccessful years as an owner, Peter O'Sullevan finally celebrated a winner as Pretty Fair won at Windsor.

12 MARCH

SIGNIFICANT EVENT
1924 Five-year-old Red Splash won the first Cheltenham Gold Cup, ridden by Dick Rees and trained by Fred Withington, the son of a parson.

STRANGEST EVENT
2008 The threat of high winds caused the abandonment of day two of the Cheltenham Festival.

OTHER EVENTS
1929 Postponed for a week, the Cheltenham Festival got under way with Royal Falcon winning the Champion Hurdle and Easter Hero the first of his two Gold Cups – neither, though, was yet a championship race.

1936 Golden Miller won his fifth successive Cheltenham Gold Cup, at 21/20.

1946 Bobby O'Ryan, enjoying a sensational spell of form, rode his seventh straight winner – Distel in the Champion Hurdle.

1964 Riding The Pouncer at Stratford, Terry Biddlecombe lost his whip. When a £100 offer failed to persuade other jockeys to lend him their own, he snatched one anyway and won the race.

1966 English-born US jockey Johnny Longden rode his 6,032nd and last winner on George Royal at Santa Anita, a world record at the time.

1991 Estimates vary, but owner Noel Furlong won up to £3m as his 6/1 chance Destriero landed a mega gamble in Cheltenham's Supreme Novices' Hurdle. On the same day, Adrian Maguire enjoyed his first British winner, on Omerta for Martin Pipe at Cheltenham.

1992 Jamie Osborne ended up with a record five Cheltenham Festival winners – the first since Fred Winter in 1959 to do that. 25/1 Cool Ground, ridden by Adrian Maguire, won a controversial Gold Cup in which Jenny Pitman's Golden Freeze stayed close to market leader Carvill's Hill, whose jumping appeared to suffer as a result. Richard Mussell, a cleaner from Havant, won £567,066.25 with a five-winner accumulator.

1996 Having been 'jocked off' favourite Alderbrook for arriving late for a training spin, Graham Bradley got on 9/1-shot Collier Bay for Jim Old in the Champion Hurdle – and won, beating Alderbrook into second.

2009 Indiana Horse Racing Commission mandated the use of a new shock absorbing riding crop, replacing the traditional jockey's whip.

QUOTE OF THE DAY
'He was wearing boots on the wrong feet,' declared Julie Williams, daughter of legendary Cheltenham bookie the late Freddie Williams, revealing that during the 2009 Festival she was interviewed by an oddly shod John McCririck.

BIRTHDAYS
1930 Arkle's jockey, Pat Taaffe.
1959 Trainer of Agnes World, Hideyuki Mori.
1977 Champion conditional jockey-turned stipendiary steward, Alan Dempsey.

DEATHS OF THE DAY
1727 Tregonwell Frampton, 86, the first great administrator and 'dictator of the turf' and 'keeper of the running horses' to William III, Queen Anne, George I and George II.

2005 Stanley T Greene, 82, trainer to wealthy Americans Alfred G Vanderbilt and Liz Whitney Tippett. Founded the Virginia Stallion Station in 1970, remarkable for housing the first 'stallion amputee', Spanish Riddle.

FIRST OF THE DAY
1997 Jamie Evans became first the Aussie jockey to win at the Cheltenham Festival when landing the Coral Cup on 16/1 Big Strand.

13 MARCH

SIGNIFICANT EVENT
2009 On the traditionally unlucky Friday 13th, in the presence of the Queen, there to see her Barbers Shop finish unplaced (seventh of 16) in the Gold Cup, Ruby Walsh became the first jockey to ride seven winners at the Cheltenham Festival – one of them a history-making triumph on the Paul Nicholls-trained 7/4 favourite Kauto Star, the first horse to regain the Gold Cup having won and then lost it. He beat the previous year's winner Denman, also trained by Nicholls, into second.

STRANGEST EVENT
2009 Gambler Graham Calvert failed in an appeal against a High Court decision to dismiss his claim for the return of £2.1m lost by betting. The 28-year-old blamed bookies for not preventing him from gambling.

OTHER EVENTS
1928 Dick Rees (né Frederick Bilbo) won the Gold Cup on Patron Saint, from elder brother Biby, on Vive.

1948 A record 58 runners contested the Lincolnshire Handicap at Lincoln, won by 33/1-shot Commissar.

1968 Bangor and Uttoxeter, the last two courses still banned from racing following a foot and mouth outbreak the previous October, were finally reinstated.

1985 Badsworth Boy completed a hat-trick of Queen Mother Champion Chase triumphs.

1986 The mare Dawn Run won the Gold Cup under Jonjo O'Neill – to add to her 1984 Champion Hurdle victory for a unique double. Cue riotous scenes after the race with the jockey carried shoulder high. Peter Scudamore rode his first Festival winner, Solar Cloud in the Triumph Hurdle.

1990 Past Glories was third to 95/40 Kribensis in the Champion Hurdle, returning 150/1, the longest priced placed horse in the history of the race.

1993 6/4 favourite Olympian was the shortest priced winner of Sandown's Imperial Cup.

1997 Tony McCoy rode 20/1 Mr Mulligan, trained by Noel Chance, to win the Gold Cup, having won the Champion Hurdle on Make A Stand 48 hours earlier. Martin Pipe became the first trainer since before World War II to send out four Festival winners.

2003 Bookies lost an estimated £20m after 10 of 20 favourites including the hugely popular Moscow Flyer won at the Cheltenham Festival.

2009 William Hill reported taking a bet on 8/1 Cheltenham Festival winner Weapon's Amnesty from a group of troops based in Basra, Iraq.

QUOTE OF THE DAY
1989 'He'll be useful if they give him a bit of time' said jockey Joe O'Gorman after Panegyrist, 14, finally got his head in front at the 39th time of asking.

BIRTHDAYS
1905 Owner Isidore Kerman who insisted his best horse, Kybo, was named after the initials of advice from his mother, 'Keep your bowels open'!

1920 Thirty-one times champion German trainer, Heinz Jentsch.

1943 Trainer of Bright Highway and Shawiya, Michael O'Brien.

1969 Flat jockey Tony Culhane.

1970 Trainer Donald McCain jr.

DEATH OF THE DAY
2001 Top Australian trainer Peter Hayes, killed in a light aircraft crash, 51. He won the 1999 Victoria Derby with Blackfriars, and sent out six winners in seven races at Balaklava in November, 1996.

CELEBRITY OF THE DAY
2009 Named in honour of the hero pilot who safely brought down a stricken airliner into the Hudson River in January, Sullenberger, 4/1, flew to victory at Wolverhampton.

14 MARCH

SIGNIFICANT EVENT
2008 Denman, 9/4, co-owned by high-rolling punter Harry Findlay, beat stablemate Kauto Star in the Cheltenham Gold Cup with trainer Paul Nicholls also saddling the third home, Neptune Collonges.

STRANGEST EVENT
1992 Just not jockey Tony Ives's day. Riding in Macau, he was weighing in after winning on Mountview when his foot caught on the scales, he tripped, hit a table and was knocked out. He came round and declared himself fit for the next, but Good Luck Snoopy played up in the stalls, trapping Ives's leg and injuring him, resulting in him missing the rest of the card.

OTHER EVENTS
1935 Traffic chaos and trains were packed as crowds poured into Cheltenham to see the Gold Cup victory by Golden Miller over his great rival Thomond III.
1976 Willie Shoemaker rode his 7000th winner, Royal Derby, at Santa Anita.
1986 Carl Llewellyn rode his first winner, Starjestic, at Wolverhampton.
1987 Laffit Pincay rode a record seven winners at Santa Anita.
1991 Jenny Pitman's Garrison Savannah, 16/1, won the Cheltenham Gold Cup, partnered by son Mark, 24, who ended the day in hospital with a cracked pelvis after riding Run To Form later in the day.
1995 A record first-day crowd of 42,875 at the Cheltenham Festival saw novice Alderbrook, 11/2, win the Champion Hurdle, ridden by Norman Williamson for trainer Kim Bailey.
1996 Ireland's Imperial Call, 9/2, trained by one-legged, trainer Fergie Sutherland, who treated the horse's legs with whisky, won the Gold Cup ridden by Conor O'Dwyer. It was a controversial Festival as ten horses died.
2000 Istabraq, 8/15, won his third straight Champion Hurdle, the fifth horse to achieve the feat.
2002 Best Mate, 7/1, won the first of his three straight Gold Cups, ridden by Jim Culloty for trainer Henrietta Knight.
2006 Tony McCoy ended a 32 race losing sequence at Cheltenham Festival by winning the Champion Hurdle on the Colm Murphy trained 8yo, 7/4 favourite, Brave Inca.
2009 A group of Scoop6 winners landed the biggest bonus fund in the history of the bet, launched in July 1999 – a total of £3,184,369.50. Seventeen winning tickets were worth £58,806 each. Harry Findlay had four and he formed a syndicate of eleven to land the Bonus the next week, delivering £227,454 for each winning ticket, including John Johnson from Fife who had laid out just £1 together with partner 'Norman'. The horse who sparked the payout was Jack Doyle-ridden 8/1 shot Russian Trigger in Uttoxeter's Midlands Grand National.

QUOTE OF THE DAY
'Happy Birthday to you,' said Jenny, wife of American Sydney Craig in 1992, giving him a horse called Dr Devious – which went on to win the Derby.

BIRTHDAYS
1933 Owner of the 1992 Oaks and St Leger winner User Friendly, Bill Gredley.
1945 Trainer Taffy Salaman.
1954 Jump jockey Paul Richards.
1960 Ace jockeys' agent, Dave Roberts.
1964 Jockey Michael Bowlby.

DEATH OF THE DAY
2007 David McHarg, 54, former clerk of the course at several Scottish tracks.

CELEBRITY OF THE DAY
1989 Buckingham Palace announced the Queen had appointed William Hastings-Bass to take over at her West Ilsley stables when Major Dick Hern's lease expired at the end of the year.

15 MARCH

SIGNIFICANT EVENT
1995 David Nicholson became the first trainer since 1942 to land a Cheltenham Festival-day treble as Viking Flagship, 5/2, won the Champion Chase, Putty Road the Sun Alliance Hurdle at 7/1 and Kadi the Mildmay of Flete Chase, 11/2.

STRANGEST EVENT
1651 A Match for 1,000 crowns was run in France at the Bois de Boulogne between Prince d'Harcourt's mount and that of the Duc de Joyeuse. The horses were fed on bread made with beans and aniseed and, for two days before the race, each was given between 200 and 300 eggs. The Duc's horse was blown to victory.

OTHER EVENTS
1978 Golden Cygnet was a 15-length winner of the Supreme Novices' Hurdle at Cheltenham – a month later Edward O'Grady's 6yo was dead after a final-flight fall in the Scottish Champion Hurdle.
1980 Seven winners from seven rides for Richard de Pass at Florida Downs, USA.
1983 Mercy Rimell became the first woman to train a Champion Hurdle winner when Richard Linley brought home 7/1 chance Gaye Brief.
1984 Jenny Pitman became the first woman to train a Gold Cup winner as Burrough Hill Lad and Phil Tuck beat Brown Chamberlin by three lengths.
1990 Norton's Coin was a 100/1 shock winner of the Cheltenham Gold Cup, for dairy farmer/trainer Sirrell Griffiths.
1994 The Richard Price-trained Flakey Dove, 9/1, became only the third mare to win the Champion Hurdle. African Sister in 1939 and Dawn Run in 1984 were the others.
1996 All Talk No Action, 4/1, belied his name by winning after a lay-off of 1,053 days at Folkestone, followed immediately in the next race by the victory of Big Ben Dun, 5/2, – after 1,019 days out.

2006 Twice winner of the Queen Mother Chase, Moscow Flyer was retired by trainer Jessica Harrington after finishing fifth behind 16/1 Newmill.
2007 Cheltenham Festival's first 'official' Ladies Day.
2009 All 17 jockeys riding in the last at Fontwell were given one-day bans for coming out on the course before being instructed to do so by the Starter.

QUOTE OF THE DAY
'I was never regarded as a great. It did worry me at one time. But I got over it.' The great, unworried Willie Carson in 1997 just after retirement from the saddle.

BIRTHDAYS
1932 Trainer Norma Macauley.
1948 Jockey Graham Sexton, who rode a winner at every Flat course in Britain.
1962 Jockey Cash – some might say by name and nature – Asmussen. Five times French champion, his real name is Brian.
1969 Perhaps Japan's greatest jockey, Yutaka Take.

DEATHS OF THE DAY
1945 Sold for a record 47,000gns in 1932, Solario who won the St Leger and the Ascot Gold Cup, died at Newmarket.
1993 John Baker, 75, who trained Star Player to win the 1991 Chester Cup.
2006 Trainer Peter Dufosee, 84, who won the 1989 Brooke Bond Oxo National at Warwick with Memberson.
2007 The death was announced of former Seabiscuit exercise rider turned top Southern California trainer, Farrel Jones, 84.

CELEBRITY OF THE DAY
1997 Willie Carson revealed to the *Daily Telegraph*'s Sue Mott that a fellow apprentice with him at trainer George Armstrong's yard in Middleham was Tony Prince, who went on to become 'Your Royal Ruler', a very popular disc jockey on Radio Luxembourg in the 1960s. Well, I remember him fondly!

16 MARCH

SIGNIFICANT EVENT
1977 Possibly the greatest ever Champion Hurdle as the previous year's winner Night Nurse beat future dual winner Monksfield, consistent top-liner Dramatist and another future dual winner and stablemate, Sea Pigeon.

STRANGEST EVENT
1999 Theatreworld finished second in the Champion Hurdle for the third successive season as stablemate Istabraq won for a second straight victory. Had his conquerors not turned up in those races he'd have been regarded as an all-time great!

OTHER EVENTS
1901 Horse racing was banned in San Francisco.

1940 Prince Regent, who became probably the best chaser of his decade, winning the 1946 Gold Cup, was unplaced on the flat in his debut at Balydoyle.

1955 Record entries for Worcester – 472 of them for an eight-race card, of which 121 finally ran.

1956 Lord Oaksey, then John Lawrence, rode his first winner under rules – Pyrene in a hunter chase at Sandown – at the age of 26.

1966 Jackie Brutton was the first woman trainer officially to train a winner over jumps in Britain when Snowdra Queen won the United Hunts Challenge Cup at Cheltenham.

1993 Montelado, 5/1, became the first horse to win consecutive races at the Cheltenham Festival. Having won the Bumper which closed the previous year's meeting at 8/1, he won the first of this, the Supreme Novices' Hurdle, ridden by Charlie Swan for trainer P J Flynn. Martin Pipe trained his first championship winner, Granville Again in the Champion Hurdle, 13/2.

1993 Founded in 1937, Spendthrift Farm, where US Triple Crown winners Seattle Slew and Affirmed stood, was sold at a foreclosure auction for a reported $7m. The Queen visited Spendthrift in 1984.

1999 Jenny Pitman announced she was giving up training.

QUOTE OF THE DAY
1995 *'I shall be able to buy the lads a new hostel,'* claimed trainer Kim Bailey after his 100/30 favourite Master Oats won the Cheltenham Gold Cup two days after the same stable's Alderbrook won the Champion Hurdle in his third race over obstacles. Bailey, rumoured to have won a seven-figure sum as a result, and Norman Williamson were the fifth trainer-jockey combination to complete the double.

BIRTHDAYS
1930 Jockey Tommy Barnes.

1942 Trainer Bill Watts, whose Teleprompter won the 1985 Arlington Million.

1949 TV commentator and occasional race sponsor, Graham Goode.

1971 Jockeys Warren Marston, and Jason Titley.

DEATHS OF THE DAY
2001 Burton Albert 'Joe' Brown, a kind of Aussie Peter O'Sullevan, who called 33 Melbourne Cups, 81. He was awarded the MBE in 1982.

2008 US trainer Dale Baird, 72 in a Indiana car crash. Record winner of over 9,400 races.

FIRST OF THE DAY
1989 The first grey to win the Cheltenham Gold Cup as Desert Orchid scored at 5/2, ridden by Simon Sherwood. On the same day Victor Chandler accepted his first on-course £90,000 bet – at 4/9 on Rusch De Farges, fourth of nine.

17 MARCH

SIGNIFICANT EVENT
1983 Trainer Michael Dickinson saddled the first five home in the Cheltenham Gold Cup – Bregawn, Captain John, Wayward Lad, Silver Buck and Ashley House.

STRANGEST EVENT
2009 Coincidence backers expecting to see twelve-times course winner Victory Quest land the 1m6f Victory Quest Handicap at Southwell were out of pocket as the 7/2 chance could manage only fifth and last.

OTHER EVENTS
1967 A *Daily Telegraph* survey suggested only 5% of those polled wanted a Tote monopoly and bookies banned.

1988 Charter Party, 10/11, won the Cheltenham Gold Cup, leaving David Barons, trainer of favourite Playschool, convinced his horse was got at.

1993 The Martin Pipe-trained Olympian, who won the Imperial Cup at Sandown on the Saturday, collected a £50,000 bonus from bookies Sunderlands when following up in the Coral Cup at Cheltenham at 4/1.

1994 Tony McCoy's first ride over jumps ended badly when he and Riszard were brought down during a Leopardstown hurdle race.

1995 21 year old Lee Ok Rue, the first female granted a jockey licence to race in South Korea, made a winning debut on Kansas, but in August, with 7 wins from 48 starts, suffered a career ending fall.

2006 Owned by Ryanair boss, Michael O'Leary, 15/2 chance War of Attrition, ridden by Conor O'Dwyer was the two and a half length Gold Cup winner, saddled by Mouse Morris. It was St Patrick's Day and the Irish had a 1-2-3, with Hedgehunter and Forget The Past chasing the winner home.

2008 Four yearlings from Lane's End Farm, Kentucky, died after bolting on to a road where they were hit by a vehicle.

QUOTE OF THE DAY
'Should the weather prevent the races coming off on the day fixed, the stewards will have the power to postpone them from day to day, or week to week, until they come off, and all entries to remain the same,' declared the racecard for today's scheduled 1859 Union Steeple Chase and Welter Race, both to be run at Market Rasen.

BIRTHDAYS
1928 Trainer Derek Kent, whose Grand Canyon won the 1976 and '78 Colonial Cups in the US.

1956 Windsurfing jump jockey-turned-starter Simon McNeill.

1958 Kiwi jockey Brent Thomson.

DEATHS OF THE DAY
1988 The 1985 Cheltenham Gold Cup winner Forgive'n Forget had to be destroyed after breaking a leg in the latest renewal.

1991 The greatest Italian jockey Enrico Camici, 78, who partnered the unbeaten Ribot during his 16-race career, and rode 4,081 winners in all.

FIRST OF THE DAY
1993 Paul Carberry rode a winner on his first Cheltenham Festival ride, on 16/1 Rhythm Section, as his father Tommy did in 1962 on Tripacer.

18 MARCH

SIGNIFICANT EVENT
1921 Six-times champion and the first jump jockey to ride over 100 winners in a season, Dick Rees won his only Grand National on Shaun Spadah, the only one of 35 starters to complete the course without falling.

STRANGEST EVENT
1875 Tommy Pickernell rode his third Grand National winner, Pathfinder – but not without a little help from his fellow jockeys who had to point the somewhat inebriated rider in the right direction after he imbibed a spot of pre-race Dutch courage.

OTHER EVENTS
1970 Persian War won his third consecutive Champion Hurdle under hurdles specialist jockey Jimmy Uttley.
1978 Something of a tall story as 6ft 2.5in jockey Chris Kinane rode his first winner, Hard Outlook at Lingfield.
1981 Willie Wumpkins, 13, won the Coral Golden Hurdle for the third consecutive year, ridden by Jim Wilson and trained by Jane Pilkington of Stow-on-the-Wold, the rider's mother-in-law.
1991 Alex Greaves was the first female to win a prestigious Willian Hill Golden Spurs Award – for Apprentice of the Year.
1993 Irish Derby winner, St Jovite, who had gone to race in the US as a 4yo, was retired after suffering tendon injury. He was runner-up in the Derby at Epsom when Dr. Devious won by a record 12 lengths.
1993 Shawiya, 12/1, became the first filly to win the Triumph Hurdle, ridden by Charlie Swan for Michael O'Brien.
1994 David Nicholson celebrated his 1,000th winner when Ramstar won at Southwell.
2000 US beat Europe in the third annual Jockey Challenge at Santa Anita making it 2-1 to the US.

2004 Welsh garage boss Mark Brilley admitted to 'forgetting to mention' to his wife the £20,000 he had placed on Best Mate, 6/4 favourite for the Cheltenham Gold Cup – which duly obliged to save the marriage.
2009 Jockey Alan 'Arthur' Daly gave up the game after 15 years and 200+ winners, hoping to become a firefighter. He bowed out with a 2/1 winner, Desert Dreamer at Lingfield, and celebrated with a perfect flying dismount – 'after all my years of ski-jumping I know how to use the landing gear.'

QUOTE OF THE DAY
2009 *'If we're going to open up our premier races to them, let's get a little reciprocity,'* demanded US trainer Ken McPeek in response as Kempton offered free admission to celebrate the first running of the £50,000 Kentucky Derby Challenge Stakes, offering entry to the US Classic as part of the prize. The race was won by the John Gosden-trained 11/2 Mafaaz.

BIRTHDAYS
1912 Trainer Lucien Laurin. On the verge of retirement, he took Secretariat to the 1973 Triple Crown. He trained 1,137 winners, collecting $6,434,303 prize money.
1946 Jump jockey Aly Branford.
1952 Pat Eddery, one of 13 children. Father Jimmy was champion in Ireland and Pat won the title 11 times in Britain.

DEATH OF THE DAY
1997 The 1978 Derby winner Shirley Heights, put down at 22.

CELEBRITY OF THE DAY
1949 One-time stable lad/apprentice jockey-turned snooker world champ, Alex 'Hurricane' Higgins born.

19 MARCH

SIGNIFICANT EVENT
2009 First run in 1519, the annual Kiplingcotes Derby is the oldest horse race in the world, run every third Thursday in March. John Thirsk rode Maisie – a hurdler really called Minster Fair – to win the event. It cost £4.25 to enter and the winner receives a trophy and £50, while the runner-up gets the purse money which usually works out at more. The race is run just off the Driffield to Market Weighton road in East Yorkshire, over a 4m (ish) course including farm tracks, road and verges.

STRANGEST EVENT
1999 Fakenham's Tote Jackpot card ended in farce when the race which would have determined the winners of a £700,000 pool became mired in controversy after stewards disqualified all eleven runners after all but one of the field went the wrong side of a dolled-off hurdle. The Ross Studholme-ridden Jamorin Dancer apparently went back and took the correct course, but no official saw him do so. The Jockey Club later said the 9/1-shot could have been awarded the race had they been satisfied he did go back and complete. As result of this the Tote had to declare a dividend of £19,638.60 rather than £500,000.

OTHER EVENTS
1880 Brothers Tommy, Harry and John Beasley finished first (on Empress), fifth (Woodbrook) and eighth (Victoria) in the Grand National.
1949 Legendary jockey Bill Shoemaker made his racing debut, finishing fourth at Gate Field, California, on Waxahachie.
1975 Mick Kinane's first winner, Muscari at Leopardstown.
1981 Martin Pipe won the Triumph Hurdle with 66/1 chance Baron Blakeney, announcing his arrival on the big stage.

1993 Red Rum just pipped Desert Orchid in their charity one-furlong walking race as part of Cheltenham's Comic Relief event.
2009 The play 'No 6 Duke Street' was presented at King's Heath Baptist Church Hall, Birmingham. The work is by Martin Becher, eldest son of the legendary Captain Becher, source of the name of the intimidating Aintree fence.
2010 Scheduled final day of Cheltenham Festival.

QUOTE OF THE DAY
'Little fish are sweet,' was the motto of trainer Arthur Stephenson, who on this date in 1987 landed a big 'un when The Thinker won the Cheltenham Gold Cup. Stephenson missed the race as he was at Hexham.

BIRTHDAYS
1935 Trainer Paddy Prendergast.
1937 Window cleaner-turned 'job' trainer, Ken Payne.
1939 David 'The Duke' Nicholson, who partnered Mill House to win the 1967 Whitbread Gold Cup and sent out Charter Party to win the 1988 Cheltenham Gold Cup.
1947 US Hall of Fame jockey Earlie Fires.
1958 Jockey Simon Sherwood. He rode eight Cheltenham Festival winners, won two Whitbreads and two King George VI Chases.

DEATH OF THE DAY
2002 Former West Country bookmaker and father to Martin, David Pipe, 78, who set his son up in Pond House stables, Somerset.

FIRST OF THE DAY
1907 Ob, (25/1, and 20/1 the year before), trained in France by Richard Carter, became the first horse to win the Lincoln twice.

20 MARCH

SIGNIFICANT EVENT

1975 Royal Cadet became the first horse in Britain ridden by a professional female jockey when partnered by Jane McDonald to finish 11th in an apprentice race at Doncaster.

STRANGEST EVENT

1948 Sheila's Cottage, the first mare since 1902 to do so, won the Grand National. Two days later during a photo session Neville Crump's inmate showed her appreciation of jockey Arthur Thompson – by biting the top of one of his fingers off.

OTHER EVENTS

1888 The Duke of Portland's Donovan won the early-season 2yo highlight, the Brocklesby Stakes at Lincoln. He ended the season with 11 wins from 13 starts and went on to win the Derby and St Leger.

1891 Four previous Grand National winners, Ilex, Gamecock, Roquefort and Voluptuary lined up for the big race, but 4/1 favourite Come Away beat a 20-strong field.

1967 Stockton racecourse was renamed Teesside Park.

1968 Jimmy Uttley rode Persian War to win the first of his three Champion Hurdles. On the same card Barry Brogan rode 20/1 and 8/1 winners.

1992 Trainer Derek Shaw's first Flat winner was 50/1 Coleridge at Doncaster.

1993 Victim of a high profile doping incident at Doncaster in 1990, Norwich won on US debut at Golden Gate, California.

1993 Uttoxeter became the first track to offer bungee jumping – whereupon Lord Oaksey dived 200 feet head first to raise £1,000 for the Injured Jockeys Fund.

2004 Japanese trainer Yasutoshi Ikee saddled his first winner, Sonic Surpass. In only his fifth season he topped the national standings and, aged 39 became the youngest ever winner of the country's 'Best Trainer (Technique)' award. Son of Deep impact's trainer, Yasuo.

2009 US website, The Record, staged an online debate asking whether horse racing should be considered a 'sport' or a 'gambling' vehicle. Surely it is both?

QUOTE OF THE DAY

'The number of times you hit them is irrelevant compared to how hard you hit them,' was the contribution to the whip debate by multiple Classic-winning Welsh jockey Geoff Lewis, rider of Mill Reef, who had his first winner (Concert Hall) as a trainer this day in 1980.

BIRTHDAYS

1915 US trainer Burly Cocks born.

1928 John Benstead, trainer of dual Cambridgeshire winner Baronet.

1929 Jockey Tommy Lowrey, who won the Derby in 1946 on Airborne at 50/1 .

1941 Twice champion apprentice, Bobby Elliott.

1945 French jockey Maurice Philipperon.

DEATH OF THE DAY

1995 73-year-old former jump jockey and trainer Mickey Browne, who saddled Kilmore to win the 1963 Munster National at Limerick.

CELEBRITY OF THE DAY

1961 Racehorse owner and chief executive of Ryanair, Michael O'Leary born. He owns Gigginstown House Stud. His War Of Attrition won the 2006 Cheltenham Gold Cup and Hear The Echo the 2008 Irish Grand National in his maroon and white colours.

21 MARCH

SIGNIFICANT EVENT
1942 The Cheltenham Gold Cup was won by Medoc II ridden by Frenchie Nicholson. The race was run in thick fog, but radio listeners weren't told that by commentator Raymond Glendenning who was mindful that the broadcast was being monitored by foreign enemy sources.

STRANGEST EVENT
1997 Having won the 471st running of the ancient Kiplingcotes Derby in East Yorkshire, 9yo mare Sunny, ridden by Sheila Ashby, died after running into a parked car.

OTHER EVENTS
1871 The Lamb, 11/2, was a dream winner for owner Lord Poulet who had 'seen' Tommy Pickernell riding the horse to victory in his slumbers, woke up, and booked him for the ride.

1899 US jockey Tod Sloan who brought the 'monkey on stick' style of riding to GB, rode five winners from five rides at Ingleside, California.

1902 Shannon's Lass won the Grand National, earning south coast village, Telscombe, a new church after the owner and local squire Ambrose Graham used his £2,000 winnings for restoration funds.

1964 They bet 100/7 the field as 18/1-shot Team Spirit won the 33-runner Grand National.

1992 Lester Piggott's bid to win the Lincoln for the first time was foiled by his son-in-law William Haggas, trainer of High Low who beat Lester on Mudaffar into second.

1994 For the third time in nine months *Daily Star* tipster Tony Lewis went through the card – this time at Plumpton with a 797/1 accumulator.

1995 Champion Japanese jump jockey Kazuya Nakatake rode 25/1-shot Fred's Delight to win a selling hurdle at Stratford for Mikey Heaton-Ellis.

1996 The instruction obliging trainers to make public any reasons emerging for the poor performance of horses came into effect.

QUOTE OF THE DAY
'They used to tie her to this wooden wheel, and then some idiot with a blindfold on would throw knives at her', explained Frankie Dettori today in 2004 to *Sunday Times* readers about his mother's circus job.

BIRTHDAYS
1944 Tim Norman, who rode Anglo to win the 1966 Grand National.

1950 Trainer Nerys Dutfield, who had the interestingly named Lady Dominatrix in her stable. She is a sun-lover whose racing hero is Bill Shoemaker.

1962 Jockey Nicky Connorton.

1963 Trainer and jockey Pat 'Shorty' Leech.

DEATHS OF THE DAY
1999 Twenty-year-old female Chinese apprentice Willy Khan, the first woman to ride in the Hong Kong Derby and who had ridden a Haydock winner in 1998, died following a fall at Sha Tin. She was only the third fatality in Hong Kong.

2003 US Hall of Fame jockey Eric Guerin, 68, who won the 1953 Preakness and Belmont Stakes on Native Dancer and the 1947 Kentucky Derby on Jet Pilot.

CELEBRITY OF THE DAY
1929 Lord Oaksey, aka John Geoffrey Tristram Lawrence, President of the Injured Jockeys Fund, was born today. In 2008 he became the 12th recipient of the annual Sir Peter O'Sullevan award for services to racing. In 2009 a statue to him was unveiled in Lambourn by the Princess Royal.

22 MARCH

SIGNIFICANT EVENT

1921 Later to ride 14 Classic winners, Charlie Elliott pulled off a double on Rakings and Golden Myth at Nottingham on his public debut.

STRANGEST EVENT

2009 Grand National-winning jockey Graham Lee was one of five riders given a twelve-day ban after taking the wrong course in an eight-runner handicap hurdle at Huntingdon – they were roundly jeered by racegoers. Tony McCoy, though, went the right way and won on 9/4 favourite Yossi.

OTHER EVENTS

1929 Easter Hero carried a massive 12st 7lb for the National – yet started favourite in a record field of 66. He gave best to 66/1 Gregalach, carrying 11-4, as he finished a six-length runner-up.

1968 When the $6000 filly Dark Mirage won the Delaware Oaks, few imagined she could sweep all before her to win the US fillies' Triple Crown that year – but that is just what happened for her and her jockey, Manuel Ycaza and trainer Everett King. Aged four, Dark Mirage won first time out but in her second outing injured a fetlock joint, resulting in her untimely death some months later.

1995 An estimated 775 people won a share of the first ever £2m+ Tote Jackpot at Exeter. There was £2,050,651 in the pool and it returned £11,931 for £1 – although the SP odds were 32,938/1 – odds at which a Glasgow barmaid was paid out for her £1 accumulator at William Hill in Thornliebank where she told staff she selected the winners because she 'liked the names.' She must have LOVED them when they won!

1997 Racing at Saint-Cloud in France was delayed by half an hour as racecourse staff went on strike over salaries and pensions.

2008 10/1 Smokey Oakey, named after the co-owner's grandson, Samuel Michael Oak Williams, won the 21 runner Lincoln – co-owner Dame Judie Dench: 'We cried uncontrollably – it was thrilling and wonderful'.

2008 US Apprentice Sebastian Morales rode four winners at Aqueduct.

QUOTE OF THE DAY

'I was excessive, but you don't think of that during the Gold Cup and I wouldn't have won otherwise' explained a chastened Adrian Maguire after his 1992 win in that race on Cool Ground. Today in 1993 he completed his first century of winners on Trendy Auctioneer , 2/1, at Plumpton.

BIRTHDAYS

1913 Trainer Peter Nelson, whose Snow Knight, 50/1, won the 1974 Derby.

1948 Trainer Bill O'Gorman, father of jockey Emma. Today in 1984 his Provideo won the first of his 20th Century record 16 triumphs as a 2yo.

DEATH OF THE DAY

1922 'Just in case' said financier Jimmy White who put £1,000 on his Granely at 20/1 when confined to his office and unable to watch it win the Lincoln on this day. Five years later his finances were wiped out on the stock exchange and he committed suicide.

CELEBRITY OF THE DAY

1948 Owner of Bacchanal, Crystal Music and others, Lord Lloyd Webber, born today.

23 MARCH

SIGNIFICANT EVENT
2009 The Irish Racehorse Trainers' Association presented Jim Bolger with a Special Achievement Award for the third successive year; it also inducted TP Burns, 84, who rode 1,200 winners including eight Classics, into its Hall of Fame.

STRANGEST EVENT
1997 A meeting at the Royal Bangkok Sports Club, Thailand, was cancelled midway through after racegoers and punters objected to the disqualification for interference of two fancied runners in favour of a 35/1 shot. Punters chanting 'Cheating, cheating' came on to the course which was soon covered in rubbish which was then set ablaze. Undeterred, stewards reviewed the tape of the race and upheld the verdict.

OTHER EVENTS
1603 Racing was recorded at Leicester.
1877 Holding on to his saddle at every jump, Fred Hobson nonetheless won the Grand National on Austerlitz, 15/1, in his only appearance in the race.
1934 Five-time Gold Cup winner Golden Miller won the Grand National.
1979 David Elsworth sent out his first winner, Fortune Cookie at Devon.
1989 Prince Charles 'lost' his first winner as owner-breeder, Devil's Elbow, who finished first in a Worcester hurdle race in December 1988, only to be disqualified following a Jockey CLub enquiry. A test revealed prohibited substances; trainer Nick Gaselee was fined £2,000 but was cleared of administering substances intentionally.
1991 Alex Greaves was the first female Lincoln winner, on 22/1 Amenable.
1991 Lester Piggott's first all-weather winner in Britain, on La Masaas at Lingfield.
1994 Following 'special instruction' from the Jockey Club, new official distances were introduced – one and quarter lengths; one and three quarters;

nine, eleven, thirteen and fourteen lengths.
1995 The biggest ever sponsorship of a single British stable, worth a 'substantial six-figure sum' was announced as Danish dairy giant MD Foods supported Mary Reveley's Saltburn yard for a year, Flat and jumps.
2008 Reports suggested Chinese authorities were planning to introduce horse racing with legal betting to the city of Wuhan following the Olympic Games.

QUOTE OF THE DAY
1840 *'In point of interest and attraction this race is second to none in the kingdom; it is a joyous and animating scene, and worthy of being paid a visit, not only by lovers of the sport but by those of the beau monde who delight in seeing and being seen, for the attendance is always numerous and fashionable,'* wrote Colburn's Kalendar of Amusements of the Leamington Grand Steeple Chase.

BIRTHDAYS
1955 Trainer Oliver (Martin Carwardine) Sherwood. Champion amateur in 1979-80.
1966 Lewes trainer Mark Hoad.
1975 Chestnut colt, Alydar who was a runner up to Affirmed in at three Triple Crown races, an unprecedented feat, unlike winning all of them!

DEATH OF THE DAY
1945 Ten-times champion jockey Steve Donoghue, in his 61st year. He rode 14 Classic winners including six in the Derby.

CELEBRITIES OF THE DAY
1968 Owner, racegoer, punter, writer, president of the Racegoers' Club – oh yes, and cricketer – Mike Atherton born today in 1968, while multiple Olympic gold medal-winning rower and owner with Rod Millman, Steve Redgrave, arrived in the world six years earlier.

24 MARCH

SIGNIFICANT EVENT
1988 Jockeys announced a ban on media interviews because of worries over 'trial by TV' amid controversy over use of the whip.

STRANGEST EVENT
1999 After winning on 2/1 favourite Rusk at Towcester, amateur Fred Hutsby was disqualified after weighing in one and a half pounds light which, he claimed, was caused by a call of nature after weighing out. He was fined £265.

OTHER EVENTS
1876 Captain James Machell trained the Grand National winner for the third time in four runnings, 25/1 Regal.

1882 Only three of 12 runners completed the Grand National course, with 6yo Seaman ridden by Lord Manners, an amateur winning at 10/1 by a head from Cyrus, ridden by pro, Tommy Beasley.

1885 The Bard claimed the first of his 16 wins as a 2yo. Trained by the Derby winning handler Martin Gurry, the 15 hand chestnut was runner-up to the classy Ormonde in the Derby, but won Goodwood and Doncaster Cups.

1911 One-eyed Glenside was the only horse to complete the National course without mishap, winning at 20/1.

1922 Only three got round and for the first time the RSPCA complained about the severity of the Grand National as 100/9 Music Hall won.

1939 Workman, trained by Jack Ruttle in Ireland, won the final pre-War Grand National at 100/8, having finished third to Battleship the previous year.

1982 Double century day as both Colin Brown (The Go-Boy) and Phil Tuck (Highland Linnet) rode their 100th winners at Southwell.

1997 Owners of US super-horse Cigar accepted a $25,000,000 payout, triggered by the horse's infertility at stud. No mares were scanned in foal from 39 covered.

2008 Trainer David Murray Smith, 53, the first English trainer to saddle the Irish Grand National winner for 57 years when Rhyme 'N' Reason won in 1985, returned to racing after a seven year hiatus to become trainer to property developer owner, Rob Lloyd's Tarporley, Cheshire, yard.

2008 Conor O'Dwyer retired after winning on 3/1 chance Mister Top Notch at Fairyhouse. Born April 8, 1966, he was a jockey for almost 25 years. He won the Champion Hurdle twice on Hardy Eustace in 2004/5, and the Cheltenham Gold Cup on Imperial Call, 1996, and War of Attrition, 2006.

QUOTE OF THE DAY
'If you only have one day to live, you should spend at least half of it in the saddle,' goes the traditional proverb from Kyrgyzstan, where on this date in 2005 President Askar Akayev was ousted on charges of corruption in the 'Tulip Revolution', marked annually afterwards by a festival of traditional horse races.

BIRTHDAYS
1947 Trainer Tony Ingham, whose career as a jockey ended when he fractured his skull at Folkestone.

1967 Former French champion jockey Thierry Jarnet.

1971 Twice Scandinavian champion jockey Fredrik Johansson.

DEATH OF THE DAY
1988 Arthur Freeman, 62, who rode Mr What to win the 1958 Grand National.

CELEBRITY OF THE DAY
1956 The Queen Mother's Devon Loch collapsed inexplicably under Dick Francis as the pair were clear on the Grand National run-in, leaving E.S.B. to take the honours. Suggestions for the collapse have varied from Francis' belief that the horse was distracted by crowd noise, to the less likely that the horse let rip with an enormous fart.

25 MARCH

SIGNIFICANT EVENT
1668 The oldest existing racing trophy known for an event in America bears the inscription '1668. wunn att hampsted plaines, march 25' It is believed to have been donated by Governor Nicholls.

STRANGEST EVENT
1997 A William Hill shop in the City of London took bets of £50,000 on Wylde Hide at 16/1 and £20,000 on 25/1 Time For A Run in the forthcoming Grand National. Both were owned by JP McManus. Neither won.

OTHER EVENTS
1799 £250,000 was gambled on the outcome of a Newmarket race between northern champ Hambletonian, the 1795 St Leger winner, and Diamond, sparkling for the south. The former prevailed by half a neck under Frank Buckle to land the odds.

1887 A huge gamble on Spati, who had never raced over obstacles, was lost when the 9/2 favourite fell in the Grand National as Gamecock won. But Spati reappeared 24 hours later to win the Champion Chase under 12st 12lbs.

1904 Legend has it that the 25/1 Grand National winner Moifaa was shipwrecked off Ireland en route to Britain from native New Zealand. 16yo Manifesto was running in the National for the eighth time, finishing eighth, having won twice and finished in the first four on four other occasions.

1938 17-year-old Bruce Hobbs became the youngest Grand National-winning jockey on 40/1 Battleship.

1961 Two Russian horses, Grifel and Reljet ran in the Grand National – unseating rider, and pulling up resectively – as 28/1 Nicolaus Silver won for trainer Fred Rimell.

1968 Former champion jockey Doug Smith sent out his first winner as a trainer with his first runner, Owen Anthony at Doncaster.

1994 For the first time live racing was shown from Nad al Sheba, Dubai, on Channel 4, as US jockey Chris McCarron won the International Jockeys' Challenge.

1999 The first racing World Series, offering $15m prize money and involving nine of the world's top races was announced. Whatever became of it?

2000 Sheikh Mohammed's favourite horse, Dubai Millennium, won the Dubai World Cup, his eighth win in nine starts.

2006 Frankie Dettori came with last to first swoop to win the $6m Dubai World Cup on Electrocutionist for Godolphin.

2006 Switched to Redcar, the Lincoln was won by 22/1 Blythe Knight trained by John Quinn, ridden by Graham Gibbons.

QUOTE OF THE DAY
'The bizarre thought of Willie Carson looking like Britt Ekland came from two separate quarters,' revealed the *Daily Mail*'s Alan Fraser, considering entries for a lookalike competition this week in 1994, while on this day in 1997 the pint-sized Scot became the associate director of Swindon Town FC.

BIRTHDAYS
1934 Trainer Peter Harris.
1946 Trainer Ben Hanbury. He rode 50 winners as a jockey, and his Midway Lady won the 1986 1,000 Guineas and Oaks.
1956 Trainer Kevin Bishop, owner of 12 chase winner Tiepolino.
1982 Jockey Nelson de Souza.

DEATH OF THE DAY
1892 Captain Roddy Owen won the National on 20/1 Father O'Flynn, but later died in Africa where a Kenyan waterfall was named in his honour.

FIRST OF THE DAY
1927 Meyrick Good and George Allison commentated as the BBC broadcast the Grand National for the first time. The 8/1 favourite Sprig won.

26 MARCH

SIGNIFICANT EVENT
1992 No-one paid very much attention to the 20/1 victory of Jim Bolger trained Legal Steps at Thurles – the first victory for unknown jockey AP McCoy.

STRANGEST EVENT
1886 Owner A J Douglas handed £1,000 of his prize money to trainer George Mulcaster and the rest to jockey Tommy Skelton after his Old Joe won the National – well, he could well afford it after winning a tidy sum on the 25/1 shot.

OTHER EVENTS
1909 Lutteur, the last 5yo to do so, won the Grand National, carrying 10st 11lb. He finished third with 12st 6lb in 1914.
1955 Vincent O'Brien's Quare Times, 100/9, was his third consecutive National winner following Early Mist, 20/1 and Royal Tan, 8/1.
1960 The Grand National was televised for the first time as Merryman II won, trained by Neville Crump, ridden by Gerry Scott, 13/2.
1968 Knotty Pine, ridden by Frank Durr, gave Michael Jarvis his first winner as a trainer at Doncaster.
1993 Gary Stevens won three out of four races at the inaugural International Jockey's Challenge in Dubai to give the US team victory.
1999 Calvin Borel, who would win the 2009 Kentucky Derby on Mine That BIrd and Preakness on Rachel Alexandra, scored his 3000th win at Oaklawn Park.
2008 The *Racing Post* reported that Jonjo O'Neill was calling for the abolition of water jumps after his East Tycoon at Ludlow six days earlier became the second horse in four weeks to die at such obstacles.

QUOTE OF THE DAY
'I'm glad I won, because if I hadn't I'd have taken my horses away from you,' the owner of 1962 Hennessy Gold Cup winner Springbok, Lord Joicey, told trainer Neville Crump who on this day in 1960 won the first televised Grand National with 13/2 Merryman II ridden by Gerry Scott.

BIRTHDAYS
1906 Northern jockey Billy Nevett, who won three wartime Derbys at Newmarket and was six times runner-up to Gordon Richards in the title race. He won the 1948 Oaks on Masaka. He partnered 2,068 winners from 12,356 British mounts in 33 seasons, trained at Ripon without distinction for a few seasons and died in May 1992.
1924 Walter Wharton, who trained Vaguely Noble to win the Observer Gold Cup before the colt was sold for a record 136,000gns at auction and went on to win the Arc, later siring Dahlia and Empery.
1933 US champion trainer King Leatherbury.
1938 Nine-times champion jockey between 1963-74 in Ireland, Johnny Roe.
1940 The jockey on Roberto when he inflicted Brigadier Gerard's only defeat, the Panamanian Braulio Baeza. He retired in 1976 with 3,140 wins to his credit.
1960 Newmarket trainer James Eustace.

DEATH OF THE DAY
1926 William Watkinson rode Jack Horner to win the Grand National on this date – but three weeks later died in a fall at Bogside.

CELEBRITY OF THE DAY
1966 Drake's Drum, bought by Paul McCartney for his father, won the 6f Hutton Plate at Aintree, the race before the Grand National, and was led in by Macca who later saw 50/1-shot Anglo win the big race.

27 MARCH

SIGNIFICANT EVENT
2000 Hayley Turner had her first public ride, on Markellis at Southwell. The horse broke a leg.

STRANGEST EVENT
1995 Two-year-old filly Wear The Fox Hat was scheduled to run in a maiden race at Folkestone for trainer David Cosgrove –until the Jockey Club stepped in and refused to allow her to do so unless her name was changed. Owner Julian Wilson – NOT the tv commentator, but a farmer from near Newmarket – had no option, changing her name to, er, Nameless. Come race time, Nameless had been withdrawn – oh, Fox!

OTHER EVENTS
1901 Ironically enough, the Initial Steeplechase was, in fact, the last such race run at Bedford.

1903 The first horse to represent a reigning monarch in the National, King Edward VII's Ambush II fell as Drumcree won.

1989 Sixteen runners filled the entire six-race card at Chepstow where Peter Scudamore rode a treble – 1/7; 1/7; walkover.

1968 Frankincense, ridden by Greville Starkey set a 20thC weight carrying record of 9st 5lb when winning at Lincoln for trainer John Oxley at 100/8. Oxley's travelling head lad of the time, one Barry Hills, launched his own training career on the back of his winnings from this race.

1993 Native Americans were brought in to perform a rain dance at parched Newbury. It didn't work.

1993 Lynda Ramsden was the first woman to train a Lincoln winner when 16/1 High Premium won under Kieren Fallon.

1996 Graham McCourt came full circle, winning on his final appearance, partnering 5/4 favourite Sister Stephanie at Chepstow, having won on his first

ride, Vulrory's Kid at Ascot in 1975. In between, there were 919 other winners.

1997 Walter Swinburn jr was fined £500 after admitting assaulting a restaurant owner and damaging a glass door. Magistrates at Newmarket ordered him to pay £600 plus compensation following an incident at Il Piccolo Mondo restaurant in the town after a dispute over the bill.

1999 A record US jumps crowd of 69,300 saw Lonesome Glory, champion jumper four times, and the first to win over $1m, win again at Camden, South Carolina.

QUOTE OF THE DAY
'What I've done is let nature take its course. I've gone to the toilet, done a number one and number two, gone out, ridden the horse, pushed and shoved away on it and got it up to win.' Jockey Andrew Thornton explaining how he weighed in 1lb 3oz light after winning on Radar Love at Fontwell in 2009. He was disqualified as a variation of only 1lb is permitted.

BIRTHDAYS
1918 Jockey Alec Russell, who rode all six winners at a meeting at Bogside in July, 1957. He retired in 1973.

1955 US Hall of Fame jockey Chris McCarron, rider of a record 546 winners in 1974.

FIRST OF THE DAY
1996 Trainer Tim Easterby sent out his first winner on the Flat, Jackson Park, 8/1 at Catterick.

CELEBRITY OF THE DAY
1996 Singer/songwriter Burt Bacharach's Soul of the Matter finished second behind Cigar, the 5/4 favourite, in the world's richest race, the Dubai World Cup, worth $4m. Trained by Bill Mott and ridden by Jerry Bailey, Cigar was winning his 14th successive race, taking his prize money total to $7,488,815.

28 MARCH

SIGNIFICANT EVENT

1884 Winner of Chester's Dee Stakes, but a failure in the Derby, Voluptuary had never run in a chase, but won the Grand National. He was subsequently put on stage at Drury Lane Theatre in a production of The Prodigal Daughter, in which he had to leap a water jump each night.

STRANGEST EVENT

1919 The Grand National was won by Poethlyn, as the big race resumed after a four-year gap during the war. Uniquely, a runner pulled up to enable the jockey to throw up. Jockey T Williams, blaming dodgy seafood, did so on All White, who then ran on to finish fifth.

OTHER EVENTS

1924 Bill O'Neill took a tumble from Libretto in the Grand National, then remounted a faller to chase after his horse, then got back on – and took another, final, tumble as up ahead 25/1-shot Master Robert won.

1931 Dual Cheltenham Gold Cup winner Easter Hero ended his career by dead heating in Liverpool's Champions Chase – just a day after being brought down in the Grand National.

1984 Michael Dickinson's final British winner over the sticks, Mister Donut at Fakenham.

1988 The first winner as a trainer for Lester Piggott's wife, Susan, as Raahin, 4/1, won at Folkestone.

1989 Such was the popularity of Desert Orchid that owner Richard Burridge launched a fan club for him.

1990 Attempting to win the See It Live in Yorkshire Handicap for the sixth successive year, the grey Gods Solution, in whose honour the race was renamed, could only finish third, behind So Careful.

1991 The *Sun* reported Shergar had been discovered in the Channel Islands.

2005 Numbersixvalverde who would win the Aintree version, a year later, took the 26 runner Irish Grand National, 9/1, under Ruby Walsh for trainer Martin Brassil. Walsh had already won the season's Welsh National at Silver Birch, and Aintree version on Hedgehunter, before finishing second on theScottish National on Cornish Rebel.

2009 Well Armed won the $6m Dubai World Cup at Nad al Sheba by a record 14 lengths, trained by Eoin Harty, ridden by Aaron Gryder, at 10/1. Apprentice Ahmed Ajtebi showed up his seniors when landing a double on the day – winning the Dubai Duty Free on 12/1 Gladiatorus and the Sheema Classic on 14/1 Eastern Anthem. He rode Regal Parade to win the Buckingham Palace Stakes at Royal Ascot in 2008, when employed by Clive Brittain, but was then ordered to leave the country because of visa irregularities. He was the first native Emirati to ride a World Cup day winner.

QUOTE OF THE DAY

'Peter O'Sullevan is the race of voicing' declared Richard Pitman once, but I'm sure Sir Pete, who had his first Flat winner with Just Friendly at Lincoln today in 1958, knew what he meant.

BIRTHDAYS

1954 Curragh trainer and former jockey, Declan Gillespie.

1966 Jockey, publican and broadcaster Luke Harvey.

DEATHS OF THE DAY

1994 Shrewd gambling trainer, Epsom-based Snowy Parker, 94. Real name Evan James Parker. Born Feb 6, 1900, he began training in 1930, having ridden over jumps until a bad fall curtailed his career in 1926.

1997 Winner of perhaps the most emotional Grand National of them all, Aldaniti, 27.

CELEBRITY OF THE DAY

1941 Owner-cricketer Jack Simmons, of Lancashire and Tasmania, born.

29 MARCH

SIGNIFICANT EVENT
2008 Robby Albarado rode Curlin to a record 73/41 win in the Dubai World Cup. 'Curlin is like a limousine and I am just along for the ride' marvelled the jockey as the horse took winnings to almost £9m, Trained by Steve Asmussen.

STRANGEST EVENT
2009 An unexpected contender jumped up alongside Just Talking, going for his fourth straight win, as the runners took the seventh fence at Maisemore Park point-to-point, but the whippet who bounded over the obstacle then dropped out of the race, leaving the 7yo horse with just equine opponents to beat – which he did.

OTHER EVENTS
1881 Amateur rider Charlie Cunningham rode in seven races at Rugby's jump meeting, winning six of them and finishing second in the other.
1901 The 2lbs of butter packed into the horse's hooves to stop him losing footing as snow fell helped Grudon, 9/1, ridden by Arthur Nightingall, win the Grand National by four lengths.
1935 For the first time the National was won by two furlongs – Frank Furlong, jockey, and owner-trainer Noel Furlong – responsible for the 22/1 Reynoldstown.
1958 Mr What, trained by Tom Taafe, ridden by Arthur Freeman won the National at 18/1, but the 8yo never won again in 33 attempts.
1969 12-y-o Highland Wedding, trained by Toby Balding, won the Grand National as rider Eddie Harty became the only person to ride at the Olympics (three-day event, 1960), and win the National.
1991 Arkle's jockey Pat Teaffe underwent successful heart transplant surgery.
1992 Tony Ives rode Let Us Famous to win the first Macau Derby, 4/6, at Taipa.
1992 Gianfranco Dettori won Italy's Premio Pisa on Worldwide. That'll Be The Day was second – ridden by Frankie Dettori – his son!
1993 Richard Dunwoody and fellow jockey Roger Marley were arrested for disorderly behavior after attending the Jockey' Association Awards Ceremony.
1994 Channel 4 celebrated its tenth birthday with the news that it had secured rights to screen the five British Classics until 1997.
1997 A torrential downpour washed out the Dubai World Cup meeting at Nad al Sheba.
2009 Charlotte Kerton won on 11/1 Spring Goddess at Doncaster – the first winner of the campaign for the 28-year-old who had already become the first professional female jockey to compete in both Dubai and Bahrain.

QUOTE OF THE DAY
2009 *'Some live on chocolate and Red Bull.'* Jenny Pitman, expressing concern that the desire to produce results adds pressure to jockeys' lifestyles.

BIRTHDAYS
1917 US superstar Man O'War, winner of 20 of his 21 races, starting odds-on every time and known as Big Red.
1949 Steve Jobar, rider of 1980 Triumph Hurdle winner Heighlin and popular chaser Combs Ditch.

FIRST OF THE DAY
1947 The Grand National was run on a Saturday for the first time – at the request of prime minister Clement Attlee 'in the interests of British industry.' 100/1 winner Caughoo did little for the interests of British punters, although his stuffed head was preserved and one owner would sit it in front of the TV to watch the race each year.

CELEBRITY OF THE DAY
1955 Amateur rider-turned MP Henry Bellingham born.

30 MARCH

SIGNIFICANT EVENT
1996 Mick Fitzgerald won the Grand National on 7/1 favourite Rough Quest, then made infamous comments about the experience being 'better than sex', later used as the title of his autobiography.

STRANGEST EVENT
1994 Hops And Pops broke a leg before the start of the Golden Eagle Novice Chase at Ascot –but still won the race. The leg she broke belonged to jockey Carl Llewellyn who had been due to ride Ghia Gneuiagh before Hops And Pops kicked him. He was replaced by Simon Earle.

OTHER EVENTS
1883 The smallest ever Grand National field, just ten. The winner was Zoedone at 100/7, owned and ridden by Bohemian, Count Charles Kinsky, who bought the horse for £800 with the proceeds of a wager on Corrie Rot winning the Cesarewitch. After the race disgruntled jockey Jimmy Adams moaned: 'Last year it was a blooming Lord (Grenadier Guard, Lord Manners at 10/1) won the National; this year it's a furring Count, and next year it'll be an old woman most likely!' Replied the Count: 'Yes, Jimmy, and I hope this old woman will be yourself'. It wasn't.
1898 The first meeting at Folkestone.
1928 Only two horses – 100/1 winner Tipperary Tim, and 33/1 Billy Barton, of the 42 starters finished the Grand National, run on very heavy ground.
1968 Pat Eddery's first British ride, finishing sixth at Liverpool on Dido's Dowry.
1974 Red Rum won his second successive Grand National, at 11/1 ridden by Brian Fletcher.
1990 Mick Channon saddled his first winner, Golden Scissors, 4/1, at Beverley.
1998 Six-times French champion jockey Freddie Head celebrated his first winners as a trainer when Mulahen, then Ta Aruf, both won at Fontainebleau.
2002 Sunline became the first horse in Australia to win over A$10,000,000 when taking the Doncaster Handicap at Randwick.
2005 The Goldenway Handicap was declared a 'no race' at Sandown, Australia, when runners rode into a flock of seagulls, dislodging five jockeys. Brandy Cross broke his arm, Darren Gauci suffered chipped teeth – and one seagull was injured!

QUOTE OF THE DAY
2007 *'Never ride out with your mobile – run around the track when you go racing – go for the bloody gap– and don't be associated with oiks – you'll go down to their level.'* Advice for aspiring jockeys from trainer Mark Tompkins.

BIRTHDAYS
1931 One of two famous trainer brothers, Mick (Michael William) Easterby. He trained Mrs McArdy to win the 1977 1,000 Guineas.
1945 Owner of The Ripleyite and Via Delta, guitarist Eric Clapton.
1951 Top trainer John Gosden.
1962 Singer and dancer MC Hammer – a successful owner who was no stranger to a wager.
1970 US Triple Crown winner Secretariat, known as 'Super Red'.

DEATH OF THE DAY
2002 Huge racing fan and owner HM Queen Elizabeth, the Queen Mother, 101.

CELEBRITY OF THE DAY
1963 Film star Gregory Peck was at the Grand National to see his 20/1 chance, the grey Owen's Sedge finish seventh to 66/1 Ayala, who was trained by Lester Piggott's dad, Keith.

31 MARCH

SIGNIFICANT EVENT
1978 Irish trainer Jim Bolger sent out his first English winner, Beparoejojo, at Liverpool.

STRANGEST EVENT
1995 A betting shop at Cressy's Corner, Hounslow became the first in Japanese ownership when Japanese financier Hajime Nakano and partner Masayuki Kawabe bought it from Ken Munden.

OTHER EVENTS
1905 Paid £300 not to ride for two weeks before the National, crack jockey Frank Mason duly won the National on 6/1 Kirkland.

1921 Gordon Richards rode his first winner, Gay Lord at Leicester, where the last horse home in the race was the charmingly named Toilet.

1973 Red Rum, ridden by Brian Fletcher, was something of a villain as he won the National for the first time, pipping gallant front-runner and superb jumper Crisp, also 9/1 joint favourite, and partnered by Richard Pitman. Red Rum was receiving 23lbs from the runner up and set a record time of 9m 1.9s.

1984 Fourth the previous year, Hallo Dandy, 13/1, ridden by Neale Doughty for Gordon W Richards, won the Grand National, the first held since the Jockey Club guaranteed the race's future by buying Aintree.

1990 East and West Germany met at a race meeting for the first time since the 1961 erection of the Berlin Wall, which had been brought down months earlier. Hoppengarten in the East held a meeting also attended by westeners who saw British jockey Peter Bloomfield win on Kassu.

1993 Tyrone Flyer at Catterick was Gay Kelleway's first Flat winner.

1997 Jenny Pitman's Mudaahim, 13/2, won the Jameson Irish Grand National at Fairyhouse. Later in the afternoon jockey Shane Broderick suffered a terrible fall which left him paralysed.

2007 Very Wise, 9/1, won Lincoln, run at Newcastle, partnered by Joe Fanning for William Haggas.

2007 The smallest field in a 12 year history, seven, contested the Dubai World Cup with Invasor going off as 5/4 favourite and winning by one and three quarter lengths.

2009 Fergal Lynch, British-based jockey who switched to the USA, landed a five-timer at Philadelphia Park.

QUOTE OF THE DAY
2009 *'Michael has got the rest of his life to concentrate on horse racing – but football should surely be his priority,'* said former England striker Ian Wright, apparently blaming Michael Owen's interest in racing for his inability to persuade Fabio Capello to select him for England squad.

BIRTHDAYS
1927 Former Carlisle trainer Stan Payne.

1933 Former 'Cock of the North', jockey Johnny Seagrave. Died in November 2009.

DEATH OF THE DAY
1979 Cheltenham Gold Cup winner Alverton, ridden by Jonjo O'Neill, broke his neck and was killed at Becher's during the Grand National, won by the first Scottish-trained winner, Rubstic 25/1, handled by John Leadbetter in Roxburghshire. The horse returned to the hamlet of Denholm accompanied by a kilted piper.

CELEBRITY OF THE DAY
1935 Owner and trumpeter with Tijuana Brass, Herb Alpert.

1 APRIL

SIGNIFICANT EVENT
1764 It may just be racing's ultimate April Fool joke from history. The first true equine superstar, Eclipse, was foaled on this date – or maybe not. Other sources suggest March 17 as the date, when a lunar eclipse took place, or even April 15. Author Nicholas Clee tried to clear matters up in his commendable 2009 book, *Eclipse* but despite exhaustive research could not conclusively settle the issue.

STRANGEST EVENT
1929 Amateur Frank Wise wore an artificial leg when winning the Irish National on Alike at Fairyhouse. He also lost the tops of three fingers during the war.

OTHER EVENTS
1926 Hamlet won over hurdles at Bournemouth – first of 355 National Hunt wins for owner Jim Joel.

1949 Newbury resumed racing after World War II, having been used as an Army depot during the conflict and covered with concrete and 35 miles of railway line. Jumping did not return until November 1951.

1972 Clive Brittain sent out his first winner, Vedvyas, at Doncaster.

1974 Linda Goodwill won the first mixed race, the Lads and Lassies Handicap at Nottingham, riding Pee Mai.

1976 Aintree's final Flat card was run.

1978 Lucius, 14/1, won the Grand National after Red Rum had been withdrawn 24 hours before with a bruised heel on the eve of his attempt to win for a fourth time. The winner, a 9 year old trained by Gordon W Richards at Greystoke, Cumbria, ridden by Bob Davies, prevailing by half a length from Ridley Lamb and Sebastian V.

1991 Trainer Peter Chapple-Hyam sent out his first winner, Noble Flutter, 11/2, at Warwick. Not much more than a year later he had 2,000 Guineas and Derby winners to his credit.

1991 19 year old Deborah Ryan became the youngest female to make a book at the racecourse, representing her father Pat Ryan at Weatherby.

1991 *The Racing Post* 'revealed' that Desert Orchid was to go show jumping, partnered by Harvey Smith.

1991 Jacqui Oliver became the first female jockey to ride a treble over jumps, with Bolshoi Boy, Noble Ben and Shu Fly at Uttoxeter.

1993 Betting shops were permitted to open until 10pm between April 1 and August 31.

2002 The Bunny Boiler, 12/1, landed 17 runner Irish Grand National for jockey Ross Geraghty, landing his first win for trainer Noel Meade, who had a 4-timer on his card.

QUOTE OF THE DAY
'Frankly, these chaps have been getting away with some pretty blatant abuses of the dress code and enough is enough. This year, jockeys will be required to wear full morning dress on arrival, in the parade ring and whilst riding.' Ascot chief executive Charles Barnett reveals sense of humour sensation! A press release from the course in 2009.

BIRTHDAYS
1941 Former champion lady rider Gaie Johnson Houghton.

1944 Handler of the popular and successful Swinging Junior and Roman Warrior, Nigel Angus.

1950 Merrick Francis, trainer son of Dick.

DEATH OF THE DAY
2003 Irish jump jockey-turned trainer, John Crowley, 61. His Hippolito lost the 1979 Triumph Hurdle in the stewards' room, having been backed from 66/1 to 20/1.

CELEBRITY OF THE DAY
1957 David Gower, cricketer, and owner with Lawrence Wells, born.

2 APRIL

SIGNIFICANT EVENT
1821 Durdham Down, Bristol staged the first officially recorded hurdle race, run in three heats of one mile with five hurdles in each heat.

STRANGEST EVENT
1925 Despite having had a leg amputated below the knee, Gerald Foljambe rode two jump winners at Melton, Leicestershire.

OTHER EVENTS
1945 13-year-old Heirdom won the Irish National.

1954 Vincent O'Brien's licence was suspended for three months following an inquiry into alleged inconsistencies of his star chasers Royal Tan, Lucky Dome, Knock Hard and Early Mist. O'Brien issued a statement – 'I am completely in the dark as to what, if any, offence I am alleged to have been guilty of.'

1987 Wayward Lad, with £217,923 in prize money, from 28 wins in 55 races, surpassed only by Dawn Run, retired on a winning note after the Whitbread Label Gold Cup Chase at Aintree, 7/1.

1988 3 yo Simply Majestic won the Golden Gates' Breeders Cup Handicap by 10 lengths under Russell Baze, setting a world record for 9f on dirt of 1m45s.

2009 Anabolic steroid use was banned by racing authorities in Michigan, USA.

QUOTE OF THE DAY
2009 *'My first ride back after that was when I broke my neck. It was the one they call the 'hangman's bone', but it didn't move and I was very, very lucky.'* Venetia Williams recalling her first outing after being knocked out, ending up in traction when Marcolo fell in the 1988 National.

BIRTHDAYS
1933 Major owner and sponsor George Ward.

1936 The trainer involved in the infamous 'Gay Future' coup, Tony Collins.

1937 Trainer Barry Hills, who sent out winners at 9/2, 5/2 and 16/1 on his birthdays in 2006, '07 and '08 but only managed a third and fourth in 2009. He won the 1973 Arc with Rheingold.

1963 Trainer of Derby winners Dr Devious and Authorized, Peter Chapple-Hyam. Also landed the 1992 2,000 Guineas with Rodrigo de Triano.

DEATHS OF THE DAY
1838 'Emperor of Trainers' Robert Robson, 73, with 34 Classics to his credit including seven Derby and twelve Oaks triumphs. He never won the St Leger. He is credited with phasing out the 'sweating' of horses by galloping them clad in heavy rugs and hood.

2009 Exotic Dancer, who collapsed after finishing second to Madison du Berlais in Aintree's Totesport Bowl Chase in which Cheltenham Gold Cup winner Denman fell. Winner of eight of his 28 races including the same race in 2007, Exotic Dancer was second and third in the 2007 and 2009 Gold Cups. He won £780,939.

FIRST OF THE DAY
1977 Charlotte Brew, 21, became the first woman to ride in the Grand National. She and 200/1 shot Barony Fort, trained by her mother, made it to the fourth from home before the horse refused, as Red Rum won for the third time, by a facile 25 lengths at the age of 12 under Tommy Stack. Rummy was 9/1 joint second favourite.

3 APRIL

SIGNIFICANT EVENT
1993 Judy Higby had dreamed overnight that the day's Grand National was cancelled. The Tring woman went to her local betting shop to ask for a bet about that happening, but the boss turned her down. That afternoon the National was turned into a farce when a false start fiasco led to the race being declared void. Jenny Pitman's 50/1 shot Esha Ness finished first, but it didn't count. She was, to put it mildly, unhappy.

STRANGEST EVENT
1970 Jockeys John Murtagh and Brian Lee were bizarrely injured during a 1m6f race at Aintree when they were struck by wires hanging down as they rode under the Grand National starting gate.

OTHER EVENTS
1840 Set to carry 13st 3lb in the Cheltenham Cup Chase, great jumper Lottery nevertheless won the 4m race.
1978 Michael Roberts, future champion jockey, rode his first British winner, Pakeha at Ayr.
1986 Two days before riding Classified in the Gold Cup, Steve Smith Eccles claimed to have been hijacked in his car. He survived to tell the tale, and finished third in the big race.
1993 Morley Street, ridden by Graham Bradley, won the Grade 1 Martell Aintree Hurdle for the fourth successive season. Yet started at 6/1.
1995 Neale Doughty retired after winning on American Hero at Kelso. He won the 1984 National on Hallo Dandy.
1998 One Man broke a leg in Aintree's Mumm Melling Chase and was put down, a month after the popular grey had won the Queen Mother Champion Chase at Cheltenham. His trainer Gordon Richards died later in the year.
1999 A senior Jockey Club official was left red-faced after being found guilty of riding a non-trier in a point-to-point race at Charing, Kent. Simon Claisse, head of the Club's racecourse department and controller of point-to-pointing, pulled up Forest Musk in a four-runner race and was fined £125 at a stewards' inquiry. 'I told them the horse was never going on the ground' he said.
2008 Bring Me Sunshine, at Taunton, was Mick Fitzgerald's final winner of a fine career of some 1,250 successes – 12 at Cheltenham Festival. He won the National on Rough Quest in the 1996; Gold Cup on See More Business in 1999.

QUOTE OF THE DAY
1958 *'I rode in six Nationals and I was pissed for three of them – the horses I rode, you had to be.'* Trainer Charlie Mann, born today, who won legendary Czech race the Velka Pardubicka on It's A Snip: *'I didn't have a licence to ride, with it not given back after I broke my neck, so I printed my own one and rode anyway.'*

BIRTHDAYS
1937 Snooker-playing Irish trainer Liam Browne who, as a jockey, was a champion apprentice.
1971 Welsh trainer Evan Williams, handler of Hennessy winner State of Play.
1976 Trainer Harry Dunlop, son of champion trainer John, brother to Classic-winning trainer Ed.

DEATH OF THE DAY
2002 Owner of 1965 National winner Jay Trump, her only horse, Mary Stephenson LeBlond died, aged 100.

FIRST OF THE DAY
1982 Geraldine Rees became the first lady to get round in the Grand National, finishing eighth on Cheers, 66/1, while Dick Saunders, 48, became the oldest winner, on Grittar, 7/1 favourite.

CELEBRITY OF THE DAY
1946 Snooker star-turned pundit, and owner of Jokist, John Virgo born.

4 APRIL

SIGNIFICANT EVENT
2009 After two false starts, which saw six jockeys handed suspensions, Venetia Williams became only the second female trainer – after Jenny Pitman – to saddle a Grand National winner as 100/1 outsider Mon Mome stormed home under 23-year-old Liam Treadwell, to whom Clare Balding suggested in a post-race interview that he might now be able to have his less than perfect teeth fixed. Cue ludicrous public complaints.

STRANGEST EVENT
1991 Mark Salvaggio rode three winners at three tracks for trainer Tim Ritchey; Broken Silence, 9/10, in the 1pm at Philadelphia Park, Barbara's Cutlass, 13/10, in the 2.50 at Delaware Park and Don't Throw Stones, 46/10, in the 9.10 at Penn National.

OTHER EVENTS
1943 Longchamp racecourse was bombed by the British just before racing began – but the meeting went ahead.
1981 One-time invalid Aldaniti, and former cancer victim Bob Champion, teamed up to win the Grand National.
1992 Five days before the General Election, topical tip Party Politics won the Grand National at 14/1.
1994 Son of War, 12/1, won the Irish Grand National, partnered by Fran Woods, whose father Paddy had won it in 1963 on Last Link and Splash two years later.
1997 For the first time in its 61-year history, Keeneland racecourse in Lexington, USA offered racegoers live commentary, by 28-year-old Kurt Becker.

QUOTE OF THE DAY
'Here happened a dispute along the greatest point of Criticall learning that was ever known at Newmarket. A match between a horse of Sir Rob. Car's, and a gelding of Sir Rob. Geere's, for a mile and a halfe only, had engaged all the Court in many thousand pounds, much depending in so short a course to have them start fairly. Mr Griffin was appointed to start them. When he saw them equall he sayd Goe and presently he cried out Stay. One went off, and run through the Course and claims the money, the other never stird at all. Most possibly you may say that this was not a fayre starting, but the critics say after the word Goe was out of the mouth his commission was determined and it was illegal for him to say Stay'. Sadly, Lord Conway did not record the verdict in this controversial race, held in 1682.

BIRTHDAYS
1929 Trainer John Winter. Brother of top jump jockey-turned trainer Fred Thomas Winter. John took over Newmarket's Highfield Stables in 1965 and won the Wokingham Stakes in 1967 with Spaniard's Mount.
1951 Trainer Michael 'Mouse' Morris, the son of Lord Killanin, who competed at the Olympic Games and went on to head the IOC. Morris won the Irish Grand National on Billycan in 1977, and twice won the Queen Mother Champion Chase on Skymas in the mid '70s. Trained War of Attrition to win the 2006 Cheltenham Gold Cup. His recreations include hang gliding

DEATHS OF THE DAY
1999 Aussie-born globe-trotting jockey Eddie Cracknell, 72 who became a trainer in India.
2007 Legendary Australian jumps trainer Jim Houlahan, 93. Inducted into the Hall of Fame and received the Order of Australia Medal for services to racing, in 2004.

CELEBRITY OF THE DAY
1991 The Queen Mother visited Aintree for the first time since Devon Loch's infamous Grand National run-in collapse in 1956, to open the £3m Queen Mother Stand.

5 APRIL

SIGNIFICANT EVENT
1997 The Grand National was abandoned and Aintree evacuated following a bomb warning from the IRA. People were left wandering the streets looking for rooms – amongst them jockeys still in silks – after police refused to allow them back to their parked cars. The Adelphi Hotel put many up and one room hosted twelve jockeys, Timmy Murphy reportedly sleeping in the bath. The race was switched to Monday at 5pm when Lord Gyllene, 14/1, was the winner in front of a 20,000 crowd including Prime Minister John Major.

STRANGEST EVENT
1970 Frankie Dettori's father, Gianfranco, was stoned when riding at San Siro. He was literally the target of stones hurled at him after he partnered outsider Furibondo to beat 1/5 shot Hogarth in the Premio d'Aprille. Punters were not best pleased at the improvement shown by Dettori's mount after a disappointing display last time.

OTHER EVENTS
1915 Oriental Park Racecourse, Havana, Cuba staged a World Heavyweight Championship clash between Jack Johnson and Jess Willard, which was won by underdog Willard – in the 26th round.
1940 25/1 Bogskar won last Grand National until 1946 when Lovely Cottage, also 25/1, won on this date.
1978 Animation at Rouen was Criquette Head's first winner as a trainer.
1999 Richard Dunwoody broke Peter Scudamore's record of 1,678 NH winners in his career, with Yorkshire Edition at Wincanton.
2008 Controversial broadcaster Jonathan Ross gave Radio 2 listeners his opinion of horse racing: 'It's rubbish, horse racing. We all know it isn't sport – its humans on the back of animals'.
2009 Limerick racecourse held a meeting dedicated to rugby union's reigning Heineken Cup champions, Munster, offering half-price admission to those wearing Munster jerseys.
2009 Trainer Howard Johnson and jockey Denis O'Regan landed a 793/1 four-fold at Hexham.

QUOTE OF THE DAY
'The racing public had a picture in their minds of Walls in one of his typical Aldwych farce roles and found it impossible to take such an accomplished comedian quite seriously.' The book, *History of the Derby Stakes,* explained why comic-cum-trainer Tom Walls staggered the racing and entertainment worlds in 1932 when he saddled the 100/6 Derby winner – called April the Fifth, and foaled on that very date in 1929.

BIRTHDAYS
1924 Brown Jack was born – winner of the Queen Alexandra Stakes at Royal Ascot an incredible six times from 1929 to 1934. Also won the Champion Hurdle. When he died, aged 25, his heart was found to weigh 19lbs, some 8lbs over the average.
1940 Jockey Brian Rouse. Won 1980 1000 Guineas on Quick As Lightning.
1941 US trainer Mike Harrington.

DEATHS OF THE DAY
1994 'Hotspur' of the *Daily Telegraph,* racing writer Peter Scott, 64.
2004 Fred Winter, 77. He was champion jump jockey four times, champion trainer eight times, and the first man to ride and train winners of the Grand National, Gold Cup, King George VI Chase and Champion Hurdle.

CELEBRITY OF THE DAY
1916 Actor, Gregory Peck was born – owner of Grand National runners, Owen's Sedge and Different Class. The latter was third in 1968.

6 APRIL

SIGNIFICANT EVENT
1967 Brenda Johnson was the first woman officially to train a winner at Liverpool when Minto Burn, ridden by Brian Surtees, won the Foxhunters Chase.

STRANGEST EVENT
1995 Jockey Steve Williams won for the first time as a professional boxer, beating Andy 'Mighty Atom' Roberts on points, having drawn his first paid scrap.

OTHER EVENTS
1854 Virago, trained by John Day for moneylender Henry Padwick, landed a double in the 1m2f City and Suburban – and the 2m2f Great Metropolitan at Epsom. A tough filly who won the 1000 Guineas on May 4 after two more successes at York.

1962 Quenn Mother's Laffy won the Ulster Harp National at Downpatrick, ridden by Willie Robinson for Peter Cazelet.

1968 Bill Watts saddled his first National Hunt winner, Prospect Pleases at Leicester – followed almost immediately after by his first flat winner, Rasping at Catterick.

1983 Fulke Walwyn saddled his 2000th winner, Noble Heir, at Ascot.

1992 Topical tip Political Issue, 9/4 won at Kelso three days before the General Election.

1995 Longchamp's meeting was abandoned after protesting racecourse staff invaded the paddock and staged a sit-in to object to a pay 'rise' of zero.

2002 Bindaree was a 20/1 National winner for jockey Jim Culloty and trainer Nigel Twiston-Davies.

2009 A family affair as former jockey Tony Dobbin landed his first winner as a trainer, Luksar at Kelso. The horse was partnered by Dobbin's wife, Rose, and owned by her dad, Duncan Davidson. The afternoon featured a race in honour of 101-year-old Isabel Archer, who was there for the occasion.

QUOTE OF THE DAY
'This day there was a race at Sapley neere Huntingdon, invented by the gentlemen of that country (sic): at this Mr Oliver Cromwell's horse won the sylver (sic) bell and Mr Cromwell had the glory of the day.' Page from the 1602 diary of John Manningham.

BIRTHDAYS
1944 Susan Nock, trainer of Senor El Betrutti.

1933 Solihull trainer of Winnie the Witch, Ken Bridgwater.

1953 Racing historian and author Chris Pitt, whose book *A Long Time Gone* chronicles the British racecourses which have closed down since 1900.

CELEBRITIES OF THE DAY
1961 Comic impressionist and owner with Lady Herries, Rory Bremner born. On the same day in 1938 magician Paul Daniels, owner of That's Magic, was born.

7 APRIL

SIGNIFICANT EVENT

1994 Robert Sangster, son of football pools magnate Vernon, died aged 67. He won the Derby with The Minstrel in 1977 and in 1982 with Golden Fleece. Owned horses since buying gelding Chalk Stream in 1960 as a present for his fiancée. Launched breeding and racing magazine Pacemaker in 1974. Owned Arc winners Alleged and Detroit, and his Beldale Ball won the Melbourne Cup. Sangster's final Classic winner was Rodrigo de Triano in the 1992 2,000 Guineas.

STRANGEST EVENT

1990 Mr Frisk, ridden by Marcus Armytage at 16/1 set a record time of 8m47.8s in the Grand National. On the same day the Santa Anita Derby was won by – Mr Frisky.

OTHER EVENTS

1951 Nickel Coin, 33/1, won the Grand National

1967 Red Rum – then trained by Tim Molony – dead-heated in the 2yo 'seller' at Liverpool, ridden by Paul Cook. Two years to the day he won over sticks for the first time, at Wetherby.

1977 Steve Cauthen rode six winners in a day for the second time at Aqueduct. Two years to the day later he rode his first winner in England – Marquee Universal, at Salisbury.

1979 David Elsworth sent out his first winner Raffia Set, at Salisbury.

1993 Peter Scudamore bowed out on Sweet Duke at Ascot, with 1,677 wins.

1994 Kim Bailey saddled the winner of Aintree's Martell Cup for the third successive year when Docklands Express completed a double. Kings Fountain won in 1992.

1995 Sydney champion jockey Jim Cassidy was banned for six months by Aussie officials inquiring into a major race-fixing incident.

1997 The rescheduled Grand National was run at 5pm on – for the first time – a Monday, after being postponed following Saturday's bomb scare. Lord Gyllene beat Suny Bay by 25 lengths, ridden by Tony Dobbin. It was Peter O'Sullevan's final National as commentator. Prime Minister, John Major was amongst the 20,000 crowd.

2009 Watching on TV, Barry Hills, 72, saw his 3,000th winner, 4/7 favourite Chapter And Verse, land the odds at Pontefract, partnered by son Michael.

QUOTE OF THE DAY

1949 *'Bookmakers are like leeches'*. Trainer Luca Cumani, born this day, who taught Frankie Dettori much of what he knows.

BIRTHDAYS

1920 William A Stephenson. Won July Cup and Gimcrack with Rapid River in 1972. First NH handler to score 100 winners in a season. Won 1987 Gold Cup with The Thinker.

1943 Trainer of perennial, record-breaking loser Quixall Crossett, Ted Caine.

1951 Newmarket trainer Mark Tompkins.

1953 French trainer Pascal Bary.

1954 Trainer Colin Tinkler.

1971 Jockey and trainer Sean Curran.

1978 Flat jockey Fergus Sweeney.

DEATHS OF THE DAY

1982 Former jockey and trainer, Rufus Beasley, 75. He won the Cambridgeshire three times as a trainer. He won the St Leger on Boswell in 1936.

1991 20yo jockey Rodney Dickens, following a fall at Sportsman's Park, Cicero, Illinois.

FIRST OF THE DAY

1993 Amateur Johnny Greenall became the first jockey to lose a claim for the third time. He first lost it when he rode his 30th winner, only for the Jockey Club to change the rule to 40 – which he achieved – only for the number to increase to 55.

8 APRIL

SIGNIFICANT EVENT
2009 Trainer Roy Cambidge, one of few racing folk to get a mention in the *Guinness Book of Records* – in 1973 his Threadbare won over hurdles, fences and on the Flat in three consecutive days – died aged 86. In 1976 Roaring Wind won him the Arkle Trophy and Java Fox the County Hurdle at the Cheltenham Festival.

STRANGEST EVENT
1995 Jockey Stephen Davis may have thought he had the race in the bag, but instead literally bagged a fine of £75 at Hereford, for carrying a yellow plastic bag whilst riding Arcticflow – winless in 41 attempts – in a hunter chase. He said it was to encourage the horse to put his best foot forward. It didn't work as the 10yo was pulled up.

OTHER EVENTS
1844 Grand National winning Lottery (1839) ran and won his final race at Windsor, but ended his days pulling a cart in Neasden.
1922 Derby-winning jockey Charlie Smirke rode his first winner, the Vitalba filly (many horses raced nameless in those days) at Derby.
1967 'He can safely be ignored even in a race noted for shocks' predicted *Daily Express* tipster Charles Benson of Foinavon, previewing the 1967 Grand National – won, at 100/1, by Foinavon.
1968 A course record of 97 runners contested a card at Edinburgh.
1972 Capt Tim Forster saddled 14/1 Well To Do, ridden by Graham Thorner, to win the Grand National, beating the previous year's winner Gay Trip by two lengths.
1985 The Gambler's Cup at Huntingdon was John Francome's 1138th and last winner. On the same day Desert Orchid raced in blinkers for the only time. He was pulled up in the Welsh Champion Hurdle.
1991 Legendary US jockey Bill Shoemaker was paralysed following a car crash in California. On the same day Buzzard's Crest won at Newcastle under George Duffield – but only after the field raced towards a group of deer grazing on the track – they scattered just in time.
1995 Two years after 'winning' the National that never was with Esha Ness, Jenny Pitman won it for real with Royal Athlete, ridden by Jason Titley.
2000 Father and son success as Papillon, backed from 40/1 to 10/1, won the Grand National for trainer Ted Walsh and jockey son Ruby.
2009 It was announced that Beverley racecourse, one of 14 to hold the Racehorse Owners' Association Gold Standard Award, would become the first to be stripped of it after refusing to supply free food for owners.

QUOTE OF THE DAY
2009 *'The Queen says we should stick him in the race and see how he is in a week's time.'* Trainer Nicky Henderson was reported by *London's Evening Standard* to have said of the possible participation in the Guinness Gold Cup at Punchestown of her Barbers Shop. 'Stick him in the race'? The Queen? Don't think so!?

BIRTHDAYS
1966 Jockey Conor O'Dwyer, rider of Hardy Eustace and War of Attrition.
1975 Jockey John Thomas McNamara, rider of recular cross country chase winner, Spot Thedifference.

DEATH OF THE DAY
2009 1973 champion apprentice Steve Perks, 54, who rode over 600 winners. He suffered a fall at home which resulted in his death. After retiring because of a back injury he owned a Chinese takeaway, learning Cantonese to help his relationship with his staff.

9 APRIL

SIGNIFICANT EVENT
1917 Many claim he was the greatest trainer of all time. Michael Vincent O'Brien, born today, sent out three consecutive Grand National winners; won the Cheltenham Gold Cup four times; the Derby six times, as well as winning every British Classic; plus nine Irish St Legers, six Irish Derbys, five Irish 2,000 Guineas, four Irish Oaks, three Irish 1,000 Guineas and three Arcs.

STRANGEST EVENT
2009 An obvious tip after the event – but few got on 8/1 Tipperary winner Lastkingofscotland, trained by Charles O'Brien and running in the colours of his legendary father, trainer Vincent – whose 92nd birthday it just happened to be.

OTHER EVENTS
1966 Classic-winning jockey Tony Murray rode his first winner, Cleodora at Warwick.
1983 Corbiere was the first Grand National winner trained by a woman – Jenny Pitman. Runner-up Greasepaint was again second next year when Corbiere was third, then in 1985 Corbiere was third with Greasepaint fourth.
1984 Chris Loreth rode eight winners from 10 rides at Exhibition Park, Vancouver.
1985 John Francome's last mount, on The Reject, a faller at Chepstow.
1991 Hong Kong trainer Peter Tse Yan-Sid was fined £44,000 following the doping of three horses in his stables.
1994 Fiddlers Pike, 100/1, the oldest runner at 13, was an admirable fifth in the Grand National, the highest placing for a woman so far, achieved by 51-year-old grandmother Rosemary Henderson. Martell sponsored both the National and Hong Kong's L'Or de Martell Cup, claiming the first same day, dual continent sponsorship deal.

1994 Uncle Ernie won the Martell Aintree Chase to give trainer Jimmy FitzGerald his 1,000th winner, Flat and jumps combined.
1999 One punter was £100,000 better off after the £4,000 North London betting shop wager he staked at 25/1 on Bobbyjo on this day to win the National, paid off the next afternoon!
2007 A.P. McCoy rode Butler's Cabin, 14/1, to win Irish Grand National, completing a unique double with Cheltenham's National Hunt Chase, for Jonjo O'Neill.

QUOTE OF THE DAY
'Horses are much happier in less open spaces,' explained master trainer Vincent O'Brien, born this day in 1917, in 1994.

BIRTHDAYS
1910 Punters' friend Phil Bull, instigator of *Timeform*, in Hemsworth, Yorkshire.
1920 Trainer George Vergette, handler of Purple Silk and King of Diamonds.
1937 Trainer Roy Bowring.
1939 Trainer Alan Bailey.
1975 Robbie Fowler, owner along with fellow Liverpool star Steve McManaman of Auetaler and Seebald, born.
1981 Jockey Brian Crowley.

DEATHS OF THE DAY
1945 Northern jockey Lawrence Brown.
1990 Irish jockey David Parnell, 24, killed in a car crash. He won the Ulster Oaks and Ulster St Leger.

CELEBRITY OF THE DAY
1994 Laughs all round on this day as comedian Freddie Starr's Miinnehoma (trained by Martin Pipe, ridden by Richard Dunwoody) – for whom he bid at auction by sticking his tongue out at the auctioneer – won the 36-runner Grand National. The owner claimed to have staked £10,000 on the 33/1-shot which returned 16/1 but I suspect that was another of his jokes!

10 APRIL

SIGNIFICANT EVENT
1999 Bobbyjo was a 10/1 Grand National winner, ridden by Paul Carberry for his trainer father, Tommy – who had ridden the last Irish winner of the race, L'Escargot, 24 years earlier.

STRANGEST EVENT
1909 For the last time a dead heat was 'run off' at Plumpton as Marcellin and Santa Claus were ruled inseparable, so they did it again – and the former, 2/7, prevailed.

OTHER EVENTS
1408 King of Tibetan province, Gyangtse, decreed that 10-28 April each year be set aside for prayer ceremonies, featuring, to this day, horse racing.

1965 Bogside in Scotland, (opened near Ayr in 1867) and Rothbury in Northumberland both staged their final meetings – the former with its richest ever day's racing; the latter with under 3,000 in attendance to see Jack Berry ride a winner.

1983 Merseyside headmaster Peter Rogers set a Grand National record, completing the course in 40 minutes – without a horse! He raised £6,000 for school funds.

1989 Labour MP Tony Banks tabled a House of Commons motion, calling for the Grand National to be banned unless the course passed animal welfare safety standards.

1992 Amateur rider William Hurst shed four stone to ride Mils Mij in the Ayr Handicap Hurdle – 36yo was rewarded with his first victory.

1993 Aged 65, Stuart Oliver won on Valoroso at the Sandon point-to-point, Staffordshire. On the same card jockey Barry Leavy was somewhat optimistic when objecting to the winner even when his own horse, Local Customer had fallen.

2009 Hayley Turner won the Professional Jockeys' Association Lady Jockey of the Year accolade at the annual jockeys' 'Lester' awards night, where Ryan Moore and Tony McCoy won the Flat and jump jockey of the year prizes.

2009 The *Irish Times* reported that the Minister of Sport's comment that 'Ireland had the most successful horseracing industry in the world'.

QUOTE OF THE DAY
1937 *'The connection between all those who have got to 1,000, considering what it takes, is that we must all be nuts,'* said Stan Mellor, MBE, born today, the first jump jockey to reach 1,000 winners, after Messrs Dunwoody, Francome and Scudamore had joined him.

BIRTHDAYS
1937 Triple champion jump jockey Stan Mellor, the first to ride 1000 winners. He became a respected trainer, winning the Triumph Hurdle, Whitbread Cup and the Welsh Champion Hurdle.

1947 Brian Fletcher, who twice won the Grand National on Red Rum, and also won it on Red Alligator. Retired in 1976 due to head injuries.

1949 Trainer Chris Popham.

1949 Amateur jockey Peter Craggs, winner of the 1978 William Hill Scottish National on King Con.

FIRST OF THE DAY
1965 Gordon W Richards – the other one – sent out his first winner, Playlord, at Bogside.

CELEBRITY OF THE DAY
1932 Film star, owner and gambler Omar Sharif born.

11 APRIL

SIGNIFICANT EVENT
1992 Jim Bolger saddled five of the seven winners at the Curragh. One of the losers was 8/11 St Jovite who made up for it by finishing runner-up in the Epsom Derby and winning the Irish version. On 12 August 1991 Bolger had also saddled five winners on a mixed card at Gowran Park.

STRANGEST EVENT
1892 Coverdale refused during the Ovingdean Chase at Plumpton, returning to the paddock – only to be taken back to the course when the other two runners both also refused, allowing Coverdale to claim an unlikely victory.

OTHER EVENTS
1770 Eclipse beat Bucephalus in a match at Newmarket. Co-owner William Wildman won a bet of 600-400 guineas.

1872 Forced out of business by competition from local fairgrounds, Metairie racecourse at New Orleans staged a final day's racing after 35 years existance.

1957 John Buckingham finished unplaced on his first ride, on Royal Oak at Stratford. He made a bigger impression when winning the 1967 Grand National on 100/1 no-hoper Foinavon.

1966 Graham Sexton rode his first winners, Calisto, at Wolverhampton.

1980 Lottie Lehmann won at Sedgefield to give permit holder Mary Reveley her first success.

1993 The first three home in a point-to-point at Dromoland, Ireland, were disqualified. The winner weighed in 6lb light; the runner-up took the wrong course; the third horse missed out a fence. Fourth placed Ballycasey Girl VI won by default.

2009 Veteran Aussie trainer Bart Cummings broke a ten-year Group One drought in his home town of Sydney when 14/1 chance Roman Emperor ruled in the AJC Australian Derby at Randwick, Cummings's fifth win in the race.

QUOTE OF THE DAY
2009 *'If I could come back to racing and help tackle its addiction problems, it would be a dream come true'* declared former jump jockey Kevin Tobin, who quit to become an addiction counsellor.

BIRTHDAYS
1946 Trainer of Champion Hurdler Monksfield, for whom he paid 740gns, Dessie McDonogh.

1955 Jockey Raymond Carroll.

1904 Keith Piggott, father of Lester, himself son of jump jockey Ernie, was born. Keith rode his first winner on his fifteenth birthday.

1974 Jockey Emma O'Gorman – daughter of trainer, Bill.

DEATHS OF THE DAY
1887 The 1866 Triple Crown winner Lord Lyon was destroyed.

1989 Five-times champion jockey Doug Smith found dead at his Newmarket home, 71. He rode Our Babu, 1955, and Pall Mall, 1958, to win the 2,000 Guines, and Hypericum, 1946 and Petite Etoile, 1959, to win the 1,000 Guineas. Trained Sleeping Partner to win the 1969 Oaks. He was champion from 1954-1959 except for '57 when Scobie Breasley won. His autobiography, *Five Times Champion*, was published in 1968, the year in which Owen Anthony, his first runner as a trainer, won the first race of the Flat season.

12 APRIL

SIGNIFICANT EVENT
1947 The Cheltenham Festival was postponed until this date, and reduced to a one-day card because of inclement weather; the Champion Hurdle, won by National Spirit, and Gold Cup, won by Fortina, were both run on the same day, a Saturday. Crowds were so huge that jockey Dicky Black, riding in the opening race, the Foxhunters, had to abandon his car and run two miles to make it in time. He finished runner up on Celtic Cross, by a neck, to Lucky Purchase – but gained compensation when partnering Fortina.

STRANGEST EVENT
2009 'I once saw a couple engaging very intimately, shall we say, behind the weighing room at York' revealed commentator Mike Cattermole in the *Racing Post*.

OTHER EVENTS
1876 The first race at Cottenham Pastures in Cambridge's final meeting was won by ... Cottenham.

1909 Little Hack won the Irish Grand National, worth £167, by 30 lengths. He won again, aged 14, four years later.

1923 Henry Cecil's stepfather, Sir Cecil Boyd-Rochfort, Royal trainer from 1943-1968, saddled his first winners, Plumb Square and Young Pole in successive races at Pontefract. Sir Cecil trained 13 Classic winners.

1993 Charlie Swan rode his first Irish National winner on 6/1 Ebony Jane.

2004 Granit d'Estruval, 33/1, saw off 27 opponents in the Irish National at Fairyhouse under Brian Harding – whose first victory in Ireland it was – for trainer Ferdy Murphy. Five days later the horse contested the Scottish National. looking a winner until falling at the last.

2008 The king of jump jockeys rode a right Royal winner – AP McCoy's first for Her Majesty as he won on Barbers Shop at Newbury.

2009 Nicky Henderson completed his first century of winners when Horseford Hill, ridden by Felix de Giles, won at Towcester.

QUOTE OF THE DAY
2009 *'I like to send the bookies on plenty of wild goose chases. It's a game of cat and mouse, and most of the time I'm the cat.'* Mixed metaphors from pro punter Patrick Veitch in conversation with the *Mail on Sunday*'s Jonathan Powell, on the eve of the publication of his autobiography, *Enemy Number One*.

BIRTHDAYS
1934 Jockey Frank Morby, champion in Kenya.

1937 Jockey Edward Hide, Cock of the North, and in the top ten of winning-most British riders. Won the 1973 Derby on Morston.

1946 Jockey Paul Cook. He once rode winners at three separate meetings in one day. Won 1,000 Guineas and English and Irish Oaks on Glad Rags in 1966.

DEATHS OF THE DAY
1992 English born apprentice Leanne Crook, fatally injured when she fell from Spotted Wonder during a race at Doomben, Brisbane, Australia.

1996 84-year-old former Epsom trainer Tom Smyth, who won the 1955 Wokingham Stakes with Plumber's Mate, 25/1.

2000 Vicente Tovar, Venezuelan champion jockey for 16 seasons in succession, between 1977 and 1992, committed suicide.

2009 Former jockey Pat 'PJ' Doyle, who rode the Willie O'Grady-trained Icy Calm to win the 1951 Irish National, aged 81.

CELEBRITY OF THE DAY
1950 Teenybopper idol rock star and racehorse owner, David Cassidy born.

13 APRIL

SIGNIFICANT EVENT
2009 Wichita Lineman, who had won so dramatically under Tony McCoy weeks earlier in the Cheltenham Festival's William Hill Trophy for trainer Jonjo O'Neill, was killed on the trainer's birthday during the Irish Grand National. The race went to 33/1-shot Niche Market, ridden by Harry Skelton for Bob Buckler.

STRANGEST EVENT
1998 Bobbyjo, 8/1, ridden by Paul Carberry (and trained by father Tommy Carberry), receiving 11lb, beat top weight Papillon, 20/1, ridden by then amateur Ruby Walsh, to win the 22-runner Irish Grand National. Next year Bobbyjo won the Grand National, followed by Papillon, in 2000. Owner Robert Burke won Bobbyjo in a game of cards. He also collected IR£50,000 bonus as his horse also won the Porterstown Chase.

OTHER EVENTS
1923 Lord Derby's Tranquil won a 7f handicap at Newbury en route to a 100/9 victory in the St Leger.
1968 Returning after breaking a leg, Jack Berry fell from Oban Bay at Carlisle, and fractured a wrist.
1968 Private trainer to David Robinson, Paul Davey sent out five winners – two at Doncaster, three at Teesside Park.
1973 Ben Hanbury's first winner as a trainer, Double Sensation at Thirsk.
1982 Bob Champion announced his retirement as a jockey after winning a hurdle on Lumen at Wetherby, and with 420 winners to his credit.
1988 Josh Gifford's 1,000th winner, Ballyhane, 11/2 at Ascot.
1989 Jockey Jimmy Moffatt landed his first winner on 12/1 Silver's Girl at Ayr. He rode over 100 more before turning to training.

1991 Martin Pipe became the first trainer to win £1m in a jump season when Colour Scheme won at Southwell.
1993 Billy Newnes completed the set when victory on Queen of the Quorn at Newcastle meant he had ridden a winner at every Flat course in Britain.
2009 After a blank spell of 705 days – his worst run in 40 years of training – David Gandolfo, with a career total of some 1,500 winners, broke the run with Glengarra at Plumpton.

QUOTE OF THE DAY
1952 'A good jockey doesn't need orders, and a bad one forgets them,' according to Jonjo O'Neill, born today. O'Neill fought an ultimately successful battle against cancer, and helped raise, in 1989, £225,000 for Christie's Hospital in Manchester.

BIRTHDAYS
1913 US trainer Charlie Whittingham, in San Diego. Sent out his first winner in 1934. Champion trainer in 1970-73,'75, '81 and '82. Sunday Silence won him the 1989 Kentucky Derby, Preakness Stakes and Breeders' Cup Classic.
1915 Trainer of 1962 2,000 Guineas winner Privy Councillor, Tom Waugh.
1928 US owner Richard Kirstein, whose 1989 Derby third, Cacoethes, was originally named Our Friend Elvis.
1946 National Hunt trainer John Edwards.
1952 Jockey-turned-trainer Jonjo O'Neill, who won the Champion Hurdle and Cheltenham Gold Cup on Dawn Run. Won the title with 149 winners in 1977-78.
1981 Jump jockey Paddy Brennan.

CELEBRITY OF THE DAY
1993 Coventry City FC manager Bobby Gould had his first winner when Homemaker won at 14/1 at Warwick.

14 APRIL

SIGNIFICANT EVENT
1812 The earliest date on which a Classic was run – the unpronounceable Cwrw, ridden by Sam Chifney jr, 7/1, won the 2,000 Guineas.

STRANGEST EVENT
2009 Racing's pin-up girl, Hayley Turner, was told by the BHA's Chief Medical adviser that she could not race again until 3 March 2010 following head injuries sustained in a March 2009 fall. She managed to return before then.

OTHER EVENTS
1858 Racing ceased at Ilsley, Berkshire, having been on-going since 1804.

1885 Fred Archer rode three winners at Northampton, a course which closed in 1904.

1891 Named in honour of dual Victoria Racing Club Newmarket Stakes winner Aspen, Aspendale racecourse near Melbourne opened. Five years later a man called Benjamin Nathan made history when becoming the first person in Victoria to be warned off, after offering a jockey at Aspendale £50 to pull a horse.

1989 Newmarket handlers Michael Bell and Alex (Archibald) Scott both enjoyed their first winners, Bell with 11/8 favouritePass The Peace in the Fred Darling Stakes at Newbury, Scott with Spoilt Son 2/5 favourite at Thirsk.

2007 33/1 Silver Birch, partnered by Robbie Power, for the youngest trainer to win the race, 29 year old Gordon Elliott; he also became the sixth Irish trained winner of the Grand National in the past nine runnings. Regulars at the Silver Birch pub, Bracknell, Berks, nearly bankrupted the local betting shop. Landlord Phil Carter was the only regular not to back the horse.

QUOTE OF THE DAY
2009 *'If you haven't the temperament for training, you shouldn't do it. I think a lot of trainers probably plod on because they don't feel qualified to do anything else.'* Charlie Brooks, trainer-turned writer, as his first novel, *Citizen*, was about to be published.

BIRTHDAYS
1914 Jockey Tommy 'T P' Burns. Rode Ballymoss, who in 1958 became the first Irish-trained winner of the Arc.

1944 Nottingham trainer Charles – aka Chuck – Spares.

1950 Ruby's Dad, Ted Walsh. He never turned pro but was an exceptional amateur jockey, before turning trainer and TV pundit.

1952 Former joint-champion lady rider Linda Sheedy.

1962 Irish trainer Eddie Lynam.

1963 Trainer Keith Reveley.

1968 Jockey Alex Greaves. She made her name on the all-weather at Southwell. The first woman to ride a Lincoln winner, she married jockey-turned trainer Dandy Nicholls.

DEATHS OF THE DAY
1969 Former jockey and trainer Tommy Dent, 65. Rode his first winner at Pontefract in 1920, and began training at Penrith in 1949.

1971 Former jump jockey and trainer, the appropriately named Johnny Gamble, 71.

2005 Former US jockey Nick Jemas, 86. He rode some 800 winners between 1940 and 1960.

2009 The 1987 Irish Derby winner, Sir Harry Lewis, 25.

FIRST OF THE DAY
1990 Former jump jockey Roger Charlton sent out his first winner, 10/11 Deploy (Pat Eddery) at Haydock. By June 6 he had won the French Derby with Sanglamore and the Epsom Derby with Quest for Fame, 7/1. He had taken over Jeremy Tree's Beckhampton Stables.

15 APRIL

SIGNIFICANT EVENT
1986 The *Racing Post* was published for the first time.

STRANGEST EVENT
1895 Only two of the seven setting out completed the 2m4f course in the inaugural Welsh Grand National at Cardiff's Ely racecourse. Winner Deerstalker, ridden by George Mawson who died two years later, was even-money favourite, and owned by Derby-winning jockey Tom Cannon.

OTHER EVENTS
1882 The Jockey Club Argentino was founded.

1950 Then Princess Elizabeth, the future Queen had her first Flat winner, Astrakhan, at Hurst Park.

1952 Trainer Jeremy Tree saddled his first winner, Court Life at Birmingham.

1980 Tony McGlone rode his first winner, Ashgayle at Wolverhampton. He won the 1983 Barbados Guineas and the 1987 Kuwait Derby.

1987 Trainer William Haggas saddled his first winner, Tricky Note, at Newmarket.

1989 Mark Birch rode his 1,000th winner, Bollin Patrick, 6/4, at Thirsk on his wife Joyce's birthday. The colt's dam Bollin Charlotte had given him his first victory in July 1968. Rounding off the day he rode a treble, but had to bail out from one of them after it refused to pull up.

1997 Kieren Fallon rode his first winner as stable jockey for Henry Cecil when 7/4 fav Street General won at Newmarket.

2009 Barry Hills passed the milestone of 300 winners at Newmarket with Redwood, ridden by son Michael and the second of three winners for Hills senior during the afternoon. Michael's twin Richard rode the other two.

QUOTE OF THE DAY
'If you mind losing more than you enjoy winning, do not bet.' Sir Clement Freud who died on this day in 2009.

BIRTHDAYS
1902 Mrs Lurline Brotherton, owner of 1950 Grand National winner, Freebooter, and 350 others, who kept and displayed plates from all of them.

1940 Old Harrovian John McCririck born. The 1979 Campaigning Journalist of the Year and divider of opinions refuses to acknowledge birthdays and does not list his in *Directory of the Turf* – and some sources believe it is 17 April.

1959 Jockey John White, rider of Esha Ness.

1964 Flat Jockey John Carroll, rider of Paris House and Halling.

1983 Amateur rider Sam Waley-Cohen.

DEATHS OF THE DAY
1990 Tim Hamey, 84, one of the few jockeys to win the Grand National (Forbra, 1932) and Cheltenham Gold Cup (Koko, 1926).

1992 Nijinsky, in USA, 25. He was buried between Secretariat and Riva Ridge at Claiborne Farm Horse Cemetery. By Northern Dancer, bred in Canada, he won the 2,000 Guineas, Derby, Irish Derby, King George VI and Queen Elizabeth Stakes and St Leger in 1970; and second to Sassafras in the Arc.

1996 Owner Stavros Niarchos.

2009 Owner – Nagnagnag was one of his best – punter, writer, broadcaster, gourmand, occasional jockey – he won on Winter Fair at Haydock in 1971 – and former MP, Sir Clement Freud, 84.

CELEBRITY/FIRST OF THE DAY
1963 The Queen Mother had her first Plumpton winner, Super Fox, partnered by Clive Chapman.

16 APRIL

SIGNIFICANT EVENT
1988 Kieren Fallon's first British winner, Evichstar at Thirsk.

STRANGEST EVENT
1994 Jockey Hans Waltl, an Austrian, was ordered to pull up his horse during a race by the stewards – communicating with him over the tannoy system! Waltl was riding a hunter, Simon, at the Braes of Derwent point-to-point meeting at Tranwell, Northumberland. After refusing twice at the second and again at the third, fourth and eighth, he was lapped by the remainder of the field – at which point the patience of officials ran out.

OTHER EVENTS
1875 Fred Archer rode Peeping Tom, owned by Captain Bastard, to win one of the earliest sponsored races, the Newmarket International Free Handicap for which the town of Newmarket put up £300 prize money and the Jockey Club contributed £100 for the runner-up.
1913 Arguably the fastest 2yo ever, and known as the 'Spotted Wonder', The Tetrarch, trained by Atty Persse, won on his debut at Newmarket.
1968 Five months after a car crash which nearly killed him and his family, Willie Carson returned to the saddle on Bikini at Newmarket, finishing unplaced.
1969 Trainer Tommy Fairhurst sent out his first winner, Brython (Brig Robson) at Pontefract.
1983 Ace French jockey Yves Saint-Martin rode a double at Thirsk.
1983 Trainer Neville Crump won his fifth Scottish National with the Kevin Whyte-ridden Canton. He once said of a candidate hoping to become a steward: 'He'd be perfect– he's deaf, he's blind, and he knows nothing about racing'.
1995 Kent Desormeaux, 25, became the youngest jockey to ride 3,000 winners,

reaching the total at Santa Anita.
2009 Thierry Gillet, 2004 Arc-winning jockey on Bago, retired at 39, with seven Group One wins to his name.
2001 Melissa Seagren made Australian racing history when riding all six winners at Einasleigh, Queensland – all trained by Brian Condon.

QUOTE OF THE DAY
2009 *'I gave them all free admission to the Grandstand purely because of their lovely attitude to the situation.'* Newmarket managing director Stephen Wallis on having to deny a family of six jeans-wearing racegoers entry to the Premier Enclosure because of the dress code.

BIRTHDAYS
1887 Five-times champion trainer and step-father to Henry Cecil, Capt. Sir Cecil Boyd-Rochfort.
1941 Trainer Michael Kauntze. He rode as an amateur from 1957-1968 with, he says, 'conspicuous lack of success'.
1944 Trainer Mick Naughton.
1949 Canadian and US Hall of Fame jockey, Sandy Hawley.
1973 Trainer Emma Lavelle.

DEATHS OF THE DAY
2003 One of the few remaining tic-tac men, Michael Stuart, 80, described by John McCririck as having 'the fastest hands in the west'.
2009 Trainer of the popular and prolific hurdles winner Limestone Lad, who eventually scored 35 victories, James Bowe, aged 77.

FIRST OF THE DAY
1993 Taunton's evening meeting, sponsored by William Hill, was the first for which Britain's betting shops were officially permitted to stay open after 6.30pm.

17 APRIL

SIGNIFICANT EVENT

1993 Frankie Dettori rode his first single-meeting four-timer. Tissisat, 20/1 for the Queen, Linpac West, 25/1, Inchinor, 7/2 and Winged Victory, 11/2 gave him a 15,969/1 accumulator at Newbury.

STRANGEST EVENT

1907 Davy Jones born; when he rode Red Rover to win the 1945 Cheltenham Gold Cup he was carrying a hefty 3st of dead weight. He reputedly rode winners over hurdles, fences and on the Flat on the same afternoon at Liverpool. His son 'Buck' Jones won the 1964 Imperial Cup on Invader.

OTHER EVENTS

1939 Fulke Walwyn rode his last winner, Mansur, at Uttoxeter.

1970 Richard Hannon saddled his first winner, Ampney Prince, ridden by Frankie Durr, at Newbury.

1982 Ken Oliver won his sixth Scottish National when David Dutton partnered Cockle Strand to victory.

2006 Philip Carberry, younger brother of Paul, partnered Point Barrow to 20/1 Irish Grand National victory for trainer Pat Hughes, who also won it in 1986 with 16/1 Insure.

QUOTE OF THE DAY

1940 'Why should I celebrate the obscenity of getting old?' asks John McCririck, rhetorically on what may or may not be his birthday. Different sources credit 15 and 17 April, but all agree that he was born in 1940. Old Harrovian, McCririck doesn't believe in birthday parties either: 'I am not a pleasant man. I have very few friends, if any. I don't go to parties.'

BIRTHDAYS

1915 Owner/trainer of top hunter chaser Flying Ace, Adam Calder.

1935 Dale Baird, from Illinois, who in 1990 became the world's most prolific winning trainer. Saddled his 6,000th winner in August 1992, at which point he could boast 4,600 winners as owner.

1962 Paul Nicholls, son of a policeman. He rode two Hennessy Cognac Gold Cup winners amongst 130 or so others as a jockey before weight problems got the better of him, then played second fiddle to Martin Pipe as a trainer before kicking on and re-writing the record books himself with the likes of Kauto Star and Denman.

1963 Jockey Tom Morgan, former Irish champion over the sticks.

DEATHS OF THE DAY

1990 Trainer Robbie Connolly, 31, of motor neurone disease.

2003 The man who recognized and nurtured Tony McCoy's ability as a jockey from a very early age, Irish trainer Billy Rock, 59.

2009 The funeral of 76-year-old former amateur rider Bob Hargreaves, one of the jockeys who rode Creggmore Boy, the oldest horse to race in Britain, competing until the age of 22.

CELEBRITY OF THE DAY

1992 Flamboyant owner P B 'Teasie Weasie' Raymond, 80. Failed actor and wrestler-turned high society hairdresser to royalty and movie stars, who owned 1963 and 1976 Grand National winners Ayala, 66/1, and Rag Trade, 14/1, (his only runners in the race). He caused a sensation by wearing coloured morning suits to Royal Ascot. Colours – ice blue and wine.

18 APRIL

SIGNIFICANT EVENT
1809 The first 2,000 Guineas was run, five years before the first 1,000 Guineas. Won by 4/5 favourite Wizard.

STRANGEST EVENT
2009 The Queen was refused admission to the royal box at Newbury as the course had let it out for commercial use – reportedly for the first time. Having been there the previous day 'the Queen was effectively evicted from her own quarters and had the ignominy of spending the day in a hospitality box' reported Richard Alleyne of the *Daily Telegraph*. Insurance broker John Finch from Denham, Bucks, had paid £10,000 to use the box and was unrepentant: 'I had arranged to rent it last July so there was no way I was going to pass it up.'

OTHER EVENTS
1947 George Boyd saddled his first winner, Backbite, at Bogside. Three days later he landed a treble at Edinburgh. He became Scotland's most successful trainer in the next 20 years, sending out Rockavon to win the 1961 2,000 Guineas at 66/1. Won the Northumberland Plate three times, and retired in 1969.

1969 Barry Hills sent out his first winner, La Dolce Vita at Thirsk.

1970 Frankie Durr's 1,000th winner, Gold Rod at Newbury.

1989 England 'keeper Peter Shilton's unraced 2yo Between The Sticks was a 33/1 winner on his debut at Newmarket but the footballer, known to enjoy the odd flutter, arrived too late to get on.

1991 Julie Cecil sent out her first winner, the Lester Piggott-ridden Golan Heights, 9/4, at Newmarket.

1991 Martin Pipe's Hopscotch won a record sixth race in a season at Cheltenham, in Park Financial Hurdle.

1997 Betting shops were permitted to advertise in print media – but not on TV and radio.

1997 A major award for Frankie Dettori, which literally went to his head. He was declared Head of the Year by the National Hairdressers' Federation.

QUOTE OF THE DAY
1977 *The Sporting Life* reported: 'John Higgins fractured a bone in his left leg in a fall from Mrs Higgins at Edinburgh on Monday, and will be out of action for a month.'

BIRTHDAYS
1915 Anne, Duchess of Westminster, owner of Arkle. Her famous colours of yellow, black belt and black cap with gold tassel were also carried by Gold Cup winner Ten Up and Grand National winner Last Suspect.

1919 Successful speedway rider-turned trainer in 1959, Ron Mason. He was noted for his successful tilts at the ring.

1947 Self-confessed alcoholic and compulsive gambler (described at the time as 'problems of weight and very highly-strung nerves') but brilliant jockey, Barry Brogan. The Irishman was never champion, but won the 1971 King George VI Chase on The Dikler, 11/2, and the 1970 Benson & Hedges Gold Cup on Even Keel and Scottish National on The Spaniard.

1951 Eponymous bookie Victor Chandler.

1964 TV and racecourse commentator, Simon Holt.

DEATHS OF THE DAY
2003 Northumberland trainer Andy Scott, 78, whose Hill's Guard won the 1984 County Hurdle at Cheltenham.

2005 The Queen's former Representative at Royal Ascot, Sir Piers Bengough, 75. A Jockey Club steward, he won four Grand Military Gold Cups. He was married to Olympic ice skater Bridget Adams.

CELEBRITY OF THE DAY
1946 TV and radio personality Henry Kelly, a great racing fan, was born, on the same day as actress and owner with Fred Winter, Hayley Mills.

19 APRIL

SIGNIFICANT EVENT
1957 Arkle was foaled at Ballymacoll stud, Co Meath. His dam Bright Cherry was useful at up to 2m4f, but sire Archive, though Clasically bred, proved hopeless on the racecourse and stood at a mere 48gns.

STRANGEST EVENT
1919 The Great Metropolitan Handicap at Epsom was run on a thick covering of snow. Tattenham Corner was so slippery from ice that a succession of snow heaps were made around it to widen the bend and lessen danger to jockeys, who were instructed to keep to the outside. Wily champion jockey Steve Donoghue stole the last race by nipping inside the heaps.

OTHER EVENTS
1770 After Eclipse won the 100gns King's Plate at Newmarket, Dennis O'Kelly bought out William Wildman's half share for 1,100gns.

1877 Fred Archer won on all six of his Newmarket rides.

1939 A fractured skull sustained in a fall at Ludlow resulted in Fulke Walwyn's retirement from the saddle.

1976 Peter Scudamore was fourth on Jack de Lilo at Chepstow on his first ride over jumps.

1978 The 5yo Ubedizzy, trained by Steve Nesbitt, was second at 20/1 to Boldboy in the Abernant Stks at Newmarket but behaved so badly in the unsaddling enclosure after, trying to savage his lad and anyone else within range, that he was banned from ever running again. It was his jockey Andy Crook's 23rd birthday.

1978 Jonjo O'Neill rode five winners from five rides at Perth, in the process passing Ron Barry's seasonal record of 125 winners, en route to a total of 149.

1984 No sniggering at the back, there, but Tit For Tat gave jockey Vicki Harris her first winner, at Southwell.

1987 Britons abroad Anthony Speelman and Nicholas Cowan visited Santa Anita in California – and won $1,627,084 with their $64 nine-horse accumulator.

1994 Gyles Parkin was banned for careless riding at Pontefract but winning mount Nordoora was allowed to keep the race – the first such decision after new interference rules had been introduced the day before. Under the previous rule horse and jockey would both have been disqualified.

QUOTE OF THE DAY
1909 'It's not good day, it's goodbye,' was the reported farewell message by jockey Mick Williams as he set off to Kelso to partner Master William in the Roxburghe Chase. Williams' premonition that the track was an unlucky one for him proved tragically accurate as he and his horse were both killed in the race.

BIRTHDAYS
1952 Native Dancer foaled. Only ever beaten once in 22 races when second in the 1953 Kentucky Derby to Dark Star.

1956 Trainer Paul Dalton; he may have been a pessimist as he named his Burton-on-Trent stables Noah's Ark – or maybe he prefers winners two by two.

DEATH OF THE DAY
2008 Hawthorne racecourse, Illinois, staged its first $200,000 Bill Hartack Memorial Handicap in memory of the five time Kentucky Derby-winning jockey who died in November 2007 and rode 4,272 winners between 1953 and 1974.

FIRST OF THE DAY
1964 French jockey Freddie Head rode his first winner, Zamboanga, at Fontainebleau.

20 APRIL

SIGNIFICANT EVENT

2008 Having missed out on April 4, March 26, March 18 and February 24 opening dates, Great Leighs, the first new racecourse since Taunton in September 1927, opened for racing, a mere 23 months behind schedule. Ed Dunlop trained Temple of Thebes won the first race – 7/4 favourite –ridden by Stephen Donohoe.

STRANGEST EVENT

1996 Having broken his neck in a fall during the 1994 Becher Chase at Aintree, 11-year-old Moorcroft Boy, trained by David Nicholson, ridden by Martin Dwyer, landed an amazing 20/1 victory in the Scottish Grand National at Ayr. He never ran again.

OTHER EVENTS

1880 Tristan won a star-studded 2yo race, the 5f Westminster Stakes at Epsom. The winner went on to land the Ascot Gold Cup; third placed Voluptuary won the 1884 Grand National; unplaced Hackness won the 1882 Cambridgeshire.

1920 Fernley was the 'first' winner for Mrs Florence Nagle at a time when women were not officially permitted to train – the horse was disqualified. In 1966 Mrs N contested a court case which resulted in the Jockey Club licensing women trainers.

1949 He'd have 8,832 more of them but US superstar jockey, Texan Bill Shoemaker, won for the first time on his third ride in public,on the filly Shafter V at Golden Gate Fields at the age of 17. He ended the year with 219 winners.

1992 Wingcommander Eats, 6/1, beat Mayfair Moss, 14/1, in a ten-runner seller at Newton Abbot, for which there were only 45 possible dual forecast combinations. The Tote dividend was £1,002.80.

1992 Martin Pipe-trained 1/2 favourite Riverside Boy disappeared before the start of the Real British Coal Novice Chase at Uttoxeter. Puzzled connections eventually discovered that the horse broke loose from his lad, found an exit gate and strolled off down the road. The race was run without him before he was discovered three miles away.

1994 Tony McCoy rode his first hurdles winner, Riszard, at Gowran Park. The horse had previously been won on by Aidan O'Brien.

QUOTE OF THE DAY

1946 'When he first came to Mr Dreaper's, his action was so bad you could drive a wheelbarrow through his hind legs,' said Arkle's jockey Pat Taaffe who rode his first winner, Ballin Corona, on the Flat at Phoenix Park for trainer Micky Gleeson on this day.

BIRTHDAYS

1915 Carlo Vittadini, whose Grundy won the 1975 Derby.

1935 Trainer Ken Ivory, best known for his handling of Dawn's Delight and Ivory's Joy.

1924 Trainer Gerry Blum, whose Venus of Streatham won 11 races.

1962 Globetrotting trainer Danny Murphy, who has worked at the Curragh, Newmarket and Singapore.

DEATH OF THE DAY

1999 Top US trainer Charlie 'Bald Eagle' Whittingham, 86. He won the Kentucky Derby with Ferdinand in 1986 and with Sunday Silence three years later.

CELEBRITY OF THE DAY

1978 Top goalkeeper and owner with Nicky Vaughan, Shay Given born.

21 APRIL

SIGNIFICANT EVENT
1989 Quick-thinking horsebox driver Ivan Hughes saved the lives of three people trapped on the roof of a blazing building in Newmarket by driving an empty box up to the building so they could jump on it to escape.

STRANGEST EVENT
1979 No Bombs won the Sean Memorial Hurdle at Worcester – only to be disqualified for failing a dope test after consuming a Mars Bar.

OTHER EVENTS
1887 Five winners at Kelso was small beer for jockey Charlie Cunningham – he rode seven at Rugby on March 29, 1881.

1924 The current track at Market Rasen opened for business.

1930 Fulke Walwyn rode his first winner, Alpine Hut at Cardiff, on his first ride under NH rules.

1990 Jenny Pitman was fined £200 by stewards at Ayr after striking unfortunate jockey Jamie Osborne in the face. Pitman's 20/1 Run To Form had collided with the rails and Jenny blamed Jamie, who was riding Dwadme.

1993 A North-east based professional punter lost £40,000 at Catterick, including £15,000 on a 1/10 shot and £18,000 on a 1/6 favourite.

1994 37-year-old Chris Grant, three times runner-up in the Grand National, retired after riding Capital Punishment to win at Perth, with 788 winners to his name.

1997 Walter Swinburn announced his temporary retirement, reportedly due to weight problems.

2003 Timbera, 11/1, carried Jim Culloty to win the 21 runner Irish Grand National. Trained by Dessie Hughes, who only allowed the 9yo triple course winner to take his chance when the heavens opened on the day.

QUOTE OF THE DAY
'That was a brilliant piece of training. I don't know why I've got empty boxes back home.' Typically immodest comment by jump jockey-turned Flat trainer Paul Kelleway, who died aged 58 on this day in 1999, to the press after a winner.

BIRTHDAYS
1918 Lord Derby, whose Alycidon – bred by his grandfather – won the Ascot, Goodwood and Doncaster Cups. His Swallow Tail was third in the 1949 Derby.

1929 US trainer Allen Jerkens, whose Beau Purple won string of important races in 1962.

1943 Owner Barry Irwin, whose Prized was the first horse to win million dollar races on turf (Breeders' Cup Turf) and dirt (Molson Million) in the same season, 1989.

DEATHS OF THE DAY
1999 Affectionately known as the most pessimistic of trainers – partly due to his instruction to Hywel Davies to 'keep remounting' before he went out to ride Last Suspect – the winner – in the 1985 Grand National, Captain Tim Forster, 65, who also won the great race with Ben Nevis and Well To Do.

1999 Paul Kelleway, 58. Father of jockey-turned trainer, Gay, he rode 392 winners including What A Myth to win the 1969 Cheltenham Gold Cup and Bula to win the 1971 and '72 Champion Hurdles. Trained 1978 Champion Stakes winner Swiss Maid, and 1981 French Oaks heroine Madam Gay, who cost 9,000gns and was sold for £1.4m.

CELEBRITY OF THE DAY
1926 The Queen was born. Racing colours: purple, gold braid, scarlet sleeves, black velvet cap with gold fringe. Her stud manager, Michael Oswald, was born on the same day eight years later.

22 APRIL

SIGNIFICANT EVENT
1989 Martin Pipe became the most successful trainer over one season when High Bid at Uttoxeter became his 181st winner of the campaign, passing the record formerly held by Henry Cecil, who set it in 1987.

STRANGEST EVENT
1899 Colonel M Lewis Clark, an enthusiast of English racing, who founded the Louisville Jockey Club and established the racetrack on which the Kentucky Derby was run from 1875, committed suicide with a pistol, 12 days before the 25th running of the great race.

OTHER EVENTS
1754 Mr Corker's bay mare was ridden 300 miles in three days on the course at Newmarket to win a £100 wager.
1783 The first recorded meeting at Catterick.
1875 The first fully enclosed course, Sandown, opened for business.
1947 The photo-finish was introduced to Britain, at Epsom.
1968 Bob Lawson, 17, rode his first winner, Portland II, at Alexandra Park.
1995 Paul Cole saddled a 41,768/1 four-timer at Newbury, all ridden by Richard Quinn – Posidonas, 16/1; Strategic Choice, 12/1; Star Manager, 20/1 and Monarch, 8/1. He flew to Paris to celebrate.
1995 Jenny Pitman's 16/1 chance Willsford won the Scottish National to add to her two Grand Nationals and three Welsh Nationals.
2006 Run For Paddy, the 33/1 winner of the Scottish National, was the first winner sent out by rookie trainer Carl Llewellyn. The 40-year-old, a trainer in his own right for just a fortnight, also rode the horse, who completed a hat-trick of Nationals for him, Llewellyn having already won the English and Welsh.

QUOTE OF THE DAY
2000 'That's it lads, I'm finished,' announced Walter Swinburn, retiring from the saddle for good.

BIRTHDAYS
1922 Allen Paulson, part-owner of Theatrical and Arazi.
1929 Part-owner of Cheltenham Gold Cup winner Alverton, Dana Brudenell-Bruce, who also won the Irish St Leger with Opale.
1952 Flat jockey Bob Weaver.
1966 Jump jockey Guy Upton.

DEATHS OF THE DAY
1916 A record-breaking purchase as a 5,500gns yearling, La Fleche proved to be a bargain when winning the 1892 1,000 Guineas, Oaks and St Leger. She died this day at Sledmere stud, Yorkshire.
1967 George 'Buster' Fenningworth, who won 52 races in 1962 from Hurgill Lodge and Belle Isle, Richmond stables, was killed in a car crash en route to Ayr races.
1990 Retired Curragh trainer Mick Connolly, 77, six days after son Robbie died of motor neurone disease.

FIRST OF THE DAY
1957 Jack Berry rode his first winner, 10/1 chance Sarsta Girl, trained by Charlie Hall, over hurdles at Wetherby.

23 APRIL

SIGNIFICANT EVENT
1994 Newmarket trainer Giles Bravery's Royal Flamingo finished second at Hexham, only to be disqualified for testing positive for a 'beta blocker', propanol. The trainer was fined £500. It was believed to be the first time any horse had tested positive for the substance.

STRANGEST EVENT
2009 Adolf Hitler came to Ludlow racecourse! Thirteen paintings by the German dictator were sold there at auction for almost £95,000.

OTHER EVENTS
1624 Joseph Strutt, whose 1801 volume *Sports and Pastimes of the People of England* chronicled many sports including horse racing, reported on this day that for the first time the prize for the St George's Bell, run at Chester on Shrove Tuesday since 1540, would be kept permanently by the winner. The prize was a silver bell worth £10.
1962 Plumpton's Glynde Novice Chase was declared void after going off four minutes early.
1971 Mark Prescott sent out his first winner, Belle Royale, at Teesside Park.
1982 Leading owner and breeder, John R Gaines, announced plans for a multi-race, multi-million dollar Breeders' Cup Series, at the annual Kentucky Derby Festival awards luncheon.
1984 Silver Buck, winner of the 1982 Cheltenham Gold Cup, ran his final race, winning a chase at Wetherby to take his prize money total from 34 wins in 48 races to £177,179.
1986 Lester Piggott saddled his first winner as a trainer, Geordie's Delight, ridden by Tony Ives, at Epsom.
1987 Trainer John Hills sent out his first winner, Sanamar, at Pontefract.
1990 Adrian Maguire's first win under rules, on Gladtogetit at Sligo.

QUOTE OF THE DAY
1994 The *Weekender* reported that trainer Neville Crump, 83, after a Yorkshire Ridings magazine declared him dead, had responded: *'Invitations to my funeral are not going out for a while yet, anyway.'*

BIRTHDAY
1846 Jockey Thomas Cannon, at Eton, son of Windsor horse-dealer. He rode 13 Classic winners, including 1882 Derby winner, the filly Shotover, and trained two more. The father of Mornington Cannon and great grandfather of Lester Piggott, he once accepted a £9,000 lump sum to ride for three seasons for Scottish millionaire Mr George Baird, for whom he partnered Busybody to win the 1884 1,000 Guineas and Oaks.

DEATH OF THE DAY
2000 Former jump jockey Jumbo Wilkinson, 67, who trained Hardy Lad to win the 1986 Scottish Grand National.

CELEBRITY OF THE DAY
1932 Racehorse owner and Coronation Street stalwart William Roache, Ken Barlow, born.

24 APRIL

SIGNIFICANT EVENT
1969 'My overwhelming feeling on passing the post was one of relief' – Pat Eddery, 17, after riding his first winner, Alvaro, at Epsom, on this day. He had ridden in his first race over a year previously.

STRANGEST EVENT
2009 It would have been his 85th birthday but the funeral of racegoer, owner, punter and writer Sir Clement Freud took place on this day, with the order of service declaring: 'BORN 24.04.24 BEST BEFORE 15.04.09.' His son, Matthew Freud, spoke of his father's love of a bet and added of his last visit to the races at Exeter before he died: 'We are grateful to the undertakers who returned the £2,000 found in his suit pocket'. Mourners speculated as to whether that meant he had had a good or bad day!

OTHER EVENTS
1855 Dubious dealings at Newmarket as James Merry's Lord of the Isles, trained by William Day, beat Henry Padwick's St Hubert by a neck in the 2,000 Guineas, the latter trained by Day's father, John Barham Day. When the Day family explained to owners that St Hubert had 'allowed' Lord of the Isles to win, in expectation of the compliment being returned in the Derby, the two owners rapidly disabused their trainers of such thoughts, and made alternative arrangements. In the event, both were eclipsed by Wild Dayrell in the big race.

1929 The last meeting held at Banbury racecourse in Oxfordshire. The final race, the Banbury Cross Local Chase, celebrating the area's most famous landmark immortalized in nursery rhyme, was won by Anchored, ridden by local man Thomas Morgan.

1945 Gordon Richards won at Newmarket, riding bareback after the saddle slipped on the Aga Khan's Leventina with two furlongs remaining.

Richards returned 'with all his gear intact'.

1961 Nick Gaselee rode his first winner, One Eyed Gunner, at Folkestone.

1967 Guy's Master, at Alexandra Park, was the appropriately named first winner as a trainer for Guy Harwood.

1985 Private Views at Worcester was jockey Andrew Adams' first winner.

1986 Trainer Alex Stewart wed Katherine Domville. Their engagement cost Stewart a £1,500 bill for dinner for friends – the cost of losing a bet by becoming the first of four to propose.

2000 Ruby Walsh won 24 runner Irish Grand National for trainer/father Ted on 14/1 Commanche Court, making Ted the first trainer to win English (Papillon) and Irish Nationals in the same year.

QUOTE OF THE DAY
'A woman standing beside me as the runners for the Champion Novice Hurdle were led around the ring said Country Pride would win. I pointed out that all ten runners carried the name Country Pride on their saddle cloths to acknowledge the Irish backers' sponsorship. She opined that I was a smart ass.' Yet another fine example of Sir Clement Freud's ability to construct and deliver an anecdote; appropriate for the date he was both born and buried.

BIRTHDAYS
1884 Jumps trainer Tom – father of Fred – Rimell born. Tom won the 1932 Grand National with Forbra and collected 15 Cheltenham Festival victories.

1924 Sir Clement Freud, whose colours were black, orange hooped sleeves, black cap with orange spots.

1940 Gloucestershire trainer David Wintle.

1958 US trainer, Englishman Ian Jory.

CELEBRITIES OF THE DAY
1973 Ryder Cup golfer and owner Lee Westwood born, as was former Wealdstone FC player, and racehorse owner, Stuart Pearce, in 1962.

25 APRIL

SIGNIFICANT EVENT

1905 British champion jockey to be, Steve Donoghue rode his first winner, Hanoi at Hyeres in France, where the Warrington-born 20 year old had gone to work for American trainer, Edward Johnson, having suffered physical abuse at John Parker's Kingsclere stables.

STRANGEST EVENT

1994 The Frank Jordan-trained Foggy's Dream became the first modern Arab racehorse to compete against thoroughbreds in Britain when the 8yo finished 19th of 21 in a maiden at Windsor, at 100/1.

OTHER EVENTS

1878 The first running of Newmarket's Craven Stakes was won by Thurio, owned by Prince Soltykoff. Runner-up Sefton gained small consolation when winning the Derby.

1978 John Francome was banned until 3 June and fined £750 for his part in the conntroversial 'John Banks affair', in which his riding of the horse and relationship with the wealthy bookie were investigated.

1984 Somjam Gold won at Saint-Cloud, giving jockey Yves St-Martin his 3,000th winner.

1992 Topsham Bay, 9/2, won the Whitbread Gold Cup for Michael Marsh, who also owned and trained Larbawn, who won same race in 1968 and '69.

2009 British-based jump jockeys Dave Crosse and Jimmy McCarthy rode a winner apiece at Mineral Springs in North Carolina, which staged one of America's biggest jump meetings of the year in temperatures of 92 degrees.

2009 44-year-old Exeter punter Tony Wonnacott won £310,000 for £2 on the Tote Scoop6. A week later 8/1 winner Confront landed him an extra £133,000 by winning the bonus race.

QUOTE OF THE DAY

1989 *'Their move was scandalous, and an insult to the public,'* harrumphed *The Sporting Life* when Another Clem beat nine opponents to win the 5.45 at Punchestown – but no-one backed the winner as bookies' clerks, Tote staff and the official timekeeper all downed tools, objecting to the eight-race card ending so late.

BIRTHDAYS

1925 Paul Davey, son of Malton trainer Ernest. He trained Yellow God, My Swallow and Deep Diver for wealthy patron David Robinson, from 1967-74 .

1941 Multiple Italian champion jockey and father of Frankie, Gianfranco Dettori.

1951 Clerk of the course at Goodwood, and at Aintree on the fateful 1993 'non-National' day, Rod Fabricius.

1968 Flat jockey Dale Gibson.

DEATHS OF THE DAY

1991 Trainer Laz Barrera, 66, who sent out Affirmed to win the 1978 US Triple Crown.

1994 Sam Burns, 74. Former MD of William Hill, who said 'betting during the day, boxing at night' as he was also a successful boxing manager. Launched his Burns and Downes chain of betting shops with boxer Terry Downes – and then merged them into the Hill chain.

1999 Former President of the International Olympic Committee, leading member of the Irish Turf Club and father of trainer 'Mouse' Morris, Lord Kilanin, 84.

CELEBRITY OF THE DAY

1969 Singer/comic Des O'Connor, whose Bermondsey won a novice hurdle at Hereford.

26 APRIL

SIGNIFICANT EVENT
2009 'Don't believe all you read in the papers' said top owner Trevor Hemmings, admitting that his string of horses would be reduced from 80 to 65 after media reports suggesting that his fortune had dropped by £730m. His Hedgehunter won the 2005 Grand National.

STRANGEST EVENT
1950 Jockey Kevan Leason born. He announced in 1990 that henceforth he would be known as Karen, and would continue his life as a woman.

OTHER EVENTS
1721 Flying Childers, who would become one of the highest rated horses of the day, beat Speedwell in a four-mile match at Newmarket on his debut, aged six. The Duke of Devonshire's runner went on to give another of the top horses around, Fox, a stone and a 360-yard beating. The horse was said to be able to cover 82.5 feet per second, 25 feet per stride, and leap 30 feet on level ground with a man on his back. Few believe these figures, but there is no doubt that he was the best of his day.
1851 Defaulter, Squire of Malton, Reindeer and Pulcherrina ran a quadruple dead-heat in the Omnibus Stakes at The Hoo.
1939 Third in the Derby ten years earlier, Brienz won the Ely Handicap Chase at Cardiff, ridden by Tommy Carey.
1943 Gordon Richards rode his 2750th winner, Scotch Mist, at Windsor, taking him clear of Fred Archer's total.
2008 Nom de Jeu won the AJC Australian Derby at Randwick, giving sire Montjeu his fourth Derby winner, following on from Authorized and Motivator at Epsom and Hurricane Run in the Irish version.

QUOTE OF THE DAY
2009 *'It will sink in shortly as it has never happened before.'* Richard Johnson, perennial runner-up to champion jockey Tony McCoy, celebrating being 3-1 up after day one of the jump season in 2009.

BIRTHDAYS
1918 John Hooton, trainer of Flosuebarb and Ginger Boy.
1936 Top amateur rider, Sir Edward Cazalet.
1943 Jockey Ron Atkins, rider of Moyne Royal and Mon Plaisir, who later became a trainer.
1953 Irish jockey Michael Furlong, rider of Bannow Rambler.
1961 Chilean-born Jose Adeon Santos, top American money-earning jockey from 1986 to 1989, with earnings of between $11m and $14.8m in each year.

FIRST OF THE DAY
1992 Sudden Blessing won the Golden Horse Cup at Wang Chuen, Canton, China, ridden by Mongolian Za Na. He was the first winner at the first meeting in China since the Communists took over in 1949. A crowd of 4,000 turned up and saw the same horse also win the Guangzhev Derby. No legal betting was permitted.

27 APRIL

SIGNIFICANT EVENT
1989 Peter Scudamore rode a four-timer at Towcester – the third of which, Gay Moore, 10/1, made him the first jump jockey to ride 200 winners in a season.

STRANGEST EVENT
1857 Emperor Napoleon II opened Longchamp racecourse. He observed proceedings along with 10,000 spectators.

OTHER EVENTS
1852 Lord Exeter's Stockwell won the 2000 Guineas under J. Norman.
1937 Superior Guard lived up to his name, winning both the second and third races at Avondale, New Zealand.
1939 The last meeting was staged at Cardiff's Ely racecourse. Grasshopper, ridden by Keith Piggott, won the last race.
1966 Trainer John (Leeper) Dunlop got off the mark with Tamino in Newmarket's Palace House Stakes, ridden by Ron Hutchinson.
1969 British trainer Sam Hill trained all six winners (all in handicaps) at Ootacamund, Tamil Nadu, India.
1971 Arthur Stephenson saddled five winners at Kelso – all ridden by different jockeys.
1992 Jenny Pitman and jockey Michael Bowlby were cleared of breaking the rules over the controversial running of Golden Freeze in the Cheltenham Gold Cup when the horse took on front-running favourite Carvill's Hill. A Jockey Club hearing ruled the horse ran

on its merits, and that the tactics were legitimate.
1992 Prosquendo was Mark Dixon's first Flat winner as trainer, at Wolverhampton.
1996 Aidan O'Brien won the Whitbread Gold Cup with the Charlie Swan-partnered 12/1 chance Life Of A Lord.

QUOTE OF THE DAY
1966 *'You don't get surprises in racing, just disappointments,'* a somewhat pessimistic philosophy expressed by trainer John Dunlop.

BIRTHDAYS
1927 Owner of Cheltenham Gold Cup winner Burrough Hill Lad, Stan Riley.
1944 Senior steward of the Jockey Club, Lord Hartington.
1981 Kempton boss Amy Starkey.

FIRST OF THE DAY
1857 The first race run at Longchamp was won by Eclaireur.

CELEBRITY OF THE DAY
1922 Actor Jack Klugman born, star of cult TV series 'The Odd Couple' and 'Quincy, M.E.' and owner-breeder of 1980 California Horse of Year Jaklin Klugman. Jaklin Klugman won the California Derby before running third in Kentucky Derby. Retired to stud in Temecula, California, which Jack Klugman bought and renamed El Rancho de Jaklin. Horse's son, Sky Jack, won 2002 Hollywood Gold Cup, but Jaklin Klugman died in March 1996.

28 APRIL

SIGNIFICANT EVENT

1994 Irish Forever (Alan Munro), 33/1, became the first US-trained filly to run in a British Classic, finishing tenth in the 1,000 Guineas for Maryland handler Billy Boniface. The race was won by the Tommy Stack-trained Las Meninas, 12/1, after a 17-minute photo finish with Dubai-trained Balanchine. Unplaced Randonneur was Ernie Weymes' first Classic runner in 36 years as a trainer. Stack became only the second Grand National-winning jockey to train an English Classic winner, after Joe Cannon who rode Regal in 1876 and won both the 1,000 and 2,000 Guineas as a trainer with Pilgrimage (1878) and Petronel (1880) respectively.

STRANGEST EVENT

1993 The Insulpak Victoria Cup at Ascot had five 11/1 co-favourites, none of which finished in the first four of 22 as 16/1 chance Tender Moment won.

OTHER EVENTS

1984 The Queen Mother's Special Cargo won what many claim was the greatest chase ever. Second in the Sandown event was Lettoch, a short head down; with Diamond Edge a short head back in third, partnered by Royal jockey Bill Smith who, riding his last race, opted for this mount in preference to the winner.
1990 The Kim Bailey-trained Mr Frisk, 9/2 fav, Marcus Armytage up, became the first horse to complete the Grand National-Whitbread Gold Cup double in the same season.
1995 Kevin Darley rode his 1,000th winner, 7/4 fav Busy Banana at Carlisle.

QUOTE OF THE DAY

2004 *'When you go out to ride him you don't feel you're going out to ride a horse; it feels like you're going to meet one of your old mates for a pint.'* Which is how so many racegoers felt about gallant stayer Persian Punch, whose rider Martin Dwyer had paid tribute to him in this way and who on this day died at the end of a race at Ascot. I was there. The eerie silence which fell over the course was extremely moving.

BIRTHDAYS

1925 Dual code trainer Harry Thomson Jones. Touching Wood, Tingle Creek and Devon Ditty were amongst his best. In 1971 on the same day his Athens Wood won the St Leger and he also sent out Ramequin to win a Fakenham novice hurdle – versatile enough for you?
1943 Trainer Adrian Maxwell, handler of Willie Wumpkins.
1949 Trainer Tony Newcombe.
1958 Trainer Mark Wilkinson, whose stable stars included Rattlin' Jack and Smart Star.
1961 Trainer John Akehurst born. Son of trainer Reg, John was a useful amateur rider and also awfully proud of a Frilford Heath Golf Club hole in one in August 1991!

DEATHS OF THE DAY

1972 Unbeaten dual Arc winner Ribot, 20, of a twisted intestine at stud in Kentucky.
1973 Jockey Doug Barrott, killed in a fall from French Colonist in the Whitbread Gold Cup, run that year at Newcastle.

CELEBRITY OF THE DAY

1909 Owned by King Edward VII, Minoru won the 2,000 Guineas, making HRH the first reigning monarch to own a Classic winner – although he had already won six whilst Prince of Wales. The horse went on to win the Derby, but retired with eye trouble next season, then exported to Russia – where he disappeared during the Revolution. However, one story has him and 1913 Derby winner, Aboyeur, jointly harnessed to a cart, being driven from Moscow to Novorossiysk, and then evacuated to a new life in Serbia.

29 APRIL

SIGNIFICANT EVENT

1994 Jumps trainer David Nicholson sent out his first Group winner with his first such runner when 20/1-shot Silver Wisp won the Jockey Club Stakes at Newmarket.

STRANGEST EVENT

2002 All the runners in Plumpton's Restart (!) Claiming Hurdle took the wrong course and were disqualified, and the race voided – only for the Jockey Club to quash the decision and award the race to Potentate, 7/1, ridden by Gerry Supple.

OTHER EVENTS

1904 1/4-shot Pretty Polly won the 1,000 Guineas by three lengths. She went on to win 22 of her 24 starts including the Oaks for which she was 8/100, and the St Leger, 2/5.
1921 The 2,000 Guineas (won by Craig An Eran) and 1,000 Guineas (Bettina) were run at Newmarket on the same day.
1935 Chelmsford racecourse closed its gates.
1967 Mill House, so often second best to Arkle, won the Whitbread Gold Cup ridden by David Nicholson, replacing broken leg victim Willie Robinson who was nonetheless introduced on crutches to the Queen Mother.
1991 There were seven 6/1 co-favourites for Hexham's 10-runner Law Society Legal Handicap Hurdle – only the second time such an event had happened. Fingers Crossed, one of the six, won.
1993 Walter Swinburn won the 1,000 Guineas for the third time in five seasons, on the Clive Brittain-trained Sayyedati, 4/1.
1994 Sam Houston Race Park opened for business in Texas – the first Grade 1 racing to be held there for 57 years. Betting had been legalized in the state just seven years earlier.
1995 Ann Moran, a 36-year-old mother of three from County Meath, became the first Irish-born rider to win America's Maryland Hunt Cup, aboard Buck Jake trained by Charlie Fenwick.
2003 Jockey Laffit Pincay jr retired with 9530 winners to his credit.
2008 Michael Scudamore, 75, who won the Grand National and the Gold Cup as a jockey, retired from training – again – handing over to grandson, Michael, 24.

QUOTE OF THE DAY

'I was too small to become a window cleaner and too big to be a garden gnome.' Adrian Maguire's explanation for how he came to be a jockey. This day in 1994 Maguire celebrated his 23rd birthday by landing his first win at Southwell with his first ride there, on Buckra Mellisuga.

BIRTHDAYS

1940 Former Royal jockey David Mould. He won two Mackesons, a Hennessy, plus the 1973 Benson & Hedges Chase on Tingle Creek. Married show-jumper Marion Coakes. He retired in 1975.
1944 International footballer-turned trainer-turned paper salesman, Francis Lee.
1947 Trainer of Cool Ground and Rooster Booster, Richard Mitchell.
1961 John Quinn, dual purpose trainer of Blythe Knight and Fantasy Believer.
1971 Jockey turned trainer, Adrian Maguire. He won 1024 races in the UK, retired from the saddle on Oct 28, 2002 following a fall at Warwick which broke his neck.

DEATH OF THE DAY

2009 *The Racing Post* reported the death of Greek shipping magnate Captain Marcos Lemos, 81, whose Pebbles won the 1984 1,000 Guineas and whose patronage did much to establish Clive Brittain as a big-league trainer.

CELEBRITY OF THE DAY

2003 Owner of Derby winners Psidium and Henbit, plus Arc winner Sassafras, six times married Austrian countess Etti Plesch, who died today aged 89

30 APRIL

SIGNIFICANT EVENT

2009 The scheduled card at Hollywood Park was cancelled because there weren't enough horses to stage the programme. Vice president Eual Wyatt jr commented: 'This isn't a bump in the road. This is a large pothole. We're not out of business. There is a shortage of horses. It may be the economy – investing in horses is an expensive proposition.'

STRANGEST EVENT

1992 Rag Time Belle, 10/1, won at Redcar to bring home the bacon for pig breeder-owner Roger Hughes, pig-keeper-trainer Malcolm Eckley and breeder Victor Wadge, a bacon farmer.

OTHER EVENTS

1894 Coalminer Nathan Richards married dressmaker Elizabeth Dean. Neither had the remotest connection with horse racing, but their son Gordon became 26 times champion jockey.
1965 Ascot staged its first jump meeting. The two-day card included Flat races. The inaugural hurdle was won by favourite Sir Giles, trained by Fulke Walwyn and ridden by Willie Robinson. The Kennel Gate Chase went to Another Scot, ridden by Tim Norman.
1969 After just 100 yards of the 2,000 Guineas, 15/8 favourite Ribofilio, trained by Fulke Johnson Houghton, was struggling. After 3f the horse was tailed off, and Lester Piggott pulled up after 4f. Right Tack, 15/2, won for Geoff Lewis. A dope test on Ribofilio proved negative.
1992 Weighing out procedures were modified so that breast plates, breast girths, martingales and neck straps would no longer count towards a Flat jockey's weight, although would still be included for jump jocks.
1994 Lochsong set a 5f record time of 56.18s in winning the Palace House Stakes at Newmarket, smashing the 57.4 record which had stood since 1938 to Knights Armour.

1994 The first Northern-trained 2,000 Guineas winner for 33 years was Middleham-based Mark Johnston's Mister Baileys, 16/1. He was ridden by Jason Weaver, having his first ride in a Classic. Martin Pipe's first Classic runner, Cotteir Chief, was unplaced.
1995 Pelder, 13/1, trained by Paul Kelleway, became first English-trained winner of the Group 1 Prix Ganay at Longchamp since Rheingold (1973).
2009 Enda Bolger saddled the winner of the La Touche Cup at Punchestown for an amazing eleventh time as Nina Carberry rode 13/8 favourite Garde Champetre to victory.

QUOTE OF THE DAY

'The Game Spirit Chase, named after Game Spirit, a lovely horse, owned by the Queen Mother, who dropped dead here after a long and distinguished career.' Broadcast gaffe attributed to veteran BBC commentator Peter Bromley, born today in 1929.

BIRTHDAYS

1944 Englishman abroad? Champion Canadian trainer Phil England born.
1956 Jockey turned sprint-training king, David 'Dandy' Nicholls.
1955 Jockey Richard Hoare. One of the few sportsmen whose entire name could be construed as an insult.

DEATHS OF THE DAY

2002 Trainer of 1987 Stewards' Cup winner Madraco and 1990 Magnet Cup winner Eradicate, Peter Calver, 68.
2005 Racing was shocked when popular Italian trainer Don Enrico Incisa died suddenly aged 70. He began his career in Milan, winning the 1972 Gran Premio d'Italia before moving to Middleham in 1981.

CELEBRITY OF THE DAY

1947 Trainer Geoff Huffer, reputedly once a member of band Mungo Jerry, and trainer of Cockney Rebel, named in honour of Steve Harley's band, born.

1 MAY

SIGNIFICANT EVENT
1994 Marildo (185/10) won the Prix Ganay at Longchamp, becoming only the third 7yo to win a European Group One race, following Drum Taps in the 1993 Ascot Gold Cup and El Badr in 1982 Prix du Cadran.

STRANGE EVENT
1939 The last meeting held at the second Pershore track, between Worcester and Evesham, attracted 1,293 paying customers. Top, ridden by Alec Jack, won the last race, a handicap hurdle. The course had been operational for less than four years.

OTHER EVENTS
1943 65,000 saw Count Fleet win the Kentucky Derby under Johnny Longden, for trainer Don Cameron. He went on to complete the Triple Crown.

1954 For the first time net prize money for the Kentucky Derby topped $100,000 and connections of Determine – the first winning grey – collected $2,050 more than that for the win over 16 opponents.

1961 Betting shops became legal in Britain.

1969 Geoff Lewis partnered the John Sutcliffe-trained Right Tack to win the 2,000 Guineas on the same day as Peter O'Sullevan's Be Friendly won the Palace House Stakes.

1975 Pickets were on duty at 1,000 Guineas meeting at Newmarket, where striking stable lads provoked ugly scenes during which Willie Carson was dragged from his horse.

1982 Gato Del Sol, 21/1, won Kentucky Derby under Eddie Delahoussaye. The grey won over $1.3m during a 39 race career, of which he won just seven.

1985 Desert Orchid unplaced in his only two mile Flat race, run at Ascot.

1990 Ascot staged first evening jumps meeting for 25 years. On the same day Pat Eddery rode a five-timer – the second of his career – at Bath.

1993 Newmarket jockey Adam Shoults won the Austrian 2000 Guineas on Cortez. The next day he added the Czech 1000 Guineas on Ajanta for a rare double.

2009 Champion New Zealand-bred mare Sunline was put down after contracting laminitis. The 14yo won 13 Group 1 races and A$11m in prize money from 32 wins in 48 starts and was Australian Horse of the Year for three straight seasons to 2002.

2009 Red-hot 3/10 favourite Rachel Alexandra won the Kentucky Oaks by over 20 lengths for jockey Calvin Borel and trainer Hal Wiggins.

QUOTE OF THE DAY
'Channel 4 will be asked to reduce the extent to which gambling features in its racing coverage.' Chris Cook of *The Guardian*, revealing in 2009 that 'racing' was looking to make the sport 'appeal to an audience beyond punters'. Mmm.

BIRTHDAYS
1960 Champion jockey, Steve 'The Kentucky Kid' Cauthen. He won the title for the first time in 1984, having won the US equivalent in 1977. He was the first jockey to to win both the British and US titles since Danny Maher in 1908.

1972 Jockey Tony Dobbin, who won the 1997 Grand National on Lord Gyllene.

1962 Jockey Wendyll Woods.

DEATHS OF THE DAY
1995 Popular member of the Channel 4 Racing team John Tyrell, 60, who read the results.

2002 Trainer of 1981 Belmont Stakes winner Summing, and who sent out future Triple Crown winner Affirmed to victory in his first outing, Luis Barrera, 80.

FIRST OF THE DAY
1971 Brigadier Gerard won his first race as a 3yo, the 2,000 Guineas, ridden by Joe Mercer at 11/2 and beating Mill Reef in the process.

2 MAY

SIGNIFICANT EVENT
2009 Mine That Bird, bought for $9,500, the only gelding in the field, and tailed off as the runners rounded the first turn in the 135th Kentucky Derby, scored an astonishing win at odds of 506-10 for trainer Bernie L ('Chips') Woolley jr (a moustachioed, former bareback rodeo rider, whose seasonal record had been one win from 34 starts) and wily jockey Calvin Borel, who had won it in 2007 on Street Sense, eventually winning by seven lengths.'It's not the first half mile that counts, it's the last', Borel observed. The day before Borel had won the Oaks on odds-on shot Rachel Alexandra. New track announcer Mark Johnson, the first Brit to get that gig. He is the first man to commentate on both Kentucky and Epsom Derbys.

STRANGE EVENT
1517 The Duke of Suffolk took on a sportsman called Nicolle Dex in a horse race in France, 'from the Elm at Auvergney to within St Clements Gate for 80 crowns'. Despite, or perhaps because of, giving his horse no hay for three days and restricting his own diet to white wine, the Duke finished second.

OTHER EVENTS
1893 Irish jockey Jim Parkinson had his first winner, Noiseless, at Birr. He was later warned off for over a year for foul riding but went on to become 23 times champion trainer.
1959 Tomy Lee became only the second English-bred to win the Kentucky Derby. The Bill Shoemaker-ridden 3.7/1 shot had to survive an objection.
1964 Northern Dancer, 3.4/1, ridden by Bill Hartack and trained by Horatio Luro, was the neck winner of the 90th Kentucky Derby in a new track record time of 2 minutes.
1970 Diane Crump, 15th of 17 on Fathom, was the first female to ride in the Kentucky Derby.

1984 Barry Hills celebrated his 900th winner as Steve Cauthen rode Gildoran to win the Sagaro Stakes at Ascot.
1985 One of the closest finishes to a modern British Classic as Sheikh Mohammed's Oh So Sharp (Henry Cecil/Steve Cauthen) got up in the final stride of the 1,000 Guineas to beat Al Bahathri (Tom Jones/Tony Murray) a short head with Lester Piggott on Bella Colora trained by Michael Stoute a further short head in arrears.
1992 Lester Piggott rode his 30th Classic winner as 6/1 Rodrigo De Triano won the 2,000 Guineas. His first was 38 years previously – the longest ever first-to-last Classic span.
1992 Record stakes of $1,460,470 were staked on 9/10 Francois Boutin-trained Kentucky Derby wonder horse favourite, Arazi – who finished only eighth, the worst placed odds-on favourite in the race's history.

QUOTE OF THE DAY
1974 *'Ten stall urinals, six WCs and three hand basins all for seven nicker, but then, to the connoisseur, racing at Wye was always a bargain.'* Sporting Life commenting on a sale of fixtures and fittings from Wye, which staged its final meeting today.

BIRTHDAYS
1962 Jump jockey Billy Morris, who rode The Ceiriog to win the Swedish Champion Hurdle. Self-nominated as the highlight of his career; 'Deciding not to get married in 1981.'
1962 Footballer/trainer, Mick Quinn.

DEATH OF THE DAY
1870 The first horse to win the Triple Crown, West Australian (1853).

CELEBRITY OF THE DAY
2009 Trainer Willie Mullins completed the Punchestown Festival with 12 winners to his credit. Jockey Ruby Walsh rode ten winners. They received their trophies from Taoiseach Brian Cowen.

3 MAY

SIGNIFICANT EVENT
1979 One In A Million was the first horse running under the name of company ownership to win an English Classic. Joe Mercer rode the Henry Cecil-trained even money chance to victory in the 1,000 Guineas in the colours of textile firm Helena Springfield Ltd.

STRANGE EVENT
2009 Former trainer Ron Sheather, whose 1984 champion sprinter Chief Singer was the first horse to win a British Group race on his debut – the 1983 Coventry Stakes under Ray Cochrane – died aged 76. After winning the Ayr Gold Cup in 1951, on Fair Seller, and having been promised a 50gns bonus from his guv'nor Ernie Davey, he went to the trainer's house to collect. Davey refused to pay his apprentice and stormed off, handing Sheather a cigarette, which he lit up, only to be confronted by Mrs Davey, telling him, 'Apprentices aren't allowed in the house and there'll be no smoking in my house. Get out.'

OTHER EVENTS
1842 Northern mare Alice Hawthorn won the Chester Cup en route to a career record of 52 wins from 71 races.

1940 Billy Nevett rode his 1,000th winner on Thixendale at Thirsk. He went on to win three Wartime Derbys, on Owen Tudor, 1941, Ocean Swell, 1944, and Dante, 1945.

1952 Ben Jones trained a record sixth Kentucky Derby winner, Hill Gail at 11/10 ridden by Eddie Arcaro, a fifth Derby for the jockey.

1954 Jockey Scobie Breasley fractured his skull in a fall from Sayonara at Alexandra Park. His eyes were paralysed and sense of balance destroyed. He returned to racing several months later despite medics predicting he would never ride again.

1978 Three years after his brother Alvaro, a top California jockey, died in a freak starting gate accident when his mount Austin Mittler reared up, Mexican jockey Roberto Pineda, 25, was killed at Pimlico in Baltimore.

1990 Willie Carson completed the English Classic set by riding Salsabil to a 6/4 triumph in the 1,000 Guineas.

1991 Lite Light won the 117th Kentucky Oaks in the record time of 1.48 4/5ths. Owners Lewis Burrell Sr and family, including rapper MC Hammer, picked up $207,285.

1992 Burst became the first filly to complete the Australian two year old Triple Crown.

2009 20/1-shot Ghanaati won a second 1,000 Guineas for Barry Hills. 'I think he had a bit of 33s the other day' said jockey and son of the trainer, Richard Hills. The horse was the first ever to win a British Classic having never raced on turf. .

QUOTE OF THE DAY
1769 'Eclipse first, the rest nowhere.' One of racing's most famous 'quotes of the day', when the legendary Eclipse made his racecourse debut at Epsom. Pro gambler owner, Dennis O'Kelly, used the phrase to strike a bet indicating that Eclipse would win easily. He won his bet.

BIRTHDAYS
1927 Jimmy Uttley, rider of triple Champion Hurdler Persian War.

1948 Former champion lady jockey-turned trainer Brooke Sanders.

1961 Newmarket trainer Maureen Haggas, daughter of Lester Piggott.

1974 Owner Princess Haya of Jordan, wife of Sheikh Mohammed.

DEATHS OF THE DAY
1971 Marion H Van Berg, who had owned a staggering 4,775 winners in North America since 1937.

2004 Owner of 'all straw' colours, first listed in 1762, The Duke of Devonshire, 84. His Park Top won the 1969 Coronation Cup and King George VI and Queen Elizabeth Stakes.

4 MAY

SIGNIFICANT EVENT

1996 The first three jockeys home in the 2,000 Guineas received whip bans, and Frankie Dettori, who rode Mark of Esteem, 8/1, was also fined £500 for jumping off the horse on the course before reaching the winner's enclosure. Dettori was given an eight-day whip ban, Philip Robinson on Even Top got four and Jason Weaver, on Bijou D'Inde, two.

STRANGE EVENT

2009 Welsh trainer David Evans brought a team of horses to contest the one five-race meeting held in Guernsey each year – and returned with three victories to his credit. The horse of his which declared 13lb overweight minutes before the off was beaten – but Evans still won.

OTHER EVENTS

1905 Belmont Park, New York opened. The main race, the Metropolitan Handicap, produced a dead heat between Synosby and Race King, watched by 40,000.

1933 They raced for the last time at Monmouth, with Fred Gurney riding Tapinois to win the final event, the Ross Maiden Hurdle.

1935 Omaha was a 4/1 winner of the 18-runner Kentucky Derby. He came to England the next year and finished second in the Ascot Gold Cup.

1953 Walter Swinburn senior rode his first winner, Metalon at Warwick.

1968 For the first time a Kentucky Derby 'winner' was disqualified. Dancer's Image, 3.6/1, passed the post in front of 2.2/1 favourite Forward Pass in a field of 14, but was later thrown out 'because of the finding of prohibited medication'.

1974 Cannonade won the 100th Kentucky Derby worth $274,000. Angel Cordero jr rode the 6/4 favourite, who beat a record 22 rivals in front of a record crowd of 163,628.

1983 Champion-to-be Richard Dunwoody rode his first winner, Game Trust at Cheltenham.

1985 Shadeed (Michael Stoute/Lester Piggott) won the 2,000 Guineas at 4/5, the shortest-priced winner since Nijinsky at 4/7 in 1970.

1988 Husband and wife Robert and Theresa Elwell raced against each other in the Audi Grand Prix Hunter Chase at Cheltenham. Theresa was second on Mister Skip; Robert fell at the 14th on White Paper.

1996 Grindstone touched off Cavonnier by a nose in the Kentucky Derby to give trainer D. Wayne Lukas an incredible sixth straight victory in a Triple Crown race. Grindstone, ridden by Jerry Bailey, was one of a record five Lukas starters in a field of 19.

QUOTE OF THE DAY

'Carrie is a grand lass, but she's a brood mare now, and having kids does not get you fit to ride Grand Nationals.' Ginger McCain, unimpressed by fancied Forest Gunner's partner for 2005 Grand National, Carrie Ford, born on this date in 1971. At 8/1, they finished fifth.

BIRTHDAYS

1946 Trainer Neville Callaghan.

1957 Trainer Dr Jon Scargill. He claimed to have no recreations - 'work all day and night'.

1974 Tony McCoy. Many people's idea of the greatest jump jockey.

1971 Jockey Carrie Ford, best known for her association with Forest Gunner.

DEATH OF THE DAY

1996 Former trainer Joe Carr, 80, who won 27 races with Lochranza.

FIRST OF THE DAY

1780 The Derby was run for the first time, over one mile. Diomed, partnered by Sam Arnull, won for owner Sir Charles Bunbury, going some way to consoling him for losing to Lord Derby in a toss of a coin to decide whose name the race should carry.

5 MAY

SIGNIFICANT EVENT

1996 Pat Eddery completed a full house of Classic winners, landing the 1,000 Guineas on Henry Cecil's Bosra Sham, the 10/11 favourite. Cecil joined Dick Hern as the modern-day leading trainer in the English Classics, on 16, while Alex Greaves became the first woman to ride in the race, finishing tenth of 13 on outsider Portuguese Lil.

STRANGE EVENT

2003 Boxer, turned film actor, turned trainer Sandy Carlos Clarke died. He won the best actor award in Canada in 1938, having boxed 19 professional bouts in France from 1933. He worked as a cowboy in Texas before becoming a commando during the war. An assistant to Fulke Walwyn and racing manager to owner Dorothy Paget before setting up as a Lambourn trainer, he won the 1957 Ascot Stakes with Widnor.

OTHER EVENTS

1950 Happy 46th birthday to Gordon Richards, whose win on Abernant at Sandown was his 4,000th, an English first.

1973 Secretariat, 6/4, won the 99th Kentucky Derby in record time, 3/5s under 2min. He won the Triple Crown.

1979 The 3/5 favourite Spectacular Bid won the 105th Kentucky Derby. He won 26 of his 30 starts.

1982 Willie Carson wed Elaine Williams, celebrated by winning the Cheshire Oaks on Swiftfoot, but was miffed at an £8 fine for forgetting to bring his medical records book to the track.

1984 Pat Eddery stormed to 2,000 Guineas victory on the Vincent O'Brien-trained El Gran Senor.

1986 Anthony Tory rode his first winner, Kilton Jim, at Fontwell.

1990 92-year-old Frances Genter, with Unbridled, became the oldest owner of a Kentucky Derby winner.

1997 Richard Dunwoody made history at Southwell as his win on Jervaulx

2/1 fav gave him an eighth successive century, one more than Peter Scudamore.

2007 Cockney Rebel – whose name was cleared by racing fan and rock star Steve Harley – came up to see the 2,000 Guineas and made connections smile by winning both it, at 25/1, and the then Irish equivalent.

2007 The Queen was at Churchill Downs to see Street Sense, favourite at just under 5/1, run out a comfortable winner of the 133rd Kentucky Derby, ridden by Calvin Borel for trainer Carl Nafzger. He became the first Breeders' Cup Juvenile winner to go on to take the Classic.

2009 Leighton Aspell, one of the few jockeys with his own fan club, rode his first winner since resuming his career after a 19-month hiatus when Saafend Rocket scored at 7/1 at Fakenham.

QUOTE OF THE DAY

'By his skill, consistency and longevity in the saddle, and his strength of character out of it, he brought more credit to his profession than any other jockey has ever done.' Turf historians John Randall and Tony Morris, in their book *A Century of Champions*, declared Sir Gordon Richards as jockey of the century.

BIRTHDAY

1904 Gordon Richards, the first jockey to be knighted. One of 12 children, he was champion jockey 26 times and rode 4,870 winners including 14 Classics.

DEATH OF THE DAY

2005 US jockey Ted Atkinson, 88, known as 'The Slasher', allegedly because of the frequency with which he won on outsiders. was the top jockey in 1944 and '46 and had a career total of 3,795 winners from 23,661 rides.

FIRST OF THE DAY

1987 Satellite Information Services began daily broadcasts to betting shops, opening up with a service to shops in Bristol and Colchester.

6 MAY

SIGNIFICANT EVENT
2009 Barry Hills' Daraahem, 7/1, won him his 150th win at the track and fourth Chester Cup. Hills told Channel 4 viewers that when he backed Frankincense to win the 1968 Lincoln he won £50,000.

STRANGE EVENT
2009 Struggling Premiership club Hull City sponsored a race at Chester and boss Phil Brown invited his first-team squad to the races for a morale-boosting day after a string of defeats, only to admit that they refused to attend, believing they should be concentrating on preparing for their vital next match at home to Stoke, which they lost 2-1.

OTHER EVENTS
1971 John Matthias rode his first winner, Garden Games at Beverley.
1972 Meriel Tufnell, 23, became the first woman to ride a winner in Britain under Rules when scoring on Scorched Earth, 50/1, at Kempton in the Goya Stakes, the first ladies' race.
1974 Jack Berry sent out his first Flat winner, 20/1 outsider Fiona's Pet, partnered by wife Jo, at Wolverhampton.
1978 Steve Cauthen rode Affirmed to win the Kentucky Derby en route to the Triple Crown. He became the first rider to complete the Kentucky-Epsom Derby double when winning the latter on Slip Anchor in 1985.
1991 Racing closed ranks when a controversial Cook Report TV programme criticised Martin Pipe's training methods. Many who had given him grudging praise rallied round him.
1995 The Andre Fabre-trained Pennekamp was the 9/2 winner of the 2,000 Guineas, beating latest 'super horse' Celtic Swing into second.
1996 Fran Berry, 15-year-old son of ten times Irish champion jump jockey Frank, rode his first winner, Loughmogue, in a Navan sprint.
2001 Davids Lad partnered by Timmy Murphy for trainer Tony Martin, was the 10/1 winner of the 19-runner Irish Grand National, postponed from its usual Easter Monday date because of the foot-and-mouth crisis.
2009 Five of the seven runners in Nash Hunter Chase at Cheltenham traded at odds-on in running while the winner, The Baillie, 14/1 traded at 1000/1!

QUOTE OF THE DAY
'One of my owners said he wanted a three-mile chaser. My reply was that you cannot buy one – you try to create one and then you wait and hope.' David Elsworth, who on this day in 1992 was the first trainer given the go-ahead to operate from two yards – Whitcombe Manor and Whitsbury.

BIRTHDAYS
1920 Jockey Club member John Henderson – something of an A-grade owner – as Acre Hill won him three races, Acquit four, Acquaint five and Accord six.
1948 French trainer Robert Collet.
1956 Trainer Tim Thomson Jones, champion amateur Flat and jump jockey.
1959 Apprentice in England, Ireland and France, jump jockey-turned sculptor Willie Newton.

DEATHS OF THE DAY
1992 Blushing Groom, sire of Arazi and Nashwan, put down aged 18.
1993 French jump jockey Roger Duchene, 37, from head injuries sustained when To Bamara fell at the Auteuil water jump. He rode 450 winners including the 1987 Breeders' Cup Chase.
1994 Steve 'Sampson' Wood, 26, who had ridden 129 winners, of internal injuries when Kalar stumbled and threw him at Lingfield.

CELEBRITY OF THE DAY
1910 Ailing monarch King Edward VII's Witch of the Air won at Kempton. When told, he expressed his pleasure with his dying words, expiring shortly after.

7 MAY

SIGNIFICANT EVENT
1995 Newmarket and Salisbury staged the first Sunday racing with betting as the majority of betting shops opened for the first time on a Sunday.

STRANGE EVENT
1990 Jockey Terry Smith failed to win a walkover. His Rossa Prince was the only 'runner' entered for a Tweseldown point-to-point race. Smith only needed to canter the horse over the finishing line, but it bolted and couldn't be caught in time. Smith was also fined £25 for declaring the wrong colours.

OTHER EVENTS
1887 Bendigo, who had won the first Eclipse Stakes at Sandown in 1886, now collected the first Grand Jubilee Handicap at Kempton under John Watts, carrying 9st 7lbs for trainer Charlie Jousiffe and owner Buck Barclay.

1914 Lester Piggott's grandfather Fred Rickaby won the opening race on the card at Harpenden's final meeting.

1949 Ponder beat Capot to win the 75th Kentucky Derby, preventing Capot from winning the Triple Crown after he had beaten Ponder in both the Preakness and Belmont Stakes.

1955 Swaps, 2.8/1, was the first of four Kentucky Derby winners for jockey Bill Shoemaker.

1977 The odds-on favourite and subsequent Triple Crown winner Seattle Slew won the Kentucky Derby, for jockey Jean Cruguet and trainer William H Turner.

1982 Chaplins Club was runner-up in his first race at Lingfield. He went on to set and then equal the 20th-century record of nine handicap wins in a season.

1988 A roan filly, Winning Colors lived up to her name in the Kentucky Derby for jockey Gary Stevens and trainer D Wayne Lukas.

1992 49-year-old Puerto Rican Angel Cordero announced his retirement, having suffered a broken elbow, broken ribs and a damaged spleen in a four-horse pile-up at Aqueduct. His tally of 7,076 career wins was bettered at the time only by Laffit Pincay's 7,758 and Bill Shoemaker's 8,833.

1997 The Lynda Ramsden-trained Top Cees, 11/2, won the Chester Cup for a second time, by ten lengths. Previously won, 1995.

2006 Pam Sly turned down a £600,000 offer for filly Speciosa – then saddled her to win the 1,000 Guineas, beating Mark Prescott's first Classic runner, Confidential Lady, into second.

QUOTE OF THE DAY
'When Lord Glasgow died in 1869 he made tacit acknowledgement of the wrong he had done Aldcroft, by leaving him £500.' A *Biographical Encyclopaedia of British Flat Racing* comment about jockey Thomas Aldcroft who died this day in 1883, and who rode General Peel to win the 1864 2,000 Guineas for owner Lord Glasgow, who erroneously accused the rider of dodgy dealings.

BIRTHDAYS
1914 Great Aussie rider Arthur Edward 'Scobie' Breasley, who went on to train in Barbados. He won the Epsom Derby twice.

1958 The 1987-88 champion lady rider Carolyn Eddery, wife of Pat.

FIRST OF THE DAY
1991 Toulon became the first French winner at Chester since 1952. Trained by Andre Fabre, he won the Chester Vase at 9/4.

CELEBRITY OF THE DAY
2009 It was revealed that the Queen's Moonlit Path, trained by Nicky Henderson, had failed a drugs test after racing at Huntingdon in February. The mare, sixth in a novice hurdle, tested positive for the anti-bleeding drug Cyklokapron.

8 MAY

SIGNIFICANT EVENT
1994 The Paul Cole-trained 7yo Snurge finished fourth in the Group 2 Gerling-Preis at Cologne to become the leading British money earner ever with £1,185,491, taking him past Pebbles' record of three grand less, set in 1985.

STRANGE EVENT
2009 A William Hill customer asked to back horse number 9 in a race at Nottingham for £1,500. When a clerk repeated the horse's name back to him, 'Say No Now', the customer said, 'Okay, then' and put the phone down, believing his bet had been refused. The horse won and Hill's contacted the client to tell him the bet on the even-money chance had been placed for him after all!

OTHER EVENTS
1788 The first Royal winner of the Derby, the Prince of Wales's odds-on shot Sir Thomas, ridden by the Lester/Frankie of his day, William South, in his 54th year.

1915 Regret, 2.65/1, became the first filly to win the Kentucky Derby; for the first time connections copped for a five-figure sum - $11,450.

1941 Gordon Richards broke his left leg after being kicked by a filly at the start at Salisbury. He was out of action for the rest of the season, so 39-year-old Harry Wragg overtook him to win the title.

1945 1,000 Guineas day at Newmarket coincided with VE (Victory in Europe) day but, noted a contemporary report, 'The stewards did not exchange hats, nor did the bookmakers pay out any bonuses.' So, business as usual as Lord Derby's 5/2-shot Sun Stream won the big race, then.

1990 Black Sapphire, 11/2 at Salisbury, opened trainer James Fanshawe's winning account.

1995 Streaker Stephen Brighton, a barman, who ran on to the course at Fontwell, was knocked flying by a horse called Boxing Match, after being walloped by Richard Dunwoody's whip for good measure as he went past on Laughing Gas. Brighton was arrested and taken, appropriately according to eye witnesses, to Littlehampton Police Station for questioning.

1996 Jonothan Lower rode Martin Pipe's The Black Monk into second at Chepstow, later broke his arm on the gallops, was diagnosed as diabetic and forced to quit in August as the Jockey Club would not licence insulin-dependant diabetics for fear they might black out.

1997 Alexandra Madigan won a claiming race at Churchill Downs on Distinctive Angel – which she also bred, owned and trained.

QUOTE OF THE DAY
2009 'The funniest race I've ever seen,' said Hayley Turner, commentating for Channel 4. It was a second bad day at the office for Johnny Murtagh at Chester. The day before on Aidan O'Brien favourite, Masterofthehorse, in the Chester Vase, he'd come late and failed to catch the stable's second string, 25/1 shot Golden Sword. Today he was on the 13/8 fav, Frozen Fire, in the three-horse, 1m 5f, Ormonde Stakes, which was run farcically slowly, in almost a minute more than standard time, with William Buick stealing the race from the front on 15/8 chance Buccellati and Murtagh returning to jeers from the crowd, admitting later that he was likely to have lost friends from his Facebook site as a result!

BIRTHDAYS
1924 US trainer Luz (aka Luis) Barrera, whose Affirmed won the 1978 Triple Crown winner.

1955 Jockey Lindsay Charnock.

1964 Trainer John Carr, who won the 2007 Champion Hurdle with Sublimity.

DEATH OF THE DAY
1994 Philippe Lallie, 68. Trained 1971 Irish Sweeps Derby winner Irish Ball.

9 MAY

SIGNIFICANT EVENT

1975 Champion trainer Martin Pipe sent out his first winner when Len Lungo rode Hit Parade to win a Taunton selling hurdle. Déjà vu kicked in 31 years later on this day in 2006 when Martin's son David sent out his first winner with a full licence, Standin Obligation at Kelso in a novice chase. David had 134 winners in his first season and 100 in his second, in the latter also winning the Grand National with Comply Or Die, who was also runner-up in 2009.

STRANGE EVENT

1936 Actor-owner Albert Finney born. He once reportedly bought all the tickets for a performance of a show he was in, so that he could take the day off to see his horse run. Come the day, it was a non-runner!

OTHER EVENTS

1800 Champion, a son of Pot-8-os, ridden by William Clift, won the Derby. He later added the St Leger.

1893 Entry was charged by Chester for the first time – 45,000 racegoers paying 1/- (5p) during the three-day meeting.

1914 The 17/20 favourite Old Rosebud won the 40th Kentucky Derby in a new track record of 2m 3 2/5s.

1955 Sir Gordon Richards sent out his first winner as a trainer when the Dorothy Paget-owned The Saint won at Windsor.

1982 Luca Cumani's first Classic winner was the Pat Eddery-ridden Old Country in the Derby Italiano in Rome.

2009 After screening racing from Haydock for five successive decades, the BBC broadcast racing from the track for the final time.

QUOTE OF THE DAY

'All I do now is sit on my tractor, drink my Foster's, smoke my fags and watch them come up the gallops' declared Abergavenny

dual-purpose trainer David Evans in 2009, after a prolific week of winners had been topped off with three more in 45 minutes this evening, reflecting that following an accident with a fallen tree a few weeks back he had been on crutches.

BIRTHDAYS

1912 Welsh jockey Evan Williams, who rode Golden Miller to win the 1936 Cheltenham Gold Cup.

1934 Former Irish champion jockey Buster Parnell.

1940 Trainer (Richard) Fulke Johnson Houghton. He won the 1967 and '68 St Leger and Irish Sweeps Derby double with Ribocco and Ribero, while his 1969 2,000 Guineas favourite Ribofilio was pulled up, sparking 'nobbling' rumours.

DEATHS OF THE DAY

1892 One of the famous jockey Beasley brothers, Willie, runner-up in the 1888 Grand National on Frigate, died from injuries sustained in a race at Punchestown. He and three brothers all raced in the 1879 Grand National.

1977 Trainer Sir Noel Murless, 77. He was knighted in 1977, the year after retiring with 19 Classic winners, including Crepello, St Paddy and Royal Palace in the Derby.

1988 Top Australian jockey Craig Wake died three weeks after a collision during a race at Perth's Ascot track. He had ridden over 400 winners.

1989 Great racemare Park Top, runner-up to Levmoss in the Arc, was put down, aged 25.

CELEBRITY OF THE DAY

Old Etonian, and MP for Plymouth, US-born Lord Waldorf Astor won his third 2,000 Guineas winner with Court Martial this day in 1945. The owner also won a St Leger, two 1,000 Guineas and five Oaks, but never the Derby, his runners finishing second five times. He never bet.

10 MAY

SIGNIFICANT EVENT
2009 Former trainer 'Ginger' McCain put aside his, shall we say, 'traditional' views on female jockeys when he watched a lady win the Ed Weetman Memorial Charity Flat Race at Uttoxeter on My Condor. She was Ginger and Beryl's daughter Joanne, landing her first ever win (and last, she 'retired' after the race) – aged 42 on a horse trained by her brother Donald.

STRANGE EVENT
1993 The title of a ladies' race sponsored at Redcar by 15 racecourse bookies sparked controversy when they opted to call it the 'Worth Laying Handicap.'

OTHER EVENTS
1905 Just three went to post for the 31st Kentucky Derby, with 1/3 favourite Agile obliging.
1919 Sir Barton won the Kentucky Derby, ridden by Johnny Loftus. The partnership went on to become the first US Triple Crown winners.
1950 Tommy Weston rode his last winner, Lindum Hill, at Doncaster. Born in 1903, he won eleven Classics including the Derby in 1924 and '33. He was torpedoed during war service, drifting on a raft in the Atlantic for days.
1977 Eddie Hide rode his 2,000th winner, Triple First at York.
1989 John Francome rode Gaasid round Chester, wearing a Channel 4 TV camera on his helmet for the benefit of viewers. Trainer Reg Akehurst was livid when he found out and sacked the member of staff who arranged it. The 5/1 second favourite Gaasid contested the Chester Cup that afternoon and finished only fifth.
1991 Jump jockey Kevin Mooney rode his 296th and final winner, By Line at Taunton. He won the Whitbread on the Queen Mother's Special Cargo in 1983/4.
1993 Frankie Dettori was cautioned by police in London 'for being in possession of a controlled drug.'

1995 Paul Eddery had ridden 4/1 Son of Sharp Shot to win the 4.10 at Chester, flew to Doncaster to win the 6.30 on 14/1 Fleet Cadet before driving to Newmarket. He rode to work this morning before flying to Prestwick and taking a taxi to Ayr where he rode Bulsara to win the 2.25 at 7/1, completing a long-range 591/1 treble.
1998 The Peter Chapple Hyam-trained Victory Note, 25/1, led home an all British first four in the French 2000 Guineas.

QUOTE OF THE DAY
2009 Six horses died in two hurdles, a chase and a bumper at a Killarney meeting. Racecourse manager Michael Lucy described the deaths as 'a freak', but top trainer Willie Mullins declared: *'To lose six horses in one day doesn't add up, and I'm not buying the freak story. Someone should ask why these horses were killed.'*

BIRTHDAYS
1943 Jockey Bruce Raymond. Off the mark at Birmingham in June 1961, his best season was 1988 with 77 wins.
1968 Twice champion apprentice, Gary 'Angry Ant' Bardwell.
1970 Jump jockey and Grand National winner, Mick 'Better Than Sex' Fitzgerald.

DEATHS OF THE DAY
1986 Amateur jockey Michael Blackmore, in a fall at Market Rasen.
1992 Billy Nevett, 86, who won wartime Derbys in 1941, '44 and '45. He rode for three generations of the Peacock training dynasty, Dobson, Matthew and Richard. His last winner was Setting Star on the final day of the 1956 season at Manchester. He later trained for a while without great success.

CELEBRITY OF THE DAY
1881 Japan's Emperor Meiji paid his first visit to Negishi racecourse, constructed for exiled Brits abroad.

SIGNIFICANT EVENT

2009 A new blueprint for the 'rebranding' of racing, carried out on behalf of the BHA and Racing Enterprises Ltd, the sport's commercial arm, by consultants Harrison Fraser at a reported cost of £250,000 decided that the sport has too many 'Brians' who are 'boring, dull, traditional, old-fashioned, out of touch and very British' and not enough 'Bens' who are 'a bit edgy, approachable, well groomed and athletic, younger minded' amongst other things, than Brian.' (No Brendas?). They also unveiled eight new steering and development groups – on which there were no women. Not everyone was impressed. 'Lacking in inspiration' grumbled William Hill boss Ralph Topping. 'As solutions go it's as convincing as the King's New Clothes' said Brough Scottt. '

STRANGE EVENT

1989 Steve Cauthen on Mountain Kingdom in Chester's Ormonde Stakes suddenly felt his nearest rival snapping at his heels – literally – as Lazaz took a bite at Cauthen's boot as they raced up the home straight.

OTHER EVENTS

1870 Formosa, who had won the 1,000 Guineas, Oaks and St Leger and dead-heated in the 2,000 Guineas two years earlier, gave 30lb to Our Mary Ann in the Chester Cup and was only just beaten. On the same afternoon, Disturbance won the Dee Stand Stakes – three years later he won the Grand National.
1955 Billy Nevett rode his 2,000th winner, Vanished Sage at Ripon.
1963 Trainer John Sutcliffe's first winner was Wayward Cous Cous at Kempton.
1968 Optimistic Pirate, 10/1, was Paul Cole's first winner as a trainer, scoring at Beverley. On the same day John Lowe rode his first winner, Pally's Double, at Kempton.

1979 Bob Champion fell from Fury Boy in a novice chase. The horse lashed out and kicked him in the testicles. The incident is believed to have led to the cancer from which Champion suffered.
1994 The BHB announced they were scrapping all-weather hurdling.
1995 The David Thom-trained Tiger Shoot became the first horse to be banned from racing under the non-triers' rule after finishing sixth at Southwell.
1999 David Pipe sent out his first winner under rules when Stacky Light won a hunter chase at Hereford.
2009 Racehorse owner and gambler Norman Jones, 50, whose horses won 19 Flat and 16 jump races, father of Newmarket apprentice Jamie was found guilty of murdering traveller John Finney, 42, whose dismembered body was found in Hertfordshire. He was sentenced to 33 years.

QUOTE OF THE DAY

2004 *'Racing today is not a married man's job. During the summer it is a full-time commitment, seven days a week. My daughter is 15. I missed a lot of her growing up and won't make the same mistake again with my five-year-old son.'* A stable lad to Paul Cole explaining why he was quitting racing to drive a tanker.

BIRTHDAYS

1957 Jockey Jimmy Bleasdale, former champion apprentice.
1960 Bawtry trainer Stewart Parr.
1964 Snooker champion, owner and BBC TV betting pundit, John Parrott.

DEATH OF THE DAY

2002 Former apprentice jockey Joe Jennings, who went on to found Jennings Bookmakers, 58.

CELEBRITY OF THE DAY

1941 One of the finest British equine artists, Susan Crawford, was born. A trademark gremlin is secreted in many of her works.

12 MAY

SIGNIFICANT EVENT
1859 Mayonaise, ridden by George Fordham, was a 20-length winner of the 1,000 Guineas – still a record margin in a domestic Classic.

STRANGE EVENT
1996 Augustin Herrera, a Colombian jockey based in Italy, was banned for 40 days by stewards at San Siro, Milan, after being discovered using batteries during a race. He finished fourth but was revealed to have two low-voltage batteries, with live points similar to cattle prods, strapped to his wrists, presumably designed to give the horse a jolt.

OTHER EVENTS
1780 Herod, champion sire for eight consecutive years from 1777 to 1784, died aged 22. His daughters won three of the first five Oaks and son Phenomenon won the 1783 St Leger. He was also thought to be the source of the tendency of many modern thoroughbreds to break blood-vessels.

1899 Fred Rickaby rode Beatitude to win Haydock's first Flat race, the Golborne Stakes.

1909 The Preakness Stakes, run at Gravesend, Brooklyn since 1890, was returned to Pimlico where it had last taken place in 1889. Effendi won.

1917 Omar Khayam, foaled in England, was the first foreign-bred Kentucky Derby winner.

1949 Reg Hollinshead owned and rode his first winner as a trainer, 2/1 favourite Shivallee in a novice hurdle at Woore.

1976 Steve Cauthen finished tenth of eleven on his public debut on 136/1 shot King of Swat at River Downs, USA.

1988 Today newspaper tipster Fred Shawcross went through the seven-race card at York.

1994 Pat McCabe, a 5lb claimer, was the first jockey found guilty of 'irresponsible riding', acquiring a four-day ban at Brighton where he partnered Hello Mister, trained by 85-year-old Jack O'Donoghue, to win the Spring Handicap. The horse was placed last.

1996 Ed Dunlop, 27-year-old son of trainer John, won a Classic at the first attempt, with 14/1 Ta Rib in the French 1,000 Guineas.

QUOTE OF THE DAY
1960 *'I'm afraid my luck is beginning to run out'* was the prescient observation of high-profile owner Prince Aly Khan, who died in a car crash in Paris today, four days after uttering those words when his Sheshoon had stumbled with a Longchamp race at its mercy. He had 65 horses in training with Alec Head, four with Noel Murless. Successful in the 59 Arc with Saint Crespin, he had six studs in Ireland, 90 broodmares in France plus 40 mares and three stallions in Venezuela in case of a nuclear holocaust.

BIRTHDAYS
1919 Irish trainer George Dunwoody.

1937 Owner-breeder Bill Shand Kydd. His Brown Windsor won the 1989 Whitbread.

1938 Trainer Don Eddy.

1964 Trainer of Cactus Ridge, Bret Calhoun.

1970 Trainer Peter Grayson.

DEATH OF THE DAY
1950 Lord Anthony Mildmay, the great amateur rider born in 1909, went for a swim in the South Devon sea, never to be seen again. He rode his first winner at Wye in 1933 and almost won the Grand National on Davy Jones in 1936, having to settle for being runner-up on the front-running 100/1-shot when the reins slipped through the buckle at the second-last, leaving Mildmay with little control. He also introduced the Queen Mother to jump racing.

CELEBRITY OF THE DAY
1929 Owner and songwriter Burt Bacharach born.

13 MAY

SIGNIFICANT EVENT

2009 Frankie Dettori's first Breeders' Cup winner, Barathea, was put down aged 19. After that win at Churchill Downs, Frankie's flying dismount made its first ever racecourse appearance.

STRANGE EVENT

1864 An unnamed colt by Vedette won the Stonehenge Plate at Salisbury. The race was ordered to be re-run – as the judge wasn't in his box. They did it all again – with the same result.

OTHER EVENTS

1851 A famous re-match between Lord Eglinton's The Flying Dutchman and Lord Zetland's Voltigeur, both Derby and St Leger winners, took place at York. The Dutchman's jockey, Charles Marlow, had been roaring drunk in the first encounter, and was beaten by half a length. The result was reversed here by a length.

1891 Kingman finally won the slowest ever Kentucky Derby, clocking 2m 52 1/4s.

1952 Choir Boy at Newmarket was the Queen's first winner since coming to the throne. He was ridden by Harry Carr and trained by Cecil Boyd-Rochfort.

1970 Mill Reef, 8/1, won on his debut at Salisbury, en route to his 1971 Derby triumph, ridden by Geoff Lewis.

1976 Luca Cumani sent out his first winner, Three Legs at York, ridden by Frankie Dettori's dad.

1977 Richard Rowe rode his first winner, Retaliation at Stratford, for Josh Gifford.

1982 Lester Piggott rode the Henry-Cecil trained Ardross, 2/5, to become the first horse to win the Yorkshire Cup in

consecutive years.

1992 Peter Niven became the first Scottish jump jockey to ride 100 winners in a season when Henbury Hall, 9/4, won at Perth.

2007 Immy Robinson, 16, won on a horse the same age – Jemaro – at Wheatley, Chaddesley Court, point-to-point.

QUOTE OF THE DAY

1991 *'I felt myself hoping that Fontwell was off. I had always loved going there. If I wanted Fontwell to be off, I had no chance of getting round Plumpton!'* Jockey Richard Rowe explaining in February 1991 why he was quitting.

BIRTHDAYS

1939 Trainer Tony Hide (Celestial Dancer) born. Middle name Gatehouse. He rode as a professional from 1954 to 1968.

1959 Jump jockey-turned stipendiary steward Robert Earnshaw, who won the 1982 Cheltenham Gold Cup on Silver Buck.

DEATHS OF THE DAY

1975 Trainer Henry Peacock who sent out 100 winners in 1932 and trained six Northumberland Plate winners.

2005 Jockey/trainer Kay Erik Jensen, 86. He did both at the same time until the US Jockey Club prohibited him from doing so. Danish-born, Virginia-based, he once rode chase and Flat winners on the same day at Belmont Park.

CELEBRITY OF THE DAY

1938 Coronation Street actor, course announcer and auctioneer Milton Johns was born.

14 MAY

SIGNIFICANT EVENT
1779 Dick Goodison rode Bridget to win the first running of the Oaks for the 12th Earl of Derby, after whose Epsom country house the race was named.

STRANGE EVENT
1807 The Earl of Egremont's Election won the Derby on his debut, and was strongly fancied despite it being his first run, starting as 3/1 favourite. However, the horse may have been a 4yo as the trainer, Bird, confessed on his death bed that he had twice won the Derby with 'ringers', but did not reveal which of his five they were.

OTHER EVENTS
1886 No bookies were on course for the Kentucky Derby after they failed to reach licence agreement with the track management. The race went to Ben Ali.
1929 The colours of Lord Rosebery – who as a young man wagered he would marry the richest woman in England, own a Derby winner and become Prime Minister – were carried to victory for the last time when Annis won the Norfolk Stakes at Newmarket. Rosebery died a week later, having won the 1894 Derby with Ladas; wed Hannah, daughter of banker Baron Meyer de Rothschild, and became Prime Minister in 1894.
1979 Saudi Arabian owner Prince Khalid Abdullah had his first winner, Charming Native, at Windsor. He won the Derby in 1990 with Quest for Fame and 1993 with Commander in Chief.
1984 Faridpour at Pontefract was Kiwi Brent Thomson's first English winner.
1991 US jockey Pat Day rode his 1,000th winner at Churchill Downs, where he was leading jockey.

1995 Godolphin won Group One races in France, Italy and Japan, worth over £750,000.
2009 Jenna Joubert won on Chloes Song at Pimlico, Prove Meguilty at Penn National, and Cover My Six at Charles Town, all in the same afternoon.

QUOTE OF THE DAY
'Johnny Murtagh, Irish champion jockey, once said to me, "Mick, if you want to do this job you've got to realize you are not a normal person."' Jockey Mick Fitzgerald recalls the words of the multiple champion Flat jockey in Ireland, born this day in 1970.

BIRTHS OF THE DAY
1932 Trainer Jumbo Wilkinson. Real name Benjamin, he rode from 1950-67.
1935 Renowned 'horse whisperer' Monty Roberts.
1946 Jump jockey Bob (Bertram Robert) Davies. He was champion in 1968/9 (77 winners, joint with Terry Biddlecombe); 1969/70 (91 winners) and 1971/72 (89 winners) and won the 1978 Grand National on Lucius.
1955 Trainer of Waggoners Walk, Caroline Clark.
1964 Trainer Clive Cox..
1979 Multiple champion jump jockey in Ireland, and rider of Kauto Star, Papillon and Hedgehunter, Ruby Walsh.

DEATHS OF THE DAY
1989 Eddie Taylor, owner-breeder of leading sire Northern Dancer, whose Derby-winning sons included Nijinsky, The Minstrel and Secreto, aged 88.
1993 Irish trainer George Spencer, 72, whose one-eyed Winning Fair won the 1963 Champion Hurdle. He was the father of Flat jockey Jamie Spencer.

15 MAY

SIGNIFICANT EVENT
1994 East of the Moon, trained by Francois Boutin, won the French 1,000 Guineas. Her dam, Miesque, also won the race – and this was her second Classic winner, following Kingmambo's 1993 French 2,000 Guineas win, with her first two foals. Only three Classic-winning mares – Queen Bertha, 1863 Oaks winner; Pilgrimage, 1878 1,000 Guineas winner, and Cobweb, 1824 Guineas-Oaks winner – had previously produced more than one Classic winner.

STRANGE EVENT
2009 'I call it the Carlburg shuffle, and it's all the latest rage in Newmarket' declared the boss of Carlburg stables, 74-year-old Clive Brittain, whose Misheer and Nashmiah's 12.5/1 double at York sent him into a lengthy, rain-soaked celebration dance in the winner's enclosure.

OTHER EVENTS
1834 Racing was first staged at Chantilly.
1839 The Derby was reportedly run in a snow flurry; it was won by 25/1 Bloomsbury.
1940 Great jockey-turned great trainer Fred Winter had his first mount in public, Tam O'Shanter for father Fred Sr at Newbury, finishing ninth of 21 in a nursery handicap.
1964 The Sporting Life front-page headline was: 'Bookmakers Are Given 10 Years To Live', reporting the 'personal' opinion of Jockey Club member Lord Halifax that racecourse bookies were an endangered species. Can't win 'em all!
1965 Three Six at Ayr was Edward Hide's 1,000th winner.
1982 16-year-old Jack Kaenel became the youngest winning rider of the Preakness Stakes when Aloma's Ruler scored, eclipsing Steve Cauthen, who was 18 when winning on Affirmed in 1978.
1990 Serious Trouble belied his name when winning at 1/33 at Brighton for Sir Mark Prescott and George Duffield.

QUOTE OF THE DAY
'I gestured to an empty chair and the chairman of the stewards, John Jenyns, told me to remain standing. I haven't been before stewards before, but it was a most unfortunate introduction' said Channel 4 Racing producer Andrew Franklin in 1997 after a Steward at York told former Yorkshire TV managing director John Fairley, and Franklin to remain standing and take their hands out of their pockets when they attempted to sit down at a meeting to discuss York stewards' refusal to allow cameras into the winner's enclosure, contrary to advice from the Jockey Club. Jenyns subsequently resigned.

BIRTHDAYS
1884 Fred Darling, who was champion trainer six times and won seven Derbys.
1931 Trainer Gordon Price, whose best horses were Stans Pride and Pearl Run.
1934 Middleham trainer Don Enrico Incisa.
1935 Top England cricketer and keen racing man/owner, Ted Dexter.
1942 Trainer Michael Cunningham, who won the Irish 1,000 Guineas with Cairn Rouge and the Champion Hurdle with For Auction. His Greasepaint was placed three times in the National.
1945 Rider of Moyne Royal, Bryan Leyman.
1965 Trainer Vince Smith.

DEATH OF THE DAY
1995 Farmer and trainer John Webber, 69, who rode over 70 point-to-point winners and handled good jumpers like The Snipe, Knock Hill and Land Afar.

CELEBRITY OF THE DAY
2009 Controversial Joey Barton, out of football for disciplinary reasons, was able to celebrate the win of one of his five 2yos, Electric Feel 15/2, at Newmarket.

16 MAY

SIGNIFICANT EVENT

2009 The favourite, Rachel Alexandra, winner of the Kentucky Oaks, became the first filly to win the Preakness Stakes since 1924, and the first to run in it since 1999, as she beat Kentucky Derby winner Mine That Bird into second place, ridden by Calvin Borel – who won on both the first two in their previous races. For the first time Pimlico banned beer cans from infield areas and only sold beer in plastic cups after a craze for throwing beer cans out of control.

STRANGE EVENT

1832 King William IV threw an eve of Derby banquet at St James's Palace for Jockey Club members, during the course of which he solemnly presented the Club with a gold-mounted hoof of the great racehorse Eclipse – as you would.

OTHER EVENTS

1884 The first maiden to win the Kentucky Derby was Buchanan, 3/1, ridden by Isaac Murphy.

1925 The Kentucky Derby was first broadcast on network radio. It was won by black colt Flying Ebony, 3.15/1.

1959 Bali Ha'i was the Queen Mother's first Flat winner, at Sandown. He was ridden by Willie Snaith and trained by Cecil Boyd-Rochfort.

1967 Jockey Richard Grubb rode seven winners from eight mounts at Woodbine, Canada.

1992 Prolific jockey Eddie Hide came out of retirement to ride 10/1 chance Charming Gift to victory at Newmarket in the Cambridge Evening News Celebrity Riders' Handicap over one mile.

2009 David and Patricia Thompson won a seventh Juddmonte Lockinge Stakes between them as their Virtual was a 6/1 winner of the Newbury feature.

QUOTE OF THE DAY

'Hang me, you see I won, that's enough for you.' Even in the 18th century there were stroppy sportsmen – not least top jockey William Clift who on this day in 1793 rode Waxy to win the Derby then in response to a question from owner the Duke of Dorset snapped tetchily at him. Tough chap, though – aged 80 he would reportedly walk from Newmarket to Bury St Edmunds - a mere 28 miles - 'just to give my legs a stretch.'

BIRTHDAYS

1935 Jockey-turned TV pundit, Jimmy Lindley. He won the 1963 2,000 Guineas on Only For Life, the 1964 St Leger on Indiana and the 1966 2,000 Guineas on Kashmir II. In 1957 Lindley finished thid on Retour de Flamme in the Champion Hurdle.

1952 Owner trainer of Lochtillum, Jamie Douglas-Home.

1956 Jockey Robert Kington.

1957 Trainer Nigel Twiston-Davies, Grand National winner with Earth Summit (1997) and Bindaree (2002).

1960 Kevin Hodgson, who rode Polly's Brother to win the 1983 Ayr Gold Cup.

1961 Trainer John Joseph Murphy.

1989 Jump jockey Brian Toomey.

FIRST OF THE DAY

1973 Eyrly won at Goodwood, giving jockey John Reid his first success.

CELEBRITY OF THE DAY

2009 The Princess Royal was at the Golden Valley Hunt's point-to-point meeting at Bredwardine, Herefordshire to see her home-bred mare Dhu Loch win a maiden race – trained by her daughter, Zara Phillips, whose second winner it was.

17 MAY

SIGNIFICANT EVENT
1969 Bill O'Gorman rode Celestial Cloud at Ripon to give Henry Cecil his first winner as a trainer, on the same day that former champion jockey Scobie Breasley sent out his first winner, Benroy, at Lingfield. And Right Tack won the Irish 2,000 Guineas at the Curragh to add to the Newmarket version, becoming the first to do the double.

STRANGE EVENT
1954 Former editor of the *Racing Post* Graham Rock was agent for South African jockey Michael 'Muis' Roberts who, born on this date, was coming to England for a crack at the 1992 title. Rock called to ask me his odds – and staked £100 at the offered 100/1. Roberts, first to ride 200 winners in a season in his native land, duly obliged.

OTHER EVENTS
1868 The first meeting at Berlin's Hoppegarten.
1924 7/4 favourite Black Gold won the 50th Kentucky Derby, ridden by John Mooney for trainer Hedley Webb.
1930 For the first time, a starting machine was used to get the Kentucky Derby field running. Gallant Fox was the winner at 6/5.
1948 Newport racecourse in Wales staged its last jumps meeting. Only pony races were staged there while the course staggered on for a further year.
1969 Henry Cecil sent out his first winner, Celestial Cloud, 5/1, ridden by Bill O'Gorman at Ripon.
1992 Culture Vulture (131/10) (Richard Quinn/Paul Cole) was the first English-trained winner of the French 1,000 Guineas since Fairy Legend in 1927.
1997 Mallow, now known as Cork, reopened after a two-and-a-half year shutdown.

QUOTE OF THE DAY
2009 *'More painful than any injury I've had from a fall. Women tell me that on the pain scale it's second only to giving birth.'* Jump jockey Noel Fehily after recovering from kidney stone treatment.

BIRTHDAYS
1945 Racing journalist and author, and sometime broadcaster, Jonathan Powell, whose book *Champion's Story* (about Grand National-winning Bob Champion and his fight against cancer) was made into one of the better racing films.
1954 Michael Roberts, 11 times South African Champion jockey with 203 wins in his best season, even before coming to England in 1992.
1962 Brian Storey, who rode Mighty Mark to win the 1988 Scottish National.
1963 Trainer Karl Burke, who rode 48 winners from 900 rides as jockey.

FIRST OF THE DAY
1875 An estimated 10,000 watched the first Kentucky Derby at Louisville Jockey Club track, later known as Churchill Downs. It was won by Aristides, ridden by Oliver Lewis and trained by Andy Anderson.

CELEBRITY OF THE DAY
1957 The Queen enjoyed her first treble as Pall Mall, Atlas and Might And Main all won at Haydock.

18 MAY

SIGNIFICANT EVENT
1959 Willie Carson's racecourse debut, fifth on Marija at Redcar.

STRANGE EVENT
2009 'I'm sitting a Spanish exam tomorrow and the headmaster thinks I'm revising' admitted 17-year-old South Wales schoolboy David Pritchard who rode his first Flat winner, Corking in an amateur riders' handicap at Bath. Corking price, too – 20/1

OTHER EVENTS
1820 Sailor won the Derby – the only horse ever to do so on his birthday.

1898 Racing began at Southwell on the Rolleston course.

1929 A 2/1 chance, gelding Clyde Van Dusen won the 55th Kentucky Derby, trained by, er, Clyde Van Dusen, but ridden by Linus McAtee.

1937 Bill Wightman saddled his first winner when Sunny Peace, ridden by Bruce Hobbs, went in at Buckfastleigh.

1965 Derby-winning Ernie Johnson's first winner, Abel, 20/1, at York.

1976 Six days after his racecourse debut, Steve Cauthen rode a River Downs hat-trick.

1985 Lester Piggott on Liquidator took on John Francome on Shangoseer in a match on the Flat at Warwick. Piggott won after Francome declared 'Whatever beats me will win.'

1988 Mtoto won the £15,000 Festival Stakes at Goodwood, but along with the other five runners was disqualified for taking the wrong course, and the race voided. Marker dolls had been left in the wrong place. No prize money was paid.

1991 US raider Fourstars Allstar, ridden by Mike Smith and trained by Irish-born Leo O'Brien, won the Irish 2,000 Guineas at 9/1. He was the first Irish Classic winner from the States.

1994 Champion Aussie trainer Lee Freedman landed his 100th Group win when Durbridge won the Hollingdale Cup on the Gold Coast.

2009 Fears that jump racing in Australia was facing extinction receded when Racing Victoria Ltd voted to lift the ban imposed on the sport after three horses died in two days. With jumping already outlawed in New South Wales a ban in Victoria would have resulted in big problems.

2009 Having sponsored the 'Will You Marry Me Jodie Baker Maiden Auction Stakes' at Southwell, Andy Simpson would have had egg on his face had his girlfriend – yes, Jodie Baker – who had known nothing about it, turned him down when he went down on one knee to propose in the parade ring. She said yes.

QUOTE OF THE DAY
2009 *'Flat racing's just a completely different category. I think we're the Manchester United compared to the relegated Southampton of Flat racing.'* Wealthy owner Andy Stewart, who went on to say of the Flat: 'The whole thing's pomposity, it's public school. They've really got no clue'. Not a fan, then.

BIRTHDAYS
1930 Jockey Liam Ward, who rode Sindon to win the 1958 Irish Derby and Nijinsky to win the same race in 1970. He was Irish champion in 1959 and '61.

1947 Brian Fletcher, who won Grand Nationals on Red Rum in 1973 and '74 and Red Alligator in 1968.

1960 Channel 4's Lesley Graham.

FIRST OF THE DAY
1882 'Hurdles, stone walls and water jumps' made up the course when Churchill Downs, USA held its first steeplechase meeting.

CELEBRITY OF THE DAY
1949 Keyboard whiz, former Yes member Rick Wakeman, born. An owner with John Webber.

19 MAY

SIGNIFICANT EVENT
1995 Former jockey Paul Cook was awarded damages of £352,000 by a High Court Judge as compensation for a fall at Doncaster which ended his career some six years earlier.

STRANGE EVENT
2009 The horse George Baker, trained by George Baker, and ridden by George Baker, contested a race at Leicester, finishing third at 33/1. Owner? Oh, Harry Findlay.

OTHER EVENTS
1928 Reigh Count beat 21 others to win the 54th Kentucky Derby at a shade over evens, then a year later came to England, winning the Coronation Cup and finishing runner-up in the Gold Cup at Ascot.

1947 With two winners at Worcester, Gordon Richards set a world record of 3,261 winners, going past Belgian champion Sam Heapy.

1994 Bootle sheet metal worker Frank Burton won £199,847.20 from Ladbrokes for a £2.86 Lucky 7 Bingo bet in which he found winners at 8/1; 4/1; 6/1; 5/1; 33/1 (dead-heat); 6/1 and 7/2.

1995 Ten punters won £21,000 each on the first ever off-course French Jackpot run on the first seven races at Chantilly.

1996 Trainer Wayne Lukas's incomparable Triple Crown winning streak was trampled in the Preakness Stakes at Pimlico by a horse named Louis Quatorze. The jockey Lukas abandoned, Pat Day, switched to Louis Quatorze only because Lukas stripped him of the mount on Prince of Thieves, rode his third consecutive Preakness winner but claimed no revenge. The past two years, Day had delivered a Preakness victory for Lukas as the trainer assembled an unmatched six-race winning streak in the Kentucky Derby, Preakness and Belmont stakes.

2009 A rally was held to draw attention to the financial crisis threatening racing in Ohio if courses are not permitted 'expanded gaming to meet competition from tracks in neighbouring states'.

QUOTE OF THE DAY
'If you want to ride for me you haven't a chance unless you come over to my place and sleep with me and the owner tonight.' Jockey-turned trainer Vicky Haigh, born today in 1970, on how it was for a young female rider in less enlightened days, after approaching an anonymous trainer about riding his horses.

BIRTHDAYS
1941 Trainer Mick Ryan, who won the Irish 1,000 Guineas with Katies, as well as every Dutch Classic. He trained for flamboyant punter Terry Ramsden.

1955 Jockey Padge – Padraic – Gill, rider of Anaglog's Daughter and Belsir. One of the few jockeys to list a fall as a highlight of his career! The tumble in question was from Royal Appointment at the 23rd fence of the 1985 Grand National.

1957 Jockey David Wilkinson.

1977 Lambourn trainer Tor (Victoria) Sturgis.

DEATH OF THE DAY
1838 Promising jockey Samuel Day, son of top trainer-jockey John Barham Day, just 19, died after taking a fall whilst out hunting. He had already won the 1837 St Leger, the youngest jockey to win the Classic.

FIRST OF THE DAY
1875 Vinaigrette was the tasty first winner of the Kentucky Oaks, then run over one and half miles, collecting $1,175.

20 MAY

SIGNIFICANT EVENT
1943 Vincent O'Brien saddled his first winner, Oversway, at Limerick.

STRANGE EVENT
1887 Aged just 13, Mornington Cannon rode his first winner, Flint, at Salisbury. Trainer Charles Morton gave him a sovereign, suggesting he use it to buy sweets.

OTHER EVENTS
1784 For the first time, the Derby was run over the current distance of 1m4f (previously a mile), with Colonel O'Kelly's 3/1 favourite Sergeant striping the ten-strong opposition.

1863 Macaroni's Derby victory re-established Newmarket as a leading training venue after criticism that the ground there was too firm in summer. The victory pleased a local vicar, who was allowed to celebrate by ringing All Saints Church bells despite the objections of winning trainer Jem Gooding, based at Palace House stables, who detested the sound.

1879 Lord Murphy, 11/10 winner of the Kentucky Derby, who became the first such to compete in England, but without success.

1930 Ron Smyth rode his first winner, Maryland Point at Newmarket.

1964 A world record for the most races won by an owner in one day, as Audley Farm, USA saw eight of its representatives win at six different tracks – Aqueduct, Ak-Sar-Ben; Greenwood; Lincoln Downs; Pimlico; Suffolk Downs.

1967 Peter Makin broke his training duck, winning the Thirsk Hunt Cup with 11/4 favourite Danella.

1974 Stuart Webster rode his first winner, Hei Land Jamie at Pontefract.

1989 Professional gambler Paul Cooper claimed winnings of £250,000 for a £16.50 Tricast at Thirsk as Miss Daisy, 20/1, Halvoya, 25/1 and Roysia Boy, 33/1 were 1,2,3.

1992 Newton Abbot trainer Gerald Penfold was stunned when hunter chaser Seal Prince, the 9/4 favourite, collapsed and died after winning at Worcester – in the same race in which Penfold's best horse, John Sam, had been killed when favourite 12 months earlier.

1997 Mark Birch, who rode 92 winners in his best season, retired.

2007 Curlin won the 132nd Preakness Stakes, beating Kentucky Derby winner Street Sense into second in a photo finish.

QUOTE OF THE DAY
1994 *'I did feel at one time that there was a vendetta against me among the stewards in the north,'* recalled trainer Mary Reveley, who sent out Lady Donoghue, her 500th winner over the sticks, at Fakenham, on this day, when she retired in 2004.

BIRTHDAYS
1935 Jockey Brian Connorton.
1940 US-based trainer Leo O'Brien.
1967 Jump jockey Jonothan Lower.
1967 Flat jockey Jimmy Quinn.
1970 Flat jockey Tom McLaughlin.
1979 Top French jockey Christophe Lemaire, rider of Divine Proportions, Pride, Natagora and Stacelita.

DEATHS OF THE DAY
1995 Breeder of two Arc winners, Trempolino, 1987, and Subotica, 1992, Paul de Moussac, 71.
2004 Eldest son of trainer Alan, Stephen Jarvis, who had ridden over 50 winners, 44.

FIRST OF THE DAY
1995 For the first time professional jockeys rode in a modern Arab race in Britain when Richard Hills, Michael Wigham, Paul Eddery and Willie Ryan took part in the Emirates Arabian Sprint at Lingfield.

21 MAY

SIGNIFICANT EVENT
1994 Willie Carson rode his 100th Group winner, Mehthaaf (5/2) in the Irish 1,000 Guineas.

STRANGE EVENT
2009 Days after image consultants had suggested racegoers were divided into traditional 'Brian' types and younger 'Bens', an owner applied to name his horse Areyouabrianoraben. Weatherbys Director of Racing, Dr Paull Khan, who you have to believe was not joking, told the owner the name had been turned down 'because there were too many syllables in it. There is a guideline that there shouldn't be more than seven syllables, and this was eight.' You couldn't ... fill in the rest with words of fewer than eight syllables!

OTHER EVENTS
1788 Both horses in a 1m match at York carried an astonishing 30st. Mr Maynard's mare ran (?) out the winner against Mr Baker's horse.

1801 Sir Charles Bunbury's Eleanor became the first filly to win the Derby. Shortly before the race Cox, her trainer, died having told the priest ministering to him 'Depend upon it, that Eleanor is a hell of a mare'. A first death-bed tip! Eleanor also won the Oaks the next day.

1949 My Babu, the 2,000 Guineas winner, won the 7f Victoria Cup at Hurst Park under 9st 7lb. He was trained by F L (Sam)Armstrong and ridden by Charlie Smirke.

1964 Lincoln racecourse closed. Bruce Hobbs saddled 9/1 Twinkle Dee (W Carr) in the final race.

1994 Recently retired jump jockey Chris Grant returned to the saddle for his first ever Flat ride, in the Subaru Handicap Celebrity Riders' Race at Newmarket, partnering Can Can Man, Ronnie Beggan won on Overpower.

1994 D Wayne Lukas sent out Tabasco Cat, ridden by Pat Day, to win the Preakness Stakes in front of a record crowd of 99,834.

1994 'If you don't win, I'll kill you' owner Clement Freud told jockey Alan Munro, as he went to ride Nagnagnag at Lingfield. they finished second – but survived.

1995 Having previously ridden just seven winners in his fledgling career, 16-year-old Italian jockey Ricardo Cangiano rode six winners from eight mounts at Florence.

2008 Ayr's first scheduled meeting of the year was called off 20 minutes before the first race after an area of false ground was discovered.

QUOTE OF THE DAY
Champion Aussie trainer Colin Hayes died this day in 1999, aged 75. He trained 5,333 winners for A$40m and won 98 Group 1 races, including two Melbourne Cups – one, Beldale Ball in 1980, for Robert Sangster. He was the subject of perhaps the shortest ever obituary, by racing writer James Underwood: *'Colin Hayes, Genius.'*

BIRTHDAYS
1933 Aussie jockey Bill Pyers.
1951 US trainer Tim Ritchey (Afleet Alex).
1962 Newmarket trainer Giles Bravery.

DEATHS OF THE DAY
1974 Owner of Classic winners Blue Peter, Ocean Swell and Sandwich, 92-year-old Lord Rosebery – aka Albert Edward Harry Meyer Archibald Primrose, sixth Earl of Rosebery.

2006 Cited by Martin Pipe as one of the major inspirations and influences on his career, trainer Les Kennard, 85. He dominated training in the west country in the 1960s and '70s.

CELEBRITY OF THE DAY
1944 Owner with Michael Grassick, and Irish President, Mary Robinson born.

22 MAY

SIGNIFICANT EVENT
1992 A jury awarded former jockey Benito Narvaez $4.4m after ruling that officials at Tampa Bay Downs in Florida were responsible for a 1990 fall which left him paralysed.

STRANGE EVENT
1844 The most scandalous of races was run. Running Rein finished first in the Derby, but was subsequently disqualified when he was revealed to be 4yo Maccabeus. The race was awarded to Colonel Peel's Orlando. In the race itself, favourite The Ugly Buck was the target of foul riding and second favourite Ratan was not only 'got at' but also pulled by his jockey. Leander was struck into and had to be destroyed – at which point evidence suggested he too was older than three.

OTHER EVENTS
1857 'We can but deeply deplore the blackguardism which, once a year, has been allowed to establish its saturnalia in the quiet village of Harpenden' ranted a local paper in Hertfordshire about the regular race meetings.
1867 It snowed before and after the Derby, won by Hermit, whose owner Henry Chaplin won £120,000 by backing the 1000-15 winner.
1989 Madraco, 12/1, Liam Codd's first winner as a trainer, won at Bath in track record time.
1990 Kawtuban, 2/1, won at Salisbury to give Willie Carson his 3,000th British winner.
1992 Yorkshire student Emily Debenham, 21, rode her first winner in America when Victory Leader won at Garden State, New Jersey.
1993 Long retired Edward Hide landed his 2,593rd winner, after coming back to ride in the Classic FM Celebrity Handicap at Newmarket.

QUOTE OF THE DAY
'My more morbid friends ask what it is like to fall in a race, but like the boxer who never talks about the knockout punch, I do not like discussing it. What goes on is between me and the dirt' declared jockey Tom Scudamore, born today in 1982.

BIRTHDAYS
1935 Malton trainer Jimmy Fitzgerald whose Forgive 'n Forget won the 1985 Cheltenham Gold Cup.
1947 Trainer Giles Pritchard-Gordon.
1955 Jim McGrath, of Channel 4 and formerly of Timeform.
1964 Trainer Graham Motion.
1973 Four-times Canadian champion jockey Patrick Husbands.
1975 Flat jockey Matthew Henry.
1977 Irish jockey Pat Smullen.

DEATHS OF THE DAY
2002 Four-time champion trainer Major Dick Hern, 81. Responsible for 26 Classic victories, winning every British Classic at least twice, he collected six St Legers and in 1974 landed the 1,000 Guineas-Prix de Diane double with Highclere for the Queen. He broke his neck in 1984 but continued to train from a wheelchair. In 1989 the racing world was divided by the news that the Queen had decided Hern should leave West Ilsley Stables at the end of the season. He was awarded a CBE in 1998.
2007 Sweden's most successful trainer, Michael Khan, 58. He was champion 15 times at Taby racecourse and Homosassas won him the 1985 Swedish Triple Crown.

FIRST OF THE DAY
1828 The Derby, run for the first time on a Thursday, produced its first dead-heat, between Cadland, ridden by Jem Robinson, and The Colonel – Bill Scott. The former won the run-off.

23 MAY

SIGNIFICANT EVENT
2009 Aidan O'Brien won an incredible ninth successive Irish Classic as Johnny Murtagh guided 6/4 favourite Mastercraftsman to victory in the Irish 2,000 Guineas, O'Brien's sixth and Murtagh's third win in the race.

STRANGE EVENT
2009 It was reported by the *Guardian* that the Brighton Cup, a trophy worth £15,000 and dating from 1924, had been 'rediscovered' by the Sussex track which began planning a race for which it could be presented.

OTHER EVENTS
1853 Lexington won for the first time, although he was then named Darley. Re-named by owner Richard Ten Broeck, he had a fine career before becoming the most successful US stallion, leading the sires list for 16 seasons.

1873 Seven runners contested the first Preakness Stakes, with Survivor winning by a ten lengths.

1955 Alexandra Park staged London's first evening meeting.

1966 Tony Murray rode his first winner, Guardian Oak at Windsor.

1984 John Francome set a career record for a jump jockey, passing Stan Mellor, when Rhythmic Pastures became his 1,035th winner.

1989 Racing was delayed at Beverley – because of a bullock on the track.

1990 Lafitte Pincay became the first jockey to take his prize money earnings past $150m in his career.

2009 Preston school 'lollipop' man Adrian Underwood, who paid 7,500 euros for Look Busy, saw the mare take her winnings to over £200,000 as she won the Temple Stakes at Haydock at 15/2, ridden by Slade O'Hara.

2009 Fifth in the jockey table at Fair Hill, USA, Irish jockey Padge Berry suffered a fall, causing the 30yo's retirement.

QUOTE OF THE DAY
'The lovely thing about having older horses like Marlborough is that you get to know them so well, like reading a favourite book. He tells you if anything isn't quite right – he can nearly talk.' Nicky Henderson in 2004 who, on this date in 1984, passed £100,000 in earnings in a season when Spartan Daisy won at Worcester.

BIRTHDAYS
1928 Willie 'Pocket Hercules' Snaith, who rode Landau to win the 1954 Sussex Stakes at Goodwood for the Queen.

1928 Trainer of triple Champion Hurdler Persian War, Colin Davies, formerly a very useful racing driver who, as a jockey, completed the 1964 Grand National on 66/1-shot Claymore in 13th place behind 18/1 winner Team Spirit.

1953 Trainer Kevin Morgan.

1973 Jump jockey Mattie Batchelor.

1977 Australian jockey Craig Williams.

DEATHS OF THE DAY
1985 Jockey Macer Gifford, 40, of motor neurone disease. He rode 230 winners including Larbawn in the 1968 Whitbread Gold Cup.

CELEBRITY OF THE DAY
1936 Owner Robert Sangster was born, son of football pools promoter Vernon Sangster. He won the Derby with The Minstrel and Golden Fleece, and his Alleged was a dual Arc winner.

24 MAY

SIGNIFICANT EVENT
2009 Aidan O'Brien's run of nine straight Irish Classic victories was ended in the 1,000 Guineas as the David Wachman-trained 5/2 favourite, Again, won – ridden by Johnny Murtagh, who had never won the race before and became the first rider since Joe Canty in 1946 to win both Guineas in the same year.

STRANGE EVENT
1993 Frankie Dettori was refused a licence to race in Hong Kong – possibly a decision related to his recent police warning for possession of drugs.

OTHER EVENTS
1798 Sir Harry was the first Derby winner sired by a previous winner, namely Sir Peter Teazle.
1848 Surplice won the Derby. He had been sold, to his great regret, by Lord George Bentinck whose original idea it was that Parliament should take a day off to attend Epsom, which they did for forty years until the political climate changed.
1918 The Jockey Club announced: 'There must be considerable curtailment of racing during the present season' – and that racing must be limited to Newmarket after May 31.
1995 John Dunlop sent out Subya, 11/2, to win at Goodwood, a fourth consecutive Lupe Stakes for him. Son Ed won the opener with Marguerite Day, 7/1, the first time they had saddled winners on the same day.
1995 The Hong Kong season of French jockey Eric Legrix ended when he was banned for six meetings for intentionally striking apprentice K C Chan with his whip. On the same card a punter took half of the biggest dividend in HK racing history – HK$48,689,015 (£4,023,886) – by finding the first three home in three set races, the Tripletrio, with the rest carried over.
2009 Aidan O'Brien's son Joseph, 16, made his racecourse debut riding unplaced Coat of Arms for his dad at the Curragh.

QUOTE OF THE DAY
2009 *'A Tyson among jockeys.'* Trainer Jean-Paul Gallorini called 15-times French champion jump jockey Christophe Pieux on this day – presumably meaning it to be a compliment – after he had to be carried into the paddock after winning his third Grand Steeple-Chase de Paris at Auteuil on Remember Rose, breaking a toe and severing a tendon after hitting a rail.

BIRTHDAYS
1929 Owner of six-chase winner April Rose and 1974 National third (behind Red Rum) Charles Dickens, the Queen's representative at Ascot Sir Piers Bengough.
1968 US trainer Doug O'Neill, whose star performers include Lava Man and Stevie Wonderboy.
1968 Jockeys John Egan and Gary Hind.

DEATHS OF THE DAY
1947 The Earl of Harewood, 64, a member of the Jockey Club since 1920 and senior steward in 1940.
1989 Great racemare Triptych, placed in the Arc, Prix de Diane, and Washington DC International, killed after running into a truck at Claiborne Farm, Kentucky.
1992 German jockey Hans Strompen, 34, in a fall at Baden-Baden when his mount Sherlock Holmes rolled on him. He had ridden over 100 winners.

CELEBRITY OF THE DAY
'John McCririck calling 'Mummy, Mummy, Mummy!' with his head in his hands when things got a little fraught a couple of seasons ago – very worrying!' Channel 4 racing presenter Alice Plunkett telling the *Racing Post* this day in 2009 about a disturbing scene she witnessed.

25 MAY

SIGNIFICANT EVENT
1887 Making his racecourse debut, George Baird's interestingly named Merry Hampton was the 100/9 winner of the Derby.

STRANGE EVENT
2009 Five racegoers were injured in a freak accident before racing at Goodwood when a car being parked by a a racecourse vet accelerated backwards through a protective rail and shot down a bank, colliding with other cars, some of which were occupied. Racing was delayed for some 30 minutes.

OTHER EVENTS
1814 England had Eclipse, and now the USA produced on this day a foal by Duroc out of Miller's Damsel, named American Eclipse, which also retired undefeated, beating all-comers including in a $20,000 three-heat showdown with Henry at New York's Union track, with $200,000 gambled on the outcome.

1864 For the last time the Derby-winning owner was required to contribute towards policing the course and paying judge's fees. William I'Anson's Blair Athol was the 14/1 winner.

1984 Peter Niven rode his first winner, Loch Brandy, at Sedgefield.

1898 Jeddah became the first 100/1 Derby winner, under German born rider Otto Madden.

1991 Joie de Soir, down the field at Southwell in November 1990, became the first horse to begin on the all-weather and go on to win a listed race when scoring at 16//1 in the Crawley Warren Heron Stakes at Kempton, trained by Fulke Johnson Houghton and ridden by Paul Eddery.

1992 Daughter of Prime Minister John, Elizabeth Major made her riding debut on Milly Black in a charity race at Huntingdon. She fell as she passed the post in sixth in the 2m race.

1997 Having enjoyed a first Classic win a day earlier in the Irish 1,000 Guineas with Classic Park, Aidan O'Brien saddled the 3/1 Irish 2,000 Guineas winner, Desert King.

2009 The last race at Leicester's evening meeting was delayed by eight minutes when five of the 13 runners proved unruly at the start and were withdrawn.

2009 41 years after first winning the Zetland Gold Cup with Castle Yard, the Queen won the Redcar feature again with Kingdom of Fife, 9/4, ridden by Ryan Moore for Michael Stoute.

QUOTE OF THE DAY
'Training with the St Helens rugby league team,' answered jockey Julie Bowker asked for her favourite recreation, and who rode her first winner, Misha, at Doncaster this day in 1985.

BIRTHDAYS
1945 Trainer Fred Watson.

1953 Trainer Kim Bailey, who won the Grand National with Mister Frisk, the Cheltenham Gold Cup with Master Oats and the Champion Hurdle with Alderbrook.

1955 Trainer John Mackie.

1957 Trainer of Sergeant Cecil, Rod Millman.

1960 Jockey Nigel Coleman, who won the 1989 Triumph Hurdle on Ikdam.

1978 Flat jockey Neil Pollard.

DEATH OF THE DAY
2009 Ted Walsh's favourite horse Commanche Court, ten times a jumps winner, including the 1997 Triumph Hurdle, was put down aged 16 after suffering a colic attack.

CELEBRITY OF THE DAY
2009 Owned and bred by Prince Charles and the Duchess of Cornwall, Royal Superlative was fourth in a maiden stakes at Chepstow.

26 MAY

SIGNIFICANT EVENT
1909 King Edward VII became the only reigning monarch to win the Derby, courtesy of 2,000 Guineas winner Minoru, ridden by Herbert Jones.

STRANGE EVENT
1994 The smallest ever Tote Jackpot dividend of 15.6/1 was declared after Brighton was abandoned after just one race because of heavy rain. I Should Cocoa was the 13/2 winner.

OTHER EVENTS
1773 'A poor wretch was detected picking a gentleman's pocket at Epsom Races, and was so severely ducked, that he could not have escaped with his life, but for the interposition of his R H the Duke of Cumberland, who displayed upon this occasion a humanity that must endear him to all considerate Englishmen' reported the *Morning Chronicle*.

1869 A rare northern-trained Derby winner, as 11/8 favourite Pretender, trained at Tupgill, Middleham by Tom Dawson, and partnered by Johnny Osborne, beat 21 rivals.

1886 Fred Archer landed his fifth and final Derby victory on 4/9 Ormonde.

1932 Doug Smith rode his first winner, Denia, at Salisbury. 11 years later he rode his first Royal winner, Knight's Daughter at Newmarket in the King George VI.

1937 Major Derrick Candy – father of Henry – trained his first winner, his mother's 5yo Mountain Ash at Bath.

1979 Hello Louis got Mary Reveley – then a livery yard owner – off the mark as a trainer.

1988 16yo Grey Tarquin won a Taunton handicap chase.

1990 Versatile trainer David Elsworth became the first to complete the Irish Grand National (Desert Orchid) – Irish 1,000 Guineas double when In The Groove , 5/1, landed the latter at the Curragh to become Elsworth's first Classic winner.

2009 Ayr clerk of the course Katherine Self, 36, announced that she was stepping down – to join the Coastguards.

QUOTE OF THE DAY
2009 *'The sight of them, probably being whipped, staggering through heavy ground at the end of a long-distance chase. I wonder if new racegoers find it appealing?'* David Ashforth nominates 'Exhausted Horses' as the top of 12 things he will not miss about British racing after relocating to Kentucky.

BIRTHDAYS
1916 Professional gambler who made fortunes betting on the outcome of photo finishes, Alex Bird, who died in 1991.

1916 Trainer-owner-breeder of Derby winners Blakeney and Morston, Arthur Budgett, the third Old Etonian of the century to train a Blue Riband winner.

1948 Jockey Martin O'Halloran, associated with Bachelor's Hall and Celtic Ryde.

1969 Jockey Declan O'Shea.

1973 BBC TV racing presenter Rishi Persad.

1978 Channel 4 racing presenter Emma Spencer.

DEATHS OF THE DAY
1933 Owner-gambler Horatio Bottomley MP, who brought off a £50,000 coup when Northern Farmer, 20/1, won the Stewards' Cup in 1899. Once asked in court, 'You keep racehorses, I believe?', he replied 'No, they keep me.'

1990 Former dual Champion Hurdler of 1973 and '75, Comedy of Errors, put down aged 24.

1992 The 1975 Derby winner Grundy, 20, who died in Japan.

CELEBRITY OF THE DAY
1908 Actor and owner Robert Morley born.

27 MAY

SIGNIFICANT EVENT
1857 Blink Bonny won the Derby – and two days later, the Oaks. She was 'pulled up' in the St Leger by her jockey.

STRANGE EVENT
1996 Starter John Leech let the field for a Redcar race out of the stalls, without realizing one of the runners, Lostris, had not been loaded. He managed to alert the recall man to call the field back. Lostris finished sixth to Adrain Spirit.

OTHER EVENTS
1846 Pyrrhus won the first officially timed Derby, in 2m 55s, winning by a neck from Sir Tatton Sykes, whose jockey Bill Scott was drunk and missed the break.

1950 Charles Cooper lost his NH riding allowance after winning his 15th race on Paricutin at Hereford. All of the other 14 had been on the same horse.

1980 Rednael, ridden by Tommy Carmody at Uttoxeter, was trainer Tony Dickinson's final winner of 562 over 13 seasons.

1985 Spend A Buck picked up record winnings for a single race of $2.6m when winning the Jersey Derby in New Jersey.

1990 196,517 paid to see the Japanese Derby at Fuchu, Tokyo.

2007 The owner of Smoakey Oakey missed a 4/1 Newmarket success – Dame Judy Dench was away filming.

2007 Holly Glover, Debbie Gray, Claire Miles and Diane Kennett, Hereford racecourse staff appeared in the Racing Post clad in hats and, apparently, nothing else, to promote the track's Ladies' Day.

2009 12yo Chabrimal Minster 8/1, won Cartmel's Grand Veterans Handicap Chase for the third year in a row – and was immediately retired by trainer Richard Ford.

2009 Czech born Natalia Gemelova, 29, was back riding competitively just nine weeks after giving birth to Nicole Margaret (her partner is jockey David Allan) on March 21. 'I've found being a mother harder than being a jockey' she said before riding fourth placed Cativo Cavallino at Lingfield.

QUOTE OF THE DAY
'Most riders beat horses as if they were guards in slave labour camps. "Shoe" treated them as if he were asking them to dance,' wrote *LA Times* writer Jim Murray of US riding legend Willie – Bill – Shoemaker, who on this date in 1981 rode his 8,000th winner on War Allied at Hollywood Park.

BIRTHDAYS
1917 Former champion jump jockey Jack Dowdeswell.

1943 Former champion apprentice David Yates.

1948 Trainer Patrick Haslam.

1950 An official starter in Hong Kong, former jockey Philip Waldron whose first winner was Aldie at Bath in 1969 and who was runner-up in the 1980 Derby on Master Willie.

1966 Moreton-in-Marsh trainer John Gallagher.

1970 Trainer Neil King.

DEATHS OF THE DAY
1835 Jockey Benjamin Smith, 65, winner of six St Legers. He once won on Ironside at York despite a broken leg after being kicked at the start.

1992 Owner Charles St George, 66. His best horses included Arc winner Rheingold, St Leger winner Bruni and Oaks winner Ginevra.

CELEBRITY OF THE DAY
1932 Writer, racegoer and punter Jeffrey Bernard, played on stage in *Jeffrey Bernard Is Unwell* by Peter O'Toole and James Bolam, born. Legend has it he once threw up close to, or perhaps even on, the Queen Mother.

28 MAY

SIGNIFICANT EVENT
1984 Mister Donut was Michael Dickinson's 374th and final British jumps winner, at Fakenham, as 1/3 favourite.

STRANGE EVENT
2009 Newcastle staged a card featuring race names such as 'Botox & Fillers Maiden Fillies Stakes'; 'Liposculpture Selling Stakes' and 'Breast Augmentation Handicap'. The programme also featured the 'Jade Goody Foundation Handicap'.

OTHER EVENTS
1839 The Grandstand at Ascot was used for the first time – admission 5s - 25p.
1879 'Because Sir Bevys was the hero of one of my early poems' beamed poet laureate Alfred Tennyson, explaining why he staked £5 on the horse of that name, who was the 20/1 winner of the 100th Derby on this date in 1879.
1884 St Gatien, 100/8, and Harvester, 100/7, dead-heated in the Derby but the owners declined a run-off. Next day, though, Harvester's owner, Sir John Willoughby, objected to St Gatien on the grounds of incorrect entry, only to think better of it and withdraw his objection.
1952 After he won the Derby on Tulyar, sparky jockey Charlie Smirke couldn't resist declaring to all and sundry of the Marcus Marsh-trained 11/2-shot, and fifth winner for the Aga Khan, 'What did I Tulyar?!'
1984 Don't Touch at Fontwell put John Francome one winner ahead of Stan Mellor's record total of 1,035.
1990 Martin Pipe saddled nine winners at six different meetings.
1994 Lester Piggott rode a double – and was fined half a million. Fortunately for him, the winners were at Capannelle, Rome and the fine, for failing to make the weight for another mount, was in lira - about £200.
1999 Trainer James Given sent out his first winner, I Cried For You 8/1, at Nottingham.
2000 Edgar Prado rode to his 4,000th victory on Thunder Breeze, at Belmont Park.

QUOTE OF THE DAY
2009 *'I approached him as if he were a horse'* explained 61-year-old trainer Bill Turner, who had achieved the rare feat of breaking in and riding a zebra, Zebedee, which he bought for £4,500. 'I have broken hundreds of horses over the years and always wanted to try my hand with a zebra.'

BIRTHDAYS
1913 Popular 'gentleman'-style TV racing presenter and writer, John Rickman, who invariably doffed his hat when coming on screen.
1937 Owner-trainer of 7/1 1983 Mackeson Gold Cup winner Pounentes, Billy McGhie.
1957 Trainer Jackie Retter.
1950 Official starter Hugh Barclay.
1982 Equine artist Nichola Eddery.

FIRST OF THE DAY
1994 Mary Reveley became the first woman trainer to send out 100 winners in a jump season when Stay Awake 4/5 won at Cartmel.

CELEBRITY OF THE DAY
2009 'Looking ahead, the prognosis is very good' – TV presenter Clare Balding, 38, revealed that she had been having treatment for thyroid cancer.

29 MAY

SIGNIFICANT EVENT
1872 The Derby was run over the modern course for the first time and was won by Cremorne, the 3/1 second favourite.

STRANGE EVENT
2009 Richard Dunwoody set off from Bedford Lodge Hotel, Newmarket in his successful bid to walk 1,000 miles in 1,000 hours to raise money for four charities.

OTHER EVENTS
1769 Legendary 'Eclipse' won the Noblemen's and Gentlemen's Plate at Ascot.

1857 Two days after winning the Derby, filly Blink Bonny also won the Oaks. Her offspring Blair Athol also won the Derby, in 1864.

1860 The first meeting to be held at Randwick in Sydney.

1939 The 16-runner Golden Apple Stakes at Hurst Park, open only to horses with female owners, was won by Mrs Thurston's appropriately named Lover's Fate, ridden by, er, Dave Dick.

1939 Blue Peter won the Derby for trainer Jack Jarvis and Eph Smith, but denied tilt at Triple Crown as St Leger fell victim to the Second World War.

1946 2 yo fillies Chakoora and Uleta became the first thoroughbreds to take a transcontinental flight, from New York to California. The 2446 mile trip took 20 hours due to adverse weather conditions.

1967 Ten year old Vulmidas clocked up his tenth win in 13 Wetherby starts.

1980 A racing wedding took place as Peter Scudamore and Marilyn Kington, sister of jump jockey Robert, tied the knot.

1982 Dawn Run made her racecourse debut, unplaced in an amateurs' Flat race at Clonmel, ridden by owner Mrs Charmian Hill.

1990 Prince's Court, ridden by Kevin Mooney, at Uttoxeter, was Fulke Walwyn's last winner as a trainer.

1993 South African jockey Basil Marcus became the first jockey since 1979 to land a five-timer at Sha Tin, Hong Kong. On the same day, Kiwi horse Rough Habit became the first to win three straight runnings of Brisbane's Doomben Cup.

2009 Aidan and Anne-Marie O'Brien's son, 16-year-old Joseph, who had been 12th on his first public ride at the Curragh a few days earlier, got off the mark at the second attempt, winning at Leopardstown on 7/4 favourite Johann Zoffany, trained by his father.

QUOTE OF THE DAY
1777 *'All persons are desired to keep their dogs at home; and if any be found upon the Race-ground, it is hoped the populace will destroy them.'* Doggone harsh warning in the racecard for this day's Silver Cup meeting at Sheffield & Rotherham.

BIRTHDAYS
1863 Jockey George Barrett, who rode Common to win the 1891 2,000 Guineas, Derby and St Leger.

1927 *Sunday Express* racing writer, Tom Forrest.

1945 Innovative and highly successful trainer Martin Pipe, son of a bookie.

1979 Jump jockey Liam Cooper.

DEATH OF THE DAY
2004 Former jockey Denis Ryan, 68, who rode over 500 winners, including two in the Indian Derby. Father of jockey Willie Ryan.

CELEBRITY OF THE DAY
2009 The John Higgins Wizard of Wishaw Stakes was run at Hamilton to celebrate third World Title (1998, 2007, 2009) triumph of the snooker player.

30 MAY

SIGNIFICANT EVENT
1992 At the close of the jump season, The Laughing Lord, 7/2, won over hurdles at Stratford to give trainer Arthur Stephenson a career total of 2,951 winners, breaking the record set by Arthur Yates who trained for 50 years from the late 19th century.

STRANGE EVENT
1943 Hitler's bombs did for Torquay racecourse as the grandstand, weighing room and stabling block were destroyed in an air raid. Three years earlier over 8,000 people had attended the races there at Easter, which turned out to have been the final meeting.

OTHER EVENTS
1962 Lester Piggott was suspended until July 28 after being adjudged to have made 'no effort to win the race' when riding Ione at Lincoln to finish second behind stable companion Polly Macaw. Trainer Bob Ward's licence was withdrawn.

1981 The whole of trainer Jack Berry's family rode in public. He raced at Kempton while wife Jo and sons Alan and Martin were in action at Ayr.

1983 Record British money winner Pebbles made her debut, finishing unplaced at Sandown. She went on to win the 1984 1,000 Guineas amongst other top prizes.

1989 Monica Dickinson saddled her last runner as a public trainer, Half Decent, unplaced at Uttoxeter.

1992 For the first time a trotting race was included in the Tote Jackpot. The 2100m Prix du Tote at Lingfield, won by Turkey, contributed to a £7,869.30 payout for one winning ticket.

1992 Mary Reveley began the day needing two winners to become the first woman to train 100 winners in a season. Watertight, ridden by Peter Niven at Market Rasen, duly obliged, but her final runner on the last day of the season, Peacework in the End of Term Chase,

shattered a hind leg and was put down.

1994 Nearco Bay won at Uttoxeter to give the Queen Mother her 400th winner.

1994 Merry Master 11/8 won the R A Chase at Wetherby to bring down the curtain on trainer Roddy Armytage's 32-year career.

2009 12yo Caracciola became the oldest horse to win a Listed Race when taking the Stowe Family LLP Grand Cup at York – removing 11yo Further Flight who won the Chester Rated Stakes in 1997 from the record books. Dale Gibson rode the Nicky Henderson-trained veteran.

QUOTE OF THE DAY
'Like Linford without the lunchbox' quipped Frankie Dettori, comparing flying filly Lochsong with the Olympic gold medal-winning sprinter Linford Christie as the 'Queen of Speed' romped home in Sandown's Temple Stakes as 4/9 favourite on this day in 1994.

BIRTHDAYS
1945 Twice champion trainer Richard Hannon, who allegedly once used infant triplets Henry, Richard and Elizabeth in a unique form of gambling game Find the Lady.

1953 Former jump jockeys, twins Mark and Richard Floyd.

1953 Former champion lady rider Franca Vittadini.

1963 Trainer Alan Berry.

1965 Jockey Tony Charlton.

DEATH OF THE DAY
1967 Captain John Fawcus, 59, champion amateur jockey over jumps before the war, died after a motoring accident en route to Uttoxeter. He won the Welsh National four times, the Scottish National on three occasions, and won the latter as a trainer with Game Field in 1958.

FIRST OF THE DAY
1877 Fred Archer rode the first of his five Derby winners, Silvio.

31 MAY

SIGNIFICANT EVENT

1764 Gimcrack raced for the first time, beating five rivals at Epsom for a £50 prize. Winner of 26 of his 36 races, he is one of the few horses commemorated by a race – the important Gimcrack Stakes for 2yos at York, founded in 1846 and which entitles the winning owner to make a high-profile, often controversial speech. Incidentally, grey Gimcrack raced only twice at York - losing each time

STRANGE EVENT

1993 Female jockey Dodie Duys, and male counterpart Carl Gambadella came to blows after a hard-fought race at Suffolk Downs, Massachussets. They were separated only for Gambadella to resume hostilities by attacking Duys in the shower. Both were suspended for 15 days.

OTHER EVENTS

1865 5/2 favourite Gladiateur was the first French winner of the Derby. Also successful in the 2,000 Guineas and St Leger, he became known as the 'Avenger of Waterloo.'

1899 2/5 favourite Flying Fox won the last flag started Derby, later going on to claim the Triple Crown for trainer John Porter and jockey Mornington Cannon – Lester Piggott's great uncle. .

1961 Bred in Ireland, ridden by a French jockey, trained in England, by a French sire out of an Italian mare, 66/1 Psidium won the Derby, but never ran again.

1975 Lester Piggott rode his 3,000th British winner, at Kempton.

1980 Bob Champion rode his first winner since defeating cancer, and his first ever on the Flat, Ripon, at Fairhill, USA.

1991 Alex Greaves became the first woman in Britain to ride out her claim, with a Hamilton Park double on 11/10 chance Love Jazz and Mac Kelty 10/1,

bringing her total of winners to 75, since her first in December 1989.

1993 Ridden as usual by Derrick Morris, St Athans Lad, 8/13, chalked up his ninth course win of the season at Fontwell – a 20th century record for one horse at one course in one season. In 1787 Rockingham won 11 times at Newmarket.

1994 Ronnie Beggan announced his retirement after riding Kinda Groovy to win at Hexham – completing the feat of riding a winner at all British racecourses and every Irish jump track.

2001 Pat Day became the third jockey to ride 8000 winners when Camden Park won at Churchill Downs.

2007 Mum-to-be Stolen Glance won at Ayr. Owner Pam Cockerill said: 'I was abetter woman wen was in foal, too.'

QUOTE OF THE DAY

'You've got to get them mentally as well as physically fit' explained trainer Mark Pitman, who had ridden his last winner, Tammy's Run, at Huntingdon, trained by mum Jenny, on this day in 1993.

BIRTHS OF THE DAY

1944 Owner of Derby runner-up Master Willie, Robert Barnett, whose Time Charter won the Oaks.

1945 *Daily Mirror* 'Bouverie' tipster, Charlie Fawcus.

1963 Trainer Sylvester Kirk.

DEATHS OF THE DAY

1970 The incomparable Arkle put down, aged 13.

2002 Agent to Frankie Dettori for 12 years, Matty Cowing, 65.

CELEBRITY OF THE DAY

1785 George, Prince of Wales, had his first Ascot runner, Rosaletta, second in a two-horse race to Colonel O'Kelly's Soldier. On the same day she contested an event run in two heats over 3m, which she won.

1 JUNE

SIGNIFICANT EVENT
2007 Barely a dry eye in the house as Light Shift 13/2 restores Henry Cecil to the Classic roll of honour, after a gap of seven years, by giving the training legend his eighth Oaks win.

STRANGEST EVENT
1984 Ken Richardson found guilty by a majority of 10-2 at York Crown Court in Flockton Grey 'ringer' affair in which better and older Good Hand ran in his place at Leicester in March 1992. He was given a nine-month suspended jail sentence and costs of £100,000.

OTHER EVENTS
1881 Iroquois became the first American-bred horse to win the Derby, ridden by Fred Archer, owned by tobacco millionaire Pierre Lorillard and trained at Newmarket's Terrace House stable by Jacob Pinkus.

1904 George Thursby, Derby runner-up on John O'Gaunt, became first amateur placed in the race – a feat that has never been emulated.

1953 Gordon Richards knighted.

1957 Nickleby, at Stratford, last winner as jockey for Bryan Marshall, who rode 517 jumps winners in Britain and was champion jockey in 1947-48.

1985 Dermot Weld sent out five winners at Phoenix Park, where Sherkhraine became the first winner sired by Shergar.

1994 Erhaab, 7/2 fav, won the Derby, partnered by Willie Carson for John Dunlop. He was the latest foaled winner of the race (May 24) but not the youngest winner, which was Sailor, who won on May 18, 1820, his third birthday. Willie Ryan broke three ribs after being thrown from Foyer, who collided with 14/1 runner up King's Theatre; Erhaab was Willie Carson's fourth Derby winner in 26 rides.

1995 Tony McCoy rode his first winner for Martin Pipe – Crosula at Hereford.

2006 The new Great Leighs racecourse missed its scheduled opening date.

2009 Portable loudspeaker system introduced, to be used by all starters for jumps racing in Ireland, having been trialled at Fairyhouse and Punchestown.

QUOTE OF THE DAY
'I now regret that decision' - John Francome, ten years after he had, on this date in 1982, ridden his 120th winner of the season to draw level with the injured Peter Scudamore, then quit for the season to share the title.

BIRTHDAYS
1931 Trainer Fergie Sutherland, handler of unusually named A.20.

1943 Former dual-purpose jockey turned trainer,Ken 'Stoker' White. Partnered 1975 Champion Hurdle winner Comedy Of Errors to victory in the Irish Sweeps Hurdle and Scottish Champion Hurdle, and also won the 1970 Mackeson Gold Cup on Chatham.

DEATHS OF THE DAY
1969 Newmarket trainer William O'Gorman, 56. Like his son, specialised in sprinters, winning 1958 Stewards' Cup with Epaulette and King's Stand Stakes with Drum Beat and Majority Blue.

2000 'We're dead, mate, this is it, we're gone,' Frankie Dettori told Ray Cochrane as their light aircraft was about to crash. They survived the impact in Newmarket, but pilot Patrick Mackay did not.

2009 Vincent O'Brien, 92. Voted top of a *Racing Post* readers' poll of racing greats in 2003. Trained six Derby winners between 1962 and 1982. Uniquely saddled three consecutive Grand National winners. Had 23 Cheltenham Festival winners; only man to land Triple Crown in 74 years (Nijinsky, 1970).

CELEBRITY OF THE DAY
1947 Ronnie Wood – Rolling Stone, equine artist, who painted Moscow Flyer among many others, racehorse owner – born.

2 JUNE

SIGNIFICANT EVENT
2007 Frankie Dettori broke his Derby duck, finally winning the great race on 5/4 favourite Authorized for trainer Peter Chapple Hyam and celebrating with the famous trademark flying dismount.

STRANGEST EVENT
2009 After 22 years with a training licence, jumps specialist Peter Beaumont sent out his first Flat winner, Golden Groom, 8/1, at Ripon.

OTHER EVENTS
1920 Major Giles Loder of the Scots Guards became the last serving officer to own a Derby winner, 100/6 chance Spion Kop.

1949 1,000 Guineas winner Musidora did the double in the Oaks for rider Edgar Britt and trainer Charles Elsey, but never won again.

1954 Lester Piggott won his first Classic, landing the Derby on 33/1 shot Never Say Die for trainer Joe Lawson.

1960 Indigenous set the fastest time recorded for 5f at Epsom, hand-timed at 53.6s.

1972 Stan Mellor's last winner as a jockey, Arne Folly, at Stratford.

1982 'The best I've ever sat on,' enthused Pat Eddery after winning the Derby on the Vincent O'Brien-trained Golden Fleece, the 3/1 favourite.

1982 Philip Blacker retired after a jumping career of 327 winners, including 1980 Whitbread Gold Cup on Royal Mail; became successful sculptor.

1984 Trainer Michael Dickinson failed to win with last British runner over jumps, Compton Lad, at Stratford.

1988 Tony Buckmaster, 42, took it into his head to streak in front of the Royal Box at the Derby.

1993 The Henry Cecil-trained Commander In Chief, partnered by Michael Kinane, won the Derby at 15/2. Punter who staked £112,000 on odds-on favourite Tenby (10th) never looked like winning. Exactly 40 years after her coronation, The Queen enjoyed an Epsom winner, Enharmonic, ridden by Frankie Dettori.

2009 *Racing Post* said that a team of Irish scientists 'have reported that they have for the first time identified genes which they believe contribute to athletic performance in thoroughbreds.'

QUOTE OF THE DAY
'Because of the money involved in the Breeders' Cup they are the roughest races of the whole year. Nobody gives you a shot, so it's ironic that we're riding for a million dollars and yet we are only covered up to $100,000,' said top rider Gary Stevens, pulling out of the 2004 event, concerned about insurance.

BIRTHDAYS
1920 Michael O'Hehir, Irish commentator whose rapid-fire delivery was popular with racing fans, and impressionists.

1930 Trainer Gay Kindersley, who broke his back in 1965 but defied doctors to return to a successful amateur riding career. Champion amateur in 1959-60.

DEATHS OF THE DAY
1871 Riding his hack up Cheltenham's Cleeve Hill, George Stevens, who rode five Grand National winners, was injured after his hat blew off and spooked his horse, which threw him off. He hit his head and died next day. He was 38.

1945 Former jockey Charles Wood, 91. He partnered St Gatien to dead-heat with Harvester in the 1884 Derby and three years later was champion jockey.

CELEBRITY OF THE DAY
2009 Jim Hogan, a former international athlete who contested the 1964 Olympic marathon in Tokyo for Ireland and won the 1966 European championship marathon, had his first winner as an owner when Marathon Leader won at Listowel.

3 JUNE

SIGNIFICANT EVENT

1950 The five-year-old Citation became the leading money-earner of all time when winning for the 32nd time in 45 starts at Albany, California, taking his total to £330,225 ($1,085,760).

STRANGEST EVENT

1824 Jem Robinson won the Derby on Cedric, launching an amazing bet he had made. He followed up by winning the Oaks and completed a treble by marrying at the weekend.

OTHER EVENTS

1840 Queen Victoria visited the Derby for the only time, watching 50/1 Little Wonder score a shock win.

1874 Big coincidence tip as George Frederick was 9/1 winner of Derby on ninth birthday of Prince George Frederick.

1885 Harry Custance became first Derby-winning jockey (Thormanby, 1860; Lord Lyon, 1866; George Frederick, 1874) to go on to act as starter for the race.

1908 100/1 outsider Signorinetta won the Derby and, two days later, at odds of 3/1, added the Oaks.

1914 Victor Smyth rode his first winner, Dick Whittington, at Manchester. He went on to win the 1923 Oaks on Brownhylda and to train the 1952 1,000 Guineas winner, Zabara.

1982 Padge Gill rode his first winner, Crest Fallen, at Naas.

1986 BBC racing presenter Julian Wilson enjoyed his first home-bred winner when Pleasure Island obliged at Beverley.

1989 Peter Scudamore completed a record-breaking season with 221 winners.

1990 US jockey Chris McCarron broke both legs and an arm in a fall at Hollywood Park.

1990: 1888 Ascot Gold Cup stolen from home of former Turf Club senior steward Major Victor McCalmont.

1992 Dr Devious, 8/1, ridden by John Reid and trained by Peter Chapple-Hyam, won the Derby, having previously run seventh in the Kentucky Derby. He was only the second horse to attempt the 'Durby'-Derby double – the first was Bold Arrangement in 1989, who was second in the States but unplaced at Epsom.

2007 Ashling O'Connor, 20, got off the mark on Miss Mason in a Listowel bumper – for trainer-father Kevin.

2009 Champion Hurdle (Hors La Loi, 2002) winning jockey Dean Gallagher retired, a day after riding a winner at Auteuil. He rode 500 British winners and 126 in France. His career was blighted by several failed drug tests.

QUOTE OF THE DAY

1952 *'Never bet odds on. If you could buy money, they would sell it at the shop down the road.'* Barry Hills who, on this day, had his first ride on Golden Chance, trained by Fred Rimell, finishing tenth at Birmingham.

BIRTHDAYS

1920 Jockey Tommy Cusack.

1975 Jockey Danny Beasley

DEATHS OF THE DAY

1947 Fearless gambler Charles Hannam, who relied solely on his own form interpretation, 88. He once lost £10,000 on a game of darts.

1992 Robert Morley, 84, actor and racehorse owner.

1993 Mita Easton, 76, who trained Cheltenham winner Martinstown. She combined training with jobs as an anaesthetist and landlady in Dorset.

1994 Former jump jockey Roy Mangan, 41, of asthma attack. He retired from the saddle in 1980 and built up a saddlery business, introducing felt-covered whips and jockey goggles that did not mist up.

CELEBRITY OF THE DAY

1971 Singer and comic Des O'Connor applied for a permit to race as an amateur.

4 JUNE

SIGNIFICANT EVENT

1993 Anne Marie O'Brien became the first woman to top the Irish trainers' list, Flat or jumps, with 53 winners during the jumps campaign. Celebrated by handing licence over to husband Aidan.

STRANGEST EVENT

1913 Suffragette Emily Davison was fatally injured as she brought down the King's horse, Anmer, when she ran on to the course during the Derby. The race was 'won' by Craganour, later disqualified in favour of 100/1 Aboyeur.

OTHER EVENTS

1918 Gainsborough, 8/13, became the first Derby winner owned by a woman, Lady James Douglas, who had already made history when the same horse won the 2,000 Guineas.

1919 106 years after Smolensko became the first black horse to win the Derby, Grand Parade was the second.

1924 Having won the Derby on 9/2 favourite Sansovino, 21-year-old Tommy Weston was handed a £1,000 tip by owner Lord Derby and celebrated with his wife – on a wooden merry-go-round horse on Epsom Downs.

1949 For the first time a photo-finish decided the Derby result as Nimbus beat Amour Drake by a head. The 7/1 winner was bred by William Hill.

1977 Chris Grant rode his first winner, Trim Lawns, at Hexham.

1982 Derek Kent left his Sussex stables to train in Hong Kong. Former stable jockey Peter Haynes took over.

1985 William Jarvis sent out his first winner as a trainer, Dorset Cottage, at Beverley.

1994 Having been runner-up in both Guineas, Frankie Dettori landed his first Classic victory on 6/1 Balanchine in the Oaks. The filly was trained in Dubai by Hilal Ibrahim and became the first horse trained in the Middle East to win an English Classic.

1995 The Peter Savill-owned 'wonder horse' Celtic Swing won the French Derby, having been runner-up to Pennekamp in the 2,000 Guineas.

2000 Hayley Turner rode her first winner, Generate, 9/2, at Pontefract.

2005 Motivator, the 3/1 favourite ridden by Johnny Murtagh, stormed to a five-length Derby victory for trainer Michael Bell and the 230 members of the Royal Ascot Racing Club who owned the horse.

QUOTE OF THE DAY

2009 *'What made me frightfully pleased about winning a Derby was that for some years I thought I had no hope of winning anything better than the Tradesmen's Selling Handicap at Bath,'* said Arthur Budgett, looking back to this day in 1969 when Blakeney won the Derby. Budgett won again in 1973 with Blakeney's half-brother, Morston. Both were named after Norfolk villages he had never visited.

BIRTHDAYS

1948 Cancer-beating Grand National-winning jockey Bob Champion, who rode 421 winners (including his famous 1981 National winner Aldaniti) under rules in Britain before becoming a trainer.

1981 French champion jockey Christophe Soumillon.

DEATH OF THE DAY

2003 Peter Bromley, 74, racing commentator for BBC radio for more than 40 years (1959-2001) and almost as celebrated in his day as Peter O'Sullevan. He commentated on 202 Classics and more than 40 Grand Nationals. Calling Shergar over the line in the 1981 Derby, he observed, 'You need a telescope to see the rest'.

CELEBRITY OF THE DAY

1844 The Emperor of Russia, Nicholas I, and the King of Saxony, attended Ascot races where they saw Alice Hawthorn, winner of 52 of 72 starts, win the Queen's Vase.

5 JUNE

SIGNIFICANT EVENT
2009 Having saddled Derby winner Motivator in 2005, trainer Michael Bell added the Oaks as 9/4 jt fav Sariska survived a stewards' inquiry, just preventing Henry Cecil's Midday giving him a ninth win in the race.

STRANGEST EVENT
1994 Paul Kallai, 60, a former professional boxer in Germany, rode the winners of four of the most valuable races on the card at Bratislava, all trained by Tibor Farkas.

OTHER EVENTS
1901 Volodyovski became first the Derby winner bred by a woman, Lady Meux.

1902 Lord Wolverton's Osboch won the first Coronation Cup, formerly the Epsom Cup, which was renamed to commemorate the coronation of King Edward VII.

1907 Orby, 100/9, from Col McCabe's Co Dublin stables, became the first Irish-trained Derby winner. On the same day at Churchill Downs, USA, Jimmie Lee rode six winners from six mounts.

1931 Lady Trace clocked 55.2s (40.76mph) over 5f at Epsom, a record for a two-year-old.

1937 War Admiral won the Belmont Stakes in a record time of 2m 28.2s.

1939 Two of the first three home in the Park Chase at Napier Park, Hastings, New Zealand were ridden by jockeys other than those who set out on them. Wykemist finished first but the second horse, Kikiroki, had fallen, only to be remounted by a spectator, Mr Marquand, while the third, Begorrah, who fell and got loose, was caught by Mr Greene, who rode him in.

1982 Henry Candy trained his first Classic winner, and jockey Billy Newnes rode his first, as Time Charter took the Oaks.

1991 Alan Munro won the Derby on Generous, a 9/1 shot, for Paul Cole. Lester Piggott rode in the race for the first time since 1985, having spent time in prison in the interim, and finished seventh on Hokusai on his 33rd ride.

1993 Richard Dunwoody became champion jump jockey for the first time.

1993 Julie Krone became the first female rider to win a US Triple Crown race as she partnered 14/1 Colonial Affair in the 125th Belmont Stakes.

1999 Henry Cecil and Kieren Fallon teamed up to win the Derby with 13/2 chance Oath, whose next race proved to be his last as he cracked a bone in his near foreleg during the King George VI and Queen Elizabeth Stakes at Ascot in which he was seventh to Daylami. Oath was sold for £8m to Japan's Yushun Farm, where he stood at stud.

2004 Fifty years after his first win in the Derby, Lester Piggott was guest of honour at Epsom as Kieren Fallon partnered 7/2 favourite North Light to Derby victory for Sir Michael Stoute, three times a previous winner.

QUOTE OF THE DAY
2009 *'You have to handle them differently, as they have a lot of character. I think basically you have to be a psychiatrist. You have to make them believe they are the bee's knees and I enjoy that challenge'* – Henry Cecil speaking before his filly Midday was narrowly beaten into second place in a bid to become his ninth Oaks winner.

BIRTHDAYS
1927 Trainer Tommy 'Squeak' Fairhurst, who was based at Middleham, North Yorkshire.

1938 Australian Hall of Fame jockey Roy Higgins.

1946 John Gorton, a South African jockey active in Britain from 1966 who partnered Sleeping Partner to win the 1969 Oaks. He retired in 1974.

CELEBRITY OF THE DAY
2009 Publication of book compiling the best writings of recently deceased Sir Clement Freud, *Freud On Course.*

6 JUNE

SIGNIFICANT EVENT
1923 Steve Donoghue won his third consecutive Derby on Papyrus, 100/15, following victories on Humorist in 1921 and Captain Cuttle in 1922.

STRANGEST EVENT
1962 Seven horses fell in the Derby as the field came down Tattenham Hill. King Canute II broke his leg and six jockeys ended up in hospital. The race was won by Larkspur, trained by Vincent O'Brien and ridden by Australian jockey Neville Sellwood, who was killed the following November when Lucky Seven fell at Maisons-Laffitte.

OTHER EVENTS
1894 The Prime Minister, Lord Rosebery, saw his Ladas win the Derby at 2/9, the shortest-ever winning odds.
1921 Gordon Richards rode his first double, on John Charles and Spiral Spin, at Lewes.
1934 Maharajah of Rajpipla's Windsor Lad, 15/2, won the Derby ridden by 27-year-old Charlie Smirke, whose licence was returned the previous October after being warned off for five years following an incident in which his mount failed to start.
1953 Sir Gordon Richards finally won the Derby at the 28th and final attempt, on 5/1 jt fav Pinza.
1979 Willie Carson rode the Dick Hern-trained Troy, 6/1, to win 200th Derby.
1987 Henry Cecil set a record for the fastest half-century of wins in a Flat season when Space Cruiser won at Haydock.
1990 Pat Eddery won the Derby for trainer Roger Charlton, former assistant to Jeremy Tree, on 7/1 chance Quest For Fame. The winner was owned by Khalid Abdullah.
1992 The Clive Brittain-trained User Friendly, 5/1, beat the smallest field (7) for 76 years to win the Oaks, giving 45-year-old jockey George Duffield his first Classic success.

1997 Reams Of Verse, 5/6, partnered by Kieren Fallon, became the fifth Oaks winner for Henry Cecil.
1998 High-Rise, 20/1, ridden by Olivier Peslier, won the Derby for Luca Cumani, who had also won it a decade earlier with Kahyasi.
2009 The Irish Field reported that Australian trainer David 'Butch' Londregan had been fined A$5,000 by Racing Victoria, having threatened to kill his horses and send a severed head to Racing Minister Rob Hulls if jumps racing was banned.
2009 The Queen attended the Derby amid controversy that she had not been invited by the French government to participate in their 65th anniversary celebrations for D-day. She saw John Oxx's Sea The Stars win the race.

QUOTE OF THE DAY
2009 *'Last year's Belmont was like swallowing a spoon sideways. What a pill to swallow. To have to go away from this game and not have a Belmont – that would have been a little scratch in my craw'* – Kent Desormeaux after Summer Bird completed his personal Triple Crown, making up for previous year's defeat with odds-on Big Brown in the same race.

BIRTHDAY
1905 Trainer Freddie Maxwell, whose Pandofell won him the Queen's Prize, Yorkshire Cup, Ascot Gold Cup and Doncaster Cup in 1961.

DEATH OF THE DAY
1993 Wilf Crawford, 77, former Scottish rugby union international, and later a trainer, handling good jumpers Final Approach and Shady Will.

CELEBRITY OF THE DAY
1945 Claude 'Punters' Pal' Duval of *The Sun*, was born. Once forced to run naked around Jockey Club HQ by his editor, having unsuccessfully predicted the outcome of an appeal to that body.

7 JUNE

SIGNIFICANT EVENT
1997 'I'd like to say to my old man, somewhere up there, that we finally got it right' – trainer John Gosden after his Benny The Dip won the 1997 Derby. Gosden, whose father Towser trained Charlottown as a juvenile, was deprived by ill health of being in charge when the horse won the 1966 Derby.

STRANGEST EVENT
1887 A mounted policeman attempting to cross the track interfered with several runners in Ascot's Prince of Wales's Stakes, including favourite Reve D'Or who ended up beaten by Claymore.

OTHER EVENTS
1808 Extraordinary quadruple dead-heat as judge could not split Honest Harry, Miss Decoy, Beningborough, Peteria in a £50 plate. Venue unrecorded.
1864 America's first Derby was run at Paterson (mile and a half), even though the Civil War was still being fought. The Jersey Derby was won by Norfolk, beating 11 rivals in front of 10,000.
1947 The Derby, run on a Saturday for the first time in peace time, was won by 40/1 chance Pearl Diver.
1969 South African jockey John Gorton rode Sleeping Partner to win the Oaks.
1975 Wally Wharton rode his first winner, Persian King, 20/1, at Warwick.
1986 Trainer Dermot Weld and jockey Mick Kinane won the first five races at Phoenix Park and had the runner-up, beaten half length, in the sixth race.
1986 Danzig Connection gave trainer Woody Stephens an unprecedented fifth straight win in the Belmont Stakes.
1989 Terimon (M. Roberts) smashed the record odds for a placed horse in the Derby - Clive Brittain's colt was runner-up to 5/4 favourite Nashwan at 500/1.
1992 Frankie Dettori's second Classic victory came on Polytain in the French Derby (the first was Temporal in the 1991 German Derby). Polytain became the first ex-claimer to win the prize.

2003 Kieren Fallon won the Derby on 6/1 shot Kris Kin, trained by Sir Michael Stoute, just holding off Pat Eddery, riding in his last Derby, on The Great Gatsby (20/1). Refuse To Bend, the 11/4 favourite, was 13th.
2008 After much prevaricating by trainer Jim Bolger over whether New Approach would run in the Derby, the colt won at 5/1 in the hands of Kevin Manning. Three million watched on BBC, 37% of the terrestrial TV audience at the time. New Approach was the first champion two-year-old to win the race since Reference Point in 1987.

QUOTE OF THE DAY
2009 *'It is such a hard race to win. It is pretty special to me. I remember the first time I followed the Prix du Jockey-Club. It was the 1966 edition, won by Nelcius, and I was eating cherries. Since then, I have always known when cherries are in season'* – French trainer Jean-Claude Rouget after Le Havre had given him his first win in the race, partnered by Christophe Lemaire on a day when the pair landed a Group treble.

BIRTHDAYS
1936 Prolific trainer Jack van Berg, whose best horse was Alysheba.
1952 Trainer Patrick Biancone, whose best horses were the Arc winners All Along and Sagace.
1960 Neil Graham, trainer of 1988 St Leger winner Minster Son.

DEATH OF THE DAY
2007 Jockey turned trainer Doug Marks, 85. He won the 1,000 Guineas and Oaks on Godiva in 1940 as an apprentice. His best-known horses as a trainer were the sprinters Fireside Chat, Shiny Tenth and Singing Bede.

CELEBRITY OF THE DAY
1957 Carrozza, leased from the National Stud, gave The Queen her first Classic win, the Oaks, ridden by Lester Piggott.

8 JUNE

SIGNIFICANT EVENT
1992 It was revealed that Cheltenham had been staging races over the wrong distances for almost 20 years. The Gold Cup and Champion Hurdle had both been run over half a furlong further than the official distances. The errors came to light during a full remeasurement of the track.

STRANGEST EVENT
2009 Disaster was narrowly averted at Pontefract when two large plastic cones, which were used to keep runners away from the inside section of the track, were left in place as runners contested a 6f handicap. Several jockeys were forced to take urgent evasive action and, although the cones were scattered, no horse or rider was injured.

OTHER EVENTS
1945 Lord Derby's Sun Stream added the Oaks to her 1,000 Guineas triumph.
1956 Greville Starkey rode his first winner, Russian Gold, at Pontefract.
1968 Green Plover (Jim Ford/Adrian Maxwell) was the 33/1 outsider of eight for the Horse and Hound Cup at Stratford, and became the longest-odds winner of the race.
1979 Spectacular Bid could manage only third when going for Triple Crown glory in the Belmont Stakes. The 3/10 favourite, who was going for his 13th successive win, stepped on a safety pin before the race and was lame next day. He raced 13 more times, losing only once - to 1978 Triple Crown winner Affirmed.
1985 Crème Fraiche, 5/2, became the first gelding to win the Belmont Stakes.
1989 The 11-year-old sprinter Rapid Lad won at Beverley for the 11th time.
1991 Jet Ski Lady, 50/1, won the Oaks by 10 lengths, equalling the longest odds returned for a winner of the race.
1991 Julie Krone became the first woman to ride in the Belmont Stakes, finishing ninth of 11 on Subordinated Debt at 4.1/1 shot Hansel won for jockey Jerry Bailey and trainer Frank Brothers.
1992 Jamie Osborne won the World Jump Jockey Championship in Australia.
1996 Alex Greaves became the first woman to ride in the Derby, finishing last on 500/1 Portuguese Lil as 12/1 chance Shaamit won for Michael Hills and trainer William Haggas.
1996 Three weeks after his unprecedented six-race Triple Crown winning streak ended in the Preakness, trainer D Wayne Lukas was back on top. In front of 40,797 at Belmont Park, Editor's Note outbattled Skip Away to win by a length, giving Lukas his third straight victory in the Belmont.
2002 Trainer Aidan O'Brien dominated the Derby as 7/2 second favourite High Chaparral, ridden by Johnny Murtagh, beat 9/4 favourite Hawk Wing. High Chaparral went on to win the Irish Derby and finish third in the Arc.
2006 Donald McCain junior sent out his first winner as a trainer, Bearaway, at Newton Abbot.

QUOTE OF THE DAY
'*Little fish are sweet*' – career-long motto of dual-purpose trainer W A (Arthur) Stephenson, whose The Thinker won the 1987 Cheltenham Gold Cup (he was at Hexham at the time) and who on this day in 1946 saddled - and rode - his first winner as a trainer, T O D at Hexham.

BIRTHDAYS
1933 Sir Eric Parker, owner of 1991 Grand National winner Seagram.
1952 French-based English trainer Jonathan Pease.

DEATH OF THE DAY
2007 Jockey Doug Page, 79. He rode 628 Flat and jumps winners, including the 1955 Irish St Leger on Diamond Slipper.

CELEBRITY OF THE DAY
1953 Bonnie Tyler, rock singer and racehorse owner, was born.

9 JUNE

SIGNIFICANT EVENT
1987 Unknown youngster Frankie Dettori rode his first winner, Lizzy Hare, at Goodwood.

STRANGEST EVENT
1962 Aged 22, Creggmore Boy became the oldest recorded runner to race, finishing fourth in a Cartmel chase.

OTHER EVENTS
1888 Brothers Phil and Mike Dwyer saddled Belmont Stakes winner for third time in a row and fifth in six runnings.

1930 Last jump meeting on the Isle of Wight was held on Whit Monday at the racecourse at Ashey, near Ryde.

1945 The Hon George Lambton sent out his final winner as a trainer, Golden Cloud, at Newmarket. His 1924 autobiography, *Men and Horses I Have Known*, is a racing classic.

1948 Ron Smyth had his first winner as a trainer, Turkestan, at Brighton.

1967 Trainer Bill Elsey landed his first Classic win as Edward Hide rode Pia, 100/7, to victory in the Oaks.

1973 Secretariat completed the US Triple Crown, winning the Belmont Stakes by 31 lengths in a record time of 2m 24s.

1979 Flamboyant trainer Rod Simpson sent out his first winner, Lady Tartown, at Warwick.

1983 Pebbles, who became the British record prize-money winner, won for the first time in the Kingsclere Stakes at Newbury, ridden by Philip Robinson.

1984 US super-jockey Willie Shoemaker rode his first Epsom winner, Royal Recourse, as Lester Piggott had his 27th British Classic winner as Circus Plume won the Oaks to help the 'Long Fellow' equal Frank Buckle's record total.

1986 Willie Carson rode his 2,500th British winner, Flower Bowl, at Leicester.

1990 Dermot Weld sent out Go And Go, partnered by Michael Kinane, to become the first European-trained winner of the Belmont Stakes.

1993 For the first time in ten years the Royal Hong Kong Jockey Club had to abandon part of a race meeting because of bad weather. The final night of the season at Sha Tin was hit by monsoon downpours, lightning and thunder, causing the cancellation of the last race.

2007 Rebecca Chomiak arrived at Newbury races a single woman and left as fiancée to golf pro Andrew Bayliss, who proposed to her on one knee in the parade ring. She accepted.

2009 'Horses make monkeys of you,' mused trainer Michael Dods after the outsider of his three runners in a 7f handicap at Redcar, 20/1 shot Jimwil, put supposedly better fancied stablemates in the shade by winning.

2009 Trainer Hughie Morrison realised a personal ambition when his Cill Rialaig won the fillies' handicap named after his late grandfather, Lord Margadale, at Salisbury.

QUOTE OF THE DAY
2009 *'English races are for prestige, foreign races are for money,'* said trainer Luca Cumani, planning campaigns abroad for some of his top horses.

BIRTHDAYS
1955 Former jockey turned tipster Steve Smith Eccles, who completed a Champion Hurdle hat-trick on See You Then.

1964 Jump jockey Eamon Murphy, whose career highlight was a Sandown treble that included the Imperial Cup on the Queen Mother's Insular.

DEATH OF THE DAY
1953 Beckhampton trainer Fred Darling, 69, who had 19 Classics, including seven Derby wins. He left an estate valued at £99,082.

CELEBRITY OF THE DAY
2009 Russell Crowe was reported as being lined up to play Joe Janiak, cabbie turned globetrotting trainer of Aussie champion sprinter Takeover Target.

10 JUNE

SIGNIFICANT EVENT
1995 Saeed Bin Suroor sent out Lammtarra, 14/1, ridden by Walter Swinburn, to win the Derby in a course record of 2m 32.31s. Lammtarra had been trained as a two-year-old by murdered Alex Scott, who had placed £1,000 at 33/1 on him. It was the first Saturday Derby since 1953.

STRANGEST EVENT
1935 Harry Beasley rode Mollie to finish unplaced in the Corinthian Plate at Baldoyle, Dublin. He was 83 at the time!

OTHER EVENTS
1871 James E Kelly had opened the first ever US ante-post market on the Belmont Stakes, which was won on this day by Harry Bassett, partnered by W Miller.

1944 Brownie, Bossuet and Wait A Bit finished in a triple dead-heat at Aqueduct, USA.

1966 Sea Cottage, who was hotly fancied for the July Handicap in Durban, South Africa, was shot in the leg by a gunman. The horse recovered sufficiently to run but finished fourth.

1989 Aliysa, 11/10 favourite, owned by the Aga Khan, won the Oaks. But 528 days later she lost the race when the Jockey Club disqualified her for having a prohibited substance in her system. The legal arguments raged for years and the Aga Khan removed his horses from Britain in protest.

1992 Jockey Dandy Nicholls was banned for two successive four-day periods after being hauled in front of the stewards following consecutive races at Hamilton. Well, it was the Saints and Sinners meeting.

1993 British Horseracing Board officially launched as the new governing authority.

1994 Frankie Dettori set the record for the quickest 100 winners in a season when Fleet Hill won at Goodwood. However, one of his winners, Dime Time, was subsequently disqualified, so he didn't officially achieve it until June 11 at Wolverhampton on Winter Coat for John Gosden. The previous record had been held by Gordon Richards, who achieved it on June 17, 1949.

1995 D Wayne Lukas trained his fifth successive US Triple Crown winner as Thunder Gulch, 6/4, won the Belmont Stakes. Tabasco Cat began the sequence in 1994 Preakness and Belmont, followed by Thunder Gulch in the Kentucky Derby and Timber Country in the Preakness.

2000 The Aga Khan's Sinndar, 7/1, won the Derby, ridden by Johnny Murtagh and trained by John Oxx.

2009 The Mark Johnston-trained Record Breaker, ridden by Royston Ffrench, lived up to his name, setting a 1m4f course record of 2m 30.52s in winning the Lanark Silver Bell, run at Hamilton.

QUOTE OF THE DAY
1902 *'If a racehorse could talk, one of the first things he'd tell jockeys would be "If you don't know where the bloody winning post is, I'm sure I don't."'* Harry Wragg, born this day, in Sheffield. Wragg, who liked to deliver a late challenge, rode 13 Classic winners and in total had 1,762 winners from 11,658 British and Irish mounts. He trained from 1947 in Newmarket and sent out five Classic winners, including Psidium in the 1961 Derby.

BIRTHDAYS
1937 Jockey turned trainer Eddie Harty, who rode Highland Wedding to win the 1969 Grand National and also competed in the 1960 Olympics.

1939 Trainer Guy Harwood, whose Dancing Brave won the 1986 Arc. He rode 14 jumps winners.

1966 Trainer and vet James Given.

CELEBRITY OF THE DAY
1966 David Platt, former England midfielder and owner of Handsome Ridge, was born.

11 JUNE

SIGNIFICANT EVENT
2009 Trainer Matt Gingell was warned off for two years after becoming the first British trainer to be found guilty of a doping offence involving sodium bicarbonate (known as a 'milkshake'). His horse Kassuta was tested at Fakenham in November 2007 after finishing third.

STRANGEST EVENT
2009 New Zealand jockey Lynsey Satherley, 25, rode her 189th winner, at Rotorua, just 15 days after giving birth to daughter Sophie Angela.

OTHER EVENTS
1944 Apprentice Hubert Jones became the first jockey to ride eight winners on a single programme, achieving the feat from 13 mounts at Caliente, California.
1977 Seattle Slew, 2/5, ridden by J Cruguet for trainer William H Turner jr, won the Belmont Stakes to complete the Triple Crown. Innkeeper John Esposito, whose tavern bordered the stable area, painted his picket fence in the winner's colours, thus starting a tradition.
1983 The Belmont Stakes was contested by a record field of 15, as 13/5 Caveat won for Laffit Pincay jr and trainer Woody Stephens.
1988 For the first time a woman saddled a placed horse in the Belmont Stakes as Diane Carpenter's Kingpost ran second behind 21/10 Risen.
1989 Scu beat Shoe as champion jump jockey Peter Scudamore defeated all-time winningmost Flat jockey Willie Shoemaker 2-1 in a best-of-three charity challenge at Cheltenham.
1990 Australian jockey Gavan Eades was suspended for six months for spitting at apprentice Ricky Maund as they pulled up after the Swan Hill Cup, won by Maund.
1993 Michael Roberts rode Alinova, 1/3, to win the 2.10 at York before dashing to Sandown to win the 5.30 on Learmont, 13/8, and then shooting off to Goodwood, where he won the 7.35 on

14/1 Contract Court.
1995 Hong Kong punters staked a record £134m on a nine-race card at Sha Tin, beating the previous best of £121m.
2004 At The Races TV channel was relaunched, having looked doomed earlier that year when live UK racing disappeared from its screens.
2009 The newly constructed open ditch at Leicester racecourse was destroyed by fire. 'It will cost between £3,000 and £4,000 to replace it,' said course chairman Nick Lees.

QUOTE OF THE DAY
1940 *'If you like to bet in France you cannot have friends. Because if you have friends and you tell them to back your horse, the price is spoilt. And if you don't tell them, well, you don't have friends any more.'* Francois Doumen, whose Nupsala and The Fellow were King George VI Chase winners, was born on this day.

BIRTHDAYS
1935 Owner Trevor Hemmings, who won the 2005 Grand National with Hedgehunter. Based on the Isle of Man, he was a major shareholder in Arena Leisure, owned an interest in Blackpool Tower and was a Jockey Club member.
1946 Jenny Pitman, who was the first woman to train winners of the Grand National and Cheltenham Gold Cup.
1949 John Forsyth, actor and racehorse owner.
1955 Jump jockey turned clerk of the course Sam Morshead, whose first ride in 1973 was a winner, whose first ride over fences was a winner, and whose first two rides for Fred Rimell were winners.

DEATH OF THE DAY
1989 Phil Bull, founder of Timeform, 79.

CELEBRITY OF THE DAY
1994 Encore M'Lady, 20/1, became the biggest winner in Britain for footballer turned trainer Francis Lee when winning the £40,000 William Hill Trophy at York.

12 JUNE

SIGNIFICANT EVENT
2009 Frankie Dettori and Sir Peter O'Sullevan were among those delivering a 184,740-signature petition to 10 Downing Street calling for racing's coverage on the BBC to be saved and intended cuts to be reduced or reversed.

STRANGEST EVENT
1992 The eight-race card at Canterbury Downs, USA, turned into something of a family affair as David Essman rode two winners but was trumped by Kokie Warhol, his wife, who won four races.

OTHER EVENTS
1825 Brazil's first meeting took place at Praia Vermelha, Botafogo.
1884 Trainer Mat Dawson declared that his great horse St Simon had more 'electricity' about him than any other. So it couldn't have been a shock to him when the horse romped home in the Ascot Gold Cup by 20l, aged three. St Simon went on to be an outstanding nine-time champion sire. After he died, aged 27, his skeleton was given to the Natural History Museum.
1940 The Derby was set to be run at Newbury, but switched to Newmarket where Pont L'Eveque, 10/1, won.
1964 Ian Balding sent out his first winner, Atholl, at Sandown.
1982 Barry Hills saddled his 800th winner, Reves Celestes, at Bath.
1993 Richard Dunwoody awarded the MBE. On the same day in 1982 Bob Champion had received one, too, while, after 23 years as Sporting Life editor, Ossie Fletcher was recognised with an OBE.
1996 Six winners in a day's racing for Frankie Dettori for the first time - three at Yarmouth in the afternoon and three more in the evening at Kempton.

QUOTE OF THE DAY
'A purse of 30 guineas was run for weight 12st, 3 guineas entrance and won by Lord Molyneaux's Bay Gelding, Tickle Me Quickly'. This happened, according to John Cheny's *An Historical List of Horse Matches Run,* at Oswestry, Shropshire, on this day in 1729.

BIRTHDAYS
1938 Trainer Lady Herries, widow of England cricketer Colin Cowdrey.
1945 Former French champion jockey Alfred Gibert, who finished third on Irish Ball in the 1971 Derby.
1967 US Hall of Fame jockey Edgar Prado.

DEATHS OF THE DAY
1999 Former Epsom trainer Dermot 'Boggy' Whelan, 80. He won the 1962 Wokingham with Elco and also trained dual Northumberland Plate winner Tug Of War.
2002 Charles Benson, 66. He was a *Daily Express* racing correspondent for 30 years, friend and colleague of Peter O'Sullevan, friend of Lord Lucan, and general bon viveur.
2006 Rails bookie Roy Christie, 80, who was proud to have worked with his son John and grandson Mike on his pitch at Newmarket.

CELEBRITY OF THE DAY
2003 Actor and racehorse owner Gregory Peck, who died aged 87. His Different Class won the 1967 National Hunt Chase at Cheltenham.

13 JUNE

SIGNIFICANT EVENT
2009 The first running of the Reg Griffin Memorial Trophy at York commemorated the former Timeform chairman, who spent 50 years with the company, retiring in 2007 and dying in October 2008, aged 79. He started the Timeform Charity Day, which has raised almost £5m in 39 years.

STRANGEST EVENT
2009 York racecourse had to send for a beekeeper when a huge swarm arrived at the track and settled on a viewing bench overlooking the paddock area.

OTHER EVENTS
1913 Prince Eugene's Belmont Stakes win was the eighth in the race for trainer James Rowe.
1954 Geordie Ramshaw rode his first winner, Fairy Princess, at Lingfield.
1969 Terry Biddlecombe won the final race of the jumps season on Golden Berry at Uttoxeter to share the jockeys' title with Bob Davies (77 winners each).
1970 Jockey turned trainer Stan Mellor was awarded the MBE.
1975 Edward Hide didn't enjoy Friday the 13th, breaking his leg in a bad fall from Bewerley at York when he was three ahead of Lester Piggott in the title race. Hide would never win the title, although he was second in 1957.
1976 Lucky Friday the 13th for Pat Day, whose seven mounts at Churchill Downs produced five winners.
1992 Wangola won at Naas to give Jim Bolger his 1,000th winner.
1993 On-course Pari Mutuel workers at Chantilly went on strike over pay, prompting punters to stage sit-down protest. The Prix de Diane (French Oaks), delayed almost two hours from the scheduled start time of 2.40pm, was won by Shemaka.
1994 The John White-trained Shikari's Son won at Brighton, equalling Operatic Society's record of seven course victories, achieved on June 8, 1966.

2009 On the eve of his 37th birthday, Darryll Holland got celebrations off to an early start with a 622/1 four-timer at Bath.
2009 Brough Scott, one of the founders of the *Racing Post*, was awarded the MBE.

QUOTE OF THE DAY
2009 *'I found that 119 of the 60,084 winners of British Flat and jump races were disqualified from 1996 to 2003, but from 2004 to date only 26 out of the 48,615 winners were disqualified. In other words the percentage of disqualified winners in Britain has dropped from 0.2% to 0.05% – a quarter of what it was.'* Interesting stat in the *Irish Field* written by Nick Mordin.

BIRTHDAYS
1948 Jockey Sandy Barclay. Once retained by Sir Noel Murless, he also rode for The Queen. Champion apprentice in 1966, he rode Caergwrle to win the 1968 1,000 Guineas and Lupe to win the 1970 Oaks.
1952 'Aussie' Jim McGrath, racing writer and BBC TV commentator.
1958 Champion jump jockey Peter Scudamore born in Hereford on Friday 13th, but claims not to be superstitious.
1961 Trainer Simon Dow. In 1976 Dow was the top UK athlete in his age group over 800m.

DEATH OF THE DAY
2009 Former trainer Tom Costello, 77, who sold on six Cheltenham Gold Cup winners, including Best Mate. Among the horses he sold on were Gold Cup winners Imperial Call, Midnight Court, The Thinker, Cool Ground and Cool Dawn as well Grand National winner Hedgehunter and the Queen Mother Champion Chase winner One Man.

CELEBRITY OF THE DAY
2006 Former Taioseach Charles Haughey died, 80. His Flashing Steel, trained by son-in-law John Mulhern, won the 1995 Irish Grand National.

14 JUNE

SIGNIFICANT EVENT
1843 The first running of the Royal Hunt Cup was won by Nat Flatman on Lord Chesterfield's Knight Of The Whistle, 5/1. Gary Owen, Epaulette and Bourra Tomacha triple dead-heated for second.

STRANGEST EVENT
1991 Gary Carter won at three racecourses in one day. Luvly Jubly, 6/1, for Jack Berry, won the 1.30 at Southwell, Romany Rye, 85/30, scored for Geoff Wragg in York's 4.00, and Able Susan, 4/1, also trained by Wragg, won the 8.15 at Doncaster. Carter was the first British jockey to achieve the feat since Paul Cook on July 4, 1981.

OTHER EVENTS
1910 The Royal meeting at Ascot began. It became known as Black Ascot as it came five weeks after the death of King Edward VII and everyone was in mourning.

1936 Shanghai's Kiangwan course held its final race meeting.

1959 Herbager, 4/5 favourite, won the Prix du Jockey-Club, partnered by Guy Chancelier and trained by Pierre Pelat. He started odds-on for the Arc but was injured during the race and managed only tenth.

1991 Chinese jockey Tse Wai-Ho was banned for four months and fined £4,685 on betting-related charges in Hong Kong. He had admitted giving tips in return for 'the services' of a prostitute.

1991 Polish-bred Serafin won the Swedish Grand National for the fourth straight year – with four different jockeys.

1994 Martin Pipe won the Ascot Stakes with 14/1 Sweet Glow, ridden by Cash Asmussen – his third winner in the race after Right Regent in 1983 and Balsaan in 1993.

1995 Willie Carson rode a 235/1 five-timer from five mounts at Beverley.

1997 It was announced that Peter O'Sullevan was to be knighted, while trainer Ken Oliver received the OBE and jockey John Reid the MBE.

2009 Jean-Claude Rouget landed his 11th Group One success of the season as Stacelita won the Prix de Diane at Chantilly.

QUOTE OF THE DAY
2009 *'At Royal Ascot a couple of years ago, a woman walked into the reception wearing nothing but a tailcoat borrowed from a man.'* On the eve of Royal Ascot, the racecourse's chief executive Charles Barnett recalled a recent abuse of the dress code for the meeting.

BIRTHDAYS
1955 Charlotte Budd, nee Brew. She was the first woman to ride in the Grand National, getting as far as the 27th fence in 1977 on Barony Fort.

1972 A popular day to be born for racing folk, with jockeys Jimmy Fortune and Darryll Holland and trainer James Moffatt all arriving into the world.

DEATH OF THE DAY
2009 Winning seven-year-old Quizzene met a tragic death in an accident with a motorbike near Lambourn, where he was trained by Alastair Lidderdale.

CELEBRITY OF THE DAY
1892 Jack Watts partnered Milford to win the Coventry Stakes at Royal Ascot for Mr Jersey, a name that concealed the identity of actress Lily Langtry, as it was not the done thing for women to own horses.

15 JUNE

SIGNIFICANT EVENT
2009 Kentucky Governor Steve Beshear said the Kentucky horse industry was 'dying'. His solution was to legalise slot machines at racetracks in order to boost revenue and prize-money.

STRANGEST EVENT
1982 There was embarrassment for Ascot when a 'jobsworth' steward refused entry to the owners' and trainers' bar to legendary trainer Vincent O'Brien, on the grounds that he did not have the correct badge.

OTHER EVENTS
1889 Five thousand racegoers attended the opening of Epsom racecourse - near Melbourne, Australia - and saw the £500 Mordialloe Cup run. The track survived until 1938.

1915 The Derby took place somewhere other than Epsom for the first time as 17 went to post at Newmarket with 11/10 favourite Pommern, partnered by Steve Donoghue, coming out on top.

1918 Johren, bred in England by Harry Payne Whitney, won the 50th Belmont Stakes.

1940 Gatwick held its final meeting.

1947 Sandjar became Marcel Boussac's eighth French Derby winner.

1963 A crowd of 48,000 watched at Aqueduct, US, as 88-year-old trainer 'Sunny' Jim Fitzsimons received a tray engraved with the names of his 148 stakes winners to mark his retirement.

1967 George Duffield rode his first winner, Syllable, at Yarmouth for trainer Jack Waugh.

1983 The David Elsworth-trained Mighty Fly won the Royal Hunt Cup under Steve Cauthen, becoming the first horse of the 20th century to complete the double with the Lincoln.

1988 Tote turnover at Royal Ascot topped £1m in a day for the first time.

1990 Peter Scudamore awarded MBE.

1991 Peter O'Sullevan was awarded the CBE. On the same day Henry Cecil had his 2,000th domestic winner, Wave Hill, at Bath.

1994 Royal Ascot's first dead-heat since 1976 saw Gneiss, Julie Cecil's first Group winner, and Paul Cole's River Deep share the honours in the Jersey Stakes.

1996 Trainers John Dunlop and Jack Berry awarded the OBE and MBE respectively.

QUOTE OF THE DAY
2009 *'The doctors said that was the best possible place if you have to be kicked.'* Paul Hanagan, kicked viciously at the top of his leg by a two-year-old in the paddock at York a couple of days earlier, reported by the *Racing Post* today in 2009, after x-rays revealed nothing was broken.

BIRTHDAYS
1955 Trainer Linda Stubbs.

1963 Trainer Tom Taaffe, who won both the Irish Champion Hurdle and Irish Grand National.

1976 Former New South Wales champion jockey Corey Brown.

1977 Dual code Irish trainer Robbie Osborne.

DEATHS OF THE DAY
1992 Trainer Will Pearce, 42, was found dead with a shotgun nearby on gallops adjacent to his yard at Hambleton, near Thirsk. He was believed to have financial problems, but two days before had landed a reported £250,000 gamble with Father Hayes, backed from 14/1 to 4/1 at Sandown.

1993 Lester Piggott's father, Keith, 89. He won the 1939 Champion Hurdle on African Star and as a trainer he landed the 1963 Grand National with Ayala.

CELEBRITY OF THE DAY
1959 Alan Brazil was born. The former Ipswich Town, Manchester United and Scotland striker forged a post-football career as Talksport presenter, tipster, punter and organiser of racing clubs.

16 JUNE

SIGNIFICANT EVENT

2009 Richard Hughes rode an 88/1 treble on the first day of Royal Ascot, partnering Paco Boy; Canford Cliffs and Judgethemoment. There was an Aussie double too as Judgethemoment's trainer Jane Chapple-Hyam was born there and sprint raider Scenic Blast, trained by Daniel Morton and ridden by Steven Arnold, blitzed the field to win the King's Stand Stakes.

STRANGEST EVENT

1988 Greville Starkey fell inexplicably from Ile De Chypre, the 4/1 second favourite, when in front in the final furlong of the King George V Handicap at Royal Ascot. Four months later a jury in a drug-smuggling case heard that Starkey fell after a blast from a high-tech ultrasonic 'stun gun' that directed a high-pitched sound at the horse. No conclusive proof was ever produced

OTHER EVENTS

1752 The first race meeting in the Haydock area was held at Golborne Heath.

1904 Alluded to in James Joyce's masterpiece, Ulysses, Throwaway won the Ascot Gold Cup.

1949 Alycidon won the Ascot Gold Cup, beating the favourite and previous year's winner, Black Tarquin, by five lengths for owner Lord Derby, ridden by Doug Smith.

1959 Cath Walwyn's Monamolin won Royal Ascot's Windsor Castle Stakes, trained by her husband, Fulke, the great jumps trainer. Exactly fifty years later she attempted to win the same meeting's Coventry Stakes with Treadwell, trained by Jamie Osborne, but was out of luck.

1981 Stockton racecourse in Yorkshire held its final meeting.

1982 Ryan Price won the Bessborough Stakes at Royal Ascot with Spin Of A Coin, ridden by Brian Rouse, and then announced he would retire at the end of the season.

1992 McBeans Nursery in Lewes, Sussex unveiled a white orchid named Dessie in honour of Desert Orchid.

1994 Mind Games became the first Royal Ascot winner for Jack Berry in the Norfolk Stakes. On the same day, spectator James Florey, 20, was hit by Mick Kinane's mount Papago when he strayed on to the course during the Ribblesdale, won by 3/1 favourite Bolas.

1994 Arcadian Heights became the first gelding to win the Ascot Gold Cup, returning 20/1 for Michael Hills and Geoff Wragg.

2005 Hayley Turner had her first Royal Ascot ride on 100/1 shot Skidrow, who was fifth in the Britannia Handicap.

2009 'My underwear is by Marks and Spencer before you ask,' revealed Britain's Got Talent judge Amanda Holden on arrival at Royal Ascot, before anyone had even thought of asking.

QUOTE OF THE DAY

2009 *'Stand on your head and bet your ass!,'* instructed American trainer Wesley Ward before his Cannonball contested the King's Stand Stakes. His optimism was misplaced as the race went to Australia's Scenic Blast.

BIRTHDAYS

1937 Trainer Peter Bailey.

1938 James Bolam, star of 'The Likely Lads' and 'New Tricks', owner of Credo's Daughter and King Credo.

1955 Jockey Colin Magnier, who won the Champion Hurdle on 40/1 For Auction in 1982 and was runner-up in the 1983 Grand National on Greasepaint.

DEATH OF THE DAY

1988 Jockey John 'Jack' Bissill, 73, who won 1937 Scottish National on Right 'Un.

CELEBRITY OF THE DAY

2009 BBC sports presenter John Inverdale's Amour Propre was tenth of 15 in Royal Ascot's King's Stand Stakes.

17 JUNE

SIGNIFICANT EVENT
1954 Riding Never Say Die in the King Edward VII Stakes at Royal Ascot, Lester Piggott was involved in a skirmish with Rashleigh on the final bend. The stewards suspended the youngster for the remainder of meeting and the Jockey Club ruled that because of his 'dangerous and erratic riding' and 'complete disregard for the rules of racing and for the safety of other jockeys' his licence would be withdrawn and he would get it back only if he spent six months working for a trainer other than his father, Keith.

STRANGEST EVENT
2009 Trainers Dandy Nicholls and William Haggas were not best pleased when their horses were withdrawn from the Royal Hunt Cup prior to the start for alleged unruly behaviour. Peter Haynes, later claiming he had been 'f****** pushed' by him, complained: 'He's the senior starter and he couldn't start his own engine.'

OTHER EVENTS
1882 Hindoo won the last of his 36 races, of which the US great won 31, including the 1881 Kentucky Derby.
1910 The first aeroplane flight in Kentucky took place, from and around Churchill Downs racetrack.
1949 Gordon Richards completed the fastest century of winners.
1982 Ardross won his second consecutive Ascot Gold Cup, ridden by Lester Piggott for Henry Cecil.
1989 Champion jockey turned trainer Josh Gifford was awarded the MBE.
1992 The Richard Hannon-trained Lyric Fantasy won the Queen Mary Stakes in record 59.72s, becoming the first juvenile to go under one minute at Ascot. On the same card, Colour Sergeant won the Royal Hunt Cup to become The Queen's first winner at the meeting since 1979.
1994 Sir Mark Prescott saddled his first Royal Ascot winner, Wizard King.

2008 Trainer John Best broke his Royal Ascot duck in style as his 100/1 shot Flashmans Papers - the longest-odds winner at the meeting since Fox Chapel in the 1990 Britannia Handicap - won the Windsor Castle Stakes. Spanish trainer Mauricio Delcher-Sanchez was a 22/1 shock winner of the King's Stand Stakes with Equiano.
2009 Jockey Tadhg O'Shea landed his first Royal Ascot win on Barry Hills's 12/1 shot Ouqba in the Jersey Stakes. Stablemate Infiraad started 5/1 favourite, partnered by first jockey Richard Hills, but finished last of 16.
2009 Jealous Again's Californian trainer Wesley Ward landed his second Royal Ascot winner in consecutive days as his 13/2 shot won the Queen Mary Stakes.
2009 Forgotten Voice, racing on turf for the first time, became the first favourite to win the Royal Hunt Cup since True Panache in 1986. The 4/1 shot was trained by Jeremy Noseda and partnered by Johnny Murtagh.

QUOTE OF THE DAY
2009 *'National Hunt for the sport, but Flat for the business.'* Willie Carson in answer to the question 'Do you prefer Flat racing or jumps' posed by the *Weekender*.

BIRTHDAYS
1937 Jockey John Cook, who turned from Flat to jumps and rode Specify to win the 1971 Grand National.
1964 Tarnya Davis, who in 1986 became the first woman to ride a winner on King George day at Kempton.

DEATH OF THE DAY
1999 Ken 'The Benign Bishop' Oliver, 85. He trained five Scottish Grand National winners, and rode one, his own Sanviuna in 1950.

CELEBRITY OF THE DAY
2009 Showbiz legend Bruce Forsyth presented the trophy for the Jersey Stakes at Royal Ascot.

18 JUNE

SIGNIFICANT EVENT

2009 New Welsh racecourse Ffos Las enjoyed a sellout opening meeting, where Tony McCoy soon established himself as the leading rider at the track with three winners, while commentator Derek Thompson entertained racegoers by referring to the course as 'Ffas Los' and 'Los Ffas'. Trainer Evan Williams sent out the first winner at the new track, Plunkett.

STRANGEST EVENT

2009 Referring to the political scandal of the day, Kamilla Klimczak, a lady raceoger at Royal Ascot, wore a hat bearing a large receipt proclaiming: 'I Paid For This On Expenses.'

OTHER EVENTS

1867 Jockey George Fordham had six winners from seven races at Stockbridge. He dead-heated in the other, but lost the run-off.

1919 Irish Elegance set a weight-carrying record of 9st 11lb for the Royal Hunt Cup, beating 25 opponents under Fred Templeman.

1930 A fierce thunderstorm hit Ascot and lightning struck and killed Mr Hobein of Southport, who was sheltering under a bookie's brolly. The course was flooded and racing was abandoned after the second race, the Royal Hunt Cup, which was won by The McNab, ridden by Freddie Fox.

1941 Trainer Fred Darling had his seventh and final Derby winner - Owen Tudor, 25/1. He also saddled the runner-up, Morogoro, 11/2.

1964 For the first time since Royal Ascot was established, the entire Gold Cup day card was abandoned, due to torrential rain.

1984 Kieren Fallon's first winner was Piccadilly Lord at Navan.

1991 After a six-year drought, Lester Piggott got back on the Royal Ascot scorecard when he won the King Edward VII Stakes on Saddlers' Hall, 7/1.

1992 Drum Taps, trained by Lord Huntingdon, won the Ascot Gold Cup. He was ridden by Frankie Dettori, who was lucky to avoid being bitten on the rear end by Walter Swinburn's mount Arcadian Heights. Trainer Geoff Wragg was ordered to equip the horse with a net muzzle in future.

1993 Mick Channon saddled his first Royal Ascot winner when Great Deeds, 10/1, landed the Windsor Castle Stakes. 12/1 Elbio, trained by Peter Makin and ridden by Walter Swinburn, became the first horse in 59 years (Gold Bridge was the last) to win two King's Stand Stakes.

1994 51-year-old Bruce Raymond handed first whip ban of his 35 year career, after winning on Superpride at Ayr.

1996 It wasn't a yankee bet, but US punter Jeff Thomasson from Barnes in London had two £1 tickets on the Tote dual forecast as 25/1 Sea Freedom beat 100/1 Mirador at Ascot, paying £8,237 per ticket. Thomasson said: 'I liked the names of the horses.'

2009 Aidan O'Brien's 6/4 favourite Yeats, ridden by Johnny Murtagh, won the Ascot Gold Cup for a record fourth successive year, at the age of eight. He was retired later in the year.

QUOTE OF THE DAY

1963 *'Five successful years with I A Balding, one and a half disappointing years with R M Whittaker and a disappointing year with N Tinkler,'* was how jockey Joey Brown, born this day, described his career.

BIRTHDAYS

1945 Broderick Munro-Wilson, rider of The Drunken Duck.

1957 Jockey Ray Cochrane, who rode Kahyasi to win the 1988 Derby.

1971 Jump jockey Ken Whelan.

DEATH OF THE DAY

2005 Racing journalist and gourmand Christopher Poole, 68, of the *London Evening Standard*.

19 JUNE

SIGNIFICANT EVENT
1867 Ruthless, a filly, won the first Belmont Stakes, oldest of the US Triple Crown races, run at Belmont Park over one and five-eighths of a mile.

STRANGEST EVENT
1996 Trainer Alan Bailey's contender for the Royal Hunt Cup was a dead loss – literally. He declared a dead horse, Reverand Thickness, who had been destroyed after breaking his off-fore at Chester on 6 June, hoping to get back his £360 entry fee. If a horse was subject to elimination rather than being withdrawn, entry stakes were refunded. The BHB announced they would investigate the rules loophole.

OTHER EVENTS
1910 Jerry M, runner-up in the Grand National earlier in the year, was injured while winning the Grand Steeplechase de Paris. He didn't appear for two years but came back to win the 1912 National.
1924 First meeting at Naas.
1968 Half-brothers and stablemates Golden Mean (Frankie Durr) and Owen Anthony (Ray Still) fought out the finish of the Royal Hunt Cup with the former, 28/1, winning by half a length.
1993 Leeds supporter Eric Wilkinson's Ooh Ah Cantona was a 12/1 winner at Redcar. On the same card Lester Piggott's daughter Maureen, 32, rode her first winner, Let's Get Lost.
1994 Christy Roche won on Hamseh at Gowran Park to post his 1,438th Irish winner and become the winningmost jockey in Ireland, supplanting Joe Canty, who scored his 1,437 from 1912 to 1952.
1997 For the first time the BBC screened all six races at Royal Ascot, after play at the Test match between England and Australia was abandoned.
2007 Aidan O'Brien trained the first three home in Royal Ascot's St James's Palace Stakes: Excellent Art, Duke Of Marmalade and Astronomer Royal. Miss

Andretti won the King's Stand Stakes – the third Australian winner of the race since 2003, following Choisir and Takeover Target.
2008 Yeats, 11/8 favourite, won a third successive Ascot Gold Cup for the Aidan O'Brien stable, ridden by Johnny Murtagh. Geordieland was second for the second time in succession, five lengths behind.

QUOTE OF THE DAY
2009 *'Others spent a fortune on paper clips, matches, milk frothers, assertiveness training courses and the Racing Post.'* Front-page report in *The Times* on what MPs had been controversially claiming for on their expenses.

BIRTHDAY
1947 Freddie Head, Arc-winning French Champion jockey-turned-trainer

DEATHS OF THE DAY
1877 Admiral John Rous, 82, who established the authority of the Jockey Club in British racing.
1958 US Hall of Fame jockey Jack Westrope, who rode 2,467 winners, was fatally injured during the Hollywood Oaks at Hollywood Park. He was 40.
1998 Jockey Richard 'Dicky' Black, 72, who partnered Fortina to win the 1947 Gold Cup and Rowland Boy to win the Scottish National. He rode more than 500 winners before taking up training.
2003 Kentucky-based trainer William E 'Smiley' Adams, 67, whose 750 career winners included Dusty Run, placed in all three Triple Crown races in 1977.

CELEBRITY OF THE DAY
2009 Henry Cecil saddled his 71st Royal Ascot winner but his first for seven years, as Father Time won the King Edward VII Stakes. The trophy was presented to him by Charlie Watts, drummer of the Rolling Stones, of whom Cecil claimed not be a fan as 'they were before my time.'

20 JUNE

SIGNIFICANT EVENT
1895 Triple Crown winner Isinglass won the Ascot Gold Cup on his final appearance, having won 11 of his 12 races and finished runner-up in the other. He earned record prize-money of £57,455 – a mark that stood until Tulyar finally exceeded it in 1952.

STRANGEST EVENT
2009 Marcus Armytage, writing in the *Daily Telegraph*, revealed that racegoers at Royal Ascot had tried unsuccessfully to smuggle a parrot and a cat into the track. The parrot on its owner's shoulder and the cat 'impeccably dressed with a bow tie'.

OTHER EVENTS
1890 Twelve fillies and eight colts from the Royal Stud, Hampton Court, sold for just over 14,000gns - little more than 700gns each.
1949 All six favourites won at Folkestone.
1952 Lester Piggott rode his first Royal Ascot winner, 100/6 Malka's Boy in the Wokingham.
1967 Royal Ascot double for Scobie Breasley on Mark Royal, 13/2, in the Coventry Stakes and Reform, 4/6, in the St James's Palace Stakes.
1984 Pat Day rode seven winners from eight starts at Churchill Downs, where he had ridden six in a day twice before.
1986 A tough day at the office for jockey Pat Eddery, who was thrown twice, by Dallas and Live In Hope, at Royal Ascot.
1991 Indian Queen became only the second pregnant mare to win the Ascot Gold Cup. La Fleche was the first in 1894.
1992 London-born South African champion jockey Jeff Lloyd, 30, became the first to ride 300 winners in a season there with a double at Clairwood.
1993 Pat Lalor, chairman of the stewards at Sandown in Melbourne, caused uproar when lodging a protest to the winner after runner-up Disrepute's

rider Danny Nikolic did not object to 7/4 favourite and first past the post, Alias Comberbache. Having lodged the protest, Lalor then upheld it and handed the race to the 25/1 outsider.
1993 The Turkish Derby at Veliefendi was won, simply enough, by The Best.
1997 US jockey Gary Stevens rode his first Royal Ascot winner, 6/1 shot Predappio in the Hardwicke Stakes.
2009 Tom Queally rode his first Group One winner as the Michael Bell-trained Art Connoisseur landed a 20/1 shock in Royal Ascot's Golden Jubilee 6f sprint, which had attracted an international field including J J The Jet Plane from South Africa, Cannonball, the runner-up, from the US, Sacred Kingdom from Hong Kong, Ialysos from Greece and Bushranger from Ireland.
2009 The Nicky Henderson-trained Caracciola won the Queen Alexandra Stakes at the grand old age of 12 to become the oldest winner at Royal Ascot. She also became the oldest horse to win a Listed race.

QUOTE OF THE DAY
'*He's a certainty.*' Lester Piggott's words, as reported by Willie Carson to BBC viewers, about big gambler Harry Findlay's contender for the 2009 Wokingham Stakes at Royal Ascot. Not a bad tip as the 6/1 High Standing swooped to take the lead almost on the line.

DEATHS OF THE DAY
1995 Paddy Powell, 67, rider of the Irish Derby and Irish St Leger winner Zarathustra.
1997 US jockey Chris Valovich, 41, who rode more than 2,000 winners, shot himself.

CELEBRITY OF THE DAY
1905 For the first time the reigning monarch, King Edward VII, arrived at Ascot races by motor vehicle, instead of the customary carriage.

21 JUNE

SIGNIFICANT EVENT
1982 Dawn Run, who went on to set a record winning prize-money total for a jumper of £259,740, scored her first victory in a £572 Flat race at Tralee, ridden by her 62-year-old owner, Charmian Hill.

STRANGEST EVENT
1832 The Eclipse Foot was run at Ascot and the 1830 Derby winner, Priam, took the prize - Eclipse's foot, or at least one of his hooves set as a snuff box in gold.

OTHER EVENTS
1944 Jockeys Jack Moylan and George Wells fought out the finish of the Irish Derby - twice. First as Moylan on 4/7 favourite Slide On prevailed from Wells on 7/2 shot Water Street by a head, then again in the weighing room when Moylan took exception to Wells' riding tactics and floored him with a single blow. One of the stewards who fined him £10 was Dermot McCalmont, owner of Slide On.

1961 A record field of 18 competed for the £7,921 first prize in the Irish Derby, with Herbert Holmes winning on 33/1 Your Highness for trainer Humphrey Cottrill.

1963 Trelawny completed a unique Ascot Stakes-Queen Alexandra Stakes double at the same Royal Ascot meeting - for the second consecutive season.

1965 The last meeting was run at Bromford Bridge, four miles from Birmingham city centre, where triple Champion Hurdle winner Sir Ken won the Champion Trial Hurdle on three occasions. Lester Piggott rode a double on the evening card on London Way and Selly Oak. The track became a housing estate.

1984 Gildoran won the Ascot Gold Cup in a record 4m 18.81s, knocking 2.55s off Tubalcain's 1966 time.

1993 Ray Cochrane rode his 1,000th domestic winner when Declassified,5/2, won at Windsor.

2002 Pat Eddery went past Lester Piggott's total of 4,493 career winners at Goodwood on Lady Pahia, becoming the second most prolific British rider, behind only Sir Gordon Richards.

2007 Racing journalist Lydia Hislop observed pre-meeting: 'Today's meeting is widely billed as Ladies' Day. To any sensible woman, it's Ascot Gold Cup day.' Yeats won the Gold Cup for the second straight time at 8/13, beating Geordieland by a length and a half.

2008 Aidan O'Brien rounded off the Royal Ascot meeting by winning the Queen Alexandra Stakes with Honolulu, 7/4, having begun it by winning the opening Queen Anne Stakes on 5/1 Haradasun – and winning four more in between, all ridden by Johnny Murtagh.

QUOTE OF THE DAY
1992 *'Who was the last jockey to ride in two Derbys without getting round in either?'* asked Ray Cochrane rhetorically on the day after his Epsom Derby mount Young Senor had been withdrawn when refusing to enter the stalls, then 24 hours later his Austrian Derby mount, Green Foot, had at least gone into the starting gate, only for the stall to remain firmly closed when the others opened.

BIRTHDAYS
1925 Owner Charles St George, who won the Arc with Rheingold and the St Leger with Bruni and Michelozzo.

1934 Clive Chapman, jump jockey turned actor.

1940 Julian Wilson, BBC commentator, Swindon Town fan and owner of 1977 Gimcrack Stakes winner Tumbledownwind.

1944 Royal jockey Richard Dennard.

1955 Mtoto's trainer Alec Stewart.

CELEBRITY OF THE DAY
1950 Comic actor Enn Reitel, voice behind many of the Spitting Image puppets, amateur rider and owner, was born.

22 JUNE

SIGNIFICANT EVENT

2009 Trainer Nicky Henderson was found guilty of rule breaches after the Queen's horse Moonlit Path was found to have run with a prohibited substance at Huntingdon in February. He was later suspended from training for three months.

STRANGEST EVENT

2009 Lingfield's 3.45 race was the Durex Pleasuremax Handicap. Make your own jokes about withdrawals, coming too early, etc.

OTHER EVENTS

1922 The Aga Khan III (Aga Sultan Sir Mahomed Shah) had his first British winner when Cos won at Royal Ascot.

1934 Brown Jack, ridden as usual by Steve Donoghue, won the Queen Alexandra Stakes for a record sixth successive year, sparking memorable scenes of celebration. Trainer Ivor Anthony had been unable to watch the race and sat under a tree in the paddock.

1955 Jimmy Eddery, father of Pat, rode Panaslipper to win the 13 runner Irish Derby at 4/1. The colt was trained by Seamus McGrath.

1960 Emotional scenes at the Irish Derby, which was won by 3/1 shot Chamour, ridden by Garnie Bougoure. The colt was trained officially by Phonsie O'Brien, who was handling the horse for his brother Vincent, who had been suspended from May that year until November 30, 1961 after the stewards of the Turf Club decided 'a drug or stimulant had been administered to Chamour' in the Ballysax Maiden Plate in April. Vincent denied it vehemently and went fishing while the Derby was run. In December the sentence was reduced by six months.

1978 Greville Starkey became only the third jockey after Lester Piggott in 1957 and Geoff Lewis in 1971 to win the Derby (Shirley Heights), Oaks (Fair Salinia) and Ascot Gold Cup

(Shangamuzo) in the same year.

1984 Dawn Run completed a unique treble of the Irish, English and French Champion Hurdles in the same season when winning the Grande Course de Haies d'Auteuil, ridden by Tony Mullins.

1992 Trainer Bill Preece celebrated his 100th career win, more than four months after the race. Baluchi was confirmed as the winner of a Ludlow chase run on February 5, after Beau Rose was disqualified due to a positive dope test.

2006 The Aidan O'Brien-trained Yeats was an unexpected 7/1 winner of the Ascot Gold Cup, partnered by Kieren Fallon. Having not quite made the Classic grade, he had been pushed up in distance.

QUOTE OF THE DAY

2009 *'It's on our radar but not our agenda'* Cheltenham's Edward Gillespie is a little coy about including Saturday as part of the Cheltenham Festival.

BIRTHDAYS

1948 Trainer Philip Mitchell, who sent out King's Glory to win the 1982 Lincoln and also trained Peter O'Sullevan's Attivo.

1959 Jockey Mick Kinane, who at the age of 50 found the horse of a lifetime in Sea The Stars, who won the 2,000 Guineas, Derby, Eclipse, International, Irish Champion and Prix de l'Arc de Triomphe.

1984 Jump jockey Sam Thomas.

DEATHS OF THE DAY

1989 French trainer Olivier Douieb, 42, of lung cancer. He trained Detroit to win the 1980 Arc.

2005 Pat Mitchell, 62, who trained Tauber, prolific winning sprinter of the late 1980s/early 1990s.

2007 Trainer Jack Ormston, 97. He sent out Le Garcon D'Or to win at least once every year from 1960 to 1972, eventually winning 34 races.

23 JUNE

SIGNIFICANT EVENT
1993 Kent Desormeaux, 23, became the youngest rider to reach 2,500 winners when landing two victories at Hollywood Park, passing the mark set by Chris McCarron at the age of 25.

STRANGEST EVENT
1990 Sister Mary Joy rode the favourite, Scrubs, to win the International Nun Race run at Trim, County Meath.

OTHER EVENTS
1744 'There was a very extraordinary horse race between a six-year-old horse and one aged 21. They ran 14 miles round the said course and performed it in 39 minutes for 100 guineas, which were won by the former, only by a horse's length. There were great wagers laid and the greatest concourse of people ever seen there,' reported the Westminster Journal of a race in Lincoln.

1880 A horse with no name won the richest Irish Derby, worth £475 to the winner. Francis Wynne rode the colt, later called King Of The Bees, for trainer Dan Broderick.

1914 J J Parkinson sent out five of the six winners on the Curragh card.

1920 He Goes did just that, landing the Irish Derby and 3,400 sovereigns for trainer Joe Butters and jockey Fred Templeman.

1926 The English-trained Irish 2,000 Guineas winner Embargo doubled up in the Irish Derby, partnered by Steve Donoghue at 4/5.

1934 Omaha won at Aqueduct for the only time in a nine-race juvenile career. He was a revelation as a three-year-old, winning the US Triple Crown, and raced in the Ascot Gold Cup as a four-year-old, losing narrowly to Quashed.

1937 Trainers Fred (Gold Cup and Grand National winner) and Mercy (Champion Hurdle winner) Rimell were married.

1945 Trainer Robert Fetherstonhaugh and jockey Jack Moylan won the Irish Derby for the second straight year as Piccadilly, 25/1, beat seven rivals.

1948 Jockey Rae Johnstone rode Nathoo to victory in the Irish Derby on his first trip to the country, having already won the Epsom (My Love) and French (Bey) equivalents that season. Nathoo was trained by Frank Butters in Newmarket for the Aga Khan.

1954 At 50/1 Zarathustra became the longest-priced winner of the Irish Derby.

1967 Jockey Doug Smith rode at Royal Ascot for the final time. He won the Wokingham on 100/6 Spaniard's Mount but was beaten on his final mount, Rose Of Tralee, in the King's Stand.

1999 The minimum win dividend on the Tote was cut from £1.10 to £1.05, in response to heavy backing of big odds-on favourites that took advantage of the over-generous minimum.

2009 Tony McCoy rode his 3,000th British jumps winner, Havenstone, at Newton Abbot.

QUOTE OF THE DAY
2009 *'He's a bit of a mongrel, but then this is a dog track.'* Even though his Penang Cinta had won at Brighton, trainer David Evans could not hide his disdain for the course.

BIRTHDAY
1982 Former US champion jockey Rafael Bejarano.

DEATH OF THE DAY
1945 Trainer Tom Leader, 66, whose 100/1 Gregalach won the 1929 Grand National two years after stablemate Sprig.

FIRST OF THE DAY
1875 Innishowen, 2/1 second favourite, saddled by G Ashworth from Staffordshire, became the first winner of the Irish Derby trained outside the country.

24 JUNE

SIGNIFICANT EVENT
1970 All-time great Brigadier Gerard won on his debut in Newbury's Berkshire Stakes at a subsequently unimaginable 100/7.

STRANGEST EVENT
1874 Breeder, owner and rider Sir Tatton Sykes was so unimpressed with Lily Agnes that he gave her away to stud groom James Snarry, who made best use of her to win the Northumberland Plate. She became dam of Ormonde, the 1886 Triple Crown winner.

OTHER EVENTS
1885 St Kevin was third yesterday to The Chicken, and would finish behind that rival again tomorrow, but on this day, ridden by Henry Saunders, he won the Irish Derby with The Chicken fourth.

1914 The Guller, trained by Johnny Osborne, 81, emerged from his Brecongill yard at Middleham to win the Northumberland Plate.

1914 Land Of Song, 3/1, made it successive Irish Derby wins for trainer Atty Persse and jockey Steve Donoghue.

1925 Harry Beasley somehow managed to don the wrong colours but still won the Irish Derby on 5/2 favourite Zionist. The Aga Khan, the winning owner, was fined two sovereigns for the mix-up.

1931 For the first time in ten years a home-trained runner won the Irish Derby as Joseph Canty partnered unbeaten Sea Serpent.

1943 Unbeaten 2/5 shot The Phoenix, trained by Frederick Myerscough of Dublin, who went on to be 1/8 favourite for Irish St Leger – and lost.

1953 Premonition (Harry Carr) and Chamier (Bill Rickaby) passed the post together in the first Irish Derby photo-finish, with the former winning by a head. Vincent O'Brien, trainer of 5/4 favourite Chamier, objected successfully on the grounds of boring and was awarded the race. Premonition was placed last to the fury of trainer Captain Boyd-Rochfort, who refused to run another horse in his native land for more than ten years.

1959 Fidalgo, runner-up in the Derby at Epsom, went one better by winning the Irish Derby under Joe Mercer.

1960 Shamrock Star equalled the 5f course record at Newcastle, having broken the 5f record at Redcar already and six days later doing the same at Liverpool; 4yo dead by end of season.

1994 Goodwood lost a day's racing due to an electric storm.

1995 Mary Reveley saddled her 1,000th winner, Hit The Canvas, at Ayr. The total comprised 608 winners over jumps and 392 on the Flat.

2009 Trainer Alan Swinbank sent out 20/1 Stevie Gee to win the stable's 400th race in the oldest event in the calendar, the historic Carlisle Bell, which dates back to 1599.

QUOTE OF THE DAY
2009 *'I hope I don't live long enough to see the Derby run over ten furlongs.'* John McCririck suggested that the way to revitalise the Triple Crown would be to leave the 2,000 Guineas alone, switch the Derby to 10f and run the Leger over one and a half miles, but his closing comment indicated that he didn't think it was desirable.

BIRTHDAY
1971 Trainer Ralph Beckett, whose Muhannak won 2008 Breeders' Cup Marathon.

DEATH OF THE DAY
2009 Ray Rooney, former senior steward of the Turf Club and owner of Supreme Novices' Hurdle winner Golden Cygnet.

CELEBRITY OF THE DAY
1994 The Birmingham Midshires Building Society Handicap at Wolverhampton was the first race to feature commercial logo sponsorship on number cloths, with owners getting £32 each.

25 JUNE

SIGNIFICANT EVENT

1930 For the last time there was a run-off to decide a race that had finished in a dead heat. The judge could not separate Ruby's Love, ridden by Jim Kirby, and Walloon, partnered by Tommy Lowrey, at the end of the 7f Berkshire Selling Handicap at Newbury. Ruby's Love prevailed by three-quarters of a length in the re-run.

STRANGEST EVENT

2004 Henry and Anne Yearley, owners with Newmarket trainer Michael Bell, were reported to have died in a bizarre suicide pact. They were 62 and 56 respectively.

OTHER EVENTS

1812 Champ De Mars racecourse in Mauritius held its first meeting.
1919 The record £3,550 first prize for the Irish Derby stayed at home as the James J Parkinson-trained Loch Lomond romped to a six-length win. Miss Cowhy became the first winning lady owner.
1924 The first Irish Derby dead-heat saw even-money favourite Haine share the spoils with 3/1 shot Zodiac.
1939 Despite being boxed in and nearly brought down, Charlie Elliott extracted Pharis to produce a devastating turn of foot to win the 1m7f Grand Prix de Paris for trainer Marcel Boussac.
1942 Windsor Slipper, 2/7, cruised to victory in the Irish Derby in a record 2m35s. He went on to complete the Irish Triple Crown.
1947 Third in the English 2,000 Guineas and Derby, Sayajirao started evens for the Irish Derby and won by a length and half for jockey Edgar Britt and trainer Frederick Lakin Armstrong, universally known as Sam.
1958 Trainer Michael Dawson, whose father (also Michael) rode three and trained four winners of the Irish Derby, won the Classic with Sindon.
1982 Former champion jump jockey Bob Davies retired, having ridden 911 winners.
1989 Former British champion jumps trainer Michael Dickinson sent out his 50th US winner, The Way It's Bin, at Philadelphia Park.
1993 Good news for jockey Richard Hills, who rode a 407/1 treble at Bath. Bad news for Richard Hills, who was short-headed on 10/1 shot Latest Flame and received a four-day suspension.
2008 Kentucky Horse Racing Authority suspended trainer Rick Durrow for 15 days and demanded return of $20,000 prize money after his Salute The Count tested positive for twice allowable level of a substance which helps burn fat and promotes mucscle growth.

QUOTE OF THE DAY

1977 *'Don't be *****ng silly. I've got to go out there and earn my £14 riding fee in the next race.'* Lester Piggott to the course doctor at Leopardstown, upon being advised to give up his remaining rides after falling from Glencoe Lights when his stirrup broke. Earlier, Piggott had won the Irish Derby on Robert Sangster's The Minstrel, the 11/10 favourite.

BIRTHDAYS

1912 Dorothy Laird, president of the Lady Jockeys' Association.
1942 Trainer Richard Whitaker, dual winner of the Thirsk Hunt Cup.
1953 Allan Keane, jockey turned equine dentist

DEATHS OF THE DAY

1949 Captain Oswald Marmaduke Dalby Bell, the Lambourn trainer whose Felstead won the 1928 Derby. He was born in Australia in 1871.
1991 Tony Dickinson, 75, father of record-breaking jumps trainer Michael. Known as 'The Boss', Tony had started training in 1967. On the same day, trainer Ryan Jarvis, whose Front Row won the 1968 Irish 1,000 Guineas, died, aged 77.

26 JUNE

SIGNIFICANT EVENT
1993 There was a Geordie-Mackem showdown in the Newcastle Brown Ale Northumberland Plate as Highflying, running in the Sunderland colours of red and white for owners Brian Batey and Ronnie Murray, stormed to a 7/1 triumph over 17 rivals including Newcastle United vice-chairman Douglas Hall's unplaced Welsh Mill.

STRANGEST EVENT
1971 Linden Tree, the 7/4 favourite, ridden by Duncan Keith for Peter Walwyn, took a stride out of the stalls as the Irish Sweeps Derby got under way, swerved to his left and stopped dead, leaving 7/2 second favourite Irish Ball to win.

OTHER EVENTS
1895 Portmarnock, 2/5, ridden by William Clayton, won the Irish Derby by a record margin of 12 lengths. Clayton's fortunes declined and he committed suicide in 1904.

1935 100/1 when winning the Irish 2,000 Guineas, Museum returned 100/8 when adding the eight-runner Irish Derby. He later collected the Irish St Leger to complete the Irish Triple Crown, all ridden by Steve Donoghue.

1954 Jockey Tommy Lowrey rode his last winner, Florient, at Doncaster.

1965 Actor-crooner Bing Crosby was part-owner of Irish Sweeps Derby winner Meadow Court, and to celebrate the Lester Piggott-inspired victory Crosby gave a rendition of 'When Irish Eyes Are Smiling' in the winner's enclosure.

1976 Joanna Morgan became the first woman to contest the Irish Derby, finishing 14th of 17 on Riot Helmet, behind 5/1 winner Malacate.

1982 Busaco won at Newmarket to give Willie Carson his 2,000th winner in Britain.

1982 Christy Roche rode Robert Sangster's Assert to win Irish Derby for trainer David O'Brien, three weeks after his mount triumphed in Prix du Jockey Club, becoming first British trained horse to complete double.

1991 Luca Cumani won the Heads Nook Maiden Fillies' Stakes at Carlisle with Shardelisada, his fifth win in the last six runnings of the race.

1992 Pat Eddery rode a British-record seven winners in a day – three at Newmarket in the afternoon and four more at Newcastle in the evening.

1994 Chris McCarron won on Andestine at Hollywood Park to become the first jockey to reach 6,000 career winners.

2009 The British Horseracing Authority banned jockey Darren Williams for three months and fined fellow jockey Fergal Lynch £50,000 over breaches of the rules in their associations with disqualified punter Miles Rodgers.

2009 'Although this has not been raised as an issue before, the message has been very clear. We like to think we are a listening racecourse, and we will be allowing ice creams in Members from now on.' Jeremy Martin, Salisbury clerk of the course, after the track was criticised for preventing racegoers in Members from consuming ice creams on a hot afternoon.

QUOTE OF THE DAY
1941 *'Is it desirable to allow these insane and unseemly spectacles to continue?'* demanded Labour MP Manny Shinwell on this day during a Parliamentary debate, following reports that 50,000 had attended the Derby, costing the country half a million hours of workers' time during WWII.

DEATHS OF THE DAY
2000 Lucien Laurin, trainer of legendary US Triple Crown winner Secretariat, died, aged 88.

2005 Richard Whiteley, Countdown presenter and a keen racing man, died, aged 61. Whiteley was honorary mayor of Wetwang in east Yorkshire and named one of his horses Mare Of Wetwang.

27 JUNE

SIGNIFICANT EVENT
1993 Henry Cecil's Derby winner Commander In Chief, ridden by Pat Eddery, beat French Derby winner Hernando into second in the Irish Derby.

STRANGEST EVENT
1969 Different times – a dead-heater in a Newcastle seller was called Nig Nog.

OTHER EVENTS
1866 The inaugural Irish Derby was won by Charles Maidment on Silem, at the Curragh over 1m6f3yds. The 5/4 chance beat two rivals.
1900 Mr Graham Wildman Lushington, aka Tommy, became the second and final amateur to win the Irish Derby, on board 6/1 chance Gallinaria.
1903 Major Eustace Loder's Pretty Polly made her debut, winning by 10l from Lily Langtry's Vergia in a two-year-old race at Sandown. She went on to win 22 of her 24 races, including the 1,000 Guineas, Oaks and St Leger.
1951 A record field of 16 lined up in the Irish Derby, won by 5/2 favourite Fraise Du Bois II, ridden by Charlie Smirke for Harry Wragg.
1970 Nijinsky won the Irish Derby at 4/11, ridden by Liam Ward for Vincent O'Brien.
1979 British-born trainer Sally Ann Bailie's Poison Ivory set a world-record 1m33s for the turf mile at Belmont.
1990 Pat Eddery completed the fastest century of winners since Gordon Richards (17 June 1949), with a double at Kempton.
2009 The racegoers' reaction at Newcastle was, to say the least, muted as the Totescoop 6 Handicap was won by Roker Park, name of the former ground of Newcastle's bitter football rivals, Sunderland, and owned by Sunderland fan Trevor Alderson, whose ambition it had been to have a winner at the track. He had another later, with Horatio Carter, named after a legendary Sunderland player.
2009 Racecourse announcements failed to find the owner of a full set of false teeth found in Windsor racecourse car park.

QUOTE OF THE DAY
1919 *'I still don't approve of women jockeys, except in point-to-points and hunter chases, of course. Really, they're not the right make or shape for it.'* Trainer Mercy Rimell who was born this day and won the 1983 Champion Hurdle with Gaye Brief, having also been assistant to her late husband, Fred.

BIRTHDAYS
1934 Jockey Keith Temple-Nidd, who partnered Space King and Ruby's Princess.
1948 Trainer Angel Penna jr.
1960 John Hammond, trainer of 1991 Arc winner Suave Dancer.

DEATHS OF THE DAY
1920 Champion jockey in 1902 with 170 winners, William Lane died at Tower House, Lingfield, still suffering from the effects of a Lingfield fall in 1904, which came just a fortnight after completing the fillies' Triple Crown on Pretty Polly.
1986 Dawn Run, the only horse to complete the Champion Hurdle-Cheltenham Gold Cup double, was killed when she fell in the French Champion Hurdle at Auteuil. She ran 35 times, winning 21 for record prize-money of £259,740.
1988 Jump jockey Arthur Thompson, 71, who won the Grand National on Sheila's Cottage in 1948 and Teal in 1952.

CELEBRITY OF THE DAY
2009 Andrew Lloyd Webber's Dar Re Mi won the Audi Pretty Polly Stakes at the Curragh, after which the composer's wife Madeleine joked with Audi boss John Hayes: 'We'll send you a CD if you send us an Audi.'

28 JUNE

SIGNIFICANT EVENT
1947 Gordon Richards was beaten on 1/20 'certainty' Glendower at Chepstow and was mortified to learn that one fan who always backed Gordon's best ride of day to win him £1,000 had lost £20,000 as a result.

STRANGEST EVENT
1882 Nicholas Behan – whose three brothers, William, Jack and Phillie, all trained Irish Derby winners – became the only family member to ride an Irish Derby winner when he partnered Sortie to a 5/1 victory.

OTHER EVENTS
1871 The Irish Derby was run over 1m6f for the last time, with Maid Of Time becoming the first filly to win

1905 Flax Park was the 5/1 Irish Derby winner, partnered by jockey Peter Hughes, who had bought a new whip for the race and drove his mount so vigorously that when he pulled up after the race, only the handle of his stick had survived.

1911 A second successive Irish Derby win for jockey John Doyle, riding 6/1 shot Shanballymore.

1969 Geoff Lewis, a hotel page boy before becoming a jockey, rode 7/2 second favourite Prince Regent to win the Irish Sweeps Derby for French trainer Etienne Pollet.

1969 Bill O'Gorman saddled his first winner as a trainer. The man who rode Henry Cecil's first-ever winner, Celestial Cloud, a month earlier, sent out Golden Masquerade for a Newmarket maiden - and won courtesy of the stewards.

1975 Pat Eddery won the Irish Derby on Grundy, having already won the Derby at Epsom, which he said was 'the ultimate test for any human or equine athlete'.

1993 Jockey David 'Dandy' Nicholls, whose 421 winners included 13 on high-class sprinter Soba, retired, aged 37.

1995 For the first time a mother-daughter combination won at a major Australian track as High Rose, trained by Dianne Wynne and ridden by daughter Sally, landed the St Kevin's Handicap at Caulfield.

2009 Coolmore, having owned the winners of the last ten Irish Classics, had six runners in the first Irish Derby to be contested only by Irish-trained runners since 1957. They won again with Fame And Glory. Trainer Aidan O'Brien took his total of Irish Derby wins to seven, one ahead of his late namesake Vincent O'Brien.

2009 Carl Llewellyn brought down the curtain on his short-lived career as a trainer, sending out his final runners at Uttoxeter before going into business partnership with Nigel Twiston-Davies.

2009 Banned from racing in Britain after playing up at the start, Sir Michael Stoute's Spanish Moon went to France for the Grand Prix de Saint-Cloud. The stalls handlers performed a minor miracle to get Spanish Moon in – and the horse went on to win.

QUOTE OF THE DAY
2009 *'I can stomach anywhere save Brighton, which I last visited in 1984,'* said Channel 4 presenter Jim McGrath when asked to name his favourite racecourse, opting for Longchamp. If forced to attend a fancy dress party, he said he would go as 'probably, Peter Easterby'.

BIRTHDAYS
1957 Phil Gleaves, an English-born trainer in the US.

1975 Jockey Martin Dwyer, devoted rider of Persian Punch.

1978 Channel 4 presenter Nick Luck.

CELEBRITY OF THE DAY
1791 George, Prince of Wales, later King George IV, reportedly won £17,000 at Ascot by backing his 20/1 winner of the Oatlands Stakes, Baronet, ridden by Sam Chifney. It was the first big race at the track, worth 2,950gns to the winner in a year when the Derby was worth £1,076.

29 JUNE

SIGNIFICANT EVENT
1993 Old Hook won at Folkestone, landing a coup for trainer Ray Smith after accomplices backed the horse in betting shops at 20/1 right at the off. The winnings were estimated at £100,000 for those 'in the know'. The horse's previous form had not been listed in many papers, and the horse had acquired an 'IRE' suffix, having arrived from Belgium for the race.

STRANGEST EVENT
2009 Trainer Ian Semple's Trade Price, returning from Musselburgh where he had finished third, shocked his horsebox driver on the M8 when he joined him in the driver's cab, having somehow climbed over an internal partition. The horse became jammed there and firemen had to be called to cut him out.

OTHER EVENTS
1769 Salisbury was graced by the great Eclipse, who won the City Free Plate.
1887 The richest prize in the history of Irish racing, £763, was on offer to the winner of Irish Derby and a record 11 runners turned out. The race was won by 6/1 third favourite Pet Fox, ridden by Terry Kavanagh and trained by his owner, Henry Linde.
1929 En route to being runner-up in the jockeys' championship behind Gordon Richards, Freddie Fox rode five winners at Sandown. Fox won the title the following year and ended up with six Classic winners including Derby winners Cameronian (1931) and Bahram (1935).
1963 Relko, the 8/11 favourite, was withdrawn not under orders after going lame prior to the Irish Sweeps Derby. The race was won by 100/7 Ragusa, ridden by Garnie Bougoure and trained by Paddy Prendergast.
1968 Sir Ivor, the 2,000 Guineas and Derby winner, was expected to walk the Irish Derby as the 1/3 favourite, but Lester Piggott on Ribero pulled off a 100/6 shock for trainer Johnson Houghton.

1974 Peter Walwyn saddled 8/1 English Prince to win the Irish Sweeps Derby, ridden by Yves Saint-Martin. Owner Vera Hue-Williams saw husband Colonel Hue-Williams finish second with 11/5 favourite Imperial Prince. The pair collected £90,993 prize-money.
1988 Mohammed Moubarak, who later moved to Qatar, saddled his first winner, Libra's Comet, 5/1, at Lingfield.
1994 The punter who placed £3,000 on 13/8 favourite Azureus at Catterick was either very loyal or very stupid, as the horse had refused to race three times. He promptly made it four.

QUOTE OF THE DAY
1982 *'Joe Mercer will go down in the annals of the turf as the best jockey never to have won the Epsom Derby,'* wrote Richard Baerlein in his biography of the pipe-smoking rider who, on this day, was partnering King's Soldier, trained by Peter Walwyn, to win a maiden race at Folkestone.

BIRTHDAYS
1946 Chris Read, who finished third in the 1977 Grand National on Eyecatcher, and later became a trainer at Pulborough.
1952 Trainer Myriam Bollack-Badel, handler of Air De Rien and Reve D'Oscar.

DEATHS OF THE DAY
1991 A 35-year-old woman was killed when scaffolding fell from the grandstand at Santa Anita during an earthquake measuring 6.0 on the Richter scale. The course was being used to train horses at the time.
2000 Top German trainer Bruno Schutz, 60, whose Caitano won the Gran Premio del Jockey Club in Milan in 1997 before finishing third in the Arc.
2000 John Aspinall, zoo owner, casino owner and racehorse owner, died. His pink colours decorated with playing card suits were carried by 1962 Portland Handicap winner Harmon. He also had a stake in Garnishee, who won the Massey Ferguson Gold Cup in 1974.

30 JUNE

SIGNIFICANT EVENT
1962 The inaugural running of the Irish Sweeps Derby attracted a field of 24 and French raider Tambourine II, ridden by Roger Poincelet and trained by Etienne Pollet, won by a short-head at 15/2. The winning sweep ticket, worth £50,000, was won by Melbourne dairy farmer and bookmaker Albert Smith.

STRANGEST EVENT
1990 Willie Carson became only the third jockey in the 20th century to ride six winners at a single UK meeting when scoring a 3,246/1 accumulator at Newcastle. He was unplaced in the third race on the seven-race card, and he later joked that had it been the last race he would definitely have won!

OTHER EVENTS
1897 Having ridden one winner during the season up to this point, Tommy Fiely rode six at the three-day Irish Derby meeting, including the big one on 4/1 favourite Wales.

1930 The patrol camera was introduced to British racing at Newmarket.

1964 Northern Dancer, who became the most influential stallion in the world, sustained an injury during training for a race at Belmont and never ran again. Bred in Canada by E P Taylor, he won the Kentucky Derby, in record time, and the Preakness Stakes.

1979 Davona Dale, the 1/10 favourite, won the American Oaks at Belmont Park to complete the fillies' Triple Crown under Jorge Velasquez.

1987 Michael Dickinson sent out his first Flat winner in the US, Bold Magestrate at Philadelphia Park.

1991 The Irish Derby set a record for the amount bet with on-course bookies on a single race in Ireland. Ir£378,000 was gambled on the race, won by Generous.

1995 A trial at Wolverhampton saw marker poles used for the first time on a British track, with riders having to maintain draw position until reaching markers placed 60-100 yards up the track.

2002 Local trainer Steve Woodman won his first race at Goodwood in 16 years of holding a licence when Common Consent won the Mail On Sunday/Tote Mile Handicap.

2009 Alan Lee, respected racing writer for *The Times*, raised the issue of horses with a propensity to bleed not being permitted to receive medication: 'The authorities have made no effort to address the "bleeding" issue even though research has shown that 90 per cent of all thoroughbreds bleed to some extent during a race.' He asked: 'How humane is that?'

2009 The Tote's Super7 bet was won for only the third time, with three tickets winning £292,931.39 each, including, for the first time, one from a punter staking a single £2 line.

2009 Australian jockey Kerrin McEvoy rode his 1,000th winner when partnering Bright Mind at Randwick, Sydney.

QUOTE OF THE DAY
'He's the all-time bravest horse I have trained and consistency is his hallmark,' was the complimentary opinion of trainer Dermot Weld on Vinnie Roe, who became a four-time winner of the Irish St Leger in 2004.

BIRTHDAYS
1929 Rex Hamey, rider of Linwell, on whom he won the 1956 Mildmay Chase at Sandown, and Vivant.

1949 Chris Thornton, trainer, six times winner of Ayr's Bogside Cup.

DEATHS OF THE DAY
2001 Jimmy Harris, 66, a jump jockey until breaking his back in a fall at Huntingdon in 1971, leaving him in a wheelchair. He became a trainer, sending out winners under both codes for thirty years. He trained Vindaloo to win 11 races on the Flat in 1995.

1 JULY

SIGNIFICANT EVENT
2009 Rule introduced in France meaning that cheekpieces must be declared in advance. On the same day, according to magazine *The Week*: 'From July 1, horse owners will have to sign a pledge not to eat their animals. The EU's horse identification regulations are designed to prevent horses which have been treated with harmful drugs from entering the food chain.'!

STRANGEST EVENT
1974 Trainer Harry Bell's Traffic Leader won the seller at Edinburgh – and was then saddled again for the ladies' race, finishing second by a length.

OTHER EVENTS
1957 Doug Smith rode at four tracks – winning at three – in a 53-hour spell ending today. He won at Lingfield, Brighton and Wolverhampton, but drew a blank at Longchamp.

1966 Panamanian jockey Laffit Pincay rode his first winner in the US, Teacher's Art at Arlington. He went on to become the sport's leading money winner.

1967 Described by Lester Piggott as the best he ever rode, Sir Ivor was beaten first time out at the Curragh but went on to win eight of his 13 races, including the 1968 Derby.

1968 Margery Nightingall, who took over the training licence at South Hatch, Epsom, when her brother Walter died the previous month, sent out her first winner, Tyronera, ridden by Piggott.

1972 The Scobie Breasley-trained Steel Pulse was a 10/1 winner of the Irish Sweeps Derby under Bill Williamson.

1978 Greville Starkey won the Irish Sweeps Derby on Shirley Heights, the 5/4 favourite, for John Dunlop.

1982 Having injured his neck in a fall at Southwell the previous October, jockey Jeff Pearce, 34, retired.

1987 Mark Johnston saddled his first winner, Hinari Video, at Carlisle.

1990 Salsabil, ridden by Willie Carson and trained by John Dunlop, became the first filly in the 20th century to win the Irish Derby and the first to complete the 1,000 Guineas/Oaks/Irish Derby treble.

1992 Epsom held its first evening meeting. .

1993 A Racehorse Owners' Association survey voted Ascot the least owner-friendly track in the UK – the best track in the survey was Uttoxeter.

1997 *Sporting Life* tipster Steve Delve went through the card at Hamilton – 6/1; 6/4; 9/1; 7/2; 2/1; 3/1 – 9,449/1.

1998 'A day at the races cost the Queen £11,843 last year – the amount charged by Railtrack to take the royal train 21 miles from Victoria to Tattenham Corner for the Derby. The cost of £564 per mile compares unfavourably to the normal day return fare of £10,' pointed out Alan Hamilton in *The Times*.

2007 Betting shops become smoke-free.

2009 After just one race, Worcester was abandoned due to extreme heat and water shortage. The Charlie Egerton-trained Highland Laddie needed hundreds of gallons of water poured over him after collapsing twice after his race.

QUOTE OF THE DAY
2007 *'She was always a bitch in the box; her eyes would change and she'd try to jump over the box walls. Pure evil,'* said Ouija Board's head lad, Chris Hinson, recalling the great filly's aversion to horseboxes.

BIRTHDAYS
1931 Epsom trainer Michael Haynes. He was a dual-code jockey from 1946 to 1959 and trained Popsi's Joy to win the 1980 Cesarewitch.

1933 Trainer Peter Tyndall Walwyn, who won the 1975 Derby with Grundy.

DEATHS OF THE DAY
1989 Former jump jockey Jack Delaney. Born in 1923, he rode his first winner, Hunting Cap, at Southwell in April 1952.

2005 Seamus McGrath, 82, trainer of the 1969 Ascot Gold Cup winner Levmoss.

2 JULY

SIGNIFICANT EVENT
2000 Sinndar earned connections the $1m bonus put up by sponsors Budweiser for adding the Irish Derby to his earlier triumph in the Derby at Epsom. John Oxx's horse went on to win the Arc as well.

STRANGEST EVENT
1947 Having retired almost 25 years earlier, J. Anderson, who rode his first winner in 1906, returned to partner Gracious Sun to victory in Trial Selling Plate at Carlisle.

OTHER EVENTS
1878 Lambourn, where racing had been held since 1804, had its last meeting.
1924 Billy Nevett, six times runner-up in the jockeys' championship between 1933 and 1944, rode his first winner, Stockwood, trained by Dobson Peacock, at Carlisle
1929 Totalisator used for the first time in England, at Newmarket and Carlisle. .
1966 An outbreak of swamp fever prevented the French challengers from travelling over for the Irish Sweeps Derby, which was won by Sodium (Frankie Durr). Trainer George Todd, of Manton House, Marlborough, refused to attend the meeting, having vowed on returning to England after World War One, in which he was wounded, never to leave the country again.
1990 Four-timer at Wolverhampton for Willie Carson, whose recent eight-day hot streak had brought 25 winners.
1993 Alan Munro became the fourth British jockey to ride three winners at three tracks in one day, at Sandown on Lomas, at Southwell on Gran Senorum and at Beverley on Parfait Amour.
1995 Peter Scudamore rode in a six-furlong race for the first time, winning on Rocketeer in the Past v Present Challenge Handicap at Chepstow.
2008 The BHA and Racing UK announced a plan for a points-based £10m Sovereign Series of ten Group 1 races designed to take racing 'to the mainstream of British sport'.
2009 They had never met before but Sheikh Mohammed walked with Richard Dunwoody on a one-mile stage of his charity bid to walk 1,000 miles in 1,000 hours at Newmarket.
2009 Windsor announced restrictions on the amount of alcohol racegoers were allowed to take into the picnic car park on race nights to 'one bottle of wine or four beers per adult'. This was nothing at all to do with the fact that Windsor has a bar next door to the car park, where people can buy as much as they want!

QUOTE OF THE DAY
'He has to have a challenge, and golf has provided it,' said wife Amy of husband Steve Cauthen, when he had just retired. On this day, though, in 1989 Cauthen completed a unique four-timer when he won the Irish Derby on Old Vic, adding to the Kentucky, Epsom and French Derby triumphs already secured.

BIRTHDAYS
1921 Former Taunton trainer Betty Kennard, who took out her licence in 1967.
1924 Bob Butchers, the Daily Mirror's long-serving 'Newsboy' tipster.
1927 Former jump jockey turned horse therapist Taffy Jenkins.
1941 Irish trainer John Crowley, who rode Herring Gull to win the 1968 Irish Grand National.
1942 (Walter) Nelson Guest, a former Newmarket trainer who moved to the United States. He began training in Denmark in 1968, sending out winners of the Danish and Dutch Derbys, and the Swedish and Danish 1,000 Guineas.

CELEBRITY OF THE DAY
1730 According to Treasury records, the manager of the Royal Stud, Richard, Earl of Stafford, was authorised to receive expenses of £10,000 per annum – and he was not even an MP!

3 JULY

SIGNIFICANT EVENT
2009 Royal trainer Nicky Henderson was hit by a record fine of £40,000 and prohibited from entering horses for three months from July 11 to October 10 inclusive, as punishment for being found guilty of administering an anti-bleeding drug to The Queen's Moonlit Path prior to a race at Huntingdon in February.

STRANGEST EVENT
1982 There was a world record starting price in Australia as the two-year-old Anntelle won the Norman Ross Handicap at Canterbury, Sydney, at 500/1.

OTHER EVENTS
1967 Geoff Oldroyd had four winners at Edinburgh's evening meeting, with Officer Kelly, Remraf, Cincinatti Kid and Some Tune.

1981 Jimmy Bleasdale had a bad fall from Maple Queen at Haydock that eventually caused his retirement ten years later. He suffered blackouts after the fall and a brain scan revealed brain tissue damage.

1992 There was drama at Hollywood Park as jockey Pat Valenzuela struck the Ted West-trained Interwit with his whip in his right hand. The horse ducked sharply into the rail, and was killed, while the rider was thrown into a pole. Another horse behind tripped over Interwit and was destroyed. West claimed he had told Valenzuela to keep his whip in his left hand.

1993 Australian trainer Jim Houlihan, 80, won the Grand National Hurdle at Flemington with Fun Verdict.

2009 In a revealing *Racing Post* interview, sometimes controversial former champion jockey Jamie Spencer told James Willoughby, 'I'm nowhere near fulfilling my ambitions in racing,' and admitted that those who have criticised his late-finish style can get to him: 'People think I couldn't give a toss but that's totally wrong. I take things to heart far more than others.'

2009 Jockey J P McNamara, who battled back from being paralysed from the neck down following a race at Bangor in 2006, walked with Richard Dunwoody, who was reaching the end of his 'one thousand miles in one thousand hours' charity challenge in Newmarket. JP completed his first mile in under 23 minutes and eventually walked 12 miles.

QUOTE OF THE DAY
'There's a big difference between being a punter and a gambler. I've been backing horses all my life, but I'm not a gambler.' Former BBC racing commentator Sir Peter O'Sullevan, who opened his first credit betting account on this day in 1939.

BIRTHDAYS
1909 Owner Stavros Niarchos, whose Miesque won the 1,000 Guineas and the Breeders' Cup Mile twice.

1938 Wantage trainer David Gandolfo.

1952 New York trainer William Badgett jr, who sent out Go For Wand to win the 1989 Breeders' Cup Juvenile Fillies.

1962 Jump jockey John Harris.

DEATH OF THE DAY
1977 Sam Hall, who was born in 1916. Training from Spigot Lodge, Middleham, he won the Manchester November Handicap and the Zetland Gold Cup four times. He also sent out Morecambe (Joe Sime) to win the 1957 Ebor, the 1958 Cesarewitch and the 1959 Timeform Gold Trophy, setting a prize-money record for a gelding.

FIRST OF THE DAY
1982 Trainer Charlie Nelson had his first treble as as Chaste Lady, Maritime England and Wiki Wiki Wheels all went in at Bath.

4 JULY

SIGNIFICANT EVENT
1954 Dual Arc winner Ribot won on his debut, over 5f at Milan. He retired undefeated in 16 races, including victory in the King George VI and Queen Elizabeth Stakes on his only appearance in Britain.

STRANGEST EVENT
1989 Jockey Allan Mackay, free on £250,000 bail accused of a £7m drug-smuggling offence, rode Bashaq to victory at Folkestone. Later he was fully cleared of any involvement.

OTHER EVENTS
1890 America's new Monmouth Park course opened in grounds covering 600 acres. The main track was 1m6f round, with a 700ft-long iron grandstand.
1952 All six favourites won at Haydock.
1972 There was little reason to suppose the fourth home in a race at Aqueduct would amount to much, but the colt, Secretariat, won the 1973 Triple Crown in stunning style.
1981 Paul Cook set a record by winning at three different courses on the same day – Prince's Gate in the 2.15 at Sandown, Ramannolie in the 5.00 at Bath and Pavilion in the 7.50 at Nottingham.
1990 South African jockey Piere Strydom rode seven winners from nine races at Newmarket, Johannesburg. Ten days later he rode seven from ten at Gosforth Park, Germiston.
1992 Milligram won the Jamaican St Leger to complete a remarkable sequence for trainer Phillip Feanny and jockey Winston Griffiths. The horse had also won the Derby and 2,000 Guineas for them.
1993 Durand was a 120/1 shock winner of the Polish Derby, on the same day as trainer Heinz Jentsch won his seventh German Derby with Lando.
1995 Richard Quinn rode his 1,000th domestic winner – Martin Pipe's 13/8 favourite, Just Fizzy, at Chepstow.
1996 Cheeky Chappy, trained by David Chapman, won at Yarmouth at 7/2, having finished second at Epsom the day before and third two days earlier at Windsor.
1997 Owner Stuart Mercer's Manileno won on the Flat at Warwick, making it 13 winners from his last 13 Martin Pipe-trained runners.
2004 Amateur rider Charlotte Towsley made history when she won in Warsaw, becoming the first British woman to ride a winner in Poland.
2009 7/2 joint-favourite Warcraft was playing up on his way to the start of the 8.00 race at Bellewstown, so jockey Adrian Heskin dismounted and trotted the horse towards the start, but as he did so he was astonished to see the race start without him as starter Derek Cullen sent off the other 11 runners, with 5/1 shot Fingers winning. The horse was deemed to have been withdrawn and all bets on him were refunded.

QUOTE OF THE DAY
2009 *'This fellow will never win by more than two lengths, he just does enough, although I admit his enough is more than good enough for me,'* said trainer John Oxx after his Derby winner Sea The Stars, 4/7, landed the Eclipse Stakes from Rip Van Winkle and Conduit.

BIRTHDAYS
1918 Tote Board chairman Lord Wyatt.
1929 Epsom trainer Reg Akehurst.
1951 Gerry Enright, jump jockey turned Lewes trainer. He rode Kybo (an acronym for Keep Your Bowels Open) to win 1977 SGB Hurdle and Kirk & Kirk Hurdle.

DEATH OF THE DAY
1997 Trainer Ron Smyth, 81. He was champion jumps jockey in 1941-42 and rode three Champion Hurdle winners.

CELEBRITY OF THE DAY
1996 Former footballer Mick Quinn saddled first winner as assistant for Mick Channon, Victoria's Dream At Haydock.

5 JULY

SIGNIFICANT EVENT
1997 Kieren Fallon was criticised for his ride on Bosra Sham in the Coral-Eclipse after the 4/7 favourite finished third. Trainer Henry Cecil was not best pleased and Fallon was sacked by owner Wafic Said.

STRANGEST EVENT
2009 Having carried a preposterous story the previous week in which 'sacked City trader' Elliott Short, 22, claimed to have won £20m a year by laying horses on Betfair, *News of the World* printed an apology, explaining: 'Betfair, while not commenting on individual accounts, say Mr Short's claims were inaccurate.'

OTHER EVENTS
1952 Owner Mrs D Crossman's Cider Apple won the London Cup at Alexandra Park for the third time.
1956 La Rinconda racecourse, Caracas, Venezuela, opened.
1969 Henry Cecil hit the big time as 8/1 Wolver Hollow, ridden by Lester Piggott, won the Eclipse, beating the odds-on, unlucky-in-running Park Top.
1983 Jockey John Snaith was forced to retire, aged 27, with 97 winners to his credit, after taking one too many blows to the head.
1990 For a record eighth time, Sandown was named Racegoers' Club Racecourse of the Year.
1992 Pik Konig won the last running of Hamburg's Deutsches Derby to be restricted to German-bred runners.
1993 Darryll Holland won on Roxonian at Windsor but became the first jockey to fall foul of new Jockey Club rules restricting use of the whip to five strokes instead of the previous nine.
1994 For the first time Jockey Club permitted details of stewards' inquiries to be filtered through to the betting shops via SIS. Club spokesman David Pipe described it as 'a small step' in the campaign to provide better information.
2008 Apprentice jockey Pietro Romero, 25, was literally set on fire in a freak accident in Haydock's weighing-room sauna, after mistakenly pouring undiluted oil on to the rocks. He suffered bad burns to the chest, but was able to return to riding towards the end of August.
2009 Asked 'what is the first big decision you would make if you took over racing?' Newmarket clerk of the course Michael Prosser responded: 'Introduce a fitting Champions' Day finale to the Flat season.'
2009 Trainer Karl Burke and jockey Jim Crowley had their first Group 1 winner as Lord Shanakill landed the Prix Jean Prat at Chantilly.

QUOTE OF THE DAY
'The flashing lights could not be seen in the bright daylight and the klaxons petrified the horses, so it was decided that the best system was still the flag system.' Vintage 1993 quote from the Jockey Club head of PR, David Pipe, describing tests of starter recall systems.

BIRTHDAYS
1923 Jockey George Moore, who won the 2,000 Guineas and the Derby in 1967 on Royal Palace, and the Arc on Saint Crespin in 1959.
1932 Irish trainer Kevin Prendergast, who sent out Nebbiolo, 20/1, to win the 1977 2,000 Guineas. Classic winners include Nikoli (Irish 2,000 Guineas) and Arctique Royal (1981 Irish 1,000 Guineas).
1956 Dual-code trainer Julia Feilden, who rode 17 winners as amateur and whose other business, Hoofbeats, organises guided tours of Newmarket.
1970 Larry Cassidy, three-time champion jockey in Sydney.

CELEBRITY OF THE DAY
1932 Joe Cornacchia, whose company marketed the board game Pictionary and who owned 1991 Kentucky Derby winner Strike The Gold, was born.

6 JULY

SIGNIFICANT EVENT

1992 For the first time, a jockey was ordered to contribute towards the legal costs of an appeal hearing. Christy Roche lost his appeal against a 15-day ban for improper riding after an incident in which he was alleged to have hit, or attempted to hit, apprentice Robbie Skelly with his whip at Naas. The Turf Club stewards ordered him to pay a maximum Ir£5,000 towards their legal costs.

STRANGEST EVENT

1995 US Hall of Fame jockey Ralph Neves died, aged 74. He had died before. On 8 May 1936, while riding Flanakins at Bay Meadows, California, he was thrown into a wooden rail and trampled on. The racetrack doctor pronounced him dead, but at the morgue another doctor injected adrenaline into his heart – and he revived. He rode again the next day.

OTHER EVENTS

1189 King Henry II died – during his reign he allowed the first organised horse racing, in 1174 at a track prepared in Smithfields, London

1719 The earliest written reference to racing at Oswestry, Shropshire (discovered in Chirk Castle archives): 'Pd my Master's subscription to ye Oswestre Race for this present year to ye hands of Mr James Betton, whose Horse won ye plate ... £1-1-0.'

1946 Closeburn and Julius won the final two races at Stockton. Both were trained by Noel Murless, bred by his wife Gwendolen, and had been foaled on the same day.

1975 Brilliant black filly Ruffian, unbeaten in ten races and believed by many to be the best ever of her sex, took on Kentucky Derby winner Foolish Pleasure in a match race at Belmont Park. She was leading when she broke down. She was humanely destroyed and buried in the infield of the track.

1983 Apprentice Tony McGlone rode a 180/1 treble at Brighton for boss Richard Hannon.

1989 Top US rider Bill Shoemaker raced in Britain for the last time, finishing unplaced on 6/1 Restless Don.

1990 Jack Berry saddled Distinctly North to win at Sandown, completing his set of winners at all 33 Flat courses.

1996 Godolphin's Halling won the Eclipse for the second successive year.

1996 Leopardstown staged Ireland's first Saturday evening meeting for 35 years.

2009 'His schedule is now that of a midweek dilettante and a weekend meandering minstrel.' *Times* writer Alan Lee wondering whether Frankie Dettori, with only 19 winners to his credit, might be considering hanging up his saddle. Frankie's eventual three figure total for the year gave its own answer.

QUOTE OF THE DAY

'We had 102 brass sprinklers to water the course, and all of them have been stolen. It's a bloody nuisance,' said Newmarket clerk of the course, Nick Lees, after being unable to water track for the final day of the 1994 July meeting because thieves had made off with the new sprinklers.

BIRTHDAYS

1911 Reg Tweedie, owner-trainer of great jumper Freddie, runner up in the 1965 and 1966 Grand Nationals.

1939 Brian Taylor, who rode Snow Knight to a 50/1 shock victory in the 1974 Derby.

1941 Jeff King, often described as the best jump jockey never to be champion. He won the 1976 Whitbread on Otter Way and went on to train from 1981.

CELEBRITY OF THE DAY

1887 Ormonde, the unbeaten Triple Crown winner, won the 6f Imperial Gold Cup (later the July Cup) at Newmarket on his final appearance for his owner, the Duke of Westminster. He was returned at 3/100 as he won for the 16th time in his career.

7 JULY

SIGNIFICANT EVENT

1989 Steve Cauthen led a deputation of jockeys to tell officials at Beverley they were not prepared to race after a heavy downpour during the first race left the track in a potentially dangerous condition. The stewards agreed to allow jockeys to refuse to race, and trainers to withdraw horses, both without penalty. Several substitute jockeys were called in for the second race, which started an hour and 18 minutes late. Three races were run and the last three were abandoned.

STRANGEST EVENT

1992 Second favourite O'Donnell's Folly, trained by Alan Bailey and ridden by Danny Wright, collapsed and died after the runners came under orders for an apprentice race at Pontefract. The dead horse was officially ruled a runner, as he had come under orders.

OTHER EVENTS

1829 Aintree held its first race meeting. The first race, the Croxteth Stakes over a mile and a quarter, was won by Mr Francis' Mufti.

1886 Fred Archer won on his final July Cup ride as Melton, the previous year's Derby winner, beat Bright by three lengths.

1967 Liam Ward rode four winners from five mounts at the Curragh.

1968 Sandy Barclay rode the Noel Murless-trained Hopeful Venture to win the Grand Prix de Saint-Cloud for The Queen.

1984 Sadler's Wells, who went on to greater glories at stud, won the Eclipse Stakes for Vincent O'Brien and owner Robert Sangster. On an eventful day, the two-year-old Provideo, who would end up with a record-equalling 16 wins, landed his 10th victory of the season at Haydock, and globe-trotting Teleprompter won the International Stakes at Phoenix Park.

1990 Police recovered 220-year-old Richmond Cup race trophy, which had been stolen from the home of Penelope, widow of the Marquess of Zetland.

1999 A two-mile novice hurdle turned into a ten-mile race for the Menin Muggeridge-trained 33/1 chance Posative, who unseated her rider and then escaped from Worcester racecourse, bolting for eight miles, hotly pursued by racecourse staff, vets and two police cars, who caught her outside a school.

2009 After heavy rain an hour before racing, Uttoxeter's evening card was abandoned when a course ambulance became bogged down.

2009 Dual Group 1 winner and leading French sire Anabaa died, aged 17. Next day his Breeders' Cup-winning daughter, Golidkova, won Newmarket's Falmouth Stakes for trainer Freddie Head.

QUOTE OF THE DAY

1993 *'He used his whip both above shoulder height and with unreasonable force.'* Stewards' judgement on Gary 'Angry Ant' Bardwell, who became first jockey suspended under new whip rules.

BIRTHDAYS

1925 Pat Samuel, owner of 1974 Cheltenham Gold Cup winner Captain Christy and dual Colonial Cup winner Grand Canyon.

1941 Michael Howard, former Conservative Party leader, racegoer, and chairman of Northern Racing.

DEATH OF THE DAY

1992 Pat Taaffe, born 1930, son of trainer Tom and jockey of Arkle.

CELEBRITY OF THE DAY

1993 Luciano Gaucci, owner of Group One winners Tony Bin, Sikeston and White Muzzle and also of Italian football club Perugia, was banned from football for three years after being found guilty of bribing a ref 'with gifts of racehorses'. Perugia were stripped of the promotion they had won.

8 JULY

SIGNIFICANT EVENT
1965 Newmarket became the first British racecourse to use starting stalls, in the 4.30, Chesterfield Stakes, won by Lester Piggott on Track Spare.

STRANGEST EVENT
1968 Trainer Mick Easterby was astonished to be told his Lucia Santa had been withdrawn from a Teesside seller by a telephone caller. An irate Easterby managed to have the horse reinstated – and she duly won. Weatherbys said it was the first time this had occurred in seven years since the current entry system was introduced.

OTHER EVENTS
1990 Jockey Carl Llewellyn launched a new venture as publican of The Star in Sparsholt, near Wantage, in Oxfordshire.
1993 Willie Carson partnered Peter Walwyn-trained 33/1 shot Hamas to the longest-priced win in July Cup.
2008 Aidan O'Brien collected his 12th Group One winner of the season as Mount Nelson, 7/2, ridden by Johnny Murtagh, won the Coral Eclipse. Violence broke out among 20 racegoers at the end of the afternoon, but no arrests were made.
2009 Flamboyant trainer Rod Simpson, plying his trade in Abu Dhabi, returned to Newmarket to saddle his top-rated pure-bred Arabian, Fryvolous, in the Abu Dhabi International Stakes.
2009 The London Philharmonic Orchestra played the William Tell Overture live during the running of the 7.20 race at Kempton, which was won by gambled-on 7/2 favourite Action Impact.
2009 Sixty soliders from the Royal Anglians, recently back from Afghanistan, paraded before racing at Lingfield. It was revealed that point-to-point winning jockey Guy Disney,

27, who rode in the previous two runnings of Sandown's Royal Artillery Gold Cup, had been flown home from Afghanistan after losing the bottom half of his right leg.

QUOTE OF THE DAY
'If I have to limp a little it's worth a trade-off for being able to ride.' Teak-hard Julie Krone, reflecting on a nine-month injury layoff. On this day in 1992, Julie rode in England for the first time, scoring a 46/1 treble at Redcar. She began by winning Julie Krone Maiden Stakes, then booted home Gant Bleu, 9/1, and Cockerham Ranger, 3/1. On the same card 10/1 Tees Gazette Girl won, ridden by Clare Balding for Mary Reveley.

BIRTHDAYS
1910 David McCall, owner in partnership of Ile De Bourbon, winner of the King George VI and Queen Elizabeth Diamond Stakes, Coronation Cup and King Edward VII Stakes. He also owned the less well-known Purchasepaperchase.
1947 Clive Eccleston, the 1969 champion apprentice, who rode his first winner at Carlisle on August 27, 1964.
1962 Former lightweight jockey, Simon Griffiths, rider of Short Sleeves, whose first winner was Lunar Wind at Ripon on 22 April 1981.

DEATHS OF THE DAY
1981 Jockey Joe Blanks, 24, was fatally injured after his mount, Sleigh Queen, clipped the heels of another runner in a Brighton sprint, causing him to fall. He was rushed to Royal Sussex Hospital but died eight days later.

FIRST OF THE DAY
1993 Mary Reveley enjoyed her first four-timer on the Flat at Redcar, all ridden by Kevin Darley.

9 JULY

SIGNIFICANT EVENT
1992 Chaplin's Club, who once ran nine times in 18 days, winning on seven occasions, won his 24th race, at Redcar, and was promptly retired, aged 12. Owned by Peter Savill and trained by David Chapman, he raced 160 times, winning £144,739.

STRANGEST EVENT
1999 Lord Howard de Walden and Seaford, who died on this day, aged 86, legendarily knocked down a pedestrian in Munich during the inter-war years. The man was shaken but not hurt – sadly, as it turned out to be Adolf Hitler.

OTHER EVENTS
1839 Crucifix, owned by Lord George Bentinck and ridden by John Day jr, made a winning 5/6 debut in Newmarket's July Stakes. She went on to win the 1840 1,000 and 2,000 Guineas, and the Oaks, before becoming dam of Derby winner Surplice.

1954 Princely Gift was Sir Gordon Richards' final winner, at Sandown - his 4,870th from 21,837 rides.

1967 A Brighton housewife finally disgorged her Kempton Jackpot ticket from her rubbish bin after discovering that there was a consolation dividend for picking the first four winners – she collected £711.30 for her £1 stake.

1982 Brian Rouse rode a 170/1 five-timer at Lingfield – for five different trainers.

1992 Lester Piggott clocked up his 10th Newmarket July Cup win when 16/1 Mr Brooks obliged for Richard Hannon.

1994 Mark Johnston had his first Irish winner as Millstream won the Curragh Stakes under Frankie Dettori.

1994 Having been told she would never ride again after suffering serious leg injuries in a baling-machine accident in 1993 Candy Morris, 29, rode her first winner since her return, at Lingfield.

1997 Khalid Abdullah owned five of the seven winners at Newmarket, four ridden by Kieren Fallon and trained by Henry Cecil.

2007 'Little Knickers on thong today' – unusually named 33/1 winner called home at Bath by Richard Hoiles.

2008 Racegoers at Worcester were ordered out of the stands as each of the first two races of the evening were being run – because of false fire alarms.

2009 Sir Michael Stoute won Newmarket's Princess of Wales's Stakes for the seventh time, with 8/1 shot Doctor Fremantle. On the same day at Warwick, Australian jockey Michelle Payne, with 400 winners back home, rode her first in Britain on Iasia for Jane Chapple-Hyam.

QUOTE OF THE DAY
1990 *'I've never known anything like it,'* said jockey Mark Birch after his mount in a Ripon race, Bescaby Boy, clashed heads with Ernie Johnson's It's Me, drawing blood on the race to the line. Following a stewards' inquiry, Birch got the race.

BIRTHDAYS
1914 Trainer Bill Wightman, whose Halloween twice won the King George VI Chase, in 1952 and 1954.

1950 Trainer Rae Guest, who as a jockey won Danish, Dutch and Calcutta Derbys.

1959 Ben de Haan, who rode Corbiere to victory in the 1983 Grand National. He also rode the winners of the Welsh and Norwegian equivalents.

DEATH OF THE DAY
2005 Richard Cohen, 70, who owned 100/1 2004 Cambridgeshire winner Spanish Don and the Philip Mitchell-trained globetrotter Running Stag.

CELEBRITY
2008 Abba star Benny Anderson, whose homebred Sibelius won the 2004 Danish Derby, explained the attraction of racehorse ownership: 'I do it because of the enjoyment. It's not a way to make money, it's a good way to spend money.

10 JULY

SIGNIFICANT EVENT
1954 Gordon Richards unexpectedly ended his glittering career in the saddle. Having ridden third-placed Landau in the Eclipse Stakes at Sandown, he was legged up to partner Abergeldie in the next, but he was thrown by the horse, breaking four ribs. The incident persuaded him to call it a day and retire.

STRANGEST EVENT
1992 Jockeys Michael Roberts and Jimmy Quinn, with trainer Barney Curley, survived a plane crash near Chester; the six-seater Cessna crashed through hedges, narrowly avoiding trees, and ended up in a water-filled dyke.

OTHER EVENTS
1786 Lord Clermont's chestnut colt, Bullfinch, 4/1, beat Bustler in the first running of Newmarket's July Stakes – now the oldest 2yo race in the world
1992 Jockey Anthony Powell, 33, who suffered hip and other injuries in an accident at Mallow racecourse three years earlier, was awarded Ir£29,000 damages and costs in the High Court.
1993 *Daily Star's* Tony Lewis went through the card at Lingfield, with odds of 2/1, 3/1, 10/1, 11/2, 5/2, 5/1 and 6/4.
1988 'I suddenly thought, it's all daftness. It was getting out of hand.' Jockey Phil Tuck ditched his superstitious ways, which included wearing the same socks and t-shirt when racing, and saluting magpies, on this day - his 32nd birthday.
2008 Trainer Tom Dascombe clinched the first Group-race victory of his career when Classic Blade triumphed in the Group 2 TNT July Stakes.
2009 Hayley Turner returned to racing at Ascot after an appeal, having completed four months of a year's medical suspension following head injuries. 'Back to normal. Just like riding a bike,' she said.
2009 Richard Dunwoody completed his fund-raising 1,000 miles in 1,000 hours walk at Newmarket racecourse, walking the last mile with Lester Piggott, hoping he had raised 'a six-figure sum'.
2009 Ten-year-old Takeover Target, the Australian sprint champion, raced for the last time when he fractured a cannonbone in the July Cup and was retired by trainer Joe Janiak. Bought for a knockdown Aus$1,400, the horse landed 21 wins for prize money of £6m.
2010 2,010 horses to be ridden from Ascot to Windsor and back pre-racing to help raise £1m for 'Help for Heroes'.

QUOTE OF THE DAY
2009 *'I don't ride for punters, I ride for Aidan O'Brien,'* declared an upset Seamus Heffernan after being handed a four-day ban for riding an 'injudicious race' at Gowran Park on O'Brien's Drumbeat.

BIRTHDAYS
1933 Trainer David Chapman, whose prolific winners Soba, Chaplin's Club and Glencroft became hugely popular.
1939 Dual-Derby winning trainer John Dunlop.
1940 John Buckingham, who booked a place in history by partnering 100/1 shot Foinavon to win the 1967 Grand National; later became a jockeys' valet.
1956 Irish jockey Tommy Carmody, who won three King George VI Chases.
1965 Richard Guest, who rode 50/1 Beech Road to victory in the 1989 Champion Hurdle.

DEATH OF THE DAY
2004 Kilkenny trainer Tom Nicholson, 82, whose Bigaroon won the Irish Cesarewitch three times.

FIRST OF THE DAY
1997 Compton Place won Newmarket's July Cup for trainer James Toller and jockey Seb Sanders - the first Group 1 win for both of them – and at 50/1 he was the longest-odds winner in the 121-year history of the race.

11 JULY

SIGNIFICANT EVENT
1984 Terry Ramsden, the legendary punter and owner, staked £70,000 on his Katies in Newmarket's Child Stakes, for which she started 8/13 favourite – and was beaten.

STRANGEST EVENT
1993 The John Dunlop-trained Alhijaz, ridden by Willie Carson, was demoted from second to fourth after his race at Hoppegarten in Berlin. On the horse's previous visit to Germany, the previous May, the horse finished first, only to be demoted to fourth.

OTHER EVENTS
1934 Prince Aly Khan, father of the Aga Khan, rode his own horse Pergomas to win the George Thursby Welter Plate at Salisbury, beating Jack, ridden by the Earl of Carnarvon.

1983 King Charlemagne won at Epsom to give Mary Reveley first Flat winner.

1990 Willie Carson booted home a four-timer at Newmarket, bringing up his fastest century in 19 seasons.

1992 Trainer Clive Brittain and jockey George Duffield landed their first Irish Classic win when User Friendly became the eighth filly to complete the English-Irish Oaks double.

1992 Michael Roberts completed his fifth successive century of winners, on 10/11 Southwell winner Foolish Heart.

2008 The Freddie Head-trained Marchand D'Or won the July Cup at Newmarket under Davy Bonilla at 5/2. Head won the race as a jockey in 1996 on Anabaa. On the same card Tom Dascombe, who had saddled his first Group winner the day before, sent out his second as Firth Of Fifth won the Group 2 Weatherbys Superlative Stakes.

2008 Having won the race in 2002, 2005 and 2006, Mine failed to land a fourth Bunbury Cup victory and was retired by owner Mike Dawson after ten wins worth £355,107 in 66 races.

2009 Hayley Turner got back on the winning trail on her second ride back after winning an appeal against her 12-month ban, scoring on Lombok at Nottingham on a card that saw Christine Dunnett send out Russian Rocket to be her 100th winner as a trainer.

2009 The Queen's Kingdom Of Fife went off 11/2 joint-favourite for the 50th John Smith's Cup at York, and finished second to become Sir Michael Stoute's eighth clear or joint-favourite to be beaten in the race since he saddled the first two in 1989.

QUOTE OF THE DAY
2004 *'The prevalence of superstition in the racing world is irritating, not endearing. Superstition is another word for stupidity.'* Racing Post's John Randall, clearly a man who walks under ladders, lives at number 13 and always avoids wood.

BIRTHS OF THE DAY
1915 Epsom trainer Syd Dale, who had jumping great Mill House in the horse's early days.

1917 Michael Pope, trainer turned author. He took out his first training licence in 1947 and had his first book published by the Sporting Life in 1992.

1932 Top US trainer Ron McAnally, who handled John Henry and Bayakoa.

1933 Robin Gray, jockey and stalwart of the racing media. The highlight of his riding career was 'not winning the 1967 Kim Muir Chase on Devon View'.

DEATH OF THE DAY
1988 Journalist David Hedges, 57, founder of the Racing Information Bureau and International Racing Bureau.

CELEBRITY OF THE DAY
1957 The Aga Khan died in Geneva in his 80th year. Owner of five Derby winners, including 1935 Triple Crown winner Bahram, six St Leger, three 2,000 Guineas, two Oaks and one 1,000 Guineas winner.

12 JULY

SIGNIFICANT EVENT
1711 The London Gazette carried an advertisement for the first meeting to be run at Ascot Common on August 6 and 7. The meeting was later postponed until August 13.

STRANGEST EVENT
1990 US jockey Chip Termini was suspended for 30 days after dropping his towel when he emerged from the shower in the jockeys' room at Louisiana Downs in full view of a 'jockette'.

OTHER EVENTS
1888 The first meeting was held at Hamilton Park's new course. The old one had opened in 1782. Wild West II, ridden by George Barrett and trained by Bob Armstrong, was the first 'modern' winner.

1955 The Royal Ascot meeting got under way, having been transferred from its usual June date because of a rail strike and an official state of emergency proclaimed by the government.

1969 Nijinsky won on the first outing of a 13-race career, scoring at 4/11 at the Curragh, ridden by Liam Ward. The Vincent O'Brien-trained colt went on to become the first Triple Crown winner since Bahram in 1935.

1972 Jockey David Dineley had his first winner, Purple Rock at Kempton.

1978 Walter Swinburn rode his first winner, Paddys Luck at Kempton.

1989 Bookmaker Stephen Little accepted what was believed to be the largest bet ever seen at Bath racecourse - £20,000 to win £32,250 on the Guy Harwood-trained Parador, which duly obliged, returning 5/4.

1992 Racing resumed at Beijing for the first time since the Communists came to power in 1949. Punters bet via lottery tickets. The Kang Xi Cup was won by Inner Mongolia champion rider Za Na.

1992 Trainer David Hayes became the first Australian to win 300 races in a season with a treble at Flemington, which was holding its first Sunday meeting and attracted a crowd of 15,000, 25 per cent up on the average Saturday turnout.

1997 Pasternak, owned by former *Racing Post* editor Graham Rock, landed a hefty gamble when winning the John Smith's Magnet Cup at York.

2008 Archipenko (K Shea), 11/1, gave South African trainer Mike de Kock his first British winner in Ascot's Plymouth Gin Summer Mile.

QUOTE OF THE DAY
1994 The racecard spoke of *'the special joy'* that racegoers felt at welcoming Lester Piggott to Taby racecourse near Stockholm in Sweden. The Long Fellow, who had won three Swedish Classics at that stage of his career, boosted the crowd from 1,500 to almost 5,000.

BIRTHDAYS
1939 French trainer Robert de Mony-Pajol, the handler of Dictus, in Margouillat

1940 Racing commentator John Hanmer.

1983 Francesca Cumani, daughter of trainer Luca; model and amateur rider.

DEATHS OF THE DAY
1992 Former trainer Ted Goddard, 84. In 1968 he won the Bessborough Stakes with Q.C. and the Queen Alexandra Stakes with Tubalcain, both at Royal Ascot. He rode winners over hurdles in the inter-war years and took out his first training licence in 1950.

1992 Czech Flat jockey Josef Dolesji, 36, broke his neck and died after a last-race fall at Munich

2002 Danny Kinane, 79, a former jump jockey and uncle of jockey Mick Kinane.

CELEBRITY OF THE DAY
2008 Comedian Mel Smith co-owned Ascot 7f winner The Cheka, making his racecourse debut.

13 JULY

SIGNIFICANT EVENT
1951 The first official evening meeting in England took place at Manchester racecourse, on Friday 13th from 6.30pm.

STRANGEST EVENT
1994 The Ulster Harp Derby at Down Royal had two false starts and all but three runners continued to race after the second one, with Imposing Time passing the post first. Even more confusion reigned after the stewards ordered a re-run, with Imposing Time's trainer Tommy Kinane – without a winner for a year – withdrawing his gelding and Willie Carson's mount also taken out after the jockey complained he would miss his plane. When the race was eventually re-run, the first three home were Nabeel, Five Little Girls and Dacani Star – the three who had pulled up in the initial 'race'.

OTHER EVENTS
1939 Blue Peter won Eclipse, having already won 2000 Guineas and Derby – Triple Crown bid foiled by outbreak of Second Word War.

1967 Lester Piggott won his third Derby of the year when he collected the Ulster Harp Derby on Dan Kano, trained by Jimmy Lenehan, to add to his wins in the Irish Derby on Ribocco and in the German version on Luciano.

1973 David 'Dandy' Nicholls rode his first winner, Hunting Tower, at Chester.

1981 Willie Hayes rode first winner, Drummer Jess, at Windsor.

1985 Former jump jockey Gerry Kelly finally got off the mark on the Flat when he partnered Always Native to win at Ayr – at the grand old age of 53.

1988 Sheep delayed the start but an Oxx won the Ulster Harp Derby. After the errant flock had been cleared from the course, the John Oxx-trained Highland Bud, 6/1 outsider came home in front.

1990 Five years after retiring, Lester Piggott was back – taking part in an invitation race at Tipperary, a course where he had never previously ridden. He finished down the field on Don Leone in the Silvermines Veteran Riders' Stakes.

1996 Cigar equalled Citation's historic winning streak of 16 on the spin, by capturing a special race created for him by Arlington racecourse. An event that looked like an easy set-up for the champion turned into a test that showed why he was rated the best American racehorse since 1980. Comparisons with such legends as Citation, who went unbeaten from 1948 to 1950, seemed warranted after this performance.

2008 Boxer Ricky Hatton was at Haydock for a race named in his honour, won by 11/2 chance Supermassive Muse.

2008 Aidan O'Brien landed his seventh consecutive Irish Classic as Moonstone, the 2/1 favourite, won the Irish Oaks.

2009 Two horses slipped, five others brought down on treacherous surface at Ayr, after which meeting was abandoned.

QUOTE OF THE DAY
1991 'As a jockey you never allow yourself to take a break because you're scared someone else will get your winners,' said Walter Swinburn, but he wasn't too upset about someone else winning on his horse as he followed Willie Carson (with 1988 St Leger winner Minster Son) by breeding a Classic winner, when Possessive Dancer won the Irish Oaks at the Curragh. Steve Cauthen was in the saddle.

BIRTHDAYS
1925 Trainer David (Trenchard) Thom, who took out his first licence in 1960.

1938 Jockey Ron Vibert, whose first winner was Perquisite in Jersey in 1956.

FIRST OF THE DAY
1986 Leading US jockey Kent Desormeaux rode his first winner, at Evangeline Downs in Louisiana. Less than seven years later he would have 2,500 to his credit.

14 JULY

SIGNIFICANT EVENT
2008 Commentator Mike Cattermole caused chaos on betting exchanges when mistaking Windsor winner Make My Dream for also-ran Brazilian Brush, giving one sharp punter the chance to back the winner for £15 at 999/1 with Betfair.

STRANGEST EVENT
1964 Lester Piggott rode winners in two different countries on the same day – probably the first British jockey to do so. He partnered a horse named after yet another country, Mexico, at Saint-Cloud in France, before involving a fourth country as he rode Prince Of Norway to win at Birmingham.

OTHER EVENTS
1951 The six-year-old Citation, the American Triple Crown hero, became racing's first equine dollar millionaire when victory in the Hollywood Gold Cup took his career earnings $85,760 past that mark.

1965 Joe Mercer rode four winners at Yarmouth in the afternoon and two more at Doncaster that evening, from a total of ten mounts during the day.

1982 Nerida Saunders became part of Australian racing history when she finished second on 50/1 Scrappy Sal at Eagle Farm, losing out to winner Cherry-Maree, 6/1, partnered by her brother, Ben.

1983 Jockey Billy Newnes was saved by the kiss of life after being pinned down when Silver Venture fell on the gallops. In 1984 he was banned for three years for accepting £1,000 from pro-punter Harry Bardsley, in return for information.

1990 A remarkable afternoon for New England Stud stallion Precocious, who was responsible for three winners in less than half an hour. Bold Starlet won the 4.30 at the Curragh, Sheer Precocity the 4.45 at Chester and Boy Emperor the 4.50 at Ayr.

1992 In his will, wealthy owner-breeder Jim Joel left his last winner, Keep Talking, to the Queen.

2008 A train re-named Red Rum, from the somewhat plain 507-021, following a vote on Merseyside, had its debut trip out of Southport station with Ginger McCain, the triple Grand National winner's trainer, in attendance.

QUOTE OF THE DAY
2007 *'You get rained on a lot at Ascot, where Above does not much care for Below.'* Sir Clement Freud, unimpressed with the 'new' Ascot 'where I paid £60 to stand in a queue and be denied access to the elevator and to get out of the rain'.

BIRTHDAYS
1919 Vic Mitchell, who won the 1939 Lincoln on Squadron Castle and became a trainer in 1964.

1943 Pat Buckley, who rode 66/1 Ayala to victory in the 1963 Grand National. He retired due to injury in 1976.

1950 John Oxx, Irish trainer of Sea The Stars.

1951 Robert Hughes, who rode Peter O'Sullevan's Attivo to win the 1974 Triumph Hurdle.

1963 Paul Eddery, brother of Pat. He rode 25/1 shot Most Welcome to be runner-up in the 1987 Derby.

1978 Jumps jockey Robert 'Choc' Thornton, whose 'facial hair' themed stag celebrations prior to 2009 wedding raised thousands for charity. He also made his modelling debut in 2009 Cheltenham Xmas gifts brochure.

DEATHS OF THE DAY
1955 Two racegoers at Royal Ascot were killed by lightning during a violent storm.

1996 Two Australian jockeys died following falls. Heidi McNeich, 24, fell at Allman Park, Warwick, and David Wilkes, 32, at Clifford Park, Toowoomba. Both were airlifted to the same Brisbane hospital.

15 JULY

SIGNIFICANT EVENT
1993 Jockeys Paul Cook and Ray Cochrane won a High Court claim that the condition of Doncaster racecourse was to blame for horrific falls that ended Cook's career and injured Cochrane at the St Leger meeting in 1989.

STRANGEST EVENT
1997 As news of the murder of fashion designer Gianni Versace was breaking, Fashion Victim won the 3.30 at Beverley.

OTHER EVENTS
1987 US trainer Jack Van Berg saddled his 5,000th winner, Arts's Chandelle, at Arlington Park in Chicago.

1989 Icona won the 30th running of the John Smith's Magnet Cup at York, the longest-established sponsored Flat race.

1989 The Wonderfuel Gas Handicap at Chester was won by ... Burnt Fingers.

1989 Sheikh Mohammed became the first person to own the first four Irish Classic winners when Alydaress won the Irish Oaks. Shaadi had won the 2,000 Guineas, Ensconce the 1,000 Guineas and Old Vic the Derby.

1990 The years rolled back as Yves Saint-Martin, 48, rode Chirkpar to win the Veterans' Race at the Curragh. Orbis, partnered by Willie Robinson, was second and third was Lester Piggott on Legal Legend.

1991 Lester Piggott made his one and only visit to Killarney and left with a treble, all trained by Vincent O'Brien.

1991 Jump jockey Shane Jennings, 25, finished last of eight on Direct Mail in the Hiskens Chase at Moonee Valley, Melbourne, but was later banned for two years after he was found to have used a hand-held metal object as an 'improper contrivance'.

1992 An 'obscenity' appeared in place of jockey Julie Krone's name during a simulcast of the Matchmaker Stakes at Atlantic City. The employee believed to be responsible was sacked.

1994 Tony McCoy won on Mollie Wootton at Kilbeggan – his last winning ride before moving to England.

1995 Sheikh Mohammed's Pembroke set a world-record 1m 0.4s for 5.5f on turf when winning the Listed Hollywood Park Budweiser Breeders' Cup race at, er, Hollywood Park.

2007 'These days you're supposed to have it in your mind about all the people betting in-running – it's like you're responsible for them. That's of no consequence to me, I just get on and do the job. If they're gamblers by nature, then they're gambling on the whole thing and it's their lookout.' Irish course commentator Des Scahill, quoted by Steve Dennis in the *Racing Post*.

QUOTE OF THE DAY
1989 '*I could feel something tugging at my leg and when I looked down he had the number cloth and the back of my boot in his mouth. I kicked out at him and luckily he let go. Anyway, I won.*' Champion jockey Michael Roberts, who rode his first British four-timer, at Newbury, recalling an incident during a race when Arcadian Heights, ridden by Walter Swinburn, took a fancy to the South African's leg.

BIRTHDAYS
1940 Jockey Eric Apter, partner of Kingfisher Blue.

1952 Alan Bates, who trained in Maisons-Laffitte and was once apprenticed to John Dunlop

DEATH OF THE DAY
2005 Jerome Meyer, 78, three-time champion trainer of Canada in 1960s.

CELEBRITY OF THE DAY
1983 Sting celebrated his tenth winner as an owner when Sandalay won at Newbury, partnered by Willie Carson and trained by Peter Cundell. The lead singer of The Police said he became an owner after being persuaded to do so by builders working on his home.

16 JULY

SIGNIFICANT EVENT

1903 The greatest bookmaker of them all, William Hill, was born in Birmingham. He started out collecting tanner and two bob flutters from local pubs, on his bike, and became the most fearless layer of bets ever to grace racecourses. He built up a huge credit betting operation, but was initially against betting shops when they became legal in 1961 and did not buy into them until five years later.

STRANGEST EVENT

1953 Good French horse, Santa Amaro, was substituted for a moderate British one, Francasal, at Bath. The horse was heavily backed and telephone wires from the course were cut to prevent word getting out. 'Francasal' strolled home at 10/1, but the perpetrators of the coup were eventually unmasked and four men were jailed.

OTHER EVENTS

1926 The present course at Hamilton Park opened for business. Bob Armstrong, who had trained the first winner at the 1888 opening meeting of Hamilton's second racecourse, did it again when his Impress won the opening race, partnered by Joe Thwaites.

1943 Michael Charles Morris, born on this date, may have enjoyed the shortest spell as an owner in the game's history. The North Devon man splashed out to acquire his pride and joy, Glentino, who, he said, 'only ran once, injured.'

1952 The Newmarket judge gave Pirouette as the winner of the Cherry Hinton Stakes, before later amending the verdict to a dead-heat with Omelia after seeing the photograph. Eight days later the Jockey Club issued a directive that in the event of close finishes judges 'shall consult the photograph before announcing their decision'.

1955 Vimy, from Alec Head's stables, became the first French-trained winner of the King George VI and Queen Elizabeth Diamond Stakes.

1969 Looking set to win, Willie Carson on Javatina had to swerve swiftly to avoid disaster as two dogs raced on to the track at Redcar. He avoided a nasty accident, but lost the race.

1990 Pat Eddery rode six winners – four at Wolverhampton in the afternoon and two more at Windsor in the evening, taking his career total to 2,815.

1992 The aptly named Mr Confusion was reinstated as the winner of the John Smith's Magnet Cup, run five days earlier, after apprentice Ollie Pears was cleared of careless riding. Mr Confusion had been demoted to third with second-placed Tell No Lies promoted to first, even though Mr Confusion had been found to have interfered with third-placed Steerforth.

2008 Polled on their 'greatest irritation', 34 per cent of responding members of the Racegoers' Club cited 'drunken and rowdy behaviour', followed by 32 per cent naming 'cost, quality and service of racecourse catering.'

QUOTE OF THE DAY

2007 *'What is it with women? Mention a day at the races, and taste seems to fall at the first hurdle.'* Daily Telegraph fashion writer Hilary Alexander, drawing on her experiences of Royal Ascot.'

BIRTHDAY

1967 Brian Meehan, trainer of 2006 Breeders' Cup Turf winner, Red Rocks.

DEATH OF THE DAY

2000 Pat Taylor, 85, who trained Bremontier to win the 1957 Scottish National and Tip The Wink to land the 1977 Arkle.

CELEBRITY OF THE DAY

1992 Owner Peter Savill enjoyed a fast treble as Second Colours (1/3) won the 3.40 at Hamilton, Night Melody (11/4) the 4.05 at Catterick and Northern Graduate (11/10) the 4.10 at Hamilton.

17 JULY

SIGNIFICANT EVENT
1903 A top-class field contested the Eclipse Stakes. Rock Sand, the 2,000 Guineas and Derby winner, was third; Sceptre, with four Classic victories, was runner-up; and the winner was the previous season's Derby winner, Ard Patrick.

STRANGEST EVENT
1990 'I obviously feel let down to some extent,' said jockey Michael Hills with commendable restraint and understatement after being sacked as stable jockey – by his father, Barry.

OTHER EVENTS
1946 Wings Ashore at Lanark was the first winner for ill-fated jockey Manny Mercer.

1952 Newmarket Yearling Sales ended with 139 lots being sold for an average of 546gns.

1960 Lester Piggott was criticised after he left hot favourite Petite Etoile, 2/5, with too much ground to make up in the straight in the King George VI and Queen Elizabeth Stakes, won by Jimmy Lindley on 100/8 chance Aggressor.

1965 Meadow Court, 6/5, was Lester Piggott's first King George VI and Queen Elizabeth Stakes winner.

1980 Matilda Cave was trainer Mark Tomkins' first Flat winner, scoring at Kempton. Tompkins remains convinced his 1993 Irish Champion Hurdle contender, Halkopous, was 'got at'.

1991 Jack Berry set a new record for training the fastest 100 winners in a Flat season when Our Fan won at Hamilton. He beat the previous record, set by Henry Cecil in 1987, by six days.

1993 George Duffield rode a Ripon four-timer, at odds of 5/4, 2/1, 5/1 and 11/8.

QUOTE OF THE DAY
2009 Jamie Spencer observed: 'Horses are like oranges – there is only so much juice you can squeeze out of them.'

BIRTHDAYS
1930 James Morrison, owner of 1975 Oaks winner Juliette Marny.

1932 Michael Scudamore, father of champion jumps jockey Peter. Michael won the King George VI Chase on Rose Park in 1956, the Cheltenham Gold Cup on Linwell in 1957 and the Grand National on Oxo in 1959. He rode in 16 consecutive Nationals before he was forced to retire from the saddle in 1966 after a fall damaged his eyesight. He became a trainer, sending out 1974 Mackeson Gold Cup winner Bruslee.

1941 Jump jockey Ernie Fenwick.

1972 Jockey Seamie Heffernan, who partnered Dylan Thomas and Frozen Fire.

1964 Marcus Armytage, amateur jockey turned racing journalist for the *Daily Telegraph*, who rode Mr Frisk to win 1990 Grand National, in record time, and Whitbread Gold Cup.

DEATH OF THE DAY
1991 Irish trainer Willie Rooney, 77, whose 401 winners as a point-to-point jockey was claimed as a world record. He sent out Bentom Boy to win the 1984 Irish Grand National.

CELEBRITY OF THE DAY
1993 Ridge Pool, running in the colours of the President of Ireland, Mary Robinson, broke a hip in a race at Leopardstown.

18 JULY

SIGNIFICANT EVENT
1997 For the first time the Audit Bureau of Circulation put the Racing Post, with 52,418 sales, ahead of its great rival, the Sporting Life, which had 51,431.

STRANGEST EVENT
1990 Hong Kong-based Australian jockey Gary Moore was banned from all racing for five and a half years and fined almost £100,000 by the Royal Hong Kong Jockey Club after being found guilty of 66 betting-related breaches of the rules of racing. The 38-year-old former French champion had been Hong Kong champion seven times.

OTHER EVENTS
1964 Santa Claus, at 2/13 the hottest-ever favourite for the King George VI and Queen Elizabeth Stakes, was beaten into second by 100/7 chance Nasram II.

1969 Jockey Derick Stansfield, 39, was terribly injured in a fall at Hamilton and died two days later. It was the first fatal accident in Britain since Manny Mercer's death at Ascot in 1959.

1989 The last son of the great stallion Northern Dancer was sold for $2.8m at Keeneland Sales, Kentucky, to Zenya Yoshida, Japan's leading breeder.

1990 Former jump jockey Micky Hammond saddled his first runner as a trainer, Eladham at Hamilton, who finished third.

1993 Even by his standards, this was an extraordinary day for Lester Piggott, who had five winners in two countries in one day. He had three in Slovakia, including the Barry Hills-trained Zimzalabim in the Slovensk Derby, and that evening rode two more in Austria.

2008 Former trainer Jack Berry raised £15,000 for the Injured Jockeys' Fund annual holiday to Tenerife with his Red Shirt Night card at Pontefract –named after his penchant for such garments.

2008 Trainer Mark Johnston issued an intriguing prediction: 'I am convinced that the day will come when Japan will be the greatest racing nation. People go to the races there to support their horses as sports stars and that's the reason racing gets such a huge following.'

2009 Richard Hughes threaded Monsieur Chevalier through the field to land the seventh Wetherbys Super Sprint at Newbury for trainer Richard Hannon.

QUOTE OF THE DAY
1997 *'The press only want to talk about doom and gloom,'* complained Jenny Pitman, who never appeared that reluctant to talk to them. She married David Stait on this day but remained Jenny Pitman, although he didn't become David Pitman!

BIRTHDAYS
1911 Sir Harry Llewellyn, who partnered Ego to finish second and fourth in the Grand Nationals of 1936 and 1937. He was one of the great riders in the show jumping arena, in partnership with Foxhunter.

1930 Trainer Major Verley Bewicke. He won the 1938 Territorial Army Cup at Sandown as an amateur rider on Noble Artist and as a trainer he sent out Kerstin to win the 1958 Cheltenham Gold Cup and Court Painter to land the 1951 Scottish National.

1953 Peter Greenall, champion amateur rider in 1975-76 and 1976-77.

DEATH OF THE DAY
1999 National Hunt trainer Reg Tweedie, 88. His great hunter chaser, Freddie, twice finished runner-up in the Grand National, each time as favourite.

FIRST OF THE DAY
1947 Britain's first evening meeting, at Hamilton Park, attracted 18,000 spectators.

19 JULY

SIGNFICANT EVENT
1957 Alec Russell went through the card at Bogside, winning all six races, and all for different trainers. His winners were Double Up, Wage Claim, Cligarry, Courtlier, Newton and Roselime. Born in 1918, he retired after being badly injured in 1973.

STRANGEST EVENT
1901 Epsom Lad, 7/1, became the only gelding to win the Eclipse Stakes, but it was a close-run thing as Argentinian jockey Pedro Gomez passed the post with the saddle in his hand after it slipped during the race.

OTHER EVENTS
1952 The King George VI and Queen Elizabeth Stakes was run under that name for the first time, having been instigated the previous year as the King George VI and Queen Elizabeth Festival of Britain Stakes. The winner was Tulyar, whose prize of £23,302 took the Aga Khan's Derby winner to just under £60,600 in career earnings, beating Isinglass's record of £57,455.
1962 Willie Carson rode his first winner, Pinkers Pond, 6/1, at Catterick.
1967 Jockey Gary Moore had his first ride in public on Barbentane at Le Tremblay, France.
1986 Jockey Steve Wood rode his first winner, Allisterdransfield, at Ayr. He was tragically killed in a fall at Lingfield in May 1994.
1985 Jockey Derek Brown won the White Horse Handicap at Newbury on Floyd, his first winner as a professional.
1990 Steve Cauthen was fined £1,000 for bringing racing into disrepute after refusing to ride the three-year-old Nicholas Payne at Leicester on May 29, having already weighed out. 'I did it because it was in my best interests, and I would do the same again,' he said.
1991 Lucky Ben hardly lived up to his name at Calder racecourse, Florida. Before the start, he threw jockey Willie Hernandez, bolted straight into the infield lake and was drowned.
2007 Cartmel's card produced winners trained in England, Wales, Scotland and Northern Ireland - believed to be a first.
2008 Jockey Richard Kingscote was pictured in the Racing Post showing off his remarkable number of body tattoos, which cost him £70 per hour to acquire.
2008 'Words were exchanged between (trainer) David Elsworth and another well-known person in racing who we aren't prepared to identify. It was a verbal exchange for which Mr Elsworth later apologised,' said a spokesman for Newmarket racecourse. Road rage was later identified as the cause of the Elsworth confrontation.

QUOTE OF THE DAY
1902 *'There were only five runners, but three with a chance to win in the sixth race, which he was very keen to win. One of the three was a 'stiff 'un' and he had the chance to buy the other two, but he would buy only one - and that was the wrong one.'* Steward George MacLachlan owned the winners of the first five races at Hamilton and had the chance to make history in the last but, as reported by Hamilton clerk of the course General Sir Loftus Bates, he blew it for financial reasons.

BIRTHDAY
1919 Racing author Peter Willett, co-author of the definitive *Biographical Encyclopaedia of British Flat Racing.*

DEATH OF THE DAY
1968 The Maharajah of Baroda, 60. He owned St Leger and Irish Derby winner Sayajirao and1948 2,000 Guineas winner My Babu.

CELEBRITY OF THE DAY
1988 Victor Morley Lawson died, aged 81. A solicitor, he rode on the Flat from 1949 to 1976 and created a stir by riding his first winner, Ocean King, at Warwick, at the age of 67.

20 JULY

SIGNIFICANT EVENT
1957 French horses took the first four places in the King George VI and Queen Elizabeth Stakes at Ascot. Montanal, 20/1, was first, followed by Al Mabsoot (100/7), Tribord (100/7) and Raphael (20/1).

STRANGEST EVENT
1990 US jockey Pedro Ortega, 26, went missing. In August, body parts washed up in a garbage bag on the New Jersey shore were identified as his remains. Ortega was believed to have become involved in a drugs ring.

OTHER EVENTS
1931 Fitzroy racecourse, near Melbourne, closed after a 40-year history.
1968 Celina, ridden by Sandy Barclay for Noel Murless, ran out the five-length winner of the Irish Oaks.
1985 Starlite Night, trained by Henry Cecil and ridden by Paul Eddery, was reckoned to be such a certainty for a race at Nottingham that no SP was returned. The horse finished fifth of six.
1991 Shane Dye became the first New Zealand jockey to ride 100 winners in a season in Australia, when Beau Channon won at Rosehill. Only five other jockeys of any nationality had ridden 100 winners in a single campaign before.
1994 Coincidence backers cleaned up as Bryan Robson was an 8/1 winner at Sandown, shortly after Middlesbrough player-manager Bryan Robson had scored for his side in a friendly.
1997 Catherine Allen became Catherine Dettori as she wed Frankie.
2008 Braille won first time out at Redcar. The horse is blind in his left eye.
2009 Trainer Karl Burke was banned from involvement in racing for 12 months after admitting passing on information to an associate who profited from betting on horses to lose. On the same day, Fergal Lynch was banned from racing in Britain as part of the same case, as well as being banned by US authorities at Philadelphia Park where he had become leading jockey.

QUOTE OF THE DAY
1989 *'I feel like putting a gun to my head,'* said apprentice John Carr after riding a dramatic finish at Catterick to put Earth Spacer's head over the line first - but after just three furlongs of a 1m5f race. They finished sixth.

BIRTHDAYS
1926 TV commentator John Penney.
1930 Former cock of the north jockey Paddy Farrell.
1931 Malton trainer William Haigh. He took out his first licence in 1957, having been a jump jockey from 1954 to 1956. His best horses include Prince Pecadillo.
1953 Lady rider Diana Henderson, first woman to win under National Hunt rules at Stratford, on Fire Fairy.

DEATHS OF THE DAY
1914 Rock Sand, the winner of the 1903 Triple Crown, died in France, aged 14.
1969 Derick Stansfield, 39, died from injuries received when High Daddy was brought down at Hamilton two days earlier. He rode 400 winners worldwide, including the 1945 Lincoln on 33/1 outsider Double Harness.
1993 Johnny Gilbert, 72, a jump jockey who concentrated on hurdles races. In a 22-day spell in September 1959, he rode ten consecutive winners.

CELEBRITY OF THE DAY
1790 Pegasus, owned by the Prince of Wales, won a four-mile race at Winchester.

21 JULY

SIGNIFICANT EVENT

1951 Charlie Elliott won the inaugural King George VI and Queen Elizabeth Festival of Britain Stakes at Ascot, marking 100 years since the Great Exhibition at Crystal Palace; 19 went to post and Supreme Court, the 100/9 winner, trained by Evan Williams, collected prize money of £25,322.

STRANGEST EVENT

1841 So thick was the fog at Cheltenham that jockey John Chapple on Tupsley thought he had won the 1m Sherborne Stakes, pulling up as he passed the winning post – except that it wasn't the winning post and Sam Rogers went past to win on The Currier. The meeting was then abandoned.

OTHER EVENTS

1931 Royal jockey-to-be, Harry Carr, 14, rode his first winner, Knights Folly, at Ayr.

1956 Dual Arc winner Ribot, who was foaled at the English National Stud, raced in the land of his birth for the first time, winning the King George VI and Queen Elizabeth Stakes.

1962 Don't think that music acts playing at racecourses is a recent innovation - Britain's first Saturday evening meeting took place on this date at Wolverhampton, with a regimental band and a skiffle group entertaining the crowd.

1990 Norton's Coin, the 100/1 Cheltenham Gold Cup winner, led a civic parade through the centre of Carmarthen, near trainer Sirrell Griffiths' stable at Rwyth Farm. Peter Hughes Griffiths, the town mayor, said: 'This is the highest award we can give and I am sure it has never gone to a horse before. Norton's Coin has brought honour and a touch of colour to the town.'

1990 Mick Channon was fined £350 by the Ayr stewards for acting in an improper and abusive manner. He was reported after one of his owners was prevented from entering the stable block without a pass.

1990 Lingfield staged trotting as a preliminary to racing.

1991 Derby-winning jockey Alan Munro was honoured by the Clan Munro, based at Foulis Castle, Rossshire, which was founded in 1937 and boasted 1,500 members.

2008 Returning to the weighing room at Windsor after finishing unplaced on a 100/1 outsider, jockey Michael Hills was slapped in the face by a youth, who then ran off.

2009 Ffos Las, the new racecourse in south Wales, held its first Flat meeting, with Our Dream Queen winning the opening race for Barry and Michael Hills at 10/11.

QUOTE OF THE DAY

2004 *'This morning I galloped 12 horses. When I got done I went home and cleaned tomatoes and juiced a dozen quarts. And tonight I'll go dancing.'* R A 'Cowboy' Jones when he rode Jarrett to win at Ellis Park, Kentucky; the 61-year-old had ridden at the track in six different decades.

BIRTHDAYS

1943 Glamorgan trainer Derek Haydn Jones. He was an amateur rider from 1959 to 1969, and the best horses he trained were Annies Edge and Melody Time.

1949 Jockey Vic Soane.

1977 Jockey Richard Johnson, who would have been a multiple champion jump jockey, but for A.P. McCoy.

FIRST OF THE DAY

1985 Leopardstown staged the first Sunday race meeting held in Britain or Ireland.

CELEBRITY OF THE DAY

1990 Then Prime Minister Margaret Thatcher paid her first visit to a Flat race meeting, at Newbury.

22 JULY

SIGNIFICANT EVENT
1991 Pat Eddery became the fifth jockey to ride 3,000 winners in Britain when Sure Victory proved just that at Bath. Eddery achieved the feat faster than the other four – in 22 years, three months. Gordon Richards took 24 years, Lester Piggott nearly 27, Willie Carson almost 28 and Doug Smith more than 33.

STRANGEST EVENT
1994 Tubed horses (those who had had an operation leaving a hole in the windpipe) were barred from running on the all-weather to prevent them suffering from track kickback.

OTHER EVENTS
1968 Jockey Tony Murray suffered a broken jaw in a fall from Windy Breeze at Windsor.

1968 George Cadwaladr, who recorded his favourite recreation as 'car designs', rode his 100th winner, Baytown Willow, at Teesside.

1978 Sue Day became the first lady jockey in New Zealand to win a race against male opposition when she rode Jaws to victory at the South Canterbury Hunt meeting.

1982 The 'worst day' of trainer Jim Bolger's career - 'I took Favourite Niece to Gowran Park. I fancied her and I backed her. She ran a poor race. When I returned home I found the stables on fire!'

2007 'The first text I got was from David Loder asking if I would like to ride some horses for him next week. You've no idea how important that was' - Jamie Spencer quoted in the Sunday Times on the aftermath of his departure from the job as Coolmore stable jockey.

2008 Work rider David McMinn was revived 17 times following a fall on the Mandown gallops at Lambourn, Berkshire. The 19-year-old, treated by Tom Lovell-Stagg of Jockey Club Estates, who was riding out for trainer Jane Chapple-Hyam, was airlifted to hospital and live to tell the tale.

QUOTE OF THE DAY
2004 *'The horse started at 16/1 only because she's married to me.'* A slightly mangled way of expressing himself, but on the basis that Luke Harvey wasn't wed to a horse one must assume that when his trainer wife Georgina Browne won at Bath with Tight Circle, he was referring to her rather than the horse. By the way, they are no longer married.

BIRTHDAYS
1941 Jockey Ron Turcotte, partner of the great Secretariat, winner of the US Triple Crown in 1973.

1949 Jockey Bob Curant, who rode his first winner at Newbury 1965 and went abroad after his apprenticeship, winning in Australia, Jamaica and Ireland. The best horse he rode was Nicholas Bill and in his best year, 1979, he rode 32 winners.

1960 Amateur jockey John Greenall.

1988 Top young rider William Buick.

DEATHS OF THE DAY
1983 Thatch, aged 13, who was fourth in the 1973 2000 Guineas and went on to win the St James's Palace Stakes, July Cup and Sussex Stakes, winning seven races in all for a total of £40,277. He became the sire of Thatching and Final Straw.

2004 Gordon Smyth, 77. From Heath House, Lewes, Sussex, he trained Charlottown to win the 1966 Derby and 1967 Coronation Cup. His father, Willie, and brothers Herbert, Victor and Monty were all jockeys who became successful trainers.

FIRST OF THE DAY
1728 Drummer, owned by Capt Hugh Collyer, became the first recorded horse to win a race at Doncaster. The third winner of the day was Mr Clapham's superbly named Sweetest When Naked.

23 JULY

SIGNIFICANT EVENT
1886 The inaugural running of the Eclipse Stakes at Sandown, which was Britain's first £10,000 race (the Derby was worth less than half that at the time). The winner was Major Hedworth T 'Buck' Barclay's Bendigo, ridden by Tom Cannon and trained at Seven Barrows, Lambourn, by Charlie Jousiffe.

STRANGEST EVENT
1985 Robert Sangster and partners paid a record $13.1m at Keeneland sales, Kentucky, for Seattle Dancer, who proved virtually useless as a racehorse.

OTHER EVENTS
1684 *The London Gazette* reported that racing had taken place at Doncaster, but no records of the meeting have been discovered.
1977 The Minstrel was Lester Piggott's sixth winner of the King George VI and Queen Elizabeth Stakes.
1983 *The Sporting Chronicle* racing newspaper closed down.
1995 Dakhir Shidakov, 18, became the youngest winner of the Great All Russian Stakes (the country's equivalent of the Derby) when winning on Gurzuf at Pyatogorsk.
1995 Yutaka Take, 26, became quickest and youngest Japanese jockey to win 1,000 races when Yale No Kobito won at Kokura. The previous youngest was Hiroyuki Gohara, 34, in 1979.
2003 Australian trainer Frank Cleary sent out all five winners at Doomben, Queensland.
2007 'It was being carried towards the river and I had to get out through the sunroof and swim,' said relieved jockey Richard Johnson, whose 4x4 was swept away in the July floods, near Worcester, as he headed for the races.
2008 Former trainer Charlie Brooks was racing correspondent for Sportsxchange, a free-to-air sports news and betting channel, which launched today but did not survive long.
2009 Twelve year old sprinter The Tatling won at Bath for trainer Milton Bradley, in his 126th race.

QUOTE OF THE DAY
'Oh, you can wipe him out, he has just been married,' said great trainer George Lambton, who died on this day in 1945. Once he got married himself, however, he altered that opinion of what matrimonial bliss did to racing men, confessing 'the rough passages of life were made smooth, and the pleasant ones delightful.'

BIRTHDAYS
1947 Jockey Dennis Letherby, whose best horses included Caterina and Barwin.
1956 Steve Davis, a useless snooker player but decent jump jockey, who partnered Jer.
1965 Jockey Tony Mulholland, whose first winner was Paddy's Dream at Devon and Exeter on May 5, 1986.

DEATHS OF THE DAY
1945 Trainer Hon George Lambton, 85, died two days after retiring and handing over the reins at Kremlin House stable, Newmarket, to son Teddy. George trained 13 Classic winners, including Sansovino and Hyperion in the Derby and Colorado in the 2,000 Guineas. He also wrote a classic of racing literature, Men and Horses I Have Known.

CELEBRITY OF THE DAY
1886 Wealthy Leopold de Rothschild, a friend of the Prince of Wales, had been persuaded by General Owen Williams, the driving force behind the newly opened and enclosed racecourse Sandown Park, to provide the cash to give the relatively new venture a focal point to the season, which was the Eclipse Stakes (*see* 'Significant Event' above).

24 JULY

SIGNIFICANT EVENT
1971 Geoff Lewis rode the Ian Balding-trained Mill Reef, 8/13, to a record-breaking six-length victory in the King George VI and Queen Elizabeth Stakes.

STRANGEST EVENT
2007 As a campaign to have his OBE restored gathered pace, Lester Piggott distanced himself from it. 'Whilst I appreciate the efforts that people are making to have my OBE returned, I'd really prefer matters to be left as they are,' said the jockey, who was jailed for financial irregularities. 'The award was for what I had done up to that time, and I can't see the point in trying to get it back now. I was saddened at the pettiness of it being removed.'

OTHER EVENTS
1806 Lewes was the scene of a match race between the 1804 St Leger winner Sancho, owned by Col Henry Mellish, and Lord Darlington's Pavilion for a 2,000-guinea stake. Mellish backed his horse to win him £20,000 but Sancho went lame, allowing Sam Chifney jr to win easily on Pavilion.

1931 Richmond racecourse, near Melbourne, closed after a colourful history during which it had also hosted boxing title matches, hurling, motor sport and political rallies.

1959 The Three Swans was a horse in a hurry, winning at Ayr to complete a quick-fire hat-trick in the space of four days. The eight-year-old, trained by Eric Cousins, had also won there on July 21 and at Lanark on July 22.

1993 Mick Kinane rode five winners for a 560/1 accumulator at Leopardstown. His other two rides both finished second.

1993 The Jack Berry-trained Laurel Queen won at Southwell, notching her 20th success – a post-war record for a mare or filly. She would win two more that season. The Mark Prescott-trained Misty Halo won 21 races between 1981 and 1985 but two of these were on the Isle of Man. Southwell had somehow managed to schedule two meetings on the same day, turf in the afternoon and all-weather in the evening. They raced from 2.25 to 8.50 with 13 races.

1999 Tote Scoop 6 launched.

QUOTE OF THE DAY
2004 *'I have lived here for 18 years and the British people have taken me to their hearts as if I was one of them.'* Frankie Dettori as he celebrated his 2,000th winner, at Ascot, winning on both Nightfall and Doyen for Godolphin.

BIRTHDAYS
1926 Winston Churchill's jockey, Tommy Gosling, was born in New Lanark, Scotland. He once played football in front of 41,000 in the first floodlit match in England, played between a team of jockeys and a team of boxers at Highbury in 1949. He died in November 2008.

1962 Jockey Mark Perrett, who won the 1989 Mackeson Gold Cup on Joint Sovereignty.

1963 Top US female jockey Julie Krone was born at Benton Harbour, Michigan.

DEATHS OF THE DAY
1992 David Swannell, MBE, former senior Jockey Club handicapper, 73, shortly after giving an address at Irish Turf Club handicapper Dick Turner's memorial service.

2001 Trainer Terry Casey, 56, who sent out Rough Quest, the 7/1 favourite, to win the 1996 Grand National.

2006 Jockey Graham Sexton, 58, who rode winners at every Flat course.

CELEBRITY OF THE DAY
1991 Winning owner Ken Wheldon refused to accept the trophy after Doncaster's Yorkshire Metropolitan Property Selling Stakes because sponsor David Blunt had bid for his horse, Vado Via, unsuccessfully offering 8,000gns, which meant Wheldon had to stump up 8,200gns to retain the horse.

25 JULY

SIGNIFICANT EVENT
1967 Lester Piggott booted home his 2,000th domestic winner on the Peter Walwyn-trained Coonbeam, 8/13, at Leicester.

STRANGEST EVENT
1993 Ephes, ridden by Alexander Chuguevets, won the Russian Derby. He was sired by Floridon, whose son Flagman sired both the runner-up and the fourth-placed horse.

OTHER EVENTS
1786 The second day of the auction of the stud of HRH Prince of Wales, 'consisting of Stallions, Horses in training, Brood Mares, Colts, Fillies, Hunters, Coach horses, Hacks etc'. Two days later *St James Chronicle* reported: 'The Stud was not sold, but given away, the two-day sale not having amounted to half the sum that was justly expected.'
1899 MP and fraudster Horatio Bottomley's Northern Farmer, 20/1, won the Stewards' Cup.
1928 Owner Jim Joel had his first winner on the Flat, Black Fly (Percy Whitaker) at Liverpool. He went on to have 804 more winners up to 1991.
1950 Lester Piggott rode his first Goodwood winner, Vidi Vici, in the Craven Stakes.
1967 John Dunlop had his first Goodwood winner, Storm Bird, in the New Ham Stakes. By the end of 2001 he was the most prolific trainer ever at the track with 154 victories to his credit.
1981 Hot favourite Shergar, 2/5, won the King George VI and Queen Elizabeth Stakes by an easy four lengths.
1990 Top US female jockey Julie Krone returned to the saddle after smashing her arm in a fall at Meadowlands the previous November.
1994 Pro punter Tommy Dodds bet £15,000 on 1/3 favourite Magnasonic in a three-horse race at Newcastle, which was beaten by a Jack Berry-trained runner. Two days earlier Dodds had bet another £15,000 on 1/5 shot Fiendish, beaten by Dom One - trained by Jack Berry.
1998 Swain, ridden by Frankie Dettori, won his second successive King George VI and Queen Elizabeth Stakes at Ascot.
2001 Princess Abassi was a 200/1 shock winner at Flemington, home of the Melbourne Cup.
2008 Nicholas Godfrey revealed in the *Racing Post* that actress and racing fan Bo Derek, whose film *Bolero* featured a sequence in which she rode a horse naked, had been appointed to the California state's racing board.
2008 Fontwell clerk of the course Edward Arkell stood in for his Chepstow counterpart, but when he turned up at the course at 5.30am with his going stick he had to scale a wall to get in, only to be spotted by a passer-by who called the police. Arkell was not charged with any offence.

QUOTE OF THE DAY
2004 *'Sorry, I ballsed up,'* admitted Darryll Holland, apologising to trainer Michael Bell after failing to get a run at Ascot on odds-on favourite Sacred Nuts, who would have been called Goldenballs had the authorities not vetoed the name.

BIRTHDAY
1923 Irish trainer Tommy Shaw, who sent out Zenobia to win the Irish 1,000 Guineas in 1960.

DEATH OF THE DAY
1994 Trainer and former jockey Ridley Lamb, 39, drowned, along with fellow rider Alan Merrigan, 30, as a result of a tragic car accident. Lamb rode 547 winners; Merrigan, 6ft 2in, rode 28 winners in the 1988-89 jumps season.

CELEBRITY OF THE DAY
1992 Channel 4 commentator Graham Goode sponsored 'Folks That Live On The Hill Handicap' at Southwell to mark his and wife Gill's 21st anniversary.

26 JULY

SIGNIFICANT EVENT
1992 Britain's first Sunday race meeting was held at Doncaster, but on-course betting was not allowed. Mother and daughter Rita and Claire Mason from Mexborough, Doncaster, were the first to pay £5 to get in. The attendance was 23,000 – 2,000 more than had paid to see the Derby. The four-year-old Savoyard, trained by Michael Jarvis and ridden by Walter Swinburn, won the first race, the Coral First Sunday Race.

STRANGEST EVENT
1973 Golden Hansel won at Limerick to give Niall Madden his first winner. The jockey became affectionately known as 'Boots' and son Niall, who followed him into the business, was given the nickname 'Slippers'.

OTHER EVENTS
1958 Great French jockey Yves Saint-Martin rode his first winner, at Le Tremblay.

1975 Nominated by many as 'The Race of the Century' (a book of that name was written by Chris Hawkins), the King George VI and Queen Elizabeth Diamond Stakes produced a breathtaking battle between the Peter Walwyn-trained Grundy, 4/5, ridden by Pat Eddery, and Bustino (Joe Mercer, 4/1), trained by Dick Hern. Grundy ,the Derby winner, triumphed by half a length over the previous year's St Leger winner. It was the first running of the race to have 'Diamond' in the title.

1991 Pat Eddery reached 100 winners for the season for the 18th time as Sun And Shade won at Ascot.

1992 Trainer Geoff Wragg forgot to declare Young Buster for the Mail on Sunday Trophy at the first British Sunday meeting at Doncaster but, after the Jockey Club re-opened the race for him, Young Buster won two days later.

1992 Alydeed, the 1/20 favourite, was beaten in the Prince of Wales Stakes at Fort Eric, Ontario. The race was won by 24/1 shot Blenburb.

1997 Swain, partnered by John Reid, won the King George VI and Queen Elizabeth Stakes at 16/1.

2008 Duke Of Marmalade was only the second horse (Brigadier Gerard was the first) to win the King George VI and Queen Elizabeth Stakes on his first attempt at the 1m4f trip, returning 4/6 for Aidan O'Brien and Johnny Murtagh.

QUOTE OF THE DAY
'Has there ever been a racing authority that was not incompetent, lacking in imagination and dynamism, or out of touch with the industry's needs?' *Guardian* racing writer Chris Hawkins, who wrote the definitive book on the 1975 *Race of the Century* (*see* 'Other Events, 1975' above), asked this rhetorical question in 1996. .

BIRTHDAYS
1920 Hurdles jockey Johnny Gilbert, who won the 1959 Triumph Hurdle on Amazon's Choice, and posted 38 winners in his best season 1959-60, finishing sixth in the title race.

1924 Tommy Robson, twice Scottish National-winning rider, who trained the 1964 Champion Hurdle winner Magic Court, 100/6.

1955 Philip Hobbs. As a jockey he rode 160 winners between 1975 and 1986 and then became a hugely successful dual-code trainer of horses such as Flagship Uberalles, What's Up Boys, Rooster Booster and Detroit City.

DEATHS OF THE DAY
1991 East Sussex-based National Hunt trainer Ben Wise.

2005 Uttoxeter-based jumps trainer Peter Bevan, whose Salwan won the 1992 Glenlivet Aniversary Hurdle at Aintree.

CELEBRITY OF THE DAY
1952 Diorama won at Warwick, giving owner Charles St George, formerly of the Coldstream Guards, his first winner.

27 JULY

SIGNIFICANT EVENT
1968 Royal Palace gave trainer Noel Murless a third successive victory in the King George VI and Queen Elizabeth Stakes, ridden by Sandy Barclay. Busted won for Murless in 1967 and Aunt Edith in 1966.

STRANGEST EVENT
1970 Punters were not happy when they discovered Lester Piggott would be putting up 14lb overweight to ride It's The Finish for trainer Richmond Sturdy in a Newcastle seller. They shouldn't have worried, though, as Lester duly won.

OTHER EVENTS
1875 The final meeting took place at Abingdon, Berkshire, where racing had been held since 1774.

1910 Magic, trained by Felix Leach at Newmarket, pulled off a shock by defeating 1/20 favourite Bayardo by a neck in the Goodwood Cup.

1955 Jim Joel's Star Of India, ridden by Eph Smith and trained by Ted Leader, won on her debut in a Goodwood maiden. She won all five of her two-year-old races and was rated a remarkable 138 by Timeform, who had previously rated only Windy City (142 in 1951) higher. However, Star Of India seemed not to train on and was unplaced in her only three-year-old start.

1965 Willie Carson won at Goodwood for the first time on Osotis, 100/7, in the Charlton Handicap.

1968 There were no tote facilities at Phoenix Park, where clerks went on strike over pay. Liam Ward rode a treble at the meeting.

1974 The great filly Dahlia, partnered by Lester Piggott, became the first horse to win two King George VI and Queen Elizabeth Stakes.

1992 Julie Krone became the first female jockey to win a meeting title in New York when she rode a double to take her score to 73 victories from 370 mounts at Belmont Park.

1996 Financial manager Tim Rogers, 34, and fiancée Julia Burn, 30, wed at Cheltenham racecourse, with Rogers declaring: 'I don't ride and I hate horses – they smell from both ends. But I love racing.'

2008 Fifty-year-old Robert Thompson equalled the record for career winners in Australia when riding Prior Baron to victory at Scone for his 3,322nd win - drawing level with his namesake, but no relation, Jack Thompson. He was presented with a pair of the other Thompson's boots by the local raceclub. He pulled clear of Jack with a winner at Port Macquarie the following day.

QUOTE OF THE DAY
2004 'I think Barney Curley would have been a better name for him,' declared Luca Cumani after his Mephisto – by Machiavellian, out of Cunning – won at Glorious Goodwood.

BIRTHDAYS
1920 Harry Sprague, who won the 1959 Whitbread Gold Cup on Done Up – his last ride. Done Up was a notably lazy horse and Sprague was so exhausted by his efforts in the saddle that he was physically sick after the race.

1923 Jockey Joe Sime, the pipe-smoking former Cock O'The North. He won a string of top races, including the Lincoln, Wokingham, Northumberland Plate, Ebor, Cesarewitch and Ayr Gold Cup.

1943 Trainer Pam Sly, whose best horse is Speciosa, winner of the 1,000 Guineas.

DEATH OF THE DAY
1796 Jockey George Herring, rumoured once to have ridden 19 consecutive winners, was killed in a race fall at Hull.

CELEBRITY OF THE DAY
1909 Dowager Lady Beaverbrook was born on this day. Her best horses usually had seven-letter names, including 1974 St Leger winner Bustino and top sprinter Boldboy.

28 JULY

SIGNIFICANT EVENT

1982 John Francome, Peter Scudamore and Steve Smith Eccles were all informed they need not apply for their licences for the forthcoming jumps season until 2 August, effectively a seven-day suspension. Francome was said to have given the other two £200 each by mutual agreement after riding Donegal Prince to win the Schweppes.

STRANGEST EVENT

1999 Kieren Fallon was sacked as Henry Cecil's stable jockey amid allegations of an affair with the trainer's wife, which were denied. Fallon's lawyer released a press statement: 'Mr Fallon understands that Mrs Cecil has recently been quoted in the national press to the effect that she has had a relationship with a top jockey. For the avoidance of doubt, Mr Fallon would like to make it clear that he is not the top jockey involved.'

OTHER EVENTS

1854 Dunstable racecourse held its final meeting.

1914 Poor Boy, owned by Solly Joel (whose Pommern won 1915 Triple Crown), made a seventh successive attempt to win the Stewards' Cup at Goodwood. The nine-year-old had been runner-up four times - beaten a neck in 1908 and 1910, and second again in 1912 and 1913 – and had been unplaced in 1909 and 1911. There was no happy ending as the horse was unplaced again.

1952 Gordon Richards rode five of the six winning favourites at Alexandra Park, London – four for owner Dorothy Paget.

1973 Dahlia, ridden by Bill Pyers, equalled Mill Reef's record six-length victory in the King George VI and Queen Elizabeth Stakes. On the same card, the first race at Ascot for lady riders was won by Caroline Blackwell on Hurdy Gurdy.

1984 French challenger Esprit Du Nord was declared to run in blinkers in the King George VI and Queen Elizabeth Stakes, but he arrived at the post without them and the stewards decided he could not run, fining trainer John Fellows £200.

1994 Racing at Yarmouth was cancelled. A fire engine was called to deal with a gorse fire at the neighbouring golf club, but, said clerk of the course David Henson, 'fire appliances trailed up and down the track several times, causing severe rutting to the full width of the track'.

1994 Jockey Jason Tate, 22, rode his first treble, at Southwell.

2009 Four-timer at Colonial Downs, US, made Rosemary Hofmeister jr summer season champion jockey.

QUOTE OF THE DAY

2004 'I have done a lot of horses before, but not many racehorses,' said artist Andrew Baynes as he worked away at his site near Goodwood's Richmond Enclosure, sculpting popular stayer Persian Punch, kneeling, full size and made of sand.

BIRTHDAYS

1923 Shropshire trainer Arthur Jones, who also owned his 1957 Champion Hurdle winner, Merry Deal.

1933 Amateur rider Dick Saunders, who rode Grittar to win the 1982 Grand National and became, at the age of 48, the oldest jockey to win the race.

1945 Welsh jockey Trevor Rogers, who moved to Germany, and then rode 39 winners to become champion in Madras in 1971-72.

DEATH OF THE DAY

1988 Renowned bookmaker John 'Jack' Swift, 74, also known as 'Chuckles' as he seldom smiled. Father of trainer Brian, who handled many of his horses, including top sprinter Never So Bold. He won the 1976 Lincoln with The Hertford

FIRST OF THE DAY

1974 Unique feat by tipster Charles Lamb of the *Baltimore News American*, who selected ten out of ten winners at a Delaware Park meeting – a world record.

29 JULY

SIGNIFICANT EVENT
1994 Women jockeys won seven of the nine races at Aussie track Warracknabeal. The Payne sisters, Therese and Maree won four and two respectively, with Christine Puls winning another.

STRANGEST EVENT
1965 Carl Llewellyn, who rode the heavily backed Party Politics to win the 1992 Grand National, was born. His first winner as a trainer was the 33/1 winner of the 2006 Scottish National, Run For Paddy, who he rode himself. He quit his short-lived training career to work with Nigel Twiston-Davies. Llewellyn once listed his favourite recreation as 'eating puddings'.

OTHER EVENTS
1952 A record 55,000 turned up for the opening day of the Goodwood meeting.
1980 Queen opened Goodwood's March Grandstand, unveiling Elisabeth Frink's life-size bronze, The Thoroughbred.
1988 Trainer Jack Berry had his first Goodwood winner when Almost Blue, partnered by John Carroll, won the Molecomb Stakes.
1990 Top Australian trainer Colin Hayes retired after sending out 5,329 winners. He was the top trainer at Moonee Valley, Melbourne, for 13 straight seasons.
1992 Trainer Richard Hannon broke the £1m prize-money barrier when 7/1 Son Pardo won the Richmond Stakes at Goodwood.
1993 For the second consecutive year owner Jeff Smith landed a double at Goodwood, with Philidor (Schweppes Golden Mile) and Lochsong (King George Stakes), both ridden by Neil Kennedy.
1990 Trainer Graeme Rogerson became the first New Zealand trainer to send out 100 winners in a season when On The Nose and Grand Coquette won at Ruakaka.
1995 Darren Beadman set a new Australian record for most wins by a jockey in a season when he took his score to 182 by riding Brawny Spirit to victory at Rosehill in his last ride of the season.
2007 'In time we'll find casinos on courses here. Racecourses are not churches; casinos are a logical fit' – trainer John Gosden made an interesting prediction to Racing Post readers.
2007 'Training was the last thing on my mind when I retired. I never gave it a thought.' Only when boredom set in did Pat Eddery change his mind, he told the Mail On Sunday on this day.
2008 Kerrin McEvoy, 27, with 321 winners in Britain since becoming understudy to Frankie Detorri for Godolphin in 2004, returned to his native Australia to ride there for Sheikh Mohammed.

QUOTE OF THE DAY
2004 *'He had it in his head that the start was 5.30pm,'* explained Michael Clower in the Racing Post of starter Peter McGouran at the Galway Festival. This was unfortunate for punters wanting a bet on the Guinness Handicap, which went off at 5.31pm but should not have done so until 5.35pm.

BIRTHDAYS
1920 Tim Fitzgeorge-Parker, trainer turned journalist and author, was born. His books included The Guv'nor, a biography of Sir Noel Murless.
1948 Dual purpose Irish trainer Dermot Weld, who in 1989 became the first trainer to win more than £1m in prize-money. He has won top races on four continents, including Melbourne Cup twice; all the Irish Classics; English Oaks, and 2,000 Guineas; the Hong Kong Bowl; and the American Oaks.

DEATH OF THE DAY
1902 Former jockey turned trainer John Watts, who had been taken ill at Sandown ten days earlier due to effects caused by regular and excessive wasting. Born in 1861, he won 19 Classics as a jockey, including four Derbys.

30 JULY

SIGNIFICANT EVENT
1994 Riding in his first chase, Tony McCoy was a faller from No Sir Rom at Galway.

STRANGEST EVENT
1991 The Hull City AFC Handicap at Beverley was 'won' by 11/1 Azubah, ridden by Kieren Fallon and trained by George Moore, only for the race to be declared void because starter John Mangles had got the race under way a minute and six seconds early. He was later fined an undisclosed sum.

OTHER EVENTS
1840 The heir to the French throne, the Duc d'Orleans, won the Goodwood Cup with Beggarman.

1931 Forty years after opening, Melbourne's Aspendale racecourse closed down.

1947 BBC Radio broadcast from Goodwood for the first time, paying a 15-guinea fee for the privilege. Frank More O'Ferrall presented, covering just the Goodwood Stakes.

1948 Jockey Pat Taaffe, who achieved fame on the mighty Arkle, rode his first double, at Tuam, Co Galway.

1959 Trainer Peter Walwyn's first Goodwood winner was Enticement in the Lavant Stakes.

1968 Sky Diver, trained by Peter Payne-Gallwey and ridden by Terry Sturrock, became the first horse to win consecutive Stewards' Cups since Lord Annandale (in 1913 and 1914, one of which was a dead-heat).

1974 Red Alert won the Stewards' Cup, giving trainer Dermot Weld his first victory at Goodwood.

1080 Mushref, trained by Tom Jones, won at Redcar to give owner Sheikh Hamdan Bin Rashid Al Maktoum his first winner.

1988 Back protectors were made mandatory for jump jockeys.

1992 The German horse Elsurimo appeared at Goodwood with jockey Mark Rimmer wearing colours emblazoned with the name of Steigenberger Hotels across the back of his silks. Such advertising was in direct breach of Jockey Club rules at a time when the Club was engaged in discussions about allowing riders to wear advertising material. The horse's owner, a certain hotel proprietor named Herr Steigenberger, was happy enough when Elsurimo finished sixth.

2008 Aidan O'Brien's Henrythenavigator won his fourth consecutive Group One race, taking Goodwood's Sussex Stakes at 4/11.

2008 Oslot won the Galway Plate for Paul Nicholls and Ruby Walsh at 11/4, becoming only the third British-trained winner in the race's 139-year history. Third was the 12-year-old Ansar, who had won the Plate twice and also won six other races at the meeting, having run at every festival since 1999. On the same card Dermot Weld landed his 200th winner at the meeting with Lady Alicia.

QUOTE OF THE DAY
'*Racing is the only sport in the world in which you can participate, spectate and socialise all at the same time,*' observed owner and racing politician, Peter Savill, born today in 1949.

BIRTHDAY
1914 Lord Killanin, former steward of the Turf Club.

DEATH OF THE DAY
1991 Jack Egan, 59, former champion jockey in Denmark.

CELEBRITY OF THE DAY
1714 Turf enthusiast Queen Anne's bay horse Star won a 40-guinea race at York. Three days later the Queen died. The new monarch, King George, was not interested in racing.

31 JULY

SIGNIFICANT EVENT
1956 BBC TV broadcast racing from Goodwood for the first time. Commentary of three races – the Craven Stakes, Stewards' Cup and Bentinck Stakes - was by Peter O'Sullevan, with Clive Graham in the paddock.

STRANGEST EVENT
1770 Leonatus, the Duke of Grafton's five-year-old, entered a £50 Plate at Huntingdon, run in two-mile heats and he ran in five. Two days later he raced there again, this time in a £50 Plate run in four-mile heats, of which he again ran five. He had run a total of 30 miles in 48 hours. He never raced again.

OTHER EVENTS
1920 Comic singer, actor and banjo/ ukelele player George Formby had his third and final ride as a jockey, finishing unplaced on Old Chris at Catterick.
1958 Vincent O'Brien saddled his first Goodwood winner, the 1/ 2 chance Gladness, ridden by Lester Piggott, in the Goodwood Cup.
1973 Tony Murray rode his 500th winner, King Frog, 11/4, at Goodwood as Alphadamus (P. Cook, 16/1) won the Stewards' Cup to give Michael Stoute his first Goodwood success.
1976 Fool's Mate, trained by Henry Cecil, won at Glorious Goodwood for the second time, adding the PTS Laurels Handicap to the Trundle Handicap won four days earlier.
1993 Willie Carson rode the John Gosden-trained King's Signet, 16/1, to win Goodwood's first Saturday running of the Stewards' Cup, in the process winning his 3,500th British race.
1993 Only four of the 14 runners in the Jif Lemon Amateur Riders' Handicap squeezed themselves around the correct course at Newmarket, with ten others neglecting to negotiate the right-hand bend into the straight, heading off instead over the Heath. Mark Buckley,

21, won on Viardot.
2008 On his 20th racecourse appearance, Aidan O'Brien's doughty stayer Yeats not only won the Goodwood Cup at 8/15, ridden by Johnny Murtagh, but also took his prize-money earnings through the million-pound barrier.

QUOTE OF THE DAY
2004 *'The crying shame is that he's imprisoned in a body two sizes too big for Flat racing,'* commented Tom O'Ryan on talented but over 6ft tall Keith Dalgleish, who failed to turn up for four booked rides at Hamilton, sparking reports that weight problems had forced his retirement, aged just 21.

BIRTHDAYS
1924 Trainer Alec Head, who won the Derby with Lavandin in 1956, and as a jockey he rode Le Paillon into second place in the Champion Hurdle.
1932 Jockey turned trainer Eric Eldin. As a jockey in 1973 he rode Knockroe to break the record for the Derby course and distance in the Weetabix Wildlife Handicap at Epsom.
1950 Derek 'Tommo' Thompson, the ubiquitous TV commentator, radio pundit and tipster As an amateur jockey he beat Prince Charles at Plumpton in 1980, riding Classified.
1958 Jockey Jimmy Frost, who won the 1989 Grand National on 28/1 shot Little Polveir and the 1991 Champion Hurdle on Morley Street, 4/1.

DEATH OF THE DAY
1999 Peter Burrell, 94, racehorse owner and director of the National Stud.

CELEBRITY OF THE DAY
2004 Mystic Meg, the all-seeing tabloid newspaper astrologist, failed to arrive at Goodwood to see her filly Astrocharm win there. Trainer Mark Tompkins explained: 'She hasn't been at the races when Astrocharm has won, and thought it would be best to stay away.' Quite.

1 AUGUST

SIGNIFICANT EVENT
1878 The great Hungarian mare Kincsem, unbeaten in a career spanning 54 races, made her only English racecourse appearance, winning the Goodwood Cup.

STRANGEST EVENT
1994 Worcester's two-mile £4,000 Dylan Thomas Handicap Chase, due to be run on Saturday, August 6, failed to attract a single entry – 'the first time in living memory that no horses have been entered for a race in Britain,' said *The Sporting Life*.

OTHER EVENTS
1898 Large bets are placed on the outcome of races at Trodmore Hunt meeting, featured in the sporting press. However, once results had appeared and much money been paid out, it was discovered that there was no such place. The whole incident was a complete scam.
1973 New Zealand racing went metric.
1974 Ray Cochrane rode the first of his eight winners over hurdles when Wanlockhead won at Newton Abbot.
1985 An anonymous punter won £227,812.50 from William Hill after staking three £2,000 doubles and a £9,000 treble on three winners. Became entry in the *Guinness Book of Records*.
1992 Ruby Tiger, 2/1, trained by Paul Cole, won Goodwood's Nassau Stakes for the second consecutive season, having also won Group races in Italy (twice), the US, Germany and Ireland.
1993 Racing returned to China, having been banned by the Communists in 1949, with meetings now reportedly legalised at Guangzhou, with betting allowed only at the track.
1993 Lingfield's first Sunday meeting attracted a record turnout of 8,736.
2004 'The first people were here at 7.15am,' said clerk of the course Ed Gretton of a 2004 Chester Sunday meeting, which attracted a record 46,137 crowd, and started at 2.20pm.

2008 The winner of Goodwood's Totesport Mile Handicap in 2007 was a horse with a tennis-themed name, Third Set, drawn 20, from Roger Charlton's stable. In 2008 a horse with a tennis name, Fifteen Love, drawn 20, again from Charlton's stable, was the 5/1 winner.
2009 Genki, ridden by the appropriately named Steve Drowne (given the damp conditions) was the 14-1 winner of the Stewards' Cup at a less than glorious Goodwood. He was trainer Roger Charlton's fifth runner in race – and third winner. Only Fred Armstrong 56 years previously ever achieved as much.

QUOTE OF THE DAY
'Hopefully, Sir Alex Ferguson can set me up with one of his nice players after that,' remarked Hayley Turner on this day in 2009 after she rode his 7-1 chance, Broomielaw, running in the colours of the Manchester Utd boss's wife, to win at Newmarket.

BIRTHDAYS
1947 Jockey Dennis Atkins, who rode Cancello to win the 1976 Mackeson Gold Cup, run that year at Haydock.
1966 Jockey-turned-trainer, turned ex-trainer-turned-trainer again, Mark Pitman. The son of Jenny and jockey-turned-TV commentator Richard, he rode Garrison Savannah to win the 1991 Cheltenham Gold Cup.

DEATH OF THE DAY
1985 Dual Grand National runner-up Freddie, 28, at the home of his devoted owners, Reg and Betty Tweedie, who owned and trained him near Kelso in Scotland.

CELEBRITY OF THE DAY
1943 Irish trainer Dennis Cordell-Lavarack was born in Brazil. As Denny Cordell, he was involved in the production of the Moody Blues' number-one single Go Now, before making Procol Harum's A Whiter Shade of Pale.

2 AUGUST

SIGNIFICANT EVENT
1995 Aidan O'Brien sent out an unprecedented 1,2,3 in the Galway Plate, with Life Of A Lord, 12-1, beating Kelly's Pearl, 16-1, and Loshian, 6-1.

STRANGEST EVENT
1991 After 35 years, it was revealed that the trophy presented by Chepstow racecourse to Sir Gordon Richards after his 1954 retirement had been recovered, having been stolen during a 1956 robbery. It was discovered in a TSB vault in Ashton.

OTHER EVENTS
1803 Eleanor, the first filly to complete the Derby-Oaks double, beat Fieldfare in two mile heats at Huntingdon.

1918 Sally Crag, at Newmarket, was the first winner for jockey Thomas Weston, born in Dewsbury, 1903. He went on to ride 11 Classic winners.

1963 Fraxinus won the News of the World Handicap to give trainer Bill Wightman his first Goodwood winner.

1969 Jimmy FitzGerald got off the mark as a trainer with Archer at Market Rasen.

1985 Kim Tinkler rode her first winner, Wow Wow Wow at Edinburgh.

1991 Paul Barton became the first former pro jockey to take charge of a meeting as a stewards' secretary at Bangor.

1991 A fall from Independent Air at Bangor resulted in jockey Sharron Murgatroyd breaking her spinal cord.

1993 Nicky Connorton, 31, rode his 500th winner, Silverlocks, at Ripon. His dad, Brian, rode more than 600 in total.

2008 Glorious Goodwood ended with Johnny Murtagh topping the jockeys' table, with a record eight wins, which only Lester Piggott in 1982 and Kieren Fallon in 1998 had previously achieved. On the final day of the meeting trainer William Haggas sent out 40-1 Conquest to win and 12-1 King's Apostle to finish second in the Stewards' Cup, a feat last achieved in 1990 by Richard Hannon

with Knight Of Mercy and Bocas Rose.

2009 Dermot Weld was top trainer at the Galway festival for an astonishing 25th time.

QUOTE OF THE DAY
'I recall one occasion, I was down at the start for the two-mile chase when the race was held up by cattle walking across the track.' Jockey-turned-trainer Jimmy FitzGerald, thinking back to the now defunct Northumberland track, Rothbury, on this date in 1969 when he saddled his first winner, Archer, at Market Rasen.

BIRTHDAYS
1927 Trainer and boxing fan Frank Menin Muggeridge. He first held a licence in 1956, having been a jump jockey from 1945-55. His best horses were Energy and Soapey Sponge. On his birthday in 1965 he sent out four winners at Newton Abbot.

1932 Actor Peter O'Toole, an owner with Bruce Hobbs, and who played the eponymous subject of 'Jeffrey Bernard Is Unwell'.

1934 Peter Beaumont, who would saddle Jodami to win the 1993 Cheltenham Gold Cup. He also rode in one race under NH rules.

DEATHS OF THE DAY
1959 Mick Pumfrey, 29, died from head injuries, having fallen in a Plumpton chase the previous day.

1980 Owner and rider Anthony Robinson, 43, whose Tied Cottage finished first in the 1980 Cheltenham Gold Cup under Tommy Carberry, only to be disqualified later. The horse's trainer Dan Moore also died within months.

1988 1972 Derby winner Roberto, 19.

CELEBRITY OF THE DAY
1983 Errol Brown, lead singer of pop band Hot Chocolate, owned his first winner as Dancing Barron (John Dunlop/Willie Carson) took a nursery at Brighton.

3 AUGUST

SIGNIFICANT EVENT
1966 An announcement appeared in the Racing Calendar: 'Mrs Florence Nagle and Miss Norah Eleanor Wilmot have been granted licences under rule 102 of the rules of racing for 1966.' At last women were free to train horses with Jockey Club approval. Pat, a winner at Brighton, became the first Flat winner to be trained officially by a woman, Norah Wilmot.

STRANGEST EVENT
1985 A horse not in a race won it. The Bill Watts-trained Handspring was inadvertently left out of the published runners for the Bradford Nursery at Thirsk. With the public largely unaware that the horse was even running, it won at 14-1, ridden by Nicky Connorton.

OTHER EVENTS
1959 The first running of Redcar's Vaux Gold Tankard and the William Hill Gold Cup took place – two of the six richest handicaps of the season.
1965 Willie Carson lost his apprentice claim on Regal Bell at Redcar.
1973 Tuam racecourse in County Galway held its final meeting.
1989 Panamanian-born jockey Jorge Velasquez rode his 6,000th winner, Maddie Bumpo, at Arlington International. He became the fifth to achieve the feat, the others being Bill Shoemaker, Laffit Pincay, Angel Cordero and Johnny Longden.
1991 Jerry Sung's Auric stables set a record for the most races won by an owner on a single card with seven winners at Bukit Timah, Singapore, all trained by The Choon Beng.
1992 Punters enjoyed a two-horse race in which they couldn't lose – Jdaayel, a 5-4 shot, was withdrawn from Ripon's Bouncing Castle Maiden Stakes, leaving two runners. Many A Quest won at 4-7, with Tip It In second at 33-1. Rule 4 deductions were 40p in the pound, but at that rate smart punters had backed both and still made a profit.
2008 Newbury staged three camel races after the normal card.
2009 England footballer Michael Owen confirmed the link with Betfair founder, Andrew Black, to recruit trainer Tom Dascombe to run the 170 acre Manor House Stables, Cheshire.

QUOTE OF THE DAY
'Fast youths, fancy men, gamblers, blacklegs and women of easy virtue.' The Airdrie & Coatbridge Advertiser of this date in 1861 was, one supposes, trying to deter people from attending the races – I can't help thinking they were actually encouraging them to go!

BIRTHDAYS
1938 Sir Terry Wogan, whose show used to feature the popular 'Wogan's Wager' item; also an owner with Nicky Henderson
1941 Four-time champion jump jockey-turned-top trainer, Josh Gifford, MBE. He rode 122 winners in 1966-67, and sent out Aldaniti to win the 1981 Grand National.
1958 Bryn Crossley, the former champion apprentice in 1981, who partnered Lester Piggott's first winner as a trainer, Latch Spring.

FIRST OF THE DAY
1988 Jump jockey Gee Armytage became the first jockey with a sponsored bed. 'I can't imagine what the sponsors expect me to do in such an enormous one – 5ft by 6ft 6in,' declared the then unattached Ms Armytage somewhat disingenuously.

4 AUGUST

SIGNIFICANT EVENT

1914 War broke out – and there were Flat meetings at Brighton, Birmingham and Ripon. Brighton's opener was won by Picton, ridden by Fred Rickaby, who would later be killed in action while serving with the Tank Corps in France.

STRANGEST EVENT

1980 Swaying Tree, ridden by Eddie Hide, set off for the Yorkshire Handicap at Ripon at 4.30 – and won it over an hour later, partnered by Jimmy Bleasdale. 14 runners went off as normal but after one furlong of the scheduled six, the red flag was waved and six jockeys stopped. Eight ran on, Wynbury passing the post ahead. At 4.35 the race was announced void; at 4.48 it was announced there had been false start; at 5.04 it was announced the race would be re-run at 5.30. Nine withdrew, and although Wynbury ran again, it was Swaying Tree, one of the six who stopped, who won. However, Hide had been kicked and therefore replaced.

OTHER EVENTS

1825 Two Cossack horses took on two English thoroughbreds over 47 miles near St Petersburg. The thoroughbred Charper won. As a consequence many more were imported to Russia and organised racing became established.

1960 Anne, Duchess of Westminster splashed out 1,150gns for a three-year-old sold by farmer's wife Mrs Henry Baker. The horse was Arkle.

1990 Aussie jockey Jeremy Hurstwitt, 35, became the first in that country suspended for a positive drug test after traces of cannabis were discovered in his urine sample following meeting at Belmont Park, Western Australia.

1993 Kevin Darley completed his first century, and the first for a northern-based jockey since Eddie Hide in 1981, when Talented Ting won at Nottingham.

1994 Laytown's meeting in Ireland, where they race on the beach, was marred by injuries to five riders and the deaths of three horses in the opening race of the day.

1996 Mark Johnston-trained Branston Abby equalled Laurel Queen's record number of wins – 22 – by a filly or mare trained in Britain since the Second World War when winning at Munich.

1997 On the Queen Mother's 97th birthday, Royal Mint, ridden by Mick Fitzgerald, finished second, behind Regal Absence, at Newton Abbot.

2000 Goodwood's Molecomb Stakes was renamed the Queen Elizabeth The Queen Mother's 100th Birthday Molecomb Stakes.

2008 The third race at Carlisle's evening meeting was delayed by eight minutes by a racegoer who walked up the course to the start, refused to move back behind the rails and stood shouting at jockeys until he was handcuffed by police.

QUOTE OF THE DAY

2004 *'That's the official explanation – if others want to read in other reasons for it, they can!,'* declared Richard Whiteley, the Countdown presenter and owner of Twice Nightly, explaining that Terry Wogan had suggested the horse's name on the basis of his double stint on hit C4 show and Yorkshire TV's Calendar.

BIRTHDAY

1929 Trainer Miles Henry Easterby – known as Peter – born, perhaps! His daughter told me: 'He says he was born on the 4th but Mum is positive it is really the 5th – she says she's seen his birth certificate.' Trained the legendary dual Champion Hurdle winners Sea Pigeon and Night Nurse.

1900 Birthday of the Queen Mother.

DEATH OF THE DAY

2004 Alec Stewart, 49, the trainer of 1988 Horse of the Year Mtoto. Mtoto won the Eclipse, Prince of Wales's Stakes, King George VI and Queen Elizabeth Stakes and Select Stakes.

5 AUGUST

SIGNIFICANT EVENT
1882 Fred Archer rode six winners from six rides at Lewes for second time.

STRANGEST EVENT
1839 Jockey John Jackson, 70, was born on this date. Winner of eight St Legers between 1791 and 1822, he was normally abstemious, but once drowned his sorrows in a pub after losing the job of stable jockey to trainer Sykes. Leaving the pub determined to fight Sykes, he instead mistakenly set about a passing chimney sweep.

OTHER EVENTS
1876 First meeting took place at Caulfield, Melbourne.
1977 Kevin Darley, who would be champion in 2000, celebrated 17th birthday with first winner, Dust Up, at Haydock for Reg Hollinshead.
1977 Gary Stahlbaum had six mounts at Fort Erie, Canada. He won on all of them.
1981 John Carroll rode first winner, Helvic, at Pontefract.
1992 Devon & Exeter renamed plain Exeter. Anthony Cottrell, former assistant to father Gerald, made a winning start to his training career with Bluechipenterprise in a novice chase.
1992 John Reid rode five winners in a day for the first time – four at Brighton, another at Kempton in the evening.
1992 Germany's most successful trainer, Heinz Jentzsch, 72, won highest award handed to racing professional in that country when presented with the Verdienstkreuz First Class zum Verdienstorden (Order of Merit). He was the 29-times champion trainer, saddling more than 3,400 winners.
1907 Apprentice Harvey Bastiman received record 16-day ban after partnering gambled-on (14-1 to 8-1) but subsequently disqualified Mybotye to 'victory' at Catterick. Ten days were for having 'no regard to consequences of his actions' after his mount drifted left, hampering other runners, and the other

six were for excessive use of the whip (17 strokes).
2000 Riding for the first time since the plane crash that almost killed him and Ray Cochrane, Frankie Dettori rode a winner Atlantis Prince, at Newmarket, but the comeback victory was soured by an injury to Dubai Millennium on the gallops, forcing his retirement to stud.
2008 Better known as a jump jockey, Mick Naughton rode his first Flat winner as a professional at the age of 34 – 80-1 shot Spiders Star at Catterick.

QUOTE OF THE DAY
'A big run from Merry Master would be a fitting finale to a 34-year career which, if nothing else, dissuaded me from ever contemplating life as a trainer,' Jockey-turned-writer Marcus Armytage contemplates his father Roddy's role in his life before the latter sent out his runner in the 1994 Scottish National. Roddy, whose Barona had won that race twice, was born this day in 1934.

BIRTHDAYS
1932 Jockey George Milburn (hobby: breeding chinchillas), for whom Hurgill Lad at Hexham in 1953 was a first winner.
1934 Willie Robinson. Irish-born jockey, who rode Mill House to win the 1963 Cheltenham Gold Cup and Team Spirit to win the 1964 Grand National.
1939 Lester Piggott's wife Susan, who trained and as a jockey twice won the Newmarket Town Plate.

DEATHS OF THE DAY
1993 Cliff Beechener, 81. Former jockey (50+ winners) and Denton, Northants trainer (300+ winners).
1993 1,000 Guineas runner-up Niche, trained by Richard Hannon, died after a collision with stable blacksmith's van.

FIRST OF THE DAY
1984 Jersey staged the UK's first Sunday race meeting at Les Landes.

6 AUGUST

SIGNIFICANT EVENT
2005 Former Foreign Secretary and great friend of both racing and John McCririck, Robin Cook died aged 59. He once said that all politicians 'should write a tipping column to teach them humility'.

STRANGEST EVENT
1956 David O'Brien, the trainer who gave up horses for wine was born. Sent out winners of English (Secreto 1984, in process beating father Vincent's El Gran Senor into second); Irish (Assert 1982) and French (Assert 1982) Derbys. Became youngest trainer of Epsom Derby winner with Secreto but, disliking the pressure of the job, gave up training in October 1988 and has been producing highly rated wine from his Chateau Vignelaure in Provence since 1994 – bottles carry the logo of a racehorse.

OTHER EVENTS
1768 The great Gimcrack, winner of 26 of his 36 starts, lost on his only appearance at York – the course where the race bearing his name is still run.

1782 Disguise, owned by the Duke of Hamilton, won first race staged at Hamilton Park, run in two four-mile heats.

1900 Current Ripon course opened.

1926 Racing began at Chepstow's Piercefield track.

1985 Princess Anne won on Gulfland at Redcar.

1991 New Jockey Club rule introduced, permitting race entries to be reopened at overnight stage when less than two overnight declarations were made.

1992 Former jump jockey Clive Cox, who rode nearly 100 winners, saddled first winner as a trainer when Ushba won at Pontefract.

2005 Robert Winston's bid for the jockeys' championship ends when he takes a fall at Ayr, having already expressed concern at the state of the ground. Winston smashed his jaw when his mount slipped up, and the remaining races were abandoned. The rider, who sustained dental bills of some £18,000, agreed an out-of-court settlement with the course.

2008 Playing at Brighton racecourse while racing was going on, cockney duo Chas & Dave had to turn their amps down. 'They got some of the two-year-olds a bit upset,' said Richard Aldous, clerk of the course.

QUOTE OF THE DAY
'It is being passionately run by former racehorse trainer David O'Brien and his Australian-born wife Catherine, and it is no exaggeration to say the wines are among the classiest in the region.' Praise indeed from a renowned wine writer in the Telegraph in 2004 about trainer-turned-wine producer O'Brien, born on this date in 1956.

BIRTHDAYS
1915 Trainer Tony Dickinson. Leading point-to-point rider in 1954, who started training in 1967-68 with horses mainly partnered by son Michael.

1928 Jockey Ray Readers, whose 100th winner came on Pigeon Vole, owned by Winston Churchill, who sent a letter of congratulation.

1947 Nadine (Dina) Smith. Rode four winners under NH rules as amateur, and her Shiny Copper won the 1982 Triumph Hurdle.

1955 Rider of 1992 Derby winner Dr Devious, John Reid, who also won the Arc in 1988 on Tony Bin.

DEATH OF THE DAY
2004 New York trainer Phil 'P.G.' Johnson, 78, whose 43-1 chance Volponi won the 2002 Breeders' Cup Classic. Inducted into Hall of Fame in 1997.

CELEBRITY OF THE DAY
1922 Budget air travel pioneer, Jockey Club member and owner, Sir Freddie Laker, born on this date.

7 AUGUST

SIGNIFICANT EVENT
1936 Sir Michael Smurfit, Irish-based owner of first northern hemisphere-trained winner of the Melbourne Cup, is born. His Vintage Crop, trained by Dermot Weld, shocked the Aussies in 1993 when winning their great race. The combination did it again in 2002 with Media Puzzle. He also won three Irish Champion Hurdles and two Irish St Legers. He is one of the 100 leading international owners as quantified by the annual Directory of the Turf.

STRANGEST EVENT
1986 Riding 11-4 shot Amantiss at Devon, jockey Anthony Charlton finished first – but his horse finished second. As they approached the line, Charlton tumbled out of the saddle and crossed the line a split second ahead of the horse. The race was awarded to the runner-up – named Slip Up!

OTHER EVENTS
1891 For the last time racing was viewed from the Georgian grandstand at Richmond, Yorkshire. It was built by public subscription in 1775.
1967 Lester Piggott rode Chestergate (Reg Hollinshead) into second place in one-mile-five-furlong race at Newmarket, steering horse by its mane after bridle broke shortly after the start.
1976 Willie Carson rode all four winners Denys Smith saddled at Redcar.
1982 Flying three-year-old filly Soba won at Haydock for trainer David Chapman and jockey David Nicholls as part of an 11-win campaign.
1993 John Harris became first jockey to fall foul of new whip rules when banned for two days at Worcester for hitting mount 'with unreasonable frequency on the run-in'
1993 Jack Berry-trained Laurel Queen equalled post-war record for wins by filly/mare when landing 21st at Lingfield to draw level with Sir Mark Prescott's Misty Halo.

1996 Les Eyre's Jambo won at Nottingham to give Kieren Fallon his debut century, and trainer his first 50.
2009 Doncaster racecourse started a three-day meeting – for tattoo enthusiasts, The Tattoo Jam.

QUOTE OF THE DAY
2004 *'Surprisingly, considering Dettori's record at the course, there was not a single bet of three figures or more seen for the winner,'* said ring reporter Kel Mansfield at the 2004 Ascot Shergar Cup event in which 10-1 shot Justaquestion came from last to first to win.

BIRTHDAYS
1932 Paul Wright, headmaster and proprietor of Slindon College born. He proudly boasted that his was the 'only school to run a National Hunt racing stable'. He bred horses called Slindon, Slindon College, More Slindon, who ran under the care of trainer/science master Nicholas Lee-Judson.
1934 Jockey Johnny Kenneally born. He rode Red Holly to win over jumps eight times.
1937 Northern-based jockey Pat McCarron, who won the 1964 Champion Hurdle on Magic Court and finished runner-up in consecutive Grand Nationals on Freddie in 1965 and 66.
1951 Jockey Ron Hyett, third in the 1980 Grand National on The Pilgarlic.
1956 Trainer Gary Moore (hobbies: squash and shopping). Ryan's dad, he rode 150 winners over jumps and one on the Flat.
1961 Walter Swinburn – the junior seems to have been dispensed with these days. Jockey-turned-trainer who won the Derby aboard Shergar in 1981 and in 1986 on Shahrastani.

DEATH OF THE DAY
1993 Ossie Fletcher, OBE (1982 for services to racing), 72. Former *Sporting Life* editor (1959-85, the longest serving editor of a daily national newspaper).

8 AUGUST

SIGNIFICANT EVENT
1812 Daniel Dawson hanged in Cambridge, having been convicted of poisoning horses to stop them winning.

STRANGEST EVENT
1967 Owner Len Colville's claim that controversial Schweppes Gold Trophy winner (11 days after running fourth in a modest handicap) Hill House's body could have produced its own cortisone was finally accepted by the stewards of the National Hunt committee and no further action was taken against him, trainer Ryan Price or jockey Josh Gifford. The horse was sold to bookmaker John Banks and raced a further 23 times without winning.

OTHER EVENTS
1783 Final meeting of Bishopsgate racecourse near Windsor.
1876 Fred Archer rode a double at Lambourn, on Major Stapylton's Sabrina and Tom Stevens' Miss Croft.
1900 Having already won the Irish Derby with Gallinaria, trainer Dan McNally added the Irish Oaks with May Race.
1970 Bill Shoemaker landed his 6,000th winner on Shining County at Del Mar.
1982 Owner Craig B Singer issued writ against Jockey Club. His filly, Cairn Rouge, finished second to 15-2 Vayrann in the previous October's Champion Stakes, and the winner failed a post-race dope test. Vayrann's owner the Aga Khan's experts claimed the colt could have produced his own anabolic steroids, and Jockey Club stewards allowed the result to stand. Vayrann is still the winner in the record books.
1990 Trainer Jack Berry became first northern handler for 58 years to saddle 100 winners in a season when Heaven-Liegh-Grey won at Brighton. As result, Berry won £100 bet at 50-1 with Leeds bookie Graham Lisle. Dobson Peacock in 1932 had been the last northern trainer to complete the century.

1990 The good news was that the Fulke Johnson Houghton-owned and -trained Akdam won for the fourth time in the season at Kempton, landing a £100,000 bonus. The bad news was as the race was a claimer, he lost the horse.
1991 After 54 penalty-free years, 77-year-old Bill Wightman, Britain's longest-serving trainer, was hauled up to face the stewards for the first time since taking out a licence in 1937 when Divine Pet won at Brighton. They demanded an explanation for the 12-1 chance's improved form, and accepted the answer that the horse needed firm ground.
2008 *Racing Post* announced jockey Mick Fitzgerald's retirement in his own words: 'When you are advised that a fall could kill you, you have to listen.'

QUOTE OF THE DAY
2004 *'He has stabled a handful of his lovers in lavish houses around the world and visited them in turn, for days or weeks at a time, in the same way that a champion stallion is taken to cover beautifully bred mares.'* A *Sunday Telegraph* revelation about owner and trainer Ivan Allan.

BIRTHDAY
1957 Jockey-turned-Cumbria trainer John Lennox Goulding. He rode Astral Charmer to win the 1981 Scottish Grand National.

DEATH OF THE DAY
1999 Trainer Mikey Heaton-Ellis, 41. In October 1982, as a promising jump jockey, he suffered a paralysing fall at Huntingdon, which left him confined to a wheelchair. Nonetheless he became a trainer in 1991, sending out winners under both codes.

CELEBRITY OF THE DAY
1991 Former snooker world champion and one-time stable lad Alex 'Hurricane' Higgins was arrested at Uttoxeter racecourse for alleged threatening and abusive behaviour.

9 AUGUST

SIGNIFICANT EVENT

1992 Johnny Kok, champion trainer of Malaysia and Singapore, was suspended for three years – later reduced to six months – after sprinter Giltedged III tested positive to stimulant Etorphine, aka 'Elephant Juice', after winning the Jubilee Stakes at Bukit Timah, Singapore. Kok was later banned for a further six months when Star Of Today and Salute For Me both also tested positive. The trainer claimed he was being set up and would retire.

STRANGEST EVENT

1983 Trainer Derek Garraton was fined £500 after his horse was found to have tested positive after racing at Edinburgh in April. The horse's name? Oh yes – Magic Mushroom.

OTHER EVENTS

1939 Racing held for last time at Derby with the £500 Peveril of the Peak Plate won by Lady Ludlow's Morwell, ridden by Sam Wragg for trainer Capt Ossie Bell's Lambourn stable. The Hartington Plate was a void race after no runners were declared – which perhaps helps to explain why the course became defunct.
1947 Tote takings of £31,550 at Phoenix Park represented an Irish record, as was the £8,652 invested on Phoenix Plate.
1994 Bath staged its first Listed race, the Upavon Fillies' Stakes, won by Island Of Silver, 4-5, ridden by Frankie Dettori for John Gosden.
1998 Seeking The Pearl became first Japanese-trained horse to win a Group 1 event in Europe, winning the Prix Maurice de Gheest at Deauville, ridden by Yutaka Take.
2007 'The only sport more crooked than tennis is British horseracing,' declared *Daily Mirror* sports betting columnist Derek McGovern, not a man to mince his words.
2008 Riding in England for the first time as part of the 'Rest of the World' Shergar Cup squad, US jockey Russell Baze, the second rider ever to reach 10,000 winners and nine-times US champion, was given a four-day suspension for overzealous use of the whip on unplaced Mac Gille Eoin at Ascot.
2009 First double for trainer Ron Barr, who boasts 14 horses and 20,000 hens, at Redcar.

QUOTE OF THE DAY

'I have a three-year-old gelding by Mtoto – he has big honest eyes, a lovely countenance and a very friendly demeanour. I had to hold him for an hour the other day while another horse was being treated. He was so patient I'm going to call him Alec.' Former trainer Charlie Brooks on this date in 2004 paying a quirky tribute to the trainer of the top-class Mtoto, Alec Stewart, who had recently died of cancer, aged 49.

BIRTHDAYS

1963 Jockey Mark Dwyer
1967 'For their employers they must be biggest price about the losers, and shortest price the winners.' William Hill spokesman David Hood sums up the vulnerable nature of odds compilers, whose job it is to price up races for punters to bet on. Hood was born on this day in 1967. His apprenticeship as a jockey was spent with Stan Mellor, and his first winner, Supergrass, came on April 11, 1985 at Cheltenham.

FIRST OF THE DAY

1991 Spy In The Sky became the first racehorse foaled in Barbados to race in Britain. The Richard Hannon-trained two-year-old finished 14th of 21 at Newmarket behind X My Heart.

CELEBRITY OF THE DAY

1969 Plumpton racecourse moved into the rock music business, hosting a concert by heavy metal legends, Ozzy 'Prince of Darkness' Osbourne and his band, Black Sabbath. A week later the Who played there.

10 AUGUST

SIGNIFICANT EVENT
1985 Tremulous won at Haydock to give trainer Barry Hills his 1,000th Flat winner in Britain.

STRANGEST EVENT
1993 After 102 days without a single winner Owen O'Neill sent out two – at odds of 66-1 (unraced Harvest Rose) and 50-1 (Miss Crusty, who had been off the course for 658 days) at Bath. Tote odds were 157-1 and 51-1 respectively.

OTHER EVENTS
1711 Jonathan Swift wrote in his diary: 'Dr Arbuthnot, the Queen's favourite physician, went out with me to see a place they have made for a famous horse race tomorrow, where the Queen will come.' 'A place' was Ascot, the Queen, Anne.

1994 Star Rage equalled record for most handicap wins in a season when landing ninth victory at Beverley for trainer Mark Johnston. Glencroft and Chaplin's Club in 1988 – the latter also in 1984 – and Framboise in 1874 were others to achieve the feat.

1991 Owner Jim Joel's 805th and final winner since 1928 was Living Image, 6-1, in Redcar's Bonusprint Handicap. His Royal Palace won the 1967 2,000 Guineas and Derby.

1991 *The Weatherbys General Stud Book* celebrated its 200th anniversary. Volume one of the book, the world's first national stud book, was produced in 1791 by James Weatherby.

1991 First Flat turf race run at Southwell, You Can't Beat Heat Handicap, won by 11-2 Kawwas, trained by William Holden and ridden by John Lowe.

1992 Michael Roberts rode treble at Windsor, reaching 150 winners in Britain in a season for the first time.

1992 Sir Andrew Lloyd Webber on song when paying 39,000gns at Doncaster Sales for five-year-old Russell Dalus, with only one race – second in Hereford bumper – to his credit.

1996 Latest US superhorse Cigar, 1-10, who had drawn level with Citation's 16-win streak of 46 years earlier, was denied a record 17th straight victory by 39-1 Dare And Go, who passed the US superstar in the stretch to win Del Mar's $1m Pacific Classic.

2008 French sprinter Marchand D'Or, trained by Freddie Head, won the Prix Maurice de Gheest at Deauville for the third consecutive year, the first time any French horse had ever won the same French Group event on three straight occasions.

2008 19-year-old apprentice David Probert rode his first treble – a 213-1 accumulator at Windsor.

QUOTE OF THE DAY
'A licence to print money,' was the phrase describing betting shops attributed to Scottish bookmaker and racehorse owner John Banks, who died on this date in 2003, aged 68. His Katmandu landed a hefty gamble from 100-8 to 7-1 when winning the 1969 Royal Hunt Cup.

BIRTHDAYS
1944 *Racing Post* breeding specialist, Tony Morris.

1965 Jockey Michael Earl Smith, in New Mexico. Twice within 17 days in 1992 he rode six winners in a day at Aqueduct.

CELEBRITY OF THE DAY
1950 Lord Astor's High Stakes scored his 34th win from 50 starts when landing mile-and-a-half Rotherham Stakes at Pontefract on this day. Lord Astor, who had won every Classic bar the Derby, in which he was five times second (three 2,000 Guineas; two 1,000 Guineas; five Oaks; one St Leger), thought so much of the gelding that when he retired from racing at the end of this year he disposed of every horse he owned except High Stakes. Astor died in 1952, in his 73rd year.

11 AUGUST

SIGNIFICANT EVENT
1711 Racing took place at Ascot for the first time, watched by Queen Anne plus courtiers. £558 19s 5d had been spent on clearing the course to provide 'the round Heath on Ascott Common', and a further £15 2s 8d was paid to mark it out with painted posts. Seven contested the first race: Doctor, Have At Al, Teague, Dimple, Flint, Grey Jack and Grim. Frustratingly there is no record of how they finished.

STRANGEST EVENT
1994 Longest odds ever offered on Australian course, 5,000-1, were laid to $20 by bookie Mark Read over seventh placed About Our Friend at Canterbury.

OTHER EVENTS
1803 Three-day meeting staged at Lewes (11-13th) with today's card featuring His Majesty's (George III) Plate of 100gns, to be run 'after dinner'.

1991 Lester Piggott won the Swedish Derby for first time since 1958, when he'd won on Flying Friendship. This time he triumphed on Jagersro.

1992 Red Rum's trainer Ginger McCain fined £1,250 by Jockey Club disciplinary committee for failing to pay correct wages to stable staff.

2007 Having won the Preakness on Curlin, jockey Robby Albarado landed the 25th Arlington Million on Jambalaya, denying runner-up Tin Man the honour of being the first winner of consecutive Millions by a 3/4 length.

2008 The *Racing Post* reported that Paul Scotney, director of integrity services and licensing for the BHA, had warned that any trainers refusing to participate in the seminars organised for them on the subject of inside information could lose their licences.

2009 It was announced that the annual Louisianna Derby, run at the Fair Grounds would be extended by half a furlong to 9f to make it more attractive to Kentucky Derby contenders, while the value was also increased from $600,00 to $750,000, and the date was moved from seven to five weeks before the big race in 2010.

QUOTE OF THE DAY
'We'd love to hear from any single men who want an evening to remember on Saturday.' Gabrielle de Brie of Rapid Romance, organisers of the first ever speed-dating session held at a racecourse, Goodwood, on this day in 2004.

BIRTHDAYS
1933 Former Irish champion jump jockey Tos Taaffe. Younger brother of Arkle's jockey, Pat, and of amateur jockey, Willie. In 1959 Pat rode Zonda to win the Irish Grand National, and Tos was second on Knightsbrook.

1956 Jockey Willie Higgins. He rode Primula Boy to win the 1979 Ayr Gold Cup.

1953 Durham-based trainer Howard Johnson, who teamed up successfully with millionaire owner Graham Wylie, saddled Ushers Island to win the 1994 Whitbread Gold Cup and Grey Abbey to win the 2004 Scottish National.

1971 Three time champion jockey in Germany, Andrew Suborics.

DEATHS OF THE DAY
1894 Popular, successful Aussie jockey Tommy Corrigan, with career total of 239 winners, died after falling from his mount, Waiter, during the Caulfield Grand National Steeplechase. Funeral went down in folklore when cortege took 30 minutes to pass massive crowds.

1988 Promising jump jockey Paul Croucher, 27, in a car accident. He won the Scottish Champion Hurdle on Positive.

LAST OF THE DAY
1984 Bedtime, a bay gelding trained by Dick Hern won the Prix Gentaut-Biron at Deauville, giving jockey Brain Taylor his final Pattern win.

12 AUGUST

SIGNIFICANT EVENT
1995 Gai Waterhouse made history as she became first female trainer in Australia to record four-timer at a city meeting – doing so at Rosehill, Sydney, with Sea Captain, Electronic, Light Up The World and Western Approaches.

STRANGEST EVENT
1993 It was announced that the start time of the St Leger on September 11 would be brought forward by 40 minutes in order to avoid a TV clash with, er, the World Chess Championship.

OTHER EVENTS
1967 The Queen's Hopeful Venture won for the fourth time in five outings, scoring by five lengths in Newbury's Oxfordshire Stakes.

1988 Klute, touted as the fastest horse in the world on time trials, but who had never competed on a racecourse, was trounced over five furlongs in a match at Haydock by Jack Berry's So Careful – not, with all due respect, anywhere near the fastest horse in the world.

1989 Jack Berry-trained O I Oyston helped raise money for charity when released into a field divided into squares, which had been raffled off, to leave his droppings in a winning square. O I Oyston kept punters waiting for 40 minutes. Winner Bob Heathcote donated £1,000 winnings to Royal Manchester Children's Hospital.

1989 Former Newmarket trainer Bill Marshall celebrated his imminent (August 14) 71st birthday by sending out Coo-Bird to win the Barbados Derby. His own horse Valial was second.

1990 Jump jockey Andy Orkney won chase at Pyatgorsk, USSR and then finished fourth, with colleague Marcus Armytage third, in Russian Grand National on same card.

1991 196.5-1 accumulator for trainer Jim Bolger, who saddled five winners from five runners at Gowran Park.

1994 The first race at Catterick was delayed by ten minutes when an accident on the A1 caused traffic jams.

1994 Pollen Count and Young Ern fought out the first dead-heat for 45 years in Newbury's Hungerford Stakes.

1996 Having suffered severe head injuries in a Hong Kong fall, Walter Swinburn returned to the saddle with a winner.

1997 After riding Marathon to win at Deauville for trainer-father Alec, jockey Freddie Head, 50, six-times French champion, announced his retirement on 2,937 winners.

2007 'There are a lot of lads now who are developing into riding robots.' Veteran rider Kevin Darley doesn't sound over-impressed as he tells the *Racing Post* what he thinks of up-and-coming riders.

2008 Kirsty Milczarek became only the fifth female jockey to ride out her claim when Ruby Tallulah won at Lingfield.

QUOTE OF THE DAY
'I've got the worst bunch of two-year-olds I've ever had. I was hoping something was wrong with them, but we had them tested and the only thing wrong with them is that they are slow.' Mick Channon in 2004, not exactly mistaking his geese for swans.

BIRTHDAYS
1956 Aussie Hall of Fame trainer, Lee Freedman.

1960 Jockey Nigel Tutty, and Newmarket trainer Grant Eden.

DEATH OF THE DAY
2003 Irish jump jockey Kieran Kelly, 25, died from injuries sustained in a fall on August 8 at Kilbeggan.

CELEBRITY OF THE DAY
1989 The Queen's first runner in the US for 35 years, Unknown Quantity, won Grade 1 Arlington Handicap (10-1), ridden by Jorge Velasquez at Arlington International, Chicago. This was Her Majesty's first US winner.

13 AUGUST

SIGNIFICANT EVENT
2008 *The Racing Post* revealed that trainer Jamie Osborne had signed up for a course in Mandarin Chinese to help sell bloodstock to China.

STRANGEST EVENT
1996 All four of the runners in Southwell's Skegness Handicap went off as 11-4 co-favourites.

OTHER EVENTS
1711 Queen Anne was again at the new racecourse of her devising at Ascot Common, this time along with writer Jonathan Swift, who noted that Her Majesty was dressed 'like a man' in a long riding coat and waistcoat. However, Swift arrived late as 'everybody's coach had gone'.

1737 An odd horserace took place between two contestants, from 'Tyler's Ferry to the bridge at Hackney March'. The notable difference was that the horses were swimming, and had no jockeys.

1888 Racing held for the first time at Wolverhampton's Dunstall Park course. The first winner, Silver Spur, was ridden by Tommy Loates, who had won the last race at the previous Wolverhampton course, Broad Meadows.

1919 Great US horse Man o'War was defeated for the only time during his career – by the aptly named Upset, who he subsequently beat six times.

1985 Hi Tech Leader gave Eddie Hide his 2,591st and final British winner as an active jockey at Nottingham.

1992 Dale Baird, holder of world record for training most winners, saddled 6,000th winner, Irish Laser, at Mountaineer Park, West Virginia.

1993 Tony Hide-trained Magnetic Point, due to race at Folkestone, was delivered to Southwell, courtesy of Hughes Racehorse Transport. The trainer was fined £105.

1994 Tony McCoy finished second on Arctic Life over hurdles at Stratford on his first ride in Britain.

2008 French trainer Andre Fabre had a runner at Salisbury for the first time with In The Light. She went off 3-1 favourite for the £50,000 mile-and-a-quarter event but could manage only fifth of eight.

QUOTE OF THE DAY
'The meeting was originally scheduled for May 3, but that was lost through waterlogging. So it was rearranged to this meeting, which was again waterlogged.' Newcastle commercial manager Kay Forster, about a second waterlogging abandonment of a 2004 charity meeting in aid of, er, Water Aid, dedicated to the provision of safe domestic water to the world's poorest countries.

BIRTHDAYS
1924 Bishop Auckland trainer Denys Smith. Became a trainer in 1961, and sent out Red Alligator to win the 1968 Grand National. In the same year he was leading trainer with 55 winners worth £37,944. Dual-purpose, he also sent out winners of the Lincoln and William Hill Gold Cup.

1925 Trainer John Webber.

1967 Jockey Tim Sprake.

FIRST OF THE DAY
1982 Trainer David O'Brien saddled first winner in England when Pas De Seul (Pat Eddery) won the Hungerford Stakes at Newbury.

CELEBRITY OF THE DAY
1994 Footballers Ian Rush and Peter Beardsley of the Footballers' Racing Club enjoyed a winner as Sky Music, 3/1, scored at Ripon, ridden by Sean Mulvey. Alan Shearer, owner with Howard Johnson, born today in 1970.

14 AUGUST

SIGNIFICANT EVENT
2009 Irish jumps trainer Janet Elliot, 60, became the first female trainer ever inducted into the US Hall of Fame, having worked there since 1968, with career earnings there of $7.6m.Also inducted was US horse Ben Nevis, winner of the 1980 Grand National, while silver-haired trainer Bob Baffert also made it in at a ceremony held at Saratoga Springs.

STRANGEST EVENT
1986 Catterick staged a Christmas meeting. Santa Claus was present for six races with titles such as Christmas Morning Nursery, Stuffed Turkey Handicap and the Queen's Speech Stakes. The meeting was switched from festive season when it had been abandoned courtesy of foul weather.

OTHER EVENTS
1865 First meeting held at Eagle Farm, Queensland.
1926 Last meeting held at West Cheshire course of Bidston, which had opened for business in October 1921.
1946 Haydock resumed racing for first time since war.
1967 Jockey Joe Mercer fractured spine in a fall at Folkestone.
1982 Lester Piggott rode 4,000th domestic winner, 1-3 favourite Ardross, in Newbury's Geoffrey Freer Stakes.
1987 Martin Pipe completed record-breaking run of seven straight winners at Devon & Exeter.
1992 Jo Berry, Jack's wife, won amateur riders' race at Wolverhampton for the fourth time in as many attempts.
1992 Southwell featured three harness races, on which course Tote turnover was £2,606 compared with £17,163 on racing.
1993 Captain Keith Brown, starter of the 1993 'National that never was' false-start fiasco, officially retired after carrying out duties at Newbury.
1993 Charlie Mann, ex jump jockey, launched training career with a winner from his first runner as Laburnum landed tree-mendous win at Bangor.

QUOTE OF THE DAY
'You couldn't choose 13 favourites to get beaten in a row. I was beginning to wish I was allowed to lay my horses to lose.' Owner-breeder Jeff Smith was relieved after his Night Rocket justified favouritism to win at Salisbury in 2008, breaking a run of 13 consecutive losing favourites running in his colours

BIRTHDAYS
1918 Trainer Bill Marshall born. Awarded DFC while serving as a fighter pilot during World War II. Made name as a trainer handling greys – Grey Mirage; My Swanee and prolific sprinter Raffingora. He narrowly escaped death in a 1972 air crash, in which he was rescued by jockey Joe Mercer.
1938 Trainer Michael Jarvis, son of jump jockey Andrew. Saddled two Classic winners – Ameerat in the 2001 1,000 Guineas, and Eswarah in the 2005 Oaks. Also won 1989 Arc with Carroll House.
1959 Basketball legend and racehorse owner, Magic Johnson.
1959 Alison Thorpe. Became Carmarthen, West Wales trainer in September 2001.

DEATH OF THE DAY
2006 Versatile Tom Fitzgeorge-Parker, 86. Trainer – sent out 50 Flat and jumps winners; chief racing correspondent for *Daily Mail*; author – wrote *Training the Racehorse*; war hero – Major in Royal Scots Greys during World War II, winning Military Cross in 1945.

CELEBRITY OF THE DAY
1992 Newcastle United striker Mick Quinn's Mighty Miss Magpie, trained by Mick Channon, won at Southwell – as former England international Francis Lee also trained a winner on the card, Must Be Magical.

15 AUGUST

SIGNIFICANT EVENT
1972 Unbeaten Brigadier Gerard, hot favourite at 1-3, suffered his first defeat in 14, and only defeat of 18-race career, finishing runner-up to 12-1 shot Roberto, the Derby winner, in the Benson & Hedges Gold Cup at York. Winning jockey Braulio Baeza was flown in specially from the USA.

STRANGEST EVENT
1992 'They'll have a lot more to check on the way back,' said Amsterdam-based businessman Dave Spencer on this day in 1992. He flew to England to see his two-year-old Palacegate Episode win Newbury's St Hugh's Stakes, only to be strip-searched by immigration officers who checked every note of currency he had, after he arrived at the airport without luggage.

OTHER EVENTS
1720 Racing resumed at Ascot after six-year gap following death of founder, Queen Anne.

1825 Racing held at Broad Meadows, Wolverhampton, with eccentric gambler Jack Mytton's Euphrates winning the feature event, the three-mile Darlington Cup. Wolverhampton races moved to Dunstall Park in 1888.

1863 First meeting at Saratoga, USA, concluded. Track became known as 'favourites' graveyard' – champions Man o'War, Gallant Fox and Secretariat all met with high-profile reverses here. Huge gambler John 'Bet A Million' Gates said to have lost $400,000 at one meeting.

1930 Eph Smith, older brother of Doug – both Classic-winning jockeys – rode first winner, Red Queen, at Windsor. He went on to ride until 1965, scoring 2,313 winners, including Blue Peter in the 1939 2,000 Guineas and Derby. He was found dead in a brook in 1972, with the verdict death by misadventure. He left £141,798.

1967 Scobie Breasley rode Windsor treble on Dear Mama, Wippip and Onward.

1989 Cricket Ball became first horse to win Group race for fourth consecutive year when taking Prix de Meautry at Deauville. Gerald Mosse rode the John Fellows-trained six-year-old.

2007 'In Britain we seem to think that jockeys are good if they whack their mounts really hard lots of times and win by a short head. The rest of the world is much more interested in jockeys who get horses to settle, run at an even pace and maximise their potential.' Tom Segal in the *Racing Post* Weekender.

2009 Sarah's Art won the 7th running of popular grey-only race at Newmarket, which attracted 166 runners.

QUOTE OF THE DAY
'I must have been mad. Stark, staring mad. It was the morning of the Derby of 1939, I had the greatest chance ever of winning on Blue Peter and there I was in the paddock at my father's farm, riding a hunter over the sticks.' Not so mad, as jockey Eph Smith, who rode his first winner on this date in 1930, also duly won the Derby on Blue Peter despite his unorthodox preparation.

BIRTHDAYS
1935 Gloucester jockey/trainer/novelist Graeme Roe. Rode as an amateur 1975-85 before training Major Owen, Dom Perignon and Broomy Bank.

1962 Four-times champion woman rider, Kim Tinkler.

DEATH OF THE DAY
1993 Former jump jockey Denis McCarthy, 52, who rode more than 50 winners.

CELEBRITY OF THE DAY
1950 Princess Royal, rider of Ten No Trumps and Insular, and recently involved in point-to-point training, was born on this date.

16 AUGUST

SIGNIFICANT EVENT
1912 AND 1986 Ryan Price, born on this date 1912, died this date 1986. In between he carved out a career as one of the greatest jump trainers, winning virtually every major race. In addition, from 1970, he turned out top Flat winners. Jump triumphs included What A Myth, 1969 Cheltenham Gold Cup; Kilmore, 1962 National; three Champion Hurdles – Clair Soleil, 1955; Fare Time 1959, and Eborneezer, 1961. He won the Schweppes Gold Trophy four times, and on the Flat Ginevra won the 1972 Oaks, and Bruni the 1975 St Leger.

STRANGEST EVENT
1993 A punter carrying a Tesco bag entered a William Hill betting shop, and removed £20,000 cash from the bag to back White Muzzle, 2-1, to win the next day's Juddmonte International at York.

OTHER EVENTS
1731 The bodies of three robbers – Joseph Askwith, and Richard and John Freeman – who had been hung that morning were cut down to enable racegoers to have an uninterrupted view of racing at York where Lord Lonsdale's Monkey won both heats of the 100gns King's Plate.
1962 Terry Biddlecombe rode Fire Raiser to win over hurdles at Newton Abbot to give Roddy Armytage his first winner as a trainer.
1971 Entertainer Des O'Connor bought Champion Hurdle runner-up Major Rose for 3,000gns at Doncaster Sales.
1989 Sixteen-year-old chaser Ken's Lake almost pulled off a 200-1 sensation when runner-up at that price in a five-runner chase at Devon.
1990 Jockey-turned-trainer Menin Muggeridge sent out a winner with his first runner over jumps, 33-1 Swingtime Belle at Newton Abbot.
1991 Former international footballer Francis Lee enjoyed first equine hat-trick as trainer when Charly Pharly, Killy and Sir Arthur Hobbs all won at Haydock.
1995 Mick Channon sent out first winner in France – Maggi For Margaret, at Deauville.
2007 Date number four for opening of new racecourse Great Leighs came and went.
2009 Pat Eddery's first runner in France as trainer, Hearts of Fire won at Deauville, under Olivier Peslier.

QUOTE OF THE DAY
'A total very close to £500,000.' The amount of winnings claimed by pro punter Patrick Veitch on this day in 2004when his horse, Exponential, trained by Stuart Williams and ridden by David Allan, won at Nottingham, having been backed down from 100-1 to 8-1, according to his autobiography, Enemy Number One.

BIRTHDAYS
1933 Jockey Jock Wilson. The best horses he rode were Polyfoto and Tribal Chief.
1955 Jockey Colin Brown, who rode Desert Orchid, Combs Ditch, Floyd, Sabin du Loir and Barnbrook Again.
1957 Jump jockey-turned-saddler, Martin Pepper.

DEATH OF THE DAY
1993 Frank Gilman, 78, the owner-trainer-breeder of 1982 Grand National winner Grittar. A friend of mine backed the horse and celebrated loudly when he won – unfortunately he was in church getting married at the time. He has since divorced.

CELEBRITY OF THE DAY
1939 Sir Trevor McDonald was born today. The newsreader was recalled by Sir Michael Stoute as a fellow radio commentator on races at Port of Spain's Queen's Park track.

17 AUGUST

SIGNIFICANT EVENT
1995 Luca Cumani sent out Larrocha to win the Galtres Stakes at York. The filly started at 4-11, possibly something to do with the extraordinary fact that Cumani was winning the event for the sixth successive year.

STRANGEST EVENT
1993 Racing was delayed by 14 minutes on Ireland's beach course, Laytown. The judge's view of the finish was blocked by a burger van.

OTHER EVENTS
1869 A crowd of 40,000 flocked to see the first day's racing at Ballybrit, Galway.
1898 The first Flat meeting was held at Folkestone.
1955 Camarero lost for the first time, after 56 successive wins in Puerto Rico.
1974 Michael Wood rode his first winner, Mary Mod (17-2) at Ripon.
1978 Pretty Cute gave Lorna Vincent her first winner – and the first NH win by a professional lady jockey in Britain – at Devon & Exeter.
1991 After trying for 20 years of training, Eddie Harty managed to book Lester Piggott to ride one of his horses. Sha's Dream (12-1) duly made the wait worthwhile, winning the Tattersalls Auction Race over six furlongs at the Curragh.
1992 The Tote announced that the £9,540.40 dividend declared two days earlier for the Placepot at Newbury should really have been £4,659.20 after a £1.10 bet in a Fulham betting shop was found that hadn't been added to the pool.
1993 White Muscle ran unplaced in the Juddmonte International, and the mystery plastic bag punter (see 16 August) lost his £20,000 stake. But the bookies had to hand it on to £1 accumulator punter Michael Charlton

of Tottenham, London, whose final selection Ezzoud, the 28-1 Juddmonte winner, landed him a £39,000 payout.
2004 'Few sons exceed the achievements of famous fathers in the same field, but Frankie has managed that rare trick and, by the beam on Gianfranco's face, he is one proud dad.' Alastair Down, marvelling at Frankie Dettori's career as, in front of his old man, the rider won the 2004 Juddmonte International at York on 3-1 shot Sulamani.
2009 Odds on favourite, New Christmas burst out of the stalls – without Jamie Spencer on board. As he removed the blindfold the stalls opened, unbalancing the rider who was left standing on the side of the Yarmouth stalls.

BIRTHDAYS
1942 The delightfully named bloodstock agent, Tote Cherry-Downes.
1954 Jockey, horse and human chiropractor, Anthony Webber.
1959 Graham McCourt, who pulled off one of the great shocks when riding Norton's Coin to a 100-1 victory in the 1990 Cheltenham Gold Cup.

DEATH OF THE DAY
1899 Born 1845, trainer Robert Peck died on this day in Scarborough. He trained four Classic winners including Oaks and St Leger winner Marie Stuart, who did the double in 1873 – and Derby winner Doncaster, who won in that same remarkable year. Thanks to his astute tilts at the ring he was able to retire.

CELEBRITY OF THE DAY
2008 Swimmer-turned-TV presenter Sharron Davies revealed that she once had a date with trainer Michael Dickinson. 'He was very charming, and I was free and single. But all he did was quiz me about training techniques and make notes in a little jotter he was carrying.'

18 AUGUST

SIGNIFICANT EVENT
1948 The 12-year-old youngster Lester Piggott rode his first winner, The Chase (10-1), at Haydock in the Wigan Lane Selling Plate.

STRANGEST EVENT
1980 George Duffield earned a place in the Guinness Book of Records when he partnered the two-year-old Spindrifter to win the Leicester City FC Stakes at, er, Leicester – the 11th consecutive victory he had chalked up on the horse that season in its 12 appearances. For its one defeat a different jockey was in the saddle.

OTHER EVENTS
1959 Noel Murless' Petite Etoile won the Yorkshire Oaks, beating Meld's record prize money haul for the filly/ mare trained in Britain. Piggott also won on Right Boy at Nunthorpe for the second straight season.

1981 Willie Carson fractured his skull following a fall from Silken Knot at York.

1989 Trainers Ian Semple (Good Mood at Perth) and Henrietta Knight (The Grey Gunner at Bangor) both won with their first runners.

1991 The latest wonder horse, Arazi, cruised to a three-length win in Deauville's Prix Morny.

1994 'She probably broke the track record going down to the start,' said Frankie Dettori of the furiously fast filly Lochsong, who boiled over during the parade for the Nunthorpe at York and finished last in the race, won by 14/1 Piccolo on the disqualification of Blue Siren, thus giving Mick Channon his first Group 1 winner.

2009 John Oxx trained Sea the Stars, 1/4, beat Mastercraftsman in the four runner Juddmonte International, breaking the course record. It is believed to be the first domestic Group 1 race run without a British runner.

2009 Frankie Dettori scored, then missed a penalty in a shoot out as Northern jockeys beat Southern counterparts in a York game which raised £15,000 for the Injured Jockeys' Fund.

QUOTE OF THE DAY
'It was the first time in 25 years Lester had asked for advice on how to ride a horse,' claimed owner Robert Sangster after his Rodrigo De Triano was the 8-1 winner of York's Juddmonte International in 1992, exactly 44 years after Piggott's first win as a 12-year-old schoolboy. Mind you, Sangster didn't say just WHO Lester asked!

BIRTHDAYS
1931 Irish-based owner Bertram R Firestone. Among his best horses were champion US two-year-old Honest Pleasure; Kentucky Derby runner-up General Assembly; Irish 2,000 Guineas winner King's Company and Breeders' Cup Turf winner Theatrical.

1940 Irish trainer John Mulhern, known for his interestingly named horses like Wolf Of Badenoch, Hungry Hur and Welcome Pin. Business interest – frozen food distribution.

1954 Jump jockey-turned-valet Steve Charlton.

1965 Jumping trainer Ger Lyons, also the rider of 50 winners as a jockey. He lists in the Directory of the Turf his stable facilities as including 'some lovely pubs in the area'.

FIRST OF THE DAY
1975 Peter Scudamore's first ride in public was on the Flat, aboard Stellemon, unplaced at Leicester.

CELEBRITY OF THE DAY
2009 The Queen's first runner at Killarny, Michael Bell-trained Far Winds, 7/4, finished runner up to Poet.

19 AUGUST

SIGNIFICANT EVENT

1931 Jockey William (Lee) Shoemaker born near Fabens, Texas. Family legend has it his grandmother incubated him in a shoebox. He won the Kentucky Derby four times and became the oldest jockey to win in 1986 on Ferdinand. He retired as the most successful jockey of all before being paralysed in car crash.

STRANGEST EVENT

1983 Having ruled that race six days earlier had resulted in dead heat, Judge, Michael Hancock took another look at rather larger version of print, after Henry Cecil appealed. Decided that Cecil's Be My Valentine had indeed beaten Gavin Hunter's Brave Advance, after all.

OTHER EVENTS

1982 Even-money favourite Sharpo completed a hat-trick of wins in the William Hill Sprint Championship at York, ridden by Steve Cauthen. He had been partnered in 1980 (3-1) and 1981 (14-1) by Pat Eddery.

1988 Lester Piggott's wife Susan was badly injured in a fall on the gallops.

1989 Thar-An-Bharr won at Hereford to give trainer John Upson his first winner.

1992 Lester Piggott, Michael Hills, Philip Robinson and George Duffield were all aboard a plane to York that missed colliding with an RAF jet by 'about 2ft'. In March 1993 an official report revealed that the Piper air taxi carrying the jockeys was almost sliced in two by a Tornado because of blunders by air traffic controllers. Nonetheless, Duffield went on to ride User Friendly to victory in the Yorkshire Oaks.

1997 Disaster was narrowly averted at Folkestone when a caterer's car appeared ahead of the runners during the third race. The jockeys managed to swerve their mounts clear.

2002 Hayley Turner rode her first double, when Blue Streak (13/2) and Timeless Chick (20/1) won at Brighton.

2008 The first two days of York's Ebor meeting are washed out through waterlogging.

2008 Mark Cleminson, 38, the racegoer who caused a delay of several minutes by walking up the course at Carlisle on August 4, abusing jockeys and refusing to remove himself from the track, was fined £188 and banned for life.

2009 Irish jumps specialist trainer Willie Mullins won Ebor with 25/1 Sesenta while huge gamble on Red Merlin failed as horse finished 12th.

2009 Channel 4's Jim McGrath, shrewd punter and U2 fan, was asked by the *Racing Post* Weekender to name his biggest fear: 'Having a losing flat season. I have never experienced one yet'.

QUOTE OF THE DAY

'It's like making love, luv!' said an excited David Nicholls after the nine-year-old Bahamian Pirate became the oldest horse to win a Group 1 in Britain in the Nunthorpe Stakes in 2004.

BIRTHDAY

1953 Europe's winningmost trainer, Frenchman Jean-Claude Rouget. Pau-based trainer's address is Chemin de la Foret Bastard.

FIRST OF THE DAY

1967 Pat Eddery's first mount, True Time, finished last at the Curragh.

CELEBRITY OF THE DAY

1934 Bookie John 'Betting shops are a licence to print money' Banks was born.

20 AUGUST

SIGNIFICANT EVENT

1853 Not many people are aware that betting shops flourished in the mid 19th century – until a large number of them fell into the hands of unscrupulous operators. So the Betting Houses Act became law today, suppressing the several hundred shops that had been operating, often ripping off customers.

STRANGEST EVENT

1966 Fifty-five of 66 licensed jockeys riding boycotted a meeting at Accra, Ghana, because the Accra Turf Club had refused a request to slaughter a sacrificial cow at the six-furlong bend of the course. Eleven accidents had taken place there and the jockeys wished to appease the fates. The riders were banned, and no cow provided.

OTHER EVENTS

1770 Eclipse turned up – but no-one else did. For the third consecutive time the great horse frightened off the opposition and the King's Plate at York was a walkover.

1817 Racing had been scheduled to begin at a new Wormwood Scrubs location. Six days earlier, an objection by the Army killed off the project.

1824 A busy afternoon for Lord Bentinck's Olive at Goodwood. Unplaced in the first race, Olive dead-heated with Swindon in the next. The two had a run-off, which resulted in another dead-heat, so they ran off again and this time Olive finished in front.

1971 Willie Carson rode a treble at Haydock, completing his first century.

1991 Terimon (Clive Brittain) led from the front to pull off a 16-1 shock in the Juddmonte International at York.

1992 Lyric Fantasy became the first two-year-old for 36 years, and the first filly of that age, to win York's Nunthorpe Stakes. Ridden by Michael Roberts for Richard Hannon.

1994 Frankie Dettori became only the third – Gordon Richards first in 1936 and Michael Roberts second in 1992 – jockey to have 1,000 mounts in a season. The 1,000th was runner-up at Ripon, but the 1,001st, Halling, at York, was a 6/4 winner – Dettori's 188th of the season.

2008 It is confirmed that the whole of the York Ebor meeting had fallen victim to waterlogging.

2010 The scheduled opening date for Fontwell's new £6.5m premier enclosure grandstand.

QUOTE OF THE DAY

1860 'A good jockey by profession, rather than a brilliant horseman by intuition.' An anonymous but contemporary assessment of first champion jockey Elnathan Flatman, who died today.

BIRTHDAYS

1925 Racing writer and trainer Ivor Herbert. In 1957 he saddled Linwell to win the Cheltenham Gold Cup, although it was credited to head lad Charlie Mallon, as the stewards of the NH Committee had ruled that Herbert's activities as a racing journalist precluded him from being a public trainer.

1941 Robin Oakley, former political journalist-turned-*Spectator* racing columnist.

1943 Tom Kelly, former *Sporting Chronicle* editor and spokesman for the Betting Office Licensees Association, and then Association of British Bookmakers.

1974 Jockey Timmy Murphy.

DEATH OF THE DAY

1860 Nat Flatman, 50. He was the first ever champion jockey, in 1846, and then for the next six seasons, and he rode ten Classic winners. Buried under the tower of All Saints Church, Newmarket.

CELEBRITY OF THE DAY

1739 Highwayman Dick Turpin put to death at York's Knavesmire, hours before racing began and Smallhopes won the King's Plate.

21 AUGUST

SIGNIFICANT EVENT

1997 Alex Greaves became the first female to ride a Group 1 winner when dead-heating on 11/1 Ya Malak, trained by David Nicholls, with Coastal Bluff, ridden by Kevin Darley and trained by David Barron, in the Nunthorpe Stakes at York. Coastal Bluff's bit broke and Darley had to ride holding the horse's mane; when he couldn't pull up afterwards, he had to jump off – fortunately uninjured. Both horses were Yorkshire-trained, and the first from the county to win the race since 1976.

STRANGEST EVENT

1897 Well-fancied two-year-old Sabine Queen finished unplaced in the Londonderry Plate at Leopardstown. The advertised distance of the race was five furlongs, but owner Lt Col F F McCabe lodged an objection on grounds that the course was too short, eventually taking the battle to the Turf Club. It was indeed discovered that the track was 100 yards short. Leopardstown was fined and forced to correct its race distances.

OTHER EVENTS

1846 The Gimcrack Stakes was run for the first time at York. Ellerdale won, owned by Capt Harcourt, ridden by Tommy Lye and trained by Tom Dawson at Middleham's Tupgill Stable.
1971 The world's most expensive yearling, $510,000 Crowned Prince, trained by Bernard van Cutsem, made his debut at Newmarket, finishing sixth.
1989 Darakah, a chestnut filly trained by John Benstead at Epsom, made her debut at Windsor. However, she turned out to be Muarij, another chestnut filly, also trained by Benstead, and owned by Sheikh Hamdan Al Maktoum, also the owner of Darakah. Muarij, really Darakah, had already raced four times, winning once. The Jockey Club said: 'The form of the two fillies will be swapped.'
1991 Jack Berry broke his personal record of 127 winners for a season when Food Of Love won at York, taking him to 128.
1991 A punter in a William Hill Sunderland branch won £163,884.16 for £81.50 when seven of his eight selections won – the other was Jet Ski Lady at York, beaten in a photo-finish.
1992 Irish champion jockey Charlie Swan had a five-week suspension reduced to one on appeal, following his ride on 6-4 favourite King Taros in Victoria, Australia where he was taking part in an international jockeys' challenge. Swan took the wrong course on the clear leader in the Hot Shot Challenge thus forfeiting all chance of winning and costing punters an estimated AUS$350,000.
2004 Someone hadn't told the *Racing Post*'s Richard Birch it is the done thing to be charitable about a certain charity day – 'It's Variety Club day at Sandown when people who once graced many a black and white TV set are wheeled out in front of a baffled public – but I'd bet 1-10 any racegoer under the age of 50 has no chance of recognising any of the celebrities.'

QUOTE OF THE DAY

'*A car emerged from the car park as we were cantering across the middle of the course, and missed us by an inch, no more,*' said a relieved Pat Eddery on this day in 1990 when he came close to death on Batshoof at York, who went on to be third.

BIRTHDAY

1918 Trainer Dermot 'Boggy' Whelan born. His Elco was the 20-1 winner of the 1962 Wokingham.

DEATHS OF THE DAY

1995 Dual Arc-winning French trainer, Charles-William 'Mike' Bartholomew, 76. His Puissant Chef and Topyo won in 1960 and 1967.
2002 Trainer Neil Adam, 70, struck down by multiple sclerosis.

22 AUGUST

SIGNIFICANT EVENT

2008 Newmarket got under way at 12.25 to ensure that its 11-race card could all be crammed in to the afternoon, with the last off at 5.45. The track had taken on three races including the Yorkshire Oaks and Nunthorpe Stakes from the York Ebor meeting abandoned earlier in the week. Newbury staged a nine-race card with the Gimcrack Stakes and an Ebor 'substitute 'race, the Newburgh, open only to Ebor-entered runners, both salvaged from York. On the same day Evangeline Downs in Louisiana staged what for it was a normal 11-race card.

STRANGEST EVENT

1832 Former sailor Dennis Collins was found guilty of high treason and sentenced to be 'hanged, decapitated and quartered' – for the offence of throwing a stone at King William IV at Ascot races. The King reprieved him – and had him transported to Australia.

OTHER EVENTS

1822 The first documented race meeting in Germany took place at Bad Doperan.
1856 Blink Bonny won the Gimcrack Stakes at York. Next season the William l'Anson-trained filly would land the Oaks-Derby double; later she became dam of Derby-winning Blair Athol.
1942 Last meeting held at Melbourne's Ascot (opened 1893) track.
1970 The 3lb apprentice Pat Eddery, 18, rode a 1,001-1 five-timer at Haydock – all for different trainers.
1989 A racegoer staked £205,000 on three races at York – and ended the day exactly level after losing £90,000 on 4-9 runner-up Cacoethes; winning £50,000 for £25,000 on Zalazl, then collecting £40,000 from a £90,000 bet on Weld.
1990 Steve Smith Eccles won on Spofforth at Fontwell – his eighth win from as many rides during the fledgling jump season.
1992 Martin Pipe's son David, 19, rode his first winner under rules when Passed Pawn, trained by dad, won at Hereford.
1996 Sir Mark Prescott landed his first Group 1 winner as Pivotal won the Nunthorpe Stakes.
2007 Grandfather Mick Easterby provided 17-year-old schoolgirl/ granddaughter Joanna Mason with her first winner, Lake Chini, 12/1 at Carlisle.
2008 Borderlescott won the Nunthorpe Stakes, run at Newmarket as York was flooded, at 12-1 for trainer Robin Bastiman, ridden by Pat Cosgrave. At Newbury, Dane O'Neill partnered Godolphin's All The Good to a 25-1 win in the substitute Ebor, alias the Newburgh Handicap.
2009 Twenty-five horses and riders were entered for probably the toughest and longest race in the world, the Mongol Derby, run over 1,000km across the Mongolian plains with riders changing mounts every 40km.

QUOTE OF THE DAY

'I danced with the devil and got burned – twice,' confessed jockey Dean Gallagher, twice suspended for drug use, after surprisingly being given the chance to resuscitate his career in 2004 when Francois Doumen invited him to succeed his son, Thierry, as stable jockey.

BIRTHDAY

1944 Frequent 'through the card' newspaper tipster, and fellow 1960s music fan, Tony Lewis of the *Daily Star*.

DEATH OF THE DAY

1984 Classic-winning jockey and trainer, Vic Smyth, 83. As a jockey he won the 1923 Oaks on Brownhylda and was a versatile trainer, winning the Champion Hurdle with Seneca, Forestation and National Spirit and the 1,000 Guineas with Zabara in 1952.

CELEBRITY OF THE DAY

2002 Tony Cooke, ITV's first racing commentator, died aged 92.

23 AUGUST

SIGNIFICANT EVENT
2008 Aidan O'Brien's Duke Of Marmalade won a fifth Group 1 race as he had Derby winner New Approach back in third when winning the Juddmonte International at Newmarket. The 4-6 favourite was taking his earnings to just under £1.4m. However, the race sparked allegations of team tactics by the O'Brien jockeys, after Duke Of Marmalade was allowed through by his pacemaker.

STRANGEST EVENT
2008 Goodwood racecourse announced that following criticism by stable staff that they had been charged £1 for a slice of toast they would provide free tea, coffee and toast for the rest of the season.

OTHER EVENTS
1770 Eclipse was 1-20 favourite and duly obliged by a distance in York's four-mile Subscription Plate.

1949 Widely rated as greatest of all sprinters, Abernant won the first of two Nunthorpes.

1982 Willie Ryan rode first winner, Will George, at Windsor.

1986 Pat Eddery failed by half a length to go through a six-race card at Phoenix Park – the distance by which Stop The Fighting was beaten.

1986 Phil Tuck rode first of a run of ten consecutive winners, the last coming on September 3. The record, 12, was set by Gordon Richards in October 1933.

1990 'He could prove himself the fastest horse in the world,' said Willie Carson after riding the Dick Hern-trained Dayjur to win the five-furlong Nunthorpe Stakes at York, in which he lowered the course record by a second-plus to 56.16sec.

1991 Martin Pipe and Peter Scudamore had the first five winners at Exeter. But Ever Smile, 5-6 favourite for the last, was beaten into second by 15-8 shot Frosty Reception – which there was! The winner, was trained by John Baker and was his fifth win from as many runners that season.

1993 Riding for the first time at Tralee, Lester Piggott won at his first attempt, on John Oxx's 4-5 Caliandak.

1997 Frankie Dettori had a winner and two disqualifications at Goodwood in the afternoon and two more winners at Windsor in the evening.

2004 After Templet won a Hamilton maiden, trainer Ian Semple remarked: 'He's disappointed us more times than the late Rock Hudson disappointed women.'

2008 Rider Craig Walker, 24, rode Bulberry Hill to a record furlong victory in Newmarket's annual traditional three-mile-six-furlong Town Plate, for which the prize is a box of Newmarket sausages.

2009 Betfair appointed executive Doug Gambling.

QUOTE OF THE DAY
2008 *'Daytime racing is rubbish when compared to evening meetings which boast live music at the end.'* Sports betting journalist Steve Palmer of the *Racing Post* showing exactly what lures him – a confirmed punter – to the races.

BIRTHDAYS
1926 Lancashire trainer Jimmy (Captain James Hume) Wilson.

1942 Roger Fisher, the Cumbria-based trainer of Ekbalco and Run And Skip.

1960 Cricket-loving trainer William Haggas, who won the 1996 Derby with Shaamit.

DEATH OF THE DAY
1992 West Country amateur John Farthing, 57, who rode 80 winners.

CELEBRITY OF THE DAY
1992 Ashes of legendary gambler Alex Bird were scattered at Haydock, where he scored many of his biggest early wins.

24 AUGUST

SIGNIFICANT EVENT
1796 Hambletonian, Sir Charles Turner's famous horse, met defeat for the only time in a 22-race career when he ran off the course in a 100gns sweepstake at York. He won the 1795 St Leger, two Doncaster Cups and a famous match against Diamond in 1799 over 4m1f138yds for 3,000gns in front of a vast crowd. He went on to sire more than 140 winners.

STRANGEST EVENT
2008 Trainer Andrew Balding revealed that he has an odd superstition – 'Eat some duck to change your luck!' – that was passed on to him by one of his owners.

OTHER EVENTS
1830 King William IV attended the races for the first time since succeeding to the throne at Ascot, where had a winner in the first race – The Colonel. He later completed a double with Frederica.

1968 The four-year-old Dr Fager, carrying 134lb, set a world record 1min 32.2sec (other than hand-timed) for a mile at Arlington Park.

1969 Brian Taylor rode Lord Lark, a colt given to Norway's Crown Prince Harald and wife as a wedding day present, to win that country's Norsk Derby in which the favourite Polar Sea, ridden by Frankie Durr, was runner-up.

1990 Willie Carson moved up to third on the all-time list of British jockeys when a double at Newmarket took his total to 3,112, better than Doug Smith but still behind Gordon Richards and Lester Piggott.

1991 As a Russian coup took place and Mikhail Gorbachev was overthrown, Bold Russian became a topical tip, Willie Carson riding the horse to a 100-30 win in the Celebration Mile at Goodwood for Barry Hills.

QUOTE OF THE DAY
'The ground has been laid out in accordance with the latest ideas, with the result that the course is one of the finest and most completely adapted for racing purposes in all England.' If Hull's new track was so good on this date in 1888, according to the local *Express*, it seems odd that it did not survive beyond 1909. But then look a Great Leighs...

BIRTHDAYS
1915 Scottish trainer Wilfred Crawford. His best horses were Mirval, Hamilcar and Final Approach

1921 Jockey Micky Greening, who rode High Treason and Magic Boy.

1941 Jockey Stan Murphy, partner of Celtic Gold and Skymas.

1946 Jockey David Munro, who rode Go Bingo and Forest King.

1949 Irish jockey Gabriel Curran. In 1977 he partnered 20-1 shot Nebbiolo to win the 2,000 Guineas. He also won the Irish 2,000 and 1,000 Guineas.

1956 Jockey Allen Webb.

DEATH OF THE DAY
1988 1965 Grand National winner Jay Trump, 31.

CELEBRITY OF THE DAY
1684 Charles II attended the races for the last time, captured in the only recorded engraving of the monarch at the sports, created by Francis Barlow in 1687, two years after the King's death, titled 'The Last Horse Race Run before Charles the Second of Blessed Memory by Dorsett Ferry.'

25 AUGUST

SIGNIFICANT EVENT
1969 Brian Connorton won an appeal against a three-day suspension acquired at Teesside Park. This was believed to be the first time the verdict of the local panel had been overturned in this way.

STRANGEST EVENT
1804 Alicia Thornton took on her brother-in-law Captain Flint, who was secretly in love with her, in a public race at York for a side-stake of 500gns. Some 100,000 reportedly turned out to see Alicia, riding Vinagrillo, beaten by Flint on Thornvile. Alicia's husband, Colonel Tom Thornton, refused to pay up, so Flint horse-whipped him. Alicia went on to challenge the top jockey of the day, Frank Buckle, to a match, which she won.

OTHER EVENTS
1869 The final meeting at Hungerford, where they had raced since 1840.
1909 British military forces in Tibet organised a race meeting complete with steeplechase and Army Cup, which took place in front of a bemused crowd of Nepalese and Tibetans, and four important Lamas.
1975 Jenny Pitman saddled her first winner, Bonidon, at Southwell.
1989 Stable lass Melody Town was leading Cotton On Quick around the parade ring at Goodwood for trainer Alan Bailey when it was discovered that Dewi Williams, the jockey of 12/1 chance Damaskeen in the Oakley Handicap, was not qualified to ride. Melody was called upon and duly won by half a length.
1992 Gay Kelleway, the only woman to ride a Royal Ascot winner, landed her first win in five years when John Rose won at Brighton, trained by father Paul.
1997 US rider Pat Day became the fifth rider to clock up 7,000 winners when Bay Harbor won at Saratoga. Bill Shoemaker, Angel Cordero, Laffit Pincay and Dave Gall beat him to it.
2006 Frankie Dettori lost his MBE and racing trophies when his home was burgled.
2008 Peter Scudamore was best known for his exploits over the jumps, and his son, 24-year-old Michael, who had already celebrated three winners on the Flat, saddled his first winners in that sphere when Dark Energy and Fourpointone (ridden by brother Tom) obliged at Huntingdon to give him a 43-1 double. The track became the first to feature a water-less water jump by replacing the liquid with blue AstroTurf over the filled-in ditch.

QUOTE OF THE DAY
'Things are going from bad to worse over there. The prize-money is gone.' After training in Italy for more than 20 years, Birkenhead boy Frank 'Italian Scouser' Sheridan explained why he was now operating in Britain, as he saddled his first winner here with Icelandic, 8/1,at Warwick in 2008.

BIRTHDAYS
1917 Dual Welsh Grand National-winning trainer Earl Jones. His best horses included Forty Secrets, Honey End, Tasco, Trespassing and Pattered.
1928 Manchester-born jockey Frank Barlow. He won the Champion Stakes on 20-1 Narrator in 1954 and the 2,000 Guineas on 50-1 Gilles De Retz in 1956.
1961 Racing writer and champion of punters via National Association for the Protection of Punters, Mark Coton.
1964 Three-times champion point-to-point jockey Polly Curling.

DEATH OF THE DAY
1988 Twice Irish champion jockey, Jimmy Eddery, 64 – father of Pat, Paul, Michael and nine other children. In 1944 he dead-heated for both the Irish 2,000 Guineas and the Cambridgeshire.

CELEBRITY OF THE DAY
1930 Sir Sean Connery, James Bond and owner of Risk Of Thunder, born.

26 AUGUST

SIGNIFICANT EVENT
2007 Dundalk launched its new Polytrack surface and Ireland's first all-weather track. A capacity crowd of 7,000 watched Johnny Murtagh ride the first winner, Ms Victoria, 14/1.

STRANGEST EVENT
1998 One of the leading amateur Flat riders in Britain, Angel Jacobs, was exposed as professional jockey Angel Monserrate, aka Carlos Castro, from Puerto Rico. He had already been banned in the US.

OTHERS
1880 Northern jockey Johnny 'Old Pusher' Osborne won the Gimcrack Stakes for the ninth and final time on Simnel.

1925 Former champion jockey Otto Madden, by then an owner and trainer, sent out Chapeau, ridden by that season's champion, Gordon Richards, to win York's Ebor by three lengths from Highbrow, ridden by future champion Tommy Weston.

1939 Legendary trainer Fulke Walwyn saddled his first winner, Poor Duke (Bruce Hobbs), at Buckfastleigh.

1967 Trainer John Edwards saddled first winner, Mons Badonicus, at Hereford.

1974 The most notorious of racing's attempted coups was launched when Gay Future, 10-1, won at Cartmel. Horse had been coupled with two other of trainer Anthony Collins' declared runners in doubles and trebles, but they were withdrawn from their races leaving all bets as singles. More than £250,000 was thought to be involved. Scotland Yard investigated and two men, one Collins, were charged with conspiracy to defraud bookmakers. They were found guilty, fined £1,000 and ordered to pay £500 towards costs.

1977 Ernie Johnson, riding Courjet at Newmarket, was thrown against a post when the horse swerved off course. He broke a leg, injured a shoulder and

missed the rest of the season.

1988 Steve Cauthen fell from Preziosa at Goodwood, suffered concussion and missed the rest of the season.

1991 Ron Smyth, champion jump jockey 1941-42 and a trainer for 44 years, announced his retirement at the end of the season. He saddled Patient Constable (1966 Stewards' Cup), Copsale (1967 Magnet Cup) and Flash Imp (1973 Cesarewitch and 1975 Great Met).

2008 Trainer George Moore, celebrating his 56th birthday, saddled Ripon winner Sorrento Moon.

QUOTE OF THE DAY
'Rather than go on holiday to Spain or France, we went to Thirsk or Ripon.' Eight-year-old Jamie Thomas, from Cardiff, was at Musselburgh on this date in 2004, visiting the last of Britain's 59 racecourses that he and father Tony had been to during a 'pilgrimage' that began when Jamie was just three months old.

BIRTH OF THE DAY
1935 Bobby Beasley. Champion jump jockey in 1958, 1959 and 1960. He won the 1959 Cheltenham Gold Cup on Roddy Owen; the Champion Hurdle on Another Flash in 1960; and the Grand National on Nicolaus Silver in 1961, emulating his uncle, Tommy, and father-in-law, Arthur Thompson. He also famously overcame alcoholism.

DEATH OF THE DAY
1999 Trainer Humphrey Cottrill, 92. He won the Irish Derby in 1961 with Your Highness, while St Pauli Girl was runner-up in both the 1967 1,000 Guineas and Oaks.

CELEBRITY OF THE DAY
2007 'When you retire, you have to have something that grips you and gives you that adrenalin thrill. I've been in racing for ten years, and it is the only thing that matches the thrill of scoring a goal,' said England's striker, Michael Owen.

27 AUGUST

SIGNIFICANT EVENT
2008 The BHA's desire 'for horses rated 40 and below to be removed from the system' was the lead story in the *Racing Post*, which suggested that some 800 hundred horses would have 'significantly fewer opportunities to race' from start of the 2009 campaign as a result of the reframing of races.

STRANGEST EVENT
2008 Jockey Joe Tizzard was fortunate to escape with his life after being trapped in a baling machine and suffering serious injuries to his scalp while working at his brother-in-law's Dorset farm.

OTHER EVENTS
1921 Derby-winning jockey Charlie Smirke finished third on his racecourse debut, riding King George at Gatwick.
1960 Last meeting held at Buckfastleigh in Devon.
1964 First winner for jockey Clive Eccleston, at Carlisle.
1966 Mrs Anne Biddle became the first of her sex granted a licence to train in Ireland.
1977 Dermot Weld saddled five winners at Tralee.
1990 Vision Of Wonder finished second at Plumpton as rider Steve Smith Eccles attempted a tenth consecutive winner – he won on his next mount, Spofforth.
1990 Frankie Dettori became the youngest rider since Lester Piggott in 1955 to ride 100 winners in a season. The 19-year-old did it on Line Of Thunder at Chepstow, beating Piggott, who reached his first ton ten days short of his 20th birthday.
1990 New trainer Ferdy Murphy made an instant impact with three winners from five runners on his first day at Huntingdon.
2002 Tony McCoy scored record 1,700th victory on Mighty Montefalco at Uttoxeter, passing former record holder Richard Dunwoody's total.
2008 Trainer Mick Channon suffered broken ribs, a broken arm, a fractured jaw and punctured lung as a result of a car accident in which his great friend, bloodstock agent and owner Tim Corby, was killed. Channon's son, Jack was injured, too, albeit not seriously in the crash on the M1 in Leicestershire.

QUOTE OF THE DAY
'Sacred to the memory of Leopardstown – finally and brutally strangled at birth by gross incompetence, bungling and mismanagement – August 27, 1888.' A spoof obituary published by an Irish sporting paper after the new course's first meeting was bedevilled by problems, threatening to make it also the last.

BIRTHDAY
1948 Andy Turnell. Highly successful jump jockey notable for short riding style, riding winners of the Massey Ferguson, Hennessy Cognac and Mackeson Gold Cups. Successful trainer who has saddled winners of Hennessy, Tote Gold Trophy, Queen Mother Champion Chase and the 1987 Grand National with Maori Venture.

DEATHS OF THE DAY
2003 Highly rated Irish jump jockey Kieran Kelly, 25, following heavy fall at Kilbeggan.
2006 Top jockey-turned-top trainer David Nicholson, 67. 'The Duke' – one of his father Frenchie's grooms, who thought he talked 'posh', gave him the nickname – rode Mill House to win the 1967 Whitbread Gold Cup, and won three Welsh Grand Nationals (1959-61); he trained Charter Party to win the Cheltenham Gold Cup, and Viking Flagship to twice win the Queen Mother Champion Chase.

CELEBRITY OF THE DAY
1970 Peter Ebdon, former snooker world champion and racing fan and breeder, was born.

28 AUGUST

SIGNIFICANT EVENT
1989 Riding Timely Column at Clairefontaine, France, Alfred Gibert was run away with after his reins broke. Sacrificing his chances, Cash Asmussen, on Glenetive rode after Gibert and brought his mount under control, saving the jockey from serious injury. Asmussen was later honoured by a national TV station for making 'the year's most sporting gesture'.

STRANGEST EVENT
1992 Newmarket jockey Allan Mackay was put out of action for two weeks after injuring his hand – while washing up.

OTHER EVENTS
1890 Top US four-year-old Salvator staged an unusual race against the clock at Monmouth Park on a straight course of 11 furlongs in an effort to beat the then mile record of 1min 39.25sec. He was 2-5 favourite to do it under Martin Bergen, carrying 110lb, and clocked 1min 35.5sec.

1943 Jockey Tommy Carey rode five consecutive winners at Ascot – making it six when he rode the first winner at the next meeting on September 11.

1967 Red Rum won a Warwick nursery handicap in a photo-finish.

1972 Roger Wernham rode first winner, Pharaoh's Call, at Chepstow.

1982 The most expensive horse in training in Britain, $3.3m Shareef Dancer, made a winning debut for Michael Stoute, ridden by Walter Swinburn at Newmarket.

1983 Luca Cumani's Tolomeo, ridden by Pat Eddery, became first the English-trained (well, in England!) winner of the Arlington Million, beating hot favourite John Henry into second, paying 38-1.

1994 Pat Day won the Arlington Million for the first time on Paradise Creek.

2008 Having begun working at the *Daily Mirror*, where he became 'Newsboy', Bob Butchers, who tipped 43,000 winners during his 39-year stint, celebrated the publication of his first book, *Silks, Soaks and Certainties* at the age of 84, saying, 'I haven't got a computer so it was all written in long hand.'

2008 Alan Jarvis's Athania won at Great Leighs to give him a full house of winners at every Flat and NH track in Britain.

2009 Sir Peter O'Sullevan officially opened Ffos Llas – although it was the third meeting. Tony McCoy rode a treble.

QUOTE OF THE DAY
'This is the last evening meeting of the year at Redcar. But we're going out with a bang because this is ladies' night.' Peter Naughton's double entendre welcomed viewers to the twilight action on this day in 2004.

BIRTHDAYS
1943 Elain Mellor, seven-time champion lady rider.

1959 Jump jockey-turned-Hong Kong TV presenter, Mark Richards.

1963 New Zealand's most prolific jockey Lance O'Sullivan.

1967 Jamie Osborne, jockey (won 1990 Hennessy Gold Cup on Arctic Call) and trainer of enigmatic stayer Geordieland. Only jockey ever punched in public by Jenny Pitman.

FIRST OF THE DAY
1989 Former champion jump jockey Jonjo O'Neill landed his first treble as a trainer when Roliad, Master Lamb and Ben Ledi all won at Cartmel.

CELEBRITY OF THE DAY
1947 England and Liverpool skipper Emlyn Hughes was born. His 100-1 Wayward Scot was a Grand National faller in 1979.

29 AUGUST

SIGNIFICANT EVENT
1923 Flint Jack, a six-year-old gelding, became the first horse to win the Ebor twice, for trainer Ossie Bell and ridden by H Gray. His odds of 10-1 were twice the previous year's.

STRANGEST EVENT
1805 A race whose conditions were advertised as restricted to those who had paid out at least £200 in 'adverse litigation' was run at Tralee. The prize was a plate donated by 'the Gentlemen of the Profession of the Law in the County of Kerry'. It was won by a Protestant clergyman, Rev Mr Dennis, of Wicklow.

OTHER EVENTS
1950 Prolific jockey Eddie Hide had first ride on Copper Wire at Birmingham.

1981 A first Goodwood training success for former jockey Geoff Lewis, as Hollow Heart won the Drawing Room Stakes.

1982 The Mick Ryan-trained Boxberger Speed completed the Dutch Triple Crown, winning the St Leger at Dunduigt.

1992 A Newmarket treble took Michael Roberts past £1m British win prize-money.

1992 The Sarah and Mike Gull Handicap Hurdle at Southwell was named in honour of that couple, who were married that afternoon. The bride, groom and guests were photographed in the winner's enclosure after Nuns Jewel won the race.

1994 Adrian Maguire rode first five-winner haul at Plumpton – for a 63-1 accumulator. He pulled up in the last.

2004 Gowran clerk of the course Paddy Graffin was pulled up by the Turf Club for describing the going as good to soft rather than the traditional Irish yielding, for what the *Racing Post* said 'could well be the first time on an Irish racecourse'. An unrepentant Graffin declared: 'I'm calling the ground as it is, and bugger convention.'

2008 His horse was slashed by 100 points prior to the off but Alan Campbell was one of very few people at Salisbury to fancy his own Bermondsey Bob, who won a maiden at 150-1, leaving Campbell some £8,000 better off for his £30 each-way bet at 250-1 after the John Spearing-trained two-year-old obliged. 'My winnings have just about paid for the horse,' said the owner.

2009 Instituted in 1665 by King Charles, the 340th Newmarket Town Plate was won by Artist's Return, ridden by Caroline Scott.

QUOTE OF THE DAY
'Things have been a bit slow,' was the masterful understatement by trainer Tony McWilliams on this day in 2008 at Hamilton where Miacarla, 14-1, won to give him his first success for, er, 1,983 days.

BIRTHDAYS
1941 US Hall of Fame trainer Carl Nafzger. Handled 1990 Breeders' Cup Classic winner Unbridled.

1957 US Hall of Fame jockey Jerry Bailey. He rode Black Tie Affair to win the 1991 Breeders' Cup Classic, and won the Kentucky Oaks on Dispute in 1993.

DEATH OF THE DAY
1988 Conditional jockey Vivian Kennedy broke his neck in a Huntingdon fall; he died two days later.

CELEBRITY OF THE DAY
1918 Sir John Astor born. Educated at Eton and Oxford, he served in the Household Cavalry and was an MP for Sutton in Plymouth. He fulfilled many roles in racing, riding under both codes; being 'one of the most active and progressive' members of the Jockey Club; steward; member of the Turf Club; member of the Racecourse Betting Control Board; member of the Horserace Totalisator Board; president of the Thoroughbred Breeders' Association; trainer of jumpers until 1975.

30 AUGUST

SIGNIFICANT EVENT
1972 The previous year's Derby winner, Mill Reef, fractured near foreleg while exercising at trainer Ian Balding's Kingsclere yard.

STRANGEST EVENT
1993 Jockey Laffit Pincay jnr, 46, arranged for his whole family to attend a meeting at Del Mar to see him hit the milestone of 8,000 winners – a feat only ever previously achieved by Bill Shoemaker. You're only partly ahead of me here – no, he didn't fail to achieve the landmark, but he was told before racing that he'd actually done it the day before, on El Toreo in the seventh race. The confusion had arisen over a win he'd had in Mexico City in 1991 that had somehow been left off the record.

OTHER EVENTS
1771 Hereford staged its second ever meeting. Lord Chedworth's bay Weazle 'won easy' over heats of four miles, reported the Sporting Calendar.
1825 Sporting annals reported a match race at Maghull, ten miles from Liverpool: 'Equestrians thronged to the scene of the action and for more than a mile the road from Liverpool to Maghull might be seen crowded with horse and foot.'
1968 Lester Piggott chalked up his 12th century of winners when Big Sir won at Goodwood.
1969 Michael Roberts, aged 15, survived an objection to win his first race on Smyrna at Scotsville, Natal, South Africa.
1969 Henry Cecil saddled first Goodwood winner, Rohays, in the Wills Embassy Mile.
1981 Bill Shoemaker partnered the great John Henry to victory in the first million dollar race, Chicago's Arlington Million.
1982 Jump jockey Gee Armytage got off the mark on Applante at Southwell.
1983 Spark Chief, trained by Frankie Durr, clocked the fastest ever electronically recorded time for five furlongs – 53.7sec – at Epsom,
equivalent to almost 42mph.
1983 Tyrone Williams' first winner was Going Going at Epsom.
1991 Sir Mark Prescott saddled his first Group winner in Britain, Chicmond, 16-1, in the Solario Stakes at Sandown.
1991 1968 2,000 Guineas and Derby winner Sir Ivor was retired from stud.
1993 Manhattan Boy won for the 14th time at Plumpton. The 11-year-old had never won anywhere else.
2006 Wolverhampton staged its 'greatest day' – well, according to clerk of the course Fergus Cameron, who said of the meeting the track acquired because of redevelopment at Doncaster: 'The occasion gave us an opportunity to wave our flag during the summer rather than the winter when we do most of our business.'
2008 Seb Sanders, the joint champion Flat jockey of 2007, broke his femur in a fall from Speed Gifted at Chester. He returned to the saddle in March 2009.

QUOTE OF THE DAY
This is the first time two Irish horses have run against each other in England with no English horse in the race in National Hunt history,' said County Tyrone trainer James Lambe, after his Caislean Ui Cuain beat stablemate Zurs in a Cartmel novice chase in 2004.

BIRTHDAY
1972 Jockey Brett Doyle. He rode Sayyedati, the 1995 Sussex Stakes winner, and won Classics in Italy, Japan, Germany and Singapore.

DEATH OF THE DAY
1991 French-trained Zino, the 1982 2,000 Guineas winner, died of colic.

CELEBRITY OF THE DAY
2008 The 50th anniversary of the Variety Club fundraising raceday at Sandown, marked by the appearance of Dancing on Ice winner Suzanne Shaw – and some horses.

31 AUGUST

SIGNIFICANT EVENT
1966 Anne Bullitt Biddle became the first female trainer in Irish racing history to saddle a winner in her own right when Liam Ward rode 6-4 favourite Flying Tiger to win the Cork Stakes at Naas.

STRANGEST EVENT
2008 Casey's Jet ran in the $75,000 Rose de Bartolo Memorial Stakes at Thistledown, USA, landing prize-money for finishing third – but the horse wasn't placed third. Due to a clerical problem at the time of entry, officials had allowed the horse to race for prize-money, but not to be placed for betting purposes.

OTHER EVENTS
1928 Charlie Smirke's mount, 4-11 Welcome Gift, refused to race at Gatwick. Even though the horse misbehaved in future races, Smirke was banned for five years. He came back triumphantly to win the 1934 Derby on Windsor Lad.
1962 Universally known as 'Taffy', Myrddin Lloyd Thomas rode his first winner, Weather Way, at Hurst Park.
1972 Vet Barry Williams, examining the suspected broken leg of Derby and Arc winner Mill Reef, was not optimistic. 'It feels like a bag of marbles,' he said. The horse was saved for stud duties.
1978 Peter Scudamore landed first winner, Rolyat, in hurdles race at Devon for trainer Toby Balding.
1982 Jack Berry, the permanently red-shirted trainer and indefatigable fundraiser for the Injured Jockeys' Fund, saddled his 100th winner when Bri-Eden won in, inevitably, a sprint at Epsom.
1993 Suluk, who had won 20 races at Southwell, was retired aged eight by trainer Reg Hollinshead.
1996 Racegoers at Klampenborg Galopbane racecourse in Denmark were initially unconcerned when a herd of 50 deer escaped from nearby State Park. That was until they invaded the racecourse, delaying the first race as

spectators and staff tried fruitlessly to shoo them away from the track. The meeting had to be abandoned.
1996 Jockey Richard Hughes rode a finish a circuit early on 25-1 Mapengo in a one-mile-seven-furlong race at Wolverhampton, believing it to be a seven-furlong race. He was banned for six days.
2004 Fergal Lynch later admitted to preventing Bond City from winning at Ripon today – he was fined £50,000 and suspended
2008 Having won the 2006 Scottish National on Hot Weld, jockey PJ McDonald decided to turn to the Flat and on this date rode out his claim when Tale Of Silver won at Musselburgh.

QUOTE OF THE DAY
2007 *'They do the job – which has become increasingly necessary – of separating those of us who go racing for its own sake, from those who go racing for other, entirely separate reasons.'* Racing writer Laura Thompson revealing herself not to be a fan of ladies' days.

BIRTHDAY
1940 Paul Kelleway, jockey-turned-Newmarket trainer, and father of jockey-turned-trainer, Gay. He rode What A Myth to win the 1969 Cheltenham Gold Cup, and partnered fast-finishing Bula to win the 1971 and 72 Champion Hurdles.

DEATHS OF THE DAY
2003 Anne, Duchess of Westminster, 88, the owner of Arkle.
2004 Ken Hussey, 75, who pioneered speed ratings for punters and published them under the byline Split Second in the *Handicap Book*, which he once edited.

CELEBRITY OF THE DAY
1968 Legendary West Indian cricketer Sir Gary Sobers reportedly backed three winners (Gipsy Bridge, 10-1; Mycropolis, 20-1 and Jubilation, 4-1) then hit six sixes in one over against Glamorgan.

1 SEPTEMBER

SIGNIFICANT EVENT
2004 The racing world was shocked when Kieren Fallon was detained in a dawn raid under suspicion of race-fixing. He was eventually cleared. 'They picked me up before five in the morning and let me out at seven in the evening. I spent most of those hours in a cell, and it was pretty unpleasant.'

STRANGEST EVENT
1992 Noel Barker, 30, popular Aussie jockey, died in hospital 12 days after a fall in a Randwick race trial. Wife Kelly, a former Hong Kong champion, wanted to scatter his ashes in the territory but was refused permission by the Royal Hong Kong Jockey Club, which said 'Local feelings on such matters are very strong'.

OTHER EVENTS
1930 Winner of a record five Cheltenham Gold Cups, Golden Miller made his unplaced debut at Southwell.
1945 Wartime racing finished at 5.02pm, Stockton.
1961 Horserace Totalisator Board and Horse Race Betting Levy Board created.
1965 Jungle Student, the shock 20-1 winner of the Seaton Handicap at Devon, collapsed and died after passing the post, while beaten favourite Galatea, who fell, galloped on riderless before also collapsing and dying.
1988 A manufactured surface is used at a US meeting for the first time as they race on Equitrack at the inaugural meeting of Remington Park, Oklahoma.
1990 Tony McCoy's first ride in public on Nordic Touch at Phoenix Park for Jim Bolger. The pair finished seventh.
1992 Antoinette 'Tiddler' Armes, 23, became the first female apprentice to ride a winner over the Derby course, on Henry Candy's Incola, 5/1. On the same card Yoshiba Okabe became the first Japanese rider to win at Epsom when 13-2 chance Shrewd Partner won.
1993 Jump jockey Lorna Vincent rode her 100th winner, Va Utu, the 15-8 favourite at Newton Abbot. Her first was 15 years earlier.
2008 Having left Britain in the wake of race-fixing allegations, Fergal Lynch rode You Bet Lily to win at Philadelphia Park, USA, for his trainer brother, Cathal.
2009 J P McManus had his first winner at Laytown, The Hamptons.

QUOTE OF THE DAY
'Blow me, if she didn't die in my arms.' The poignant recollection by Dick Francis of his wife of 53 years, Mary, in a *Daily Mail* interview in 2000.

BIRTHDAYS
1913 Woodford (Woody) Cefis Stephens, in Kentucky. He trained 1974 Kentucky Derby winner Cannonade, and 1982 Belmont winner Conquistador Cielo.
1981 Emma-Jayne Wilson who, in June 2007, became the first woman rider to win $1m Queen's Plate at Woodbine.
1982 Jockey George Baker, who has ridden the horse George Baker for the trainer George Baker.

DEATHS OF THE DAY
1990 George Boyd, 83, the most successful Scottish Flat trainer of his day. He won the 1961 2,000 Guineas with 66-1 shot Rockavon, the only Scottish-trained horse to win an English Classic.
2003 Up-and-coming female jockey Sandrine Boisnier was killed as a result of a fall at the beach racecourse of Plouescat.

CELEBRITY OF THE DAY
2008 Long-standing owner David Sullivan, best known for his involvement with Birmingham City and the *Daily Sport* newspaper, threatened to review his involvement in the sport as a result of receiving no compensation after his Jack Junior was left several lengths behind in a race at Great Leighs, when the horse's stall malfunctioned.

2 SEPTEMBER

SIGNIFICANT EVENT
1991 Martell announced it was to sponsor the Grand National in a £4m package.

STRANGEST EVENT
1978 Dulcify, who went on to win the Victoria Derby, AJC Derby and Cox Plate in Australia, began his career at Morphettville, Adelaide with a win – at 300-1.

OTHER EVENTS
1975 Roche Noire, at Brighton, was Joe Mercer's 2,000th winner.

1995 Aidan O'Brien saddled nine runners in the 29-runner Tattersalls Breeders Stakes at the Curragh – and had four of the first five home, winning with 9-1 shot No Animosity.

1997 Waregem racecourse in Belgium attracted 32,000 spectators to its 150th anniversary meeting.

2008 Plan to revive Lincoln racecourse unveiled. The circuit at Carholme had been disused since 1991, having previously been used for point to points.

2009 Frankie Dettori partnered Godolphin and Sheikh Mohammed's first winner in Turkey – Balios – in the valuable Anatolia Trophy.

2009 Ian Carnaby, broadcaster, journalist and racing sentimentalist, handed over a stick of Brighton rock to trainer Christine Dunnett after Scruffy Skip won 15th runner of his sponsored seller at a seaside track.

QUOTE OF THE DAY
'PC Plod kept an eagle eye on Lester Piggott at Epsom as a safety precaution as the racecourse received a telephone call saying that an attempt would be made to kill the champion jockey,' was how the *Sporting Life* reported in 1968, semi-humorously, on a threat to the great Lester. Imagine how the tabloids and news channels would report a similar threat to Frankie Dettori now. Piggott was not fazed – he rode a treble.

BIRTHDAYS
1917 Irish trainer, Clem Magnier.

1920 Maurice Zilber, trainer of Dahlia and Youth.

1935 D Wayne Lukas, US Hall of Fame trainer. In 1978 he had six horses; he sent out 343 winners in 1987, worth $17m. Winning Colors won him a first Kentucky Derby in 1988.

1952 Leading Aussie trainer Gai Waterhouse, well on the way to 100 winners.

DEATHS OF THE DAY
1969 Lewes trainer Tom Masson, 71. He sent out 33-1 shot Kami to be third in the 1947 Grand National, while Pindaric won the 1962 Lingfield Derby Trial, but failed in the real thing.

1988 John Hughes, aged 61. The youngest clerk of the course when he took on the job at Haydock at 33, he went on to help revitalise Aintree and the Grand National, and later became clerk of the course at Chepstow. He also helped launch the Arlington Million.

1990 Robert Holmes a Court, 53. Born in South Africa, and once the richest man in his adopted Australia, he owned 1984 Melbourne Cup winner Black Knight.

2001 Horace A 'Jimmy' Jones, aged 94. He trained three Kentucky Derby winners, including Triple Crown winner Citation in 1948.

2007 Carlo Vittadini, 92, owner of Grundy, who won 1975 Derby and King George VI and Queen Elizabeth Stakes.

FIRST OF THE DAY
1953 Having given Gordon Richards his first – and only – Derby victory earlier that year, Pinza was found to have developed an injury and was retired to stud.

3 SEPTEMBER

SIGNIFICANT EVENT

1986 Jump jockey Phil Tuck completed a sequence of ten consecutive winners, equalling Johnny Gilbert's 1959 record, on even-money favourite Doronicum at Southwell.

STRANGEST EVENT

1992 Irish-born Stephen Hillen, 22, became Britain's youngest trainer after being granted a Flat licence.

OTHER EVENTS

1770 Once again, Eclipse walked over, this time in the King's Plate at Lincoln, his seventh appearance of the year.

1889 First meeting held at Koln, Germany.

1931 Second day of two-day jump meeting at Chelson Meadow, Plymouth, went the way of the first – abandoned due to flooding. The course, first used in 1828, never reopened.

1939 As Britain and France declared war on Germany following the Nazi invasion of Poland, racing was cancelled in Britain and France, resuming on October 18 that year at Newmarket and at Auteuil on Febraury 25, 1940.

1982 Levy Board chairman Lord Plummer opened a new £2.5m stand at Haydock.

1992 Lester Piggott presented with first grandson when elder daughter Maureen, wife of Newmarket trainer William Haggas, gave birth to a second child, a boy, weighing almost 9lb.

1992 Former jump jockey Richard Rowe saddled first Flat winner when 11/2 L'Uomo Classics won at Salisbury.

1994 Jimmy Fortune rode first five-timer – three from six at Thirsk and a double at Wolverhampton.

1995 Love was in the air as jockey Adrian Maguire married Sabrina Williams and trainer Ed Dunlop tied the knot with Rebecca Mallen.

2008 Towcester racecourse put up for sale at £10m. Perhaps letting people in for nothing wasn't profitable enough!

2009 Europe's richest mile race was won for the second straight year by the Michael-Jarvis trained Neil Callan-ridden Pressing, who collected £600,00 by landing Istanbul's Topkapi Trophy. Lester Piggott had won the inaugural running in 1991.

QUOTE OF THE DAY

'I did my brains on her last week ... I was really scratching my head. I decided that if the bloody thing didn't win, we'd drop her into a seller.' And that is what Gay Kelleway did for Avoca Dancer, who duly won that seller at Brighton this day in 2008, enabling Gay not only to win her money back but to receive a bottle of bubbly and a stick of rock from the track.

BIRTHDAY

1932 Mick Batchelor, who rode Fincham to win the 1960 Scottish National.

DEATH OF THE DAY

1990 1977 Derby winner The Minstrel was put down in Kentucky.

CELEBRITY OF THE DAY

1987 Cnoc Na Cuille, trained by David Nicholson, won at Worcester, giving Princess Anne her first winner over fences, at 7-2, in the Droitwich Handicap Chase.

4 SEPTEMBER

SIGNIFICANT EVENT
1990 Timeless Times won at 11/2 at Pontefract to equal the record 16 wins as a two-year-old held by The Bard, 1885, and Provideo, 1984. He didn't manage to exceed the record despite racing the next day at York when third, and unplaced at Laurel Park in the States, in October.

STRANGEST EVENT
1826 Certainly 18, maybe 19 at the time, Marksman won the Yeoman's Plate at Ashford, Kent, losing the first two-and-a-half-mile heat, but winning the next two. There appears to be no other claim for a horse of 19 to have won a race.

OTHER EVENTS
1930 Lester's dad, Keith Piggott, rode a treble at the final meeting at Chelson Meadow, Plymouth.

1945 Racing resumed at York following the war. The course had been used as a prisoner-of-war camp.

1967 George and Dennis Ware were found guilty of running a ringer in a point-to-point race. The verdict was no great surprise – one horse had a large star on its head, the other was unmarked.

1982 Five winners from as many rides at Leopardstown for Pat Eddery.

1987 Stock Hill Lass won for a third time at Kempton in a single season to net a £50,000 bonus.

1992 1991 Arc winner Suave Dancer retired.

2002 Tony McCoy achieved his fastest century of winners in a season when 2/5 favourite Toi Express won at Newton Abbot.

2009 Kieren Fallon was free to ride following a ban for failing a drug test. He had seven mounts, four at Lingfield, three at a Kempton evening meeting, but no winners.

2009 Pat Eddery landed his first Group winner as a trainer when 2yo Hearts of Fire took Baden Baden's Zukunfts Rennen.

QUOTE OF THE DAY
2004 *'Oh, yes – he has no balls, so he definitely will,'* trainer Tim Easterby, confirming his Somnus, winner of Haydock's Sprint Cup in 2003 and runner-up today, would keep on trying – fourth in 2005 and 2006, ninth in 2007.

BIRTHDAYS
1894 Owner Jim (real name Harry) Joel, whose Maori Venture won the 1987 Grand National and Royal Palace won the 1967 2,000 Guineas and Derby.

1919 Trainer Harry Blackshaw, also a successful dual-code jockey. He rode Pappatea to win the 1948 Northumberland Plate, and also won the Danish and Swedish Derbys.

1933 Jockey Roy Edwards, who won the 1967 Champion Hurdle on Saucy Kit. And on the same day, Stan Hayhurst, who won the 1958 Cheltenham Gold Cup on Kerstin.

CELEBRITY OF THE DAY
2008 It was reported that the first and only horse to win the Coventry, July and Richmond Stakes, stallion Primo Dominie, had been put down aged 26.

5 SEPTEMBER

SIGNIFICANT EVENT
1994 Paul Carberry rode a notable treble at Galway's evening meeting – hurdler Dardjini at 8/13; followed by 8/1 chaser Foilaclug Furry, then Jakdul 8/1 on the Flat.

STRANGEST EVENT
1989 All four runners in the Chilton and Windlestone Working Mens Club Handicap Chase at Sedgefield either fell or refused at the final fence. Jockey Andy Orkney dragged Grange Of Glory, who had landed on top of the fence, off the obstacle and remounted, and the 5-4 favourite went on to win by a distance.

OTHER EVENTS
1862 Trainer T S Dawson completed a run of seven successive victories in races at the two-day Ayr meeting, with horses he both owned and trained, four of which were won by his runner Tommy Jones.

1945 Chamossaire (11-2), ridden by Tommy Lowrey, won the last wartime substitute St Leger, run at York.

1966 Lester Piggott rode first five winners at Warwick.

1981 Sheikh Ali Abu Kamsin received the trophy for Migrator's win in the Garrick Jubilee Handicap Hurdle at Stratford – only for jockey Sam Morshead to object on behalf of third-placed Space Ship, who was then moved up to second, while the winner was demoted to third. Runner-up Sir Eamon therefore won the race and the trophy had to change hands.

1990 Mick Channon's first double at one meeting when Lorna Vincent won on Dear Miff 5/1 and Golden Scissors, 5/2, at Fontwell.

1990 Timeless Times came third at York in his attempt to set record two-year-old tally of 17 wins in a season.

2004 'That's total bollocks,' declared trainer David Nicholson, contradicting Cheltenham's managing director, Edward Gillespie, who justified a change of name for the Festival's Stayers' Hurdle because

'we always thought the word 'stayers' implied plodders'.

2008 Ayr racecourse put up for sale with no guide price, although it cost £9m when sold five years earlier.

2009 Kieren Fallon's first comeback winner, Our Kes, at Wolverhampton.

QUOTE OF THE DAY
'When a jumper I had wouldn't take a fence, the trainer seriously told me the horse would need a psychiatrist. I knew that was enough, and got out,' said owner and impresario Lord Delfont, born this day in 1909.

BIRTHDAYS
1908 Matt Feakes, jump jockey from 1927-46 turned trainer.

1931 Jockey Kit Stobbs.

1975 Former champion apprentice Royston Ffrench.

DEATH OF THE DAY
2009 Racing mourned as apprentices Jamie Kyne, 18, and Jan Wilson, 19, died when fire broke out in flats at Norton, near Malton.

FIRST OF THE DAY
1992 Mary Reveley reached the 50-winner mark when Corn Lily, 10-1, won the Hambleton Cup at Thirsk, in doing so becoming the first female – and only third of either gender – to reach the half-century in consecutive Flat and jump seasons, following Denys Smith (1969-70 jump and 1970 Flat season) and Peter Easterby (1977-78 jumps and 1978 Flat season). She achieved the feat for seven consecutive seasons in all.

CELEBRITY OF THE DAY
1899 Tod Sloan rode Democrat to win the Champagne Stakes at Doncaster. Another rider, Field Marshal Lord Kitchener, was given the horse when he was no longer good enough to race, and used it as a charger when Commander-in-Chief in India.

6 SEPTEMBER

SIGNIFICANT EVENT
1893 Thomas Loates rode 40-95 Isinglass to win the seven-runner St Leger, completing the Triple Crown. Isinglass created a new record for career winnings of £57,285, of which £5,300 was won in the Leger.

STRANGEST EVENT
1854 1,000 Guineas winner Virago won the Warwick Cup – over three miles. She had the Oaks winner well behind, last of four.

OTHER EVENTS
1692 A *London Gazette* advertisement confirmed: 'A plate, as has been usual, will be run for on Langton Wolds, near Malton, and another on the Thursday.'
1899 Flying Fox, trained by John Porter, ridden by Mornington Cannon, completed the Triple Crown by winning St Leger at 2-7, beating five opponents.
1939 Outbreak of war claimed St Leger – first ever cancelled British Classic.
1971 Tommy Stack saddled first winner, Good Reason, at Hexham.
1990 A sigh of relief for jockey Dale Gibson after winning on 9/1 shot Takenhall at York, breaking a run of 102 consecutive losers.
1990 Simon Sherwood saddled first runner as a trainer – and Murphy duly won at Newton Abbot.
1991 Oldest active jockey Willie Clark, 69, rode for the final time at Charles Town, US. He began his career in 1945, and rode 1,143 winners from 10,631 mounts.
1991 Perfect Circle won at Kempton to give Walter Swinburn his 1,000th British victory.
1991 Having jumped the final hurdle at Sedgefield, Skolern, ridden by Jason Callaghan, looked all over winner – until More Swag, coming the other way, charged towards him, causing Callaghan to fall, leaving Lawrence Mullaney on Nishkina to claim an improbable victory.

1991 A US two-year-old making its debut at Del Mar finished fifth, but it may not have been permitted to run in Britain under its name – Honk A Wanker.
1992 Gay Kelleway became the first non-US female to ride in the Arlington Million, finishing last on father Paul's John Rose. She was also the first to ride wearing a jockeycam, a four-inch camera mounted on the rider's helmet to give a jockey's-eye view of the action.
1995 Runaway Pete at Exeter was Martin Pipe's 2,000th winner as a trainer.
2007 'I've nothing against the principle of wind turbines, but they don't mix well with horses, and this is horse country,' declared Tony McCoy, supporting a campaign against proposals to erect a 265ft wind turbine overlooking the Lambourn valley.

QUOTE OF THE DAY
2007 *'Britain doesn't offer the best prize-money in the world, but it probably offers the best experience of ownership in the world.'* David Ashforth, *Racing Post*.

BIRTHDAYS
1911 Tommy Lowrey born at Ryton on Tyne. He rode Chamossaire to win the 1945 St Leger, and won the 1946 Derby and Leger on the grey, Airborne.
1949 Former cock of the north jockey Mark Birch, whose first winner was Bollin Charlotte in July 1968.

DEATH OF THE DAY
1991 Trainer Tom Corrie, 73. Trained Champion Hurdle winner Comedy Of Errors to win four Flat races.

CELEBRITY OF THE DAY
1997 All five scheduled race meetings – Epsom, Haydock, Stratford, Thirsk and Wolverhampton – were off and all betting shops shut, because of the funeral of Princess Diana.

7 SEPTEMBER

SIGNIFICANT EVENT
1967 Garage proprietor, bus driver, part-time post-mistress and, ultimately an official trainer, Louie Dingwall gained her first victory since the Jockey Club grudgingly permitted women trainers when Dennis Ryan rode Olympic Boy to a 33-1 win at Folkestone.

STRANGEST EVENT
1994 Student James Florey, 21, from Bracknell, was warned off for five years by the Jockey Club for running on to the track during Royal Ascot, bringing down a runner.

OTHER EVENTS
1764 Joseph Rose completed a tough stint when riding Bachelor at Manchester. The day before, he rode Young Davy at York, and the day before that had been on Favourite at Lincoln – commuting between meetings on his own hack, carrying a racing saddle on his back.

1892 La Fleche, already a 1,000 Guineas winner and Derby runner-up, won the 11-runner St Leger at 7-2 for trainer John Porter and rider John Watts.

1968 17yo Vindicated lived up to his name after being insulted by bookies and punters who let him go off at 33-1 in a six-runner, two-mile chase at Market Rasen – he won by a short head.

1970 Bill Shoemaker passed John Longden's previous all-time record of 6,032 winners on Dares J at Del Mar.

1990 Little doubt about coincidence nap of the day as a Spitfire flypast is held at Kempton to commemorate the Battle of Britain shortly before the running of the Spitfire Handicap – 11-2 shot Blue Aeroplane duly obliged.

1994 Tony McCoy landed his first British winner, Chickabiddy, at Exeter.

1994 Eighty-seven-year-old trainer Jack O'Donoghue landed his biggest win when 12-1 Hello Mister won Doncaster's Tote Portland Handicap, ridden by Pat McCabe.

1996 Pat Eddery rode a 10,984-1 five-timer at Haydock.

1997 Hong Kong staged its first racing under Chinese rule – 32,000 turned up at Happy Valley.

2008 Having broken his leg five times, 31-year-old jump jockey Barry Fenton called it a day. He also broke ankles, ribs, sternum, collarbone (six times), eye socket, shoulder blade and needed 38 stitches to his ear. He won a Welsh National, Whitbread Gold Cup and Coral Cup.

2008 British runners, headed by 8-1 chance Pressing, giving jockey Neil Callan his most valuable winner, land a 1-2-3 in Turkey's £512,000 Topkapi Trophy at Veliefendi, Istanbul.

QUOTE OF THE DAY
2008 *'I am a dyslexic Satanist – I worship the drivel.'* Typical remark from always entertaining trainer Charlie Mann.

BIRTHDAY
1930 Jockey-turned-trainer Gordon 'The Boss' Richards, whose Lucius and Hallo Dandy won the 1978 and 1984 Nationals. Inserted a W between the two parts of his name to differentiate himself from the prolific champion Flat jockey.

FIRST OF THE DAY
2008 Jockey-turned-trainer David Bridgwater saddled his first winner, Neutrino, and then his second, Runshan, both at Fontwell for a 44-1 double

DEATH OF THE DAY
1969 Jockey Anthony Lehane, 34. Won 1958 Irish Grand National on Gold Legend. Known as 'Tumper' reputedly due to willingness to 'tump' either man or horse should he deem it desirable.

CELEBRITY OF THE DAY
1932 Four of the first five home in the St Leger were owned by the Aga Khan, including winner Firdaussi, trained by Frank Butters.

8 SEPTEMBER

SIGNIFICANT EVENT
2008 Lot 127, a colt by A.P. Indy and first foal out of Horse of the Year Azeri, became the highest RNA (reserve not attained) ever at Keeneland September Yearling Sales when failing to make $7.7m.

STRANGEST EVENT
1897 Jockey Charles Wood, champion in 1887 but warned off soon after for owning horses (against the rules) and running them to suit his own betting purposes, having recently been allowed to ride again at the age of 41, partnered the Sam Darling-trained 1-10 favourite Galtee More, the 2,000 Guineas and Derby winner, in the St Leger. The pair duly won by three-quarters of a length to clinch the Triple Crown.

OTHER EVENTS
1820 Biggest field yet of 27 for the St Leger, won by 7-1 St Patrick, ridden by Bob Johnson.
1897 The Sam Darling trained Galtee Moore completed the Triple Crown in the St Leger.
1955 Meld's St Leger win made Capt Cecil Boyd-Rochfort the first trainer to clock up total winnings in excess of £1m.
1955 Yearling Ballymoss fetched 4,500gns at Doncaster, being bought by Vincent O'Brien for US owner J McShain. He was bred at Naul Stud, County Dublin, by Richard Ball, who was known as the Poet, having once published a volume of verse. Ballymoss went on to become the record European prize-money earner, and won the 1958 Arc, having been runner-up in the 1957 Derby. He also won the Irish Derby and was the first Irish-trained colt to win the St Leger.
1959 Jump jockey Johnny Gilbert rode a record ten straight winners between this date and September 30.
1991 Latest 'wonderhorse' Arazi boosted his reputation by winning Longchamp's Prix de la Salamandre.

1992 Burooj won at Lingfield to complete 49-year-old Willie Carson's 21st century of winners in 22 seasons. A fall in Milan in 1984 had prevented the clean sweep.
2001 Frankie Dettori rode Godolphin's Fantastic Light, 9/4, to a head victory over Aiden O'Brien's dual Derby winner, Galileo, 4/11, in the Irish Champion Stakes. Reversed King George VI – Queen Elizabeth Diamond Stakes outcome.

QUOTE OF THE DAY
'That place wanted bombing. It still amazes me how horses used to race round there, ridiculous, really. There's no way I'd be calling for it to reopen, it wants to stay closed. It was dangerous, it wasn't good for horse or rider, they were always falling over.' Unlike John McCririck, who wants to be buried there, Willie Carson was no fan of 'the frying pan' track at Alexandra Park, which closed on this date in 1970. 1999 plans to re-open came to nothing.

BIRTHDAYS
1941 Yves Saint-Martin, French ace whose first English Classic win was on Monade in the 1962 Oaks. Won the 1963 Derby on Relko. Sassafras was his first Arc winner in 1970, and he repeated the feat on Allez France in 1974.
1960 Controversial jump jockey Graham Bradley, whose autobiography was called *The Wayward Lad*, also the name of one of the best chasers he ever rode.
1980 Former champion apprentice Paul Hanagan. Objected to Derek Thompson calling him 'that man again' but the winners dried up until he changed his mind and gave his blessing to the nickname.

FIRST OF THE DAY
1990 Dayjur (Willie Carson/Dick Hern) became the first sprinter to complete the King's Stand-Nunthorpe-Sprint Cup hat-trick when winning the last-named at Haydock.

9 SEPTEMBER

SIGNIFICANT EVENT
1994 Epsom announced that Derby would be run on Saturday from 1995.

STRANGEST EVENT
1992 For the first time a race was run over six and a half furlongs at Doncaster. The EBF Fillies' Nursery Handicap was won by Steve Cauthen and Michael Stoute with 7/1 chance Falsoola.

OTHER EVENTS
1754 Driver, owned by Mr Lamego, won the Give and Take Plate at Maidenhead – a three-heat event in which he was ridden by a different jockey in each. Thomas Brett fell off during the first heat, to be replaced by David Newcomb, who rode so badly he was replaced by Thomas Arnold – who rode the horse to victory.

1882 Racing took place for the first time at Newcastle's High Gosforth Park. Jump racing was introduced there in 1951.

1891 Common, 4-5, ridden by George Barrett and trained by John Porter, won the nine-runner St Leger, completing the Triple Crown.

1896 66-1 bar two as seven St Leger runners lined up, and 2-11 shot Persimmon, the Derby winner owned by the Prince of Wales, won from 6-1 Labrador. The winner, trained by Richard Marsh, was the last of jockey John Watts's five Leger successes.

1968 Winston Churchill's jockey-turned-trainer Tommy Gosling sent out his 50th winner when Chasmerella, with Lester Piggott up, completed a double on the day for him at Windsor.

1991 Known Ranger, five-year-old half-brother to Derby winner Reference Point, equalled world record of 1min 32.4sec for a mile on turf at Belmont Park, USA.

1992 Gaelic Frolic won at Exeter to give trainer Peter Cundell his 400th winner, at the same track where he had his first winner, Irish Word.

1995 Eight years, 92 days after his first success Frankie Dettori landed his 1,000th British winner when Classic Cliche won the St Leger, making him the second fastest to the total behind Fred Archer, who took seven years 307 days.

2004 Jockey Club head of security Paul Scotney commented on BBC Radio 5 Live: 'In general, racing is clean. I said that when I started 12 months ago. I stand by that – but there is a core of people who are trying to cheat. I'm putting structures in place to catch those people or persuade them not to do what they are doing. I'm talking about people both inside and outside racing.'

2008 Henry Cecil broke a losing run of four years with his Lingfield runners when 6-4 I'm Sensational won. On same date, striker turned trainer Mick Quinn sent out the mare Angus Newz, owned by his father, who owns Liverpool's Newz Bar, at Leicester to win her 12th race.

QUOTE OF THE DAY
'As far as I know, no-one has done something like this before, and that's part of the challenge,' declared trainer Mark Wallace, best known for his sprinter, Prix de l'Abbaye winner Benbaun, announcing in 2008 that after five years in Newmarket he was heading off to train at Warwick Farm in Sydney, Aus.

BIRTHDAYS
1958 Former jockey Eddie King.
1958 Trainer of Shinko's Best, Axel Kleinkorres.

DEATHS OF THE DAY
1817 Richard Goodisson, who rode the first three Oaks winners from 1779-81, died in Newmarket. He was reputed to always carry £500 cash after being refused a credit bet on a horse who won.
2008 Robin Barwell, 59; Tiverton trainer for 12 years. His best horse was eight-times winner Special Account.

CELEBRITY OF THE DAY
1943 Pink Floyd member and racehorse owner Roger Waters born.

10 SEPTEMBER

SIGNIFICANT EVENT

1969 The Fulke Johnson Houghton-trained Ribofilio, already beaten favourite in three Classics – 2,000 Guineas, Derby and Irish Derby – was again market leader at 11-10 for St Leger, but once again even Lester Piggott could not win on the horse, who finished second to the Ron Hutchinson-ridden, Harry Wragg-trained Intermezzo.

STRANGEST EVENT

1993 Women won seven races in a row at Delaware Park, USA.

OTHER EVENTS

1879 French horse Rayon D'Or, owned by Comte de Lagrange, also owner of Triple Crown winner Gladiateur, won the 17-runner St Leger, ridden by Jem Goater.

1890 Oaks winner Memoir won the St Leger at 10-1 for trainer George Dawson.

1972 Great French mare Allez France won on debut under Yves Saint-Martin in the Prix de Toutevoie at Longchamp.

1977 Rare 400-1 winner recorded at Cheltenham, Australia as Zulu Gold won.

1981 Jump jockey Malcolm Batters announced retirement – to become a deep sea diver.

1988 Willie Carson rode Minster Son to win the St Leger – uniquely having also bred the horse, who was trained by Neil Graham.

1989 Some 2,500 people were locked out as racing began at Taipa Island, Macau. £1.5m was bet on the Tote.

1992 Channel 4 announced it was dropping live coverage of the Prix de l'Arc de Triomphe – for Italian football.

1994 The St Leger was a family affair as Barry Hills trained 40-1 winner Moonax, ridden by Pat Eddery. Broadway Flyer, 6-1, finished second, trained by Hills's son John and ridden by other son, Michael.

1994 Alywow won the first race on new turf course at Canada's Woodbine track.

1995 Lester Piggott retired. For the second time.

2008 Tote launched new Totesuper7, inviting punters to pick winners of seven races selected from three meetings.

2008 French-born, Israel-based jockey Vanessa Allouche was revealed as a contestant on Israel's first Big Brother show.

2008 Vince Smith, 43, former jockey-turned-Newmarket trainer who sent out 54 Flat winners and two over jumps, gave up his licence.

QUOTE OF THE DAY

The government announced in 1942 that because of war it was *'unable to sanction NH racing'* any longer. It was January 1945 before it returned.

BIRTHDAYS

1906 Newmarket trainer Humphrey Cottrill. Trained Narrator, 20-1 winner of 1954 Champion Stakes and 1955 Coronation Cup at 10-3.

1938 Trainer Dan Combs.

1950 Channel 4 racing producer Andrew Franklin.

1961 Upper Lambourn trainer Stan Moore.

1965 Gee Armytage, who partnered namesake Gee-A in the 1988 National. Landed double at 1987 Cheltenham Festival on The Ellier and Gee-A. Became Tony McCoy's PA.

DEATHS OF THE DAY

1922 John Osborne, 89. He rode 12 Classic winners, including the Derby on Pretender in 1869. Still training successfully at 81 when The Guller won the Northumberland Plate.

1982 Jumps trainer Bob Turnell, 67. His Pas Seul won the Gold Cup, and Salmon Spray the Champion Hurdle.

CELEBRITY OF THE DAY

1983 Cash Asmussen became the first American to ride a winner for the Queen when partnering Reflection at Chepstow.

11 SEPTEMBER

SIGNIFICANT EVENT
1878 Fourteen went to post for the St Leger, one fewer than intended – jockey F Sharpe (no relation as far as I know – author) would have ridden Yagar, but broke his leg in the preliminary canter when kicked by another runner. Fred Archer won his second consecutive Leger, bringing Lord Falmouth's 5-2 favourite and Oaks winner Jannette home in front of the same owner's Childeric – the second straight year he'd owned the first two.

STRANGEST EVENT
1991 Farfelu, ridden by Simon Whitworth, fell in the Portland Handicap at Doncaster – two years after a similar incident in the same race resulted in Paul Cook's retirement.

OTHER EVENTS
1867 Tom Chaloner rode filly Achievement to a 7-4 win over 6-5 favourite and Derby winner The Hermit in the St Leger.
1889 The Duke of Portland's Donovan, a winner of 11 of his 13 two-year-old starts who went on to win the Derby, wins the St Leger as the 8-13 favourite in a field of 12, ridden by Fred Barrett.
1990 Del Mar grandstand demolished.
1993 Michael Kinane clocked up the fastest century of winners in Ireland, as the eight-times champion won on Saibot at Leopardstown.
2004 Aussie jockey Craig Agnew rode six winners at Kembla Grange, NSW. On the same day an Aussie jockey based in England, Kerrin McEvoy, won his first Classic, the St Leger, on 3-1 joint-favourite Rule Of Law. 'This is heaven!' enthused the rider, adding: 'You need to be a horseman as well as a jockey over here.' Kieren Fallon, yet to win, was runner up on Quiff.
2008 Doubles all round at the Laytown beach meeting where jockey Declan McDonogh, trainer Gordon Elliott, owner Jim Morrow and jockey Nina Carberry all enjoyed double success.
2009 Steve Asmussen became the fifth North American trainer to saddle 5000 winners via Passion Rules at Woodbine.

QUOTE OF THE DAY
The *Post Boy* newspaper carried an advertisement on this day in 1711 for a race appearing to be a forerunner of today's sellers, to be run *'on 9th October next on Coleshill Heath, Warwickshire, a plate of 6gns value. The winning horse to be sold for £10, to carry 10st if 14 hands high, if above or under to be allowed weight for inches. Also a plate of less value to be run for by asses'.*

BIRTHDAYS
1917 Daniel Wildenstein. The writer of 50 books on art, he also owned top horses like 1974 Arc winners Allez France (1974), All Along (1983) and Sagace (1984) plus Pawneese, Flying Water and Crow.
1936 Former Irish champion jockey Tommy Murphy. Won the Irish 1,000 Guineas on Lady Capulet in 1977.
1941 Paul Cole. He trained Generous to win the 1991 Derby at 9-1 and Snurge to win the 1990 St Leger.
1954 Jump jockey turned chief inspector of race courses, Richard Linley. In 1987 Linley dislocated his shoulder during the Arkle Chase at the Cheltenham Festival but shrugged (!) off the pain to ride a successful driving finish on Gala's Image.
1973 Jockey Robby Albarado. He began riding aged 12 at bush tracks in his native Louisiana. He suffered a skull fracture in both 1998 and 99 and had the repairs carried with titanium. a regular rider of Curlin, he landed his 4000th win on Keertana at Churchill Downs on May 30, 2009.

LAST OF THE DAY
1909 Hull racecourse closed its gates, staging a final Flat fixture.

12 SEPTEMBER

SIGNIFICANT EVENT
1900 The Prince of Wales's Diamond Jubilee (2-7) completed the Triple Crown, winning the St Leger under stable lad Herbert Jones for trainer Richard Marsh.

STRANGEST EVENT
1894 Mornington Cannon rode 50-1 St Leger winner Throstle. Even owner Lord Arlington had despaired of the filly, once trying to give her away – but the prospective recipient didn't turn up to collect her.

OTHER EVENTS
1843 Second-place money was doubled to £200, and third saved stake for the first time as nine went to post for the St Leger, won by Nutwith (Job Marson) at 100-7.Connections collected £3,070 4/6d.

1855 Objection made to St Leger runner BEFORE the race started – on grounds that the owner was in default for bets. Stewards disallowed objection and all 12 started, with 40-1 outsider Saucebox winning.

1877 Fred Archer won his first St Leger, on Lord Falmouth's Derby winner Silvio, the 65-40 favourite defeating 13 rivals.

1888 Jack Robinson won his second successive St Leger on Lord Calthorpe's 5-2 second favourite Seabreeze, the Oaks winner. Trainer James Jewitt also scored for the second successive year.

1966 Former jockey Tim Brookshaw, who broke his neck in a Liverpool fall in 1963 but who had taught himself to walk and ride again, had his first success as an owner with What A Yarn at Wolverhampton.

1970 Nijinsky, 2/7, (Lester Piggott – Vincent O'Brien) won the St Leger, completing the Triple Crown.

1981 Derby winner Shergar was only fourth of seven behind 28-1 winner Cut Above in the St Leger.

1985 Five-timer for jockey Greville Starkey at Salisbury.

1990 Artist Max Brandrett fined £1,200 and ordered to pay £2,000 compensation after forging Lester Piggott's signature on a painting of the maestro on Teenoso. Piggott himself instigated action.

1991 Champion Hurdle winner Morley Street, 33/1, just touched off by Great Marquess in the Doncaster Cup.

1992 George Duffield rode Oaks winner User Friendly (7-4) to win the St Leger for Clive Brittain.

2008 Racegoers wearing rugby shirts received £5 reduction in entrance fee to Sandown, staging a Rugby and Racing day.

2009 The Curragh scheduled a celebration of the late Vincent O'Brien's life at the track where he saddled 27 Irish Classic winners, highlighted by the first running of the Vincent O'Brien National Stakes, won by the Kevin Prendergast-trained Kingsfort.

QUOTE OF THE DAY
'Vincent O'Brien was undoubtedly the most influential person in horseracing history and we are delighted to be able to put together a fitting tribute to remember his remarkable career.' Curragh manager Paul Hensey announcing the track's O'Brien day on this date in 2009.

BIRTHDAYS
1917 Capt Bill Edwards-Heathcote, the owner of dual Champion Hurdle winner Bula (1971 and 72).

1934 Paddy Osborne, trainer of Brown Lad and Deep Idol.

1952 George Margarson, trainer of Barathea Guest and Young Mick.

1969 Richard Gibson, trainer of Lady Of Chad and Doctor Dino.

CELEBRITY OF THE DAY
1937 Lightning-fast West Indian bowler and racehorse owner Wes Hall was born.

13 SEPTEMBER

SIGNIFICANT EVENT
1997 Pat Eddery's 4,000th winner just happens to be the St Leger winner, too. He partnered 5/4 Silver Patriarch to the vital victory.

STRANGEST EVENT
1842 Jockey Tommy Lye, who had staked £200 on his St Leger mount, 8-1 chance Blue Bonnet, was so keen to win the 17-runner race that he gave the filly such severe punishment that despite winning, trainer Tom Dawson never used him again – and she never won again.

OTHER EVENTS
1682 A large crowd turned up at Leasowe, Cheshire, to see the Duke of Monmouth ride in a race worth £60, which he won on his own horse, Young Whisky.

1848 Surplice won the St Leger – at the second attempt. The 9-4 shot, ridden by Nat Flatman, won after a false start when the field set off without the starter's permission, resulting in all jockeys being fined.

1865 Gladiateur survived claims that he was older than three to win the St Leger, ridden by Hary Grimshaw. He clinched the Triple Crown, plus, uniquely, won the Grand Prix de Paris as well.

1871 Hannah, who won the 1,000 Guineas and Oaks, completed her Classic treble when 2-1 winner of St Leger.

1882 Fred Archer won his fourth St Leger on 40-1 Dutch Oven.

1948 After three wins over fences and four on the Flat, young Fred Winter's riding career looked as though it could be over when a fall at Wye left the 21-year-old with a fractured spine.

1950 Joe Mercer, then just 15, rode first winner, Eldoret, at Bath.

1989 Paul Cook suffered an horrendous fall at Doncaster that ended his career. Three jockeys were injured when the Cook-ridden Madraco fell in the Portland Handicap. Ray Cochrane broke his collarbone; Ian Johnson suffered a hurt lower spine; while Cook fractured his right foot, right thumb, two ribs, and a broken collarbone.

1992 English Derby winner Dr Devious just got the better of Irish Derby winner St Jovite in Leopardstown's Champion Stakes.

1992 Gianfranco Dettori, who began his career with a winner for Sergio Cumani 31 years earlier, bowed out with a double on Only Royale and Inner City for that trainer's son, Luca, at San Siro, Milan. Dettori's retirement was short-lived – he returned a fortnight later.

2008 Conduit, 8/1, became Sir Michael Stoute's first St Leger winner after 34 years of trying – and went on to Breeders' Cup glory later in the year. On the same day Aidan O'Brien completed an Irish Classic grand slam as Septimus (1-3) won the St Leger by 13 lengths, the longest winning margin in an Irish Classic since Turtle Island's 15-length romp in the 1994 2,000 Guineas.

QUOTE OF THE DAY
'Even though I'm Australian it's taking me a while to adjust back to the Australian style of racing,' said Kerrin McEvoy, who had just returned from England to ride in his native Oz – and on this date in 2008 collected his fourth riding ban since returning under a month earlier.

BIRTHDAYS
1947 Jockey Gerry Faulkner, who partnered prolific winner Supermaster.
1961 Trainer Tim Easterby

DEATHS OF THE DAY
1967 First Californian equine prize-money dollar millionaire, Native Diver, winner of 37 of 81 starts.
1999 Newmarket trainer Jack Waugh. His Arabian Night was runner-up to Never Say Die in the 1954 Derby. In 1956 his great sprinter Matador won both the July Cup and Stewards' Cup.

14 SEPTEMBER

SIGNIFICANT EVENT

1853 West Australian, the 6-4 favourite, owned by John Bowes, made history by becoming the first Triple Crown winner as he took the St Leger, trained by John Scott at Malton and ridden by Frank Butler.

STRANGEST EVENT

1994 Kieren Fallon, 29, reportedly dragged fellow rider Stuart Webster from his mount as the pair finished a race at Beverley. Fallon accused Webster of causing the hampering of a number of runners. After the incident both jockeys emerged from the weighing room sporting facial wounds. Fallon was suspended for six months at a Jockey Club hearing.

OTHER EVENTS

1725 A 'Ladies' Plate' run for by female riders on Ripon Heath, Yorkshire.
1841 William 'Glorious Bill' Scott won his fourth successive St Leger on Satirist, 6-1, beating Derby winner Coronation.
1864 Ten contested the St Leger, won by 2-1 favourite Blair Athol, the Derby winner, ridden by Jim Snowden.
1881 Iroquois, the 2-1 favourite, becomes Fred Archer's third St Leger winner, beating14 opponents, including Voluptuary, who finished last but went on to win the 1884 Grand National.
1887 4-1 favourite Kilwarlin, trained by James Jewitt, stood still as eight other St Leger runners set off, losing a good 150 yards. William 'Jack' Robinson's mount made up ground to win by a length and a half.
1937 Bill Wightman saddled his first winner, Autumn, at Warwick.
1959 America's latest track, Aqueduct, opened with Willie Shoemaker riding Four Lane to win the first race, trained by T M Waller.
1964 Lewes racecourse staged final meeting, with Miss Rhonda winning the last race, ridden by R P Elliott.
1975 The great French mare Allez France won for the 13th and last time in the Prix Foy at Longchamp.
1989 Weld won the Doncaster Cup at 1-5, becoming Lord Howard de Walden's 400th winner as an owner.
1991 After two furlongs of the St Leger, the field was confronted by a 35-year-old man, Alan Davis, and an eight-year-old boy, both sitting on the track. The runners somehow all managed to avoid them and Pat Eddery won on the Andre Fabre-trained Toulon.
1992 Surprise Offer won at Bath to give trainer Richard Hannon his 1,000th British Flat winner.
1996 Frankie Dettori, who won on Shantou (8-1), and runner-up Pat Eddery on Dushyantor were both banned for overuse of the whip after the St Leger.
2003 Sandown abandoned, as jockeys refused to race in protest at mobile phone ban.
2008 Flying French filly Zarkava won the Prix Vermeille, prior to her first race against colts in the Arc.

QUOTE OF THE DAY

1964 *'I thought it was a terrible track. The pull up wasn't much good, there was no rail to ease the horse after the finish. If you were on a real puller, you went down the hill and finished up by Lewes prison. And, thinking back, I know one or two jockeys who should have been in it.'* So said Willie Snaith, who rode at Lewes's final meeting.

BIRTHDAY

1919 Tim Molony. Champion jump jockey for five consecutive seasons from 1948 to 52, he won the Champion Hurdle from 1951 to 1954.

DEATHS OF THE DAY

1983 Meld, 1955 Triple Crown winner, died in Ireland aged 31 – a record for longevity among English Classic winners.
1994 One of the greatest chasers never to win the Cheltenham Gold Cup, Pendil, who raced 47 times, winning 21 chases and six hurdles, is put down.

15 SEPTEMBER

SIGNIFICANT EVENT
1835 Queen Of Trumps became first Oaks winner to complete St Leger double, starting 11-8 and beating ten opponents.

STRANGEST EVENT
1979 Steve Cauthen chalked up the 1,000th win of his career at Doncaster on Thousandfold.

OTHER EVENTS
1697 *The London Gazette* reported on an abandoned race meeting due to be held in the north-west of the country: 'Whereas there was notice given, that on the 15th and 16th inst there would be two Plates run for on Barlow Moor near Manchester. These are to give notice that the said Plates will not be run for till the Monday and Tuesday after Michaelmas Day next ensuing, by reason that great Rains hath hindered the repairing of the said course as was intended.'

1840 7-4 favourite Launcelot, ridden by Bill Scott, won the 11-runner St Leger, but only courtesy of 4-1 runner-up Maroon, on whom J Holmes allowed the favourite to win as they were both in the ownership of Lord Westminster, who had 'declared to win' with the market leader.

1842 Known as 'The Pride of Northumberland', Bee's-wing won the Doncaster Cup for the fourth time.

1886 Fred Archer landed his sixth and final St Leger victory on the Duke of Westminster's Ormonde, completing the Triple Crown.

1970 Mrs Hauksbee won the Plantation Stakes to give Pat Eddery his first Goodwood winner, while trainer Guy Harwood achieved his with Early Session in the Harroways Stakes.

1984 Lester Piggott set a new record of 28 Classic victories, riding 7-4 favourite Commanche Run to a neck victory in the St Leger for Luca Cumani, taking him one past Frank Buckle.

1984 Monica Dickinson sent out her first runner as a trainer – Salgar, seventh in a Cartmel novice hurdle.

1989 For the second time in three days a horse fell without apparent reason at Doncaster's St Leger meeting. The oldest Classic was abandoned for only the second time since 1776 (previous occasion in 1939 was due to outbreak of war). Billy Newnes fell from Able Player in the first race, and the Leger was later rescheduled for Ayr on September 23.

1990 Snurge (7-2) became the first maiden since 1913 to win St Leger. He was ridden by Richard Quinn for trainer Paul Cole.

1990 Confusion in the betting ring and betting shops as the Doncaster stewards waited a full seven minutes before announcing enquiry into a nursery, later disqualifying 'winner' Jenufa and handing the race to Tiber Flow.

1994 The state of the ground at Lingfield meant the usual Flat starting stalls could not be used for the seventh race, so it was decided to use a flip-start. Problems with the tape meant a flag start was eventually used.

2007 Yeats won the Irish St Leger to complete Aidan O'Brien's set of British and Irish Classics.

QUOTE OF THE DAY
2007 *'When a jockey retires he becomes just another little man.'* Former US champion jockey Eddie Arcaro's remark, recalled by Robin Oakley in *The Spectator*.

BIRTHDAYS
1910 Racing writer Richard Baerlein, of the *Guardian* and *Observer*, who was one of the earliest and most insistent advocates of Shergar's Derby-winning abilities..

1949 Arthur Moore. He won the 1971 Irish National on King's Sprite.

1956 Willie Mullins. Champion jumps trainer and champion amateur rider from 1985-89.

DEATH OF THE DAY
1993 Jockey Eric 'Monkey' Morris, 88.

16 SEPTEMBER

SIGNIFICANT EVENT
1927 1928 Champion Hurdle winner and six-times winner of Queen Alexandra Stakes, Brown Jack made his hurdling debut, finishing third at Bournemouth.

STRANGEST EVENT
1994 A case of 'air we go' at Ayr as On Air won EBF Fillies' Handicap, won the previous year by Tap On Air.

OTHER EVENTS
1834 Derby winner Plenipotentiary (10-12 favourite) finished last but one in the 11-runner St Leger; he was later proved to have been poisoned.

1863 Left at the post, trailing the leader by 50 lengths and being quoted 50-1 in running, Lord Clifden, the 100-30 favourite ridden by John Osborne, came through to win the 19-runner St Leger and £4,975 prize-money for Lord St Vincent.

1869 First meeting at Douglas, Isle of Man.

1885 The Bard set a new record with his 16th success as a two-year-old in the Tattersalls Sale Stakes for trainer Martin Gurry of Newmarket.

1972 Meriel Tufnell won on Hard Slipper at Newbury, in the 11th of 12 ladies' races, clinching the first champion lady jockey on the Flat title.

1982 Paul Cole celebrated his 500th training success in his 15th season as Brandon Creek (Richard Quinn) won at Brighton.

1989 Two horses trained by Ron O'Leary failed to arrive at Bangor. It was reported that the horsebox carrying them had gone to the seaside town of Bangor instead of racecourse town of Bangor-on-Dee. The trainer claimed the box had broken down.

1993 Racing history made as Jack Berry's mare, Laurel Queen, won her 22nd race, at Lingfield, on her 53rd start, passing the previous best, achieved by Sir Mark Prescott's Misty Halo.

1994 Trainer Sue Bradburne sent out three of the six runners in an Ayr amateur riders' stakes – husband Johnny, 48, finished fourth on Dante's Inferno (100-1); daughter Lorna fifth on Musket Shot (400-1); and son Mark, 18, last on 50-1 Templerainey.

1994 Last in the previous June's Derby, Plato's Republic won for first time in five subsequent attempts – in the Novices' Selling Hurdle at Huntingdon.

2008 BBC viewers watched Uttoxeter racecourse general manager David Macdonald win £1,380 on the Anne Robinson-presented The Weakest Link.

QUOTE OF THE DAY
'What! Ride such a cripple as that?' was the reported comment of jockey John Jackson upon learning that unfancied Theodore would be his 1882 St Leger mount. The horse was actually lame and one layer struck a bet of £1,000 to a walking stick about the 200-1 shot. Theodore shocked everyone with victory over 22 rivals.

BIRTHDAYS
1941 Tommy Carberry, the trainer of Bobbyjo, 1999 Grand National winner. He rode L'Escargot to win the 1970 and 71 Gold Cups, and the 1975 Grand National.

1945 Flamboyant trainer Rod Simpson.

1955 Champion Irish jump jockey, Joe Byrne.

1979 Moscow Flyer's jockey, Barry Geraghty, in County Meath. He won the 2003 Grand National on Monty's Pass and RTE's Sports Person of the Year.

DEATH OF THE DAY
1996 Four horses died in a fire at trainer Jim Old's Wiltshire stables.

CELEBRITY OF THE DAY
1925 Former Irish prime minister Charles Haughey born. Best horses included The Chaser (eight victories), Miss Cossie (six) and Aristocracy (five).

17 SEPTEMBER

SIGNIFICANT EVENT
1994 Vintage Crop won the Irish St Leger – becoming the first dual winner.

STRANGEST EVENT
2008 Beverley racegoers had to move sharply as a horse jumped out of the pre-parade ring and charged through crowded enclosures, knocking over a pushchair whose occupant had only just been removed, then ending up actually inside the grandstand. Bespoke Boy, trained by Patrick Haslam, escaped without injury.

OTHER EVENTS
1711 Ascot staged its second ever meeting with just one race: a Plate of 50gns; three runners went to post.
1839 First St Leger dead-heat saw 4-7 Charles XII and 13-1 Euclid pass the post together in a 14-runner event. Charles XII won the run-off by a head.
1845 The Baron, ridden by Frank Butler, was the 10-1 winner of the 15-runner St Leger, the first in which jockeys drew lots for position and went off in two ranks.
1856 Derby winner Ellington was unplaced at 8-13 as Warlock, 12-1, partnered by Nat Flatman, beat eight rivals in the St Leger. In 1857 Warlock beat Fisherman, winner of 67 races, in York's Queen's Plate.
1862 Ridden by Tom Chaloner, 100-30 shot The Marquis beat 14 others in the St Leger – and was sold off to Russia.
1963 Guy Harwood saddled first winner, Springmount at Fontwell.
1968 Goodwood lost a second successive day's racing due to localised flooding.
1973 Tracona at Wolverhampton was jockey Willie Higgins' first winner.
1979 Tina's Gold at Wolverhampton was jockey Nicky Carlisle's first winner.
1984 Monica Dickinson saddled her first winner – State Case, ridden by Graham Bradley, in a Southwell novice chase.
1989 Previously unbeaten 2,000 Guineas and Derby winner Nashwan finished third in Longchamp's Prix Niel and never raced again.
1994 Alberto Paz Rodriguez, champion trainer of Panama, saddled five of the first six in the Clasico Cerveza Panama at Hipodromo Presidente Redmon – missing out only on third in this feature event.
1994 Mysterious Ways, winner of the MacDonagh and Boland Stakes under Christy Roche at the Curragh, was Vincent O'Brien's last runner as a trainer.
1996 Two horses called Tart won on the same afternoon. One with suffix (Fr) was 15-8 favourite at Yarmouth; the other, British-bred, scored at 11-2 at Doncaster. A third horse, Tart And A Half, was also active on the circuit at the same time.

QUOTE OF THE DAY
'He's a natural in the air, and can nod the ball across to adjoining boxes,' said Richard Hannon on the heading skills of his runner Right Win, for whom he rigged up footballs on strings from the ceiling of his box to keep him alert. On this day in 1992, Hannon saddled his first winner in France, Central City, 29/1, at Maisons-Laffitte.

BIRTHDAYS
1942 TV presenter and racing fan Des Lynam.
1958 Maxine Juster, champion lady jockey 1986; winner of Ascot's Ladies' Diamond Race 1983, 86, 89.
1963 Jeremy Noseda, trainer of Sixties Icon.
1976 At The Races presenter Zoey Bird.

DEATHS OF THE DAY
2007 Martha Gerry, 88. Owner of Lazy F Stable, where her champion, Forego, was based. Became first woman named as Exemplar of Racing by the National Museum of Racing and Hall of Fame.

CELEBRITY OF THE DAY
1992 A personal best for the Queen as Zenith won at Beverley to become her 23rd home-bred winner of the season.

18 SEPTEMBER

SIGNIFICANT EVENT
1968 Red Rum made NH debut after ten Flat races, of which he won two outright and dead-heated for first in another. He finished second at Cheltenham.

STRANGEST EVENT
1835 1-10 favourite Queen Of Trumps, who had won the St Leger three days earlier, looked all over the winner of Doncaster's Scarbrough Stakes – until a large dog appeared on course, causing Tommy Lye's mount to swerve dramatically, allowing Ainderby to come through, landing a £2,000 bet for owner Capt Frank Taylor who, legend has it, found the dog's owner, bought the pooch and gave it a life of luxury.

OTHER EVENTS
1794 The Mayor of Doncaster staged the public burning of gaming tables, which had proliferated at the racecourse, where Beningbrough, 2-1 winner of the previous day's St Leger, won the Gold Cup.
1827 After seven false starts the Honourable Edward Petre's filly, Matilda, 11-1 and ridden by Jem Robinson, beat Derby winner Mameluke into second to win the 26-runner St Leger.
1838 Smallest field since 1802 as seven contested the St Leger, with Don John winning by 12 lengths in record time of 3min 17sec, ridden by Bill Scott.
1850 Voltigeur, ridden by Job Marson, won eight-runner St Leger at 8-13, having already won the Derby. Had to beat Russborough in a run-off after dead-heat.
1861 1,000-15 outsider Caller Ou, ridden by Tom Chaloner, beat favourite and Derby winner Kettledrum to win St Leger. He went on to win 51 of 101 races.
1948 Freddie Maxwell saddled first of 425 winners as a trainer when Dance Away (Davy Jones) won at Bogside.

1975 Graham McCourt rode first winner, Vulrory's Kid, at Ascot.
1982 George Duffield rode the final four winners at Catterick.
1991 Aiden Wall rode Release The Beast to win at Dundalk carrying 10st 4lb. Nine days previously the same combination had won at Roscommon when the rider weighed 11st 6lb.
2008 Former jockey-turned-trainer Brendan Powell had his first winner as an owner when 8/1 Princess Flame won at Pontefract. She was also the first winner he had trained there.

QUOTE OF THE DAY
'We are happy to say this gay scene was attended with only two accidents. Lord Macartney's groom in running had his left leg broke from his horse falling. And Mr Maxwell, his lordship's secretary, had a narrow escape of his life, having tumbled into a pond, coming from the Ball.' The London Morning Chronicle's report of an eventful race meeting in Cape Town this day in 1797.

BIRTHDAYS
1931 Trainer Mick O'Toole, whose Davy Lad won the 1977 Cheltenham Gold Cup.
1940 Ogden Phipps, the chairman of the USA Jockey Club, whose Quick As Lightning won the 1980 1,000 Guineas.
1946 Jockey Geoff Baxter.
1983 Champion jockey Ryan Moore.

FIRST OF THE DAY
1989 Credit bookies H Backhouse ventured into sponsorship at Bath – awarding a prize for best turned out – owner!

CELEBRITY OF THE DAY
1949 Birth of punter Peter Shilton, also England keeper, all-time-record cap winner, and owner of Between The Sticks.

19 SEPTEMBER

SIGNIFICANT EVENT
1992 Lochsong (10-1), ridden by Francis Arrowsmith, trained by Ian Balding and owned by Jeff Smith, completed unique treble when winning Ayr Gold Cup, run on a Saturday for the first time in 189 years, adding it to her Stewards' Cup and Portland Handicap victories.

STRANGEST EVENT
1995 After irate racegoer Michael Clarke gave jockey Gary Hind a verbal blasting for the ride he gave Clarke's wife Jennie's horse, The Deaconess, at Nottingham, Clarke was found guilty of improper conduct and fined £275.

OTHER EVENTS
1769 Eclipse made ninth and final appearance of year, starting 1-7 and beating Mr Freeth's Tardy in both of 3m heats.

1801 1799 St Leger winner Cockfighter took on highly rated Sir Solomon in a famous 500gns match over four miles. Cockfighter was odds-on, but lost by a length and a half.

1826 For the first time the St Leger is run over modern-day distance of 1m6f132yds. Tarrare, 20-1, defeated 25 opponents, and was partnered by George Nelson for Lord Scarbrough.

1967 Doug Smith rode two winners at Yarmouth – the second, the Geoffrey Brooke-trained Monte Carlo, was the 20,000th ride of his career.

1969 Having done it in 1960 with Dawn Watch and Faint Hope, Eric Cousins again saddled first and second in the Ayr Gold Cup – with Brief Star and Salan.

1978 Phil Tuck rode his first chase winner, Gay God, at Hereford.

1989 Alastair Limont, MBE, senior veterinary surgeon, retired after 41 years of service to Epsom, Kempton and Sandown.

1991 John Lowe rode his 1,000th British winner, Lobinda (3-1), at Beverley, on the same day as US rider Charles Woods recorded his 2,000th.

1992 Steve Cauthen rode Mashaallah to win Irish St Leger as British raiders occupied the first four places.

1992 The Town Council Novices' Chase at Market Rasen is won by Corrupt Committee, ridden by A Tory!

1992 Vincent O'Brien saddled Fatherland, ridden by Lester Piggott, to land his 15th win in the Smurfit National Stakes at the Curragh.

1997 US jockey Chelsea Zupan, 22, emulated Frankie Dettori, albeit over two days, when she rode four successive winners at Emerald Downs, Washington, on September 18, then added three more on this date.

2008 Newmarket's Sefton Lodge, where Henry Cecil and David Loder had trained, was offered for sale at £4m.

2009 Jimmy Styles, 14/1, Frankie Dettori's first Ayr Gold Cup winner.

QUOTE OF THE DAY
2004 *'Most men lack courage when they have to tell their wives something, so I said "I've brought you a racehorse, darling". That went down like a lead balloon.'* Sir Stanley Clarke, who died today, 71, explained how he broke the news he was going into racing. Eventually took over the running of nine racecourses, floated on the stock exchange as Northern Racing.

BIRTHDAY
1963 Trainer and well-known mimic of racing folk, Richard Phillips.

DEATHS OF THE DAY
1984 Silver Buck was killed after getting loose on the gallops and running into a barn wall. He won 34 of 48 starts including the Cheltenham Gold Cup and two King Georges, winning £177,183.

FIRST OF THE DAY
1992 Britain's youngest trainer, 22-year-old Stephen Hillen, based near Cheltenham, saddled first winner, 25-1 Dr Lechter, at Catterick.

20 SEPTEMBER

SIGNIFICANT EVENT
2008 18-1 shot Regal Parade, ridden by William Carson (achieving what grandfather Willie never did) was a fifth Ayr Gold Cup winner for trainer David Nicholls, whose Tajneed, 8-1, was second.

STRANGEST EVENT
1993 Many racegoers didn't realise that 7/2 chance Cezanne beating Bold Stroke was the perfect finish to Pontefract's Dalby Screw-Driver Stakes – until it was pointed out that David Dalby was the 19th century artist who painted the horse Screw-Driver winning at Pontefract in 1824, and that the picture hangs at the track.

OTHER EVENTS
1825 A record 30 came under orders for the St Leger, Bill Scott riding 11-4 favourite Memnon to win. There was so much interest in the result that the news was rushed to London by carrier pigeon, and to Manchester by a team of dogs.
1836 Elis (7-2) dumbfounded the bookies who fielded against him in the St Leger by winning the 14-runner race by two lengths, after three false starts. Rumours that Elis would not even make it to the course were quashed when trainer John Kent snr transported the horse from Goodwood to Doncaster, some 250 miles, in a van drawn by relays of post horses – the horsebox had been invented. 'The result was expressed to Manchester by J Richardson Junior in the short space of 2 hours and 20 minutes!' boasted the *Yorkshire Gazette*.
1950 Lester Piggott, 14, lost apprentice allowance when riding Zina to win at Brighton.
1989 Diane Clay, 25, reigning champion lady jump jockey with 12 wins in 1988-89, announced her retirement.
1989 After 31 years training at Malton, Pat Rohan sent out his last British runner, 25-1 chance Integrity Boy, who was second to Kildonan at Beverley. He left Britain to train in Bahrain.
1989 Ayr was the first British course to install sectional timing facilities.
1995 A middle-aged Brighton racegoer was injured when the ambulance following the runners ploughed through rails and into him. He was taken to hospital for x-rays but allowed home. The ambulance made a full recovery.
1996 Willie Carson suffered liver damage when he was kicked in the back by the two-year-old filly Meshhed at Newbury.
1997 Lester Piggott came briefly out of retirement, aged 61, to ride, unsuccessfully, in a Curragh charity race
2009 'Trainers and jockeys are absolutely useless when it comes to assessing draw,' opined *Racing Post*'s Tom Segal.

QUOTE OF THE DAY
It took more than two weeks to decide who won the 1819 St Leger. The 19-runner race was 'won' by Antonio, 100-30, but five runners missed the start and the stewards ordered a re-run. Only ten lined up this time, and Antonio was absent. Bill Scott rode Sir Walter to win. An appeal was made to the Jockey Club, which, on October 4, announced *'the stewards should not have allowed a second race'*, and gave the race to Antonio.

BIRTHDAYS
1926 Fred Winter, legendary champion jump jockey-turned legendary champion trainer. He was the first jumps trainer to win more than £100,000 in one season. He won two Nationals, two Gold Cups and three Champion Hurdles as a jockey. He saddled Midnight Court to win the 1978 Gold Cup, Jay Trump and Anglo to win the National, and Bula (twice) and Lanzarote to win the Champion Hurdle.
1951 Colin Astbury, the champion jump jockey of 1977 – in Norway.

FIRST OF THE DAY
1976 Jim Bolger saddled first winner as Peaceful Pleasure won at Roscommon.

21 SEPTEMBER

SIGNIFICANT EVENT
1927 Taunton racecourse opened for business – the next British course to open would be Great Leighs, on 20 April 20 2008.

STRANGEST EVENT
1969 Guy Harwood saddled his 100th winner, as Springmount (Jeff King) won a three-mile chase. The same horse was also his first winner.

OTHER EVENTS
1812 100-1 shot Otterington won 24-runner St Leger.

1818 Reveller was the 7-2 winner of 21-runner St Leger for jockey Bob Johnson. In 1822 the same horse prevented Dr Syntax from winning the Preston Cup for the eighth consecutive year.

1830 Sam Chifney, the top rider of the day, finished runner-up for the fourth time in the St Leger on Priam, behind winner Birmingham, ridden by Patrick Connolly.

1923 Dinkie, Dumas and Marvex triple dead-heated for the Royal Borough Handicap at Windsor.

1968 Bill Rickaby, a Major in the war, who also won three Classics including Sweet Solera in the 1961 1,000Guineas and Oaks, rode a winner on his final ride, Silver Spray, at Newmarket.

1989 Willie Carson complained he was beaten on Aradu at Lingfield in the Creative Design Advertising Handicap because his mount 'shied away from an advertising hoarding'!

1991 The three-runner Nalgo Novices' Chase at Market Rasen saw Sudbrooke Park fall at the tenth, bringing down Vantard. Cairncastle refused, leaving the by now remounted Vantard in the lead. Vantard fell at the 12th;. Cairncastle refused again. Then again. Mark Sharratt remounted Vantard and went on to win.

1991 French-trained 3-1 shot Turgeon (Tony Cruz) beat favourite Patricia in the Irish St Leger.

1993 Kempton staged first arab race to be part of a thoroughbred card.

1994 Diskette won at Brighton to give Michael Roberts his 1,000th British winner.

2004 Sixteen jockeys squeezed into a Mini to raise cash for charity at Chester on this day – but were five short of equalling the world record.

2008 After 6,470 victories, leaving him ninth on the US all-time list, jockey Earlie Fires, 61, retired after 44 years.

2009 Trainer Ian Balding revealed he'd backed William Buick at 500/1 ever to become champion jockey.

QUOTE OF THE DAY
'I'd picked Kicking King up off his nose at the last, had my head down and was going for the line when I saw this little red lad ahead of me for a couple of seconds,' jockey Barry Geraghty on this day in 2008, recalling the time in the 2004 King George VI Chase at Kempton when he nearly mowed down Father Christmas!

BIRTHDAYS
1930 Donald 'Ginger' McCain, who saddled the winners of four Grand Nationals, three by the legendary Red Rum, plus Amberleigh House.

1951 US Hall of Fame jockey Eddie Delahoussaye (6,384 career wins).

1981 Cathy Gannon, Ireland's first female champion apprentice in 2004, also voted country's Sportswoman of the Year.

DEATHS OF THE DAY
2000 Owner Joy Valentine, 94, whose Cahervillahow was second in the 1993 National that never was, and disqualified after 'winning' the 1991 Whitbread two years previously, died aged 94.

2007 Trainer Tom McGovern, 76. Olympian won four races for him.

2009 Trainer John Manners, 83, once fined for chasing the winner up run-in.

FIRST OF THE DAY
1950 Lester Piggott rode first Ascot winner, Tancred.

22 SEPTEMBER

SIGNIFICANT EVENT
1778 For the first time the St Leger, now in its third year, is actually run as the St Leger Stakes. It took place, also for the first time, on Doncaster Town Moor, and was run over two miles. It was won by George Herring (sometimes Hearon) on 5-2 shot Hollandaise.

STRANGEST EVENT
1978 'If he was drawn behind the stalls, he'd still win,' predicted Greville Starkey before riding 5/1 Vaigly Great to win the Ayr Gold Cup.

OTHER EVENTS
1789 John Mangle was deprived of a fourth consecutive St Leger victory, winning on Zanga, only to be disqualified for jostling. The race was awarded to the favourite, the filly Pewett.
1817 Ebor, 25-1, beat hot favourite Blacklock into second in the St Leger, for jockey Bob Johnson and owner Henry Peirse.
1951 Eddie Hide rode the first of 2,500+ winners, Ritornello, at Chepstow.
1966 Terry Biddlecombe rode five winners from five mounts at Ludlow.
1975 Michael Wigham rode first winner, Highland Jig, at Leicester.
1989 Johnny Burns watched the Ayr Gold Cup yet again, never having missed one since first seeing it in 1920, when his jockey brother Tommy 'T.P' Burns, won on 6-1 Forest Guard, which Johnny trained. This year's winner was 50/1 Jimmy Fortune-ridden Joveworth.
1990 Paul Cole became the first trainer to complete the English-Irish St Leger double in the same season when Ibn Bey, six, became the oldest horse to win a Group 1 race in Ireland. Cole had won the English St Leger with Snurge; Ibn Bey completed the first clean sweep of Irish Classics by British trainers since 1956.
1992 Lester Piggott rode first Nottingham double since 'retirement' seven years earlier. He won on Snowy

River 2/1 and Jumaira Star 3/1. The former was his first ride for Jon Scargill and that trainer's 50th Flat winner.
1997 Infamous won at Hereford to give Tony McCoy his 500th winner in Britain only three years and 15 days after his first, smashing Adrian Maguire's record of three years 333 days between 1991 and 95.
1997 Charlie Swan rode 1,000th winner, Rainbow Frontier, at Listowel.
2008 Ruth Carr, who took over from her grandfather David Chapman earlier in the year, scored her first double, with Sunley Sovereign, 50-1, and 7-2 Moheebb, both at Hamilton.
2009 Irish-based trainer Gordon Elliot was handcuffed and put in a cell for having the wrong licence as he drove horses to run at Perth. He later had three winners.

QUOTE OF THE DAY
'They always give me these things, but I haven't touched a drop for three and a half years. I'll give it to the staff.' Former alcoholic Henry Cecil on receiving a case of John Smith's Extra Smooth after Multidimenional, 5/2, won a race at Newbury on September 22, 2007.

BIRTHDAYS
1911 Owner Mrs Enid Boucher, whose chaser Killiney won 14 of 19 races before having to be destroyed, aged seven, at Ascot in 1973 after a fall.
1940 Trainer Mary Reveley.
1951 Multiple Japanese champion trainer Kazuo Fujisawa.
1954 US champion jockey Darrel McHargue.

DEATH OF THE DAY
1996 Former jockey-turned-trainer Frank Muggeridge, 68.

CELEBRITY OF THE DAY
1944 Emmerdale actor and sometime jockey Frazer Hines, owner of Escapism and Joe Sugden, born.

23 SEPTEMBER

SIGNIFICANT EVENT
1989 For the first time a Classic was run in Scotland as Ayr hosted the St Leger, moved from Doncaster after a series of falls caused the abandonment of the meeting. The Henry Cecil-trained 6-4 chance Michelozzo, ridden by Steve Cauthen, was the winner.

STRANGEST EVENT
1989 Champion US lady jockey Julie Krone was involved in an altercation with fellow rider Joe Bravo during and after a race at Meadowlands, New Jersey. She whacked him with her whip after he crowded her. She was later suspended for 15 days and fined $500, while he was suspended for five days and fined $250.

OTHER EVENTS
1777 Bourbon, ridden by John Cade, won the second running of the St Leger, run over 2m, returning 3-1. Ten ran.

1788 The first properly organised race meeting to take place in Middlesex was held on marshes at the bottom of Green Street, Enfield.

1800 Champion became the first horse to land Derby-St Leger double when Frank Buckle partnered the 2-1 chance to triumph at Doncaster.

1948 One of the hottest favourites ever to be beaten, 1-25 Royal Forest is defeated by 33-1 Burpham in the Clarence House Stakes, Ascot.

1975 L'Escargot, the first horse since Golden Miller to complete the Gold Cup-National double, raced for the final time when second at 12-1 in a three-mile chase at Listowel.

1989 US jockey Chris Antley removed from all his mounts at Belmont Park. He later announced he would seek help for 'substance abuse' problem.

1990 Jockey Club announced that two runners at the St Leger meeting, Bravefoot (Dick Hern) and Norwich (Barry Hills), were doped with 'relatively quick acting tranquilliser'. Both were beaten.

1991 Still suffering the after-effects of a 1981 fall, jockey Jimmy Bleasdale retired with 414 winners to his credit.

1994 Peter Scudamore came out of retirement to win Ascot's Shadwell Estates Handicap on Dick Hern's 4-1 shot Wajih. 'It's a bit like going back to school,' he said of the race, for which Hamdan Al Maktoum supplied all eight runners.

2009 Princess Haya announced as Patron for Retraining Racehorses.

QUOTE OF THE DAY
Jockey Graham Gibbons received a 35-day ban in 2007 after becoming the first jockey found over the drink-drive limit when breathalysed at Hamilton Park. *'It's been a wake-up call about whether I wanted to be a pisshead or a jockey. I am a far better jockey than I am pisshead, and it's time to realise I make a lot more money riding horses.'*

BIRTHDAYS
1906 Jockey Charlie Smirke, in Lambeth. Rode 11 Classic winners.

1936 Gerald 'Toby' Balding, trainer of 1992 Gold Cup winner Cool Ground, 1969 and 1989 Grand National winners Highland Wedding and Little Polveir.

1944 Trainer Jeremy Glover, whose Balthus and Rambo's Hall (twice) won the Cambridgeshire.

1970 Channel 4 presenter/exchange betting guru Tanya Stevenson.

FIRST OF THE DAY
1980 Bob Champion rode first winner in England for 16 and a half months after beating cancer when Physicist scored at Fontwell. This was Josh Gifford's 500th winner as a jump trainer.

CELEBRITY OF THE DAY
2000 Twenty-four years after her most recent win there, the Queen Mother had another – her 14th and final – winner at Plumpton as Mick Fitzgerald partnered Brandy Snap to win a novice hurdle.

24 SEPTEMBER

SIGNIFICANT EVENT

1977 English born Sally Ann Bailie became first woman trainer to win $100,000 stakes race when Tequillo Boogie won New York Breeders' Futurity at Finger Lakes, USA. Five years later she became the first woman to saddle $200,000 stakes winner when Fast Gold won the Pegasus at Meadowlands.

STRANGEST EVENT

1994 All race meetings in the south-east of Queensland, Australia postponed after nine of 49-year-old trainer Vic Rail's horses, and five from a nearby yard, died of a mystery disease. The trainer and his foreman were left in a coma in a Brisbane hospital, suffering from a disease believed to be related to that affecting the horses. Rail died on September 27.

OTHER EVENTS

1793 Coincidence backers, if such existed, must have cashed in as the horse with the same name as the year, Ninety Three, was a 15-1 winner of the eight-runner St Leger under William Peirse.

1795 Owner Sir Charles Turner dominated the three-day St Leger meeting, winning the big race itself with Hambletonian, 4-6, on first day. He also landed all but one of seven events held over three days, missing out only in the Corporation Plate, won by Capiscum.

1837 Jockey George Fordham, who went on to ride 16 Classic winners, born in Cambridge. He reportedly weighed just 3st 10lb when winning the 1852 Cambridgeshire on Little David, for which feat he was given a Bible and gold-mounted whip. Died 1887.

1959 Open Goal at Perth was Arthur Stephenson's first winner as a licensed trainer.

1968 Those convinced hotly fancied Honey End was hard done by in the shock 1967 Grand National when 100-1 Foinavon beat the Josh Gifford-partnered runner, felt vindicated when Honey End beat Foinavon in Plumpton's Kingston Chase.

1981 Baronet was given a narrow verdict over Heron's Hollow by judge Michael Hancock, after the two passed the post locked together. Bookmakers and the Tote paid out, then, half an hour later, Hancock reversed the decision, making Bruce Raymond's mount the winner over Brian Rouse's.

1982 Bill Shoemaker rode a double at Ascot, beating Lester Piggott in a match on Prince's Gate, then partnering Rose Du Soir to win a handicap.

1994 Win L F Chung became the first woman to ride a winner in Hong Kong, on 37-1 Free Zone at Sha Tin.

1994 66-1 shot Maroof, the only runner in the race without a Group 1 success, became the biggest priced winner of the Queen Elizabeth II Stakes at Ascot, partnered by Richard Hills, trained by Robert Armstrong.

1995 Champion US jockey Corey Nakatani won on first ride in Britain – Cool Jazz, in Ascot's Diadem Stakes.

QUOTE OF THE DAY

1990 Pas De Reef was brought down during a Hamilton race – by a golf ball from an adjacent course. *'It must have wedged in her foot,'* said shocked jockey Michael Wigham.

BIRTHDAYS

1944 French trainer Alain de Royer-Dupre.

1951 Richard Burridge, scriptwriter, and owner of Desert Orchid.

DEATHS OF THE DAY

1967 Tom Taaffe, father of jockeys Pat and Tos, and trainer of 1958 Grand National winner Mr What.

1992 Japanese rider Takeshi Tamanoi, 20, the 17th jockey fatally injured in Japan since 1954.

25 SEPTEMBER

SIGNIFICANT EVENT
2008 Aidan O'Brien found guilty of breaching rules of racing and fined £5,000 after inquiry into whether team tactics were used when his Duke Of Marmalade won the Juddmonte International at Newmarket. Colm O'Donoghue, riding O'Brien pacemaker Red Rock Canyon, seemed to move off the rail to leave a gap for Johnny Murtagh on Duke Of Marmalade to go through. O'Donoghue and Murtagh were suspended for seven days.

STRANGEST EVENT
2008 Racegoers – myself included– held their breath at Fontwell as a loose horse ran back up the home straight and just missed the mounts of Tony McCoy and Willie McCarthy, driving for the finish.

OTHER EVENTS
1766 First running of a, if not the, Doncaster Cup took place in four-mile heats of four runners. Lord Hamilton's six-year-old Charlotte came out on top after three heats.
1792 Fifth St Leger victory for jockey John Mangle, on Lord Hamilton's Tartar from ten rivals at 25-1.
1793 Mr John Hutchinson's Oberon achieved a feat remarkable even for those days when horses were less mollycoddled than now, winning the four-mile Doncaster Stakes at 4-1, then, an hour later, also winning the four-mile Gold Cup at 2-1, defeating useful opponents, including the previous day's St Leger winner, Ninety Three.
1804 An eventful St Leger saw Vesta fall, seriously injuring jockey Spencer; Sir Bertrand also fell, as did Witchcraft. Sancho, 2-1 favourite, beat the other seven who managed to stay upright.
1849 Perhaps the least interesting race meeting ever, as Kelso's card consisted of one race – a walkover for Elthiron in the Produce Stakes.
1989 BBC Radio 2 listeners were startled to hear the announcement that 2,000 Guineas and Derby winner Nashwan was to run in the Champion Hurdle! The next bulletin corrected the announcement – to Champion Stakes.
1992 Brough Scott broke a losing run of more than 20 years when winning for the first time since 1971 on 9/1 Kitaab.
1993 After 32 years and 56 suspensions, one of Australia's most colourful characters, jockey Malcolm Johnson, bowed out at Randwick, Sydney.
2002 Best known in the jumps sphere, Jonjo O'Neill had a 100 per cent record at Goodwood during the year after Spectroscope won the Merbury Catering Consultants Handicap, having won another race there on August 24.
2004 'If he was human he'd be having serious medication for schizophrenia,' said Alastair Down of Rakti, winner of Ascot's Queen Elizabeth II Stakes.
2009 Ginger Tosser and Naked Ladies complemented racing at Ascot's Beer Festival.

QUOTE OF THE DAY
2007 *'Racing can afford to be indulgent about the picaresque flavours in its reputation, so long as they are confined to Dick Francis or 19th century memoirs.'* Chris McGrath, writing in the *Independent*, on the opening of the Kieren Fallon corruption charge trial.

BIRTHDAYS
1960 Trainer John Hills. He also rode 21 winners as an amateur.
1962 Jockey-turned-trainer Micky Hammond.
1963 Trainer Charles Egerton.
1971 Champion jockey Seb Sanders.

DEATH OF THE DAY
2005 Bloodstock agent Keith Freeman, 88, who bought both Blushing Groom and Grundy.

CELEBRITY OF THE DAY
1978 Birth of model and racing enthusiast Jodie Kidd.

26 SEPTEMBER

SIGNIFICANT EVENT
1814 William gave the Duke of Hamilton his seventh St Leger victory in a race of which it was said in a contemporary report that 'more roguery was practiced by transactions relative to the race previous to the time of running than was ever known'.

STRANGEST EVENT
1990 Ann Boleyn lost her head – when she threw jockey Steven Porter, who ended up in hospital after she crashed through rails at Brighton en route to the start. She ended up at Roedean School for girls being fed bread by pupils.

OTHER EVENTS
1781 No member of the St Leger family ever won that Classic, founded by sportsman Lt General Anthony St Leger. On this day Mr St Leger's brown colt and Colonel St Leger's brown filly – both unnamed – were St Leger also-rans behind winner Serina, ridden by Richard Foster.

1905 Newbury racecourse opened.

1927 Subsequent Champion Hurdle winner Brown Jack won for the first time over those obstacles at Wolverhampton.

1933 Gordon Richards reached 200 winners in a season for the first time on Nevertheless at Newmarket.

1957 Toby Balding sent out first winner, Bowerchalke, at Ascot.

1968 Mill House scored his 17th and last victory, winning at Wincanton.

1987 First British Festival of Racing Day held at Ascot.

1994 17-year-old Alan Eddery rode first winner, Greek Gold, at Southwell, on same day as Uncle Pat rode a Bath treble.

2008 Wolverhampton staged the final of the inaugural William Hill Pacing Championship with 60-year-old Ian Pimlott partnering winner Crown Manhattan, 12-1, to victory in the £12,000 race.

2009 Richard Dunwoody voted off Strictly Come Dancing.

QUOTE OF THE DAY
1848 *'There's three things I can confess to. Since I was 21 I have been drunk almost every night; I never sold a race, which is more than some can say; and I never kissed a lass against her will.'* The recorded last words of 50-year-old jockey Bill Scott, who died today at Highfield, Malton, having ridden 19 Classic winners. Contemporary records suggest that at least the second of those claims was somewhat suspect.

BIRTHDAY
1948 Ian Fry, founder of Horse Racing Abroad travel company.

DEATHS OF THE DAY
1959 Manny Mercer, who rode Happy Laughter to win the 1953 1,000 Guineas, and Darius to win the 1954 2,000 Guineas, died after being thrown by Priddy Fair at Ascot. Born 1930, he was the elder brother of Joe Mercer.

1984 Popular chaser The Dikler put down, aged 21.

1991 Ravinella, 1988 winner of English and French 1,000 Guineas, died at stud while in foal to Nashwan.

2000 Promising Hong Kong apprentice Philip Cheng Cheong-tat, with 25 wins to his credit, died after being kicked in the head and chest by his mount, My Fourth Wishes, three days earlier.

2004 North American jockey Dean Kutz, who rode 2,835 winners, died aged 48.

CELEBRITY OF THE DAY
1982 The Queen completed the purchase of West Ilsley Stables from Sir Michael Sobell and son-in-law Lord Weinstock. The deal was believed to be financed by the sale of Her Majesty's filly Height Of Fashion to Sheikh Hamdan for an estimated £1.4m.

27 SEPTEMBER

SIGNIFICANT EVENT
2008 Curlin became biggest prize-money earner in US history, crashing through $10m barrier in winning Jockey Club Gold Cup at Belmont.

STRANGEST EVENT
1901 US jockey Lester Reiff, English champion in 1900 with 143 winners, was beaten by a head on De Lacy by brother John, riding Minnie Day, at Manchester. Stewards reported Lester to Jockey Club, who subsequently withdrew his licence, and warned him off.

OTHER EVENTS
1791 Young Traveller, who won the Doncaster Gold Cup at the same meeting, beating former Leger winners Spadille, Ambidexter and Pewett, landed the St Leger at 3-1.

1796 Ambrosio, 4-5, won the St Leger for Joseph Cookson, ridden by John Jackson. The next day the horse was beaten in the Gold Cup.

1803 Benjamin Smith rode the first of six St Leger winners when Remembrancer was the 5-4 all-the-way winner against seven rivals.

1813 Run over 1m6f193yds for the first time, the 16-runner St Leger suffered ten false starts before 11-5 favourite Altisidora won, ridden by John Jackson.

1894 Aqueduct's original track opened in Queen's, New York, attracting just 700 people and half a dozen bookies.

1894 The previous season's Triple Crown winner, Isinglass, started at 2-5 for the inaugural Jockey Club Stakes, and carried 10st 2lb to a two-length victory over French challenger Gouvernail.

1926 Bob Lyall enjoyed a good day at Market Rasen, riding four winners and a runner-up. When he died, his ashes were scattered near the winning post at the track.

1966 Trainer Lt Col Wilfred Lyde, in business since end of World War II, announced retirement.

1968 Sandy Barclay rode outsiders in two matches at Ascot and won both, firstly on King Bob, so unfancied that no SP was returned, and Hardiesse, for Noel Murless.

1992 Having 'retired' a fortnight earlier, Gianfranco (Frankie's dad) Dettori turned up to ride at the Capannelle, to bid Roman racing fans farewell. He won his first race there in 1961.

1995 Aidan O'Brien saddled four winners at Listowel en route to setting highest season's total of 177 winners.

1997 After riding all seven winners at the corresponding 1996 Ascot meeting, Frankie Dettori had to make do with just one – Jaseur in the last race.

2003 Aussie trainer John Hawkes sent out five of eight winners at Randwick.

2008 Noel Meade saddled his 2,000th winner when Rinroe won at Navan. His first was Tu Va at Wexford in 1971.

QUOTE OF THE DAY
1993 *'You've got to get them mentally as well as physically fit,'* declared Mark Pitman who, aged 27, announced his retirement from after 267 winners to assist his mother, Jenny Pitman.

BIRTHDAY
1949 Jump jockey-turned-sculptor and steward Philip Blacker. He won the 1979 Triumph Hurdle on Pollardstown.

DEATHS OF THE DAY
1994 Australian trainer Vic Rail, 49, who was based in Queensland, died in unique circumstances. He suffered a heart attack brought on by a virus passed to him that also affected 14 of his horses.

2008 *Racing Post* edition dedicated to Alex Lawrence, a member of the paper's internet team who had died, aged 35, after a short illness.

CELEBRITY OF THE DAY
1957 TV and radio broadcaster John Inverdale born. Part-owner of Champion Hurdle winner Make A Stand, before it won a big race!

28 SEPTEMBER

SIGNIFICANT EVENT
1996 Frankie Dettori smashed and set all kinds of records as he won all seven races at Ascot, nearly putting the nation's bookmakers out of business – punters backing Dettori cost them the best part of £50m. His winners were Wall Street, 2-1; Diffident 12-1; Mark Of Esteem, 10-3; Decorated Hero, 7-1; Fatefully, 7-4; Lochangel 5-4; Fujiyama Crest, 2-1.

STRANGEST EVENT
1993 After 'hiding' his mount in fog in a race before rejoining the action and winning, US jockey Sylvester Carmouche was convicted of perjury after trying to get his licence back. Handed a three-year suspended jail sentence, two years' probation, 720 hours' community service, a $500 fine and payment of court costs.

OTHER EVENTS
1790 George Searle won his third St Leger on Henry Goodricke's 5-1 shot Ambidexter, defeating eight others.

1802 John Singleton jnr partnered Orville to a 5-1 victory in St Leger, beating six others. The 26-year-old jockey died three months later.

1870 Fred Archer rode his first winner under Jockey Club rules, Athol Daisy, at Chesterfield.

1932 Fire destroyed members' stand at Kempton, and with it many of the course's records.

1982 Owner Edwin Johnson caught a flight to Peru – and missed seeing his first winner for 20 years as La Perricholi obliged at Nottingham.

1985 Chester's County Stand, built in 1899, burned down.

1990 Ray Barratt, riding Ruda Cass at Redcar, was suspended for eight days for excessive use of the whip. Two days earlier he was suspended for four days at Pontefract for the same offence on the same horse; on August 29 Gary Hind was suspended for three days for improper use of the whip – on the Roy Robinson-trained Ruda Cass.

1991 US challenger Forty Niner Days finished fifth in Queen Elizabeth II Stakes at Ascot, won by Selkirk.

1992 Owners Ken Higson and Barney Curley protested at Fontwell's 'despicable' prize-money, by withdrawing 9-4 favourite Across The Card, and 2-1 favourite Torwada at the off. Both owners and jockeys Gary Moore and Jason Twomey were fined £1,200 each.

1992 On the final scheduled day of flat racing on turf at Wolverhampton, Steve Cauthen rode last winner, 9-1 shot Iota in West Midlands Handicap.

2008 'Impatient, irritable, opinionated, overweight, misunderstood.' Trainer Mark Johnston in his own words, also admitting to having dressed up as Ozzy Osbourne to attend a fancy-dress party.

QUOTE OF THE DAY
'I've had worse days,' said Richard Hannon, after winning the 2008 Parknasilla Hotel Goffs Million at the Curragh with 5-2 favourite Soul City; and the Parknasilla Hotel Goffs Fillies Million with Minor Vamp, 10-1, from stablemate Baileys Cacao, 9-1. The prize-money from the two races was approximately £1.85m.

BIRTHDAY
1928 Leonard John 'Jack' Holt, trainer of Quortina and Epsom Imp.

DEATHS OF THE DAY
1973 Jockey Joseph Marshall, 65. Rode 33-1 Trigo to win 1929 Derby.

1994 'Jolly' Jim Stanford, 69, of the *Daily Mail*, writing as Captain Heath.

CELEBRITY OF THE DAY
1992 Owner Christine Goulandris, 44, listed by *Business Age* magazine as the wealthiest woman in Britain with a £290m fortune, married the millionaire head of Heinz, Tony O'Reilly, who had horses with Francois Boutin, including the top French performer of Priolo.

29 SEPTEMBER

SIGNIFICANT EVENT
1948 Six horses owned by the wealthy eccentric, Dorothy Paget, and trained by Fulke Walwyn and ridden by Bryan Marshall, ran at Folkestone. Five won – Legal Joy, Langis Son, Jack Tatters, Endless and Loyal King. Loyal Monarch was beaten half a length in the last race.

STRANGEST EVENT
1994 Six horses were withdrawn from a five-furlong sprint at Newmarket when the gates twice broke open by mistake due to an electrical fault. The race had to be started by flag.

OTHER EVENTS
1879 W R Brockton had a good day at Market Rasen, winning three of four races and finishing third in the other – even though he rode only two horses all afternoon. He won twice on Moorhen, then on the impolitely named Hopeless, before finishing third on the same horse.
1967 Ascot's first charity day, run in aid of St John Ambulance, also featured the course's first sponsored Flat race, the five-furlong Joynson Commodity Stakes, won by 5-1 So Blessed, ridden by Frank Durr and trained by J Thompson.
1979 Henry Cecil trained Kris, 8/11, who won 14 of 16 starts, won the Queen Elizabeth II Stakes under Joe Mecer at Ascot.
1984 Robert Williams rode eight winners from ten rides at Lincoln, Nebraska.
1984 Met Officer won at Market Rasen to open the career account of jump jockey Simon Cowley.
1989 Sheikh Hamdan Al Maktoum owned all six runners turning out for the Shadwell Estate Sweepstakes at Ascot. The race was run to raise cash for charity; the riders were ex-jockeys then on BBC and C4. The 8-11 shot Wabil, ridden by Jimmy Lindley, defeated Polemos, 7-1, ridden by Bill Smith; third was Hateel, 8-1, ridden by Lord Oaksey.
2009 David Nicholls saddled Amenable, 100/1, to win at Southwell. In 1991 Nicholls' wife Alex Greaves was the first woman to win Lincoln – on a horse called Amenable.

QUOTE OF THE DAY
One of the best colts of the day, Escape, made his debut in 1788, winning a match with Feenoli at Newmarket. He was originally sold by the Prince of Wales for 95gns to a Mr Franco, and was named when the owner exclaimed, *'Oh, what an escape!'* on being told by a groom that the horse had been extricated after kicking out in his box and embedding his fetlock in the woodwork. He was re-purchased two years later by the Prince for 1,500gns.

BIRTHDAYS
1920 Somerset trainer Les Kennard, known for training Cantlie, Highland Abbe, Stradivarius and Walnut Wonder.
1922 Roy Cambidge, the trainer of Roaring Wind and Java Fox.
1937 Jockey Jock Skilling.
1973 Marchand D'Or's jockey Davy Bonilla.

DEATHS OF THE DAY
1997 Trainer George Owen, 89. He trained Russian Hero to win the 1949 Grand National, and also rode Brendan's Cottage to win the 1939 Cheltenham Gold Cup.
1998 Gordon W Richards, 68, trainer of popular chaser One Man.

FIRST OF THE DAY
1721 A race took place at Annapolis, Maryland for which the first prize was eight silver spoons, and four of the same for second.

30 SEPTEMBER

SIGNIFICANT EVENT
1961 The first jockey to break the 10,000-winner barrier, Brazilian Jorge Ricardo, born in Rio de Janeiro.

STRANGEST EVENT
1897 The Welter Handicap at Newmarket became first race in Britain started by means of starting gate – a single strand tape barrier. The race was won by Meditation, trained by classic winning John Watts.

OTHER EVENTS
1959 Johnny Gilbert set the winning sequence record for a jump jockey of ten consecutive winners, having ridden first on September 8.

1978 Stetchworth reared and nearly threw jockey Taffy Thomas as the runners came under orders for the first at Redcar. Thomas held on and the combination won. After the race gunshot marks were found on the horse's rump – he had been shot at by youths hidden in long grass.

1982 English-born trainer Sally Ann Bailie became first woman to train $200,000 stakes race winner when Fast Gold won Pegasus Stakes at Meadowlands.

1983 Seventeen-year-old apprentice Ian Shoemark became the first jockey to ride a winner in the royal colours in his first race when partnering Insular to a Newmarket victory.

1984 George Rhodes picked all seven winners in his 5p ITV7 bet, landing world record odds of 1,670,759-1. His winnings were £86,056.42 and I visited his Aldershot home to present his William Hill cheque. 'What will you do with the money?' I asked. 'Buy a new Rolls-Royce,' said the retired businessman. 'Mine is getting on a bit.'

1990 Bill Shoemaker trained first Graded stakes winner when Baldomero won Golden Harvest Handicap at Louisiana Downs.

1992 Blyton Lad, owned by John and Jenny Addleshaw, won Rous Stakes at Newmarket for third straight year, each time with a different trainer.

1993 Record Tote Jackpot of £273,366 won for £1 stake. On the same day, Annie Elsey, daughter of trainer Charlie, rode first winner, Rapporteur, who was winning for the 17th time at Lingfield.

1995 Further Flight became the first horse to win same Pattern race five times, winning the Jockey Club Cup at Newmarket.

1995 Cap Juluca, 11/1, trained by Roger Charlton and ridden by Richard Hughes, set record weight-carrying performance in Cambridgeshire under 9st 10lb.

QUOTE OF THE DAY
'*Wrestling, hang-gliding, skiing and stamp collecting.*' The extraordinary collection of recreations listed in the *1990 Directory of the Turf* by Northampton amateur jockey Julia 'Tik' Saunders, born this day in 1961.

BIRTHDAYS
1937 *London Evening Standard* racing writer and famed trencherman, Christopher Poole.

1958 600 winner jockey turned trainer Michael Wigham.

1958 Meath trainer Suzanne Finn, the first woman elected to the Irish Racehorse Trainers' Committee.

DEATHS OF THE DAY
1962 The week before he was due to partner Val De Loir in the Arc, jockey Georges Chancelier was killed in a car accident.

1994 Trainer Alex Scott, 34, in a shooting incident at Glebe House Stud, Newmarket.

CELEBRITY OF THE DAY
2000 Holiday camp proprietor Sir Fred Pontin died, 93. His Specify – Pontin was refused permission to rename the horse Specify Pontins – won the 1971 National as he became a champion owner.

1 OCTOBER

SIGNIFICANT EVENT
2000 Sinndar added the Prix de l'Arc de Triomphe to his Derby and Irish Derby victories for the Aga Khan. The horse was immediately retired.

STRANGEST EVENT
1885 Mr Robert Vyner's Minting was fancied to win the Produce Stakes at Newmarket, starting 1/100 to defeat his two rivals. Ridden by Fred Archer, the horse scrambled home by three-quarters of a length from Charioteer. Trainer Mat Dawson still considered him unbeatable but suffered a rude awakening when Minting was defeated by Ormonde in the 2,000 Guineas. Dawson stormed from the course and retired to bed, sulking.

OTHER EVENTS
1765 The Marquis of Rockingham's Bay Malton beat Lord Bolingbroke's Gimcrack in a match for the 1,000 Guineas at Newmarket. Gimcrack later twice avenged that defeat and raced until the age of 12, winning 26 of her 36 races.
1843 The very first edition of the *News of the World* contained details of betting on the Cesarewitch and of October meetings due to take place at Wrexham, Welshpool and Ashby-de-la-Zouch.
1873 The final meeting was held at Bedford, where they had raced since 1774.
1891 W Sharp became the first New Zealand jockey to ride six winners in a day, at Kurow.
1901 The reigning champion jockey, the American Lester Reiff, was warned off by the Jockey Club after they decided he had stopped De Lacy at Manchester so his brother might win on Minnie Dee for US politician/owner 'Boss' Croker.
1979 Gordon W Richards saddled five winners at Carlisle.
1990 Ferret fan Michael Hammond saddled his first treble – Choice Challenge, Azusa, Tignanello at Carlisle – which paid 76/1
1991 Willie Carson rode five winners at Newcastle for a 539/1 accumulator.

1993 Races with only three declared runners at the overnight stage will henceforth be reopened, announced the BHB, with horses declared at the five-day stage invited to re-enter.
1994 Prince Edward opened the new £2m grandstand at Uttoxeter.
1994 Random drug testing of jockeys began.
1995 Frankie Dettori won the Arc on Derby winner Lammtarra, who was then retired undefeated. On the same card, the Joe Naughton-trained Hever Golf Rose won the Prix de l'Abbaye to set a post-war record of eight wins in a season for a British-trained filly/mare aged four or above. Her win extended France's losing run in the Abbaye to 17 years.
1995 Brighton staged the first meeting sponsored by a political party when Labour backed the meeting to launch their party conference, which was being held in the town. Jockeys were offered a £1,000 bonus if they used the newly invented 'equine-friendly' air-cushioned latex whip in Brighton's 11-runner Daily Mirror Handicap. None of the 11 jockeys took up the offer.
2008 Nottingham's meeting was delayed by an hour as only one of the requisite two medical officers had turned up.

QUOTE OF THE DAY
'The considerations of the punter come second. It's the owner who pays my wages,' declared Lynda Ramsden (born today 1949), the Thirsk-based trainer of controversial Top Cees, in a 1997 interview.

BIRTHDAYS
1934 John Tyrrel, Channel 4 commentator and racing historian.
1947 Hugh Collingridge, dual-purpose trainer of Buzzards Bay (1982 Royal Hunt Cup) and Stormont.

CELEBRITY OF THE DAY
1925 Former US President Jimmy Carter, a keen owner, was born.

2 OCTOBER

SIGNIFICANT EVENT
2005 Even by Kieren Fallon's standards this was a spectacular day as he won three straight Group 1 races at Longchamp, with Rumplestiltskin, Horatio Nelson and culminating in Hurricane Run's win in the Arc. 'I was lucky. I was on good horses. That's really the top and bottom of it.'

STRANGEST EVENT
1990 Veteran owner Frank Hill, 87, celebrated his 114th winner, Saysana at Brighton. Racegoers were astonished to see him at the races, as *The Daily Telegraph* had just printed his obituary.

OTHER EVENTS
1911 Laurel racetrack, in Maryland, USA, held its first meeting.

1965 Irish jockey Tommy Stack rode his first winner, New Money, at Wetherby.

1972 Having waited since 4 August to achieve it, Pat Rohan finally saddled his 500th winner when 9/1 shot Persian Palm won at Wolverhampton.

1981 The BBC dropped its Triella bet, which had required punters to find the first and second in three selected consecutive races.

1991 Darren O'Sullivan rode Karakter Reference, trained by his uncle Roland, to win the first race on Cheltenham's new park course, a handicap chase.

1991 The Geoff Wragg-trained Young Senor, 14/1, landed a £500,000 bonus by winning Newmarket's Highflyer Stakes.

1992 All five runners in the Keilder Handicap Chase at Hexham took the wrong course and ended up on the spur of track used only on the final circuit of the chase course. Lorcan Wyer, on Chain Shot, was the first to realize and shouted to the others, and they all retraced their steps. Spree Cross, ridden by Kenny Johnson, won the race.

1993 Further Flight won the same Pattern race, the Jockey Club Cup, for a third successive year, matching Sagaro's achievement in the Ascot Gold Cup

and Sharpo's in the William Hill Sprint Championship at York.

1993 Michael Kinane broke the record for most wins by a jockey in an Irish Flat season when riding a double at the Curragh to set a new mark of 114.

1994 French-trained horses filled the first three places in the Arc, with victory going to Carnegie, ridden by Thierry Jarnet and trained by Andre Fabre. Carnegie's dam, Detroit, was the first Arc winner to give birth to an Arc winner.

1994 Punters yelled abuse at trainer David Hayes and jockey Grant Cooksley after a horse owned in partnership by Robert Sangster was the 25/1 winner of the A$450,000 Metropolitan at Randwick, Sydney, having run last of 18 on its previous outing. Police intervened as the protests became unruly.

1996 Martin Pipe saddled five of the six winners at Exeter.

2004 Mark Johnston was impressed by his Sun Chariot Stakes winner, Attraction, who he described as, 'The best horse I've ever trained – there's no shadow of a doubt.' Earlier in the season, she had won the 1,000 Guineas.

QUOTE OF THE DAY
2008 '*The committed racing people might cut back, but they don't drop out. The ones that drop out are the ones who were looking for an excuse to get out.*' Trainer Chris Wall considering the effects of the recession.

BIRTHDAYS
1952 US trainer Steve Penrod.

1985 Jockey Alan Garcia.

DEATH OF THE DAY
1990 Pioneer female jump trainer Posy Lewis, 83. Her father, Capt Morel, was a founder of Chepstow racecourse.

CELEBRITY OF THE DAY
1951 Owner Gordon Sumner, whose Sandalay won several times, was born. He is better known as rock star Sting, lead singer with The Police.

3 OCTOBER

SIGNIFICANT EVENT
1995 Sheikh Mohammed took his horses away from Henry Cecil after a row over an injury to Mark Of Esteem.

STRANGEST EVENT
1946 Jockey Dick Black and trainer John de Moraville won with King Penguin at Ludlow – the first winner for the pair after they agreed a partnership while together as German POWs.

OTHER EVENTS
1770 Eclipse started at 1/70 and beat his sole rival, Corsican, who was owned by Sir Charles Bunbury. It was the last time Eclipse actually competed against another equine.

1810 Maria, a bay filly owned by W R Johnson, raced an astonishing 20 miles in winning a race. The Fairfield Jockey Club Purse of $500 at Richmond, USA, attracted five runners and produced two dead-heats in a row before it was necessary to run three further four-mile heats to reveal a winner.

1933 Gordon Richards rode the fifth-race winner Barnby at Nottingham, then rode all six at Chepstow the next day and the first five on the following day to set a record of 12 consecutive winners.

1934 Mr Theo West of Louth put up 33lb overweight in partnering Cornafulla at Market Rasen. He had wagered that he would complete the course and, weighing out at 13st 2lb – he came in third.

1948 Charlie Smirke rode the Aga Khan's Migoli to win the Prix de l'Arc de Triomphe.

1954 Sica Boy won the Arc, ridden by the oldest jockey in the race, Rae Johnstone (nearly 50), and trained by the youngest handler, Pierre Pelat.

1981 Baronet, the Cambridgeshire winner in 1978 and 1980, was runner-up this time to 50/1 shot Braughing, trained by Clive Brittain and ridden by Steve Cauthen.

1992 Jeremy Glover trained the Cambridgeshire winner for a third time as 9/2 favourite Rambo's Hall landed his second win in the race (he had won at 15/1 in 1989), partnered by Dean McKeown. Balthus, 50/1, also won for Glover in 1987, and the trainer won it again in 1996 with Clifton Fox, 14/1.

1993 Eric Saint-Martin, son of the great Yves, won his first Arc on Urban Sea, on his first ride in the race.

2004 After his Bago had won the Arc, trainer Jonathan Pease settled a score with the *Racing Post*'s James Willoughby. 'Willoughby poured cold water on it, but I should know my horses better than he does. He is the best I have trained,' Pease said.

2008 Johnny Murtagh rode his 19th Group 1 winner of the season as 15/8 favourite Bushranger won Newmarket's Middle Park Stakes for trainer David Wachman.

QUOTE OF THE DAY
2009 '*I have to say a big thank you to the chafer bugs,*' said Simon Dow after his Kaleo won at Epsom in 1m 2f race which was only scheduled when insect infestation of grass caused cancellation of all sprints at the track.

BIRTHDAYS
1922 Three-times champion apprentice, Ken Mullins.

1951 Jockey turned agent, John Suthern, who twice rode the winner of the Belgian National.

DEATH OF THE DAY
1995 Hampshire-based trainer Jack Holt, aged 67. He won the Cornwallis Stakes at Ascot with Argentum, the joint-top two-year-old of 1989, and his grey filly Quortina was a prolific winner at Windsor in 1970.

CELEBRITY OF THE DAY
1981 The Prince of Wales enjoyed his first success as an owner when Richard Linley rode the Nick Gaselee-trained Good Prospect to victory at Chepstow.

4 OCTOBER

SIGNIFICANT EVENT
1871 John Scott, born 1794, perhaps the greatest-ever northern trainer, died this day. In 46 years at Whitewall Stables at Malton, he sent out 16 St Leger winners, five Derby winners, nine Oaks winners, four 1,000 Guineas winners – oh, and seven 2,000 Guineas winners. He boasted an odd souvenir of his 1829 Leger winner, Rowton – a knife with a handle made from the shank bone of the horse.

STRANGEST EVENT
1986 Morning Star tipster Cayton – Alf Rubin – breated a sigh of relief as 4/9 Suhailie won a three-horse race. His first after 57 consecutive losers!

OTHER EVENTS
1770 Eclipse made his final racecourse appearance, which resulted in his 21st victory in as many races, albeit in a walkover after he scared off all opposition. Hordes turned out to see the first equine superstar for the last time. He went to stud at Clay Hill, near Epsom, at a fee of 50 guineas and sired the winners of 862 races worth £158,047.
1927 One of the world's most prolific jockeys, John Longden, rode his first winner – Hugo K Asker, at Salt Lake City.
1953 La Sorellina became the first filly to win the Arc since Corrida in 1937. Dam of the winner and runner-up, Silnet, was Silver Jill.
1959 Lycaste II was the first runner trained by a woman – Sweden's Brita Strokirk – to contest the Arc and finished 18th of 25 at 120/1, behind 17/1 winner St Crespin (ridden by George Moore, trained by Alec Head and owned by Prince Aly Khan). Midnight Sun had dead-heated for first place but was disqualified for bumping.
1964 One million francs, plus 78% of the entry fees, was the reward for Prince Royal II's 16/1 Arc win.
1970 Nijinsky (Lester Piggott) suffered his first defeat, beaten in the Arc by Yves Saint-Martin's 19/1 winner Sassafras.
1992 Arazi, whose reputation had become somewhat tarnished, managed a win in the Prix du Rond-Point at Longchamp on the same day as Subotica, trained by Andre Fabre and partnered by Thierry Jarnet, won the Arc.
1994 Tony McCoy landed his first winner over fences on Bonus Boy at Newton Abbot.
1996 Chief Gale, 6/4 favourite for a race at Hexham, paid £20.20 on the Tote – for a place, after finishing second of five.
1997 Having landed a huge gamble in the Magnet Cup in July, Pasternak landed an even bigger one, a six-figure coup, by winning the Cambridgeshire for owner Graham Rock, of the Racing Post, and trainer Sir Mark Prescott. Backed from 11/1 to 4/1 favourite.
2008 John Gosden saddled his third Cambridgeshire winner as 25/1 outsider Tazeez came home under Richard Hills.
2008 Five-year-old mare Peppers Pride, 1/5, trained by Joel Marr, set a new record for consecutive US victories since 1900 when winning for the 17th straight time at Zia Park, New Mexico.

QUOTE OF THE DAY
'Joe Mercer will go down in the annals of the turf as the best jockey never to have won the Epsom Derby,' wrote Richard Baerlein of the eminent pipe-smoker, who was aboard the first female-trained Arc runner on this day in 1959.

BIRTHDAY
1945 Trainer Gavin Pritchard-Gordon. Ardoon won 1975 Royal Hunt Cup.

DEATHS OF THE DAY
1866 Jockey Henry Grimshaw, 25, who rode Gladiateur to win the 1865 Triple Crown, was killed, when the trap he was driving home to Newmarket, after racing, overturned in the dark.
1989 Secretariat, the 1973 Triple Crown winner and one of the all-time greats of American racing, was put down, aged 19.

5 OCTOBER

SIGNIFICANT EVENT
1933 Gordon Richards completed his record 12 consecutive winners, begun on 3 October at Nottingham. His final winner at Chepstow was an unnamed filly by Hurry On in the Hughes-Morgan Nursery.

STRANGEST EVENT
1950 The gallops at Maisons-Laffitte were littered with broken glass as a French stable lads' strike raged for three days before the Arc was due to take place. One head lad was kidnapped by strikers and locked up, but tempers cooled in time for the Arc to be run.

OTHER EVENTS
1952 Lester Piggott, 16, had his first ride in France, finishing unplaced on Bagnoles De L'Orne on Arc day.

1958 Ballymoss, ridden by Scobie Breasley and trained by Vincent O'Brien, won the Arc at 39-10. He was the first Irish winner of the race and victory took his total earnings to £98,650, surpassing the previous record of £76,417 by Tulyar.

1969 Lester Piggott was second on Park Top in the Arc behind Bill 'Weary Willie' Williamson on Levmoss.

1970 Trainer Michael Kane was disqualified from training for life following positive drug tests on three of his horses – Ayr winner Jynxy, Hamilton winner Golden Duck and Teesside winner Sontana. All tested positive for caffeine. Kane denied any wrongdoing.

1970 Owner David Robinson equalled the 1873 record of C J Lefevre when a Wolverhampton double gave him 105 winners for the season.

1991 Peter Niven rode the first five winners at Kelso and was offered the ride on the favourite, Rawan, in the last, but the stewards refused to allow the switch. Graham McCourt kept the ride on Rawan, and won.

1991 The first three home in the 29-runner Cambridgeshire were all trained by women, for the first time.

Mary Reveley saddled Mellottie, 10/1, to win from High Premium, 14/1, and Vague Dancer, 40/1, who were both trained by Lynda Ramsden.

1991 'Arazi is not just the best horse I have ever owned – he's the best horse anyone has ever owned,' claimed Allen Paulson after his colt won for the sixth successive time in the Grand Criterium at Longchamp.

1992 Sue Causton, 35, made history when she became the first female member of the starting stalls team.

1994 Having saddled his final winner on September 17, legendary trainer Vincent O'Brien confirmed his retirement.

1994 Ed Dunlop, who took over the licence at Oak Stables, Newmarket, following the murder of Alex Scott, sent out his first runner, Lynton Lad, who was unplaced at York.

1994 Lester Piggott rode his final British winner, Palacegate Jack, at Haydock.

1997 Peintre Celebre, ridden by Olivier Peslier, won the Arc by five lengths in record time.

2008 Zarkava, the 13/8 favourite, became the first filly to win the Arc since Urban Sea in 1993. The unbeaten filly's win heralded the end of Andre Fabre's 21-year domination as French champion trainer, as Zarkava's trainer, Alain de Royer-Dupre, 63, took his year's total prize-money to more than E5m.

QUOTE OF THE DAY
2008 'This jumps well,' Mick Fitzgerald's response to the question, 'What's the worst thing anyone's ever said to you?'

BIRTHDAY
1939 Barney Curley – owner, lapsed priest, trainer, confidant to Frankie Dettori, self-styled punters' champion, coup organiser and charity fundraiser.

DEATH OF THE DAY
2007 Jockey Roddy Reid, 63. He won the County Hurdle at the Cheltenham Festival on Cool Alibi in 1967.

6 OCTOBER

SIGNIFICANT EVENT
1963 The Arc was run for the final time without starting stalls as 36-10 second favourite Exbury won by two lengths under J Deforge for trainer G Watson and owner Baron Guy de Rothschild, who collected F900,000 plus 78% of entry fees. Exbury never raced again, having won eight of 16 races and a European record £156,161.

STRANGEST EVENT
1957 Despite serving in the French army at the time, Serge Boullenger rode Oroso to a 52/1 Arc victory.

OTHER EVENTS
1956 Eddie 'Banana Nose' Arcaro, 40, and fellow US rider Sam Boulmetis, 29, with 5,500 winners between them, acclimatised themselves to French racing by riding in the Prix des Fortifications, with Arcaro falling, while Boulmetis finished third. The following day Arcaro was fourth in the Arc on Career Boy with Boulmetis ninth on Fisherman.
1979 Triple Crown winner Affirmed ended career with 22nd win in 29 starts in Belmont's Jockey Club Gold Cup
1989 A mystery punter arrived at Hexham by helicopter and backed 4/5, 2/5, 1/4 and 1/4 losers, dropping £100,000 in the process, before flying off again.
1991 Suave Dancer, 37/10, partnered by Cash Asmussen, won the 14-runner Arc for trainer John Hammond. Derby winner Generous was eighth, despite starting 9/10 favourite.
1993 Haydock's meeting was cut short after two races when groundsman Alan Fyles spotted a large hole in the middle of the track, believed to be caused by subsidence. Earlier on the card Philgun was trainer Bill Elsey's 800th career winner on the Flat.
1997 Seb Sanders rode 100 winners in a season for the first time.
2004 'He was like a father to me. Without him I probably wouldn't still be

in the game – he was always there when I went off the rails.' Kieren Fallon paying tribute to mentor and trainer Jimmy FitzGerald (see below).
2006 The second scheduled date for the opening of Great Leighs racecourse in Essex. The date was missed and the opening was put back until 22 February 2007.

QUOTE OF THE DAY
'I anticipate we will not only see Group 1 horses running on artificial surfaces in Britain, but will also be staging Group 1 races on these surfaces,' predicted Ian Renton, representing the racecourse group that operated three all-weather tracks in the UK, looking ahead seven years on this day in 2008.

BIRTHDAYS
1867 Thomas Loates, champion jockey in 1889, 1890 and 1893. He rode six Classic winners, including 1893 Triple Crown winner Isinglass, and also rode, astonishingly, 222 winners in 1893.
1941 Trainer Gavin Hunter.
1947 Newmarket trainer Jeff Pearce.
1966 Niall Quinn, international footballer turned Sunderland supremo, and owner of Cois Na Tine.

DEATHS OF THE DAY
1949 Col Matt J Winn, 88, credited with making the Kentucky Derby one of the world's great races as Churchill Downs president from 1938 to 1949. He witnessed the first 75 runnings.
2004 Jimmy Fitzgerald, 69. Born in Ireland, he rode 223 winners, including Brasher, winner of the last Scottish National run at Bogside, in 1965. He twice fractured his skull. In 1985 he trained the Cheltenham Gold Cup winner, Forgive 'N Forget.

CELEBRITY OF THE DAY
1930 Top cricketer turned commentator Richie Benaud, an owner with Syd Dale, was born.

7 OCTOBER

SIGNIFICANT EVENT
2007 Kieren Fallon rode Dylan Thomas to win the Arc for Aidan O'Brien, beating Mick Channon's Youmzain into second – the position he would occupy again in 2008 and 2009. The pair had finished in the same positions in Ascot's King George and Queen Elizabeth Stakes earlier in the season.

STRANGEST EVENT
1992 At York, Fetchinni collapsed and died in the stalls prior to the start of the Micklegate Selling Stakes. The horse came under orders, so was officially a runner. He was trained by Alan Bailey; incredibly, the last time there had been a similar incident, on 7 July at Pontefract, it was another Bailey horse, O'Donnells Folly, who had died in the stalls.

OTHER EVENTS
1816 Eperston, owned by Lord Queensberry, won the first race held at Edinburgh racecourse – a four-mile event run in three heats.

1951 Tantieme, the 17-10 favourite, again ridden by Jacques Doyasbere, trained by Francois Mathet and owned by Francois Dupre, won the Arc for the second successive year.

1956 Ribot, ridden as usual by Enrico Camici, won his 16th successive race and his second successive Arc at 6/10. He was then retired undefeated.

1962 Six Classic winners from five countries were among 24 runners in the Arc. None won as 40/1 Soltikoff, ridden by Marcel Depalmas, won by a length.

1973 Chris Collins partnered Stephen's Society, his own horse, to become the first Englishman to win the fearsome Czech marathon chase, the Velka Pardubicka, founded in 1874 and also known at the time as the 'Iron Curtain Grand National'.

1978 Hong Kong's Sha Tin racecourse staged its first meeting. The course was built on a 250-acre site reclaimed from Sha Tin Bay.

1978 Six-year-old Baronet won the Cambridgeshire for trainer John Benstead – and would do so again two years later. On the same card Paul Kelleway's Swiss Maid won the Sun Chariot Stakes and Buckskin, recently moved from Peter Walwyn to Henry Cecil by Daniel Wildenstein, won the Jockey Club Stakes.

1981 Lumen won at Cheltenham, giving rider Bob Champion his 400th winner.

1989 Cash Asmussen rode five winners at Longchamp – a record four of them in Group races – and was second twice.

1989 Trainer Roger Curtis saddled Androbote to win the Isle of Wight Stakes at Goodwood at 100/1.

1989 Jockey Dean McKeown won the Cambridgeshire on 15/1 Rambo's Hall to celebrate daughter Hayley's second birthday.

1991 There was a triple dead-heat at Belmont Park, USA, when Scorecard Harry, Space Appeal and Café Lex proved inseparable in a 6f race – the first such result in New York since 1944.

QUOTE OF THE DAY
2007 *'I've eaten horse. We eat lamb and chicken, after all. If it's legal, why not?'* A peckish Frankie Dettori.

BIRTHDAY
1937 Jack Berry, in Leeds. Among the best-known winners for the red-shirted trainer were Touch Boy, Paris House and O I Oyston. He was the first to carry commercial advertising on his horsebox, and is an indefatigable fundraiser for racing charities.

DEATH OF THE DAY
2005 Richard Stone Reeves, 85, the noted American equine artist.

CELEBRITY OF THE DAY
1949 The Queen's first runner, Astrakhan (Willie Smyth-Tommy Burns), was runner-up in the Sandwell Stakes at Ascot.

8 OCTOBER

SIGNIFICANT EVENT

1939 Owner, trainer and gambler Robert Sievier, whose self-trained Sceptre won four Classics in 1902 and finished fourth in the Derby, died, aged 79. In 1902 he had become the first owner-trainer to head the list of winning owners with earnings of £23,686. He ran a newspaper called *Winning Post*, in which he poked fun at, and made sinister allegations about, racing figures of the day.

STRANGEST EVENT

1967 Bill Pyers rode Topyo for trainer Mick Bartholomew to land an 81-1 shock Arc triumph. Pyers ended up in prison after a TV viewer recognised him as the driver of a car that had collided with her vehicle 15 months earlier. The rider had failed to attend the court hearing and was jailed in his absence for three months.

OTHER EVENTS

1950 Tantieme, 5/2, won the Arc for the first time, before following up in 1951.
1961 Sir Winston Churchill's High Hat, 60/1, partnered by Duncan Keith, finished fourth in the Arc. The race was won by Enrico Camici on the Italian-trained Molvedo, 18/10, who was sired by the great Ribot.
1985 Misty Halo, trained by Mark Prescott, set a then record of 21 wins by a filly or mare on the Flat when winning at Brighton. The previous record-holder was Granville Greta, with 18 wins between 1959 and 1965.
1991 Walter Swinburn was about to pass the post in front on 3/1 Hamanaka in a maiden at Redcar when his saddle slipped and he fell, breaking his wrist and collarbone; three months earlier he had done the same at Yarmouth.
1995 Charlie Mann won the Velka Pardubicka on It's A Snip, which he also trained, in the Czech Republic. The 37-year-old then retired from the saddle, having ridden 149 winners in 14 years.

He had retired before, after breaking his neck in a fall at Warwick in 1989.
1998 New racecourse betting regulations were introduced, to be phased in by 2000. The measures required bookmakers to display maximum liabilities, put up prices at least 10 minutes before the race, and tape-record bets.
2008 A report revealed that during 2007, 233,161 horses contested 154,498 Flat and jump races, with 1,500 racecourses producing a betting turnover of €19bn.

QUOTE OF THE DAY

1939 '*I may be pure, but I'm damned if I'm simple,*' stormed bookie/gambler/trainer/owner Bob Sievier, a Barney Curley-style maverick who died on this day. He was responding to a newspaper description of him as 'a gambler pure and simple'.

BIRTHDAYS

1940 Des Cullen, who won the 1967 Stewards' Cup on Sky Diver and the 1971 Cambridgeshire on King Midas. He was forced to retire in 1977, and became a jockeys' valet.
1952 Jim Ryerson, trainer of Unbridled's Song.
1984 Jockey Tom Queally.

DEATHS OF THE DAY

1998 Former jockey Johnny Haine, 55, was found dead.
2003 Trainer Ken Cundell, 88, a big early influence on Lester Piggott. Cundell began to give him rides – in 1951, aged 15, Piggott rode Barnacle to win the Great Metropolitan Handicap.
2007 US great John Henry, 32, winner of a record 25 Graded stakes, 16 of them Grade 1 races. He retired with earnings of $6,597,947.

CELEBRITY OF THE DAY

1941 Rev Jesse Jackson, firebrand US politician, was born. He became the joint manager of the US Jockeys' Guild.

9 OCTOBER

SIGNIFICANT EVENT
1992 Richard Hannon sent out 20/1 Brigante Di Cielo to win at Ascot, where Bold Pursuit in the Mayflower Apprentice Stakes made him the first Flat trainer to have 1,000 runners in a season.

STRANGEST EVENT
1889 Signorina, 4/6, won the Middle Park Stakes. He was later mated with a horse called Chaleureux because the eccentric Italian Chevalier Ginistrelli believed they were in love. He must have been right, because their offspring, Signorinetta, won the Derby and Oaks.

OTHER EVENTS
1955 Ribot, partnered by Enrico Camici, was the first Italian Arc winner since Crapom in 1933, though he had been born in Britain. Lester Piggott won for the first time in France, riding Patras, 17/1, to victory in the Prix St Moran.
1990 The two-year-old Sacque smashed the all-age record time for 5f at Folkestone, beating the previous mark of 58.5s by 0.1s.
1991 Mikey Heaton-Ellis, who had been paralysed in a 1981 Huntingdon fall, was granted a licence to train.
1991 Darryll Holland set a post-war record of 76 winners in a season for an apprentice, when Merryhill Maid won at York.
1992 Golden oldies day at Belmont Park, where 82-year-old owner Thomas Mellon Evans' Pleasant Tap won the Jockey Club Gold Cup, 85-year-old Paul Mellon's Sea Hero took the Champagne Stakes and 95-year-old Fred Hooper's Roman Envoy landed the Kelso Handicap.
1994 Carolyn Poland, wife of owner-breeder Michael, won on her first race, partnering Sea Buck to victory in the 325th Newmarket Town Plate, over three and three-quarter miles, to claim the famous prize of Newmarket sausages.
2008 Returning to the saddle after suffering a serious head injury seven weeks before, which required four hours of surgery, Joe Tizzard was back on the winning trail on Rudivale at Wincanton.
2008 Frances Crowley, the first female trainer to saddle an Irish Classic winner (Saoire in the 2005 Irish 1,000 Guineas), announced she was retiring.

QUOTE OF THE DAY
2008 *'If, for example, the fees are £1,000, the scamster wants to send the trainer £10,000 and then what ultimately comes is that he asks for the balance to be sent to him, or be picked up by one of his representatives. In the meantime the cheque, money order or whatever is made worthless.'* The National Trainers' Federation issued a warning to members about an internet scam emanating from the African Republic of Benin. Trainers would be approached to train a horse for scamster, who then said that because of problems moving money out of the country he would send them a cheque for far more than the cost of training the horse. The trainer was then told to send back the excess but, once he did so, the scamster's cheque was stopped, leaving the trusting trainer out of pocket.

BIRTHDAYS
1948 Ian Watkinson, who rode Sea Pigeon to win the 1977 Embassy Handicap Hurdle and the 1978 Fighting Fifth Hurdle.
1949 Somerset trainer Gerald Ham, who was also a pig farmer – really.

DEATH OF THE DAY
1991 Former jump jockey Bryan Marshall, 75. He rode consecutive Grand National winners for Vincent O'Brien (Early Mist and Royal Tan in 1953 and 1954) and was champion jockey in 1947-48 with 66 winners.

CELEBRITY OF THE DAY
1966 David Cameron, Conservative Party leader and occasional racegoer, was born.

10 OCTOBER

SIGNIFICANT EVENT
1866 An early example of race sponsorship as William Blenkiron, of Middle Park Stud, Eltham, Kent, put up £1,000 to support the Middle Park Stakes at Newmarket, which was won on its first running by 4/1 The Rake, ridden by Jack Loates.

STRANGEST EVENT
1993 Peter Scudamore rode 48 horses, only two of them more than once, en route to covering 200 miles (50 times round a four-mile circuit at Newmarket) in 8h 37m 51s to smash by 4m 9s the historic record of eccentric 19th century racing legend, Squire Osbaldeston.

OTHER EVENTS
1950 Ayr held its first jumps meeting.
1973 Peter Walwyn saddled Deliverance to win at Lingfield, giving the trainer his 84th winner of the season, beating Capt Charles Elsey's post-war record. Walwyn ended up with 87.
1974 Jockey Sandy Hawley rode seven winners from nine rides at Woodbine, Canada. He had achieved the same feat on May 22, 1972.
1990 Trainer Karl Burke saddled his first winner, Temporale at Towcester. On the same day Pat Eddery booted home a 1,028/1 five-timer at York, all for different trainers.
1992 Richard Dunwoody won the Breeders' Cup Chase on Jonathan Sheppard's Highland Bud, who had also won the race in 1989.
1992 South African jockey Michael Roberts announced he would take out British citizenship during 1993.
2008 Two plates from Ladbrokes World Hurdle winner Inglis Drever were sold for £220 in a charity auction raising cash for the Roy Carroll Lung Cancer Foundation.

QUOTE OF THE DAY
'A cocky little bastard,' was trainer Noel Meade's description of the young lad who arrived raw at his stables, before blossoming into a Grand National-winning jockey. That lad was Barry Geraghty, who enjoyed a four-timer at Kilbeggan on this day in 2008.

BIRTHDAYS
1943 Irish jockey Dessie Hughes, who won the 1979 Champion Hurdle on Monksfield. As a trainer, he sent out Hardy Eustace to win Champion Hurdle.
1944 Maurice Camacho, whose Clear Cut won the 1975 Mackeson Gold Cup.
1959 Mark 'Always Trying' Johnston, outspoken and successful trainer and cycling enthusiast.
1959 Trainer Conrad Allen, who saddled the first Flat winner on an all-weather track in Britain, Niklas Angel at Lingfield on October 30, 1989.
1960 Trainer Michael Bell, who won the 2005 Derby with Motivator after holding a licence for only four years.

DEATHS OF THE DAY
1989 Trainer Les Hall, 82, who won the 1954 Stewards' Cup with 50/1 Ashurst Wonder.
2001 George Sloan, a Tennessee-based amateur rider, bought a string of horses, trained by Josh Gifford, in a bid to win the 1977/78 British amateur jump jockey championship. Sloan achieved his ambition with a total of 23 winners, having commuted to Britain from the States to take part in the races.
2004 Champion Australian jockey Bill Pyers, 71. He won the 1964 2,000 Guineas on Baldric and the 1967 Arc on Topyo.

CELEBRITY OF THE DAY
1949 Monaveen, owned jointly with the then Princess Elizabeth, was the first winner for the Queen Mother, scoring at 3/10 over fences at Fontwell, ridden by Tony Grantham for trainer Peter Cazalet. He was the first horse to win for the Queen of England since Queen Anne's Star 235 years earlier.

11 OCTOBER

SIGNIFICANT EVENT

1981 Bookie Herbert King, operating as Jack Warner, deliberately flouted the law to bet in public on a Sunday, taking bets on the Newmarket Town Plate to demonstrate to the Jockey Club and the government that there was demand for Sunday racing with betting. Police turned a blind eye as Warner took £1,000 and divided the profits between New Astley Club and the Injured Jockeys' Fund.

STRANGEST EVENT

1992 The Czech-trained Quirinus won the Martell Velka Pardubicka in Czechoslovakia, ridden by Josef Brecha. The race was disrupted by animal rights' protestors as runners approached the third fence. Protestors had already delayed the start by 30 minutes, objecting to 'The Taxis', a formidable 1.5m high, 8ft wide fence with a 7ft ditch.

OTHER EVENTS

1877 The Jimmy Ryan-trained Springfield, 11-8, won the first Champion Stakes at Newmarket, beating Derby winner Silvio by a length.

1945 As three runners – Second Thought, Idle Knight and Palkin – went past the post together at Wheeling Downs, Virginia, the two placing judges and the track steward all gave a different winner. They eventually compromised by calling a triple dead-heat.

1958 The first edition of BBC TV's Grandstand programme featured racing from Ascot, with commentaries by Peter O'Sullevan and Clive Graham.

1977 Rockeater, 4/1, won at Redcar to give jockey Greville Starkey his 1,000th British win.

1990 Lester Piggott was granted a full Flat riding licence by the Jockey Club, clearing the 54-year-old for a sensational comeback, having officially retired on October 29, 1985.

1992 Kent Desormeaux, 22, fell from Judge Hammer at Hollywood Park, sustaining 14 hairline skull fractures, haemorrhaging and hearing loss. He returned to the saddle on 22 January, winning on his first ride back.

1993 Chris Brasher, the former top athlete and early driving force behind the London Marathon, celebrated his first win as an owner when River Lossie won at Fontwell. The runner-up was Princess Hotpot, owned by Brasher's wife, Shirley.

1995 A revolutionary air-cushioned whip was launched amid fanfare, but it was virtually consigned to history after one broke and marked a horse while Graham Bradley was using it.

2008 Paul Nicholls and Ruby Walsh had a 119/1 four-timer at Chepstow.

QUOTE OF THE DAY

2004 *'The transformation whereby Nearly-man became Been-everywhere-man took place on Monday,'* reported Sir Clement Freud, celebrating the fact that his visit to Roscommon completed his set of every British and Irish track.

BIRTHDAYS

1932 Former Middleham and Hong Kong trainer Eric Collingwood.

1933 Jockey Tommy Kinane, who won the 1978 Champion Hurdle on Monksfield.

1953 Former amateur rider, and former wife of John Francome, Miriam.

1965 Jump jockey Russ Garritty.

DEATHS OF THE DAY

1887 George Fordham, 50, who rode 16 Classic winners and was champion jockey for the first time in 1855, surrendering the title only twice up to 1871. Continual wasting led to his early death.

1984 Geoff Barling, 83, who trained for 41 years until 1973.

CELEBRITY OF THE DAY

2004 The death was reported of Australian cricket great and racing and betting enthusiast, Keith Miller, 84, a great friend of top jockey Scobie Breasley.

12 OCTOBER

SIGNIFICANT EVENT
2003 Legendary US jockey turned trainer Bill Shoemaker died, aged 72. The Texan, whose first ride was in March 1949, had 8,833 career winners, winning 15 North American jockeys' championships. In 1955, on Swaps, he scored the first of his four Kentucky Derby wins. He retired from the saddle in 1990 and trained successfully, despite being confined to a wheelchair after an accident in 1991.

STRANGEST EVENT
1837 Jockey Thomas Lye won the first race at Northallerton, in Yorkshire, on Alzira, having won on Abraham Newland and Modesty at far-off Edinburgh the day before – and he had no private jet to get him there.

OTHER EVENTS
1920 US equine superstar Man O'War, also known as 'Big Red', ran his 21st and final race, winning the Kenilworth Park Gold Cup at Kenilworth racetrack in Windsor, Ontario, Canada. Man O'War took on the four-year-old Sir Barton and came home the seven-length winner. It was the first horserace to be filmed in its entirety.

1948 Abernant, one of the all-time great sprinters, won the Middle Park Stakes. Trained by Noel Murless, he was beaten only three times in 17 outings.

1982 Chaplins Club, who was to become one of the most popular Flat handicappers in racing history, won for the first time, at the sixth attempt over 5f at Folkestone. By the time he retired in July 1992, Chaplins Club had raced 114 times, winning 24 and being placed in 38, earning £146,665.70.

1991 The Toby Balding-trained Morley Street became the first horse to win two Breeders' Cup Chases, and only the third to win two Breeders' Cup races of any description, following Miesque, twice winner of the Mile (1987-88), and Bayakoa, the Distaff in 1989 and 1990.

1991 John Gosden saddled his second York treble within three days, taking him past the £500,000 prize-money mark in Britain.

1992 Richard Quinn completed his first century of winners on Young Ern, 6/1, at Leicester, having been stuck on 99 for 53 rides.

1995 Sean McCarthy, 22, had his licence taken away for two months after becoming the first jockey in Britain to test positive for drugs.

1995 Newmarket staged its first 'leasing race' in which 15 of the 20 runners were leased for amounts from £50. The highest was £600 and Les Ward, of race sponsors Milcars, collected the £3,000 prize when 3/1 favourite Tarawa won.

QUOTE OF THE DAY
2004 *'He surrendered dignity and respect by confronting photographers who were merely doing their job,'* wrote The Times racing writer, Alan Lee, about Kieren Fallon, who was unable to resume riding following the fall he took the previous day, and took out his frustrations on the assembled snappers.

BIRTHDAY
1959 Nicky Carlisle, Flat jockey turned course inspector. He won the 1988 Ayr Gold Cup on So Careful.

DEATHS OF THE DAY
1894 Robert Sherwood died, four days after suffering a fit. He rode French Derby-Oaks double on Jouvence in 1853, and in 1855 he partnered Wild Dayrell to win the Derby. Trained two Classic winners.

1997 John Rickman, 84, the first TV racing presenter, who was famous for doffing his hat to viewers.

CELEBRITY OF THE DAY
1992 The Princess Royal officially opened Jackdaws Castle, the £1.8m training complex in the Cotswolds that became the new base for David 'The Duke' Nicholson.

13 OCTOBER

SIGNIFICANT EVENT
1951 Racing at Ascot was televised for the first time as King George's Good Shot, ridden by Gordon Richards, won the Tankerville Nursery Stakes.

STRANGEST EVENT
1837 There was a triple dead-heat in the Cesarewitch at Newmarket, with Pryoress, El Hakim and Queen Bess inseparable at the line. Before the run-off, bookie George Hodgman organised a betting coup. Seeing that Pryoress has been given a poor ride in the first race, he grabbed crack jockey George Fordham to take the ride, then plunged in to back the new combination before word got round. Pryoress duly obliged.

OTHER EVENTS
1927 Arlington Park, Chicago, held its first meeting.

1984 US superstar John Henry won at Meadowlands, taking the nine-year-old gelding's earnings to a record $6,597,947.

1984 One punter clearly decided jockey Steve Smith Eccles was a load of rubbish – why else would he have thrown a dustbin at him while he was riding Green Dolphin in a Uttoxeter chase? Smith Eccles didn't win.

1989 Friday the 13th was unlucky for trainer Jonjo O'Neill when Hit The Ceiling slipped up on the flat when leading at Carlisle; then Roliad broke down badly when going well and Ben Ledi had to be withdrawn before the start of his race. Things improved somewhat when Paco's Boy won the last race for O'Neill.

1990 Phoenix Park, in north west Dublin, held its last meeting after 88 years of racing. Wild Jester, 12/1, won the final race, the Irish Independent Handicap, ridden by Christy Roche.

1991 Zeleznik, a 13-year-old Czech-trained chaser, won the gruelling Velka Pardubicka for an amazing fourth time, in the 101st running of the testing marathon chase.

1991 Richard Hannon saddled Fair Crack and Autocracy, to finish first and second in the Goffs Million at the Curragh, taking his European earnings past £2m.

1992 Trainer Geoff Lewis landed a reported £90,000 gamble when Dare To Dream at Leicester became his 50th winner of the season. Lewis had struck a 40/1 bet at the start of the season that he would reach that target. The previous season he reportedly won £100,000 for training 40 winners, which makes one wonder which bookie would willingly be stung twice in the same manner!

1992 Jockey Geoff Baxter rode his last winner, Falcons Dawn at Leicester, which was his 942nd in 30 seasons.

1997 Richard Dunwoody rode his 1,500th winner, Ashwell Boy, 8/11, at Newton Abbot.

QUOTE OF THE DAY
2004 *'The French have always done the Breeders' Cup well. Their horses don't bust their guts in midsummer the way ours still do,'* opined the *Racing Post*'s Paul Haigh.

BIRTHDAY
1953 Top US rider Pat Day, who rode Easy Goer to win the 1989 Belmont Stakes and won the Kentucky Derby for the first time in 1992 on Lil E.Tee.

DEATH OF THE DAY
1988 New York jockey Mike Venezia, with 2,313 wins to his credit, was thrown from Mr Walter K and fatally trampled by another runner during a race at Belmont Park. On December 7, 1984, he had won six races at Aqueduct.

CELEBRITY OF THE DAY
1925 Occasional racegoer Margaret Thatcher, Prime Minister from 1979 to 1990, was born. Clement Freud named a horse Weareagrandmother after her memorable remark

14 OCTOBER

SIGNIFICANT EVENT
1972 The great Brigadier Gerard won on his final racecourse appearance, in the Champion Stakes. The 1/3 favourite, who ran in the name of owner-breeder John Hislop's wife, Jean, was ridden as usual by Joe Mercer for Dick Hern. 'The Brigadier' won 17 of his 18 starts from 5f to 1m4f and collected £212,319 in prize-money.

STRANGEST EVENT
1862 William Chifney, who trained five Classic winners, died in poverty, aged 76, despite having won £18,000 when landing the 1830 Derby with his own horse, Priam. Losing bets and badly organised coups wrecked his finances.

OTHER EVENTS
1885 Ormonde, the 1886 Triple Crown winner, won on his first appearance, in the Post Sweepstakes at Newmarket.
1886 Ormonde started at a prohibitive 1/100 as the Triple Crown hero won the three-runner Champion Stakes.
1967 Teesside Park held its first jump meeting. King Tarquin won the first race, the Harold Dawson Hurdle, at 6/1, ridden by G Lee and trained by G Vergette.
1978 Trainer Nicky Henderson saddled his first winner, the Bob Davies-ridden Dukery, at Uttoxeter – exactly 30 years later on the same date in 2008 he celebrated with a Huntingdon double.
1989 The three-year-old Hawkster, carrying 121lb, claimed a new world record of 2m 22.8s for one and a half miles at the Santa Anita Netlon turf course.
1992 Ingenuity, 14/1, won at Redcar to give The Queen a record 24th winner of the season – Her Majesty's previous best had been achieved in 1957.
1993 For only the third time in Britain a race had seven 14/1 co-favourites, Newmarket's 28 runner Fordham Handicap, won by 16/1 Norfolk Hero.
1993 Trainer Alf Smith of Beverley won the Tote Two-Year-Old Trophy at Redcar with the only juvenile in his yard, 33/1 Cape Merino. Including bonuses, he collected £188,900.
2008 Yorkshire-based trainer Richard Fahey reached a first-time century of Flat winners in a season when Trumpstoo, 9/2, won at Newcastle, ridden by stable jockey Paul Hanagan.

QUOTE OF THE DAY
2004 'I know some of the jockeys can't wait to get skating,' said Lingfield's Kate Hills, announcing that the track would boast a 'customised, under-cover ice rink' for six weeks between late November 2004 and early January 2005.

BIRTHDAYS
1908 William Behrens, owner-breeder of 1973 St Leger winner Peleid, who was sent off at 28/1.
1941 Hampshire trainer John Bridger, trainer of serial loser Amrullah.
1946 Justin Hayward of the Moody Blues, rock star and owner-breeder.
1956 Jockey Chris Grant, who was second in the 1986 Grand National on 66/1 shot Young Driver, runner-up again in 1988 on Durham Edition, and again on the same horse in 1990. Grant was also runner-up in the 1987 Cheltenham Gold Cup on 25/1 Cybrandian.
1960 Newmarket trainer William Jarvis.

DEATHS OF THE DAY
2002 Meriel Tufnell, 53, the first lady jockey to ride a winner in England.
2004 Double US champion (1983 and 1984) Slew O'Gold was put down at the age of 27.
2009 Four fatalities at first Wetherby meeting of the winter.

CELEBRITY OF THE DAY
1671 King Charles II rode his first winner as a jockey at Newmarket in the Town Plate – he remains the only reigning monarch to have ridden a winner.

15 OCTOBER

SIGNIFICANT EVENT
1982 The highly touted Gorytus, trained by Dick Hern and ridden by Willie Carson, put in a bafflingly poor performance in the Dewhurst Stakes at Newmarket. Starting at 1/2, he finished last of four, sparking all kinds of rumours that he had been got at, which were never satisfactorily resolved. (See 'Quote' below)

STRANGEST EVENT
1990 Lester Piggott made his comeback to race-riding on board Lupescu – five years after his original retirement. Piggott was beaten in a photo-finish, and he drew a blank on his other two rides at, obviously, Leicester. Walter Swinburn rode five winners on the afternoon and was then asked by a well-informed radio presenter: 'Are you worried about Lester's return?'

OTHER EVENTS
1929 Fairway won second Champion Stakes, adding it to Eclipse and St Leger
1963 Geoff Baxter rode his first winner, Jules, 25/1, at Wolverhampton.
1980 Jonjo O'Neill rode five winners from six mounts at Wetherby.
1982 John Dunlop saddled his 1,000th winner in 16 years as a trainer when John Lowe rode Prince Elo to victory at Catterick.
1984 Needles, who won the 1956 Kentucky Derby, died aged 31 – the second greatest age ever achieved by a winner of that race.
1991 Lester Piggott rode Shafouri, 9/2, into second place in the Lester Piggott All Aged Stakes at Chepstow. The race was won by Afif, 11/2, partnered by David Harrison.
1992 High-profile owner Bill Gredley called for a one-day strike of owners on November 2 in protest at government deductions from betting. He later withdrew his call when racing's authorities showed a lack of support.
1994 Two hours after Absalom's Lady was announced as a dead-heater in the last race at Ascot, the Captain Quist Hurdle, judge Jane Stickels declared the horse the outright winner by a short-head. 'Amateurish and desperate public relations,' fumed Oliver Sherwood, whose Large Action lost his share of first place and was placed second.
2009 Ocean Countess at Brighton was trainer Julia Feilden's 100th winner.

QUOTE OF THE DAY
'I once backed a horse that was doped. I have never backed a horse since,' wrote Simon Barnes in *The Spectator* in 1998, referring back to Gorytus's defeat this day in 1982 (see 'Significant' above). Barnes added: *'Everyone was certain that the horse had been doped, destroyed for the profits to be made on this one race; for all the long-range bets people had struck for the colt's future races, the 2,000 Guineas, the Derby. But nothing was ever proved. Racing, basically, pretended that it had never happened.'*

BIRTHDAYS
1946 Theatre-going Sussex trainer James Bryan Sayers, whose best horses included Hoorah Henry and Bigee.
1948 Sussex jockey Roger Rowell, who rode his first winner, Vaux-le-Vicomte, at Plumpton in February 1968. The best horses he rode included Avec Moi and Brantridge Farmer.

FIRST OF THE DAY
1994 The opening race at Newmarket produced a record Tote dual forecast of 4,608/1 as Chinour, 33/1, beat Royal Hill, 25/1. The previous best was 3,997/1 at Ascot in 1988.

CELEBRITY OF THE DAY
1950 Pop singer Chris De Burgh was born. He named his horse Missing You after one of his hit records.

16 OCTOBER

SIGNIFICANT EVENT
1920 Gordon Richards was unplaced on Clockwork at Lingfield on his race-riding debut.

STRANGEST EVENT
1804 Chancellor, owned by Lord Cassillis, beat two opponents to win the first running of the Ayr Gold Cup, which then consisted of two 2m heats and was confined to horses born and trained in Scotland. The horse then competed in the Ayr Subscription of £50, consisting of four 4m heats, finishing second. Chancellor had completed more than 20 miles, carrying 8st 10lb, in a single afternoon – farther than many modern horses will run during an entire career. Chancellor won again in 1805, after which heats were scrapped.

OTHER EVENTS
1891 Fitzroy racecourse, near Melbourne, Australia, opened for business – staging only five-furlong sprints.
1990 Lester Piggott rode the first two winners of his shock comeback. He won at Chepstow on 4/6 Nicholas, trained by his wife Susan, and 11/1 Shining Jewel.
1991 Derby winner Generous was retired to Banstead Manor Stud.
1992 Zafonic, the latest two-year-old 'wonder horse', won the Dewhurst Stakes to become hot favourite for the 2,000 Guineas, which he duly won the following May by three and a half lengths, breaking the 45-year-old course record at Newmarket.
1993 US trainer Shug McGaughey won four stakes races on the Belmont Park card, including three Grade Ones.
1993 Blythe Miller became the first female jockey to ride a Breeders' Cup winner when Lonesome Glory won the Breeders' Cup Chase at Belmont Park.
1993 Lester Piggott was fined a startling five million for taking the wrong course on Formato Uni. Fortunately he was riding at San Siro, Milan, and the fine was in lira, amounting to £2,115.
1996 Frankie Dettori and Pat Eddery were among 21 jockeys who went on strike after the first race at Haydock, claiming the course was too dangerous after heavy rain made the sharp final turn unsafe. The meeting was abandoned.
2004 In a classic example of 'Colemanballs', Frankie Dettori, without a win in the Champion Stakes, declared: 'I've got beaten on some great horses in the Champion – Daylami, Halling, Noverre, Best Of The Bests.' After recalling all those horses, he added: 'I don't even want to remember them.'

QUOTE OF THE DAY
1976 *'Of all the things I could have been fired for – usually people criticise me for trying too hard.'* Willie Carson lost his job riding for owner Marcos Lemos after steering his Derringo, a 6/1 chance, into sixth place in Newmarket's Highflyer Handicap on this day. Lemos had also been upset that Carson was leaving trainer Clive Brittain for Dick Hern, replacing Joe Mercer, the Queen's jockey.

BIRTHDAYS
1921 Mack Miller, the US trainer for Mill Reef's owner Paul Mellon.
1957 Scottish jockey Sandy Dudgeon, who partnered, naturally enough, Peaty Sandy, on which 13-year-old he won the 1987 Tote Eider Chase.

DEATHS OF THE DAY
1989 A fire at Randwick racecourse in Sydney killed 11 horses worth Aus$1m.
2009 Triple World Hurdle winner Inglis Drever, 10, from colic.

FIRST OF THE DAY
1973 Victor Morley Lawson won the Corinthian Amateur Riders' Maiden Stakes on Ocean King at Warwick. It was his first win – at the age of 67 – and made him the oldest jockey to record a debut victory.

17 OCTOBER

SIGNIFICANT EVENT
1991 Angel Cordero joined Bill Shoemaker and Laffit Pincay in the 7,000-winner club when Don't Cross The Law won at Belmont Park. That total excluded his 258 winners in Puerto Rico.

STRANGEST EVENT
1992 Not the best day in career of trainer Sue Bradburne, from Fife, as she sent five horses to Kelso. Ayia Napa and Dante's Inferno were pulled up, Stagshaw Belle unseated at the first and was injured, Off The Bru finished last, and a vet's certificate was produced for Rogany, which became a non-runner – her best result of the afternoon.

OTHER EVENTS
1966 Denys Smith saddled his 100th winner as a trainer – Wife's Choice, ridden in a handicap hurdle by Terry Biddlecombe. He won the 1968 Grand National with Red Alligator.
1970 Triple Crown winner Nijinsky's career ended in defeat as he started 4/11 for the Champion Stakes, only to finish second behind 100/7 winner Lorenzaccio, partnered by Geoff Lewis and trained by Noel Murless. Nijinsky won 11 of his 13 starts, suffering his only other defeat in the Arc behind Sassafras. He won £246,132 in Britain and Ireland and Ff480,000 in France.
1989 An earthquake hit the San Francisco area, causing damage to Bay Meadows and Golden Fields racecourses.
1990 Pat Eddery reached a career-best 198 winners for the season, going on to log 209.
1992 Comeback king Lester Piggott added to his legend by partnering Rodrigo De Triano to victory in the Champion Stakes at Newmarket by a neck from Lahib, having also won the 2,000 Guineas on the same horse at 6/1.
1992 Paul Cole saddled Zoman to win the Budweiser International, worth $750,000 at Laurel, Maryland, ending a 23-year drought for British raiders.
2004 With his unerring talent for tact and charm, Kieren Fallon surrendered the jockey title to Frankie Dettori a little, should we say, ungraciously. Quoted in *The Sunday Times*, he said: 'Put it this way, I think I've got more championships left in me than Frankie. Frankie knows he's got a gift this year ... A lot of people didn't want me to be champion. I was getting silly little suspensions and Frankie was getting away with a lot.'
2009 Akmal in the Jockey Club Cup was John Dunlop's 250th Newmarket winner.

QUOTE OF THE DAY
'Having come back and found I was riding as well as ever, I have nothing left to prove,' said jockey Declan Murphy shortly after winning on Jibereen at Chepstow on this day in 1995 on his comeback ride after 18 months off from near fatal brain injuries sustained in a Haydock fall. Murphy, who joined BSkyB's Racing Channel, denied his decision to quit had anything to do with rumblings about betting patterns and jockey tactics associated with his returning win, which proved to be his last.

BIRTHDAYS
1919 Wyn Griffiths, vet, owner, former Arsenal, Derby and Cardiff soccer star, TV and radio racing broadcaster.
1962 Top US rider Pat Valenzuela, who partnered Kentucky Derby, Preakness and Breeders' Cup Classic winner Sunday Silence, as well as Breeders' Cup Juvenile sensation Arazi.

LAST OF THE DAY
1997 Trainer Paul Kelleway announced his retirement after sending out Dovedon Star, 6/1, to win at Newmarket.

CELEBRITY OF THE DAY
1946 Theatre producer Sir Cameron Mackintosh, an owner with Simon Sherwood, was born.

18 OCTOBER

SIGNIFICANT EVENT
1966 Auriol Sinclair became the first woman officially to train a double when Ladino, 8/1, and Golden Gloves, 11/4, won at Folkestone.

STRANGEST EVENT
2008 The Nicky Henderson-trained Caracciola scored a shock 50/1 victory in the Cesarewitch, becoming the first 11-year-old to win the race and the oldest to win a race of such importance. Among those who cheered the outsider home was racing journalist Sean Magee, who had staked £10 each-way at 66/1 to land his biggest-ever payout.

OTHER EVENTS
1917 A match race at Laurel, Maryland, pitted that year's Belmont Stakes winner Hourless against Kentucky Derby winner Omar Khayyam, over one mile. Hourless won by a length.

1938 Apprentice Dougie Marks, 16, rode Brescia to win at Newcastle.

1939 Six weeks after the outbreak of the Second World War, a two-day Newmarket meeting began, including the two-division Cambridgeshire, which was won by Gyroscope, 100/6, and Orichalque, 25/1. It was the first race meeting to take place since the announcement on September 4 that there would be no more racing that year.

1945 Priam II, the first French raider since 1940, went close to winning the Champion Stakes at Newmarket, but was beaten by 4/1 favourite Court Martial, the 2,000 Guineas winner.

1966 Henry Cecil married Sir Noel Murless's daughter, Julie, who later became a trainer in her own right.

1975 Contesting the race for a second time, the great French mare Allez France again finished runner-up in the Champion Stakes, losing out to Rose Bowl.

1977 Lanark racecourse closed.

1991 Dr Devious, who was to win the Derby the following year, won the Dewhurst Stakes under Willie Carson.

Petite-D-Argent won on the same card, giving Alan Munro his first century of winners.

1991 Sheikh Mohammed paid a reported $8.5m to owner Allen Paulson for a half-share in Arazi.

1992 The Paul Cole-trained Snurge won Canada's Rothmans International, following the disqualification of Wiorno.

1997 Anthony Middleton gave those who thought he'd win at Kelso a bum steer – literally. As he passed the post in fourth place on Tellaporky, he was trying to tug up his breeches, which had slipped over his rear end during the race.

QUOTE OF THE DAY
1995 *'I think granddad planned this. I think my granddad is riding Red Rum again up there. It's no accident that they died on the same day.'* Three-time Grand National winner Red Rum died, aged 30, and on the same date in 2004 his devoted lad, Jackie Grainger, died, aged 84.

BIRTHDAY
1937 New York trainer Frank Allen Alexander.

DEATHS OF THE DAY
1994 Jockey Pat Colville, 49, who rode Willie Wumpkins to victory at the 1973 Cheltenham Festival.

1983 Kelso, one of the great US horses of the 1960s, died of colic, aged 26. He won 39 of his 63 starts and was Horse of the Year on five occasions.

2002 General Sir Cecil 'Monkey' Blacker, 86, former deputy senior steward of the Jockey Club. A world-class pentathlete, he won the 1954 Grand Military Gold Cup on Pointsman, his own horse.

CELEBRITY OF THE DAY
1952 The Washington DC International was run for the first time, at Laurel racecourse, Maryland. In 1954 it became the first race outside Britain in which a runner carried the royal colours when The Queen's Landau took part.

19 OCTOBER

SIGNIFICANT EVENT
1989 The Buckenham Selling Stakes at Newmarket made history when the photo-finish print was the first to be displayed in public in colour, revealing that Sister Sal had beaten Gabbiadini by half a length. The pair were 5/1 joint-favourites.

STRANGEST EVENT
1932 Harry 'Head Waiter' Wragg was thrown from Donatia in a race at Newcastle. His right leg was smashed, but doctors just managed to save him from amputation. He returned to the saddle early the next season.

OTHER EVENTS
1964 Ron Barry, twice champion jump jockey and later a Jockey Club inspector of courses, rode his first winner, at Ayr.

1989 A crowd of 15,000 at Moe, Melbourne saw legendary US jockey Bill Shoemaker ride his first Australian winner on Cosign in the Moe Cup.

1989 Super Tony completed an unusual Hexham double – for the second time taking a handicap chase on a walkover.

1990 Generous, 50/1, became the longest-priced winner in the 115-year history of the Dewhurst Stakes. The Paul Cole-trained colt went on to win the Derby in 1991.

1990 Jack Berry equalled the 1905 record for winners by a northern-based trainer – 124 by William Elsey – when Time For The Blues and Doublova won at Catterick.

1991 Dancing Brave, the European champion of 1986, was sold to stand at stud in Japan.

1992 Michael Roberts broke Gordon Richards' record of 1,000 domestic rides in a season when unplaced Aalu at Folkestone was his 1,001st mount.

1994 Ed Dunlop, who took over the training of Alex Scott's horses after the trainer was shot dead, sent out his first winner, Lynton Lad, 3/1, at Yarmouth.

1994 The retirement was announced of Snurge, the Paul Cole-trained European record-holder for win and place prize-money of £1,283,794.35.

QUOTE OF THE DAY
1964 *'I wanted to go out on a winner rather than on a stretcher.'* Dual champion jump jockey Ron Barry, who landed his first winner on this day, on quitting after partnering Ayr winner Final Argument in 1984.

BIRTHDAYS
1914 Frank Gilman, owner, breeder and trainer of 1982 National winner Grittar.

1915 Joe Carr, trainer of Lochranza. He rode successfully as a jump jockey until a fall at Ludlow in May 1940, as a result of which he lost his right leg.

1953 Jockey turned trainer Joanna Morgan, who handled the prolific One Won One.

1984 Jockey Kirsty Milczarek – aka Milkshake – who has reportedly enjoyed a close relationship with Kieren Fallon.

DEATHS OF THE DAY
1969 Hector Christie, 62, trainer of 1947 Cheltenham Gold Cup winner Fortina.

1988 Former Irish champion jockey Martin Quirke, 89. He rode nine Irish Classic winners, and set a record of 86 winners in 1923, which stood until 1972.

2001 Joe Allen, 92, founder of specialist equine bookshop, The Horseman's Bookshop in London's Victoria area. He sold the shop in 2000.

2008 Owner-breeder Harry T Mangurian jr, who founded Mockingbird Farm in Florida, died of leukaemia, aged 82. A native of New York, he bred or raced more than 150 stakes winners, including Desert Vixen and Breeders' Cup Juvenile winner Gilded Time.

CELEBRITY OF THE DAY
2009 Gamcare announced their first 'Ambassador' – ex-boxer Chris Eubank

20 OCTOBER

SIGNIFICANT EVENT
2007 The ten-year-old McDynamo scored a fifth straight victory in the $300,000 Breeders' Cup Grand National at Far Hills, New Jersey.

STRANGEST EVENT
1945 Overcrowding at Worcester racecourse resulted in the collapse of the Tote building, injuring 25 spectators

OTHER EVENTS
1841 Catherina set a British record by winning the 79th race of her career at Leek, Staffordshire. She ran 176 times between 1832 and 1841, and was unplaced third favourite in the 1833 Oaks.
1917 Thomas Weston, who would ride 11 Classic winners, rode in public for the first time, on Black Crag at Stockton.
1923 US champion Zev, Kentucky Derby winner, scored a five-length win over the English Derby winner, Papyrus, trained by Basil Jarvis and ridden by Steve Donoghue, in a $100,000 match at Belmont Park. Papyrus's cause was not helped by the unsuitable shoes with which he was fitted.
1962 John Sutcliffe saddled his first winner as a trainer, Little Smokey, ridden by Fred Winter at Huntingdon.
1984 Slew O'Gold won $1 million bonus after adding Jockey Club Gold Cup to Woodward Stakes and Marlboro Cup.
1990 Sizzling Saga gave trainer Jack Berry a record score of 125 winners in a season when winning at Catterick.
1990 The two-year-old Timeless Times, already a 16-time winner, went to Laurel in the United States in a bid to land a record 17th in Maryland's Futurity. But the Bill O'Gorman-trained juvenile finished last of 13.
1990 Peter Alafi rode his 2,218th winner on Noveka at Gelsenkirchen-Horst, to equal the record number of winners for a German-based jockey, held by Otto Schmidt.
1990 Morley Street travelled from Britain to win the $250,000 Breeders' Cup Chase by ten lengths at Belmont Park.
1992 George Duffield completed his first century of winners, aged 45, as the Mark Presscott-trained Two Left Feet won at Chepstow. That brought Duffield's career total to 1,652, making him the only jockey to have ridden so many winners yet never been champion. Later, Duffield raced over hurdles in the Flat Versus Jump Jockeys' Challenge Hurdle, won by the Flat's Michael Hills on Silver Age.
2009 Trainer David Gandolfo retired after 50 years, with over 1,500 winners.

QUOTE OF THE DAY
2008 Writer Marcus Armytage proposed a way of interesting children in racing, urging Legoland to introduce a scale model of Ascot racecourse. He told *Daily Telegraph* readers: '*Ascot, built to a 1:35 scale, would be 11.4 metres long, 1.1 metres deep and would have the same wow factor that the actual grandstand has. You could have Lego horses racing round the course and "sound files" of colleague Jim McGrath calling them home to the backdrop of thundering hooves.*' The model would cost an estimated £106,000 to construct.

BIRTHDAYS
1915 Warwickshire trainer Michael Marsh, who saddled his own Larbawn to win 1968 and '69 Whitbread Gold Cups.
1957 Neale Doughty, who rode Hallo Dandy to victory in the 1984 Grand National.

DEATHS OF THE DAY
2002 Glen Kelly, 86, jump jockey with more than 100 wins to his credit.
2003 Jumps trainer Chuck Spares, 59, who handled Ibn Majed.

CELEBRITY OF THE DAY
1964 The Queen Mother reached 100 winners over jumps when Bobby Beasley rode the Jack Donoghue-trained Gay Record to victory at Folkestone.

21 OCTOBER

SIGNIFICANT EVENT

1791 Having been a beaten favourite the day before, the Prince of Wales's Escape won at long odds at Newmarket. A stewards' inquiry was held and the Prince was told: 'If Samuel Chifney [his jockey] were suffered to ride the Prince's horses, no gentleman would start against him.' Controversial Chifney was suspected by many of pulling Escape in the first race, but the Prince stood by his rider and refused to race again at Newmarket.

STRANGEST EVENT

1995 In an odd ageist cull, Newbury dismissed 123 raceday staff, with an average age of 73.

OTHER EVENTS

1965 Doug Smith became the second British jockey to ride 3,000 winners with a Newbury double on Soft Collar and As Before.

1991 Trainer Lord John Fitzgerald announced he was to quit Newmarket to train in Germany.

1992 Jasoorah, trained by Alec Stewart, won at Chester to make Michael Roberts only the fifth jockey to ride 200 winners in a British season.

1993 John Reid rode a century of winners in a season for the first time when Googly, 9/1, won at Newbury. The horse was the last winner for retiring trainer Bill Wightman, 79, whose first was in May 1937.

1995 A riot forced the abandonment of a race meeting at Gosforth Park, Johannesburg, after punters objected to the upholding of an objection after the sixth race, which resulted in the disqualification of the well-backed winner. Windows were broken, the jockeys refused to go out for the next race and the police were called.

1997 BBC TV racing presenter Julian Wilson announced his retirement from the role after 32 years.

2003 It was announced that in memory of the great Bill Shoemaker the outstanding performance by a jockey on Breeders' Cup day would in future be honoured with the Shoemaker Award. The winner would be selected by the racing media.

2009 Apprentice Daryl Byrne, 18, won on Mid Mon Lady at Navan – his fifth ride and fifth win since his debut at the Curragh on 12 October.

QUOTE OF THE DAY

1966 *'Since gaining a licence the biggest single thing I've learned is patience.'* Jane Chapple-Hyam, former wife of Classic-winning trainer Peter, was born in Australia on this day. She won the 2006 Ebor with 100/1 Mudawin. Pro punter Dave Nevison called her, 'someone to take seriously on the Flat'.

BIRTHDAYS

1925 Swiss-based owner Gerry Oldham, who won the 1950 Irish 2,000 Guineas with Lucero; while Irish Derby winner Talgo was runner-up in the Arc, as was Salvo. Fidalgo was another Irish Derby winner for Oldham, as well as runner-up in the Derby and St Leger.

1936 Trainer Owen O'Neill, who rode 100 winners as a dual-purpose jockey.

1939 Former jockey Dinah Nicholson, daughter of trainer William Holman and widow of champion trainer David Nicholson.

1954 Jockey Gerry Newman.

DEATH OF THE DAY

1992 Jockey Club member Tommy Wallis, 69, who owned 1962 Grand Military Gold Cup winner Cash Desire.

FIRST OF THE DAY

1981 Richard Quinn rode his first winner, Bolivar Baby (trained by Paul Cole), at Kempton.

22 OCTOBER

SIGNIFICANT EVENT

1984 The Breeders' Cup, which was inaugurated in this year, unveiled its permanent trophy – a 1,850lb bronze and marble reproduction of the Torrie horse, an ecorche or flayed horse designed by 16th-century sculptor Giambologna.

STRANGEST EVENT

1855 Overreach, Unexpected, Gamester and Lady Golightly finished in a quadruple dead-heat in a £10 sweepstake for two-year-olds at Newmarket.

OTHER EVENTS

1912 Dramatic photos show 'soldiers stopping horseracing' at Mineral Park track in Indiana, but reason for action is unrecorded. See www.rootsweb.ancestry. com to view pictures

1964 Bill Shoemaker rode his 5,000th winner on Slapstick at Aqueduct.

1982 Tony Murray rode his 1,000th career winner on Guy Harwood's Northern Adventure at Doncaster.

1991 The *New York Times* reported on end of season Belmont Park, gloomily noting 'attendance was down 3.2%, wagering by 5%, continuing the decline that has afflicted racing in recent years'. Course still operating today, though.

1992 Japan acquired Classic winners Dr Devious for $6m and Rodrigo De Triano for $6.2m, both for stud duty.

1994 Lady Herries-trained Celtic Swing, partnered by Kevin Darley, sauntered to a 12 length win in the Racing Post Trophy en route to second place in 2000 Guineas.

1994 Bob Champion, out of the saddle for four years, finished second on Elegant Isle at Down Royal as he had a preparatory run while considering whether to make a Grand National comeback in 1995 for charity. He didn't.

2009 After Kamakhya 'refused to raise a gallop' at Delhi, the horse was banned until 'its behaviour improves to satisfaction of the Stewards in two mock races on race days.'

2009 Chip Woolley jnr, trainer of this year's Kentucky Derby winner, Mine That Bird, finally threw away the crutches he'd been using for eight months after breaking his leg in a motorcycle accident: 'I didn't have another scratch on me. It didn't even hurt me, other than breaking my leg.'

2009 Lemon Cream Pie almost licked 'em in $106,500 'Knickerbocker' at Belmont Park, US, only to be collared by Operation Red Dawn.

QUOTE OF THE DAY

'There is only one place worth being, and that is at the top' – Michael Stoute, born on this day in 1945, who has managed to live up to that aspiration for many years.

BIRTHDAYS

1945 Michael Stoute, in Barbados, where his father was the Commissioner of Police. He trained Shergar to win the 1981 Derby and completed the set of British Classics when Conduit (also a dual Breeders' Cup winner) won the 2008 St Leger, having won every other Classic at least twice.

1950 Jockey Gary Old

FIRST OF THE DAY

2009 Golden Gates Fields, the largest track in North California, was the first racecourse to receive annual 'Stop Waste Partnership Business Efficiency Award' for 'excellence in enviromental performance'.

23 OCTOBER

SIGNIFICANT EVENT
1990 Lester Piggott rode four winners from four rides for Vincent O'Brien at the Curragh – Legal Profession, Passer By, Fairy Folk and Classic Minstrel.

STRANGEST EVENT
1987 Lester Piggott was jailed for three years after being found guilty of alleged tax fraud of more than £3m. The 51-year-old was stony-faced as he was sentenced by Mr Justice Farquharson at Ipswich Crown Court. Piggott's wife, Susan, collapsed in tears as he was taken to Norwich prison. Piggott had failed to declare income to the Inland Revenue of £3.25m. The biggest sum on the charge sheet related to an omission of £1,359,726 from additional riding income. Another charge was that for 14 years, from 1971, he omitted income of £1,031,697 from bloodstock operations.

OTHER EVENTS
1950 The Turkish Jockey Club was founded, based in Istanbul.
1955 Ribot won Italy's Premio del Jockey Club by an impressive 15 lengths.
1966 Controversy erupted at the Preis von Europa in Cologne when, in the absence of a photo-finish, the Russian horse Anilin got the nod over Salvo, ridden by Joe Mercer, who was convinced the Harry Wragg-trained runner had won.
1989 Following controversy over safety, the new-look Becher's Brook was unveiled at Aintree. The ditch was raised by 30 inches and the slope on the landing side was levelled off. The fence remained 4ft 10in high, but the drop to the water was reduced to 8ft and the ditch was 15 inches deep. The area beyond the fence was widened to enable horses to jump straight ahead. Changes to the Mildmay course were also unveiled.
1990 Pat Eddery joined Fred Archer, who did it eight times, Tommy Loates, who managed it in 1893, and Sir Gordon Richards, who achieved it 12 times, when he rode his 200th winner of the season, Miranda Jay. 12/1, at Chepstow.
1991 A new Jockey Club ruling on walkovers, introduced in July, was used for the first time when Arthur Stephenson re-entered Palm Reader to take on Old Applejack in the Durham Handicap Chase at Newcastle. The other seven five-day entries were also invited to re-enter. Old Applejack, 6-4, beat 1-2 favourite Palm Reader. On October 21, 1992, the same pair met again in the same race – with the same outcome.
1991 Steve Cauthen completed his tenth consecutive century of British winners when Knifebox won at Chester.
1993 Staff from the Halifax Building Society in Lewisham invested their money well when teaming up for a £1 each-way accumulator on six horses, which all won, giving them a windfall of £101,000 from bookie A R Dennis.
1994 Moonax became the first St Leger winner to take the French equivalent when he landed the Prix Royal-Oak at Longchamp.

QUOTE OF THE DAY
1992 *'Spillage of aviation fuel on the course,'* was the bizarre reason for the abandonment of racing at Newbury with one race remaining on the seven-race card. A light aircraft carrying racegoers back to Hampshire crashed on to the Flat course, but luckily the occupants of the plane were not seriously injured.

BIRTHDAY
1927 Miles Gosling, Jockey Club member and owner of Master Eye, winner of 21 races.

FIRST OF THE DAY
1990 Walter Swinburn rode 100 winners in a season for the first time when Lilian Baylis scored at Chester.

CELEBRITY OF THE DAY
1935 Charles Benson, racing writer and friend of Lord Lucan, was born.

24 OCTOBER

SIGNIFICANT EVENT
1988 Lester Piggott was released from prison, just over a year after being jailed for three years for tax offences.

STRANGEST EVENT
1826 Under the hammer went horses belonging to eccentric owner 'Mad' Jack Mytton, who would saddle up and ride a pet bear and once allegedly set fire to his own nightgown, while wearing it, to cure himself of hiccups. He named his son after his favourite horse, Euphrates. The best price at the auction was 860gns for Longwaist, by Whalebone, while a two-year-old bay colt by Sceptre fetched a mere 43gns.

OTHER EVENTS
1851 St Helier, ridden by triple Grand National-winning jockey Tom Olliver, won the Grand Annual Free Handicap Chase at Hereford by eight lengths.
1876 The four-year-old Rosebery completed the autumn double, winning the Cambridgeshire at 4/1, despite carrying a stone more than in the Cesarewitch when 100/14. He was owned by brothers James and Sidney Smith, who won £250,000 over the two races.
1947 Phantom Bridge and Resistance shared honours in Doncaster's Beechfield Handicap, the first photo-finish dead-heat in Britain.
1953 Impney caused a major upset when beating 1-7 favourite Sir Ken at Uttoxeter, breaking the dual Champion Hurdle winner's run of 16 consecutive victories. Sir Ken landed a third Champion Hurdle the following year.
1974 Brighton jockey Gary Moore's first winner was Jamie's Cottage at Plumpton. He won more than 150 jump races and one on the Flat before becoming a trainer in 1993. He once listed his favourite recreations as 'squash and shopping'.
1988 Peter Scudamore completed the fastest 50 winners in a jump season, winning on Wolfhangar at Fakenham.

1992 Super Impose, trained by Lee Freedman, became the biggest earner in the southern hemisphere when winning the A$1.7m W S Cox Plate at Moonee Valley, Melbourne, to take his career earnings to A$5,659,358.
2000 Death of dual Champion Hurdler, Sea Pigeon, 30.
2004 A South African website reported that Rev Deric Derbyshire, 56, had baptised a racehorse, Running Reverend, in front of his congregation, offering the horse as first prize in a fund-raising raffle for St Peter's Congregational Church near Port Elizabeth. 'I did a scripture reading and a prayer, then sprinkled the horse's forehead. The Lord's hand is definitely on this horse – he's going to be a champion,' he said.
2009 Victoria Cartmel, second at Newbury on Mista Rossa, was suspended for trying too hard – four day ban for excessive use of the whip; then suspended for not trying hard enough – 28 day ban for dropping her hands! Victoria announced she was giving up riding.

QUOTE OF THE DAY
1776 *'It is surprising to think what a height this spirit of horse-racing is now arrived at in this kingdom, where there is scarce a village so mean that has not a bit of plate raised once a year for the purpose,'* The Post, reporting on the spread of racing.

BIRTHDAYS
1906 Sir Fred Pontin, holiday camp king and owner of 1971 Grand National winner Specify.
1942 Jockey Tony Kimberley, four-time winner of the Barbados Guineas.

DEATH OF THE DAY
1982 Former trainer Percy Vasey, 92, who sent out more than 300 winners from his Wetherby base, headed by Trimbush in the Doncaster Cup and Mad Carew, 33/1, in the 1943 Manchester November Handicap.

25 OCTOBER

SIGNIFICANT EVENT
2008 Golidkova gave trainer Freddie Head his eighth Group winner of the year when taking the Breeders' Cup Mile. On the same card Sir Michael Stoute's first St Leger winner, Conduit, landed the $3m Breeders' Cup Turf (both won again in 2009), returning 5/1, as European horses enjoyed an excellent afternoon, with Ralph Beckett saddling Breeders' Cup Marathon winner Muhannak.

STRANGEST EVENT
1968 Ribofilio ended his career unplaced in Newbury's St Simon Stakes, for which he was favourite. Bookies loved the horse, who started favourite for four Classics – the 2,000 Guineas, Derby, St Leger and Irish Derby – and was beaten every time.

OTHER EVENTS
1852 West Australian was runner-up at Newmarket on the first of his ten racecourse appearances. He won the other nine, becoming, in 1853, the first Triple Crown winner.

1881 US-bred Foxhall, 10/1, completed the autumn double, winning the Cambridgeshire to add to his 9/2 Cesarewitch triumph. He was owned by US financier J R Keene.

1893 Ascot racecourse near Melbourne opened, with 3,000 racegoers present to see the meeting, which boasted a 'new starting apparatus'. Entry was 3/- (15p).

1947 Ireland's first triple dead-heat was recorded when Colomb's Kingdom, Hisway and Lilting Lady were inseparable for second place at the Curragh.

1967 The last meeting took place at Le Tremblay, France, which had been appropriated by President de Gaulle for a new sports stadium.

1985 Steve Smith Eccles rode his 500th winner, Dhofar, at Newbury.

1986 Tony Murray rode his last winner in Britain, Jupiter Island, in Newbury's St Simon Stakes.

1990 Jockey Steve Perks was fined £150 at Pontefract – for changing boots. The problem was that he'd weighed out in a different pair to ride Grace Card, on whom he finished last.

2003 Julie Krone became the first female jockey to win a Breeders' Cup race when she took the Juvenile Fillies at Santa Anita on Halfbridled.

2008 Teenager Kosei Miura, a first-season jockey in Japan, reached 70 winners for the year, passing the previous record set in 1987 by Yutaka Take and believed to be unbeatable. Miura went on to score 91 that season.

QUOTE OF THE DAY
2008 *'It's the first time I've ever seen it. Why would he throw a $100 whip away?'* asked baffled steward Albert Christiansen when, after winning the $5m Breeders' Cup Classic on the John Gosden-trained Raven's Pass at Santa Anita, Frankie Dettori hurled his whip into the crowd in celebration.

BIRTHDAY
1934 Joe Mercer, the 1979 champion jockey, who partnered the great Brigadier Gerard in all his races. On retiring from the saddle, Mercer worked as jockey's agent for Brent Thomson and Tony McGlone before becoming racing manager for Maktoum bin Rashid Al Maktoum's Gainsborough racing operation in 1987. He retired in 2006.

DEATH OF THE DAY
1949 Harry Straus, the American who invented the Totalisator, was killed in a plane crash in Maryland.

CELEBRITY OF THE DAY
1992 Flamboyant racecourse tipster Prince Monolulu was remembered when relatives and admirers attended a celebration on what would have been his 111th birthday, at a pub with his name in London. The Prince, who died in 1965, was famous for his cry, 'I've gotta horse'.

26 OCTOBER

SIGNIFICANT EVENT

1996 Michael Dickinson saddled Da Hoss to win the Breeders' Cup Mile at Woodbine, Canada. On the same card Michael Stoute's Pilsudski won the Turf, under Walter Swinburn.

STRANGEST EVENT

1992 The race conditions of Leicester's Wysall Stakes made it a little surprising that Paul Cole entered Run Don't Fly. With 1lb allocated for each £500 won in first-place prize-money, the horse, with £91,154 in such earnings, would have been allocated 21st 3lbs!

OTHER EVENTS

1933 Having been refused a licence for more than five years after an incident where a horse he was riding took no part in a race, Charlie Smirke, now 27, was allowed to ride again as he partnered Equidistant at Newmarket.

1955 Lester Piggott completed his first century of winners on Ragd at Newmarket, ending up third behind Doug Smith in the title race, reaching 103 in all.

1963 Brough Scott rode his first hurdles winner, Arcticeelagh, in Chepstow's Monmouth Handicap Hurdle.

1966 Later to win three Champion Hurdles, Persian War beaten on his hurdling debut at Ascot.

1982 Jockey Tom Grantham rode his first winner, Peyton Pearl, at Plumpton.

1991 Lester Piggott won the Gran Criterium at San Siro, Milan, on Alhijaz for trainer John Dunlop.

1992 Trainer Charlie Nelson quit after his last runner, Awesome Power, won at Lingfield.

1993 Pat Muldoon, owner of the great dual-purpose horse Sea Pigeon, was given a one-year prison sentence for a £1m merchant bank fraud, at Edinburgh High Court, reported *The Sporting Life*.

1994 After winning over £250,000 in place money, maiden Needle Gun finally won a race at the 14th time of asking – a 9/1 shot at Yarmouth, ridden by Michael Roberts for trainer Clive Brittain.

1996 Tempting Prospect, 8/1, won at Newbury, giving The Queen her 600th winner.

2004 Newmarket-based bloodstock agent Rick Dale put the Rae Guest-trained three-year-old winning filly, Magic Verse, up for sale on eBay at £10,000, pointing out: 'For a cost of £2.70 for a ten-day listing it is a bit cheaper than Tattersalls.' But eBay took the ad down, declaring that the website prohibited the sale of live animals.

2007 Top US trainer Carl Nafzger addressed the reality of life with racehorses, telling the New York Times: 'You cannot fall in love with a horse in this day and age because the good ones are going to be taken from you because of the money.'

QUOTE OF THE DAY

'In places like that you didn't bet horses to win. You bet them to live' – late US trainer Sonny Hines, reported by Star Ledger on this day in 2007 discussing his early experiences at racetracks like Wheeling Downs and Narragansett, where *'some of the guys standing around the racing secretary's office made the joint look like the exercise joint at Alcatraz'*.

BIRTHDAY

1950 Andre Pommier, rider of 1987 King George VI Chase winner Nupsala.

DEATH OF THE DAY

1989 John Kenny, MBE, 74. He was manager of Stratford racecourse and owned Milford Grove, who won 11 races in the 1970s.

FIRST OF THE DAY

1986 Patricia Cooksey became the first female rider to partner a stakes winner at Churchill Downs when guiding Bestofbothworlds to victory in the Pocahontas Stakes.

27 OCTOBER

SIGNIFICANT EVENT
1870 Preakness won the first stakes race run at Pimlico racetrack in the US. Three years later the Maryland Jockey Club honoured the colt by naming a one-and-a-half-mile race after him, which became part of the coveted US Triple Crown, along with the Kentucky Derby and Belmont Stakes. Preakness's own future was not too bright as he went to stud at the Duke of Hamilton's in England, where the irascible Duke shot him in a fit of anger.

STRANGEST EVENT
1990 For the first time in Britain all of the runners in a race – four of them – were supplemented entries after all the original entries for Doncaster's Racing Post Trophy were withdrawn. Steve Cauthen rode 2/1 favourite Peter Davies to victory.

OTHER EVENTS
1909 Gamble on Christmas Daisy, for the shrewd 'Druid's Lodge Confederacy' owners, landed Cambridgeshire at 100/7 – and did it again in 1910 at 7/1.
1951 Newcastle held its first National Hunt meeting.
1983 Jockey Ben de Haan rode his first treble, winning on three Fred Winter-trained runners at Wincanton.
1989 Martin Pipe saddled six winners from seven runners at three meetings – four winners at Devon and Exeter, and one each at Hereford and Newbury.
1990 Lester Piggott produced the Vincent O'Brien-trained Royal Academy with a dramatically timed late run to snatch the Breeders' Cup Mile at Belmont Park, worth $450,000 to the winner. Not so fortunate was Willie Carson, who was set to win the Breeders' Cup Sprint on Dayjur, only for the horse to jump a shadow as he approached the line and lose by a neck to Safely Kept.
1991 Turgeon, who had won the Irish St Leger, added the French equivalent, the Prix Royal-Oak at Longchamp.

1992 Former jockey and trainer Dermot Browne was disqualified for ten years by the Jockey Club after being found to have breached six rules of racing, including giving information to a bookmaker in return for monetary reward. He had been exonerated on charges relating to being aware of the doping of Norwich and Bravefoot at Doncaster in September 1990.
1994 Tim Forster's Celtino won at Stratford – the first winner from his new yard at Downton Hall, Ludlow.
1996 Branston Abby, the winning-most British-trained filly or mare since the Second World War, gained her 25th victory, at Cologne.
2001 Tiznow, ridden by Chris McCarron, beat Frankie Dettori on Sakhee into second as he won the Breeders' Cup Classic for the second consecutive year.

QUOTE OF THE DAY
2001 'Not many horses are truly great, but this one is,' declared Mick Kinane, who won a Breeders' Cup race on Johannesburg today, referring to his dual Derby winner of the same year, Galileo.

BIRTHDAYS
1943 Trainer Mel Brittain, who named a bar and restaurant after one of his best horses, Grey Desire.
1963 Jump jockey Penny Ffitch-Heyes.

DEATH OF THE DAY
2007 Aidan O'Brien's George Washington was killed at the Breeders' Cup at Monmouth Park when he broke his off-fore towards the end of the $5m Classic, won by Curlin, and had to be put down. He was the tenth horse to be 'euthanised' at Breeders' Cups.

FIRST OF THE DAY
1946 El Lobo won a handicap at Bay Meadows, San Francisco, having five days earlier been one of the first two horses flown to the races when arriving with Featherfoot from Los Angeles.

28 OCTOBER

SIGNIFICANT EVENT
1973 American equine superstar Secretariat raced for the final time, winning the Canadian International Championship on turf at Woodbine. He won 16 of his 21 races, including the 1973 Triple Crown, and earned $1,316,808.

STRANGEST EVENT
1989 Lady Winner won the Washington Handicap at Laurel, ridden by Kent Desormeaux, who went on to set a record 597-winner total for the season. But did he? Lady Winner was disqualified and placed last – then in March 1990 was reinstated by the Maryland Racing Committee, only to be disqualified again in January 1991 by the Baltimore circuit court.

OTHER EVENTS
1864 Jockey George Fordham booted home six of the nine winners at Newmarket.

1935 Jimmy King had five rides and five winners at Churchill Downs.

1989 Highland Bud won the Breeders' Cup Chase by ten lengths.

1992 National Stud announced the purchase of a half-share in Arc winner Suave Dancer.

1993 Ladbrokes offered to settle with punter Philip Tilson for £33,870, after accepting they had taken a bet from him that they weren't actually offering on the Derby. Tilson, who was unhappy because he thought he should have more, appealed to Tattersalls Committee, which ruled that he was due just £728.64. He did not get even that, as it was revealed he was only 17 and so was under the legal betting age.

1995 Cigar, ridden by Jerry Bailey, won the Breeders' Cup Classic at Churchill Downs.

1995 On-course bookmakers went on strike at Leopardstown in protest at a new on-course betting shop that was allowed to take bets on races at the track.

QUOTE OF THE DAY
2004 Prokofiev supplied Tony McCoy with his tenth career century of winners, with the *Racing Post*'s Lee Mottershead describing his mount as: *'The sort of horse who would much rather sit at home watching daytime television than compete in a three-and-a-half-mile chase around Stratford.'*

BIRTHDAYS
1942 Moreton-in-Marsh trainer Sally Gill, whose best horses included Mr Mole and Eventime. She was confined to a wheelchair after breaking her back in a hunting fall in November 1985.

1944 Classic-winning Wantage trainer Henry Candy, who learned his trade in Sydney and Chantilly.

1950 Lord Hesketh, owner of Towcester racecourse, which introduced free entry for racegoers.

1951 Jockey Dick Marshall, who won the 1976 Northumberland Plate on Philominsky.

DEATHS OF THE DAY
1958 Jockey Charles Spares, who rode Arctic Prince to win the 1951 Derby, died in his 41st year. His health failed shortly after his Classic win and he retired, but he had returned to race-riding shortly before dying.

1981 Sir Randle Feilden, 77, one of modern racing's great administrators. He was responsible for the introduction of starting stalls, camera patrols and regular dope testing.

1994 Lady Beaverbrook, 85, who gave most of her horses seven-letter names. Her St Leger winner Bustino was just beaten by Grundy in the 1975 King George VI and Queen Elizabeth Stakes, which became known as 'the race of the century'.

2005 Canadian-born Michael Lapensee, 58, who rode 2,678 winners, the majority of them in New England, died from injuries sustained during a race at Suffolk Downs, Massachusetts.

29 OCTOBER

SIGNIFICANT EVENT
1886 Fred Archer rode his 2,748th and final winner when the two-year-old Blanchard won at Newmarket for owner Lord Falmouth. Ten days later, on 8 November, Archer was dead – he shot himself. .

STRANGEST EVENT
2008 The funeral took place of 83-year-old former jockey Doug Fisher, who was denied a place in racing history by a broken collarbone. He should have partnered 1951 Grand National winner Nickel Coin, but the injury cost him the ride. He retired in 1966.

OTHER EVENTS
1875 The Dewhurst Stakes was run for the first time, over 7f at Newmarket, with £300 prize-money supplied by Tom Gee, the owner of Dewhurst Stud at Wadhurst, Sussex. Hungarian-bred Kisber, the 10/1 winner, went on to win the Derby.

1926 Phar Lap, the greatest of Australasian horses, was foaled in New Zealand.

1936 Tenby racecourse staged the second day of its final jump meeting.

1980 Arthur Moore saddled his first British winner, Royal Bond, at Ascot.

1983 Desert Orchid won for the first time, in a novice hurdle at Ascot.

1985 Lester Piggott officially retired after taking his total of British winners to 4,349 with victory on Full Choke at Nottingham.

1988 The British-bred Jimmy Lorenzo, ridden by Graham McCourt, won the third running of the $250,000 Breeders' Cup Steeplechase at Fair Hills, Maryland.

1990 Jim Bolger set an Irish record with 138 wins in a year when Latin Quarter obliged at Galway, breaking Senator Jim Parkinson's 1923 record.

1991 Very Dicey was third at Salisbury as trainer Ron Smyth signed off after 45 years. He was champion jump jockey in 1941-42 and won the Champion Hurdle three times

1994 Midland businessman John Graham made history at Newmarket, as the first person to lease a horse for the day under new BHB regulations. The 49-year-old took over ownership of the William Jarvis-trained Lap Of Luxury, who finished second in the Asko Appliance Marshall Stakes. The real owners got the place money.

2005 Saint Liam, the 11/8 favourite, won the Breeders' Cup Classic under Jerry Bailey for trainer Richard Dutrow.

QUOTE OF THE DAY
1975 *'He got a pretty severe kicking but couldn't wait to get back into the weighing room to hear the end of the joke.'* Steve Smith Eccles, who got off the mark on this day, recalling how he was telling Jonjo O'Neill a risque joke during a 1986 Cheltenham race just as the Irishman parted company with his mount.

BIRTHDAYS
1881 Jockey Danny Maher, in Hartford, Connecticut. He won the British championship in 1908 with 139 winners and again in 1913 with 115. He was retained by Lord Rosebery for £4,000 in 1910. He rode nine Classic winners, three in the Derby.

1961 Dermot Browne, champion amateur jump jockey in 1981-82 and 1982-83, who would be warned off in 1992.

1966 Guy Landau, who partnered Lean Ar Aghaidh to finish third in the 1987 Grand National and win the same year's Whitbread Gold Cup.

DEATHS OF THE DAY
1989 Brigadier Gerard found dead in paddock, aged 21.

1992 Set Free, the only broodmare of the century to produce three Classic winners in Britain, was put down, aged 28. She produced Juliette Marny, the 1975 Oaks winner, Julio Mariner (1978 St Leger) and Scintillate (1979 Oaks).

30 OCTOBER

SIGNIFICANT EVENT
1989 All-weather racing made its debut in Britain as Lingfield staged a 12-race card, beginning at 11am, on the Equitrack surface. Niklas Angel, ridden by Richard Quinn and trained by Conrad Allen, won the first race. As a child actor, he fronted TV ads for Smarties and Jaffa Cakes.

STRANGEST EVENT
1948 Jump jockey Bill Smith, who was born on this day, joined Fred Rimell's stable at the age of 15 but lasted only a month before leaving to work in a branch of Moss Bros. He came back via point-to-point and amateur races and rode his first winner under rules in 1968, turning pro shortly after. He rode more winners – 65 – for the Queen Mother than anyone other than David Mould.

OTHER EVENTS
1856 The three-year-old colt Fisherman landed a record-breaking 23rd win in a single season, scoring over distances ranging from four furlongs to three miles. Owned and trained by Tom Parr, the horse went on to win 22 races in 1857 and 21 more in 1858.

1903 One of the great betting coups was landed when Hackler's Pride won the Cambridgeshire, netting connections the equivalent of £10m at modern-day rates. Backed on the day from 8/1 to 9/2, the horse had been laid out for the race all season by the 'Druids Lodge Confederacy' operating from Druids Lodge Stable, Salisbury Plain, where Jack Fallon was trainer.

1981 Fulke Walwyn had a field day when all six runners from his stable won – four at Kempton and two at Devon and Exeter.

1984 Seventy-seven horses were pre-entered for the seven races at the inaugural Breeders' Cup, held at Hollywood Park in Calfornia.

2004 A crowd of 53,717 at Lone Star Park, Texas, saw Ghoszapper lead all the way to win the $4m Breeders' Cup Classic. Frankie Dettori won the Juvenile on 28/1 Wilko, screaming 'I love America' as he came back in, while Kieren Fallon was less emotional after winning the Filly & Mare Turf on 10/11 Ouija Board. 'She done it nice,' said Fallon.

2009 The New York Racing Association banned trainer Jeff Mullins from its tracks for six months: 'for giving one of his horses an unknown substance in the Aqueduct monitoring barn in April and repeatedly lying about it,' reported the *New York Times*.

QUOTE OF THE DAY
2007 *'You can be as shrewd a judge when you're 16 as when you're 86, but you can love it as much when you're 86 as when you're 16, and there's not many things you can say that about.'* Gambler and owner Harry Findlay on his favourite occupation – punting.

BIRTHDAYS
1944 Heather Alwen, owner and Charlton Athletic fan. Spot the link in the names of her horses: Sir Percy Yeoman, Reggae Yeoman, Yeoman Metro, Noble Yeoman, Bold Yeoman, Wily Yeoman, Charlton Yeoman, Steel Yeoman.

1945 Trainer Con Horgan, whose Western Dancer won the 1985 Ebor at 20/1 and the Chester Cup at 14/1 in 1986.

1978 Jump jockey Jamie Goldstein, who rode his first winner in 1997. His biggest winner was King's Road in the 2000 Hennessy Gold Cup.

FIRST OF THE DAY
1845 Newmarket had the first recorded example of a triple dead-heat.

CELEBRITY OF THE DAY
1961 Mike Cattermole, 'heartthrob' racing writer turned TV presenter and commentator, was born.

31 OCTOBER

SIGNIFICANT EVENT
1945 Gordon Richards became the first English jockey to ride 3,000 winners.

STRANGEST EVENT
1791 Cash became the first yearling to compete on a British racecourse, beating a three-year-old conceding 3st in a match at Newmarket. Five days later, renamed Ariel and with a new owner, the horse ran and won again on the same track. Yearling racing was banned in 1860.

OTHER EVENTS
1947 Edgar Britt rode his 100th winner of the season, joining Gordon Richards, brothers Eph and Doug Smith, and Billy Nevett. It was the first time in 48 years that five riders had completed a ton.
1987 US jockey Chris Antley rode nine winners – four at Aqueduct and five more at Meadowlands, New Jersey.
1990 Australian rider Malcolm Johnston was ordered to pay damages, plus interest and costs, over a claim resulting from injuries suffered by apprentice Glenn William Frazier in a fall during a race the previous year. Frazier suffered a broken thigh and back injuries and Johnston was found to have been negligent in the way he handled his mount, which crossed two horses. He had to sell his house to settle the claim.
1991 Ray Cochrane rode 100 winners for the fifth consecutive season when Navarra won at Newmarket.
1992 Lester Piggott ended up in intensive care, after falling from fatally injured Mr Brooks in the Breeeders' Cup Sprint at Gulfstream Park, Florida.
1994 Aidan O'Brien, 24, set a record for the number of winners trained in Ireland in a calendar year when Holiway Star won at Leopardstown to become his 151st of the year, beating the mark set by Dermot Weld in 1991.
1996 Cigar, one of the world's most dominant racing thoroughbreds of the past half-century, was retired by owners Allen and Madeleine Paulson.

1997 Dick Hern's final runner as a trainer, Ghalib, dead-heated for third place at Newmarket.
2009 Barry Geraghty supsended for 12 days after taking wrong course at Wetherby.

QUOTE OF THE DAY
1950 *'I wasn't disappointed when it closed. Even though I rode the last winner there I wish it had closed before I started riding.'* John Lowe, born on this day, was no fan of Lanark, which closed in 1977.

BIRTHDAY
1948 Irish trainer William Roper, whose horses included Kinky Lady, Cabinet Meeting, Elevate and In The Dock – almost a short novel in themselves.

DEATHS OF THE DAY
1765 Owner Duke of Cumberland, 44, whose stud included Herod, the great sire, and the famous Eclipse, then 18 months old. His death was blamed on 'corpulence' and effects of an old war wound.
1982 Tony Murphy, 52, the brains behind 1974 Gay Future coup.
1995 Trainer Ron Mason, 79, once a leading speedway rider. His Petite Path won the Ayr Gold Cup.
2005 Trainer Bill Marshall, 87. He was awarded the DFC during the Second World War for shooting down a German V1 flying bomb en route to London. After a brief riding career, he took up training and handled top sprinter Raffingora, who broke the 5f world record at Epsom with a time of 53.89s.
2007 Alderbrook, 1995 Champion Hurdle winner, was put down aged 18.

CELEBRITY OF THE DAY
1920 Dick Francis, novelist and champion jockey, was born. He is best remembered as the jockey of Queen Mother's Devon Loch, who had the 1956 Grand National at his mercy when, inexplicably, he spreadeagled on the run-in.

1 NOVEMBER

SIGNIFICANT EVENT
1938 Seabiscuit v War Admiral. The two equine heroes from either side of the US met at Pimlico over 1m 1.5f for a $15,000 purse. In a showdown hyped as 'East v West', George 'Iceman' Woolf deputised for the injured Red Pollard on Seabiscuit with usual rider Charlie Kurtsinger on War Admiral, and 40,000 watched as a nip-and-tuck race unfolded with Seabiscuit finishing the stronger to win by three lengths over the 1937 Triple Crown winner.

STRANGEST EVENT
2008 'A couple of tinpot Hitlers,' said jockey John Egan, referring to vets in Melbourne who were taking an interest in the health of his intended Melbourne Cup mount, Yellowstone. It cost him Aus$8,000 (£3,340), when he was fined for his remarks.

OTHER EVENTS
1939 Run over a shortened course for the first time in 101 uninterrupted renewals, the 35-runner Cesarewitch was won by 7/2 favourite Cantatrice II, partnered by Doug Smith.
1947 US equine great Man o'War died, aged 30. Odds-on for all his 21 races, he lost just once, and won $249,465.
1966 Michael Scudamore, father of Peter, took a fall that finished his career as a jockey, from Snakestone at Wolverhampton. He broke his jaw, the top of his palate and cheekbone, and his eyesight was affected.
1975 Allez France, the great French star, finished unplaced in the last of her 21 races, on dirt at Santa Anita. She won 13 races, including the Arc.
1977 After 99 years, trainer Etienne de Mestre's record five Melbourne Cup winners was beaten when Adelaide's Bart Cummings produced Gold And Black, the 7/2 favourite, to beat 23 rivals.
1984 Provideo set a record, landing his 16th win as a two-year-old, at Redcar. The Bard also won 16 in 1885, but that included a walkover. Provideo had three more races during the season but failed to win again and was retired.
1985 Desert Orchid, 4/5, won his first chase, at Devon, ridden by Colin Brown.
1989 Southwell became the first racecourse to hold jump racing on an artificial surface, Fibresand.
1991 Jump jockey Paul Nicholls took out a training licence.
1993 Starting poles, set back five yards from the tapes, were introduced for jump jockeys to line up alongside, before moving in to start. By December 20 they had been dropped: 'They proved counter-productive, jockeys were revving up when they passed the poles,' explained Jockey Club spokesman David Pipe.
2005 Makybe Diva, foaled in England in 1999, made history as she won the Melbourne Cup for the third consecutive year. Trained by Lee Freedman, she won 15 of her 36 starts and collected prize-money of more than Aus$14m.
2008 Claire Lindop, the first female to ride in an Australian Group 1 race when Exalted Time won the 2006 Adelaide Cup, added the Australian Derby, the Victoria version, on 75/1 shot Rebel Raider.

QUOTE OF THE DAY
2008 *'Quite rightly, not one person was complimentary. I wasn't amused and found it all very embarrassing,'* trainer Paul Nicholls made his displeasure about a *Racing Post* front page depicting him on a Monopoly board quite clear on this date.

BIRTHDAY
1892 Sir Michael Sobell, owner of 1979 Derby winner Troy, who was still around to celebrate his 100th birthday.

DEATH OF THE DAY
1988 Florence Nagle, 94, the first woman officially recognised as a trainer.

CELEBRITY OF THE DAY
1935 Gary Player, South African golfer, and joint-breeder of Broadway Flyer.

2 NOVEMBER

SIGNIFICANT EVENT
1993 Vintage Crop, who earlier in the season finished sixth in the Champion Hurdle, became the first horse from outside Australasia to win the Melbourne Cup. He was trained in Ireland by Dermot Weld and ridden by Michael Kinane, who had never seen the course at Flemington until 24 hours earlier.

STRANGEST EVENT
2008 Jockey Darryll Holland revealed an hilarious Hong Kong incident: 'Richard Hughes rode out with a pair of trainers on, as he'd forgotten his riding boots. It was hysterical. It made front-page news.'

OTHER EVENTS
1936 Ryan Jarvis saddled the first of his 1,010 winners when Alexdream (Harry Blackshaw) scored at Birmingham.
1985 The Clive Brittain-trained Pebbles won her final race, the Breeders' Cup Turf at Aqueduct, under Pat Eddery, no doubt boosted by her diet supplement of a pint of Guinness a day. Her prize of £775,862 took her earnings to a record £1,182,140, beating Teleprompter's previous best for a British-trained horse.
1988 Tote Gold Trophy, Queen Mother Champion Chase and Melling Chase winner Deep Sensation was third on his debut at Newbury.
1989 Royal trainer Dick Hern, confined to a wheelchair following a 1984 hunting accident, was named Man of Year by the Royal Association for Disability and Rehabilitation. That year, Hern had trained Nashwan to win the 2,000 Guineas, Derby, Eclipse and King George VI and Queen Elizabeth Stakes.
1991 Bradbury Star became the first horse to benefit from a Jockey Club rule designed to prevent matches and walkovers, when he won at Warwick for Josh Gifford. The trainer had previously withdrawn him, only to put him back in the race when it was reopened after only two horses were declared to run from the original 23 entries.

1991 Sportscast, a new company, began beaming live racing to Britain's pubs and clubs, starting with action from Wolverhampton.
1991 Dance Smartly won the Breeders' Cup Distaff at Churchill Downs, passing Lady's Secret as racing's all-time leading female money earner, with $3,083,456.
1991 Nobody who saw the unbeaten two-year-old Arazi annihilate 13 rivals in the Breeders' Cup Juvenile at Churchill Downs would ever forget the way in which Pat Valenzuela brought the colt through, picking off runners one by one, going round, past and inside horses before cruising down the straight to a five-length win.
1992 Frankie Dettori and Ray Cochrane both reached 100 winners for the season with doubles at Newcastle.
2009 Duc de Regniere at Kempton was Barry Geraghty's 1,000th winner. New rule was brought in that banned re-mounting horses.

QUOTE OF THE DAY
2004 'Makybe Diva is the legend, I'm just the lucky b*****d who is sitting on her back,' declared Glen Boss on this day, after partnering her to become the first mare to win back-to-back Melbourne Cups.

BIRTHDAYS
1939 Jockey John 'Kipper' Lynch.
1963 Jockey Patrick Farrell, who won the 1984 Schweppes Hurdle on Ra Nova.

DEATH OF THE DAY
2004 Mick Gordon, 90, an Irish jockey who rode 600 winners under both codes, and once had five winners out of six at Bellewstown.

CELEBRITY OF THE DAY
1990 Personal form books compiled by Timeform's Phil Bull were sold at auction for £18,000. The books covered 1935 to 1989, the year in which he died, aged 79.

3 NOVEMBER

SIGNIFICANT EVENT
1991 Sign of things to come as Frankie Dettori's plane dash from Churchill Downs to Saint-Cloud produced his first French winner, John Gosden's Susurration.

STRANGEST EVENT
1989 Racegoers at Bangor had to make do without closed circuit TV, and stewards without camera patrol films, after a camera crew went to Bangor, North Wales, instead of Bangor-on-Dee.

OTHER EVENTS
1841 Lottery, the best chaser of the day, carried 13st 6lbs over four miles at Newport Pagnell, starting 4/5 favourite but finishing second.

1864 Lantern won his fourth Melbourne Cup, 15/1. The next day he won the Victoria Derby by six lengths. He is the only horse to complete the double in that order. On 6 November, he came out again to win 1m Publican's Purse, despite losing 100 yards at the start.

1990 William Hastings Bass fined £700 for failing to allow royal filly Chestnut Tree to run on merits at Newmarket. On the same day Jim Bolger had a double at Down Royal that gave him a record 121 winners in the Irish Flat season. And Australian David Hayes, a trainer for just three months, sent out a world record six Group and Graded winners in a single day, at Flemington.

1997 Bill Shoemaker retired from training after turning out 90 winners from 913 runners to add to his 8,883 winners as a jockey.

2004 Four days earlier, 75-year-old Jack Lee from Newcastle thought he had won £957,714 from his £2 accumulator as final selection Babodana passed the post at Newmarket in front. Then disaster struck, as stewards relegated the horse to second, making Jack's bet only a place accumulator – worth £90. Revealing his identity today, he was in philosophical mood: 'That's gambling for you.'

2009 Kerrin McEvoy rode Crime Scene, third straight British-trained Melbourne Cup runner up. The winner was 9/1 Shocking, ridden by Corey Brown.

QUOTE OF THE DAY
2008 *'A winning owner who had just dropped his cut-glass trophy.'* At The Races presenter Robert Cooper recalling his most memorable interview on this day.

BIRTHDAY
1947 Jockey Robert Street.

FIRST OF THE DAY
1993 For the first time in modern-day racing, free admission was offered to racegoers – and 4,000 responded by flocking to Kelso.

CELEBRITY OF THE DAY
1956 Gary Ross, producer of Oscar-nominated film *Seabiscuit*, was born.

1973 'Castaway' star turned TV presenter Ben Fogle, an owner with William Haggas.

4 NOVEMBER

SIGNIFICANT EVENT
1968 Lester Piggott was in court at Uxbridge, where he admitted trying to take £686 more out of the country in April than exchange regulations permitted. He was fined £750.

STRANGEST EVENT
1998 Amateur rider Marco Alliata won a race at San Siro, Milan, on Musharak – at the age of 77.

OTHER EVENTS
1886 Fred Archer, beaten on favourite Tommy Titlemouse at Lewes – his last ride.

1908 Jerry M won the Becher Chase at Aintree by 12 lengths. He went on to win the 1912 Grand National under 12st 7lb.

1930 Phar Lap won the Melbourne Cup, despite being shot at on the way back from morning exercise three days earlier.

1967 Peter O'Sullevan's Be Friendly won Haydock's Vernons Sprint Cup for the second straight year.

1972 Trainer Sam Armstrong– real name Frederick Lakin – who had saddled winners at every Flat course, sent out his last two winners at Haydock.

1982 Starawak, winner at Redcar, took Clive Brittain's first place earnings past £1million.

1984 The first Sunday meeting at Churchill Downs attracted 8,791 fans.

1989 A Florida record crowd of 51,342 attended Gulfstream Park for the sixth Breeders' Cup as Sunday Silence beat Easy Goer by a neck in the Classic.

1997 Bill Watts bowed out as a trainer with his last runner, the unplaced Hurgill Dancer at Redcar.

1998 Kieren Fallon followed Fred Archer, Gordon Richards and Frankie Dettori to become the fourth Flat jockey to ride consecutive double centuries of winners as he booted home a 32/1 treble at Musselburgh.

1998 Sixteen-year-old Thomas Scudamore – son of multiple champion jump jockey Peter Scudamore – rode his first winner, Young Thruster, at Newton Abbot.

2000 Spain triumphed in America as the horse of that name scored a 55/1 shock win in the Breeders' Cup Distaff.

2006 A record crowd of 129,089 at Melbourne's Flemington racecourse saw Efficient surge to a sensational victory in the AJC Victoria Derby. I backed him to win the 2007 Melbourne Cup, which he did in breathtaking style, swooping on the line to collar Luca Cumani's Purple Moon. He was the first horse since Phar Lap to achieve that double.

2008 Jockey Dean McKeown, riding newcomer Rascal In The Mix, was found in breach of the non-triers' rule at Southwell and had his licence withdrawn with immediate effect, just 12 days after being warned off for his part in a conspiracy involving the laying of 11 horses.

2008 Viewed was a 40/1 winner of the Melbourne Cup at Flemington for trainer Bart Cummings, who was landing his 12th winner in the race.

QUOTE OF THE DAY
1993 Racegoers had almost all departed from Musselburgh after racing when cleaners heard plaintive cries from commentator Raleigh Gilbert, stuck in the commentary box. He had finally called for rescue over the track's pa system: *'If anyone can hear me, please come and rescue me, I'm stuck.'*

BIRTHDAY
1950 Champion UAE trainer, Dhruba Selvaratnam.

DEATH OF THE DAY
2009 Seven times champion trainer of Malaysia and Singapore, Ivan Allan, 68.

CELEBRITY OF THE DAY
1997 The Queen's Arabian Story, 25/1, finished sixth in the Melbourne Cup behind winner Might And Power, the 7/2 favourite.

5 NOVEMBER

SIGNIFICANT EVENT
1935 Lester Piggott was born, on the anniversary of the date in 1831 that Frank Buckle – the jockey whose Classic record Piggott would ultimately break – had his final mount on Conservator, 50 years to the day since joining Richard Vernon's Newmarket stables as an apprentice. Buckle rode five Derby winners, among 27 Classic winners in all, and three months after retiring he was dead.

STRANGEST EVENT
1968 Rookie trainer Mick Robins was so excited as his first runner in the Melbourne Cup, Rain Lover, 7/1, came to win the race that he fell down the steps of the trainers' stand.

OTHER EVENTS
1831 Squire George Osbaldeston won £1,000 after proving he could ride 200 miles in under 10 hours on circuits of a round course at the Newmarket Houghton meeting. He used 29 horses, completing the 200 miles in 8h 42m. On the same day five time Derby winner Frank Buckle retired as a jockey exactly 50 years after first joining a Newmarket stable.

1950 Fulke Walwyn sent out four winners at Stratford, all owned by Dorothy Paget.

1955 A record 166 runners competed on a six-race card at Windsor. The previous highest turnout had been 157 at Leicester in 1949.

1963 Eighty-one-year-old Malcolm Reid from Adelaide owned the 25/1 Melbourne Cup winner, Gatum Gatum (reportedly Aboriginal for boomerang).

1988 A Breeders' Cup record crowd of 71,237 attended the fifth running of the event at Churchill Downs. Personal Ensign won the Distaff by a nose and retired undefeated in 13 career starts. Great Communicator won the Turf to become the first gelding to win a Breeders' Cup Flat race.

1991 Bart Cummings made it nine Melbourne Cup winners, saddling 3/1 favourite Let's Elope, who survived a stewards' inquiry. Even if she had been disqualified, runner-up Shiva's Revenge was also trained by Cummings.

1994 Frankie Dettori won the Breeders' Cup Mile in a record 1m 34.2s on Luca Cumani's Barathea at Churchill Downs. Cumani's Saxon Maid (Jason Weaver), made it a unique double, winning the November Handicap at Doncaster.

1999 Al Capone II, trained by Bernard Secly, under Jean-Yves Beaurain, won Prix la Haye Jousselin chase at Auteuil for incredible seventh consecutive year.

QUOTE OF THE DAY
1997 *'There is no malice at all. I hope she finds the whole thing funny.'* This was probably wishful thinking by racing fan John Milton, who, on this day, sponsored a race in honour of his former wife – the J C Milton She's Finally Gone Handicap Hurdle at Newton Abbot.

BIRTHDAYS
1928 Cath Walwyn, widow of great trainer Fulke Walwyn.

1946 Tom Foley, trainer of the top-class and much-loved Irish jumper Danoli.

1950 US Hall of Fame trainer Richard Mandella.

DEATHS OF THE DAY
1969 Lionel Vick Memorial Chase at Newbury paid tribute to the jockey, who had died in a car crash that May, aged 45. He had retired after being paralysed following a Sedgefield fall in 1951 and was one of the early driving forces behind the Injured Jockeys' Fund.

1998 Night Nurse, 28, the popular hurdler and chaser.

2002 Barbara Holbrook, 52, a trainer in the American Midwest, was found shot dead. She saddled 179 winners from 1,239 starts.

6 NOVEMBER

SIGNIFICANT EVENT
2004 For the first time the Tote Scoop6 win fund dividend broke the £1m barrier, paying £1,132,657.40 to Stuart Bolland, a software engineer from Greater Manchester.

STRANGEST EVENT
1993 Andre Fabre's Breeders Cup Classic winner, Arcangues, was returned at 133/1 and was backed – I know, I was there when he did it – by *Racing Post* golf expert Jeremy Chapman. By the way, Chappers, it was us who added those drinks to your tab.

OTHER EVENTS
1990 'B.B.' Shoemaker, father of top US jockey Bill Shoemaker, died, aged 81.
1991 Juvenile US superstar Arazi underwent a successful operation to treat an arthritic knee, in Lexington, Kentucky.
1995 The Racing Channel, a new satellite TV service, was launched.
1995 Jockey Declan Murphy announced his retirement after being badly injured in a fall while racing. In 2002 his home was ransacked; in 2004 he was robbed at gunpoint; in 2007 accused 'flashing' in New Zealand.
1998 A world record was claimed as 11 horses started 12/1 co-favourites for the 23-runner Curragh Carpets Celestial Apprentices Handicap at the Curragh. Only four starting prices – 12/1, 14/1, 16/1 and 20/1 – were returned. Charlton Spring, one of the co-favourites, won.
2009 Henry Cecil broke Breeders' Cup duck as Tom Queally won the 1m 2f Filly and Mare Turf, worth £750,000, with Midday. Aiden O'Brien's Man Of Iron won the Marathon, the stable's first Breeders' Cup winner since 2003. He was the only one of the the stable's runners

to run on Lasix medication. – all their others were beaten.

QUOTE OF THE DAY
1978 'Confessions of a Master Fixer' was the front-page headline of *Sports Illustrated*, the esteemed US magazine. Jockey Jose Amy confessed he had 'restrained' seven horses for $1,500 a time. He was banned, but in October 2004 allowed to return to riding, with a comeback winner in February 2005, aged 51.

BIRTHDAYS
1935 Nigel Clark, owner of 13 chase-winner Carrigeen Hill, and Jockey Club member.
1942 York trainer Donald Lee.
1938 Tony Biddlecombe, champion amateur rider in 1961-62.
1948 Former French champion trainer Criquette Head, whose Three Troikas won the 1979 Arc and Ma Biche the 1983 1,000 Guineas.
1948 Jocky turned trainer Ferdy Murphy, whose best jumpers include Anaglogues's Daughter, Sibton Abbey and French Holly.

DEATHS OF THE DAY
1992 Blakeney, the 1969 Derby winner, put down at the National Stud, aged 26.
2000 David Cecil, 57, twin brother of Henry (David was the younger by ten minutes). He trained in Lambourn for three years from 1969, going on to become a successful restaurateur.

FIRST OF THE DAY
1970 Red Rum, the Grand National winner in 1973, 1974 and 1977, won his first chase, at odds of 100/7 in the Town Moor Novice Chase at Doncaster, ridden by Tommy Stack.

7 NOVEMBER

SIGNIFICANT EVENT
1998 British-born trainer Michael Dickinson staggered US racing observers by bringing Da Hoss back to win his second Breeders' Cup Mile, two years after the first. Da Hoss, the first horse to win non-consecutive Breeders Cups, had been off the track for virtually all of the intervening period and had just one prep race before regaining his title. Race commentator Tom Durkin called it: 'the greatest comeback since Lazarus'.

STRANGEST EVENT
2006 Australian racegoers – and there were more than 100,000 of them at Flemington – were stunned as the Melbourne Cup produced a Japanese one-two, with Delta Blues, a 16/1 shot ridden by Yasunari Iwata, just holding off Pop Rock, partnered by Damien Oliver. Amazingly, both horses were trained by Katsuhiko Sumii.

OTHER EVENTS
1873 Fred Archer rode Sterling to win the Liverpool Autumn Cup and, as a present, owner Thomas Roughton gave him a short-barrelled gun – the weapon with which Archer would take his own life.
1981 King Hustler, ridden by John Francome at Chepstow, was trainer Nicky Henderson's 100th winner.
1992 Grand National-winning jockey Richard Dunwoody had his first five-timer, at Chepstow. On the same day trainer John Gosden's 11/4 November Handicap favourite Daru finished runner-up to 10/1 Turgenev - trained by John Gosden. And Michael Roberts rode the final winner of his first title-winning season on the Flat when Branston Abby won at Doncaster, taking him to 206 winners.
1993 Punters at Auteuil showed their disapproval of shock winner Bitwood after the £47,790 Grand Prix d'Automne. Annoyed that a horse with poor form

had triumphed, punters dumped tens of thousands of pari-mutuel tickets in the parade ring. Stewards called in trainer Jean Lesbordes and accepted his explanation that lack of blinkers was responsible for previous pulled-up display.
1995 Vintage Crop, the 1993 Melbourne Cup winner, ran third in this year's race, winning £89,109 to become the first equine millionaire in Irish racing history.
1998 Paul Nicholls saddled seven winners and three seconds from ten runners – three won at Chepstow, three at Sandown and one at Wincanton.
2009 Unbeaten filly Zenyatta won 14th straight race in $5m Breeders' Cup Classic, beating a field of top colts in sensational style, under Mike Smith.

QUOTE OF THE DAY
2004 *'If I unexpectedly came into £5m I would buy a thoroughbred racehorse for £1m and aim for a Derby win,'* vowed Cockney Rebel pop star Steve Harley.

BIRTHDAYS
1922 Jane Pilkington, owner-trainer of triple Cheltenham Golden Hurdle winner Willie Wumpkins (1979-81).
1928 Rosemary Lomax, trainer of 1970 Ascot Gold Cup winner Precipice Wood.
1938 Ian Balding, trainer of the great Mill Reef and the popular sprint filly Lochsong, was born in New Jersey.
1955 Geraldine Rees, first female jockey to complete the Grand National course.

DEATH OF THE DAY
1962 Australian jockey Neville Sellwood, who rode Larkspur to win the 1962 Derby, was killed when riding Lucky Seven at Maisons-Laffitte.

FIRST OF THE DAY
1861 The Melbourne Cup was run for the first time, in front of a crowd of 4,000, and was won by a horse which, according to legend, walked 475 miles in 28 days to reach Flemington for the 2m race.

8 NOVEMBER

SIGNIFICANT EVENT
1886 'The rumour was discredited, but when enquiry had proved it to be true, the news spread like wildfire, and furnished an absorbing topic for discussion and comment' – the *Newmarket Journal* reporting on the suicide by shooting on this day of 13-time champion jockey Fred Archer who had 2,748 winners from 8,084 mounts. He left an estate worth £60,000.

STRANGEST EVENT
1989 No starting prices were returned for a 14-runner 1m handicap at Southwell during the first all-weather meeting at the track. SP reporters said only one bookie displayed a full list of odds and no market was formed. Admiralty Way (paying £9.80 on the Tote) won the race.

OTHER EVENTS
1933 Gordon Richards won on Golden King at Liverpool to overtake Fred Archer's record 246 winners in a season, going on to register 259 – which he beat by ten in 1947.
1993 Having passed Henry Cecil's record 180 wins in a season when Art Tatum won at Yarmouth three days earlier, Richard Hannon added number 182 when Gallant Spirit won at the final Flat meeting of the season, Folkestone. Hannon did it from almost 1,200 runners, Cecil from 445.
1995 US jump jockey Chip Miller, battling against sister Blythe to become US champion, rode for the first time in Britain, winning on his father's Storm North at Worcester – but picked up a two-day ban for careless riding.
2008 Ryan Moore became British champion Flat jockey with 186 wins, while William Buick and David Probert shared the apprentice title with 50 apiece. Aidan O'Brien was top trainer with £3,276,097 in win and place money,

and the top owner was Princess Haya with £2,161,396.
2008 Paul Nicholls saddled five of the seven winners at Wincanton and also had two at Sandown.
2008 Aussie training legend Bart Cummings won his 251st Group race with Swick in the Patinack Farm Classic at Flemington, beating Turffontein, trained by his son Anthony.
2009 Tony McCoy rode third treble at fledgling track, Ffos Las.

QUOTE OF THE DAY
'People rarely believe us, but we can't afford to bet,' said trainer Roger Spicer after sending out Malenoir and Rural Lad, both 20/1 winners, in successive races at Southwell on this day in 1993.

BIRTHDAY
1910 Trainer Fulke Walwyn and twin Helen Johnson Houghton, at Wrexham. Helen was the first woman responsible for a Classic winner when Gilles De Retz won the 1956 2,000 Guineas. Fulke trained four Cheltenham Gold Cup winners.

DEATHS OF THE DAY
1895 Teddy Weever, trainer of Grand National-winning sisters Emblem and Emblematic
1981 Tim Brookshaw, 52, the champion jump jockey of 1958-59, died from injuries sustained in a fall a week earlier.
2004 Harry Bell, 76, trainer of three Scottish National winners – Quick Reply in 1972, Sebastian V in 1977 and Astral Charmer in 1981. In 1989 he was convicted of cruelty to horses and served a six-month jail term.

CELEBRITY OF THE DAY
1996 England footballer David Platt had his first winner as an owner, Handsome Ridge, 20/1, at Doncaster.

9 NOVEMBER

SIGNIFICANT EVENT
2008 The Joel Marr-trained five-year-old Peppers Pride won her 18th consecutive race when scoring at Zia Park, New Mexico, setting the longest winning sequence of any US horse since 1900. The all-time US record is believed to be 23, set in 1801 by Leviathan.

STRANGEST EVENT
1883 Harry Beasley rode Too Good to win the City Cup at Liverpool. Eight years later he won the Grand National on Come Away, and 44 years after that he became the oldest man to win a race when winning the Corinthian Plate at Baldoyle, aged 85.

OTHER EVENTS
1963 Manchester racecourse closed.
1985 Joe Mercer rode 20/1 Bold Rex to win the November Handicap at Doncaster, his last mount before retiring.
1987 Plumpton saw first 100/1 winner, Stargaze, ridden by Ray Goldstein in Sid Lanaway Memorial Chase.
1989 Richard Dunwoody teamed up with Desert Orchid for the first time, winning a two-horse race at Wincanton.
1991 Another Coral won the Mackeson Gold Cup, after trainer David Nicholson had made an unusual request to a jazz band that was entertaining racegoers between races. He asked them to stop playing, as his horse hated music.
1991 Geraldine Rees, who nine years earlier became the first woman to complete the Grand National, rode her first winner on the Flat, I Perceive.
1991 Rookie trainer Charlie Egerton saddled his first winner with his first runner, Torrent Bay at Windsor.
1992 It was not clear who celebrated Michael Roberts' first championship the most – the South African-born Flat jockey, who rode 206 winners, or his agent, Graham Rock, who backed him with £100 at 100/1 with William Hill to do so.

1993 Clifton Chase, a winner on the Flat at Southwell the previous day, won again at the track for trainer Jimmy Harris – on his hurdles debut.
1995 Tony McCoy was one of six jockeys suspended for taking the wrong course in a race at Taunton.
1995 Mark Sharratt became the first jockey to ride a winner using the new air-cushioned whip, on Seatwist at Towcester, where the 13/2 shot was one of only three to complete the course.
2004 Derby-winning jockey Alan Munro was reported to be planning a comeback after a four-year sabbatical, explaining: 'In the middle of 2000 I decided to leave the industry and do something I really wanted to do. I spent a lot of my time learning karate.' He became a black belt.
2008 After a 31-day strike over a threatened reduction in prize-money, which stopped both Flat racing and trotting, racing returned to Italy, at Rome's Capannelle course.
2009 Exeter's £2m grandstand opened.

QUOTE OF THE DAY
2008 *'You only get as excited as that once in a blue moon,'* said Seb Sanders, on winning the Oaks on Look Here.

BIRTHDAY
1959 Jump jockey turned trainer Richard Rowe, who rode 550 winners.

DEATHS OF THE DAY
1916 Connecticut-born jockey Danny Maher, 35. Rode nine Classic winners and British champion in 1908 and 1913.
1928 Peter (Valentine Purcell) Gilpin, in his 70th year. Trained great filly Pretty Polly, winner of the 1,000 Guineas, Oaks and St Leger, and had Derby wins with Spearmint and Spion Kop.

CELEBRITY OF THE DAY
2004 Emlyn Hughes OBE, the former England and Liverpool skipper, whose horses were trained by Martin Pipe, died aged 57.

10 NOVEMBER

SIGNIFICANT EVENT
1984 The inaugural Breeders' Cup Championship was run in front of a crowd of 64,254 at Hollywood Park, California. Chief's Crown won the first race, the Juvenile, and longshot Wild Again claimed the Classic. The first Breeders' Cup disqualification was outsider Fran's Valentine, who passed the post first in the Juvenile Fillies, with the race awarded to Outstandingly. Eilio, winner of the Sprint, was retired to go to stud, but died four weeks later.

STRANGEST EVENT
2008 Having been off the track because 'all her hair fell out, she was completely bald,' according to trainer Jonathan Jay, his three-year-old Azabu Juban returned from a seven-month layoff to win at Wolverhampton.

OTHER EVENTS
1909 All eight fell in Aintree's Becher Chase – Moorside was remounted to win.
1947 Gordon Richards broke his own record 259 winners in a season when he rode Twenty Twenty to victory at Leicester. He finished the season with 269 winners.
1992 Barbara Holland of Coral was voted the first female Racing Post Betting Shop Manager of the Year.
2007 Kevin Darley, champion Flat jockey in 2000 with 155 wins, retired at the age of 47. Born in 1960, he was apprenticed to Reg Hollinshead and had his first winner, Dust Up, at Haydock on August 5, 1977. He won the St Leger on Bollin Eric in 2002 and the 2004 1,000 Guineas (and the Irish version) on Attraction. He rode 2,451 British winners and had five winners in a day on three occasions (July 23, 1993, August 1, 1998, and July 23, 2001).
2008 'In the space of less than three weeks I won over £50,000 … the wins took me off the straight and narrow, ultimately towards founding Betfair.'

Revealing his best-ever bet in the *Racing Post*, on this day in 2008, Betfair co-founder Andrew Black told how he won £25,500 by backing the 1992 Lincoln and National winners, High Low and Party Politics, in a double. Then on June 1, 1992, trainer John Hills had three winners at Redcar: Glide Path (5/1), Gilderdale (9/2) and Eternal Flame (100/30). Black, who owned Glide Path, backed the lot and won £30,000.

QUOTE OF THE DAY
2007 *'The lucky bugger got to do all the whooping and punching the air, so it is bittersweet,'* reflected Seb Sanders, as he and Jamie Spencer finished level in the 2007 Flat jockeys' championship; Spencer won the last race of the season on 9/4 Inchnadamph at Doncaster to tie the title at 190 wins each.

BIRTHDAY
1926 Jockey turned trainer Frank Durr. The Liverpudlian rode his first winner in 1944 and went on to win Classics on Sodium (1966 St Leger), Mon Fils (1973 2,000 Guineas), Peleid (1973 St Leger) and Roland Gardens (1978 2,000 Guineas).

DEATHS OF THE DAY
1868 Owner-gambler the Marquis of Hastings, 26. He lost an estimated £102,000 betting against Hermit in the 1867 Derby, and just before his death he said: 'Hermit's Derby broke my heart. But I didn't show it, did I?'
1986 Sir Gordon Richards, 82. He won 4,870 races from 21,837 rides and was British champion Flat jockey 26 times. He rode 14 Classic winners but won only one Derby, 1953, on Pinza. He was knighted in 1953 for services to racing.
1995 Sir Ivor, the 1968 Derby winner, was put down aged 30.

CELEBRITY OF THE DAY
1944 Sir Tim Rice, a former owner with Tom Marshall, was born.

11 NOVEMBER

SIGNIFICANT EVENT
1958 Ballymoss, the Arc winner and record British and Irish prize-money earner, ran his final race, in the Washington International. He was baulked and jostled but finished third, bringing his career earnings to £107,166. He went on to sire Derby winner Royal Palace.

STRANGEST EVENT
1995 For the first time a race had a telephone number in its title – the 0990-11-11-45 Royal Star and Garter Chase at Windsor, sponsored on behalf of a refuge for disabled servicemen.

OTHER EVENTS
1874 Thameside racecourse at Reading held its last meeting.

1904 Manifesto ran his last race, finishing unplaced in Liverpool's Valentine Chase, aged 16. He won two Grand Nationals and placed in four more.

1955 Pappa Fourway, who cost just 150gns, won the eighth race of his three-year-old career, the Tetrarch Stakes at Manchester. On the same card 12 year old Robin Langley rode a winner.

1968 Trainer Ken Oliver and jockey Barry Brogan had five winners from five runners at Wolverhampton.

1968 Sir Ivor won the Washington International at Laurel Park for Lester Piggott and Vincent O'Brien.

1975 For the first time in England, there were seven 8/1 co-favourites, in Haydock's Blackburn Nursery. The race was won by one of the co-favourites, the Richard Fox-ridden Hargrave Rogue.

1978 Seattle Slew won his final race at Aqueduct, to end his career with 14 wins in 17 races. In 1977 he uniquely won the US Triple Crown when still undefeated.

1986 A *Daily Telegraph* obituary paid tribute to recently deceased jockey Gordon Richards, quoting racing writer Quintin Gilbey: 'The most beautiful sight in the world is Gordon Richards two lengths in front and his whip still swinging, when you have bet twice as much as you can afford.'

1991 Pat Eddery won ninth British Flat jockeys' championship with 165 winners.

2008 'I owe Newcastle racecourse an apology. I said the fences were too stiff, but after the pre-season inspection they have taken some birch out of them and they're fine now.' Rare apology from a trainer, by Len Lungo, in the *Racing Post*.

QUOTE OF THE DAY
2007 *'You should have to work for it and be at your best all year, whether you're riding Group One winners at Ascot or sellers at Catterick. You probably need more ability to win on the seller at Catterick.'* Seb Sanders, joint-champion Flat jockey, gives his view on whether the basis for deciding the jockeys' title should be changed from number of winners to total prize-money.

BIRTHDAYS
1911 Trainer Jack Waugh, who had a notable major handicap double in 1956 with Matador in the Stewards' Cup and Light Harvest in the Wokingham. Matador, 100/8, won under a record weight for a three-year-old of 9st 2lb.

1985 Jockey Niall 'Slippers' Madden, son of jockey Niall 'Boots' Madden. He rode Numbersixvalverde to victory in the 2006 Grand National.

LAST OF THE DAY
1989 Greville Starkey rode for the last time in Britain, on Osric, unplaced in the November Handicap at Thirsk. He rode 1,989 British Flat winners, plus three over jumps, including London Gazette in the 1964 Champion Hurdle.

CELEBRITY OF THE DAY
2008 Entertainment entrepreneur Howard Spooner paid £24,000 for the rights to the famous 'crazy quilt' patchwork racing silks once registered to Chesney Allen, a Crazy Gang member from the heyday of music hall.

12 NOVEMBER

SIGNIFICANT EVENT
1878 A riot took place at a Shrewsbury race meeting. Welshing bookies were attacked by irate punters, then a mob from Birmingham rushed the paddock in an attempt to murder the course security man, ex-Sergeant Ham, and to rob course bookies. Ham was knocked out but a group of racegoers fought off the attackers.

STRANGEST EVENT
2008 The Matthew Ellerton-trained five-year-old sprinter Sunburnt Lad, winner of eight of his 18 starts, was killed by a lightning strike in a paddock at his owner David Moodie's property in Woodend, Victoria, Australia. 'There are burn marks on the wither and at the bottom of one of his legs where it exited,' said the devastated Moodie.

OTHER EVENTS
1886 Newmarket closed down for the day to pay tribute to Fred Archer at his funeral. Poet Edgar Lee wrote: 'Farewell, best jockey ever seen on course; Thy backers weep to think by Fate's decree; The rider pale upon his great white horse; Hath Beaten thee'
1948 Miss Grillo, aged six, carrying 118lb, set a world-record time of 4m 14.6s for two and a half miles at Pimlico, USA.
1959 A record 171 runners turned out for a six-race card at Manchester.
1988 The Princess Royal fell at the first on Canon Class at Windsor in a handicap chase.
1988 Rats chewed through the mains cable at Huntingdon, shutting down the entire Tote system.
1994 Bradbury Star, 5/1, won his second successive Mackeson Gold Cup.
1994 Jason Weaver rode Magna Carta to win at Wolverhampton, landing his 200th winner from 1,073 rides. Frankie Dettori had already reached a double century – the first time two jockeys had

achieved the feat in the same season.
1995 Cheltenham unveiled its new cross-country circuit and McGregor The Third won the inaugural Sporting Index Chase winner over the course.
1997 US jockey Jose Calo claimed a record as he partnered two horses in two dead-heats on the same day at Beulah Park, where Princwee dead-heated in the first and Royal Secret two races later.
2002 Trainers had to declare cheek pieces, blinkers, visors and tongue straps.
2009 Long retired Willie Carson had a Ludlow double as an owner, with Wallace Moment and Moghaayer. Trainer Ron Hedges saddled his first treble in 40 years – at Taunton

QUOTE OF THE DAY
2008 *'We came to think about the fact that condoms – just like Ladbrokes – are all about safe transactions. It's about excitement and safety at the same time'* – Ladbrokes' boss in Sweden, Andreas Gillberg, on this day, as the company handed out Ladbrokes-branded condoms to students there.

BIRTHDAYS
1931 Jockey Cliff Parkes.
1948 Errol Brown, Hot Chocolate lead vocalist and owner of Grand National runner Gainsay.

DEATH OF THE DAY
2004 Frank 'Dooley' Adams, 77, a Hall of Fame US jockey who rode 301 winners and won seven National Steeplechase Association titles between 1941 and 1956. He rode in the 1947 Grand National, finishing seventh on Refugio.

LAST OF THE DAY
1994 Carlingford Lakes won at Windsor – the last of 868 domestic winners for Steve Smith Eccles. In 1991 he had become the ninth post-war jump jockey to reach 800 winners.

13 NOVEMBER

SIGNIFICANT EVENT
1993 Josh Gifford became the first man to both ride (Charlie Worcester, 1967) and train a Mackeson Gold Cup winner, saddling Bradbury Star to do so under 11st 8lb.

STRANGEST EVENT
1996 Celebrating a winner at Budapest racecourse, jockey Csaba Lakatos was shot and seriously wounded in the head, back and thigh. He was believed to be connected to an underworld criminal murdered earlier in the month, but he survived the shooting.

OTHER EVENTS
1889 Racing at Derby descended into farce when fog came down. In order to stage the second race, police were stationed round the course with whistles to direct jockeys. The plan didn't work, as the horses went off course and ran round the back of a nearby cricket pavilion, with two crashing into a set of hoardings. Racing at Derby ended in August 1939.
1897 Tod Sloan rode Phenomenon to win the Carandini Starting Machine Plate, for which the field was sent off using a contraption of that name. The rest of the races on the Liverpool card had a traditional flag start. Starting stalls were introduced on British racecourses in 1965.
1985 Air pellets were fired at first-aid officers prior to the first race at Wolverhampton. There were only 180 in the crowd, but no-one was caught.
1992 Peter Niven rode a five-timer at Ayr, four trained by Mary Reveley. One of the winners, Robbo, was Reveley's 1,000th.
1993 Frankie Dettori rode a 2,570/1 four-timer at Lingfield.
1999 Jockey Graham Bradley, 39, retired after riding televised winner Ontheboil at Haydock.
2009 Sam Twiston-Davies, 17 years old, went one better than dad Nigel - best effort second on Royal Frolic in the Gold Cup – by winning at Cheltenham on Razor Royale.
2009 The BHA launched a trial, putting stewarding decisions online with minutes.

QUOTE OF THE DAY
2005 *'He's Damon Runyon, out of a Dan Rickles [US comic/actor] mare,'* was actor and race fan Jack Klugman's description of trainer John P. Campo, 67, who died today. He saddled 1981 Kentucky Derby and Preakness Stakes winner, Pleasant Colony, and had a total of 1,431 winners, worth $25.75 in prize money.

BIRTHDAYS
1938 John Kempton, trainer of Foinavon, the 1967 100/1 Grand National winner. He was so convinced Foinavon could not win that he went to Worcester to ride another of his horses, Three Dons, which also won.
1958 Jump jockey Stuart Shilston who rode for the Queen Mother and won Charisma Gold Cup three times.

DEATHS OF THE DAY
1990 Irish trainer Philip McCartan, 33, in a road accident.
2001 Kentucky-based jockey Sam Maple, 48, brother of jockey Eddie.
2001 Graham Rock, 56, founding editor of the *Racing Post*. He acted as agent for South African jockey Michael Roberts, who became British champion on the Flat, and owned Pasternak, the heavily backed 4/1 favourite and winner of the 1997 Cambridgeshire.

CELEBRITY OF THE DAY
2006 Desert Orchid died at just after 6am, aged 27. His ashes were buried at Kempton Park, where a statue now pays tribute to him – as does the Desert Orchid Chase.

14 NOVEMBER

SIGNIFICANT EVENT
2008 Of 16 jockeys in the Cross-Country Chase at Cheltenham, only Davy Russell had taken the trouble to check out the course in detail and it paid off when he took a short cut inside the laurel bushes on the course – quite legitimately – and won on Dix Villez at 28/1. The winning margin was three lengths, less than he 'stole' with his smart move. On the same card, when Jason McKeown lost his whip, he grabbed one from fellow rider Donal Devereux, whose mount was already beaten, and went on to win the amateur chase on Hoopy.

STRANGEST EVENT
1994 A high-roller turned up at Leicester and staked £10,000 on 11/10 Royal Derbi, who finished last of three. The punter pulled out eight grand and backed 9/4 Do Be Brief, who was pulled up. He dug deep for £14,000 on 15/8 Magellan Bay, who fell. Down to small change, the punter put a mere £4,000 on 9/4 Black Church, who was pulled up. Down £36,000, the punter found – or possibly borrowed – another £10,000 to back even-money shot Punters Overhead, who finished third.

OTHER EVENTS
1949 Fred Winter rode his first hurdles winner – Dick The Gee at Plumpton for trainer George Archibald.

1973 Captain Mark Phillips wed Princess Anne – bookies were cleaned out as Windsor's Royal Wedding Chase was won by 11/10 Royal Mark.

1978 Peter Scudamore rode his first chase winner, Majestic Touch, for John Yardley at Ludlow.

1984 Oliver Sherwood saddled his first winner, The Breener, at Newbury.

1987 A 'Pick Six' pool of $1,190,876 built up at Churchill Downs, Kentucky; 28,396 turned up – three winners pocketed $390,958.60 each.

1989 Britain's third all-weather race meeting was abandoned – because of the weather, as fog made it impossible to race at Southwell.

1993 Steve Smith Eccles rode Declare Your Wish, trained by Janet Elliot, to win the $100,000 Colonial Cup Chase at Camden, South Carolina.

2008 Friends and family of deceased Sussex racing fan Jim Malone decided to back a horse in his honour. They chose the 1.50 at Cheltenham, taking place just after his funeral, and placed the proceeds from a whip-round on Golan Way, trained in nearby Lewes. The horse galloped home at 8/1, rewarding mourners to the tune of £600, which they donated to a local charity.

2009 Tranquil Sea (Edward O'Grady) first Irish trained winner of Mackeson-turned-Paddy Power Gold Cup at Cheltenham since Bright Highway (1980).

QUOTE OF THE DAY
2008 *'I have only taken cocaine once – I did it because I believed it would help my weight problems,'* admitted German-based jockey Torsten Mundry, on this day. He was about to retire and become a trainer, but instead he was immediately suspended.

BIRTHDAYS
1917 Tom Corrie, who saddled Champion Hurdle winner Comedy Of Errors to win four times on the Flat.

1927 Twelve-times Melbourne Cup-winning trainer Bart Cummings.

DEATHS OF THE DAY
1986 Jayne Thompson, 21, the first female jockey killed on a British track. She died of injuries sustained on November 8 in a Catterick novice hurdle.

1997 US jockey Eddie 'Banana Nose' Arcaro, 81. He rode 4,779 winners in 31 seasons between 1931 and 1961 for career earnings of $30,039,543.

CELEBRITY OF THE DAY
1948 Prince Charles, who rode over jumps as an amateur, was born.

15 NOVEMBER

SIGNIFICANT EVENT
1992 The first-ever Sunday jump meeting took place at Cheltenham, where the first race, the 3m1f Racegoers Remittance Man Amateur Riders' Chase, was won by Sibton Abbey, ridden by Paul Murphy and trained by Ferdy Murphy. The attendance was approximately 15,000.

STRANGEST EVENT
2007 'Among the bizarre experiences life has brought with it, standing outside an entrance to a toilet at Market Rasen racecourse, unveiling a plaque with my name on it, ranks highly' - David Ashforth, writing in the *Racing Post* this day in 2007. Ashforth's study of on-course facilities on his jaunt around the country's racetracks led to the erection of said plaque after he nominated Market Rasen as the best for bogs.

OTHER EVENTS
1873 Literally a 'run for gold' took place at Ocean View Park, San Francisco, where four-mile heats were run for a prize of $20,000 in gold. Four top horses contested the event, with 15,000 turning up to watch, gambling $100,000 on the race, which was won by popular California-based Thad Stevens.
1883 Perdita II, who produced Derby winners Persimmon and Diamond Jubilee for the Prince of Wales, won the Chesterfield Nursery at Derby.
1984 Leading US jockey Pat Day rode six winners from seven mounts at Churchill Downs.
1988 Cometti Star, a hurdler, made history by becoming the first horse to be entered for a race under Britain's new five-day entry system.
1989 Peter Scudamore equalled John Francome's record of 1,138 winners, on Regal Ambition at Worcester.
1990 Three times the usual crowd numbers turned up to see Lester Piggott ride a comeback winner at Ippodromo, Livorno, Italy, on Ghilly Du.

1995 Oliver Sherwood sent out his 500th winner, Myland, at Kempton.
1997 Senor El Betrutti, 33/1, won the Murphy's (formerly Mackeson) Gold Cup at Cheltenham. He was one of just three horses trained by Susan Nock.
2004 Noble Action at Folkestone was Paul Nicholls 1,000th British winner.'
2008 Jockey Ruby Walsh had his spleen removed after being kicked in the stomach in a fall from Pride Of Dulcote at Cheltenham.
2008 Frankie Dettori rode – unsuccessfully – at Argentina's Palermo track for the first time.
2009 Kieren Fallon won at Hollywood Park – on High Court Drama.

QUOTE OF THE DAY
'That was the plan, and it's lovely when a plan comes right,' said Nigel Twiston-Davies after his 13/2 shot Imperial Commander won the Paddy Power Gold Cup at Cheltenham on this day in 2008.

BIRTHDAYS
1915 Jump jockey Dick Black, who won the 1947 Cheltenham Gold Cup on Fortina, when still an amateur.
1945 Jockey turned trainer Tommy Stack. He was champion jump jockey in 1974-75 and 1976-77 and rode Red Rum to win the 1977 Grand National.

DEATHS OF THE DAY
1990 Alydar, runner-up to Affirmed in the 1978 US Triple Crown, was destroyed after fracturing a hind leg in a stable accident that left Lloyds of London facing a $50m payout.
2007 Irish former jockey and trainer Christy Kinane, 72. He won the 1960 Powers Gold Cup on Owen's Sedge.

CELEBRITY OF THE DAY
1999 Sir Harry Llewellyn, 88, the Olympic show jumping gold medallist in 1952 and an amateur rider and trainer. He finished second in the 1936 Grand National on Reynoldstown at 50/1.

16 NOVEMBER

SIGNIFICANT EVENT
2008 Hayley Turner won her first Pattern race, the Lando Trophy at Hanover on Lady Deauville, and also became the first female to win a German Group race.

STRANGEST EVENT
1983 Racecourse worker Edwyn Barnes, 75, was replacing divots at Kempton – during a hurdles race – when he suddenly realised the runners were heading towards him. He was bowled over by Knowing Card, the horse who finished second. Barnes survived the incident.

OTHER EVENTS
1946 On his final day as a jockey, Harry Wragg rode a treble, including 20/1 Manchester November Handicap winner Las Vegas. He rode 1,762 winners from 11,658 races.

1982 Having failed to ride a winner since New Year's Day the previous year, having broken his leg in consecutive seasons, point-to-point jockey Carroll Gray took a fall from Sue Lark at Haldon and punctured a lung.

1991 Jenny Pitman saddled one-third of the 24-runner field for the Grunwick National Hunt Flat Race at Warwick, but the best she could manage was second with Mailcom.

1992 Jockey Michael Bowlby announced his retirement to concentrate on his horse-bedding business. He rode his first winner, Emperor Napoleon, aged 28, at Bangor in 1983. His biggest win came in the 1989 Whitbread Gold Cup on Brown Windsor.

1994 Certainly Strong won a novice hurdle at Haydock, giving trainer David Nicholson his 1,000th British winner. On the same afternoon, ace sprinter Lochsong was officially retired.

1996 The first Murphy's (formerly Mackeson) Gold Cup, at Cheltenham, was won by Richard Dunwoody on Challenger Du Luc, for Martin Pipe.

1998 Tony McCoy was banned for 14 days for repeated breaches of whip rules.

2004 Walter Swinburn had first winner as trainer with Grand Show at Lingfield.

2007 Katie Walsh, sister of leading jump jockey Ruby, won at Cheltenham for the first time, riding Hordago to victory in the amateurs' handicap chase.

2008 Hungarian sprint sensation Overdose, who had 'won' the Prix de l'Abbaye at Longchamp the previous month, only for the race to be declared void due to a false start, took his winning streak to 11 with victory in Italy's 6f Premio Carlo e Francesco Aloisi.

QUOTE OF THE DAY
2007 *'We've never revealed where the grave is. Almost every day in summer it's cared for and the flowers are laid out in our colours in the shape of a jockey'* – John Hales, owner of Queen Mother Champion Chase winner One Man.

BIRTHDAY
1942 Willie Carson OBE, five-times champion jockey.

1968 Godolphin trainer, Saeed Bin Suroor.

DEATHS OF THE DAY
1989 Batu Pahat, trained by Bill Turner, was put down after hitting the third-last hurdle in the opening race at Lingfield's first all-weather hurdles meeting.

1990 Canadian-born Northern Dancer, probably the greatest modern thoroughbred, was put down at the age of 29 at the Northern Stallion Station, Maryland. The 1964 Kentucky Derby winner sired the winners of 99 European Pattern races from 605 foals. Three sons won the Derby – Nijinsky (1970), The Minstrel (1977) and Secreto (1984).

2009 Bobby Frankel, 68, five times US champion trainer.

FIRST OF THE DAY
1957 Mandarin won the first Hennessy Gold Cup, run at Cheltenham. The race was moved to Newbury in 1960.

17 NOVEMBER

SIGNIFICANT EVENT
1994 Patrick, Bernadette, Andrew, Marie and Therese – five members of the racing Payne family – all rode in the same race at Ballarat, Australia. Therese and Marie finished second and third as brother Patrick won the race.

STRANGEST EVENT
2007 Lady Maria Coventry died, aged 76. It was reportedly her dying wish that her Admiral Peary should still run 24 hours later in the Grade 2 Independent Newspaper Novice Chase at Cheltenham – which it did, finishing fourth at 200/1.

OTHER EVENTS
1954 None of the seven runners completed the course in Plumpton's Cuckfield Novice Chase

1956 Jockey Billy Nevett rode his final winner, Setting Star, at Manchester. He won the Derby three times – on Owen Tudor (1941), Ocean Swell (1944) and Dante (1945) and was four-times runner-up to Gordon Richards.

1969 First edition of the *Sun* with front page headline: Horse Dope Sensation.

1979 Birds Nest won Newcastle's Fighting Fifth Hurdle for the third straight year.

1990 Lester Piggott rode a comeback winner in France – Bashful Boy, at Parc Borely, Marseille.

1990 Christy Roche equalled Michael Kinane's Irish record, set two years earlier, when he rode Topanoora to victory at Leopardstown, his 113th winner of the season.

1991 William Hill were surprised no punter wanted to back 33/1 Champion Hurdle contender Mounamara – until it was pointed out that the horse had died several months earlier.

1993 Peter Scudamore came out of retirement to win the 1m5f William Hill Golden Oldies Stakes at Hereford on 11/10 Missy-S.

1997 Punters were not best pleased after Norman Williamson dropped his hands too soon on 4/11 Herbert Lodge at Leicester, losing the race. He was banned for 14 days.

1997 An unusual hazard at Plumpton led to the last two flights of hurdles being missed out during the November Hurdle, after the course ambulance got bogged down on the track.

2004 Senior jumps handicapper Phil Smith revealed his idea of what makes a winning horse: 'We are thought to have a decisive influence, but in reality there are far more important factors in a horse's performance than the weight it carries. Key things are its health, the ground and the trip.'

2008 Sheikh Mohammed was presented with the Cartier/Daily Telegraph Award of Merit.

2009 Sea The Stars named Cartier Horse of the Year.

QUOTE OF THE DAY
2008 *'My outfit is two years old because Derek is too tight to buy me a new one,'* the unembarrassable Derek Thompson, recalling an excerpt from his most memorable interview at York – with his wife!

BIRTHDAY
1965 Darren Beadman, Australian Hall of Fame jockey. On the same date, trainer Jamie Poulton and jump jockey Tony Quinn, who rode his first winner, Measure Up, at Sedgefield in 1985.

DEATHS OF THE DAY
1996 Starter Alec Marsh, 88, who sent off runners for 101 Classics. He retired after 26 years in the job when Ginevra won the 1972 Oaks.

1999 Ken Bridgewater, 66, who trained Winnie The Witch to land the 1991 County and Swinton Hurdle double.

CELEBRITY OF THE DAY
2008 Hull City manager Phil Brown was recruited by the Tote to promote their Scoop6 bet.

18 NOVEMBER

SIGNIFICANT EVENT
1989 Peter Scudamore set a record for the number of winners ridden by a jump jockey when Arden won at Ascot, giving him his 1,139th success. Scu passed John Francome's record total.

STRANGEST EVENT
1988 Listed as dead in official scratchings published two days earlier, We're In The Money ran at Ascot in a novice hurdle. On the same day, English River, listed in the Form Book as having died after falling in a previous race, ran at Nottingham. A case of two dead certs?

OTHER EVENTS
1975 William Hill announced they were to take over sponsorship of York's 5f Nunthorpe Stakes, renaming it the William Hill Sprint Championship, under which name Sharpo won it three times from 1980 to 1982.

1981 The Worcester winners' board looked rather repetitive when Roy Davies won on Milliondollarman, followed by Hywel Davies on Rogairio and then Granville Davies on Santoss.

1982 John Francome completed the fastest 50 in a jumps season when he landed a treble at Kempton, beating Jonjo O'Neill's record, set on 5 December 1978.

1992 Barnstaple trainer John Hill celebrated his first treble, at 377/1, as Tendresse, Golden Klair and Klairover won at Southwell.

1997 Reg Akehurst sent out his last runner, 5/1 winner Whispered Melody at Lingfield.

2008 Harry Findlay's Woodfall Treasure made heavy weather of justifying odds of 1/5 at Folkestone, after which trainer Gary Moore declared: 'He'll have his balls off tomorrow – that's what he gets for jumping like a prat.'

2009 *Sun* racing writer Claude Duval's 40 years in the job was recognised by a sponsored race in his honour at Lingfield. At the same meeting, Royaaty was Godolphin's 200th winner globally.

QUOTE OF THE DAY
'Deep down, we consider that the price is worth paying. That is the unfettered truth' – James Willoughby of *Racing Post* gets to the heart of the debate over equine fatalities on the racetrack on this day in 2007.

BIRTHDAYS
1914 Ken Cundell, who trained Stalbridge Colonist, winner of four hurdles and 13 chases including the 1966 Hennessy Gold Cup, in which he became one of the few horse to beat the mighty Arkle. Cundell retired at the end of the 1974 season, handing over to son Peter.

1914 Bob Turnell, a jump jockey from 1926 to 1957 and later a trainer, as well as the father of twins, Andrew and Robert. He trained Pas Seul to win the 1960 Cheltenham Gold Cup and Salmon Spray to take 1966 Champion Hurdle.

1915 Ron Smyth, champion jump jockey of 1941-42 and a triple Champion Hurdle winner, and later a trainer. He won the 1975 Great Metropolitan with Flash Imp and the 1966 Stewards' Cup with 33/1 shot Patient Constable.

1965 US champion trainer of Curlin, Steve Asmussen.

FIRST OF THE DAY
1978 Sea Pigeon scored the first of his two Fighting Fifth Hurdle victories at Newcastle, beating Bird's Nest, a triple winner of the race.

CELEBRITY OF THE DAY
2007 'One moment the horse is a soaring athlete with wings on its heels and the big race at its mercy, the next it is just a broken-necked sack of meat.' Jockey turned journalist Brough Scott writing in *The Sunday Telegraph*.

19 NOVEMBER

SIGNIFICANT EVENT
1973 Mirabel Topham, whose family had owned Aintree since 1949, sold the racecourse to property developer Bill Davies for £3m.

STRANGEST EVENT
1991 Stewards at Newmarket, in South Africa, were alerted to a race-rigging attempt, when the turf was deliberately cut short along the complete length of the outside rail, evidently to enhance the chances of Ringelman, odds-on favourite for a valuable sprint race. The stalls were moved and Ringelman was beaten into second.

OTHER EVENTS
1958 Jump jockey David Mould rode his first winner, Straight Hill, at Plumpton.
1965 Ascot staged its first sponsored race, the Kirk and Kirk Handicap Chase, won by Rupunini, 5/1, trained by A. Thomas and ridden by Bobby Beasley.
1979 Wayward Lad, who by his retirement had won more prize-money than any jumper bar Desert Orchid, won on his racecourse debut, landing a Leicester novice hurdle.
1982 A record low crowd of 362 turned up at Ayr in awful weather.
1992 It was announced that Sheikh Mohammed had bought out Allen Paulson's half-share in Arazi, who had been retired to stand at Dalham Hall Stud for £20,000.
2004 Best Mate's seasonal reappearance at Exeter in a four-horse race attracted a crowd of 6,000 – three times the usual turnout, leading Alan Lee of *The Times* to conclude: 'It was a day of very public derision for the po-faced view that racing can only be about field sizes and betting turnover.' The 4/7 favourite ran out a narrow winner from Seebald, 12/1, owned by footballers Robbie Fowler and Steve McManaman.
2009 Racing UK's Nick Luck declared Top Racing Broadcaster of the Year by www.sportinglife.com.

QUOTE OF THE DAY
2008 Betting reporter and tipster Angus Loughran left his on-course role with BBC TV. *'Given the choice I would rather work for people that want me, rather than people that don't,'* he said.

BIRTHDAYS
1913 Trainer Ryan Jarvis, whose notable horses included 1952 Stewards' Cup winner Smokey Eyes and 1968 Irish 1,000 Guineas winner Front Row.
1918 Trainer Auriol Sinclair, whose best horses included Magic Boy and Wilhelmina Henrietta. One of the first female NH trainers, the first to win major races and to record 100 winners. She loved a gamble and once hit headlines when apprehending an escaping prisoner from Lewes jail, next to her yard, with a pitchfork.
1956 Jump jockey Ted Waite.
1965 Four time champion Irish lady poin-to-poiner Liz Doyle.

DEATH OF THE DAY
2004 Former jump jockey Ian Cocks, 62.

CELEBRITY OF THE DAY
1974 Lydia Hislop, outspoken TV broadcaster and journalist, was born.

20 NOVEMBER

SIGNIFICANT EVENT
1990 Aliysa had been disqualified from first place in the 1989 Oaks. Trainer Michael Stoute was fined £200 and ordered to pay the costs of the legal and scientific advisers retained by the Jockey Club's disciplinary committee. Snow Bride, the runner-up, was awarded the race. The affair centred on the Aga Khan's filly having hydroxy-camphor, a prohibited substance, in her system. The owner today launched a series of counter-actions and refused to race in Britain until 1995, when he believed drug testing had improved.

STRANGEST EVENT
1991 Only in Oz? After Gary Murphy rode Mercator to win the Ballarat Cup at the Melbourne track, he offered to buy the entire crowd – all 13,000 of them – a beer. Chaotic scenes ensued in the bars!

OTHER EVENTS
1899 Herbert Randall, a Northampton bootmaker's son and an amateur rider at the time, defeated crack US jockey Lester Reiff in the Stonelight Plate at Warwick. Randall decided to turn pro and went on to win the 1902 1,000 Guineas, 2,000 Guineas and Oaks on the great filly Sceptre, but was blamed for her Derby defeat. Born in 1877, he retired on the outbreak of World War One.
1991 Arazi won the inaugural Horse of the Year prize at the Cartier Awards.
1992 The BBC announced that it was scrapping Trainer, the racing-based drama/soap.
1993 Indian Tonic, 4/1, won Aintree's Becher Chase, ridden by Chris Maude for trainer Nigel Twiston-Davies.
2008 Forest Heath District Council admitted that its effort to honour two prominent racing figures, owner Lady Beaverbrook and triple 1,000 Guineas-winning jockey Dick Perryman, had misfired as they had managed to spell both names incorrectly – Periman Close and Beavorbrook Road.

QUOTE OF THE DAY
'A diplomatic sensibility borrowed from Pol Pot and a vocabulary that makes Gordon Ramsay sound like Mavis from Coronation Street' – the *Racing Post*'s Peter Thomas on this day in 2007, on just retired trainer Neville 'Nasty Nev' Callaghan, who had said of his career: *'We went to Portman Square with a few, but always managed to scramble out. We'd do it more or less within the rules, but racing would lose its sparkle if there wasn't a certain amount of that.'*

BIRTHDAYS
1948 Ian Carnaby, racing writer, sometime Brighton race sponsor – victory prize a stick of rock – and former SIS presenter.
1962 Jump jockey Simon Cowley BA, former president of the Oxford University Turf Society.

DEATH OF THE DAY
1999 Jump jockey Paddy Farrell, 69, who rode more than 300 winners including State Secret in the 1956 Queen Elizabeth Chase at Hurst Park, but was left paralysed by a fall from Border Flight in the 1964 Grand National. His personal tragedy sparked a response that resulted in the formation of the Injured Jockeys' Fund, which since 1964 has spent £16m-plus supporting more than 1,000 jockeys.

FIRST OF THE DAY
1986 William Haggas took out his first training licence. Ten years later he scored his biggest win when Shaamit landed the 1996 Derby.

21 NOVEMBER

SIGNIFICANT EVENT
1992 Aintree held its first jump meeting (apart from the Grand National card) for 20 years, attracting 11,301 to see Kildimo win the Crowther Homes Becher Chase.

STRANGEST EVENT
1918 The second day of a two-day meeting took place at Basra, Iraq ('Irak' in the racecard), with seven races, featuring British military personnel as the jockeys in all bar the final race, which was for 'natives of this country'.

OTHER EVENTS
1950 The seven-year-old gelding Bistor went mad and savaged trainer Bill Marshall after winning at Fontwell.
1978 Lucky backers of Gold And Rubies at Churchill Downs could afford to buy their own gems after the horse returned a record dividend for the track of $246.80 for a $1 stake.
1979 Sea Lane gave little-known jockey Peter Scudamore his first winner as a pro, at Worcester.
1987 A Breeders' Cup Championship crowd of 57,734 at Hollywood Park saw Ferdinand defeat Alysheba by a nose after a thrilling duel in the Classic, earning him Horse of Year honours.
1988 *The Sporting Life* was banned in Dubai after running an article about Arab influence on British racing.
1988 Jump jockeys were given a 1lb weight allowance to compensate for having to wear body protectors.
1990 Equinoctial, ridden by A Heywood and trained by N Miller, won a ten-runner novice hurdle at Kelso, returning a British record SP of 250/1. On-course bookie Alex Farquhar, known as Macbet, laid £1 each-way at 300/1.
1990 Having announced a three-year sponsorship of the Champion Hurdle from 1991, increasing the value of the race to £120,000, the Bank of Ireland pulled out of the deal.
1991 Michael Oliver, trainer of 1986

Grand National winner West Tip, handed in his licence to concentrate on his bloodstock agency.
2008 Curlin, the highest prize-money earner in US racing history ($10.5m), was retired. He won 11 of his 16 starts, including the Preakness, Breeders' Cup Classic and Dubai World Cup.
2008 Brilliantly named conditional jockey Ryan Mania landed a treble at Kelso, at odds of 11/8, 15/2 and 7/4.
2009 Mick Channon received honorary degree from Southampton Solent University.

QUOTE OF THE DAY
2008 *'The lad who rides him every day is on this stuff. Putting two and two together, it's not rocket science.'* Trainer David Arbuthnot, who was fined £500 after one of his horses, Soviet Cat, tested positive for a metabolite of propranolol, more normally used for treating humans. Arbuthnot was convinced that the positive test arose because a member of staff had passed water in the horse's box.

BIRTHDAYS
1938 Epsom-based rider Brian Jago, first jockey to Bruce Hobbs.
1943 Jockey turned trainer Robert Alner, who was badly injured in a car accident in November 2007.

DEATHS OF THE DAY
1949 Coronach, 26, the 1926 Derby and St Leger winner, died in New Zealand.
1988 Former jockey and trainer Derek Leslie, 59. He won 173 races over jumps between 1949 and 1961, and trained from 1967.

FIRST OF THE DAY
1991 A plan was unveiled to turn Wolverhampton, where they first raced in 1825, into Britain's first floodlit racecourse; it came to fruition on January 8, 1994, when 3,000-plus turned up to watch all-weather racing under lights.

22 NOVEMBER

SIGNIFICANT EVENT
1947 Gordon Richards rode his 269th winner of the season on Campanelle at Lingfield – a Flat record yet to be broken.

STRANGEST EVENT
1910 Lois Duffey, the American owner of 1990 Grand National winner Mr Frisk, was born on this day. She was wearing trainers when she went up to collect the winner's trophy at Aintree, but she had an excuse – a fractured ankle.

OTHER EVENTS
1990 US jockey Pat Day rode Screen Prospect to win the Falls City Stakes at Churchill Downs, the 5,000th win of his career. To commemorate achievement, the track donated $5,000 to a local hospital and children's hospital fund.
1966 Merryman II, winner of the 1960 Grand National, collapsed and died, aged 15, while out hunting.
2004 Amateur rider Jim Lawless won a bet that he would learn to ride, then contest a race, when partnering Airgusta at Southwell over a mile, finishing seventh of 14. With coaching help from Gee Armytage, he collected on the wager struck a year earlier. Celebrating, he said: 'This is not a one-off. It took far too much work.'
2008 A punter from Thatcham, near Newbury, won £437,011 for a £2 stake on the Tote Scoop6, which attracted a record £4m pool.
2008 Kauto Star looked to have Haydock's Betfair Chase at his mercy, but the 2/5 shot stumbled and slithered after the last, unseating Sam Thomas. That left 33/1 Snoopy Loopy to win for trainer Peter Bowen, ridden by Seamus Durack.
2008 Top French-based Flat rider Christophe Soumillon revealed: 'It's one of my ambitions to win over jumps.'

QUOTE OF THE DAY
1970 'In interests of simplicity,' explained *The Sporting Life*, straight faced, on this day, as bookies announced the scrapping of odds like 100/8, 100/7 and 100/6, replacing them with 12/1, 14/1 and 16/1. Shrewd punters still managed to 'take the fractions', though.

BIRTHDAYS
1922 Owner Chris Barber-Lomax, whose Pee Mai won 13 times, Panglima six and Pandu five.
1928 John Gaines, mastermind behind the Breeders' Cup.
1958 Charles Elsey, the son of 1956 champion trainer Captain Charles Elsey. He handled Lingfield specialist Rapporteur – who won on all-weather and Turf there 19 times, but never elsewhere: 'Rapporteur definitely knows when he's at Lingfield. When they repainted the old yard there he had a right freak-out.'

DEATHS OF THE DAY
1994 Trainer Arthur 'Fiddler' Goodwill, 82. Apparently he got his nickname when he arrived, carrying a violin, while apprenticed to trainer Harvey Leader.
2005 Bruce Hobbs, 84, the youngest jockey (17) to ride a Grand National winner. He landed the race in 1937 on 40/1 shot Battleship, trained by dad Reg, and later revealed he had fellow jockey Fred Rimell to thank for pushing him back into the saddle after he nearly came to grief at the fence after Becher's. As a trainer he sent out Tyrnavos to win the Irish Sweeps Derby and had placed horses in ten other Classics.

LAST OF THE DAY
1930 Freddie Fox and Gordon Richards went into the final day of the British Flat season level pegging in the title race. Richards won the November Handicap on 25/1 Glorious Devon to go one up, but Fox took the title by winning the fourth and fifth races. Fox, killed in a car crash in 1945, was born in 1888 and won the Derby in 1931 on Cameronian and in 1935 on Bahram.

23 NOVEMBER

SIGNIFICANT EVENT

1973 Fulke Walwyn sent out his first winner for the Queen Mother, who had transferred horses to him following the death of Peter Cazalet, when Game Spirit won at Newbury.

STRANGEST EVENT

1951 The Fulke Walwyn-trained French-bred Mont Tremblant, owned by wealthy Dorothy Paget, was beaten six lengths by Rose Park in a Sandown novice chase, only to come out and win the Cheltenham Gold Cup later that season.

OTHER EVENTS

1968 Spanish Steps, owned and trained by Edward Courage, won Ascot's Black & White Gold Cup by eight lengths. He went on to finish third in the Cheltenham Gold Cup and Grand National. On the same afternoon, Courage's Royal Relief, who would become a dual Champion Chase winner, won at Warwick.

1989 Racing at Haydock was delayed by 55 minutes because one of the two ambulance crews refused to work during the national ambulance dispute. Another ambulance crew was eventually located.

1989 Jockey Brian Rouse revealed his secret weapon to combat 'kickback' effect of all-weather tracks – he put a stocking over his face.

1990 Richard Dunwoody completed the fastest 50 of his career when winning on Another Coral at Newbury.

1992 Jockey Richard Guest broke his left leg in a fall at Wolverhampton.

1993 Sixteen-year-old schoolboy Matthew Kneafsey missed a mock O level science exam at Huntington Comprehensive in order to partner Sporting Spirit at Southwell, finishing fourth. On the same card Kevin Darley landed a double to set a new record of 138 winners in a season for a northern-based jockey.

1997 Pilsudski, trained by Michael Stoute, rounded off sparkling career, worth 2.8m, with victory in Japan Cup.

2004 Marcus Armytage, the amateur rider who won the 1990 Grand National on Mr Frisk, made this observation about his fellow jockeys: 'The weighing room is something of a cultural desert. This is not a criticism, because the ability to recite poetry is bugger all use to you as you sail down to Becher's.'

2008 Jump jockey Choc Thornton revealed that if he was invited to a fancy dress party he would go as 'Doc Holliday from the gunfight at the OK Corral'.

2008 Jim Dreaper, who won the race on his father's Black Secret in 1970, landed his second Troytown Chase at Navan when, appropriately, Notre Pere came home a 6/1 winner under Andrew Lynch.

QUOTE OF THE DAY

2007 *'I like a bet, but I always seem to break even. One minute I'm up two grand, the next I'm down two grand and I think, "This is boring".'* Ronnie Wood, owner, punter, artist and Rolling Stone.

BIRTHDAYS

1937 Trainer Reynaldo Nobles.
1962 Trainer Eoin Harty.
1965 Sarah Kelleway, trainer and champion arab horse rider.

DEATHS OF THE DAY

1969 Jack Pearce, 70, who rode on the Flat and over jumps before taking up training. In 1952 Vatellus and Signification, both owned by pro punter Alec Bird, won the Ayr Gold Cup and Ebor for Pearce.

1991 Ten Up, 24, winner of the 1975 Cheltenham Gold Cup, was put down.

1994 Colonel Bill Whitbread, 93, who began his brewing company's sponsorship of the Whitbread Gold Cup at Sandown in 1956.

CELEBRITY OF THE DAY

2007 'I got thrown out of the Royal Enclosure at Royal Ascot for not having a top hat,' revealed Ronnie Wood.

24 NOVEMBER

SIGNIFICANT EVENT
1950 The Queen Mother celebrated the first win by a horse running in her own name when Manicou, trained by Peter Cazalet and ridden by Tony Grantham, won the Wimbledon Chase at Kempton.

STRANGEST EVENT
1989 *The Racing Post* revealed that the Queen Mother's favourite chaser, Special Cargo, supposedly a gelding, was thought to have got a mare, On The Hill, pregnant. There was speculation that Special Cargo was actually a 'rig', a horse in which one testicle has not descended.

OTHER EVENTS
1972 Michael Eddery, brother of Pat, suffered an accident while riding Grimsby Town in a hurdle race at Newcastle. Tragically, his leg had to be amputated. His son, Ciaran, became a jockey, aged 17, in 1998.

1990 Julie Krone became the first female rider to win a race in Japan.

1990 All five runners came to grief in a novice chase at Newcastle, but Tropenna was remounted to win for trainer John Goulding.

1991 Pat Day set a North American record for stakes victories in a single season when taking his total to 58 on Blacksburg in Hawthorne Juvenile. He exceeded the 1986 record set by Jorge Velasquez and equalled in 1990 by Craig Perret.

1991 US raider Golden Pheasant, ridden by Gary Stevens, won the Japan Cup from the French-trained Magic Night.

1992 Racing in Hong Kong was suspended due to a virus epidemic.

1994 Charlie Swan set a record for Irish racing when Calmos won at Naas to give him his 110th winner since January 1, taking him past his own record, set two years earlier, for number of winners in a calendar year.

1996 Frankie Dettori rode Michael Stoute's Singspiel, 66/10, to victory in the Japan Cup, taking the horse's earnings to £1,904,321 – a record for a horse trained in Britain.

2002 A horse who would play a big part on the chasing scene for several years won on his debut over fences, in the Morris Oil Chase at Clonmel. Beef Or Salmon never managed to win the Cheltenham Gold Cup in four attempts, nor did he manage ever to win in Britain. He won 13 times in Ireland, though, including three wins in both the Hennessy Cognac Gold Cup and the Lexus/Ericsson Chase, both at Leopardstown. He was retired in 2008 after finishing sixth in the Punchestown Gold Cup.

2008 Seven of the eight finalists for the *Racing Post* Betting Shop Manager of the Year were female, with Coral's Andrea Baker coming out on top. On the same day, the Plough Inn at Ford won the *Racing Post* Racing Pub of the Year.

QUOTE OF THE DAY
'Stephane Pasquier at Lingfield, mistaking him for the winning jockey, Christophe Lemaire' – TV racing presenter Emma Spencer reveals her most memorable interview experience on this day in 2008.

BIRTHDAYS
1965 Angus 'Statto' Loughran, tipster and former BBC betting expert.

1971 John Velazquez, the former US champion jockey from Puerto Rico.

DEATHS OF THE DAY
1875 Hannah, winner of the 1871 fillies' Triple Crown (1,000 Guineas, Oaks and St Leger) died after having slipped twins.

1996 Michael O'Hehir, 76, the Irish racing commentator renowned for his machine-gun style of rapid-fire delivery.

CELEBRITY OF THE DAY
1955 Sir Ian Botham, England cricketing hero and owner of Rely On Guy.

25 NOVEMBER

SIGNIFICANT EVENT
1967 Racing suffered a total shutdown due to an outbreak of foot and mouth disease, resuming on January 5 at Sandown. The last winner before the shutdown was Pony Express, 9/1, in the Speen Novice Hurdle at Newbury, ridden by Willie Robinson and trained by Fulke Walwyn.

STRANGEST EVENT
1939 Derby-winning Flat jockey Charlie Smirke made his debut over hurdles at Windsor on Ella A, who fell.

OTHER EVENTS
1926 Taking advantage of Gordon Richards' absence since May with tuberculosis, Tommy Weston rode his 95th and final winner of the season, Lord Derby's Schiavoni at Manchester, to clinch the British Flat jockeys' title.
1933 Gordon Richards won on Celestial City in the last race of the Flat season at Manchester to take his season's total score to a record 259. On the same day at Lingfield, Golden Miller beat Thomond and Kellsboro Jack – the trio went on to fill the same places in the 1935 Cheltenham Gold Cup.
1990 The Japan Cup was run at Fuchu racecourse in front of a crowd of 164,328 – a record paying attendance, who gambled 22m yen (£90m) on the Cup alone. The Australian-trained Better Loosen Up won the big race.
1991 David Hayes completed the fastest century of winners by an Australian trainer when he landed a treble at Sandown. The season began on August 1.
1992 Desert Orchid survived a life-threatening emergency operation on a twisted gut.
1993 The Jockey Club introduced a rule banning the changing of a horse's name once it had run.
1993 Trainer Nick Walker saddled his first winner, Noblely, ridden by Norman Williamson, at Taunton.
2000 Jamie Goldstein steered King's Road through the heavy ground at Newbury to land the Hennessy Cognac Gold Cup for trainer Nigel Twiston-Davies. The horse suffered injury problems afterwards and never raced again at the same level.
2006 The Evan Williams-trained State Of Play won the 50th Hennessy Cognac Gold Cup at Newbury, racing's longest continuous commercial sponsorship.
2009 Former Irish champion jockey Paul Carberry began a 30 day ban for failing a breath test.

QUOTE OF THE DAY
2004 *'He may not be the best amateur around but I can assure you he is better at riding than I am at bomb disposal.'* Trainer Len Lungo paid tribute to Guy Willoughby, who rode his first winner under Rules, Inn From The Cold, at Carlisle, before going back to his day job as an explosives expert.

BIRTHDAYS
1916 Long-serving Morning Star racing tipster Alf Rubin, alias Cayton.
1926 Owner Donald Fairbairn, whose Stock Hill Lass won three races at Kempton, picking up a £50,000 bonus.
1921 Stanley Ho Hung-sun, multi-billionaire racehorse owner from Macau.
1949 Jockey Richard Hutchinson.
1961 Jockey Jorge Chavez.

FIRST OF THE DAY
1988 Cash Asmussen became the first jockey to ride 200 winners in a season in France, when he won on Forest Angel at Maisons-Laffitte.

CELEBRITY OF THE DAY
1907 Owner Raymond Guest OBE was born. A former US Ambassador to the Republic of Ireland, Guest won the 1968 Derby with Sir Ivor, having earlier won the race with Larkspur, and he went on to win two Cheltenham Gold Cups and the Grand National with L'Escargot. He is the only owner to complete that treble.

26 NOVEMBER

SIGNIFICANT EVENT
1995 The German-trained Lando, 13/1, ridden by Michael Roberts, won the Japan Cup, the world's richest race, worth £1,101,928 to the winner. A record crowd of 180,760 watched.

STRANGEST EVENT
2008 Jamie Osborne revealed he had named a dozen yearlings, shared by a 12-member syndicate, after the 12 days of Christmas – Three French Hens, Six Geese A-Laying etc.

OTHER EVENTS
1880 An extraordinary sequence of nine races in two months, with eight wins, ended for 1878 Irish Derby winner Madame Dubarry with victory in the Manchester November Handicap at 12/1. Two days earlier she won the November Cup at the same track. On November 5, she won over 2m at Lincoln, having been unplaced the previous day. On October 13, she won at Newmarket, having scored at Perth over 9f on October 1 only to be disqualified. Prior to that, she had won over 10f at Perth on September 30 and at Ayr on September 28, having started the sequence at Manchester on September 25 over 12f.
1927 The last race of the Flat season, the Final Plate at Manchester, was won by the 5/2 joint-favourite – All Over.
1949 Martin Molony rode five jump winners at Navan.
1966 Stalbridge Colonist, 25/1, upset odds-on Arkle to win the Hennessy Gold Cup at Newbury.
1988 After five weeks out with a broken collarbone, 25-year-old Chris Warren returned to ride Allied Force in a Newbury novice hurdle, only to fall at the first and break his collarbone again.
1989 New Zealand's first Sunday meeting took place at Tauherenikau. On the same day, Kiwi mare Horlicks set a record time of 2m 22.2s in winning the Japan Cup.
1991 Desert Orchid was beaten at Huntingdon by Sabin Du Loir.
1993 The Tote Jackpot became a daily bet with a guaranteed pool of £5,000.
2005 Mick Fitzgerald, just back after months off with a broken neck, rode Trabolgan, the 13/2 second favourite, to victory in the Hennessy Cognac Gold Cup for Nicky Henderson.
2006 Ed Dunlop's Ouija Board signed off with Japan Cup 3rd, taking prize money from 22 races and ten wins to £3.5m.
2008 After a members' badge for Doncaster racecourse, dating from 1777, was sold at auction for £4,680 to an anonymous buyer, the course announced that the winning bidder would be offered free admission for life.

QUOTE OF THE DAY
'I never had a good day at the racetrack, not one, it wasn't conducive to enjoying yourself. But who cares. That was my job. I didn't enjoy it.' The slightly jaundiced view of five-times Kentucky Derby-winning jockey Bill Hartack, who was found dead of an apparent heart attack in a hunting cabin near Loredo, Texas, on this day in 2007, aged 74. The coal miner's son rode 4,272 winners from 21,535 rides.

BIRTHDAYS
1943 Preston trainer Eric Alston, whose best horses include Tedburrow.
1951 Jockey Bob Mann, who partnered Flash Imp.

FIRST OF THE DAY
1993 Josh Gifford had first runners at Bangor, landing a double as Philip Hide won on Jumbeau and French Charmer.

CELEBRITY OF THE DAY
2008 Reflecting on his Andrew Lloyd Webber-owned Black Humour's fourth place in the 1993 Hennessy, former trainer Charlie Brooks revealed: 'I sat on the kitchen floor and hit my head against the fridge door all night.' Two years later, though, he won the race with dour stayer Couldnt Be Better.

27 NOVEMBER

SIGNIFICANT EVENT
1996 Charlie Swan rode his 900th career winner, Ballymacrevan, at Downpatrick.

STRANGEST EVENT
1993 Daniel Fortt became the first conditional jockey to win the Hennessy Gold Cup, on the Andy Turnell-trained 10/1 shot, Cogent – it was only the 12th winner of the jockey's fledgling career.

OTHER EVENTS
1897 US jockey Tod Sloan, famed for his 'monkey up a stick' style, rode four winners at Manchester on the final day of the Flat season – in all, he had 254 winners from career 801 mounts. He was deprived of his licence for disregarding a rule forbidding jockeys to bet. He died in the charity ward of a Los Angeles hospital in 1933, aged 59.

1990 Lester Piggott rode Dear Doctor to win at Maisons-Laffitte, his first French winner since his comeback.

1990 After the finish of a Newton Abbot seller, third-placed Bore Hill Princess and the riderless Thrintoft collided. The former was knocked over, along with jockey Dale McKeown, and both horses collapsed and died.

2004 Timmy Murphy won the Hennessy Cognac Gold Cup, for the second time, on 9/4 favourite Celestial Gold. It was a third victory in the race for trainer Martin Pipe.

2004 The Mackenzie & Selby Hunter Chasers and Point-to-Pointers annual was published and the comment on a horse called Knickers was 'never looked like coming down' and of Centurion, 'having the speed of a 100-year-old.'

2008 Lord Oaksey, rider, writer and founder of the Injured Jockeys' Fund, received the 12th Sir Peter O'Sullevan award at the former BBC commentator's annual lunch, following the likes of Michael Dickinson and the Aga Khan. Oaksey joked: 'As long as Carruthers and you [O'Sullevan] keep going I think I may last a bit longer.' Via his journalist pal, Sean Magee, I laid Oaksey 1,000/1 that Carruthers, a horse he bred, would ever win the Cheltenham Gold Cup.

QUOTE OF THE DAY
2008 *'The BHA financially have done me a favour, as I will earn more betting on the all-weather than riding on it.'* Risible claim in a 'tipping' letter sent to gullible punters by warned-off jockey Dean McKeown.

BIRTHDAYS
1865 Trainer Richard Dawson, in Ireland. He sent out eight Classic winners from Whitcombe and Newmarket, including the Derby winners Fifinella (1916), Trigo (1929) and Blenheim (1930). A serious-minded man with drooping moustache and pince-nez, he also trained the supremely fast filly Mumtaz Mahal and was leading Flat trainer in 1916, 1924 and 1929.

1912 Lord Howard de Walden, owner of 1974 Champion Hurdle winner Lanzarote and 1985 Derby winner Slip Anchor, who legendarily knocked down Adolf Hitler in his car.

1962 Jockey Rodney Farrant.

1968 Jason Callaghan, jump jockey turned starter.

DEATHS OF THE DAY
1949 Tom Walls, 66, owner, trainer and renowned actor. He trained April The Fifth to win the 1932 Derby.

1999 Etienne Pollet, 88, trainer of the great Derby winner Sea-Bird. In 1953 he saddled the first and second – La Sorellina and Silnet – in the Arc, the first to achieve that feat.

CELEBRITY OF THE DAY
1993 Even though he won Wimbledon in 1952, owner Frank Sedgman was as delighted when his Hareeba broke the 6f track record at Moonee Valley in Australia.

28 NOVEMBER

SIGNIFICANT EVENT
1989 Jonjo O'Neill – a former patient – handed over a cheque for £225,000 for Cancer Research to Prof Derek Crowther of Christies Hospital in Manchester, saying: 'In the darkest days when I was very low I vowed I'd do something to help.'

STRANGEST EVENT
1992 Newbury silver ring bookies went on strike in protest at poor facilities in the enclosure. The ring had been moved, following completion of course's new Berkshire Stand, to a site one and a half furlongs before the winning post. One bookie, Frank Morrad, said: 'There were no official spots for us to pitch up and bet from. We cannot see the finish.'

OTHER EVENTS
1968 Bill Smith, later the royal jump jockey, rode his first winner, Silver Meade, 11/2, at Taunton.
1990 At the very moment her father John officially became Prime Minister, Elizabeth Major was x-raying a sedated racehorse at a veterinary surgery near Huntingdon, as part of her studies at the Animal Health Trust.
1992 Adrian Maguire rode the longest-priced Hennessy Cognac Gold Cup winner, Sibton Abbey, 40/1, for trainer Ferdy Murphy.
1993 Home contender Legacy won the Japan Cup, but the US-trained runner-up Kotashaan might well have done had jockey Kent Desormeaux not mistaken the winning post. He was fined £300.
2008 Ninety-four-year-old Tom Wellman's 50/1 shot Song Of Praise won at Lingfield.
2008 Sam Houston Race Park in Houston, Texas, cancelled its 65-date race meeting because of damage inflicted in September by Hurricane Ike to the grandstand and stable area.

QUOTE OF THE DAY
2007 'A male escort. With my charm and charisma, I'd have been a natural' – jockey Mattie Batchelor on his possible alternative career, quoted in the *Racing Post* on this day.

BIRTHDAYS
1948 Mick Channon, England international footballer turned international-standard trainer. Saddled first runners in 1989, and became regular saddler of 100+ winners per season. Owner of Cathy Jane, his first winning horse (at Ascot in 1973), declared: 'I prefer racehorses to footballers – they don't talk back.'
1952 Trainer Michael Grassick.
1979 Robert Winston, talented Flat jockey with a colourful CV. Banned for one year after a racing fixing enquiry in early 2007. Found to have misled HRA Security Department investigators. Returned to ride 64 winners in 2008, and over 100 in 2009.

DEATH OF THE DAY
1983 Leading New York apprentice Eric Beita died as a result of a gunshot wound suffered a week earlier. A memorial award, to be presented to the leading apprentice on the New York circuit, was won in its first year by Declan Murphy.

CELEBRITY OF THE DAY
1961 Actor Martin Clunes, an owner with Brendan Powell and formerly a man behaving badly, was born. Also born on this day, in 1929, was Motown founder and racehorse owner, Berry Gordy.

29 NOVEMBER

SIGNIFICANT EVENT
1997 Legendary BBC commentator Sir Peter O'Sullevan called it a day after 50 years, after calling home 9/4 favourite Suny Bay as the winner of the Hennessy Cognac Gold Cup at Newbury. Later in the afternoon O'Sullevan's Sounds Fyne won at 12/1. 'The Voice' was still being heard on TV in 2009 in trailers for the Glorious Goodwood meeting, and for Dubai tourism.

STRANGEST EVENT
2008 Vets Jack Murphy and Sean Arkins of the University of Limerick issued the results of a study that convinced them 'the hair on a horse's head curls can tell you whether it is right- or left-hoofed, which in turn can help determine the direction a horse favours to race.'

OTHER EVENTS
1966 Capt. Andrew Parker Bowles won on his first ride over fences, on Fulke Walwyn's Brown Diamond at Warwick.
1992 Charlie Swan broke Martin Molony's Irish record of 92 winners in a calendar year, established in 1950, when he rode Atone at Fairyhouse for number 93.
1993 Frankie Dettori had an all-weather four-timer at Lingfield.
1997 Satish Sanan, a Florida-based computer magnate, paid 2.5m guineas – the highest amount paid at a Newmarket public auction – for lot 1154, a ten-month-old full-brother to 1991 Derby winner Generous.
2003 Ruby Walsh took the honours in the Hennessy Cognac Gold Cup on the Paul Nicholls-trained 5/1 joint-favourite, Strong Flow. Nicholls won the race as a jockey in 1986 on Broadheath and in 1987 on Playschool.
2008 Inglis Drever, the only horse to win three straight World Hurdles, was pulled up with a potentially career-ending leg

injury on his seasonal reappearance at Newbury. He never won again. On the same day George Baker completed his first century of winners, probably the first jockey never to ride below 8st 13lb to do so.
2008 A reserve system, introduced for three Royal Ascot handicaps in this year, was scrapped after the BHA and bookies decided it was not cost-effective.

QUOTE OF THE DAY
'It's great fun coming into a bookie's, there's nothing quite like it.' The 2004 *Racing Post* Betting Shop Manager of the Year, Anita Graham. She was the first winner for the Tote, for whom she worked in Eastleigh, near Southampton.

BIRTHDAYS
1932 Steve DiMauro, trainer of Wajima and Dearly Precious.
1956 Martin Fetherston-Godley, who started training in Britain in 1986, after a couple of years in the United States.

DEATHS OF THE DAY
1988 Death reported of 77 year old Willie Stephenson, cousin of Arthur. Aged 16, he dead-heated in the Cambridgeshire on Niantic. He went on to saddle Oxo to win the 1950 Grand National and Arctic Prince the 1951 Derby; also Sir Ken, who won three Champion Hurdles between 1952 and 1954.
1991 Respected racing writer Roger Mortimer, 82. He wrote an exhaustive *History of the Derby Stakes*.

CELEBRITY OF THE DAY
2008 Interviewed on Channel 4 Racing, author Salman Rushdie, who first went racing while growing up in Bombay, told viewers that, in his twenties, he enjoyed backing a run of 'seven or eight' Grand National winners. Yeah, Salman, and I suppose you wrote a Booker Prize winner, too!

30 NOVEMBER

SIGNIFICANT EVENT
1968 Fulke Walwyn landed the fifth of his seven Hennessy Gold Cup victories (a record total) when Willie Robinson urged 20/1 shot Man Of The West home in front.

STRANGEST EVENT
2008 Mexican and Guatemalan drug traffickers who fell out over a horse race run in a rural border town began a series of gun battles, in which 17 people died, said police. Spokesman David Gonzalez said the traffickers had been drinking in a bar in a small town in Guatemala, 'when an argument broke out over bets on a horse race, leading to a pursuit in which the gunmen shot at each other with automatic weapons from trucks.'

OTHER EVENTS
1929 Coole was returned at just over 3,410/1 for a 2/- (10p) stake on the Tote at Haydock – a record return won by Catherine Unsworth of Liverpool.
1963 Mill House and Arkle, two of the greatest chasers, clashed for the first time in the Hennessy Gold Cup. Mill House won, but never again got better of his arch-rival.
1964 Leading jump jockey Josh Gifford fell from Reverando at Nottingham, breaking his thigh, and was ruled out for the remainder of the season. On his return he broke his leg again in a car accident and was out for 14 months. Did not ride a winner until January 1966.
1985 John Francome sent out his first winner as a trainer when 25/1 That's Your Lot won at Sandown.
1989 Melody Town, 17, became the first woman to ride a winner, Beechwood Cottage, on Lingfield's Equitrack course.
1989 US jockey Kent Desormeaux set a world record for number of winners in a single season – 548.
1990 Lester Piggott rode on an all-weather track in Britain for the first time, at Southwell.
1993 Top Australian jockey Darren

Beadman was given a nine-month worldwide ban by the Royal Hong Kong Jockey Club for 'not permitting Better Choice to run on his merits' at Sha Tin. It was the harshest ban handed out in the British colony for seven years.
2002 David Casey drove Be My Royal past the post first in the Hennessy Cognac Gold Cup at Newbury, only for the 33/1 chance to be disqualified after testing positive in a post-race drugs test. Gingembre, trained by Lavinia Taylor, was eventually given the race at a hearing, 14 months after the race.
2007 Gillian Dawson, from Armagh, became the first female rider to win on Dundalk's all-weather track, riding the Pat Delaney-trained Libras Child, 6/1.

QUOTE OF THE DAY
2008 *'He has terrible trouble getting up in the morning – he'd have three alarms going off at the one time and wouldn't hear any of them.'* Jockey Andrew McNamara dishes the timekeeping dirt on weighing-room colleague Davy Russell.

BIRTHDAYS
1916 Royal jockey Harry Carr, at Clifton, near Penrith. He partnered Meld to win the 1955 1,000 Guineas, Oaks and St Leger; won the Derby on Parthia in 1959.
1946 George Duffield, a jockey famed for his association with Sir Mark Prescott. He won 11 consecutive races on Spindrifter in 1980.

DEATHS OF THE DAY
1968 Billy Bow, trained by Ken Oliver, won under 12st 4lb at Newcastle – and then dropped dead.
1988 Findon trainer Diane Oughton, 62.

CELEBRITY OF THE DAY
2008 Jockey turned trainer Tommy Gosling, 82. He was jockey to Sir Winston Churchill, for whom he won regularly on Colonist II, and once drunk champagne with Winnie and the King after a Kempton win.

1 DECEMBER

SIGNIFICANT EVENT

1989 Alex Greaves rode her first winner, Andrew's First, at Southwell. On May 31 1991 she became the first woman to ride out her claim as she landed a double on Love Jazz, 11/10, and Mac Kelty, 10/1, at Hamilton.

STRANGEST EVENT

1989 The Aga Khan resigned honorary membership of the Jockey Club because of his 'strong opposition' to the Club's current drugs-testing procedures.

OTHER EVENTS

1990 The mare Sinzinbra was responsible for four runners on the same day – Young Snugfit, the only winner, Peanut's Pet and Cashew King, all at Sandown, and Snuggle at Nottingham.

1994 Having finished seventh on Ship of the Line at Windsor, three times Champion Hurdle-winning jockey Steve Smith Eccles announced his retirement. His first winner was Ballysilly at Market Rasen in 1975.

2001 Fourteen went to post for the Hennessy Cognac Gold Cup and 14/1 What's Up Boys proved a winner for jockey Paul Flynn and trainer Philip Hobbs. The grey went on to be runner-up in the next year's Grand National.

2006 Jockey Russell Baze broke Laffit Pincay's record for most lifetime wins, aboard Butterfly Belle at Bay Meadows. Perennial leading jockey in Northern California, Baze is a member of the Racing Hall of Fame and has been riding for almost 35 years; this win moved him to 9,531 wins and counting.

2008 Launceston's Mowbray Racecourse officially reopened after a A$10 million upgrade. The track closed in February to allow for new irrigation and drainage works to be installed. Tote Tasmania agreed to fund the installation of lights at the track at a cost of A$6 million to enable night racing to be held. Minister for Racing Michael Aird said the changes made Mowbray one of the best all-weather tracks in Australia.

2008 It was announced that Oscar Urbina had returned to ride in his native Spain after 15 seasons based in Britain which produced 326 winners.

2008 To celebrate twinning with French course Pompadour, Folkestone staged a race for amateurs – won by French jockey Cyril Coste on Doctored, his first UK winner at the first attempt. On the same day, groom Michelle Eve, 49, travelling in a horsebox to Wolverhampton with Spider Silk, ended up in hospital when her horse crushed her in a freak accident. The Michael Jarvis-trained horse was 12th of 23.

QUOTE OF THE DAY

'And why does Graham Goode always sound as though he thinks every race he commentates on could be of interest only to intellectual pygmies?' An odd question from writer Paul Haigh, who clearly regarded himself as an intellectual pygmy on this day in 2004.

BIRTHDAYS

1936 Trainer Robin Blakeney, who was first licensed in 1971.

1939 Jockey Jacky Taillard.

1946 Malton trainer Malcolm Jefferson.

1947 Jockey Nigel Wakley, who rode his first winner in 1969 at Newton Abbot and partnered Royal Toss and Indianapolis.

DEATHS OF THE DAY

1990 Leading French jumps trainer Henri Gleizes, 78.

1993 Wiltshire trainer David Jermy, 53.

2008 The 1993 Cheltenham Gold Cup winner Jodami, put down aged 23.

FIRST OF THE DAY

1993 David 'Dandy' Nicholls saddled his first runner, Sharp Sensation, at Southwell. It was ridden by Alex Greaves, who became his wife, but who received a £400 fine for not giving the horse every opportunity to win.

2 DECEMBER

SIGNIFICANT EVENT
1992 African Chimes, ridden by Emma O'Gorman, won for the eighth time in the Flat season giving trainer Bill O'Gorman the most prolific winner of the season for a record fourth time in his career – Abdu won nine times in 1978, Provideo won 16 in 1983 and Timeless Times also won 16 in 1990.

STRANGEST EVENT
1993 The British Turkey Federation included the '93 Grand National debacle in its nominations for 'Turkey of the Year', awarded for being 'the most ridiculous person or event of the last 12 months'. In the event, the National was voted only second, behind England football manager Graham Taylor.

OTHER EVENTS
1933 A seven-race card was the first run at Charles Town, West Virginia, under the auspices of the Shenandoah Jockey Club. An estimated 4,000 attended, betting $44,000 of which the State of Virginia helped itself to $1,300.
1970 John Francome, 17, rode his first winner, Multigrey at Worcester.
1988 Champion Hurdler-to-be Morley Street won on his hurdles debut at Sandown.
1990 Top French Flat jockey Freddie Head, 43, made his debut over jumps, at Auteuil, partnering Avaleur to commemorate the 100th anniversary of the birth of his grandfather, Louis. Head finished second.
1992 The Richard Hannon-trained Lyric Fantasy, a flying filly who won five of her six 2yo starts, when owned by Lord Carnarvon, was sold for 340,000gns at Newmarket sales to Paul Shanahan of Ashtown House stud who made the purchase for a 'Kuwaiti consortium.'
1993 Britain's top three jump jockeys – Richard Dunwoody, Adrian Maguire and Peter Niven – found guilty of rushing tapes at Uttoxeter; fine £110 each.
2001 Trainer Brian Cox saddled six winners and a short-head runner-up at Wodonga, Australia.
2007 Soy Conquistador, trained by Maximo Gomez, was the ninth Puerto Rican-bred winner of the Caribbean's richest and most valuable prize, the $300,000 Clasico del Caribe, run at Hipodromo Camarero over 1m1f.

QUOTE OF THE DAY
1933 *'The revolt against paying heavy retainers to jockeys, which began three or four years ago, has become more pronounced,'* declared the *Irish Field*, adding *'A sum of £1,000 a year for a first claim is regarded as a good figure in these days.'* Gordon Richards was still *'able to command his own figure'* said the paper, but some of the other *'fashionables'* have had to accept reduced sums, it having been gently conveyed to them that they could choose between *'take it or leave it.'*

BIRTHDAYS
1923 Trainer Martin Tate, who also rode 25 winners under NH rules.
1940 US Hall of Fame trainer Jonathan Sheppard.
1941 Jockey Brian Procter.
1961 (Thomas) Richard Quinn, in Stirling. Won 1990 St Leger on Snurge.

DEATHS OF THE DAY
1983 Former trainer Jack Waugh, 82, who won the 1950 Ascot Gold Cup with Supertello at 10/1 and the 1956 Stewards' Cup with Matador, 100/8.
2000 California-based jockey Chris Antley, whose glittering career was interrupted by personal problems, was found dead at home 'in suspicious circumstances' aged 34. In 1985 he rode 469 winners, two years later he rode nine in one day – four at Aqueduct, five at Meadowlands; in 1989 he rode at least one winner on 64 consecutive racing days; in 1991 he won the Kentucky Derby on Strike The Gold. He quit in 1997 but was back in 1999 and won the Kentucky Derby again, on Charismatic.

3 DECEMBER

SIGNIFICANT EVENT
1992 (William) Arthur Stephenson – cousin of Willie – died, 72. He spent his whole training career at Crawleas Farm, Bishop Auckland and won the 1987 Cheltenham Gold Cup with The Thinker. Held his first licence in 1959; in 1969-70 he became the first NH trainer to saddle 100 winners in a season. Trained Supermaster to win 34 races; on the Flat Rapid River won him the 1972 Gimcrack and Tudenham the Middle Park. 'Little fish are sweet' was his motto.

STRANGEST EVENT
1791 A very early example of floodlit racing at Ireland's Baltinglass meeting was reported on this date by the Irish Racing Calendar – 'The last heat was not over at 6 o'clock when lights were erected at each corner of the course, to direct the riders.'

OTHER EVENTS
1969 The Queen Mother's 200th winner over jumps was Master Daniel at Worcester for jockey Richard Dennard and trainer Peter Cazalet.
1988 Owner-trainer Robert Waley-Cohen's wife was probably the only punter who fancied their The Dragon Master who won a Sandown novice chase at 100/1 – carrying her £100 bet which won £10,000.
1990 Magomed Tokov became the first Russian jockey to win a race in Britain, partnering Macho Man at Kelso during an international challenge event, the Maxwell Glasnost Handicap Hurdle.
1995 That's My Man won the Royal Bond Novice Hurdle at Fairyhouse to give Charlie Swan the fastest century in Irish jump racing history, taking him six months and three days of the campaign.
1998 8/1 chance Charlie Banker, saddled by Karl Burke and ridden by Norman Williamson, won the last jump race run at Windsor – until it came back temporarily in 2004/5 – the Norwegian Blue Handicap Hurdle. Sovereign was the last horse to jump the final hurdle, but Nordansk finished last. Stepaside Boy won the last chase, the Huggy Bear Novice Chase, partnered by J Leech and trained by Roger Curtis at 14/1.
2008 Melbourne Cup-winning jockey Chris Munce, who served a 20-month jail sentence for his part in a 'tips for bets' scandal in Hong Kong, was cleared to ride again in his native Australia, despite the Hong Kong Jockey Club imposing a further nine-month ban on him.

QUOTE OF THE DAY
1981 *'When I ring trainers and they ask "who do you have available?" I say "Frankie Pickard" and they say "we'll have him". It's not until she gets in the paddock that they realise.'* Agent Sarah Metcalfe's tactics of calling Frances Pickard, Frankie Pickard, suddenly boosted the rides for the up-and-coming-jockey, born on this day.

BIRTHDAYS
1915 Kit Patterson, former clerk of the course at Ayr and Carlisle.
1925 US Hall of Fame trainer Frank 'Pancho' Martin.
1949 Irish champion jockey Christy Roche, who won the Irish Derby on St Jovite in 1992 and the Epsom version on Secreto in 1984.

DEATHS OF THE DAY
1973 The 1943 Kentucky Derby winner at 2/5, Count Fleet, 33 – the greatest age recorded for a winner of the event.
1988 Aged 13, 1983 Grand National winner Corbiere, put down after suffering circulation problems.
1999 Long-serving starting price reporter, returning the odds for over 45,000 races, Geoffrey Hamlyn of the *Sporting Life*, aged 89.

LAST OF THE DAY
1996 Evry racecourse in France – opened in 1973 – staged its final meeting.

4 DECEMBER

SIGNIFICANT EVENT
2008 Australia's Racing Victoria announced that following an extensive safety review of jump racing, sparked by a recent high rate of equine fatalities, the sport would be permitted to continue. However, Melbourne's Flemington was ruled 'no longer suitable' for jump racing.

STRANGEST EVENT
2006 It was revealed that the Canadian Horse Racing Hall of Fame Museum had received trainer David Cross's Kentucky Derby trophy for his 1983 win with Canadian-bred Sunny's Halo. Cross was forced to sell the trophy due to a family medical emergency, but two former owners purchased it back and donated it to the museum.

OTHER EVENTS
1895 Recorded only as 'Walley', that gentleman became the first jump trainer of the year to saddle a treble – doing so at Sheffield.

1963 Former champion jump jockey – in 1958-9 with 83 winners – Tim Brookshaw broke his back in a Liverpool fall. Brookshaw had been runner-up to Oxo in the 1958 National on Wyndburgh after losing his stirrup leathers.

1973 Jump jockey Jeff Barlow launched his career with a flourish, landing a double at Huntingdon with Quintus and Capuchin.

1990 Out of action through injury, Peter Scudamore was able to take the time to receive his MBE at Buckingham Palace without having to risk losing winners.

1990 Lester Piggott received his first ban – four days – of his recent comeback, at Saint-Cloud where he was found guilty of not riding third-placed Lady Isis to full potential.

1991 With 83 jump winners to her credit, Lorna Vincent rode her first on the Flat when Grog, trained by Mick Channon and backed from 25/1 to 6/1, won on the all-weather at Southwell.

1992 Three Court of Appeal judges found that the Jockey Club's decision to disqualify the Aga Khan's 1989 Oaks 'winner' Aliysa was not subject to judicial review.

2008 Trainer Luca Cumani was relieved to learn that his Bauer was allowed to keep second place in this year's Melbourne Cup. Racing Victoria Ltd held an investigation after it was revealed the horse had shock-wave therapy on the Thursday prior to the race. Such treatment is banned for seven days leading up to a race, but RVL found one of its vets suggested the treatment. RVL ruled Cumani was entitled to assume the vet was familiar with the rules, and was therefore not responsible for the breach.

2008 New Zealand champion jockey Michael Walker, who suffered serious head injuries in a pig-hunting accident in May which left doctors convinced he would never ride again, won on his second comeback ride.

QUOTE OF THE DAY
'*Sleeping*' answered jockey Hywel Davies, born on this day in 1956, when asked his favourite recreation. He won the 1985 Grand National on Last Suspect.

BIRTHDAY
1946 Newmarket jockey Ray Still – who rode his first winner in 1966 and partnered Zardia, 25/1, to win the 1968 Manchester November Handicap.

DEATH OF THE DAY
1967 Former trainer Hugh Barclay, 81, grandfather of jockey Sandy. On a Perth card in 1949 he sent out three winners ridden by sons Hugh, Andrew and John.

CELEBRITY OF THE DAY
1930 Comedian and racehorse owner Ronnie Corbett born.

5 DECEMBER

SIGNIFICANT EVENT
1993 Singapore staged its first international race, the Argyle Diamonds Magic Millions Classic at Bukit Timah. Sixteen 3yos ran for £460,000, five trained in Malaysia and Singapore and eleven in Australia. The locally trained Magic Guest won.

STRANGEST EVENT
1978 Three times on his morning radio show, which included a racing bulletin, Terry Wogan announced that Newton Abbot was abandoned due to freezing fog. This was news to clerk of the course Carl Nekola, who rang the BBC to explain they'd been hoaxed. The meeting went ahead, but with a smaller crowd than expected.

OTHER EVENTS
1883 'The first brick of the Grand Stand at Ascot was laid on December 5, 1838' noted a contemporary report, believed by the Oxford English Dictionary to be the first time the term Grand Stand had been recorded in a British publication.

1947 13yo Schubert, a winner there before the war, returned to Worcester to win the 3m Kingham Chase, ridden and trained by Cliff Beechner.

1964 Arkle won the Hennessy Gold Cup by ten lengths.

1991 The BBC announced that a second series of Trainer, the racing soap-drama, was commissioned despite mixed reviews.

1992 Martin Pipe saddled the first three home in Chepstow's Rehearsal Chase in which Run for Free beat Miinnehoma and Bonanza Boy.

2008 Looking forward to his return to the saddle in September 2009, Kieren Fallon vowed: 'My ambition is to win the championship, to get it back. My target

is to ride 200 winners, which is what I did four of the six years I was champion.'

2009 Today marked the end of the 48th consecutive year of thoroughbred racing at Finger Lakes. Located in the heart of the Finger Lakes region in Western New York, the track has hosted over 62,000 races and entertained over 19 million fans since opening in 1962.

QUOTE OF THE DAY
2007 *'Within racing, punters are routinely treated as, at best, something to tolerate and, at worst, parasites.'* Lydia Hislop, writing in *The Times*.

BIRTHDAYS
1919 Jersey-based owner of Twigairy, who won 19 races, Lord Matthews.

1920 Champion jockey and trainer in Germany, Hein Bollow.

1953 Northumberland trainer and Newcastle Gosforth rugby player, Brian McLean, who handled Jack of Clubs and Worthy Knight.

1963 Jump jockey Tom Grantham.

DEATHS OF THE DAY
1911 Isinglass, 1893 Triple Crown winner, who belonged to owner-breeder Harry McCalmont, MP, at Cheveley Park Stud.

2007 Dual-code trainer Harry Thomson (Tom) Jones, 82. He won the 1962 Whitbread Gold Cup with Frenchman's Cove, who also won the 1964 King George VI Chase. Thomson Jones also handled the great two-mile chaser Tingle Creek and won the 1971 St Leger with Athens Wood and the 1982 version with Touching Wood.

CELEBRITY OF THE DAY
2007 Owner-breeder and businessman behind Bob The Builder and Thomas the Tank Engine, Peter Orton, died aged 64.

6 DECEMBER

SIGNIFICANT EVENT
1993 Horses raced under floodlights for the first time in Britain in a trial at Wolverhampton, which was due to reopen for racing shortly.

STRANGEST EVENT
1989 Texas Blue became the last horse to race twice in one day in Britain. The 2yo filly, trained by Mel Brittain, took part in consecutive races at Southwell's all-weather meeting, running ninth and last respectively. This is now banned.

OTHER EVENTS
1895 Prince Frederick, 5/4 favourite, under G Williamson, beat five rivals to win Sandown's 2m Grand Annual Hurdle.
1946 After a lengthy absence since 1911, jump racing resumed at Doncaster.
1993 Richard Dunwoody became the fourth jump jockey to ride 1,000 winners, with a Ludlow double.
1995 Peter Schiergen, Germany's champion jockey, equalled Sir Gordon Richards' record for most wins in a season in a European country when riding two winners at Dortmund's all-weather track to make his total 269. He increased the record to 271 later in the month.
1997 A racegoer's arm-waving antics distracted Adrian Maguire's mount Mulligan at Sandown, resulting in the jockey breaking an arm as they fell.
2008 Master Minded headed up a four-timer for Tony McCoy as the Paul Nicholls-trained 'good thing' was the 4/7 winner of Sandown's Tingle Creek Chase by ten lengths. McCoy told his wife he thought he'd ride a four-fold: 'She

thought I was being an obnoxious prick'. At Navan, Davy Russell also scored a four-timer, only the second of his career.

QUOTE OF THE DAY
1996 *'The letter A did not appear in the names of horses in the racecards. This was due to a computer error. The problem has been dealt with and we are assured it will not happen again.'* The *Daily Express*, with perhaps the oddest ever newspaper readers' apology.

BIRTHDAYS
1920 Former BBC racing commentator, Peter Dimmock.
1928 Provocative racing columnist and editor of the *Sporting Life*, Monty Court, whose 'Court Circular' was required reading.
1936 Devon trainer David Barons, who always believed his Playschool was 'got at' prior to the Cheltenham Gold Cup. He won the 1991 Grand National with Seagram, 12/1.
1959 Jockey Billy Newnes, who won the 1982 Oaks on Time Charter at 12/1.
1977 Flat jockey Eddie Ahern.

DEATH OF THE DAY
1921 Trainer William Jarvis, whose Ravensbury was second in the 1893 2,000 Guineas, Derby and St Leger, to Isinglass each time. Jarvis won the 1899 Ascot Gold Cup with 6/4 shot Cyllene.

FIRST OF THE DAY
2002 Crosswind won the first race run at Indiana Downs racetrack in Shelbyville, Indiana, which hosts thoroughbred and quarter-horse racing.

7 DECEMBER

SIGNIFICANT EVENT
1984 Trainer Dick Hern broke his neck in a hunting accident in Leicestershire.

STRANGEST EVENT
1983 Chris Brownless rode On Leave to win at Carlisle. His next winner, Candy Cone at Hexham, did not arrive until March 21, 1992. In between he retired to assist handler Bobby Brewis, who also trained his comeback winner.

OTHER EVENTS
1963 Native Diver won the San Francisco Mile Handicap at Golden Gate Fields. It was Bill Shoemaker's 326th Stakes Race winner.

1967 The eagerly awaited sale of Observer Gold Cup winner Vaguely Noble took place at Park Paddocks, Newmarket. There was high excitement as the horse was bought for plastic surgeon Robert Franklyn for 136,000gns. Vaguely Noble went on to win the Arc and become a leading sire.

1968 Fulke Walwyn saddled 8/1 chance Tassilo to win the Massey-Ferguson Gold Cup at Cheltenham, ridden by Aly Branford. Calling the trainer a genius, Lord Oaksey reported: 'Walwyn only took over Tassilo this summer – a 10yo with fired forelegs and two highly unsuccessful seasons behind him. He has at a conservative estimate improved Tassilo by two stone.'

1985 Fulke Walwyn saddled his 200th Cheltenham winner when 2/1 shot Arctic Stream won a novice chase.

1991 Peter Niven set a record by riding five winners at Doncaster for the second time in the season.

2006 France Galop's six-month ban on Kieren Fallon for failing a drugs test began.

2008 Up-and-coming trainer Tom Dascombe saddled his first treble, at Lingfield.

QUOTE OF THE DAY
'If I could go back and do it all again, I'd appreciate everything that came my way.' Jockey Robert 'Choc(olate)' Thornton, aged 29, on this day in 2007, thinking back to his 18-year-old self, a *'snotty-nosed kid'* who *'got a bit too big for my boots'* after a string of early successes for trainer David Nicholson. *'You see some lads who get so involved in racing, to the exclusion of everything else, and you wonder if one day they'll wake up and wonder where their lives went'.*

BIRTHDAYS
1924 Devon trainer Gerald Cottrell, who didn't take out a licence until 1971.
1964 Newmarket jockey who moved to Australia, Richard Lines.
1965 Six-times Canadian champion jockey, Todd Kabel.

DEATHS OF THE DAY
1989 Forbes Spirit made unfortunate history, becoming the first horse to fall on Lingfield's Equitrack – the Paul Howling-trained runner later died.
2001 Inventor of the air-cushioned whip, Jim Mahon, aged 84.

FIRST OF THE DAY
1907 A Santa Anita racecourse opened for the first time with Elias Jackson 'Lucky' Baldwin, one of the great pioneers of American racing and driving force of the new track, saying proudly, 'I desire no other monument. This is the greatest thing I have ever done and I am satisfied.' His monument, though, vanished and the current Santa Anita course opened on Christmas Day, 1934.

8 DECEMBER

SIGNIFICANT EVENT
1953 The Vincent O'Brien-trained triple Cheltenham Gold Cup winner Cottage Rake (1948, '49, '50) – ridden every time by Aubrey Brabazon – ran his last race, finishing third, partnered by Dick Francis, in the 3m Shrewsbury Chase at Wolverhampton. He was 14.

STRANGEST EVENT
1997 Mick Quinn's first runner as a trainer, Fairy Domino, finished last at Southwell; his second, Katie's Cracker, was beaten into second by fellow footballer turned trainer Mick Channon's Cutting Anshake.

OTHER EVENTS
1937 Fulke Walwyn rode French Mandate to win the 3m Pegasus Chase at Gatwick, where the course consisted of part of the current airport.

1984 Jockey Paul Croucher rode a treble at Nottingham. Less than four years later he died in a car crash.

1995 Willie Carson won on Lord Carmelo at Siracusa in Sicily's first meeting. A crowd of 9,000 attended, although the track's stands had yet to be built. The last Flat racing on the island had been at Palermo in the fifties.

2008 Barry Geraghty, who was riding regularly in Ireland and England, revealed an unexpected problem with so much travel – 'It is harder to control your weight when you travel because you are sitting in airports for hours and not eating as well as you might do normally.'

QUOTE OF THE DAY
1997 'What I'd really like is a Royal Ascot winner. Not sure if they'd let me in the Royal Enclosure in a shellsuit, though,' joked ex-footballer turned trainer Mick Quinn who got his second career underway this day.

BIRTHDAYS
1921 Malton trainer Bill (Charles William Carlton) Elsey. First licence 1961; won the 1973 St Leger with Peleid, 28/1, Frank Durr up, and the 1967 Oaks with Pia (Eddie Hide). He won the Ebor with Phil Bull's Sostenuto in 1962.

1942 Jockey (over 100 winners, including the 1973 Hennessy Gold Cup on Red Candle) turned Salisbury trainer Jimmy Fox. He handled Hill-Street-Blues and Fortune Cookie.

1947 Limerick trainer Michael Hourigan, responsible for the hugely popular Beef or Salmon, brilliant in Ireland, unlucky in England, and Dorans Pride, 27 wins.

DEATHS OF THE DAY
1945 Irish jump jockey John Lynn, 38, having suffered a fall from Red World at Southwell the previous day.

1975 Trainer Bernard van Cutsem, born 1916, whose High Top won the 1972 2,000 Guineas. He also handled the top filly/mare Park Top and had in his yard world record purchase ($510,000) 2yo Crowned Prince, who won two top juvenile races but developed a soft palate and failed to live up to his potential.

1992 Aintree clerk of course John Parrett, 45.

FIRST OF THE DAY
1935 San Isidro racecourse in Argentina staged its first meeting.

9 DECEMBER

SIGNIFICANT EVENT

2007 'Someone of such profound stupidity and rank ingratitude that he could fail a drugs test within two months of serving a cocaine ban.' Alastair Down in the *Racing Post* on Kieren Fallon, who had justified Coolmore's faith in him when his race-fixing trial was halted in December 2007, only for it to be confirmed the next day that he had tested positive for a prohibited substance after a random drugs test in France in August.

STRANGEST EVENT

1992 A run-of-the-mill 2m hurdle race took longer than the Grand National to complete at Haydock. The runners mistakenly missed out the second obstacle, which ground staff had closed off. The field completed almost a full circuit before being warned they would have to return to jump the missed-out flight, or the race would be voided. They went back and virtually re-started, with Richard Dunwoody and Mighty Mogul prevailing in 12m 19.6s.

OTHER EVENTS

1949 Prince Regent, the greatest chaser of the 1940s, reckoned by trainer Tom Dreaper to be almost a match for Arkle, raced for the last time, falling at Lingfield; on the same date, but 12 years earlier, Arkle saw a racecourse for the first time, running third in a £133 maiden plate at Mullingar, returning 5/1, ridden by Mark Hely-Hutchinson.

1961 The Queen Mother landed a treble at Lingfield with Laffy, evens; Double Star, 4/1, and The Rip, 8/13.

1978 Bird's Nest – who won it the previous year, and would do so again the next, claimed his second Bula Hurdle at Cheltenham – more ammunition for those who dubbed the Bob Turnell-trained, Andy Turnell-ridden horse 'the best hurdler never to win the Champion Hurdle'.

1984 Jockey Brian Taylor suffered a terrible fall at Sha Tin; he was left in a coma in intensive care with neck and brain injuries. He had been riding Silver Star, whose antics had been responsible for career-ending injuries to French jockey Philippe Paquet.

1989 Run For Free set a record time for a 2m hurdle at Cheltenham – 3m 56s. One hour, ten minutes later he was the ex-record holder as Cruising Altitude clocked 3m 55.4s.

2002 Melbourne Cup-winning jockey Damien Oliver landed his 1,500th career winner – Legend of Ace – at Sandown, Australia.

2008 It was reported that Wild Again, inaugural winner of the Breeders' Cup Classic in 1984, had been put down at Three Chimneys Farm aged 28.

QUOTE OF THE DAY

'Jockeys don't eat, they survive on a diet of winners.' Racing reporter Geoff Lester in the *Sunday Telegraph* in 2007.

BIRTHDAYS

1945 Champion trainer in France over 20 times, Andre Fabre.

1952 French champion jockey Philippe Paquet, who partnered Trepan, Nureyev and April Run.

1967 Jump jockey Roger Marley, who partnered probably the best horse he rode, Nohalmdun, to victory at Doncaster on his 21st birthday.

FIRST AND LAST OF THE DAY

1989 Jump jockey Stuart Shilston, 31, won at Towcester on Slightly Gone – and was immediately completely gone, announcing his retirement – having ridden his first of 131 winners, Mr Linnet, at the track in 1976.

CELEBRITY OF THE DAY

1929 Australian Prime Minister and racehorse owner Bob Hawke born.

1934 Owner of Smokey Oakey, Dame Judi Dench, was born.

10 DECEMBER

SIGNIFICANT EVENT
1999 Laffit Pincay, 52, overtook Bill Shoemaker's record of 8,833 winners, which had stood since 1970, when winning on Irish Nip at Hollywood Park.

STRANGEST EVENT
1988 An extraordinary plunge on Zusrab saw her odds tumble from 100/1 to 6/1 throughout Australia as she started in the Savoir Handicap at Moonee Valley. Layers on course faced a AUS$1m payout, while Sydney bookies had $600,000 more riding on the outcome, Brisbane's $400,000. Zusrab finished second, beaten by inches.

OTHER EVENTS
1954 Mandarin, who would become one of the best-loved chasers, winning over £50,000 in prize money, landing the Hennessy and Cheltenham Gold Cups in 1961-62, made his racecourse debut, when third at 20/1 in the Fisherman's Hurdle at Newbury.
1991 Bravefoot, Norwich and Flying Diva, victims of a 1990 doping scandal, were finally officially disqualified from their races by the Jockey Club. All proved to have been doped with a prohibited tranquilising drug. Norwich finished fourth at Doncaster on September 13, while Bravefoot was last of five at Doncaster; and Flying Diva last of three, both at Yarmouth on 20 September.
1992 German trainer Jurgen Albrecht, 32, sentenced to 10 years for cocaine smuggling, was reported to have escaped from jail, although Yorkshire-born jockey Nick Woodall, jailed as a result of the same case, was not involved.
1994 Irish champion jockey Charlie Swan set a new record for most wins – Flat and jumps combined – in a calendar year, when Common Sound won at Punchestown, his 118th winner, beating Tom Canty's 1925 record haul of 117.
2008 The BBC decision to slash its racing coverage was made the subject of an early-day motion placed before the House of Commons: 'That this house regrets the proposals being discussed by the BBC to reduce the number of days of British horse racing it intends to cover from the present level of 27 days per year to just 13 days by 2010.'
2008 *Racing Post* letter writer Alan Brown from Tottenham launched a one-man campaign – 'He won the Gold Cup, the Champion Hurdle; was top trainer at the Cheltenham Festival... also won the Hennessy and Whitbread... he won everything except the National which, ironically, his son managed to do. So why' he asked rhetorically, 'has there never been a race named after the legendary Bob Turnell?'

QUOTE OF THE DAY
2007 *'He is not so much a magnet for trouble as a black hole. Incomprehensible forces of gravitation tug every possible aspect of strife and destruction towards him.'* Simon Barnes of *The Times* writing about Kieren Fallon.

BIRTHDAYS
1937 David Oldrey, owner of Oats, third in the 1976 Derby; Crozier, who won 13 times; and 14/1 1981 Cesarewitch winner Halsbury.
1944 Champion amateur jockey in 1963 and '64, Steve Davenport.
1950 Lambourn trainer Nicky Henderson. He was responsible for triple Champion Hurdler See You Then.
1971 Steve Drowne, rider of Queen's Logic and Sakhee's Secret.

DEATHS OF THE DAY
1924 The man who launched Belmont Park racecourse, August Belmont II.
1982 Former trainer Geoffrey Scudamore, 76, grandfather of Peter.

FIRST OF THE DAY
1983 Trainer Mark Pitman rode his first winner, Queen's Ride at Nottingham, for mother Jenny.

11 DECEMBER

SIGNIFICANT EVENT
1849 If you ever doubted racing was in Lester Piggott's blood, this day in 1849 his great uncle Joe Cannon was born – he rode Regal to win the 1876 Grand National, then turned to training and landed the 1878 1,000 and 2,000 Guineas double with Pilgrimage. His brother, Thomas, rode or saddled 15 Classic winners.

STRANGEST EVENT
1993 A storm of protest erupted after the Senior Steward of Ireland's Turf Club, Sam Waller, announced that from March 1, 1994 all Irish racecards would show weights in pounds only, even though Irish schools were teaching the metric system.

OTHER EVENTS
1895 Twenty Irish horses arrived for a two day jumps meeting at Manchester – winning three of six races with Crosslegs, First Dragoon and The Jew.

1936 The Champion Hurdler, Victor Norman, carried 12st 7lbs to win Sandown's Annual Handicap Hurdle, ridden by Frenchie Nicholson.

1948 Citation completed his US Triple Crown season with a win in the Tanforan Handicap at 1/20, his 19th win in 20 starts during the year. In 1951 he became the first horse to earn $1m prize money.

1971 Tom Dreaper won the Massey-Ferguson Gold Cup with Leap Frog, ridden by Val O'Brien, who beat The Dikler. It was his last British runner before he handed over to son Jim.

1993 Arc-winning trainer Seamus McGrath (Levmoss, 1969) announced his retirement after 40 years, aged 60, with nephew and former assistant Neil succeeding him.

1993 Lester Piggott rode a treble at San Isidro, Buenos Aires.

1999 Tony McCoy won on Majadou to become the fastest (5 years 95 days) jump jockey to 1,000 winners, beating

Peter Scudamore's 10 years 167 days.

2008 Huntingdon's John Harper 100th Birthday Handicap Hurdle paid tribute to the Nottinghamshire man claimed by the Tote to be Britain's oldest active punter, who celebrated his 100th birthday on December 5.

QUOTE OF THE DAY
2007 *'A fairly mundane eight-race card, but one of great significance. It was the return of racing to Southwell for the first time since the summer floods – our previous fixture had been held on June 5.'* Southwell's Nathan Corden welcoming racing back after a six-month lay-off while the course was refurbished after floods. Weet A Surprise ridden by local girl Hayley Turner won the first race.

BIRTHDAYS
1928 *'As a general rule we cannot have people going into the winner's enclosure and biting the jockeys' arses.'* Can't really argue with this observation by Cartmel clerk of the course Major Tim Riley, born this day in 1928, who was officiating at the track when waitress Chrissie Kent celebrated a winner for her favourite jockey Phil Tuck by nipping at his rear end.

1947 Trainer Neil Drysdale, who moved to the USA.

1949 Three-time champion trainer in Canada, Bob Tiller.

DEATHS OF THE DAY
1993 Former jockey and trainer Peter Edwards, 65.

1994 Jockey James Thornton, 54, from head injuries sustained as a result of a fall at Charles Town racecourse in West Virginia two days earlier. Ironically, this was the final day's racing for the track, which had opened in 1933.

FIRST OF THE DAY
1982 Colin Hawkins rode his first treble, at odds of 828/1, when Quay Man, Sparkie's Choice and Mulata won at Catterick

12 DECEMBER

SIGNIFICANT EVENT
2007 After riding beaten favourite Marsam at Southwell, Eddie Ahern received a three-month suspension for his use of the whip after being found guilty of deliberately flouting the rules to trigger a suspension – and Animal Aid director Andrew Tyler wrote to Nottinghamshire's chief constable asking for Ahern to be prosecuted under the Animal Welfare Act. On Christmas Eve, 2008, it was reported police were to take no further action.

STRANGEST EVENT
1964 Lord Oaksey – then plain John Lawrence – jumped clear at the second-last in Plumpton's Amateur Handicap Chase on Pioneer Spirit. Oaksey feared he had taken the wrong course and turned back – only to find French Cottage (Bill Tellwright) approaching at pace, passing him and going on to win. Lawrence was fined £25, went home, ran a bath and forgot about it – until the ceiling collapsed.

OTHER EVENTS
1984 Owner Gwyn Griffiths was warned off for 15 years after admitting his Spare Wheel, a Newmarket winner in the summer, had been 'flapping'.
1990 Trainer Mohammed Moubarak was fined £8,000 by the Jockey Club disciplinary committee over the administration of anabolic steroids to six horses.
1993 Peter Schiergen established a record of 144 wins in a German season, breaking Otto Schmidt's 1924 record.
1999 Frankie Dettori was fined £240 after kicking Golden Choice in the belly after dismounting from the Peter Ng-trained runner, which had finished mid-division at Sha Tin.
2008 Back in the saddle just 27 days after having his spleen removed following a Cheltenham fall, Ruby Walsh returned to action at the same track, finishing second on odds-on Mahonia.

QUOTE OF THE DAY
1999 'Docksider and Olivier Peslier won the Hong Kong Mile. He had been beaten two heads in the Breeders' Cup Mile and we trained him for the race from Calder in Florida.' Trainer John Hills nominated today as the best of his racing life.

BIRTHDAYS
1911 The owner-breeder of Brigadier Gerard, John Hislop. A leading amateur rider on the Flat from 1946 to 1955, he was third in the 1947 Grand National on 33/1-shot Kami.
1921 Eric Cousins, who sent out the winner of Kempton Park's Jubilee Handicap four years in succession from 1961-64 and twice won the Lincolnshire.
1922 Aussie jockey Bill 'Weary Willie' Williamson. He rode his first winner at Flemington in 1937 and came to England in 1960. He won the 1,000 Guineas on Abermaid in 1962 and Night Off in 1965, and the 1972 Irish Sweeps Derby on Steel Pulse.
1939 One-time nightwatchman David Elsworth, former champion jumps handler and Desert Orchid's trainer.
1942 Jockey turned TV commentator/writer, Brough Scott MBE.
1948 The first female champion Flat jockey, Meriel Tufnell.
1958 Irish jump jockey Niall 'Boots' Madden.

DEATHS OF THE DAY
1945 Freddie Fox, in a car accident. In 1930 he beat Gordon Richards to become champion jockey; he won the 2,000 Guineas and Derby on Bahram in 1935.
1991 Author of 1985's *The Life and Secrets of a Professional Punter*, self styled king of the pro gamblers, Alex Bird, 75.

FIRST OF THE DAY
1992 Pennsylvanian Bruce Miller sent out Lonesome Glory, ridden by his daughter Blythe, to win the Sport of Kings Hurdle at Cheltenham – becoming first US-trained winner in Britain.

13 DECEMBER

SIGNIFICANT EVENT
1952 Jump jockey turned trainer turned TV commentator John Francome born. Champion jump jockey seven times, he won the 1978 Gold Cup on Midnight Court and the 1981 Champion Hurdle on Sea Pigeon.

STRANGEST EVENT
1968 'Dark Jet is so far in front he can fall down and still win' declared the Sandown racecourse commentator as Terry Biddlecombe's mount of that name came to the last in a novice chase and, inevitably, fell, but he slithered along the ground on his belly, with Biddlecombe somehow staying put. The horse was galvanized back into action and went on to win by five lengths.

OTHER EVENTS
1951 Simonsez won Tanorfan Handicap at the track of the same name, giving Bill Shoemaker his 27th Stakes Race winner.
1969 A new TV accumulator bet, the ITV Saturday Seven, invented by William Hill director Roy Sutterlin – or so he told me – was launched. It proved an instant hit, Hills taking 75,000 bets and opening 400 new telephone accounts, while Ladbrokes were 'busier than Derby day.'
1990 Julie Cecil granted training licence.
1996 Despite being Friday the 13th Martin Pipe set a new record for the fastest 100 in a season when Daraydan won at Cheltenham, beating the previous record by a day.
1997 Senor El Betrutti, from Susan Nock's three-horse stable, landed another big prize, the Tripleprint Gold Cup at Cheltenham.

2008 Despite being one of the best draining tracks in the land, Cheltenham was abandoned due to waterlogging for the first time since April 1985, when 30mm fell in six hours prior to 10 a.m.

QUOTE OF THE DAY
1998 *'I nearly took all four out at the overnight stage, fearing the ground would be too firm,'* said Jenny Pitman, after saddling four winners at Plumpton.

BIRTHDAYS
1930 Red Rum's breeder, Martyn McEnery.
1948 Newmarket jockey John Higgins, who had three Trinidad Derby wins to his credit and also partnered top sprinter Raffingora.
1966 Champion 2008 Hurdler Katchit, trainer Alan King.
1979 Jump jockey Joe Tizzard. He rates his 1998 Christie's Foxhunters win at Cheltenham on Earthmover as the highlight of his career.

DEATHS OF THE DAY
1982 Former jockey Len 'Titch' Grantham, 82.
1992 The Peter O'Sullevan-owned Triumph Hurdle winner Attivo, 22.
1992 C V 'Sonny' Whitney, one of the leading owners in the US for over 50 years, 93. His Counterpoint was the 1951 Horse of the Year.

CELEBRITY OF THE DAY
1936 Shergar's owner, Prince Karim, the Aga Khan born. He also owned Derby winners Shahrastani, Kahyasi and Sinndar.

14 DECEMBER

SIGNIFICANT EVENT
1966 Arkle won for the 27th and final time in the 3m SGB Chase at Ascot, ridden by Pat Taaffe, carrying 12st 7lbs and starting at 1/3.

STRANGEST EVENT
1870 Lord Poulett, owner of chaser The Lamb, dreamed that his horse won the Grand National, ridden by Tommy Pickernell. Upon waking he set about engaging that jockey to ride the horse – they duly won the 1871 National.

OTHER EVENTS
1895 The first Indian Grand National was run at Tollygunge, won by the Maharajah of Patiala's Prince Imperial, ridden by J.D. Scott.
1936 21-year-old Ron Smyth landed a double at Plumpton on Jocund, trained by brother Willie, and Blue Shirt, saddled by father Herbert.
1983 A bad day for champion chasers at Haydock, as Gold Cup winner Bregawn fell, Gold Cup winner Little Owl was runner-up and champion two-miler Badsworth Boy unseated at the first.
1989 Martin Pipe lopped 15 days off his own record when he became the first trainer to send out 100 winners before Christmas. Kings Rank, Peter Scudamore up, brought up the record at Haydock.
1999 Richard Dunwoody retired with a record 1,699 career winners to his credit. He also had an estimated 669 falls.
2008 Stewards fined jockey Kevin Shea, who had just ridden a big Sha Tin winner, £420 for taking a sip of soft drink on his way to weigh-in.
2008 Reminiscing about the funniest thing he had seen on a racecourse, Terry Biddlecombe recalled 'Josh Gifford trying to pull me off my horse after he'd come off Out and About in 1963.'
2008 Peppers Pride, unbeaten 5yo filly, won US modern day record 19th straight win under Carlos Madeira, at Sunland Park, New Mexico, taking her winnings past $1m.

QUOTE OF THE DAY
'My saving grace as a jockey was determination, backed up by bravery bordering on stupidity – I fell off more times that I stayed on, yet doggedly refused to let go of the reins. As for race riding, I admit I lacked the basic skills.' Training genius Martin Pipe (see under 1989) won just one race as a jockey.

BIRTHDAYS
1927 Aussie jockey Ron (Robert) Hutchinson. Rode his first winner, Mentone, in Victoria in 1943. He came to Britain in 1960 and rode Martial to win the 2,000 Guineas in the same year for P J Prendergast. He also won the 1,000 Guineas on Full Dress II and the St Leger on Intermezzo in 1969. Retired in 1977.
1939 Welshman Sirrell Griffiths, owner-trainer of 1990 100/1 Cheltenham Gold Cup winner Norton's Coin.
1942 Former chairman of the Tote, Peter Jones.

DEATHS OF THE DAY
1967 Former trainer Henry Golightly, 85, whose biggest triumph was Dropitin's 1925 Carlisle Bell success.
1989 Five-times champion jump jockey between 1949-55, Tim Molony, 70. He rode 726 British winners incuding the 1953 Gold Cup on Knock Hard and four straight Champion Hurdles on Hatton's Grace, 1951, and Sir Ken 1952, '53 and '54. He began training in 1960.
2008 The death was reported of the only Australian to be Irish champion jockey – in 1960 – Garnet 'Garnie' Bougoure, 85. In 1963 he won the Irish Derby and Doncaster's St Leger on Ragusa, Epsom's Oaks on Noblesse and the Irish St Leger on Christmas Island.

CELEBRITY OF THE DAY
2007 England football star Michael Owen celebrated his 28th birthday at Wolverhampton – where his Four Tel, trained by Nicky Vaughan, was a winner.

15 DECEMBER

SIGNIFICANT EVENT
1970 Charismatic jockey Frankie Dettori born today. He rode his first winner, Billy Pitt, on 16 November 1986 at Turin.

STRANGEST EVENT
1918 The Duque d'Alberquerque born – a man obsessed with winning the Grand National. He fell and cracked a vertebra on his first attempt in 1952; 11 years later he fell at the 21st. In 1965 he came down at the 9th and broke his leg; he reached the 26th in 1966 – but no further; in 1973 he pulled up; in 1974, aged 55, he got round in eighth on Nereo. In 1976 the Duque fell at the 13th and was unconscious for 48 hours; the Jockey Club banned any more attempts.

OTHER EVENTS
1956 Bill Shoemaker won Bay Meadows Handicap at Bay Meadows – his 117th Stakes Race winner, on Holandes II.
1983 Willie Carson's son Anthony made his debut as a jockey in a hurdle race at Haydock. He was stretchered away when Brockley Belle came down at the second, but was not seriously injured.
1988 Peter Scudamore completed the fastest century of jump winners in a season – but one of the winners was subsequently disqualified so he didn't actually do it until December 20.
1988 1/14-shot Arum Lily was beaten at Haydock.
2008 Jockey Christophe Soumillon became involved in a 'brief pushing match' after George, son of trainer John Moore, criticized Soumillon's behaviour in a rough race for the Hong Kong Cup.

QUOTE OF THE DAY
'I get to 70 and suddenly start learning things. Watch out for me in ten years

– I could be dangerous'. Trainer Clive Brittain (first licence 1972) made this comment on this date in 2003 as he reached his three score years and ten – and has certainly continued to remain competitive in the big league ever since.

BIRTHDAYS
1938 Trainer Alan Jarvis. Best horses include Derring Rose, Hill of Slane and Kildimo.
1945 Jockey George (Elfred) Cadwaladr, who won both the Wokingham (My Audrey) and King's Stand (Roughlyn) at Royal Ascot in 1966.
1946 Half of racing's 'odd couple', Henrietta Knight, wife of Terry Biddlecombe and trainer of Triple Gold Cup winner Best Mate.

DEATHS OF THE DAY
1969 Former dual-purpose jockey Arthur Smith, 71. He rode Caligula to win the 1920 St Leger and won five races at Royal Ascot in 1919 as an apprentice.
1992 Owner-breeder Vera Hue-Williams, who escaped with her family from Russia during the Bolshevik Revolution. Born 1902, she won the first first King George VI and Queen Elizabeth Stakes (run as the Festival Of Britain Stakes) in 1951, with Supreme Court.
2006 Dual-purpose trainer David Cosgrove, aged 43.
2008 Former trainer and amateur rider John Fowler, 62, killed whilst felling a tree. He trained 1989 Irish Grand National winner Maid of Money.

CELEBRITY OF THE DAY
1994 The Aga Khan announced he was to end his four-year boycott of British racing, sparked by the banning of his 1989 Oaks winner Aliysa for testing positive.

16 DECEMBER

SIGNIFICANT EVENT
1969 A red-letter – well, red shirt – day as Jack Berry saddled his first winner, Camasco, Tony Potts riding, over hurdles at Kelso.

STRANGEST EVENT
2007 'I told the cameramen that I ate my chips out of the wife's knickers. It was just to give them a laugh, but the next thing you know it's on the telly and in the papers'. John Francome, admitting in the *Racing Post* that 'the things I regret are all the times I've opened my mouth thinking I'm keeping people amused.'

OTHER EVENTS
1851 Racing took place for the first time at Canterbury, New Zealand, with a four-race programme at Hagley Park.
1974 In his first season, Chris Hawley rode Ohmylove at Laurel, USA, for his 516th win of the season, beating the record set by Sandy Hawley a year earlier.
1989 Lester Piggott became a grandfather for the first time when daughter Maureen, 29, wed to trainer William Haggas, gave birth to a 9lb girl, Marianne. On the same day, Lester was reportedly in Peru, returning to the saddle after a three-year absence and finishing third at Monterrico on Sulieman, winning $20 prize money.
1990 Western Australia's first Sunday meeting took place. In an effort to please critics – of whom there were many – a non-denominational church service was staged in front of the grandstand before the first race. On the same date Clonmel in Ireland also held its first Sunday meeting but, to the disappointment of many, the bar was dry.
1993 93-year-old Brigadier Roscoe Harvey achieved an ambition when Relkeel, the first winner he bred, won at Towcester.

1993 A convicted serial killer who had escaped from jail was recaptured at Ascot. Kenneth Erskine, dubbed the 'Stockwell Strangler' after killing seven pensioners in 1986, was cornered in the members' enclosure.

QUOTE OF THE DAY
2007 *'When you're in a race, and especially when it gets tight, you're out there for yourself. You don't give a shit who's besides you, whether they go down or stand.'* Richard Edmondson recalling the comments of Kieren Fallon in an interview in the *Racing Post*.

BIRTHDAYS
1946 Abba's Benny Andersson, also a racehorse owner.
1954 Lightweight jockey Compton Rodrigues.
1955 Cricket-loving Worcestershire trainer, Neil Painting.

DEATHS OF THE DAY
1894 Jockey Billy Sensier in Lewes Hospital, having fallen from Topthorn at Plumpton the previous day.
1991 Northern Dancer's trainer Horatio Luro, 90, in Miami.
1996 Eponymous bookie Joe Coral, 92.
2000 Dual Irish Grand National-winning trainer, and former Classic-winning jockey, Georgie Wells, aged 81.
2008 Jump jockey Charles King, 83.

CELEBRITY OF THE DAY
2007 On this day, radio presenter and writer Sandi Toksvig recalled waking up and looking out on to her Surrey premises and observing: 'Either I'm not well, or there's a racehorse in my garden'. The pyjama-clad humorist ended up 'assisting with the corralling of a beautiful mare which had escaped from stables nearby.'

17 DECEMBER

SIGNIFICANT EVENT

1983 It was announced that racing at Down Royal, founded in 1685, but which had been under threat, had been guaranteed for the next 35 years at least as the course had been sold, albeit with a 35-year lease-back arrangement.

STRANGEST EVENT

1892 Despite at one point during the race being returned to the paddock after refusing to go any further, 20/1 outsider Covert Side managed to win the three-runner Ovingdean Chase at Plumpton – the other two respectively fell and refused. Jockey Mr Thompson then persuaded Covert Side back on course where they jumped round to win.

OTHER EVENTS

1895 Worth £355, champion jockey and trainer William Halsey rode Scottish National winner Nepcote to win Nottingham's two mile Great Midland Chase.

1934 Racing legends Keith (father of Lester) Piggott – on Crafty Captain – and Fulke Walwyn, on board Dusky Troubadour, rode a dead-heat in Derby's £73 Ashbourne Hurdle.

1975 Nineteen-year-old Phil Tuck rode his first winner, Persian King, at Catterick.

1983 Jockey Gerry Kelly, 52, rode his first winner for 11 years when Bluebirdino won over hurdles at Doncaster.

1993 Trained by Terry Caldwell at Warrington, Playful Juliet was a 100/1 winner in a novice chase, and Neltegrity, 25/1 in a hurdle race, both at Uttoxeter, and ridden by Caldwell's sons Pat and Peter respectively. On the same card Francois Doumen became the first French trainer to saddle a winner at the track, via Man To Man.

1997 Tony McCoy set a new record for the fastest 150 winners in a season – beating the previous record held by Peter Scudamore for over ten years.

2008 Jenny Pitman called for action to counter the BBC's threat to cover far less racing: 'Let's stop paying our licence fees.'

2008 Oasis Dream broke the record held by Danehill Dancer for siring most individual 2yo winners in a year when Pezula Bay at Lingfield was the 37th winner for the stallion.

QUOTE OF THE DAY

'He was opinionated to the point of being cantankerous,' said *Biographical Encyclopedia of British Flat Racing* of wealthy owner Major Lionel Holliday, who had three Classic winners between 1951 and 1965. He died on this date in 1965, in his 85th year.

BIRTHDAYS

1905 James Henry 'Tim' Hamey, who partnered Koko to win the 1926 Gold Cup, and Forbra to win the 1932 Grand National.

1911 Newmarket trainer Arthur 'Fiddler' Goodwill.

1940 The late, much respected racing writer George Ennor, now remembered via the George Ennor Trophy for Outstanding Achievement awarded annually at the Derby Awards Luncheon.

DEATHS OF THE DAY

1912 Common, winner of the 1891 Triple Crown – in which he won the 2,000 Guineas on his debut – at Boyce Burrow's stud near Chelmsford.

1966 Jockey Don Morris, 28, in a car crash.

CELEBRITY OF THE DAY

1937 Media tycoon and cricket revolutionary Kerry Packer born. He reputedly lost so much to his bookie that that worthy was able to retire as a result.

18 DECEMBER

SIGNIFICANT EVENT
1968 Trainer Sir John 'Jack' Jarvis died, 81; he was knighted for services to racing in 1967. He trained nine Classic winners, including the 1939 2,000 Guineas and Derby winner Blue Peter, who was denied a Triple Crown attempt by the outbreak of war. One of his owners was the similarly named Tory MP Sir John Jarvis, who decided to buy a horse when he erroneously received a cheque from a bookie intended for the trainer!

STRANGEST EVENT
1991 Owner Leonard Seale was in the winner's enclosure at Lingfield, awaiting the outcome of a three-way photo finish involving his 11/4 shot Super Sally in the European Gold Patrons Handicap. Before the official announcement that Super Sally was the winner, Mr Seale collapsed and died of a heart attack.

OTHER EVENTS
1846 A race meeting announced in the *China Mail* is believed to have been the first held at Happy Valley.

1991 Fifty-year-old jockey Takemi Sasaki, who rode his first winner in 1960, rode two winners in Japan, taking his career total to a record-breaking 6,500.

1991 Trainer Ken Oliver, 77, visited Bangor for the first time in his 30-year career – and duly saddled a 12/1 winner, Kinlet Vision.

1999 33/1 winner Coralpha returned 915/1 on the racecourse tote at Navan.

2002 Four licensed racing figures were disqualified following a brawl in the Members' Bar at Newcastle racetrack in Australia. One, trackwork rider Paula Beagan was found guilty of biting and kicking a security guard in the testicles and banned for six months, jockey Paul Falvey got four months, stable hand Kristy Ostle three months and farrier Jamie Carruthers 12 months.

2008 Dressed as Santa Claus, Barnstaple trainer Tom Newcombe announced he was giving away a dozen yearlings to potential new owners, and charging them only training fees.

QUOTE OF THE DAY
2007 *'Our view ... is that announcing equine deaths over the public address represents too much of a blunt instrument.'* Cheltenham communications manager Andy Clifton, speaking in the *Racing Post* today, on why the track could be construed to be dodging its responsibilities after the death of high profile Macs Joy in a hurdle race at the track three days previously was not conveyed to racegoers other than on a notice board.

BIRTHDAYS
1951 Trainer Noel Chance, who won Cheltenham Gold Cups with Mr Mulligan and Looks Like Trouble.

1956 One of the tallest of jockeys, and later a trainer, 6ft 2.5ins Chris Kinane.

1964 Jockey David Leadbitter.

1965 Former jump jockey Declan Murphy.

1973 Jockey Jim Culloty, rider of Best Mate and Bindaree.

DEATHS OF THE DAY
1926 Ex-jockey Charlie Maidment, 82. He won the Derby twice, on Cremorne, 1872, and Kisber in 1876; was twice joint-champion jockey, in 1870 and '71, and on Hannah won the 1871 1,000 Guineas, Oaks and St Leger.

2008 Maurice Zilber, aged 88. Trainer of the great filly Dahlia, he was Egyptian born to a Turkish mother and a French-Hungarian father. He won the 1976 Derby with Empery and, in the same year, the Prix du Jockey-Club with Youth.

CELEBRITY OF THE DAY
1947 Film director and racehorse owner Steven Spielberg born.

19 DECEMBER

SIGNIFICANT EVENT
1991 Mary Reveley became the first woman to train 100 winners in a calendar year when Festival Fancy, 20/1, won at Kelso.

STRANGEST EVENT
2008 It emerged that 21-year-old amateur rider Ryan Mahon, attached to the Paul Nicholls stable, had received what amounted to a seven-month ban after attempting to mislead drug testers when he supplied a 'substitute urine sample' after being tested whilst attending a course at the British Racing School in Newmarket.

OTHER EVENTS
1977 A rare US accolade for the Sport of Kings as the prestigious *Sports Illustrated* magazine featured jockey Steve Cauthen as their front cover feature, and declared him their 'Sportsman of the Year'.

2002 Australia's Cox Plate winner Northerly was amongst those moved to safety as a bush-fire raced across a 100-acre paddock on trainer Fred Kersley's property near Forrestdale, outside Perth. The fire was extinguished within hours. Other horses, including 40 broodmares, were also moved to safety. No horses suffered injury, and there was no damage to the farm's stables or Kersley's home.

2002 Calder Race Course, USA, issued a second Laffit Pincay 'bobble', in the late Fred Hooper's silks, and 7,500 were given away. Bobblehead dolls, wobbly headed caricatures of famous racing figures, first given out as racetrack promotions in 2001, rapidly became collectors' items, soaring in value.

2008 New York was the last of the states where Triple Crown races are contested to confirm that anabolic steroid use would be strictly restricted in horses – from January 1 2009.

2008 New Jersey website nj.com reported: 'The sports authority will allow horse-racing fans to place bets using internet-enabled mobile devices next year, as it attempts to increase revenues for the troubled racing industry.'

QUOTE OF THE DAY
'Although I achieved several firsts, I never felt as if I was accepted as a jockey in the eyes of the public. Male jockeys were the first to accept me; after a few dirty tricks they saw that I was serious, and although in 1987 some still did not like being beaten by a woman, it had become accepted.' Gay Kelleway, born today in 1963, paved the way for Alex Greaves and Hayley Turner.

BIRTHDAYS
1931 Wiltshire trainer from 1979, Peter Hayward, also assistant to David Elsworth for two years.

1934 Canadian Hall of Fame trainer David Cross.

1945 Jockey Dennis McKay, who rode his first winner in 1968. He won the Cesarewitch in 1969 on Floridian, 20/1, and in 1970 on Scoria, 33/1.

1946 Jump jockey Jimmy O'Grady.

FIRST OF THE DAY
1981 Jump jockey John Harris rode his first winner, Mandy's Time, at Southwell.

CELEBRITY OF THE DAY
1989 Actor Edward Underdown, who appeared with Humphrey Bogart in comedy movie Beat The Devil, and also dead-heated with John Hislop as 1938's leading Flat amateur, died aged 81.

20 DECEMBER

SIGNIFICANT EVENT
1982 Dawn Run, 4/6, won over hurdles for the first time in a maiden race at Navan.

STRANGEST EVENT
1971 All six runners in Plumpton's Keymer Chase fell – but David Barrons-trained Major Share, who fell at the last, remounted to win.

OTHER EVENTS
1895 First jump card at Bromford Bridge, Birmingham.

1958 It was confirmed that the famous Druids Lodge stables near Salisbury, from which many huge gambles – such as the one on Hackler's Pride to win the 1903 Cambridgeshire – were launched, was closing down. The stables and the 3,500 acre estate were sold for sheep farming.

1988 Sayfar's Lad was the horse to give Peter Scudamore the fastest NH 100 winners in a season when he won at Ludlow. Disqualification of an earlier winner, Norman Invader, had lopped one off Scudamore's total.

1989 Peter Scudamore rode his 100th winner of the season on the same day as last year when Redgrave Devil won at Bangor. He did it in just 242 rides – having taken 291 the year before.

2001 Tony McCoy rode his 1,500th winner over jumps in Britain, on Celtic Native at Exeter.

2007 Amateur rider Sarah Gaisford, 39, broke her back in a fall from Festival Flyer at Exeter.

2008 Nicky Henderson saddled the winners of Ascot's three successive big hurdle races – Binocular, evens, won the Boylesports International Hurdle; Punchestowns, 3/1, the Long Walk Hurdle, and Sentry Duty, 12/1, the Ladbroke. It was the third consecutive Ascot Saturday meeting at which the trainer had enjoyed a treble.

QUOTE OF THE DAY
'When he came to run, every horse beat him.' A rather forlorn comment by the Duke of Newcastle referring to this day in 1605 when King James I paid £154 for an Arabian horse of which he had high hopes, which were soon dashed.

BIRTHDAYS
1943 John Leadbetter, trainer of the first Scottish winner of the Grand National, Rubstic in 1979, his first runner in the race.

1945 Trainer David Barron, winner of the Stewards' Cup (twice), Ayr Gold Cup, and the Lincoln.

1948 Newmarket jockey turned Malton trainer, Chris Dwyer. On the same day, dual-purpose Compton handler, Peter Cundell, who became President of the National Trainers' Federation.

1959 Rider of Spectacular Bid, Ronnie Franklin.

1969 Jockey Thierry Gillet, rider of Arc winner Bago.

DEATHS OF THE DAY
1923 Trainer of 1887 Derby winner Merry Hampton, Martin Gurry, 82. He built Newmarket's Abingdon Place stable, later occupied by Geoff Wragg. Gurry's The Bard won 16 times as a 2yo in 1885, while La Sagesse took the 1895 Oaks.

1993 Controversial but talented jockey Charlie Smirke, aged 87. He won 11 Classics including four Derbys, but was suspended for five years after an odds-on favourite he was riding refused to start at Gatwick.

FIRST OF THE DAY
1989 Tarnya Davis became the first lady jockey to ride a jumps winner on the all-weather at Southwell, Olympus Reef.

21 DECEMBER

SIGNIFICANT EVENT

1925 Trainer Jeremy – real name Andrew – Tree born in London. Only For Life, 1963 and Known Fact, 1980 both won the 2,000 Guineas for him, while Juliette Marny, 1975 and Scintillate, 1979, landed the Oaks. He also won the 1985 Arc with Rainbow Quest. He died March 6, 1993.

STRANGEST EVENT

1985 Not one punter backed the runner who finished fourth in Lingfield's 2.15 – because it was Yankee the greyhound, who escaped from owner Mrs Violet Cohen, and overtook all but three of the 17-strong field.

OTHER EVENTS

1993 Kevin McAuliffe, former assistant to Paul Cole, won with his first runner as a trainer, 20/1-shot Sweet Whisper at Lingfield.

2001 Trans World International brokered a deal to place races from France on the BBC. The Corporation signed a five-year deal with France's Flat and steeplechase promoter France Galop for terrestrial rights to key events in the French racing calendar such as the Arc and the Prix du Jockey Club.

2007 Horse Racing Alberta, the TV company that produced the live telecast of the Alberta Derby, won the 2007 Media Eclipse Award for best local television, the National Thoroughbred Racing Association announced on this date. 'This year's broadcast was bittersweet for us, because it was to be the last Alberta Derby to be run at Stampede Park, which has been conducting racing for 117 years', said producer Jeff Robillard.

2008 Odds-on favorite Vacare, ridden by Jose Valdivia Jr., passed Gotta Have Her and In My Glory in the stretch to score a one-length victory in the $150,000 Dahlia Handicap at Hollywood Park as trainer Christophe Clement notched career win number 1,000.

2008 Solwhit, 1/3, became second straight long-odds-on loser in the Hotel Hurdle at Thurles, which has a reputation for upset results. Trainer Charles Byrne still had a 407/1 double with Dromin Hill Echo, 7/1 and 50/1 Bit of a Devil, the first winner for jockey Justin Murphy.

QUOTE OF THE DAY

'Bill got to the last fence minutes after the rest had finished – and fell. He got back on and tried again, but the crowd cheered and Sam (the horse) swerved violently right, causing Bill to fall off again. Next time, they got over the last only for Sam to swerve and jump out over the running rail. Bill got him back and trotted him over the line.' Prolific point-to-point rider Polly Gundry on this day in 2008, recalling an eventful race for rider Bill Tuck and horse Sam.

BIRTHDAYS

1935 Arc winner Mill Reef's jockey, Welshman Geoff Lewis, one of 13 children. A former hotel pageboy, his first Classic winner was Right Tack in the 1969 2,000 Guineas.

1939 Famous for his imitation of a barking dog, oh, and for riding 1978 Derby winner Shirley Heights and 1986 runner-up Dancing Brave, Greville Starkey. He won the 1975 Arc on 110/1 Star Appeal.

1946 Jockey of Roman Warrior, turned trainer, Geoff Oldroyd.

DEATHS OF THE DAY

1933 Innovative and controversial US jockey Tod Sloan, 59, who was successful around the turn of the century in England, but was warned off in 1900, penniless in a Los Angeles hospital.

1936 Prolific Puerto Rican horse Galgo Jr, who won won 137 of 159 starts.

1994 77-year-old former trainer Stuart Murless, who won the 1975 1,000 Guineas with Nocturnal Spree.

2006 Four-time British champion jockey, Australian Scobie Breasley, who twice won the Derby, aged 92.

22 DECEMBER

SIGNIFICANT EVENT
1975 Ladbrokes announced a deal with Bill Davies, owner of Aintree, under which they would pay an annual fee for the right to manage the Grand National for seven years.

STRANGEST EVENT
1962 Last racing in the UK, at Fontwell and Uttoxeter, before all racing was abandoned because of frozen ground. There would be just one further day's sport – 5 January at Ayr – before March 8 when racing resumed at Newbury.

OTHER EVENTS
1946 Owner-rider Major Victor McCalmont – Jockey Club and Irish Turf Club member – partnered his own, Neville Crump-trained Bluetit (would that name be passed today?) to win Catterick's Killerby Hurdle.

1982 Jockey Gerry Gracey – best horse ridden, Colonel Christy – was forced to retire, having been out of action since falling at Ludlow in September. His first winner was in 1969.

2007 Jerry Hollendorfer, 58, became the fourth North American trainer to send out 5,000 winners when Michael Baze rode Political High to win at Hollywood Park. Ahead of him in the standings were Dale Baird with 9,445, Jack van Berg on 6,378 and King Leatherbury, 6,227.

2008 Up-and-coming Amy Baker, 23, rode her first mainland double at Lingfield (first two races; 12/1 and 11/4) – but had already scored one at Les Landes, Jersey, where she had been champion lady rider for three straight years.

QUOTE OF THE DAY
'I feel I've had my best days as a jockey and the right thing to do is to be honest with myself and the people I ride for.' Honest signing-off comments of Derby-winning (Benny The Dip) jockey Willie Ryan, born this day in 1964 and who retired in October 2004.

BIRTHDAYS
1931 Jockey Sammy Millbanks.

1939 Trainer Peter Hedger, who rode 16 winners as a jockey before breaking his neck at Kempton in 1965.

1957 Jockey Randy Romero.

1961 Pro punter and columnist Dave Nevison, whose autobiography *A Bloody Good Winner* was a best seller.

1964 Newmarket Flat jockey Willie Ryan. On his 28th birthday he joined the 100 winners in a season club when landing a 236/1 four-timer at Lingfield – all of which won by a short head.

1966 Non-political jockey Anthony Tory, who partnered Docklands Express, Cool Ground and Kings Fountain.

DEATHS OF THE DAY
1968 Promising 18-year-old rider Nigel Thorne, son of John, killed in a car crash near Newmarket.

2003 Perhaps the most successful point-to-point rider ever, David Turner, champion eight times, rider of 343 winners and 50 more under rules, aged 59.

CELEBRITY OF THE DAY
1900 Owner of dual Scottish National winner Barona, Colonel Bill Whitbread born. In 1957 he inaugurated the Whitbread Gold Cup, the first major commercially sponsored race. He rode in two Grand Nationals, falling from his Ben Cruchan in 1925 on whom he remounted to finish 13th the next year.

23 DECEMBER

SIGNIFICANT EVENT

2007 Paul Nicholls gave an insight into his methods on this day in a *Mail on Sunday* interview: 'More horses I rode as a jockey were beaten for lack of fitness than for any other reason. My mantra is work them hard to get them fit, then work them hard again to keep them fit.'

STRANGEST EVENT

2007 Tony McCoy explained in a *Sunday Times* interview how high-profile jockeys should keep on the straight and narrow: 'Some people, you might enjoy their company, but if it's going to interfere with your career, then it's a no.'

OTHER EVENTS

1982 Irish jockey Tommy Carberry announced that injury was forcing him to give up riding to commence training at Ratoath, Co. Dublin. He rode L'Escargot to win both the Gold Cup and Grand National.

1992 Vaal's race meeting was shown live on SIS and broadcast into British betting shops, the first time South African racing alone featured on a day with no British racing in opposition.

1995 German champion jockey, Peter Schiergen, beat Gordon Richards' record 269 domestic winners in a season.

2007 'I think I'd have given up if it wasn't for the yard. You're not going to bust your arse to get back for an office job, are you?' Stable lass and groom to Henrietta Knight-trained Racing Demon, Katie Clark, on her fight back from depression and cancer to return to work.

2008 It was announced that all horses tested by Racing New South Wales as part of a check for Erythropoietin (EPO) returned negative results. At least 100 horses were tested for the blood agent that can improve stamina and recovery from injuries. The move came in response to news reports in Victoria that EPO was being used.

QUOTE OF THE DAY

'Racing has been rescued by the acknowledgement that Britain is more a nation of punters than of racegoers.' Wray Vamplew, a lecturer in economic history and racing historian, born this day in 1943, discussing the Levy Board in his 1976 *Social and Economic History of Horse Racing*.

BIRTHDAYS

1921 Owner Noel Hetherton, also a steward at Ripon, Redcar and Wetherby. He owned 1983 Yorkshire Cup winner Line Slinger, St Leger third Cold Storage and Champion Hurdle third Past Glories.

1943 Racing historian Wray Vamplew.

1953 Trainer of In Excess, Bruce Jackson.

DEATHS OF THE DAY

1958 Bill Dutton, 57, who rode the 1928 Grand National winner Tipperary Tim, 100/1, and trained 1956 Cheltenham Gold Cup winner Limber Hill.

1999 Lewes-based trainer Auriol Sinclair, aged 81. She was the second woman to be granted a licence by the Jockey Club, in 1966, although she had been training in reality, if not in name, for many years previous to that.

2007 US trainer Dale Baird, holder of the record for the total number of victories – 9,445 – was killed in a car crash aged 72. He never trained a Graded-stakes winner but was renowned at his home track, Mountaineer Park in West Virginia, where he operated for 35 years, winning his first race in 1961.

CELEBRITY OF THE DAY

1999 Formerly plain old Ronnie Strutt, a prominent amateur rider of the 1930s who twice completed the Grand National, who later became Lord Belper, died aged 87. He had lost an eye in a shooting accident – and a one-eyed horse which won the City and Suburban Handicap, Belper, was named after him.

24 DECEMBER

SIGNIFICANT EVENT

1945 Without the birth today of Jeff Smith, Frankie Dettori might never have completed his historic Magnificent Seven – for Smith owned the sixth winner that day, Lochangel, a half-sister to his famous sprinter Lochsong. He also owned great stayer Persian Punch and The Geezer, and owned Littleton Stud.

STRANGEST EVENT

1986 Students from Widnes Sixth Form College were blamed for damaging the stuffed remains of great racehorse Brown Jack, which stood at the Stable Grill Restaurant, Widnes. The horse was found lying on the ground minus one ear.

OTHER EVENTS

1960 The Countdown to racehorse ownership with trainer James Bethell began for Carol Vorderman, born this day.

1973 Jackie Stewart, World F1 Champion driver, was awarded the coveted *Sports Illustrated* Sportsman of the Year Award, just beating 'Secretariat, the winner of the Triple Crown whose triumphs focused a degree of public attention on horse racing that it had not received in a quarter century.' The other runner-up was, er, pro footballer O J Simpson.

2002 Melbourne Cup-winning trainer Sheila Laxon – New Zealand's Racing Personality of the Year 2002 – underwent four hours of surgery after suffering major hip, rib and pelvic injuries when thrown from a filly during track-work at Macedon Lodge, Victoria, Australia.

2002 Lightweight jockey Franny Norton claimed his failed drugs test was due to 'drinking a brand of exotic tea to help control riding weight.'

2007 Racing New South Wales chief executive Peter V'Landys was not concerned about the prospect of small fields during the festive season, instead reiterating what a relief it was just to be racing in the wake of equine influenza. Only 73 nominations were lodged for an imminent Rosehill meeting, but: 'You've got to expect smaller fields given we've just had the biggest crisis ever to hit racing. With the after-effects of EI you've got to expect that we are going to have a problem.'

2008 Although still adamant that he will never turn to training, it was revealed that planning consent for a 60-box training complex on Tony McCoy's estate overlooking Lambourn Valley had been granted.

QUOTE OF THE DAY

'It was that awful you could have heard a pin drop. Absolutely shocking. I've never experienced anything like it. So we said goodbye to him there and then, and left the track as soon as we possibly could.' Born today in 1945, owner Jeff Smith on the spring day in 2004 when the great Persian Punch dropped dead at the end of an Ascot race.

BIRTHDAYS

1924 Gosforth Park trainer Ronald Robson, whose Charlie Proper won 16 times, while both King Eider and Why Tell won 15 races.

1943 Trainer Jeremy Hindley. He won the 1975 Ascot Stakes and Doncaster Cup with Crash Course, and the 1977 Cambridgeshire with 18/1 Sin Timon.

1946 Jockeys' agent, Dave 'Shippy' Ellis.

1956 Hong Kong jockey turned trainer Tony Cruz.

FIRST OF THE DAY

2008 For the first time Coral and Ladbrokes opened all of their betting shops on Christmas Eve, with William Hill opening 75% of theirs.

CELEBRITY OF THE DAY

1932 Racehorse owner, husband to trainer Lady Herries, and England cricketer, Colin Cowdrey, born this day.

25 DECEMBER

SIGNIFICANT EVENT
1941 Trainer Jim 'Bolshie' Bolger – accountant by trade – born. Saddled St Jovite to win the 1992 Irish Derby and won the 1991 Oaks with Jet Ski Lady. As a rider he won three of his 12 races. He landed the 2008 Derby with New Approach while 20/1 Intense Focus that year was his third straight Dewhurst winner.

STRANGEST EVENT
1833 Born this day, jockey John 'Tiny' Wells, at Sutton Coldfield. He won 20 times on Fisherman in 1857, and died in 1873 having amassed eight Classics including the Derby in 1858, '59 and '68. Something of a dandy, he once turned up to ride out wearing an Alpine hat with feathers, a suit in Gordon tartan, and a pair of red Morocco slippers.

OTHER EVENTS
1753 The Godolphin Arabian, one of three horses from which all of today's thoroughbreds descended, died and was buried at Gog Magog, Cambridgeshire.
1907 Trainer George Owen born; he rode Brendan's Cottage to win the 1939 Cheltenham Gold Cup and trained 1949 Grand National winner Russian Hero. Three champion jockeys started out at his Tiverton stable as amateurs – Dick Francis, Tim Brookshaw and Stan Mellor.
1934 *The Los Angeles Times* ran an article by Paul Lowry entitled 'Horse Racing Has Its Own Peculiar Jargon.' The article was to help first-time racegoers by providing a glossary of terms they might encounter at the track, such as: Goat: A poor racing horse; Impost: The total weight carried by a horse; Morning Glory: A horse which looks like a champion in the morning and can't click in the afternoon; Rail Lugger: A horse which bears to the left for the inner rail.
2008 California-based jockey Sam Thompson jnr, 36, died five days after being thrown from 2yo filly Harems Dynasty at Los Alamitos. Thompson was on life support, but the decision was made to turn it off. 'Sam wanted his organs to be donated,' said Kristen Watanabe, his girlfriend, eloquently describing how his death affected people: 'His kidneys were removed and someone will be getting those. His mother, (trainer) Donna McArthur, and I were there with him. It was very peaceful. On the night of the accident I was torn apart. If he would have passed away on that night, it would have been so difficult. They resuscitated him twice and I feel like he came back to give us an opportunity to prepare. '
2008 Trainer Paul Nicholls offered punters a Christmas tip for Kauto Star in the next day's King George VI Chase at Kempton: 'If you can get 11/8 my advice is to lump on'. Kauto duly collected his third win in the race, at 10/11.

QUOTE OF THE DAY
'Christmas Day has never even been considered before,' said the BHB's Alan Delmonte on hearing October 2004 news that the government's new Gambling Bill made provision for racing to take place on this day of the year.

BIRTHDAYS
1917 Dual-purpose Hambleton trainer Jack Calvert. He won 17 races with Dieppe and 14 with Mannion.
1922 Noel Whitcomb, owner of 14 times winner Even Up and founder of the *Daily Mirror* Punters' Club.
1961 Three-time UAE champion trainer, Satish Seemar.

DEATH OF THE DAY
1991 Great Aussie champion, Vain, 25. One of the best sprinter-milers, he won the 1969 Golden Slipper Stakes.

FIRST OF THE DAY
1934 Las Palmas won the first race, the 7f California Bred Handicap, as the inaugural meeting took place at Santa Anita, California.

26 DECEMBER

SIGNIFICANT EVENT
1987 Nupsala, 25/1, trained by Francois Doumen, became the first French chaser to win in Britain for a quarter of a century, winning the King George VI Chase at Kempton.

STRANGEST EVENT
1899 A grand old chestnut was born as Good Friday fell on Boxing Day – a horse of that name capsizing in the Thorneycroft Chase at Wolverhampton.

OTHER EVENTS
1936 Bruce Hobbs rode as an amateur for the last time, completing a double on Circourt and Abbot's Glance at Wincanton. The next day he rode his first double as a professional, on Baccharis and Eliza at Wolverhampton – while also celebrating his 16th birthday.

1953 Lester Piggott rode even-money chance Eldoret to victory at Wincanton – his first hurdles winner.

1970 Arkle's jockey Pat Taaffe rode his final winner, Straight Fort, trained by Tom Dreaper, at Fairyhouse.

1972 The first Australian Derby was run at Ascot, Perth.

1973 Aged 15, Nigel Tinkler rode his first winner, Nimble Joe, at Sedgefield. Before he was 16 he had ridden winners on the Flat, over hurdles and fences.

1983 Angel Cordero rode Jacksboro to win at Aqueduct, becoming the first rider to reach $10m in prize money.

1989 Jenny Pitman sent out 14 runners, seven of which came back as winners.

1991 Desert Orchid fell at the third-last in his final race, the King George VI Chase, won by 10/1-shot The Fellow under Polish-born Adam Kondrat.

1994 15 lengths clear at the last, 100/30 favourite Barton Bank unseated Adrian Maguire in the King George VI Chase at Kempton, leaving prize to Francois Doumen (his 4th win in eight runnings with Algan); jockey Philippe Chevalier was having his first ride in England.

1994 George Duffield rode five winners – at Santa Rosa Park, Trinidad.

2006 Apprentice jockey Tamara Gillis, albeit at the unusually elderly age of 36, a chef by trade, had ridden just 15 mounts in her six-week career when she went to ride at Australia's Sapphire Coast meeting – and promptly booted home first four winners on the five-race card.

2008 Victory Gunner failed in a gallant attempt to win the Lincolnshire National at Market Rasen for the fourth consecutive year, following 11/4, 3/1 and 10/1 victories.

QUOTE OF THE DAY
1996 *'We'll have to sort out whether young Andrew can claim two losing fees for one race,'* quipped head steward at Caulfield, Australia, Des Gleeson, after a race in which apprentice Andrew Payne was riding Hon Kwok Star. Jon Patton on Cogitate was thrown from his mount, which cannoned into Hon Kwok Star, knocking Payne into the air – only for him to land in Cogitate's saddle and ride the horse to the finish.

BIRTHDAYS
1965 Former Melbourne champion jockey, Darren Gauci.

1966 Trainer Noel Wilson.

DEATHS OF THE DAY
1994 Former Irish jump jockey turned trainer Mick 'M.J.' Prendergast, 80.

1992 The only horse disqualified as winner of the Kentucky Derby, Dancer's Image, in Japan, 27. He passed the post ahead in 1968 but was thrown out after the discovery in his system of then forbidden Butazolidin.

2005 Tycoon Kerry Packer, 68, whose Mahogany won the 1983 Victoria Derby.

CELEBRITY OF THE DAY
1994 Liverpool striker Ian Rush scored the winner for his club at Leicester minutes after his horse, Great Marquess, owned together with team-mate Jan Molby, won over hurdles at Hereford.

27 DECEMBER

SIGNIFICANT EVENT
1993 Wolverhampton staged the country's first floodlit meeting, with Petraco winning the first race of its type at 4/1, ridden by Steve Williams for trainer Nigel Smith. A crowd of 10,000 attended.

STRANGEST EVENT
1999 Kempton Park evacuated following a bomb threat. Nothing was found.

OTHER EVENTS
1890 The winning jockey of a race at Calcutta was disqualified for carrying 4lb OVERweight.

1923 Captain Tuppy Bennett, who won the National earlier in the year on Sergeant Murphy, fell from Ardeen in the Oteley Chase at Wolverhampton. Kicked on the head as he lay on the ground, he died 17 days later.

1966 Arkle ran his final race. Fracturing a bone in his hoof, he still finished second in the King George.

1982 Michael Dickinson sent out 12 winners from 21 runners on the day, a world record. They were Marnik and Thornacre (at Huntingdon); W Six Times, Fearless Imp (Market Rasen); Londolozi, B Jaski (Sedgefield); Wayward Lad (Kempton); Delius, Happy Voyage (Wetherby); Brunton Park, Prominent Artist, Slieve Bracken (Wolverhampton).

1990 Aged 45, Martin Pipe became the youngest trainer to saddle 1,000 winners when Catch The Cross won the Quicksilver Hurdle at Kempton.

1991 Dermot Weld broke Jim Bolger's record of 148 Irish winners in a year when Vintage Crop won at Leopardstown.

1997 Welsh National at Chepstow won by 25/1 Earth Summit, who had previously won the Scottish National, ridden by Tom Jenks for trainer Nigel Twiston-Davies. Earth Summit went on to win the Aintree National, completing a unique treble

2001 Exonerated after being caught up in long-running race-fixing investigations, Leighton Aspell returned to the top of the sport as he partnered the Pat Murphy-trained Supreme Glory to a 10/1 triumph in the Welsh National.

2008 For the first time in its 113-year history, an Irish raider won the Welsh National, Notre Pere, 16/1, obliging for trainer Jim Dreaper and jockey Andrew Lynch.

QUOTE OF THE DAY
1910 *'He hated wearing jackets, finding them too tight under the armpits, and would refuse dinner invitations unless allowed to wear a sweater. He was also reluctant to go out if Emmerdale Farm was on TV.'* Little-known facts in a *Daily Telegraph* obituary of National-winning trainer Neville Crump, born today.

BIRTHDAYS
1921 Owner-breeder Sir Gordon Brunton was born; ten years later Sir William Purves, former chairman of the Hong Kong Jockey Club; 20 years after that, owner Viscount Astor; and six years on from that, Baron Edouard de Rothschild, president of France Galop.

1920 Bruce Hobbs, in America. The youngest rider, just 17, to win the Grand National, on Battleship in 1938. He won the Military Cross during World War II – and the Palestine Grand National.

DEATHS OF THE DAY
1991 Philip Barnard, 24, from serious head injuries after falling from Sayyure at Wincanton the day before.

1991 Ambulanceman Bob Corfield, 55, after falling from his vehicle whilst tracking the runners in the first race at Wolverhampton.

CELEBRITY OF THE DAY
1993 Racing journalist/owner Richard Evans of *The Times* won £5,000 from Ladbrokes who had been incautious enough to offer 100/1 that his Northern Saddler would win five times in the year.

28 DECEMBER

SIGNIFICANT EVENT
1992 Martin Pipe saddled the first four in the Welsh National at Chepstow – Run For Free, 11/4 joint-favourite, won from Riverside Boy, 50/1, Miinnehoma, 11/4 and Bonanza Boy. Pipe had previously won the race in 1988, '89, and '91.

STRANGEST EVENT
1905 The last jump meeting took place at Newmarket.

OTHER EVENTS
1938 Following a race meeting earlier in the day, the grandstand of Melbourne's Epsom racecourse burnt down – accidentally, by all accounts. The track, opened in 1889, would never host another card of its own.

1940 Derby-winning jockey Charlie Smirke rode his first winner over the sticks on Ladylove at Leopardstown.

1948 The Vincent O'Brien-trained Cottage Rake became the first horse to add the King George VI Chase at Kempton to a Cheltenham Gold Cup win.

1955 Lester Piggott's only jump winner of season, Dessin, at Wolverhampton.

1981 The highest odds in Irish Tote history – £289.64 for a 10p stake on Gene's Rogue at Limerick.

1992 Mighty Mogul won the Bonusprint Christmas Hurdle at Kempton – the twelfth consecutive win for owners Bill and Shirley Robins, with Mighty Mogul, Wonder Man and Baydon Star, all of which were later moved from Jenny Pitman to David Nicholson.

1993 Murphys all round: brothers Declan and Eamon rode winners at Kempton and Pat saddled 12/1 Sylvia Beach to win at Chepstow, while sister Kathleen rode a winner at Limerick.

1998 Nigel Hawke, who won the 1991 Grand National on Seagram, had had Kendal Cavalier in his yard for just ten days when the 14/1 chance, ridden by Barry Fenton, snatched the Welsh National by half a length.

1999 The first three from the previous year were in a 16-strong Welsh National field but only third-placed Forest Ivory went close, finishing runner-up behind the Henry Daly-trained Edmond, ridden by Richard Johnson, who sported bright yellow hair to raise cash for stricken fellow jockey Scott Taylor.

2008 Proudinsky won $150,000 San Gabriel Handicap, giving trainer Bobby Frankel a record 900th career win at the Santa Anita winter-spring meeting.

QUOTE OF THE DAY
'When he first came to Mr Dreaper's his action was so bad you could drive a wheelbarrow through his hind legs.' Jockey Pat Taaffe about Arkle. He quit the saddle this day in 1970 after a Fairyhouse fall from Proud Tarquin.

BIRTHDAYS
1946 Panama-born Jorge Luis Velasquez. Rode Pleasant Colony to win the 1981 Kentucky Derby.

1948 The *Racing Post's* drollest writer, David Ashforth.

DEATHS OF THE DAY
1787 Owner of the immortal Eclipse, Colonel Dennis O'Kelly, died at Piccadilly, leaving the horse to his brother Philip.

1987 Arthur Balding, 81, Britain's oldest trainer until retiring on 1 January.

1993 Twenty-nine thoroughbreds worth $2m were killed in a fire at Manor House Farm, New Jersey. One saved was the previous year's Belmont Stakes runner-up My Memoirs, once trained by Richard Hannon.

2002 Former jockey Peter Ashworth, 78, who rode for music hall star Bud Flanagan and turned trainer to send out the winner of the 1961 Irish 1,000 Guineas, Lady Senator.

2002 Known as 'the selling plate king', Hednesford trainer Bob Ward, 95. He was once suspended for ten years for running an alleged non-trier in a seller, partnered by a young Lester Piggott.

29 DECEMBER

SIGNIFICANT EVENT
1990 Alex Greaves rode her 50th winner – Andrew's First at Southwell – the horse on which she rode the first winner of her career a year and four weeks previously.

STRANGEST EVENT
1989 Brother and sister Marcus (Major Match) and Gee Armytage (Bold King's Hussar) both rode a winner at Warwick – but Gee was suspended for four days for a whip offence.

OTHER EVENTS
1951 Vincent O'Brien wed Jacqueline Wittenoom. They had five children – David, Charles, Elizabeth, Susan and Jane.

1988 Martin Pipe set the fastest time for training 100 winners in a season when Mareth Line won at Taunton.

2007 The turbulent career of 45-year-old jockey Pat Valenzuela took a downward turn when the California Horse Racing Board terminated his conditional riding licence after learning of his arrest for driving under the influence of alcohol.

2008 William Hill racing PRO Kate Miller revealed that a £2.50 each-way bet at 16/1 on Double Trigger in the Goodwood Cup as a teenager set her off on a love affair with racing. 'It was the bet that turned me from a mere fan to a racing devotee.'

2008 Garrett Gomez, who would finish the year as US leading jockey in earnings, returned to the saddle two days after being injured at Santa Anita, unseated from Back at You when the 2yo attempted to jump the rail in the stretch during the Eddie Logan Stakes. Gomez suffered broken teeth, a gashed knee and a swollen hand. He led the nation's riders with $23,246,319 in North American earnings that year, just shy of the all-time record $23,354,960 set by Jerry Bailey in 2003. Gomez won with his first mount of the day, Suit Yourself in the third race.

QUOTE OF THE DAY
1951 'My idea of the greatest trainer who ever lived,' Hugh McIlvanney's opinion of Vincent O'Brien, who was married today.

BIRTHDAYS
1934 Trainer Tim 'Jimmy' Etherington, who rode two winners as a rider.

1946 Jockey Laffit Pincay jr, former US champion, in Panama City.

1950 Jockey-trainer Steve Holland, whose first winner was in 1968.

1972 Trainer Andrew Balding, who won the Oaks in 2003 with Casual Look.

DEATHS OF THE DAY
1968 Jockey Gerry Wilson, 65, who rode Golden Miller to win both the Gold Cup and Grand National in 1934.

1988 Former jockey and trainer Tommy Cross, 75. He trained over 300 winners, mostly over the sticks.

1990 Former barrister, jockey and trainer, John Harty, a sufferer from motor neurone disease. He rode Daletta to win the 1980 Irish National.

2008 Owner Lady Anne Bentinck, 92. She had horses for many years, trained at her home, Welbeck Abbey in Nottinghamshire, firstly by Jeremy Glover then John Quinn. Her Speaker Weatherill won the 1998 Great Yorkshire Chase and Strath Royal the 1998 Charlie Hall Chase. She gave the skin of the great 19th century racehorse St Simon, owned by her grandfather, to Sir Mark Prescott, who hung it at his home.

FIRST OF THE DAY
1982 Grand National winner-in-waiting, West Tip, won at the first attempt, at 50/1 in a Warwick novice hurdle for trainer Michael Oliver and jockey Philip Hobbs. He went on to win the Grand National in 1986 under Richard Dunwoody. He was fourth in 1987 and 1988, second in 1989.

30 DECEMBER

SIGNIFICANT EVENT
1933 The Irish Field reported that the first claim on the Irish Jockeys' Accident Fund, administered by the Turf Club and the Irish NH Steeplechase Committee, was paid to dependents of jockey M. Hynes, 'the capable rider who succumbed to injuries received while riding in a steeplechase.' Payment, made in trust for Mrs Hynes and child, was £600. The premium to the fund was 2/- for each jockey's mount, the owner paying half and the jockey half.

STRANGEST EVENT
1986 Manhattan Boy won a hurdle race at Plumpton – he ran 64 times there, winning 14 times, more than any other horse. He ran 24 times elsewhere, winning none. He won five Peacehaven Hurdles at Plumpton.

OTHER EVENTS
1905 King George V, then Prince of Wales, went racing at Calcutta for the first time.

1982 Trainer Fulke Walwyn was made a Commander of the Victorian Order (CVO) 'for personal services' in the New Year's Honours List, while Willie Carson received an OBE for 'services to racing'.

1987 Gee Armytage won on her final mount as an amateur, Silent Echo at Warwick, riding for Alan Blackmore in a race named after his son Michael, killed in a 1986 racing accident.

1989 Ross Carson, son of Willie, had his first mount in public on Pointer Man at Leicester, which was pulled up.

1992 China, which only weeks previously permitted racing to recommence, announced a renewed ban on the sport and a strengthening of anti-gambling laws.

1993 Andy Orkney, a unique combination of jockey and optician, saw the light and retired aged 32, after finishing sixth on Dizzy at Carlisle. He rode 103 winners – one in Russia.

2008 Hayley Turner became the first female jockey to ride 100 winners in a calendar year, reaching 99 on Newlyn Art, 5/4, at Lingfield in the afternoon then hitting the ton on Mullitovermaurice, 7/1, at Wolverhampton.

QUOTE OF THE DAY
1992 *'When he took his hand out of his pockets I just swung at him with my left hand,'* explained US jockey Alex Solis after a Santa Anita spectator accused him of riding a bad race. He broke his critic's nose

BIRTHDAY
1942 Jockey turned trainer Johnny Haine, who rode 30 winners on the Flat before switching to jumps, winning 1966 Champion Hurdle on Salmon Spray.

DEATHS OF THE DAY
1981 Major-General Sir Reginald Peregrine 'Perry' Harding, DSO, in his 76th year – one of only two amateurs to win the Champion Hurdle – on Our Hope in 1938.

1945 Charles 'Hellfire Jack' Trigg, 62. He won 843 races over 17 seasons from 7,221 mounts and was runner-up to champion Frank Wootton in 1911 with 111 winners.

1991 John 'Jackie' Power, 72, leading Irish jockey for 30 years from the early 1940s. He rode two Irish Classic winners – Solferino in 1943 Irish St Leger, and Valoris in 1966 Irish 1,000 Guineas.

1992 Reigning Champion Hurdler, Royal Gait, collapsed and died after a Leopardstown race.

2007 Former North Yorkshire trainer Richie – JR – Kettlewell, 85.

CELEBRITY OF THE DAY
1946 Davy Jones, former apprentice jockey turned pop star with The Monkees, born today. He declared an ambition to ride in the Grand National – making him a 'Daydream Believer'?

31 DECEMBER

SIGNIFICANT EVENT
1990 Michael Stoute announced he would not be renewing his retainer with Walter Swinburn – they had teamed up in September 1980.

STRANGEST EVENT
2007 All 14 riders in the Newtown Handicap Chase at Tramore finished the race a circuit too early. Five realised and set off out again with 9/4 favourite Mr Aussie, ridden by Andrew McNamara, eventually winning.

OTHER EVENTS
1896 Both horses fighting out the finish of a chase at Keele Park were named Lambton. Commented racing historian Chris Pitt, 'A good thing neither was ridden by Mr W. Lambton who scored a double at the course in February 1898.'
1954 Johnny Kenneally rode his first winner, Evening Paradise at Manchester.
1993 Jockey Mike Smith set a record for the number of Stakes victories in a year when he won the Ticonderoga Handicap at Aqueduct on Hey Baba Lulu, his 61st, surpassing Pat Day's 1991 tally.
1994 Switched to Newbury because Chepstow was under water, 5/2 joint-favourite Master Oats won the 99th running of the Welsh National by 20 lengths for Norman Williamson and Kim Bailey, with next year's winner Earth Summit second and 1992 National winner Party Politics third.
1994 Frankie Dettori had a record 1,317 mounts in the course of the year – the first during which two domestically based jockeys both rode 200 winners or more – Frankie 233, Jason Weaver 200. It didn't happen again until Seb Sanders and Jamie Spencer rode 213 and 207 reseptively during 2007.
1997 The National Association for the Protection of Punters was disbanded.
1998 Racecourse bookies were required to issue tickets detailing horses' name or number, odds, bet type and potential return.

2000 J A Allen equine bookshop in Lower Grosvenor Place, London, which had been open for 75 years, closed down.
2007 'A lot more fun than riding a winner on the all-weather at Lingfield,' declared Flat jockey Eddie Ahern who partnered World Wide Web to win the Hayes Golden Button Challenge, run to re-enact steeplechasing's origins, by the River Severn in Gloucestershire.
2008 Charlie Mann revealed his 2009 resolution: 'Not to take life seriously, otherwise I'll never get out of it alive.'

QUOTE OF THE DAY
1998 Riding in Dubai, Gary Hinds was fined £500, when reported by an owner for whom he'd just ridden a winner at Nad al Sheba, for swearing. *'I asked Gary why he had been so far back on Susu and he used a swear word in his reply. It was not directed at me, or at anyone else. It was the first time he has done it, he has apologized, and I can forgive him. But I do not think a swear word should be used in the paddock'* explained trainer Satish Seemar.

BIRTHDAYS
1954 SNP Leader, tipster and racing fan, Alex Salmond.
1969 Trainer Amanda Perrett, daughter of Guy Harwood.

DEATHS OF THE DAY
1991 Raymond Guest, 84, the only man to own Derby, Grand National and Gold Cup winners. Also former US ambassador to Ireland.
2005 Ludlow-based trainer Malcolm Eckley, aged 68.
2005 Racing writer George Ennor, 65, of both *The Sporting Life* and *Racing Post*. He was President of Horserace Writers' Association for 20 years.

CELEBRITY OF THE DAY
1992 The Queen's Abbey Strand won at Lingfield in the Any Post Maiden Stakes to crown her most successful year to date as an owner, taking her score to 26.